THE DESIGN HISTORY READER

THE
DESIGN

HISTORY READER

Edited by
Grace Lees-Maffei and Rebecca Houze

Oxford • New York

English edition
First published in 2010 by
Berg
Editorial offices:
First Floor, Angel Court, 81 St Clements Street, Oxford OX4 1AW, UK
175 Fifth Avenue, New York, NY 10010, USA

Berg is the imprint of Oxford International Publishers Ltd.

Library of Congress Cataloging-in-Publication Data

The design history reader / edited by Grace Lees-Maffei and Rebecca Houze.
   p. cm.
  Includes bibliographical references and index.
  ISBN 978-1-84788-388-9 (hc) — ISBN 978-1-84788-389-6 (pbk.) 1. Design—
Historiography. I. Lees-Maffei, Grace. II. Houze, Rebecca.
  NK1175.D475 2010
  745.409—dc22

                                       2009052459

British Library Cataloguing-in-Publication Data

A catalogue record for this book is available from the British Library.

ISBN 978 1 84788 388 9 (Cloth)
      978 1 84788 389 6 (Paper)

Typeset by JS Typesetting Ltd, Porthcawl, Mid Glamorgan
Printed in Great Britain by the MPG Books Group, Bodmin and King's Lynn

www.bergpublishers.com

For Students and Teachers
of Design History,
and especially Nic Maffei,
Jay and Laurel Lees-Maffei,
Peter, Gabriel, and Lucian O'Leary

CONTENTS

Section 8
Objects, Subjects and Negotiations

Section 9
Gender and Design

ACKNOWLEDGEMENTS

Our primary thanks go to the authors whose work is represented here and to the students and teachers of design history, past, present and future: this book is for you all and without you there would be no *Design History Reader*. Thanks to the publishers, museums, archives and collectors who have shared their texts and images with us; they are named throughout the book. We are very grateful to Jessica McTague, Tara Quell and Brooke Stover for their help with the complex task of obtaining permission to reproduce the texts and images that make up *The Design History Reader*. We appreciate the input of Tristan Palmer, our editor, who has been unfailingly encouraging and prompt in his responses to our questions, in the years that extended between the conception and publication of this book.

Grace Lees-Maffei registers an important note of thanks to the executive committee of the Design History Society, for supporting the project through the Society's Research Award, and to the University of Hertfordshire's erstwhile Faculty for the Creative and Cultural Industries for its Faculty Research Award. Grace thanks her teachers, especially Tim Putnam, Penny Sparke, Jeremy Aynsley, John Styles, Chris Breward, Gillian Naylor, Clive Wainwright, Helen Clifford, and her students at the University of Hertfordshire, especially Marina Emmanouil and Barbara Brownie. Grace's biggest debt of gratitude is to Nic: husband, father, design historian.

Rebecca Houze would especially like to thank the School of Art, College of Visual and Performing Arts, and Division of Research and Graduate Studies at the Graduate School of Northern Illinois University for their generous financial support for this project. In addition she thanks the staff, students and colleagues at Northern Illinois University, as well as the community of editors, designers, artists, art, architecture, and design historians who through their collective energy and collaborative spirit over the years have inspired and sustained her own interest in the history of design and design history. She is very grateful to Connie Rhoton for all of her work in helping to prepare the manuscript. Most of all, she would like to thank her family for their tireless and unending support.

GENERAL INTRODUCTION

What *is* design history and what *should* it be? These are questions that every conscientious design historian should constantly pose, and many will acknowledge that the answers to each are not the same. To some extent, each text in this *Reader* can be seen as answer, and a sample of the debates surrounding such questions is provided in section 7. *The Design History Reader* employs inclusive definitions of design and of design history, which as a discipline is interested in all aspects of designed objects and images. To study design and its histories is to study processes of thinking, problem solving, drawing, talking, consulting and responding to a range of practical and aesthetic constraints to create – ideally – the most appropriate solution(s) under the given circumstances. Design history seeks to understand design in historical context, as conditioned by, and bearing evidence of, the time and place in which it was undertaken and produced. This approach is common to design histories that focus on objects from the distant and near past, as well those design histories that focus on contemporary design practices and are similarly contextualized.

The Design History Reader encompasses the history of design, the development of design history and contemporary issues in design history, relevant to design practice. While there are anthologies that address discrete aspects of design history such as interior design, or industrial design, and anthologies drawn from one stable, such as the various *Design Issues* readers and the *BLOCK* reader (see the Guide to Further Reading in section 7), *The Design History Reader* is distinguished by a concern for *all* fields of design history and a holistic approach to common debates. The authors brought together here are not all design historians, and by including them we do not propose to convert them to design historians. Rather, the range of authors shows how design history is multidisciplinary in its interests, methods and sources. In fact, it is impossible to represent the discipline of design history without including texts from adjacent disciplines. While a number of the texts selected for this *Reader* derive from other disciplines and fields, all of them have been chosen for their core contribution to, or use within, design history.

Is design history a discipline or a field? This issue is further explored in section 7, 'Foundations, Debates, Historiography, 1980–95'. We can turn to Clive Dilnot, who in 1984 thought it too early to claim disciplinary status for design history because it had not yet developed its own methodologies. In 1989, John A. Walker argued that design history was a discipline, as a way of beginning the textbook that elaborated his point. Walker lucidly distinguishes between design history, as an academic discipline, and the field of study, which is the history of design. Although the relationship between design history and design studies has been much debated, with some arguing that the former should be subsumed within the latter, the two fields have progressed side by side over several decades and inform one another in a positive manner. The first organization for design history was formed in 1977, when a group of sympathetic scholars came together at the annual conference of the British Association of Art Historians to form what became the Design History Society. However, it is not accurate to view design history as a field of art history, because it has developed in contradistinction from art history.

Recent conceptions of visual culture as a field are inadequate for the understanding of design, which is not merely visual but also material, tactile, temporal, experiential, appealing to more of our senses than sight alone. Design history might be seen as a field of cultural history, but design history is not *only* composed of those characteristics affiliated with cultural history. In addition to art history and cultural history, design history shares interests, methods and sources and literatures with business history, economic history, cultural studies, history of technology, material culture studies and so on. It is through its distinctive blend of interests, methods and sources that design history warrants disciplinary status, rather than being seen as a field of some larger discipline, as none of the potential contenders present themselves as an adequate catch-all into which an holistically conceived design history might be placed. The status of design history as a discipline is further supported by the health and growth of its various fields, including fashion history, craft history and interior design history. Design history is now more than thirty years old and any notion of pursuing a history of styles has been replaced by a more contextualized understanding of the role of design and designed objects within social and cultural history. The *Reader* demonstrates the importance of three concurrent concerns within the discipline: a concern for studies of designers and their production, a concern – informed by literary theory, cultural studies, gender studies, and economic and business history – for issues of consumption and a concern for processes of mediation. Much recent work examines the ways in which design is mediated to consumers by producers, marketers, advertisers, the media, taste experts and so on, reflecting the need for a reconsideration of the object as the defining unit of design historical analysis.

In the UK, design history has much of the infrastructure of a distinct discipline, such as validated degrees, a research culture and research degree students, and a scholarly society with an annual conference. The maturity of the discipline is indicated by the fact that design history has recently celebrated several big anniversaries: the UK's Design History Society was thirty years old in 2007. *The Journal of Design History* reached its twenty-first volume in 2008, just as The Bard Graduate Center for Studies in the Decorative Arts, Design, and Culture in New York turned fifteen. The *Scandinavian Journal of Design History* was launched in 1991, and vol. 15 appeared in 2005. Both the North American journal *Design Issues,* and the History of Design programme run by the Victoria and Albert Museum and Royal College of Art in London, celebrated their twenty-fifth anniversary in 2009. Just as significant, however, if not more so, are the smaller anniversaries that the discipline has been celebrating: the first of an annual series of meetings of the Design History Workshop Japan was held in 2002. In 2008, the sixth International Conference for Design History and Design Studies took place in Osaka. The US-based Design Studies Forum launched its journal, *Design and Culture* in 2009. *The Design History Reader* reflects both the maturity of the discipline and emergent currents of scholarship indicated by these activities.

The Design History Reader encompasses almost three-and-a-half centuries of the history of design. It begins with an account of a basket dating from 1676, and the earliest text in the book is Adam Smith's 'Of the Division of Labour' of 1775. Both appear in section 1, which explores the long eighteenth century as a point at which design and manufacture separated. Much of the material in the *Reader* has been published only recently and informs current issues for contemporary designers and design historians, such as gender, sustainable design and globalization. *The Design History Reader* not only documents what has been written within design history and adjacent fields; it aims to contribute to the further development of the discipline of design history.

This *Reader* reflects what design history *has* been, not what it *should* have been, both in terms of what has been published and where the audiences are. Design history has been dominated, until recently, by a relatively narrow definition of design. As a result, work in the discipline has dwelt on the period of industrialization, and the industrialized West. Consequently, one of the most pressing issues facing design history today is the need to globalize the discipline. This situation is reflected in the *Reader,* which bears evidence of the places where design history has been taught most extensively and strikes a balance between including the most influential texts and some of those that are needed to redress various imbalances in the discipline's coverage. Therefore, while the core texts reproduced here largely concern the UK, the US and Western Europe, the *Reader* closes by heralding future work in design history with its dedicated section 'Local/Regional/National/Global', on issues of globalizing design history. Section 12 also provides suggestions for further reading and points out the range of material in other sections of this book which extends beyond the UK/US focus. We would welcome the publication of another reader, on global design history. There is certainly enough material to fill such a book, but this is not that book. Design history has only recently woken up to the global imperative, and *The Design History Reader* reflects that fact.

DESIGN HISTORY IN TEXT

Design *as a process* is variously documented in letters, sketches and notes, plans, briefs, company records and writings by designers as well as – crucially – in the objects and images that result from this process. These form the objects of study for the design historian. *The Design History Reader* presents a wide variety of texts, including selections from book-length studies, scholarly research articles, exhibition catalogues and magazines, plus a selection of images. In this way, a variety of sources for reliable information about design history and exemplary instances of design historical work are referenced. 'The New Citroën' by Roland Barthes was one a series of pieces in which he demonstrated for the readers of literary magazine *Les Lettres Nouvelles*, that mass culture was worthy of analysis (1954–7). Examples of design journalism in the *Reader* include Reyner Banham's 'All that Glitters is not Stainless' and Steven Heller's 'Advertising, Mother of Graphic Design'. *The Green Consumer Supermarket Guide* is consumer guidance, instructional literature with a campaigning zeal, which intends to inform and persuade. Thomas Hine's *Populuxe* is a popular history of popular culture. The remainder of the texts in the *Reader* fall into two main groups: primary – such as the writings of designers and design reformers – and secondary, in the form of key works of design history and associated disciplines.

Primary sources are sometimes defined as unpublished, archival sources, but in fact *The Design History Reader* contains no previously unpublished sources. Here, the important distinction is made between sources that seek to understand the present and those that seek to understand the past. For example, Adam Smith's 1776 text was intended by its author to explain the present situation in which he and his readers found themselves. Since Smith's text was published, it has been used as a historical source but Smith did not have the benefit of hindsight and therefore his writing sets up different expectations from those relating to secondary material. Primary sources are *of* the past, and as such they are extremely useful in understanding the past, which helps to explain their prevalence in Part I of this *Reader*. Other examples of primary sources in *The Design History Reader* include the texts by Semper, Ruskin, Morris, Wright, Loos, Muthesius and van de Velde, Banham, Venturi, Scott-Brown and Izenour, Baudrillard, Buckminster Fuller, Packard, Papanek, Marx, Veblen, Barthes and Benjamin. Some secondary sources achieve the status of primary sources in that they gather their own histories, which must be negotiated by current readers. An example is Pevsner's *Pioneers of Modern Design* (1936, revised 1949, 1975). It is crucial to recognize that different texts have different histories, function differently and must be read with an awareness of their different status.

Finally, there is another distinction to be made between the texts as they are included here and their original forms. The majority of the texts presented here were previously published in longer versions. Material cut from the texts is indicated with an ellipsis […]. In a very limited number of instances, where only a word or two has been cut from the original, the ellipsis has been omitted in order to avoid impairing the clarity of the reading experience.

THE BOOK'S STRUCTURE AND ALTERNATIVE READING ROUTES

The Design History Reader accepts John A. Walker's distinction between the history of design (what happened in the past, the subject of study) and design history (the discipline within which study takes place) and is structured into two parts accordingly. Part I is loosely chronological, and provides texts that chart histories of Western design over the last 300 years. Part II adopts a thematic approach to work in design history during the twentieth and twenty-first centuries. This arrangement renders the *Reader* suitable both for historical survey courses and methods courses. The extracts are generally reproduced in chronological order within the sections. However, we do not intend that the parts of the book should be definitive or isolated; rather we hope that themes will be traced across the parts and constituent sections.

The Design History Reader employs a range of strategies for learning about design history without simply reproducing a linear understanding of the development of the subject. In addition to the two parts, which provide both chronological and thematic arrangements, we have selected texts that contribute to knowledge and understanding of the past *and* to the methods and practice of design history. Each part and each section has an introduction to explain thematic connections, juxtapositions and debates among and between the extracts. It offers a modulated reading experience through the use of both primary and secondary sources. Finally there is an index for cross-referencing.

We have not included sections grouped by medium, such as graphic design history, fashion history and so on, although each of these fields is represented in the *Reader*. Treatments of graphic design history in the *Reader* include: Morris's 'The Ideal Book'; 'Deconstruction and Graphic Design' by Lupton and Miller; Benjamin's 'The Work of Art in the Age of Mechanical Reproduction'; Baudrillard's 'The Ecstasy of Communication'; Heller's 'Advertising, Mother of Graphic Design'; '"From Baby's First Bath:" Kaō Soap and Modern Japanese Commercial Design', by Weisenfeld and 'Swoosh Identity: Recontextualizations in Haiti and Romania' by Bick and Chiper. The latter could equally inform an examination of fashion, alongside Linthicum's 'Integrative Practice: Oral History, Dress and Disability Studies', Bakare-Yusuf's 'Fabricating Identities: Survival and the Imagination in Jamaican Dancehall Culture', Breward's *The Hidden Consumer: Masculinities, Fashion and City Life 1860–1914* (1999) and Gregson and Crewe's 'Redefining Rubbish: Commodity Disposal and Sourcing' from their book *Second-Hand Cultures*.

The significance of furniture is examined in a variety of ways in the *Reader*, as shown by a comparison of Denney's 'Utility Furniture and the Myth of Utility, 1943–1948'; Hine's *Populuxe*; 'The Most Cherished Objects in the Home' by Csikszentmihaly and Rochberg-Halton; 'Faith, Form and Finish: Shaker Furniture in Context' by Burks; Kirkham's 'Humanizing Modernism: the Crafts, "Functioning Decoration," and the Eameses', Crowley's 'Finding Poland in the Margins: the Case of the Zakopane Style' and Avery's 'Furniture Design and Colonialism: Negotiating Relationships between Britain and Australia, 1880–1901'.

While the crafts merit their own reader (Glenn Adamson, *The Craft Reader,* Oxford: Berg, 2009), this book contains several instructive examples of craft analysis: the whole of section 1 is of interest in terms of its examination of production methods and the watershed of industrialization in the long eighteenth century, and especially Laurel Thatcher Ulrich's analysis of 'An Indian Basket, Providence, Rhode Island, 1676' and Darron Dean's similarly focussed account of 'A Slipware Dish by Samuel Malkin: an Analysis of Vernacular Design,' which contrasts with another study of ceramics in that section, Mary Guyatt's study of the Wedgwood Slave Medallion. The writings of John Ruskin and William Morris are, of course, central to understanding the aims of the Arts and Crafts Movement, while also informing broader discussions about the meaning and role of crafts in industrial society. Both authors are represented here in section 2, 'Design Reform 1820–1910'.

Interesting comparisons related to the gender of automotive cultures are raised by the juxtaposition of Dick Hebdige's 'Object as Image: the Italian Scooter Cycle' (1981), Bengry-Howell and Griffin's 'Self-Made Motormen: The Material Construction of Working-Class Masculine Identities through Car Modification' (2007) and van Eeden's 'Land Rover and Colonial-Style Adventure' (2006), while each sits in contrast to Barthes's 'The New Citroën' (1957) and Packard's concerns expressed in 'How to Outmode a $4,000 Vehicle in Two Years' (1960).

Alternative pathways through the book are found in the section introductions and guides to further reading: the introduction to Part II outlines texts on domesticity in the *Reader*, and the guide to further reading for section 12 suggests a route around the *Reader* exploring Western Europe.

WHO IS *THE DESIGN HISTORY READER* FOR?

The range of texts and the editorial matter in this book is designed for students coming to design history for the first time – that is first and second year students of design history and design practice. It is intended to be a core resource for courses that survey the history of design, which students of art, design and media disciplines encounter in their contextual studies, just as much as students of design history and histories of art encompassing a design historical interest. It is also intended as a resource in the teaching of design historiography, the history of design history and research methods training for design historians at both undergraduate and postgraduate levels. It therefore engages students of cultural studies, the sociology of culture, material culture studies and art history, in addition to design history. The book has further uses for teachers and scholars, in terms of the way it considers the definition, practice, historiography and methodology of design history. This book will contextualize design and its histories for students of all subjects. This is for you.

PART I

HISTORIES

INTRODUCTION

Rebecca Houze

The first part of the *Reader* takes as its point of departure John Walker's understanding of 'the history of design' as the material from which design history is written – that is, the fabricated, constructed, produced, planned and envisioned objects and images of the past and the institutions, communities, and frameworks from which they emerged. In its broadest definition 'history of design' constitutes a vast realm of human activity. It is the discipline of 'design history' that seeks to organize and understand this rich material.

We have organized Part I chronologically beginning with the long eighteenth century as a point at which design and manufacture separated. The subject of our first selection, an Algonquin basket from 1676, will certainly appear to some as an odd example of 'design'. It was not produced by industrial means and we do not know whether its construction was planned in any way. It was described by its collectors as a spontaneous production, and has been valued over the centuries for its evocation of a special relationship between white settlers and indigenous peoples in seventeenth-century North America, as much as for the materials and techniques of its woven fabrication. This little basket, as we see in Ulrich's analysis, is rich material indeed, laden with unexpected meaning.

Three of the authors in Section 1, Laurel Thatcher Ulrich, Darron Dean, and Mary Guyatt, begin by examining a single object. What does it look like? What is the shape, texture, colour? How was it made? What was it used for? And by whom? Who decided to preserve it? Why? What does this tell us about the social, political and cultural contexts from which the object emerged? The objects themselves, and our curiosity about them, mobilize broader and more complex issues such as the mechanism of production and consumption, discussed in that same section by Adam Smith and John Styles. Mary Guyatt's reading of the Wedgwood Slave Medallion points ahead to post-colonial discourse. Ideas flow between Part I and Part II of the *Reader*. Whereas 'Consumption' is given a section of its own in Part II, issues of identity, race, and colonialism are treated in various ways throughout the *Reader*, for example, by Bibi Bakare-Yusuf, in her examination of Jamaican dancehall culture in Section 5, and by Jeanne van Eeden, in her critique of racist modes of advertising by Land Rover in South Africa in Section 12.

The uneasy relationship between 'craft' and 'design', between ethnographic object and accoutrement of culture, revealed throughout Section 1, foreshadows the problems that emerge in Section 2, Design Reform 1820–1910, when critiques of industry by Gottfried Semper, John Ruskin and William Morris lay the groundwork for the innovative and experimental turn of the twentieth century that would come to be known as 'Modernism' but which we have presented as modern*isms* in order to draw attention to the plurality of movements, productions and ideologies of that period, which cannot be uniformly categorized. The juxtaposition of design historian John Heskett's reading of American responses to industrialization with the poetic exuberance of architect Frank Lloyd Wright demonstrates that modernist responses to industry were ambivalent and often contradictory.

Debora Silverman, Nancy Troy and Christopher Breward, although represented in different sections of the *Reader*, each demonstrate how ambivalences towards commerce and industry compelled designers, such as Eugène Gaillard, Henry van de Velde and Charles Edouard Jeanneret, as well as consumers in the vein of Oscar Wilde, to engage with complex styles of interior furnishings and dress at the turn of the twentieth century. The embrace of decoration and pleasure by those designers and consumers offers a sharp contrast to Nikolaus Pevsner's picture of modernism, which was inspired by the ascetic functionalism of Adolf Loos, Hermann Muthesius, and the teachers and students of the Bauhaus. The championing of the International Style by Pevsner and others in the first half of the twentieth century has made it difficult to reconcile the various strains and tendencies of the period – a problem that Paul Greenhalgh addresses in his essay for that section. More experimental and decorative modes of modernism that sought to merge art and industry are noted in the selections by Gillian Naylor, who traces the work of Laszlo Moholy-Nagy at the Bauhaus, and Nicolas Maffei, who offers a new reading of American 'streamlined' design of the 1930s.

Section 4, which examines design in the period surrounding the Second World War, offers provocative connections to other areas of the *Reader* as well. The Utility furniture investigated by Matthew Denney might be seen as a precursor to ecologically and environmentally responsible purchasing practices, such as those advocated in *The Green Consumer Supermarket Guide*. Becky Conekin's study of the futuristic models displayed at the Festival of Britain invites us to think critically about the processes of mediation that are explored in greater detail in Section 11.

The section on postmodern*isms* – also plural – deals primarily with tendencies and movements of the 1980s and 1990s, with its roots in 1970s literary theory, but its celebration of popular culture reaches further back in time to converse with the work of Reyner Banham in the 1960s and the mid-century love of consumption identified by Thomas Hine as 'Populuxe'. Many of the issues raised in this section are relevant to the readings in Part II of the *Reader*. Gert Selle's theory of German popular design in the 1980s, for example could be compared to the many analyses of national identity in Section 4, to Pierre Bourdieu's ethnographic study of the French middle-class consumer in the 1960s and 1970s in Section 10, and to David Crowley's case study of early twentieth-century Polish design in Section 12. Postmodernism has been a much-debated concept in critiques of design over the years and its complexity can be seen in the different attitudes expressed, for example, by Robert Venturi, Denise Scott-Brown, and Steven Izenour, and Jean Baudrillard, reproduced in Section 5. But 'postmodernism' has been an especially useful tool for pointing out the ruptures within 'modernism'. The period dealt with in section 6, Sustainable Futures, one might argue, preceded postmodernism, with its concern for environmental and consumer responsibility that emerged in writings of Buckminster Fuller, Vance Packard, and Victor Papanek in the 1960s and 1970s. We have positioned it at the end of Part I, however, because its project is ongoing, and all the more relevant today.

SECTION 1

New Designers, 1676–1820

INTRODUCTION

Grace Lees-Maffei

This opening section of *The Design History Reader* invites reflection on definitions of design and the role of the designer, within the context of industrialization. Much consideration has been given by design historians, art historians, economic historians and others, to identifying a point in history at which design and manufacture separated. Arguably the search for such a moment is fruitless when there have always been instances in which design and manufacture have existed separately: the age-old practice of copying, for example, involves little design and much manufacture, and the sketching of plans never realized involves design to the exclusion of manufacture. Nevertheless, design historians have tended to regard processes of industrialization as significant for providing the conditions necessary for the emergence of a distinct practice of design. The shift from a society in which goods were made by the people who devised their form and function to a society in which design was a discrete practice performed by a specialist prior to manufacture, has preoccupied design historians. The design of proto-industrial, industrial and post-industrial society has formed the primary object of study within design history, including not only machine-made goods, but also the hand-crafted, the small scale, the pre-industrial methods of production. These have persisted throughout industrialization to form highly significant objects of study in the post-industrial age.

The first extract is from a richly detailed analysis by American historian Laurel Thatcher Ulrich of 'An Indian Basket, Providence, Rhode Island, 1676'. Ulrich demonstrates how much archival research can tell us about an individual, but representative, object, as she uses the basket to explore relations between Native Americans and English settlers in seventeenth-century New England. As she explains:

Baskets are hard to find in early records because they resisted commodification. As manufactured products they were less valuable to the English than furs and skins, nor were the materials of which they were made of particular interest to colonists. Where Indian women found abundant fibres for weaving, the English saw only dark forests, waste fields, and dismal swamps. But baskets were there, and they, like blankets, were essential props in the unfolding events that led to misunderstanding and war.

While each basket refers to others of its type, the pattern was devised by the person who made it, and therefore the object under scrutiny here represents pre-industrial production within a particularly contested context.

Next, British design historian Darron Dean uses a slipware dish by Samuel Malkin to broaden definitions of 'vernacular' design to encompass a range of production, marketing and consumption practices beyond purely local materials and methods. Section 1 therefore begins with two extracts that explore examples of localized design and production as a negotiated and complex phenomenon, feeling the effects of modernity spearheaded in Britain and the US. Indeed, the UK was the first country to industrialize with rapid movement among the expanding population from the rural areas of agricultural production to industrial manufacture in the cities.

The methods of manufacture employed by Malkin vary quite considerably from those examined in 1776 by contemporary thinker, Adam Smith. The juxtaposition of extracts 2 and 3 dramatizes something of the effects of industrialization. Smith's importance as a commentator on his period is exemplified by the fact that his name recurs in the other texts in this section: Ulrich refers to his distinction between civilized and uncivilized economies and British curator Mary Guyatt discusses Smith's anti slavery sentiments as representative of an important strain of discourse for understanding Wedgwood's slave medallion. Smith's account of the ramifications of the division of labour, extracted here, helps us to understand the context in which design, too, was detached from other aspects of production.

Section 1 goes on to examine the mutually dependent phenomena of the industrial 'revolution' – although such a term is hardly appropriate any longer as a description of a process which historians have shown to have been attenuated over a long period of time – and the development of consumer society. Guyatt continues the interest in consumption demonstrated by Dean's text in this section, and explores issues of gender raised by Ulrich. Wedgwood has received a great deal of attention from design historians and economic historians for the way in which he harnessed the larger scale of production enabled by industrialization, to develop a name for his work. The carefully recorded technical experiments through which Wedgwood developed new ceramic techniques and finishes such as Jasperware are as significant, design historically, as his use of marketing methods to promote what would now be called a designer brand. Guyatt shows how the ceramicist exploited his name, his technical skill, his market and his influence, to create an object through which political ideas could be communicated in a fashionable way. As an exemplar of what Guyatt terms 'the now much-debated "conflict" between philanthropy and commerce', Wedgwood's medallion can be seen as a forerunner of the slogan t-shirt, which can be harnessed to political ends.

In the closing text, British historian John Styles questions the application of terms such as 'mass production', 'standardization' and 'consumer revolution' to the development of design in the eighteenth century. Styles's account helps us to understand what was significant and distinctive about eighteenth century design and it forms a precursor to the examination of nineteenth-century debates about design, culture and technological developments in section two, when design was regarded by some as the saviour of a society split apart by industrialization. Like Dean, Styles shows that design during this period was not always localized; and a web of communication channels and travel circulated ideas across the UK.

The blend of texts presented here has been chosen to represent debates of the period and more recent ones. Three of the five texts are object analyses; they focus on one object in order to explore wider themes. With the exception of the primary text from Smith, the other texts have a revisionist emphasis and seek to change the record in relation to the various issues they engage.

The 250-year period from the production of an Indian basket in Rhode Island to the end of what historians term 'the long eighteenth century' (1680 to 1820) was one of unprecedented social change. During that time, the motives, methods and meanings of design were continually developing in ways that remind us how ambiguous is the term 'progress', as subsequent generations of design reformers made clear.

1

AN INDIAN BASKET, PROVIDENCE, RHODE ISLAND, 1676

Laurel Thatcher Ulrich (2001)

Figure 1. Wampanoag/Algonkian. Basket. Field's Point, RI. C.1676. Bark. RHI X3 2660. Courtesy of the Rhode Island Historical Society.

The basket is four and a half inches high and four inches in diameter, about the size of a large tomato can, though smaller at the top than the bottom. When new it could have held a generous pound of meal or beans or twenty-four fathoms of wampum. Now light leaks through a weft ravaged by time and insects. The basket holds its shape through hundreds of invisible mends, the unseen art of a conservation lab. Tiny twists of rice paper

bonded with unpronounceable adhesives like polyvinyl acetate and polymethyl methacrylate fill gaps in a fragile fabric strengthened by multiple infusions of soluble nylon in ethyl alcohol. Would the basket be as precious without its story?

It came to the Rhode Island Historical Society in 1842 with a label carefully written by the donor:

> This little basket, was given by a squaw, a native of the forest, to Dinah Fenner, wife of Major Thomas Fenner, who fought in Churche's Wars; then living in a garrison in Providence, now Cranston, R.I. The squaw went into the garrison; Mrs. Fenner gave her some milk to drink, she went out by the side of a river, peeled the inner bark from the Wikup tree, sat down under the tree, drew the shreds out of her blanket, mingled them with the bark, wrought this little basket, took it to the garrison and presented it to Mrs. Fenner. Mrs. Fenner gave it to her daughter, Freelove, wife of Samuel Westcoat, Mrs. Westcoat gave it to her granddaughter, Wait Field, wife of William Field at Field's Point, Mrs. Field gave it to her daughter, Sarah. Sarah left it to her sister, Elenor, who now presents it to the Historical Society of Rhode Island. (Field's Point, September, 1842)[1]

The reference to 'Churche's Wars' led nineteenth-century antiquaries to date the basket to 1676, the year Captain Benjamin Church of Little Compton, Rhode Island, led New England troops in victory over the Wampanoag leader Metacomet, or King Philip. No one since has doubted the attribution.[2] Displayed in the late nineteenth century alongside other relics of Rhode Island's first century, the basket quieted a troubling history of frontier conflict. Exhibited today as an icon of native art, it fulfills much the same purpose, shifting attention from the violence of the late seventeenth century to our own generation's hopes for multiculturalism.[3]

The details in Field's description line up like clues in a mystery: a garrison, milk, a Wikup tree, shreds from a blanket, and those evocative names – Dinah, Freelove, Wait. There was a Dinah Fenner who lived in Rhode Island in 1676, though in that year her name was Dinah Borden, and she was only eleven years old. She did eventually marry Thomas Fenner, a man who helped to defend Providence in King Philip's War, and they did have a daughter named Freelove who had a granddaughter named Wait. Yet there is much in the story that remains puzzling. If the basket was made by 'a native of the forest,' why would she have come to an enemy garrison in time of war seeking milk, a food repulsive to a people known today to be lactose intolerant? Was she a refugee? So desperately hungry she was willing to accept any food offered? If so, how does one explain the basket? The exposed warp is indeed rough, but the twined pattern is intricate and artful. Could its maker have stripped and soaked fibers from the inner bark of a tree, gathered husks from an abandoned field, then patiently sat on the bank of a river weaving in a time and place where even friendly Indians were in danger? That hardly seems likely, yet laboratory analysis tells us there are fragments of red and blue wool still clinging to the interior of the basket.[4] Could they have come from an English blanket?

[…]

The English who came to the coast of what is now New England in the early 1600s were not all alike. Some came to fish, some to pray, and among those who prayed there were enough differences to keep them squabbling and sometimes hounding one another from colony to colony for generations. The people they found here also differed. Although scholars sometimes refer to them collectively as Algonkians, they spoke different dialects, inhabited different river basins, and assigned a bewildering array of names to one another. In terms of textile history, however, Englishmen and Algonkians differed more from each other than they did among themselves. The English came from a wool-producing country proud of its blankets. Algonkians were renowned for their basketry.[5]

Archaeological sites on coastal New England are littered with lead seals once attached to bolts of fabric. As the Englishman Richard Hakluyt expressed it in a 1584 treatise, the second purpose of colonization, after advancing the 'kingedome of Christe' was the vending 'of the masse of our cloths and other commodities.' The English did that with a vengeance.[6] Yet the first Englishmen to visit North America were fascinated with the unfamiliar fabrics they found in Indian villages. Among the Algonkians, textile production was women's work. Men worked in stone, metal, and wood, producing impressive tobacco pipes, knot dishes, pendants, and other ornaments. Women made netted, twined, sewn, and plaited textiles to cover their houses, dry corn, trap fish, store provisions, carry produce, and line graves. In the words of one English observer, they made baskets of 'rushes, some of bents; others of maize husks; others, of a kind of silk grass; others of a kind of wild hemp; and some of barks of trees, many of them, very neat and artificial, with the portraitures of birds, beasts, fishes, and flowers, upon them in colours.' Men hunted and cared for tobacco fields. Women planted, hoed, and harvested food crops, storing them in containers of their own manufacture. Rhode Island's Roger Williams described heaps of maize 'of twelve, fifteene, or twentie bushells a heap' drying on woven mats by day, covered with tarps of basketry at night.[7]

[...]

Although Europeans had their own basketry traditions, basketry was far more varied among the Algonkians. Thomas Morton wrote of mats made by stitching together long strips of what the English called 'sedge' with 'needles made of the splinter bones of a Cranes legge, with threeds, made of their Indian hempe.' In preparation for netting or weaving, women spun fine fibers between their fingers or across their thighs. William Wood said that Indian cordage was 'so even, soft, and smooth that it looks more like silk than hemp.' Other writers admired the 'curious Coats' or mantles of turkey feathers that women wove together 'with twine of their owne makinge, very prittily.' John Josselyn, who spent much of his time in northern New England, described 'Delicate sweet dishes ... of Birch-Bark sowed with threads drawn from Spruce and white Cedar-Roots, and garnished on the outside with flourisht works, and on the brims with glistering quills taken from the Porcupine, and dyed, some black, others red.'[8] Wigwams were also a form of basketry. Wigwams moved because work moved. Coastal groups cultivated fields of maize, beans, squash, and tobacco in summer, moving to warm interior valleys in winter where game and fuel were more plentiful.

[...]

Nothing survives that can fully convey the complexity of seventeenth-century Algonkian textiles, but Dinah Fenner's basket read alongside archaeological fragments helps us to understand some of the techniques and materials used. The warp is of bark, the wefts of wool and of a flatter material that may have been cornhusk. The construction is complex. The weaver began with a plaited base, using three strands of bark for each warp, then moved to simple twining and finally to a technique called 'wrapped twining' in which two wefts, one active and one passive, intersect the warp. By changing the color as she wrapped,

she produced the pattern.[9] The technical details are important because they locate the basket in an ancient textile tradition. Shreds of twining very similar to that in Dinah's basket have been found in northern Vermont in archaeological sites dating from the Early Woodland period (1000–100 B.C.). One fragment even revealed a faint chevron created by weaving animal hair in two colors. Except for the wool in its weft, Dinah's basket could have been made a thousand years before the first European excursion to North America. It only hints at the variety of early textiles. [...]

Archaeological evidence documents the similarities and differences between European and indigenous fabrics. At a Wampanoag site on the west side of Narragansett Bay, archaeologists found sixty-six fragments of native basketry alongside seventy-three relics of European cloth. The European fabrics ranged from bits of a white wool blanket with end stripes of red, blue-green, and brown to a long coil of a trimming called 'galloon' woven in yellow silk with twists of silver thread. The Algonkian textiles included ordinary matting as well as fabrics too complex and individual for an English loom – a belt of glass beads woven with sinew, a wampum collar skillfully shaped to fit the curve of a neck, and fragments of matting that incorporated as many as three techniques in a single swatch.[10]

[...]

What was different about the two sets of textiles was not their structural sophistication or the abilities of their makers, but their mode of production. In the Middle Ages, Europeans had perfected a method of producing large quantities of fairly simple fabrics through the use of spinning wheels and looms. Equally important were changes made in the early modern era in the division of labor. English fabrics traded in North America were made in an economy that divided work into many parts. A hierarchy of workers performed a small set of tasks over and over again, middlemen in one part of the kingdom selling wool, spun yarn, or undyed cloth to intermediaries in other towns who passed them along a production chain that stretched from one end of the British Isles to another and across the Atlantic to America.

[...]

This was the division of labor Adam Smith theorized nearly a century later in *The Wealth of Nations* but the general direction of change had been established much earlier. Seventeenth-century writers would have understood Smith's contrast between civilized and uncivilized economies. Hence, an industrious peasant in an advanced society was more wealthy than an 'African king' who was the absolute master of 'ten thousand naked savages.'[11] American Indians were among the earliest models for the European notion of the 'naked savage.' An icon of a man dressed only in leaves was impressed in wax on the earliest official documents of the Massachusetts Bay Colony. Although the details of clothing and even the sex of the Indian on the colony's seal changed over time, most versions included the plaintive cry 'Come over and help us,' an adaptation of a passage in the Book of Acts describing the apostle Paul's vision of a man praying, 'Come over into Macedonia, and help us.' In the English view, New World 'savages' needed both spiritual and material clothing. Christianity and good English cloth came together.[12]

[...]

When Daniel Gookin wrote that the 'Indians'' clothing in former times was of the same matter as Adam's was,' he wasn't referring to the nakedness of the first couple or to the aprons of fig leaves they constructed for themselves but to the 'coats of skins' God gave them when he banished them from the Garden of Eden.[13] The English wanted these coats. The makers of high-style hats eagerly sought American beaver since it was the only fiber that when felted was both strong and supple enough to sustain its shape when wet. Thomas

Morton reported that in the 1630s beaver sold for ten shillings a pound. Presumably that was the price given to the English broker, not the Algonkian supplier, but at ten shillings, a single pound of beaver would have purchased two and a half pounds of broadcloth, the most expensive of the English fabrics. Algonkians gave up Adam's clothing not because it was inferior to English cloth but because it had become too valuable to wear. The half-naked Indian on the Massachusetts seal obscures the interconnectedness of Adam's and Adam Smith's clothing.[14]

[...]

While it is more dramatic to think of two women practicing peace in the midst of war, it is more credible to imagine Dinah Fenner's basket as an artifact in a less visible but far more enduring stream of trade, one that stretches backward to the 'gifts' of fish and berries William Wood wrote about in the 1620s and forward to the Indian basket-makers who peddled their wares all over New England in the late eighteenth century. There is nothing qualitatively different between the exchange Eleanor Field described and the exchange the Maine midwife Martha Ballard wrote about in 1809 when she described a 'little indien girl' who came to her house several times, bringing the gift of a basket and receiving potatoes in return. The baskets, however, changed. By the middle of the eighteenth century, twined basketry declined as Algonkian families began to manufacture and sell woodsplint baskets, brooms, ax handles, and other forest products adapted to English tastes. During this transition, some basket makers surely continued to work in more traditional forms, making twined baskets for their own use or for gift-giving.[15]

[...]

The Rhode Island Historical Society began adding Indian relics to its collections in 1835.

It accessioned, among other things, several sets of arrowheads, an 'original deed from King Philip,' a 'String of Beads washed out from an Indian Grave' in Tiverton, and 'Indian remains dug up on the Rail Road near the SW corner of the State,' including a thigh bone and hair.[16] The registrar neatly wrote the nature of each acquisition on the right side of the page and the name of each donor in the ruled column to the left. But when he came to Eleanor Field's contribution, he left the name column blank. She was the society's first female donor, or at least the first woman to contribute something without the cover of a husband's name. He copied her description of the basket with its coy allusion to herself but did not identify her further. Later, in pencil, another person wrote 'Eleanor Field' in the margin, drawing a small hand with a finger pointing to the right.[17]

NOTES

Reproduced from Thatcher Ulrich, L., *The Age of Homespun: Objects and Stories in the Creation of an American Myth*, New York: Knopf, 2001, pp. 41–74. Copyright © 2001 by Laurel Thatcher Ulrich. Used by permission of Alfred A. Knopf, a division of Random House, Inc.

1. Basket with associated manuscript dated Field's Point, 1842, Rhode Island Historical Society, Providence, 1842.2.1; Dennis V. Piechota, Conservation Report, 30 Sept. 1977, Curatorial Files, Rhode Island Historical Society. The story of the basket's origins has been published repeatedly and uncritically. See H. M. Chapin, 'Indian Implements Found in Rhode Island,' *Rhode Island Historical Society Collections* 18 (1925): 23–25; Charles Willoughby, *Antiquities of the New England Indians* (Cambridge, Mass.: Peabody Museum, 1935), 251, 252, figure 135; Jonathan L. Fairbanks and Robert F. Trent, eds., *New England Begins: The Seventeenth Century* (Boston: Museum of Fine Arts, 1982), 1:77, figure 68; Sarah Peabody Turnbaugh and William A. Turnbaugh, *Indian Baskets* (West Chester, Pa.: Shiffer, 1986), 121.

2. Russell Bourne, *The Red King's Rebellion: Racial Politics in New England 1675–1678* (New York: Oxford Univ. Press, 1990), 38–39, finds in Field's story evidence that 'fundamentally important dramas of reconciliation went on among the peoples' even as the war 'was staggering toward a hateful, mutually ruinous halt.'

3. Ibid., 39. A description of an early exhibit is in *Rhode Island Historical Society Museum Illustrating the History of the State* (Providence, 1916), 5–6.

4. Willoughby, *Antiquities*, 254; Piechota, Conservation Report; Cameron McDonald, a University of Connecticut archaeology student, personal communication, 30 July 1997.

5. Despite their seeming differences, both baskets and blankets are textiles. Both have warps and wefts, vertical and horizontal elements that intersect to form a continuous surface. I. Emery, *The Primary Structures of Fabrics: An Illustrated Classification* (Washington, D.C.: Textile Museum, 1966), 210; Turnbaugh and Turnbaugh, *Indian Baskets*, 70; James B. Petersen, 'The Study of Native Fiber Industries from Eastern North America: Resume and Prospect,' in *A Most Indispensable Art: Native Fiber Industries from Eastern North America*, ed. James B. Petersen (Knoxville: Univ. of Tennessee Press, 1996), 8–9. Emery divides fabrics into two primary groups, those that are felted (pressed or matted into coherence) and those that are produced by the interworking of previously prepared elements. Among the latter, one large group is composed of 'two-or-more-sets-of-element structures' in which 'a transverse set (the weft)' is inter-worked with 'a longtitudinal set (the warp)' (17, 27). Blankets and many baskets fit the latter category.

6. E. Lipson, *The History of the Woollen and Worsted Industries* (London: Cass, 1965), 102–3; Francis Jennings, *The Invasion of America: Indians, Colonialism, and the Cant of Conquest* (Chapel Hill: Univ. of North Carolina Press, 1975), 98; Leon E. Cranmar, *Cushnoc: The*

History and Archaeology of Plymouth Colony Traders on the Kennebec (Augusta, Maine: Maine Historic Preservation Commission, 1990), 97–98; Christina B. Johannsen, 'European Trade Goods and Wampanoag Culture in the Seventeenth Century,' in *Burr's Hill: A Seventeenth-Century Wampanoag Burial Ground in Warren, Rhode Island*, ed. Susan Gibson, (Providence: Haffenreffer Museum of Anthropology, Brown University, 1980), 30; D. C. Coleman, 'Textile Growth,' in *Textile History and Economic History*, ed. N. B. Harte and K. G. Pouting (Manchester, U.K.: Manchester Univ. Press, 1973), 1–12.

7. Roger Williams, 'A Key into the Language of America' (1643), repr. *Rhode Island Historical Society Collections I* (1827): 91, 93; Daniel Gookin, 'Historical Collections of the Indians in New England,' in *Collections of the Massachusetts Historical Society for the Year 1792* (Boston, 1806), 151.

8. Thomas Morton, *New English Canaan* (New York and Amsterdam: Da Capo, 1969; facsimile of Amsterdam, 1637) 25, 28–29; William Wood, *New England's Prospect*, ed. Alden T. Vaughan (Amherts: Univ. of Massachusetts Press, 1977) 108; John Josselyn, *Colonial Traveler: A Critical Edition of Two Voyages to New-England*, ed. Paul J. Lindholdt (Hanover, N.H., and London: Univ. Press of New England, 1988), 101–2, 93; Gookin, 'Indians in New England,' 152; Williams, 'Key,' 107. Williams said that their old men made the turkey feather mantles, which were 'as velvet with us.'

9. Turnbaugh and Turnbaugh, *Indian Baskets*, figures 4, 76, and Joanne Segal Brandford to Sarah Peabody Turnbaugh, 1974, copy provided by Turnbaugh.

10. William Scranton Simmons, *Cautantowwit's House: An Indian Burial Ground on the Island of Conanicut in Narragansett Bay* (Providence: Brown Univ. Press, 1970), 87, 81, 97, 101, 44; Paul Robinson and Gail Gustafson, 'Partially Disturbed Seventeenth-Century Indian Burial Ground in Rhode Island: Recovery, Preliminary Analysis, and Protection,' *Bulletin of the Archaeological Society of Connecticut* 45 (1982): 41–50; Paul A. Robinson, Marc A. Kelley, and Patricia E. Rubertone, 'Preliminary Biocultural Interpretations from a Seventeenth-Century Narraganset Indian Cemetery in Rhode Island,' in *Cultures in Contact*, ed. William W. Fitzhugh (Washington, D.C., and London: Smithsonian Institution Press, 1985), 107–30; Eric Kerridge, *Textile Manufactures in Early Modern England* (Manchester, U.K.: Manchester Univ. Press, 1985), 24; Phyllis Dillon, 'Trade Fabrics,' in *Burr's Hill*, ed. Gibson, 104 and figures 99, 105; Gibson, ed., *Burr's Hill*, catalog entries for accession numbers MAI 8/5237b, MAI 8/5234a, MAI 8/5209; MAI 8/5215, 142, 158, 160.

11. Adam Smith, *The Wealth of Nations* (1776; repr. London: Penguin, 1986), 104–5, 112–17. On the relation of Smith's ideas to the economic thought of New England Puritans, see Stephen Inner, *Creating the Commonwealth: the Economic Culture of Puritan New England* (New York and London: Norton, 1995) 39–63.

12. Acts 16:9; Matt B. Jones, 'The Early Massachusetts-Bay Colony Seals,' *American Antiquarian Society Proceedings*, 44 (1934) 13–44; John D. Cushing, 'A Note Concerning the Massachusetts-Bay Colony Seal,' *American Antiquarian Society Proceedings* 76 (1976) part 1, 171–77; William S. Simmons, 'The Earliest Prints and Paintings of New England Indians,' *Rhode Island History* 41 (1982): 75–76; Karen Ordahl Kupperman, 'Presentment of Civility: English Reading of American Self-Presentation in the Early Years of Colonization,' *William and Mary Quarterly*, 3d ser., 54 (1997): 199–204; Jill Lepore, *The Name of War: King Philip's War and the Origins of American Identity* (New York: Knopf, 1998), xvi–xvii, 79–83; Neal Salisbury, 'Introduction: Mary Rowlandson and Her Removes,' in *Mary Rowlandson, The Sovereignty and Goodness of God, Together with the Faithfulness of His Promises Displayed*

(Boston: Bedford, 1997), 20; Morton, *New English Canaan*, 29, 30; Williams, 'Key,' 106, 107.

13. Gookin, 'Indians in New England,' 152; Genesis 3:7, 21.

14. Morton, *New English Canaan*, 78; *Plymouth Colony Records*, C. H. Simmons, Jr. (Camden, Maine: Picton Press, 1996), 1:27, 59, 61, 69, 78. In this computation, I assumed that an average broadcloth would weigh twenty ounces per yard. The best English hats, called 'beavers' or 'casters,' sold for from thirteen to twenty shillings in late-seventeenth-century Massachusetts. In the same accounts, blankets cost from three to ten shillings. Elspeth M. Veale, *The English Fur Trade in the Later Middle Ages* (Oxford: Clarendon, 1966), 175–76, 147. Kerridge, *Textile Manufactures*, 134, 138, 65; Florence M. Montgomery, *Textiles in America 1650–1870* (New York: Norton, 1984), 160; Emery, *Primary Structures of Fabrics*, 22; George Francis Dow, *Everyday Life in the Massachusetts Bay Colony* (1935; repr., New York: Dover, 1988), 5–6, 60–61; *John Josselyn*, 14; Thomas Willett Inventory, 25 Nov. 1674, typescript, Plimoth Plantation, Massachusetts.

15. Laurel Thatcher Ulrich, *A Midwife's Tale: The Life of Martha Ballard Based on Her Diary, 1785–1812* (New York: Knopf, 1990), 322; Ted Brasser, *A Basketful of Cultural Change* (Ottawa: National Museum of Man, 1975).

16. Accession Book, 1835–1880, Rhode Island Historical Society, Providence, entries for 1835, 1836, 1838, and 1843.

17. Ibid., entry for 1842.

2

A SLIPWARE DISH BY SAMUEL MALKIN: AN ANALYSIS OF VERNACULAR DESIGN

Darron Dean (1994)

INTRODUCTION

The term 'vernacular' derives from the Latin word 'vernaculas', meaning native or indigenous. It first appears in the English language in the early seventeenth century, though is not used with frequency until the nineteenth.[1] George Gilbert Scott was the first to apply the term to design in 1857,[2] and used in this sense it has since developed a substantial literature.[3] The historiography of vernacular design consists of many diverse works, ranging across rural history, popular culture studies, archaeology and a large body of collectors' literature, although these diverse treatments of vernacular material culture do not always use the term to describe their subject.[4] The way vernacular design has been understood has almost always been bound up with the way rural society and culture have been viewed. By the late nineteenth century, when the word 'vernacular' started to be increasingly used as a descriptive term, it became almost synonymous with what has been called the 'English rural myth'.[5] This conception of vernacular design, although it has undergone many subtle changes, has remained remarkably intact up to the present day.

The construction of this 'English rural myth' can be seen in much nineteenth-century literature, for example in the novels of Thomas Hardy, Jane Austen, or George Eliot;[6] or in the social critiques of Thomas Carlyle or William Morris.[7] Peasants were believed to live in harmony with and have an innate feeling for nature.[8] Similarly the work of the country craftsmen was believed to have evolved 'naturally', as the direct and 'honest' expression of simple functional requirements and solid virtues. This vernacular tradition was construed as something static and timeless, in contrast to the dynamic and progressive modern world.[9]

[…]

This article sets out to discuss vernacular design by analysing in detail a slipware dish [Figure 2] made in Burslem, North Staffordshire (c.1720–30) by the potter Samuel Malkin (1668–1741).[10] The particular example of Malkin's work which has been selected for study is a round ceramic dish, seventeen inches in diameter, approximately three inches deep, with a rim of one and a half inches; the body of the dish is uniformly half an inch thick. The clay is of a common earthenware type, fired to about 1150 degrees centigrade, finely textured, high in iron oxide (judging from its deep red colour), and considerably refined, being relatively free from impurities such as stones or other foreign matter. The dish has no base, its underside is completely rounded, so that it does not easily sit flat. It has no evidence of throwing rings or turning marks, but there are various scratches on its underside where it has been shaped, which indicate that the dish was press-moulded.[11]

The underside of the dish is left unglazed and undecorated, while the top side is elaborately

Figure 2. Samuel Malkin, slipware dish (c. 1730). Diameter 17 inches. Victoria and Albert Museum, C.125–1930, in Dean, D. 'A Slipware Dish by Samuel Malkin: An Analysis of Vernacular Design', *Journal of Design History* 7(3) (1994), pp. 153–67, p. 155. Reprinted by permission of V&A Images.

and carefully decorated. It has first had a layer of white slip poured over it. The original colour of this white slip can be seen at the edges where the glaze has failed to cover it. Different colours of slip, from the lightest to the darkest, have subsequently been added for decoration. Three different colours, light brown, red and dark brown, have been used. The pot was then glazed with powdered lead ore, which has turned the white slip base to a warm yellow colour.[12] The dish has been fired once, in an oxidizing atmosphere (the red clay retaining its original colour), and there

are signs that it was slightly overfired because the brown slips in particular have run, and the glaze has an exceptionally fluid and glassy appearance. These dishes, uniform in size, were stacked up on top of each other, edge to edge. The glaze has run inwards on this particular example indicating that it was fired face up. It has been suggested that the piecrust edge, which is a distinctive feature of these dishes, was to allow the dishes to be more easily prised apart after the firing if the glaze ran.[13]

Much of the decoration is in slight relief, indicating that it was pressed from an engraved mould. This pattern is partly drawn with a rou-lette effect and partly straight-line engraved. The pattern on the rim is freely trailed in a traditional way, using a funnel instrument. Since the pat-tern is in relief, the slip has been used to colour areas in, rather than delineate the design itself, which gives a somewhat flattened effect to the image. The main part of the decoration is drawn in a highly formalized way, carefully arranged in a highly ordered symmetrical composition. It consists of a large three-pronged flower motif in the centre, on which three sunflower faces, with somewhat ambiguous expressions, are attached at equal distances from each other, and two singing birds of equal size, facing inwards, are symmetri-cally perched.

The quality of finish is high for this type of ware, with good, consistent colour, and a bright, even glaze. The white slip has a few patches show-ing small cracks where it has crawled away from the body. This indicates that the clay used for decorating is of a similar type to the body, hav-ing contracted more on drying due to its higher water content. The dish has evidently been well looked after, however, since there is very little dirt in the cracks in the glaze. Further, the glaze is only very slightly worn in the centre, which suggests that this dish has probably been used for display, rather than used at the table, for most of its life.

AN INDIVIDUAL ARTISAN POTTER?

[…] Wedgwood values Richard Malkin's weekly production at £2 10s.[14] This figure makes Mal-kin's one of the smallest potteries working in this area at the time, but not untypical of its kind. Over half the potteries listed by Wedgwood were producing less than £3 worth of ware a week. Six men and four boys are recorded as necessary to produce £4 5s. worth of work a week, so to pro-duce about £3 worth took perhaps four men and two or three boys.[15] As contemporary accounts show, a fairly rigorous division of labour existed

in these small potteries even at this early date. […] Simeon Shaw, in the first historical account of the Potteries (1829), gives us this valuable insight: 'The potter who could then throw, stouk, lead and finish was a good workman; very few indeed being more expert at more than two or three of these branches.'[16] The product range of each pottery in the area was already specialized in 1710.[17] Whilst Malkin's pottery concentrated on 'Black and Mottled' wares (chamber pots, mugs, apothecaries' wares, cooking vessels), others, such as Thomas Taylor, made 'Moulded' wares, Aron Shaw 'Stoneware and Dipped', and H. Beech 'Butter pots'.[18]

The dish discussed here would have repre-sented a small part of Malkin's total production, as Allman found when he excavated the site. […] Dishes of this sort were obviously special pieces, more labour-intensive, more expensive, and more individual since they are signed, when the rest of the ware remains unsigned. But it is unlikely that Malkin would himself have done all the work on any one single piece. If Malkin decorated, another workman would glaze, or another, the 'Presser' perhaps, would make the dish.

To summarize, the kind of pottery that pro-duced this dish would have been organized as a small production unit in which tasks were divided and the object passed through the hands of a sequence of specialist workers. In other words, Malkin's pottery was not dissimilar in organiza-tion to later, so-called 'industrial' potteries. Lorna Weatherill has estimated that an average piece would be sold at 1d. each, which means that several hundred good pieces would have to be made and sold each week to make £3 worth of output.[19] This seems a fair estimate given the average kiln size which, according to Plot, was forty-two cubic feet.[20] Samuel Malkin, and this slipware dish, were then far from the individual, artisan craft tradition usually associated with his type of country pottery. They were, rather, part of a highly organized, subdivided trade, even though one of the smallest potteries in what was still a small, rural community.

The materials and techniques employed by Malkin demonstrate a combination of local and external influence. [...] The clay Malkin used would have been dug and prepared by himself at the pottery (or, at least, by his workmen), which he was entitled to do by common law at this time, so long as he filled the hole afterwards.[21] Coal, essential for firing, and lead for glazing, were also mined and prepared locally, and could be obtained by the potter cheaply.[22] [...] The kiln Malkin used would have been locally constructed, probably by the potter himself. [...] Staffordshire kilns were different from those in other parts of the country. The London Delftware kilns, for example, were built essentially on Dutch technology; they were more sophisticated technically than those in Staffordshire, being much larger and firing at considerably higher temperatures.[23] The Staffordshire kilns were, however, more sophisticated than many others in provincial England at the time.[24] We can conclude that the materials and many of the processes used in making this dish were 'local' to Burslem which gives this type of slipware its peculiar visual and material qualities.

The use of press-moulding by Malkin for this dish was, however, new to Staffordshire in this period and indicates the area's technical links to other dynamic areas of ceramic production, particularly London.[25] [...] The use of press-moulding indicates the flexible and dynamic nature of these small potteries which have conventionally been seen as conservative or static. This is confirmed by the results of Allman's archaeological excavations at Massey Square, which showed that various salt-glaze, fine earthenwares and stonewares were being experimented with and produced in the early 1700s. These findings suggest a far more gradual and smooth transition at the Malkin pottery to those features usually associated with an 'industrial' pottery than is normally assumed.[26] The increased application of moulds directly foreshadowed the techniques of later industrial potteries. Moreover, as will be emphasized later, these developments are a response to technical developments elsewhere, particularly London, and to changes in the markets served by the Burslem potteries. In this context, Malkin's dish can be seen not as the product of an isolated country practice, but part of a rapidly developing industry.

LOCAL POTS FOR LOCAL MARKETS?

It has conventionally been understood in the writing on vernacular ceramics that the type of ware Malkin's dish represents was produced to satisfy 'an entirely local demand'.[27] On examination, it can be shown that this was rarely the case. [...] Inventories of small potteries like Malkin's show that, unlike the larger London potteries, little stock was kept for order.[28] There were no shops selling pottery in Burslem that we know of, and no local fairs, so most of the pottery had to be sold elsewhere. Some may have been bought directly from the potter by local people but, as Weatherill has shown, the population of Burslem was very small in the early eighteenth century (about 1000 in 1700) and could not have supported the numbers of potters known to have been working in Burslem even at this early date. Furthermore, Weatherill argues, few people in and around Burslem owned much pottery because of its relative expense and the availability of cheaper alternatives, such as wooden household wares.[29]

[...]

Staffordshire ware from this period was in fact transported all over the country; some even reached North America, exported from ports such as Liverpool, Bristol, Hull, and Portsmouth.[30] Before 1730 the majority of ware was probably carried on foot out of Staffordshire by cratemen, along routes that are now virtually impossible to trace. In other words, even though the roads were too bad even for horses and carts before about 1730,[31] a fairly extensive sales network had been established before the canals. [...] The cratemen fulfilled another important function, as far as the design of these wares is concerned, in providing a constant flow of goods and information. The cratemen, and other small traders, ensured that such communities were not isolated from events and information from around the country.[32] Moreover, by working in between the manufacturers or wholesale agents and the consumer, they were able to inform both about how the market was developing. [...] Few, if any, communities remained isolated from other regions at this period, and it is essential that this is borne in mind when considering so-called 'local' or vernacular traditions.

[...]

Nor is it adequate to say that in rural areas only 'local' pottery was available. As the William Taylor example shows, if people in rural areas wanted to buy imported porcelain from China, they could do so. The pattern of consumption suggested for the kind of ware represented by the Malkin dish is not one that is defined in terms of simple geographical boundaries, that is, as a vernacular, rural, or 'local' market, as opposed to a fashionable, urban, or national one. Rather, the market for these dishes appears to have been associated with a set of socio-economic values which are linked to occupation, class, and location, but were not exclusive to any one group or type of person. Evidently a more complex model of consumption, beside that based on fashion, is necessary to understand why these dishes were bought and by whom.

[...]

STYLISTIC VOCABULARY: ITS RANGE AND INTERPRETATION

[...] The central motif on the Malkin dish is typical of the symbol known as 'The Tree of Life', distinguished by a central trunk or stem with foliage of a formalized kind. It had its origins in a number of ancient cultures but emerged as a common motif in England in the seventeenth century. [...] Chintzes, particularly those imported from India in the seventeenth century, commonly exhibit this motif and can be seen to influence much English textile and other forms of design of this period.[33]

[...] Similarly, the tulips, fashionable in the middle of the seventeenth century in Britain, were ubiquitous as a decorative motif by the eighteenth. They could be found on much of the English and imported delftware that was popular at this time, as well as many other types of objects such as wallpapers, hangings, and firebacks.

[...]

Appropriately the closest precedents for this type of slipware are the large pewter dishes made throughout Britain from the middle of the seventeenth century.[34] The stylization and exaggeration of form, and the occurrence especially of certain animal designs, floral patterns, and depictions of the monarchy found on this kind of pewter, have almost direct parallels in ceramic. Moreover, a deliberate attempt seems to have been made by Malkin to imitate 'wriggle-work' decoration, by engraving the mould in a particularly laborious way to create this roulette-effect.[35] [...] This offers an interesting illustration of the possible transferences between different media, from delft to pewter, and then to slipware. The stylistic language develops as it is transferred to and appropriated by each medium. It was also common [...] for pewterers to sign their initials in boxes which they incorporated into the design. The same kind of signature appears on decorative ceramic wares from the time of Thomas Toft, the Staffordshire slipware potter working in the 1660s who perhaps started the trend.

[...]

Since belief and symbolism in the eighteenth century were highly localized, it is difficult to interpret what the image on this dish might have meant to an eighteenth-century audience in any precise way.[36] [...] The birds perhaps refer to those 'Two Birds in a Bush' of proverbial folklore. They occur on another dish by Malkin in exactly the same position, dated 1726, and inscribed 'A Bird in the Hand is Worth Two in the Bush'. As Reay has written, 'Proverbs were important. They provided rough guide lines to popular ethics and morality'.[37]

[...]

Malkin's ornamental imagery is, then, a hybrid form, created from a multitude of historical and contemporary sources, but subject to a local process of selection and reinterpretation. [...] In this way 'local' traditions achieve a certain uniformity, or homogeneity. This helps to explain the consistency of style and character in Malkin's work and the similarities between it and that of other Staffordshire slipware produced at this time.

CONCLUSION

[...] An object's vernacularity is, therefore, a product of the varying ways appropriated forms, materials, and processes are reconstituted in and for a locality, rather than being an organic and unproblematic manifestation of local culture. The way various elements are appropriated is a complex process, dependent on the individual craftsmen, the nature of the locality, and material and cultural resources available, and the broader conditions of trade and communication at the time. [...] In this way, vernacularity is defined spatially and not by arbitrary notions of taste, or social and economic status. [...]

NOTES

Extracted from Dean, D. 'A Slipware Dish by Samuel Malkin: An Analysis of Vernacular Design',

The Journal of Design History, 7(3) (1994), pp. 153–67. Reprinted by permission of the Design History Society.

1. *Oxford English Dictionary*, Oxford, 1989, vol. XIX, p. 549.
2. G. G. Scott, *Domestic and Secular Architecture*, London, 1857
3. In 1972 Robert De Zouche Hall was able to compile a bibliography of vernacular architecture alone consisting of several hundred titles: *A Bibliography of Vernacular Architecture*, London, 1972.
4. For example, R. G. Cooper's *English Slipware Dishes 1650–1850*, London, 1968, provides a catalogue for collectors; there is the archaeological study by R. Coleman & T. Pearson-Phillimore, *Excavations in the Donyatt Potteries*, Chichester, 1988; Peter Burke's *Popular Culture in Early Modern Europe*, London, 1978 is a social history of regional cultures; and material culture studies, such as Henry Glassie's *Folk Housing in Middle Virginia*, Knoxville (USA), 1975, all deal ostensibly with the explication of what is termed here as 'vernacular' culture in one way or another.
5. Gillian Bennett, 'Folklore studies and the English rural myth', *Rural History*, vol. 1, 1993, pp. 77–91.
6. Raymond Williams, *The Country and the City*, London, 1973.
7. T. Carlyle, *Past and Present*, London, 1848; W. Morris, *News from Nowhere*, London, 1892.
8. Interestingly the term 'peasant' starts to be used in England to describe the rural working poor only from the late eighteenth century, which reflects the distinction being made from this time between urban and rural society and its population.
9. Typical amongst this literature is George Sturt's *The Wheelwright's Shop*, Cambridge, 1923.
10. H. Tait, 'Samuel Malkin and the "SM" slipware dishes', *Apollo*, Jan.–Feb. 1957, pp. 48–51.
11. Press-moulding is an early moulding technique for flatwares, consisting of a simple convex mould made from clay, which was

then fired. Over this a slab of clay was pressed and shaped, lifted off when leather-hard, and then decorated.

12. Lead was the traditional type of glaze for slipware and most common up until the mid-nineteenth century when its hazards to health became known.

13. Cooper, op. cit. p. 118.

14. Wedgwood's list of potters working in Burslem between 1710 and 1715. Reproduced in E. Meteyard, *The Life of Josiah Wedgwood*, London, 1865 (reprinted 1970), vol. 1, pp. 191–2.

15. Josiah Wedgwood's estimate of an average pottery's weekly cost around 1710–15. Reproduced in Meteyard, op. cit., p. 190.

16. S. Shaw, *History of the Staffordshire Potteries*, Hanley, 1829, p. 104.

17. Archaeological evidence suggests many pottery communities were specialized in this way by the early seventeenth century, and perhaps earlier. P. Brears, *The English Country Pottery*, Devon, 1971, p. 14.

18. Meteyard, op. cit., pp. 191–2

19. 1 *d.* refers to the cheapest wares made; the more elaborately decorated pieces are estimated to cost as much as two shillings, L. Weatherill, *The Growth of the Pottery Industry*, New York, 1986, p. 85. Without knowing how many of these more expensive pieces were made each week it is impossible to estimate more precisely Malkin's weekly output.

20. R. Plot, *The Natural History of Staffordshire*, Oxford, 1686, p. 123

21. Shaw, op. cit., p. 174

22. L. Weatherill, *The Pottery Trade and N. Staffordshire 1660–1760*, Manchester, 1971, chapter 2.

23. F. Britton, 'The Pickleherring Potteries: an inventory', *Post-Medieval Archaeology*, vol. 24, 1990, pp. 61–92.

24. The Staffordshire kilns were larger and multi-flued which enabled an easier and more efficient firing, and a smoother dispersion of heat in the pottery chamber, providing greater control and more even and consistent results. See P. Mayers, 'Excavations of the kilns at Pottersbury, Northants.', *Post-Medieval Archaeology*, vol. 2, 1968, pp. 67–71.

25. Press-moulding was used in London from the mid- to late sixteenth century, Brears, op. cit., 1971, p. 110.

26. For example, Weatherill, op. cit., 1986, p. 45,

27. B. Rackham & H. Read, *English Pottery*, London, 1924, p. 21.

28. Britton, op. cit

29. Weatherill, 1986, op. cit., p. 92.

30. I. N. Hume, *Guide to Artefacts of Colonial America*, New York, 1982.

31. E. J. D. Warillow, *A Sociological History of the City of Stoke-on-Trent*, 1960, p. 19.

32. M. Spufford, *Small Books and Pleasant Histories*, London, 1981.

33. Imported textiles of this kind became so popular in England that they were banned in the early eighteenth century to encourage home production. See K. B. Brett & J. Irwin, *Origins of Chintz*, 1970, London, Cat. Nos 6–40.

34. R. F. Homer & D. W. Hall, *Provincial Pewterers*, London, 1985.

35. This is a decorative technique which appeared from around the middle of the seventeenth century, derived from engraving on metal; small marks are carved into the surface of the pewter out of which a pattern is built up.

36. K. Thomas, *Man and the Natural World*, Penguin, Suffolk, 1983, p. 76.

37. B. Reay, *Popular Culture in Seventeenth Century England*, 1988, p. 5.

3

OF THE DIVISION OF LABOUR

Adam Smith (1776)

The greatest improvements in the productive powers of labour, and the greater part of the skill, dexterity, and judgment, with which it is anywhere directed, or applied, seem to have been the effects of the division of labour.

The effects of the division of labour, in the general business of society, will be more easily understood, by considering in what manner it operates in some particular manufactures. It is commonly supposed to be carried furthest in some very trifling ones; not perhaps that it really is carried further in them than in others of more importance; but in those trifling manufactures which are destined to supply the small wants of but a small number of people, the whole number of workmen must necessarily be small; and those employed in every different branch of the work can often be collected into the same workhouse, and placed at once under the view of the spectator. In those great manufactures, on the contrary, which are destined to supply the great wants of the great body of the people, every different branch of the work employs so great a number of workmen, that it is impossible to collect them all into the same workhouse. We can seldom see more, at one time, than those employed in one single branch. Though in such manufactures, therefore, the work may really be divided into a much greater number of parts, than in those of a more trifling nature, the division is not near so obvious, and has accordingly been much less observed.

To take an example, therefore, from a very trifling manufacture, but one in which the division of labour has been very often taken notice of, the trade of a pin-maker; a workman not educated to this business (which the division of labour has rendered a distinct trade), nor acquainted with the use of the machinery employed in it (to the invention of which the same division of labour has probably given occasion), could scarce, perhaps, with his utmost industry, make one pin in a day, and certainly could not make twenty. But in the way in which this business is now carried on, not only the whole work is a peculiar trade, but it is divided into a number of branches, of which the greater part are likewise peculiar trades. One man draws out the wire; another straights it; a third cuts it; a fourth points it; a fifth grinds it at the top for receiving the head; to make the head requires two or three distinct operations; to put it on is a peculiar business; to whiten the pins is another; it is even a trade by itself to put them into the paper; and the important business of making a pin is, in this manner, divided into about eighteen distinct operations, which, in some manufactories, are all performed by distinct hands, though in others the same man will sometimes perform two or three of them. I have seen a small manufactory of this kind, where ten men only were employed, and where some of them consequently performed two or three distinct operations. But though they were very poor, and therefore but indifferently accommodated with the necessary machinery, they could, when they exerted themselves, make among them about twelve pounds of pins in a day. There are in a pound upwards of four thousand pins of a middling size. Those ten persons, therefore, could make among them upwards of forty-eight thousand pins in a day. Each person, therefore, making a tenth part of forty-eight thousand pins, might be considered as making four thousand eight hundred pins in a day. But if they had all wrought separately and independently, and without any of them having been educated to this peculiar business, they certainly could not each of them have made twenty, perhaps not one pin in a day; that is, certainly, not the two hundred and fortieth, perhaps not the four thousand eight hundredth, part of what they are at present capable of performing, in consequence of a proper division and combination of their different operations.

In every other art and manufacture, the effects of the division of labour are similar to what they are in this very trifling one, though, in many of them, the labour can neither be so much sub-divided, nor reduced to so great a simplicity of operation. The division of labour, however, so far as it can be introduced, occasions, in every art, a proportionable increase of the productive powers of labour. The separation of different trades and employments from one another, seems to have taken place in consequence of this advantage. This separation, too, is generally carried furthest in those countries which enjoy the highest degree of industry and improvement; what is the work of one man, in a rude state of society, being generally that of several in an improved one. In every improved society, the farmer is generally nothing but a farmer; the manufacturer, nothing but a manufacturer. The labour, too, which is necessary to produce any one complete manu-facture, is almost always divided among a great number of hands. How many different trades are employed in each branch of the linen and woollen manufactures, from the growers of the flax and the wool, to the bleachers and smoothers of the linen, or to the dyers and dressers of the cloth? The nature of agriculture, indeed, does not admit of so many subdivisions of labour, nor of so com-plete a separation of one business from another, as manufactures. It is impossible to separate so

entirely the business of the grazier from that of the corn-farmer, as the trade of the carpenter is commonly separated from that of the smith. The spinner is almost always a distinct person from the weaver; but the ploughman, the harrower, the sower of the seed, and the reaper of the corn, are often the same. The occasions for those different sorts of labour returning with the different seasons of the year, it is impossible that one man should be constantly employed in any one of them. This impossibility of making so complete and entire a separation of all the different branches of labour employed in agriculture is perhaps the reason why the improvement of the productive powers of labour, in this art, does not always keep pace with their improvement in manufactures. The most opulent nations, indeed, generally excel all their neighbours in agriculture as well as in manufactures; but they are commonly more dis-tinguished by their superiority in the latter than in the former. […] The silks of France are better and cheaper than those of England, because the silk manufacture, at least under the present high duties upon the importation of raw silk, does not so well suit the climate of England as that of France. But the hardware and the coarse woollens of England are beyond all comparison superior to those of France, and much cheaper, too, in the same degree of goodness. In Poland there are said to be scarce any manufactures of any kind, a few of those coarser household manufactures excepted, without which no country can well subsist.

This great increase in the quantity of work, which, in consequence of the division of labour, the same number of people are capable of performing, is owing to three different circum-stances; first, to the increase of dexterity in every particular workman; secondly, to the saving of the time which is commonly lost in passing from one species of work to another; and, lastly, to the invention of a great number of machines which facilitate and abridge labour, and enable one man to do the work of many.

First, the improvement of the dexterity of the workmen, necessarily increases the quantity of the work he can perform; and the division of labour, by reducing every man's business to some one simple operation, and by making this operation the sole employment of his life, necessarily increases very much the dexterity of the workman. A common smith, who, though accustomed to handle the hammer, has never been used to make nails, if, upon some particular occasion, he is obliged to attempt it, will scarce, I am assured, be able to make above two or three hundred nails in a day, and those, too, very bad ones. A smith who has been accustomed to make nails, but whose sole or principal business has not been that of a nailer, can seldom, with his utmost diligence, make more than eight hundred or a thousand nails in a day. I have seen several boys, under twenty years of age, who had never exercised any other trade but that of making nails, and who, when they exerted themselves, could make, each of them, upwards of two thousand three hundred nails in a day. The making of a nail, however, is by no means one of the simplest operations. The same person blows the bellows, stirs or mends the fire as there is occasion, heats the iron, and forges every part of the nail: in forging the head, too, he is obliged to change his tools. The different operations into which the making of a pin, or of a metal button, is subdivided, are all of them much more simple, and the dexterity of the person, of whose life it has been the sole business to perform them, is usually much greater. The rapidity with which some of the operations of those manufactures are performed, exceeds what the human hand could, by those who had never seen them, he supposed capable of acquiring.

Secondly, the advantage which is gained by saving the time commonly lost in passing from one sort of work to another, is much greater than we should at first view be apt to imagine it. It is impossible to pass very quickly from one kind of work to another, that is carried on in a different place, and with quite different tools. A country weaver, who cultivates a small farm, must lose a good deal of time in passing from his loom to the field, and from the field to his loom. When the two trades can be carried on in the same workhouse, the loss of time is, no doubt, much less. It is, even in this case, however, very considerable. A man commonly saunters a little in turning his hand from one sort of employment to another. When he first begins the new work, he is seldom very keen and hearty; his mind, as they say, does not go to it, and for some time he rather trifles than applies to good purpose. The habit of sauntering, and of indolent careless application, which is naturally, or rather necessarily, acquired by every country workman who is obliged to change his work and his tools every half hour, and to apply his hand in twenty different ways almost every day of his life, renders him almost always slothful and lazy, and incapable of any vigorous application, even on the most pressing occasions. Independent, therefore, of his deficiency in point of dexterity, this cause alone must always reduce considerably the quantity of work which he is capable of performing.

Thirdly, and lastly, everybody must be sensible how much labour is facilitated and abridged by the application of proper machinery. It is unnecessary to give any example. I shall only observe, therefore, that the invention of all those machines by which labour is so much facilitated and abridged, seems to have been originally owing to the division of labour. Men are much more likely to discover easier and readier methods of attaining any object, when the whole attention of their minds is directed towards that single object, than when it is dissipated among a great variety of things. But, in consequence of the division of labour, the whole of every man's attention comes naturally to be directed towards some one very simple object. It is naturally to be expected, therefore, that some one or other of those who are employed in each particular branch of labour should soon find out easier and readier methods of performing their own particular work, whenever the nature of it admits of such improvement. A great part of the machines made use of in those manufactures in which labour is most subdivided, were originally the invention of common workmen, who, being each of them employed in some very simple operation, naturally turned their thoughts towards finding out easier and readier methods of performing it. Whoever has been much accustomed to visit such manufactures, must frequently have been shewn very pretty machines, which were the inventions of such workmen, in order to facilitate and quicken their own particular part of the work. In the first fire-engines, a boy was constantly employed to open and shut alternately the communication between the boiler and the cylinder, according as the piston either ascended or descended. One of those boys, who loved to play with his companions, observed that, by tying a string from the handle of the valve which opened this communication to another part of the machine, the valve would open and shut without his assistance, and leave him at liberty to divert himself with his play-fellows. One of the greatest improvements that has been made upon this machine, since it was first invented, was in this manner the discovery of a boy who wanted to save his own labour.

All the improvements in machinery, however, have by no means been the inventions of those who had occasion to use the machines. Many improvements have been made by the ingenuity of the makers of the machines, when to make them became the business of a peculiar trade; and some by that of those who are called philosophers, or men of speculation, whose trade it is not to do any thing, but to observe every thing, and who, upon that account, are often capable of combining together the powers of the most distant and dissimilar objects. In the progress of society, philosophy or speculation becomes, like every other employment, the principal or sole trade and occupation of a particular class of citizens. Like every other employment, too, it is subdivided into a great number of different branches, each of which affords occupation to a peculiar tribe or class of philosophers; and this subdivision of employment in philosophy, as well as in every other business, improve dexterity, and saves time. Each individual becomes more expert in his own

peculiar branch, more work is done upon the whole, and the quantity of science is considerably increased by it.

It is the great multiplication of the productions of all the different arts, in consequence of the division of labour, which occasions, in a well-governed society, that universal opulence which extends itself to the lowest ranks of the people. Every workman has a great quantity of his own work to dispose of beyond what he himself has occasion for; and every other workman being exactly in the same situation, he is enabled to exchange a great quantity of his own goods for a great quantity or, what comes to the same thing, for the price of a great quantity of theirs. He supplies them abundantly with what they have occasion for, and they accommodate him as amply with what he has occasion for, and a general plenty diffuses itself through all the different ranks of the society.

Observe the accommodation of the most common artificer or day labourer in a civilized and thriving country, and you will perceive that the number of people, of whose industry a part, though but a small part, has been employed in procuring him this accommodation, exceeds all computation. The woollen coat, for example, which covers the day labourer, as coarse and rough as it may appear, is the produce of the joint labour of a great multitude of workmen. The shepherd, the sorter of the wool, the wool-comber or carder, the dyer, the scribbler, the spinner, the weaver, the fuller, the dresser, with many others, must all join their different arts in order to complete even this homely production. How many merchants and carriers, besides, must have been employed in transporting the materials from some of those workmen to others who often live in a very distant part of the country? How much commerce and navigation in particular, how many ship-builders, sailors, sail-makers, rope-makers, must have been employed in order to bring together the different drugs made use of by the dyer, which often come from the remotest corners of the world? What a variety of labour, too, is necessary in order to produce the tools of the meanest of those workmen? To say nothing of such complicated machines as the ship of the sailor, the mill of the fuller, or even the loom of the weaver, let us consider only what a variety of labour is requisite in order to form that very simple machine, the shears with which the shepherd clips the wool. The miner, the builder of the furnace for smelting the ore, the feller of the timber, the burner of the charcoal to be made use of in the smelting-house, the brickmaker, the bricklayer, the workmen who attend the furnace, the mill-wright, the forger, the smith, must all of them join their different arts in order to produce them. Were we to examine, in the same manner, all the different parts of his dress and household furniture, the coarse linen shirt which he wears next his skin, the shoes which cover his feet, the bed which he lies on, and all the different parts which compose it, the kitchen-grate at which he prepares his victuals, the coals which he makes use of for that purpose, dug from the bowels of the earth, and brought to him, perhaps, by a long sea and a long land-carriage, all the other utensils of his kitchen, all the furniture of his table, the knives and forks, the earthen or pewter plates upon which he serves up and divides his victuals, the different hands employed in preparing his bread and his beer, the glass window which lets in the heat and the light, and keeps out the wind and the rain, with all the knowledge and art requisite for preparing that beautiful and happy invention, without which these northern parts of the world could scarce have afforded a very comfortable habitation, together with the tools of all the different workmen employed in producing those different conveniences; if we examine, I say, all these things, and consider what a variety of labour is employed about each of them, we shall be sensible that, without the assistance and co-operation of many thousands, the very meanest person in a civilized country could not be provided, even according to, what we very falsely imagine, the easy and simple manner in which he is commonly accommodated. Compared, indeed, with the more extravagant luxury of the great, his accommodation must no doubt appear extremely simple and easy; and yet it may be true, perhaps, that the accommodation of an European prince does not always so much exceed that of an industrious and frugal peasant, as the accommodation of the latter exceeds that of many an African king, the absolute masters of the lives and liberties of ten thousand naked savages.

NOTE

Reproduced from Smith, A., 'Of the Division of Labour', Book I, Chapter I, in *An Inquiry into the Nature and Causes of the Wealth of Nations*, 5th edn, London: William Allason and J. Maynard, 1819, pp. 5–17.

4

THE WEDGWOOD SLAVE MEDALLION: VALUES IN EIGHTEENTH-CENTURY DESIGN

Mary Guyatt (2000)

Figure 3. The Wedgwood Slave Medallion of 1787. Actual height approximately 35 mm. Victoria and Albert Museum, 414:1304-1885, in Mary Guyatt, 'The Wedgwood Slave Medallion: Values in Eighteenth-century Design', *Journal of Design History* 13(2) (2000), pp. 93–105, p. 94. Reprinted by permission of V&A Images.

Some had them inlaid in gold in the lids of their snuff-boxes. Of the ladies, some wore them in bracelets, and others had them fitted up in an ornamental manner as pins for their hair. At length the taste for wearing them became general, and thus a fashion, which usually confines itself to worthless things, was seen for once in the honourable office of promoting the cause of justice, humanity and freedom.[1]

The above words refer to the 'slave medallion' [Figure 3] produced in 1787 by one of the most famous of British potters and businessmen, Josiah Wedgwood (1730–95), as his very personal contribution to the campaign for the abolition of the slave trade. Originally intended to be worn by abolitionists as a means of identifying them with the cause, the medallion was essentially a ceramic cameo depicting a black male in chains below the words 'AM I NOT A MAN AND A BROTHER?' Given the popularity of neo-classical decoration at the time, ceramic cameos of numerous designs were familiar decorative items, based on the carved gemstone miniatures of antiquity. These ceramics, frequently set into furniture and jewellery, were also a product particularly associated with the Wedgwood firm, made possible by their development of a requisite pure-white 'jasper' clay in the early 1770s. By the end of that decade, their customers could choose from a total of 1,733 different cameos, depicting everyone and everything from Oliver Cromwell to a mad, drunken fawn.[2] But whilst some members of this enormous group of ceramic goods have since disappeared into obscurity, the slave medallion is now firmly established as a 'museum piece' – considered by Wedgwood experts and biographers as a technically brilliant piece of jewellery representative of the man's magnanimity, and by historians of the abolition movement as a piece of propaganda central to the impassioned campaign for the ending of the transatlantic slave trade in the closing decades of the eighteenth century. [...] Though in part this may be explained by the object's pertinence to two distinct and polarized fields, it has without a doubt been compounded by the long-standing and lamentable disinterest in non-white subjects that existed in historical discourse prior to the relatively recent advent of post-colonial criticism and the reassessments which this has produced.[3] [...]

THE ABOLITION MOVEMENT IN LATE EIGHTEENTH-CENTURY BRITAIN

If eighteenth-century Britain is to be viewed as an age of tea-sipping politeness it should also be seen as a time of extreme cruelty and barbarity, as slave-traders, slave-owners and the consuming public all benefited, either financially or materially, from the exploitation of over eleven million African lives. Arguments in favour of what now seems such an obscene practice ranged from the theory espoused by plantation owners and slave-traders that blacks were an entirely separate species, to the assumption that the British economy was dependent on colonial trade and the slave labour that that entailed. Both science and theology were used to support these views.[4]

However, by the second half of the century slavery was beginning to be questioned by a vociferous minority.[5] The impetus appears to have come from moves in Enlightenment philosophy away from the above modes of thinking and towards a pervasive sense of man as a social being whose own happiness would ultimately depend on his living in a thriving community, a state which in turn depended on the liberty of all its members, whatever their class, creed or colour.[6] Though not all contemporaries had access to the learned writings of men such as Montesquieu, Hutcheson and Smith, anti-slavery sentiment was also to be heard at the pulpit.[7] It was members of the non-conformist churches who particularly concerned themselves with abolition, that is, Quakers, Baptists, Methodists and Unitarians.[8] Nor should the individual's ability to be moved against the slave trade by events quite outside the arena of religious rhetoric be underestimated – reading Thomas Day's epic *The Dying Negro*, or through seeing Aphra Behn's dramatic romance *Oroonoko*, for instance.[9] And whilst only travellers might have observed the horrors of the slave trade at first hand, shackles and thumbscrews used for restraining slaves were openly displayed for sale in Liverpool shop windows.[10]

JOSIAH WEDGWOOD'S PERSONAL CONTRIBUTION TO THE ANTI-SLAVERY CAUSE

As a result of these various currents, anti-slavery, formally manifested in the Society for the Abolition of the Slave Trade, was a popular cause by the late 1780s.[11] As a Unitarian acquainted with other leading abolitionists and as a businessman with contacts in Liverpool (the foremost slave port of the day), it was not surprising that Josiah Wedgwood should have been one of the thousands to join the Society at its inauguration in 1787. Presumably because his name carried much weight, within months he was invited to join the Society's Committee. [...] His major contribution to promoting the cause was a material one, in the form of the slave medallion. The existing literature indicates that the sculptor Henry Webber drafted the figure and that his design was subsequently modelled at the Wedgwood factory at Etruria, Staffordshire by the jasper specialist William Hackwood. However, given Josiah Wedgwood's very personal involvement in the project, it is fair to suggest that he would have had some influence over the eventual design. In any case, since he is popularly credited as the originator of the motto 'Am I not a man and a brother?', the piece is now firmly established as a Wedgwood 'original'.[12] [...] It may be assumed that the medallions were distributed through the Society network, as it is recorded that Wedgwood sent parcels to both Clarkson and Benjamin Franklin, then President of the Philadelphia Society for the Abolition of Slavery.[13] It is generally accepted that Wedgwood

himself bore the production and distribution costs, and of these it can only be said that medallions of a similar size were commercially retailing at three guineas each.[14]

[...]

WEARING THE SLAVE MEDALLION

Though it is no longer possible to identify the individuals who received the medallions, it is apparent from Clarkson's account that they were worn by both sexes. He also describes how both men and women took it upon themselves to customize the piece at their own expense, with men setting theirs in plain metal mounts or snuff-boxes, and with women having theirs inlaid in hair-pins and bracelets. Although it may at first seem startling that such an image of human suffering was used to decorate a lady's hair ornament or bracelet, Clarkson's description does in fact show a mutually advantageous reciprocity between two objects of unequal moral worth: frivolous jewellery was lent moral value by the incorporation of an image associated with a popular and honourable cause, whilst the rather stark medallion was made more accessible to women by its transformation into a recognizably feminine decorative luxury. And perhaps because the image itself is unashamedly masculine, the process of feminization would have also helped to lessen the potential embarrassment experienced by women wearing images of semi-naked black males.[15] This is not to deny that the romantic exoticism contained in such an image could be part of the attraction for women wearers (something that will be discussed further on): rather that the slave's masculinity had to be correctly 'dressed up', not only by drapery but also through the addition of further ornamentation.

Male wearers, meanwhile, would not have encountered such problems. The simple mount into which the medallions were usually set was already a recognizably 'male' ornament, derived from the Renaissance medal. Despite literature suggesting that 'male abolitionists were generally agreed that the petitioning of Parliament was the province of adult males',[16] and although his company had long been manufacturing products aimed specifically at the female market [...] there is no sense that Wedgwood only intended men to make use of the medallion. On the contrary, he considered his female acquaintances perfectly worthy converts to the abolitionist cause.[17]

READING THE MEDALLION

At first glance, the figure on the medallion is a simple depiction of human suffering designed to communicate the abolitionists' humanitarian concerns. An immediacy of understanding is facilitated both by the moulded motto 'AM I NOT A MAN AND A BROTHER?', and the fact that the figure is shown shackled hand and foot. In terms of communicating its subject, the designer's eventual decision to use a black relief on a white ground was particularly successful in that it presented the slave 'in his own native colour',[18] whilst at the same time drawing out his characteristically African features – two things that enabled the viewer to grasp in an instant that the figure portrayed was an African slave.[19] More subtly, the silhouette effect heightened the slave's shadow-like existence and depersonalized him to the extent that he could represent his entire race and thus remind the audience of the scale of the 'crime' abolitionists felt slavery to be.[20]

Reflecting the fact that several centuries of captivity had left many slaves speaking European languages and worshipping as Christians, the slave depicted on the Wedgwood medallion shares characteristics with his audience in that he is clearly a Westernized figure: as well as speaking their language, the words he utters are themselves strangely reminiscent of the language of scripture. Indeed, given the fact that Clarkson described the slave as 'kneeling with one knee upon the ground, and with both hands lifted up to Heaven',[21] it seems probable that the designer intended him

to resemble supplicating figures from Christian iconography. After all, 'when the Negro was categorized simply as a black, a heathen, or a savage, he could be no more than an impersonal object that men manipulated for certain purposes.'[22]

[...]

If, on the one hand, the slave was to be pitied, it also appears that the abolitionists wished to present him as an eminently dignified figure: rather than breaking out of his chains through his own brute force, he is shown patiently waiting for his white master to liberate him via an act of Parliament. Paradoxically, then, though a victim, the slave is elevated to the status of a hero. This reading is substantiated both by the fact that the slave on the medallion takes his place in a line of eminent contemporaries and past heroes whom the Wedgwood company had been depicting in commercially sold miniatures since the 1770s, and also by the enormous presence of the 'noble savage' in contemporary art and literature.[23]

Essentially a fictional entity held up to white society as a model of innocence, happiness and virtue, the noble savage was a stock character who first appeared in European literature in the seventeenth century. Wearing a range of racial guises from the African to the Polynesian, over the following century the savage was to appear in writing as far apart as Rousseau's *Origins of Inequality* of 1761 and Thomas Day's sentimental poem *The Dying Negro*, before being adopted by the abolition movement as an appropriately sympathetic figure to be featured in their propaganda.[24] However [...] the eighteenth century also fostered a savage of another temperament entirely – this second character a 'terrifying avenger ... demanding as many drops of blood as he had shed through centuries of oppression.'[25] And in spite of the obvious inconsistency, this belligerent savage could also be a hero, 'for this would be how the European should want to act if he were a Slave.'[26] In terms of abolitionist propaganda, this second figure only began to appear once it became clear that slaves could assert their rights to freedom, for instance after the 1791 slave revolt at St. Dominique. Henry Fuseli's painting, *The Negro Revenged*, executed in 1807 (perhaps significantly, this was also the year the slave trade was finally abolished), is one such piece. [...]

Furthermore, as the European country most deeply embroiled in the transatlantic slave trade, British guilt was such that as the abolition movement gained ground, witnesses for the cause were claiming that Africans were 'really all born Heroes ... there never was a rascal or coward of that nation.'[27] In fact, so great was the tendency to apologize that even such rational thinkers as Adam Smith were drawn into describing slaves in unreservedly favourable terms:

> There is not a Negro from the coast of Africa who does not ... possess a degree of magnanimity which the soul of his sordid master is too often scarce capable of receiving. Fortune never exerted more cruelly her empire over mankind than when she subjected those nations of heroes to the refuse of the gaols of Europe.[28]

[...]

PHILANTHROPIST OR OPPORTUNIST?

Through Neil McKendrick's analysis of Wedgwood's marketing strategies, the latter has come to be known as a notoriously subtle and expert self-publicist, reputedly using all available means to advertise his firm and increase its profits.[29] Even the slave medallion is identified as just another manifestation of the ongoing campaign against the 'helpless' consumer:

> No public event ... lacked its commercial opportunities for Wedgwood ... the rise of Methodism, the Slave Trade controversy, and the Peace with France were all given ceramic expression: Wesley, printed in black by Sadler and Green, on a Wedgwood teapot; slavery on

the famous jasper medallion of the kneeling slave, asking 'Am I not a man and a brother?'[30]

Although the detail of the above extract is vitiated by McKendrick's misconception that the medallion was sold for profit, the argument contained therein – that Wedgwood would sink to any depths in the pursuit of commercial gain – is not necessarily weakened. For it could be argued that by producing the medallion for free, Wedgwood both gained publicity and enhanced his reputation as a philanthropist. In view of the great range of marketing tools used by his company, it might be fair to say that he was perfectly capable of such a subtle publicity device. In fact, the entire abolition movement has been seen as a convenient 'emblem of national virtue', [...][31] appropriated by middle-class businessmen like Wedgwood as a means of securing moral authority as a substitute for the titles they were born without. [...][32] Such an appraisal of Wedgwood's motivation is, however, questionable: [...] because abolition was still a minority cause even in the 1790s, the medallion may have actually lost him customers, especially those at the upper end of the market who relied on slavery to maintain their overseas interests.

Although there is little doubt that Wedgwood engaged in the anti-slavery movement for genuine moral reasons [...] Wedgwood sold out-of-date stock to suppliers in the West Indies, whilst in 1775 he accepted a commission to make a 'nest of baths' for an African king, a man who was in all likelihood a slave-trader.[33] This commission was communicated to him in a letter from his agent, Thomas Bentley, who was then responsible for the export wares leaving Liverpool:

> The above are to please the fancy of a black king of Africa to wash himself out of. They scoop the water upon them and like to have room and plenty of water – pray do this if you can and as soon as you can – and be moderate in the charge for if above should please his majesty perhaps his subjects may fancy the same kind – which will be no bad thing for the pot trade.[34]

At first it may seem highly fanciful, not to say unjust, to imagine that the king was a slave-trader. But the circumstantial evidence in favour of such a reading is inescapable. First, statistical research into shipping records reveals that around this period over ninety-five per cent of ships travelling from Liverpool to Africa were slave-trading vessels.[35] This makes it extremely likely that the order, as well as the basins themselves, were carried between the two continents aboard a slaveship. Second, when European slave-ships moored along the coast of West Africa there was a 'stock' of slaves ready and waiting for them, captured and held in specially built forts by fellow Africans. Of these African slave-traders most were tribal leaders or their intermediaries, precisely because power was needed to sustain such a constant supply of human captives. [...] It is clear that African slave-traders had expensive taste [and ...] 'were often highly Europeanised.'[36] Given what has been said of the social status of Africans involved in the slave trade, their taste for European luxuries and Liverpool's economic dependency on slave trading, it seems perfectly tenable that Wedgwood's customer was a slave-trader who would ultimately pay for the goods with human capital.

NOTES

Extracted from Guyatt, M., 'The Wedgwood Slave Medallion: Values in Eighteenth-Century Design', *The Journal of Design History,* 13(2) (2000), pp. 93–105. Reprinted by permission of the Design History Society.

1. T. Clarkson, *History of the Abolition of the Slave Trade*, Frank Cass, 1968 (first published 1808), pp. 191–2.
2. From a transcript of the 1779 Wedgwood and Bentley catalogue reproduced in W. Mankowitz, *Wedgwood*, Barrie & Jenkins, 1980.
3. David Dabydeen terms this neglect a 'pervasive colour-blindness'. See D. Dabydeen, *Hogarth's Blacks: Images of Blacks in Eighteenth Century Art*, Manchester University Press, 1987, p. 9.
4. R. Blackburn, *The Making of New World Slavery*, Verso, 1997.
5. For an extensive discussion of slavery and the British abolition movement, see R. Anstey, *The Atlantic Slave Trade and British Abolition 1760–1810*, Macmillan, 1975 and R. Blackburn, *The Overthrow of Colonial Slavery 1776–1848*, Verso, 1988, chs. I and IV.
6. For instance, in the first half of the eighteenth century Hutcheson wrote: 'Permanent power assumed over the fortunes of others must generally tend to the misery of the whole ... we must therefore conclude that no endowments, natural or acquired, can give a perfect right to assume power over others without their consent.' (Francis Hutcheson, *System of Moral Philosophy*, 1755, quoted in Anstey, op. cit., p. 100).
7. Anstey, op. cit., p. 139.
8. For an analysis of why non-conformists were particularly active in the abolition movement, Anstey, op. cit.; Blackburn, *The Overthrow of Colonial Slavery*, op. cit.; and D. B. Davis, *The Problem of Slavery in Western Culture*, Cornell, 1966.
9. First published in 1773, *The Dying Negro* was based on the true story of a London slave who ran away to marry a white woman, but was recaptured and imprisoned in a ship on the Thames, whereupon he committed suicide. Meanwhile, *Oroonoko*, a play first performed in 1688, told the story of an enslaved African prince. Towards the end of the eighteenth century the script was revised to communicate a more explicitly anti-slavery message.
10. T. Clarkson, op. cit., vol. 1, pp. 375–7.
11. Having established an exclusively Quaker pressure-group in 1782, by 1787 this was incorporated in the non-sectarian Society for the Abolition of the Slave Trade. From this point on the organization will be referred to simply as 'the Society'.
12. *The Oxford Dictionary of Quotations*, 1979.
13. R. Reilly, *Josiah Wedgwood*, Macmillan, 1992, p. 287; G. Blake Roberts, 'Josiah Wedgwood and his connections with Liverpool', *Proceedings of the Wedgwood Society*, 1982, p.130.

14. *Wedgwood Catalogue*, 1787, p. 29.
15. For a discussion of the contemporary reception of images of male nudity, see N. McKendrick, 'The commercialisation of the Potteries', in McKendrick, J. Brewer and J. H. Plumb *(eds.) The Birth of a Consumer Society*, Europa, 1982, p. 113.
16. See C. Midgley, *Women Against Slavery: The British Campaigns, 1780–1870*, Routledge, 1992.
17. In Robin Reilly's recent biography, the author details the correspondence that passed between Wedgwood and the anti-abolitionist, Anna Seward, as the one attempted to persuade the other of the evils of the slave trade. For a detailed discussion of Wedgwood's attitude to women, see S. Gater, 'Women and Wedgwood', *Women in Industry and Technology*, Museum of London, 1994, pp. 171–8.
18. Clarkson, op. cit., p. 191.
19. Since the slave medallion appears to be the only Wedgwood miniature to be modelled in monochrome, there is little doubt that this was a conscious decision on the part of the designer.
20. For this reason, I argue that the Wedgwood slave should not be considered as an example of the 'grotesque approximation of a formulaic ape', which Annie Coombes identifies as the more typical representation of the black in British art during the colonial period. See A. Coombes, *Reinventing Africa: Museums, Material Culture and Popular Imagination*, Yale University Press, 1994, p. 21.
21. Clarkson, op. cit., p. 450. Though this comment was made with reference to the Society's Seal, it is clear that this object utilized the same design as the medallion.
22. D. B. Davis, *The Problem of Slavery in Western Culture*, Cornell, 1966, p. 473.
23. Whether intentionally or not, this reading has been preserved by the curators at the Victoria and Albert Museum, who have their slave rubbing shoulders with such notables as Frederick the Great, William Shakespeare and George Washington.
24. For a greater discussion on the noble savage, see P. A. Curtin, *The Image of Africa: British Ideas and Actions, 1780–1850*, Macmillan, 1965.
25. Davis, op. cit., pp. 480–1.
26. Ibid.
27. Anonymous source quoted in Davis, op. cit., p. 477.
28. Adam Smith, *Theory of Moral Sentiments*, 1759, quoted in Anstey, op. cit., p. 118.
29. McKendrick., op. cit., pp. 100–45
30. Ibid, p. 122.
31. L. Colley, *Britons: Forging the Nation 1707–1837*, Vintage, 1996, p. 375.
32. Davis, op. cit., p. 333
33. *Letters of Josiah Wedgwood 1762–1770*, Morten, 1903, Josiah Wedgwood to T. Bentley, 18 July 1766.
34. J. Wedgwood to T. Bentley, quoted in Blake Roberts, op. cit., p. 127.
35. S. Drescher, *Econocide: British Slavery in the Era of Abolition*, University of Pittsburgh Press, 1977, p. 209.
36. A. van Danzig, 'The effects of the Atlantic slave trade in some West African societies', *The Atlantic Slave Trade*, Société francaise d'histoire d'outre-mer, 1976, p. 264.

5

MANUFACTURING, CONSUMPTION AND DESIGN IN EIGHTEENTH-CENTURY ENGLAND

John Styles (1993)

[…]

THE DICTATES OF THE MARKET AND THE IMPLEMENTATION OF DESIGN

Eighteenth-century manufacturers of batch-produced consumer goods faced markets that were often keenly attuned to the visual appearance of their products. Novelty and fashion could be important, although not necessarily dominant, at every level in the market. […]

The manufacturers of products such as these were often geographically distant from the final consumer. Moreover, they were, more often than not, distant from the metropolitan high society which was so influential on eighteenth-century fashionable taste. Two questions arise regarding the design of their products. First, how did such manufacturers determine the way their products should look in order to enjoy success in a variety of markets? Second, how did they ensure that their workers, often using hand techniques in their own homes, produced goods that accorded with the desired and often very precise visual specifications?

Most existing work on these subjects has focused either on the activities of those producing high design goods for the elite market, or on the distinctive ways design was exploited by Josiah Wedgwood and Matthew Boulton. Particular emphasis has been placed on the latter's initiation of new designs (both in the sense of new products and new forms of decoration) in accordance with or in advance of changes in fashionable taste, in order to secure a privileged place in the market. By making products to original designs, Boulton and Wedgwood were simply doing what had long been established practice in the London luxury trades. Not all metropolitan producers of luxury goods developed new designs, but it could be an important element in the success of such a business. In his discussion of cabinetmaking in *The London Tradesman* of 1747, Campbell emphasized that

> A youth who designs to make a Figure in this Branch must learn to Draw; for upon this depends the Invention of new Fashions, and on that the Success of his Business: He who first hits upon any new Whim is sure to make by the Invention before it becomes common in the Trade; but he that must always wait for a new Fashion till it comes from Paris, or is hit upon by his Neighbour, is never likely to grow rich or eminent in his Way.[1]

The fruits of innovation were similar in many of the other luxury trades. The Spitalfields silkmakers, for example, systematically commissioned novel designs in order to pre-empt changes in fashion.[2]

Producers of more modest consumer goods did not generally exercise the same degree of initiative in staying ahead of fashion. They simply adapted the broad trend of prevailing London high fashion to the prejudices and pockets of their intended customers. As in many aspects of eighteenth-century industrial innovation, a process of copying combined with small incremental adjustments was the norm. Stanley Chapman has pointed out the importance of systematic piracy of expensive London designs by Lancashire cotton printers producing for the lower end of the market in the 1780s.[3] During the same decade, the Leeds merchant house of Horner and Turner often arranged for their manufacturing suppliers to imitate woollen and worsted cloths sold by their competitors in continental Europe.[4] Manufacturers were often secretive, but successful copying and adaptation required information about what other producers, and particularly fashion leaders, were doing, as well as information about what different markets were anxious or prepared to accept.[5] Hence the constant monitoring by manufacturers of what producers of similar goods were up to, hence the desperate efforts to secure information on changes in London taste, hence the voluminous advice from agents and wholesale customers on market trends.

If design depended for most producers on copying and adaptation, precisely how was visual information on what was to be copied communicated? One way was simply to acquire an example of the product to be pirated. This was common. In textiles, for example, it was fairly easy to secure a small piece of a competitor's fabric. A 1787 parliamentary committee was informed that a print of a new design from a Surrey printworks had been sent by a London warehouseman to the Peel printworks in Lancashire to be copied. Within a fortnight it was on sale in London at two-thirds of the price of the original.[6]

Another means of communicating visual information was to use two-dimensional depictions of an object or its ornament. One of the most striking new features of late seventeenth-and eighteenth-century manufacturing in England was a dramatic increase in the use of two-dimensional paper plans for subsequent three-dimensional execution. Designs on paper had been employed long before the mid-seventeenth century, by architects and goldsmiths for example, but over the next century and a half there was a massive expansion, at first concentrated in London, but later more extensive, of activities reliant on sophisticated design and ornament, such as cabinetmaking, coachmaking, cotton printing, silkweaving and the manufacture of decorative metalware. At the same time, there were important technical innovations in two-dimensional and low relief ornament: for example, copper plate printing on fabrics, stamping on the softer metals, the use of transfers on ceramics. The consequence was a vastly increased use of both printed and hand-drawn two-dimensional designs in the manufacturing of consumer goods, for a variety of purposes. They were used as sources of visual ideas, as instructions for the execution of the work, for recording information about products and as a means of visualizing products for customers.

As two-dimensional design became more important, designer and pattern drawer emerged as distinct occupational designations. The term designer was first used early in the eighteenth century to describe those who performed the highly specialized task of providing new designs for fine patterned textiles, often on a freelance basis, but by mid-century it was being used more extensively.[7] The demand for drawing and associated skills like engraving grew apace. By the middle years of the eighteenth century there was much complaint about skill shortages in this area. Some of the deficiency had to be made up from overseas and considerable efforts were mounted to provide training. In 1759 it was claimed 'that there are two or three drawing schools established at Birmingham, for the instruction of youth in the arts of designing and drawing, and 30 or 40 Frenchmen and Germans are constantly employed in drawing and designing'.[8]

From the later seventeenth century, the London book and print trade catered to the expanding industrial market for two-dimensional designs with prints and subsequently illustrated source books. As early as the 1660s, the London bookseller and print dealer Robert Walton stocked prints which he advertised as 'extraordinarily useful for goldsmiths, jewellers, chafers, gravers, painters, carvers, drawers, needlewomen and all handicrafts'.[9] In the eighteenth century, design source books were often targeted at particular trades, like Smith and Linnell's *A New Book of Ornaments Useful for Silver-Smith's Etc.* of 1755 or Chippendale's *The Gentleman and Cabinet Maker's Director* of 1754, although designs for one material could be transferred to another, given the ubiquity of certain types of classical and rococo ornament within elite material culture.[10] From mid-century, if not before, printed designs also circulated in the illustrated trade catalogues issued by some manufacturers of ceramics, light consumer metalwares and even tools.[11] These were unabashed marketing devices, for use in showrooms, by travelling salesmen and by wholesale customers, similar in purpose to the pattern cards and books which were widely employed by textile manufacturers and merchants to circulate samples of fabric.

Clearly the increasing availability of drawing and design skills and the growing circulation in various guises of design illustrations facilitated the acquisition of design information by manufacturers and its adaptation for use in their products (legitimately or otherwise).[12] It is therefore surprising to realize the extent to which manufacturers in many eighteenth-century industries producing batches of relatively modest products on a large scale secured design information by means of the written or spoken word. This was partly because in these industries the crucial design changes were often quite simple – a new range of colours here, a different width of stripe there. In textiles, for example, weaving simple patterned cloths did not necessarily require the painstakingly prepared patterns on point paper used in weaving elaborate designs on unwieldy draw looms in the Spitalfields silk industry. One should not, however, underestimate the richness of the information that could be communicated by means of the written word. The degree of complexity is indicated in a letter that Matthew Boulton wrote to his London buckle agent in 1793 on the need to settle on a terminology for describing changes in fashion: 'As you and I shall often have occasion to speak of forms and proportions of buckles, it is necessary we should settle a distinct language that our definitions may be precise.'[13] In most trades, however, an appropriate language of visual description already existed. Indeed, it was a fundamental aspect of that elusive but much prized knowledge of the trade which was essential to participation in it.[14] But it was also possible for non-specialists to use a verbal language of visual description in the same way. For example, information about new fashions in clothes sufficiently precise to instruct a local mantua maker was sent to a Lancashire gentlewoman from a London relative mainly through the medium of words, not drawings or illustrations.[15]

The importance of a verbal language of visual description was not confined to the process whereby manufacturers secured information about design innovation. It was also central to their ability to adapt that information to their own advantage; to get their workers successfully to produce goods which incorporated those innovations. In other words, it was crucial to communication within the firm. For example, the late eighteenth-century London hat-maker Thomas Davies was accustomed to communicate the design of new hats to the manager of his manufacturing operation in Stockport, Cheshire by letter along the following lines: 'a short napp, almost like a French hat but not so bare, pleasant stiffen'd, rather smart, by no means raggy and not a heavy hat; they are to be from 71/4 to 71/2, 31/4 to 33/4 high, not quite upright, a little taper.'[16] Here we observe the use of a specialist vocabulary in combination with a system of standard sizes to communicate precise specifications for a batch of goods.

[...]

Even when two-dimensional information was transmitted, words were often an essential accompaniment, because manufacturers did not simply want their workers to copy, but to adapt, adjust and elaborate in ways appropriate to their markets, their materials and their skills. The partners in one Lancashire cotton printing firm at the beginning of the nineteenth century sent samples of other firms' prints to their pattern drawer with accompanying verbal instructions, usually to vary the ground or the motifs, or to change the direction, the emphasis or the size of the pattern. For example, 'Enclosed you have a pattern of one of the Bury House's plate furnitures. Joseph Peel desires you will draw up and engrave two or three patterns similar, they must be showey and full of work.'[17]

Success in the consumer industries depended not only on the products being of a marketable and therefore often a fashionable design, but also on each individual item conforming strictly to a precise visual specification embodying that marketability. Distant wholesale customers who bought on the basis of samples and illustrated trade catalogues expected the goods delivered to them to conform to the look of the sample or the illustration. Uniformity was crucial, but was often extremely difficult to achieve, especially when making adaptations of more expensive products in large batches using inferior materials and cheaper, less skilled and more pressured labour.[18] Consequently manufacturers, agents, wholesalers and retailers were constantly monitoring the appearance of batch-produced goods and chiding their workers and suppliers about visual deficiencies. This kind of visual policing was conducted mainly in words.

[…]

Implementing design in large-batch manufacturing of consumer goods in the eighteenth century depended on the dexterity and adaptability of the individual worker, and on the employer's capacity to direct and instruct a workforce. The initiative in specifying design flowed predominantly from master manufacturer to worker, but the ability of workers autonomously to interpret and adapt the manufacturer's instructions was also essential. Much turned on the capacity of employees, frequently working in their own homes within an intense division of labour, to use what were often general purpose tools to produce the required specification uniformly across hundreds or thousands of objects. Much also turned on the ability of the employer to communicate his requirements to such employees with sufficient precision. All sorts of devices for specifying, transmitting and reproducing visual information could play a part here, including moulds, models, dies, transfers, scale patterns and paper designs. In the course of the eighteenth century the use of two-dimensional designs probably increased, but their importance should not be overestimated. In many of these industries a specialized and sophisticated verbal language of visual description remained crucial.[19]

CONCLUSION: DESIGN PRACTICE AND DESIGN TRAINING

Eighteenth-century England witnessed considerable efforts to improve the quality of design in manufacturing. As Charles Saumarez Smith has demonstrated, the central thrust of these efforts was to teach drawing and other artistic skills to workpeople.[20] If, as has been argued in this chapter, two-dimensional designs were of restricted importance in many of the industries producing humble consumer goods, why was there such concern to promote drawing?

Part of the answer lies in the rapid expansion during the late seventeenth and eighteenth centuries of those forms of production which relied on the most sophisticated ornament and design, especially for the luxury market. The consequence of this expansion and the technical innovations of the same period in two-dimensional and low relief ornament was a real increase in the need for drawing and engraving skills, a need that some-times had to be supplied by foreign immigrants. The design debate was conducted principally in London. The metropolitan area was by far the largest manufacturing centre in the country, and it was distinguished by a disproportionately large luxury sector, which made heavy use of both printed and hand-drawn two-dimensional designs.

Another important consideration behind the promotion of drawing skills was the persistent eighteenth-century English obsession with French competition. This was made clear in 1756 by one of the protagonists of design training, William Shipley, the founder of the Society of Arts and owner of a drawing school.

> The money given for the encouragement of boys and girls to apply themselves to drawing has not, 'tis hoped, been misemployed, since drawing is necessary in so many trades, that the general knowledge of it must conduce greatly to the improvement of our manufactures, and give them an elegance of air and figure, which a rival nation (where drawing is much encouraged) has found, to its great advantage, capable of setting off even indifferent workmanship and mean materials.[21]

The English worried throughout the eighteenth century about French superiority in the manufacture of luxury goods. Efforts to improve design reached their height in the middle decades of the century, when such anxieties were at their most intense. In the second quarter of the century, before the rapid pre-revolutionary expansion of the North American colonial market, foreign markets for the humble products in which the English excelled (especially woollen textiles) appeared to stagnate.[22] Worries about England being priced out of these markets by its high wage costs prompted the belief that it was necessary for English manufacturing to compete more effectively at the top of the market, a belief reinforced by the perceived buoyancy of luxury imports from France, despite heavy duties and prohibitions. French success in the manufacture of luxury goods seemed to owe everything to the quality of French design.

Such fears receded later in the eighteenth century, as doubts about the success of English products in the middle and lower levels of the markets for consumer goods waned. In the aftermath of the commercial treaty of 1786, which reduced trade restrictions between Britain and France, it was the British who appeared to benefit and the French who complained.[23] What happened to the promotion of drawing skills for manufacturing is less clear. There is no doubt that at the middle and lower levels of the market drawing skills could be very important. The Birmingham toy makers and the Lancashire cotton printers, for example, depended on specialist engravers and draughtsmen. As we have seen, however, such expertise was mainly required for copying and adapting designs to be implemented in large volume by other workers within an intense division of labour, rather than for initiating original designs to be produced in very small numbers. Copying and adaptation did not necessarily entail a high degree of proficiency in drawing and, on the evidence of the early years of Sir Robert Peel's Bury printworks, it required only very small numbers of workers with the appropriate skills. There was no drawing shop at Bury and only one draughtsman employed there.[24] It is therefore questionable how relevant schemes for the encouragement of formal drawing skills, like those promoted in mid-century London, were to manufacturing of this sort, compared with on-the-job training involving some sort of apprenticeship.[25]

In so far as the process of design in the eighteenth century has been explored in detail by historians, the focus has usually been on the part played by the compilers of pattern books in the making of extremely expensive and often bespoke products. The precise role of visual design in the making of many humble consumer goods remains obscure. Understanding it will demand a great deal more attention to the mundane drawing skills required for successful industrial piracy, but a narrow focus on drawing will not suffice if what is to be explained is the changes in appearance of the consumer products discussed in this chapter. That will also require study of the specialized languages of visual description used in the various manufacturing trades; indeed it will require investigation of all aspects of what might loosely be termed their and their customers' visual culture. The history of eighteenth-century design in this wider sense has yet to be written.

NOTES

Extracted from Styles, J., 'Manufacturing, Consumption and Design in Eighteenth-century England,' in John Brewer and Roy Porter (eds), *Consumption and the World of Goods*, London: Routledge, 1993, 1994, pp. 527–54. Copyright © 1993, Routledge. Reproduced by permission of Taylor & Francis Books, UK.

1. R. Campbell, *The London Tradesman* (London, 1747), p. 171.
2. N. K. A. Rothstein, 'The silk industry in London, 1702–1766' (University of London, M.A. thesis, 1961), passim.
3. S. D. Chapman and S. Chassagne, *European Textile Printers of the Eighteenth Century* (London, 1981), pp. 78–81.
4. For example, Public Record Office, C108/101: letter books of Horner and Turner, merchants, of Leeds; letter to Mr George Darby, merchant in Naples, 30 December 1789.
5. For secrecy see M. Berg, *The Age of Manufactures, 1700–1820* (London, 1985), p. 296. For similar practices in the nineteenth century see Toshio Kusamitsu, '"Novelty, give us novelty", London agents and northern manufacturers', in M. Berg (ed.), *Markets and Manufacture in Early Industrial Europe* (London, 1991).
6. Referred to in Chapman and Chassagne, *European Textile Printers*, 81, from *Journal of the House of Commons*, xlii (1787), pp. 584–5; see Public Record Office, C108/101: letter books of Horner and Turner, merchants, of Leeds for similar activities.

7. Information from Charles Saumarez Smith. See his 'Design and economy in mid-eighteenth century England', paper presented at Oxford University, 1987, and 'Eighteenth-century man', *Designer* (March 1987), pp. 19–21. For designers in the Spitalfields silk industry, see Rothstein, 'The silk industry in London', passim.
8. *Journal of the House of Commons*, xxviii (1757–61), pp. 496–7. For a discussion of the whole issue of skill shortages and training, see Saumarez Smith, 'Eighteenth-century man'.
9. Quoted in Leona Rostenberg, *English Publishers in the Graphic Arts* (New York, 1963), p. 45.
10. S. Lambert (ed.), *Pattern and Design: Designs for the Decorative Arts, 1480–1980* (London, 1983), sect. 2.
11. See D. Towner, *Creamware* (London, 1978), Appendix 2; M. B. Rowlands, *Masters and Men* (Manchester, 1975), pp. 152–3; N. Goodison, 'The Victoria and Albert Museum's collection of metal-work pattern books', *Furniture History*, xi (1975), pp. 1–30; S. Ashton, *An Eighteenth-Century Industrialist: Peter Stubbs of Warrington, 1756–1806* (Manchester, 1939), p. 60.
12. The law on design copyright was extremely weak at this period.
13. Quoted in E. Robinson, 'Eighteenth-century commerce and fashion: Matthew Boulton's marketing techniques', *Economic History Review*, xvi (1963–4), p. 49.
14. See D. Defoe, *The Complete English Tradesman*, vol. 1 (London, 1745), pp. 19–23.
15. Elizabeth Shackleton of Alkincoats, Colne, who is discussed at length in 'Women and the world of goods: a Lancashire consumer and her possessions, 1751–81', in Brewer, John, and Roy Porter, eds., *Consumption and the World of Goods*, (1993) London, New York: Routledge, 1994, pp. 274–201. I would like to thank Amanda Vickery for this information.
16. Public Record Office, C107/104: Davies letter book, letter dated 3 February 1785.
17. Letter of 1807, quoted in Chapman and Chassagne, *European Textile Printers*, p. 84.

Also see H. Clark, 'The anonymous designer', in *Design and Industry: the Effects of Industrialisation and Technical Change on Design*, ed. Nicola Hamilton (London, 1980), pp. 33–8 and idem, 'The design and designing of Lancashire printed calicoes during the first half of the 19th century', *Textile History*, xv (1984), pp. 109–10.

18. A witness before a 1787 parliamentary committee claimed that the Lancashire cotton printers who copied southern firms' design executed 'them in a much inferior style, and consequently are not at the same expense in cutting their blocks', as well as using cheap colours that ran; *Journal of the House of Commons*, xlii (1787), 584.

19. This calls into question the extent of the contrast identified by Craig Clunas between the 'visual' design practice of Europe and the 'verbal' design practice of China during the seventeenth and eighteenth centuries; C. Clunas, 'Design and cultural frontiers: English shapes and Chinese furniture workshops, 1700–90', *Apollo*, cxxvi (October 1987), p. 259.

20. Saumarez Smith, 'Design and economy in mid-eighteenth-century England' and 'Eighteenth-century man'.

21. *Gentleman's Magazine* (February 1756), quoted in Saumarez Smith, 'Design and economy'. For the Society of Arts, see D. G. C. Allen, *William Shipley: Founder of the Royal Society of Arts* (London, 1979), chs. 3, 4.

22. M. Jupp, 'Economic policy and economic development', in J. Black (ed.), *Britain in the Age of Walpole* (London, 1984), pp. 124–5.

23. J. Black, *Natural and Necessary Enemies: Anglo-French Relations in the Eighteenth Century* (London, 1986), p. 152.

24. Chapman and Chassagne, *European Textile Printers*, p. 79. Also see Clark, 'The anonymous designer' and 'Design and designing of Lancashire printed calicoes'.

25. We have here, in an incipient form, the disjuncture that dogged design education in nineteenth-century Britain between fine art sensibilities and the limited skill requirements of manufacturers producing for the middle and lower sections of the market.

GUIDE TO FURTHER READING

The extensive specialist literature on eighteenth-century design is beyond the scope of this *Reader*; here we will point to some texts that will provide a working understanding of what was distinctive about design in the period prior to 1850, and what points of continuity can be discerned in the later nineteenth-century and beyond.

Ulrich provides a broader discussion of war and trade in her chapter on 'An Indian Basket', as well as charting in detail the lives of the individuals related to the basket. It may be compared with Sarah H. Hill's *Weaving New Worlds: Southeastern Cherokee Women and Their Basketry* (1997). Ulrich's book, *The Age of Homespun*, provides similarly developed analyses of a range of other examples of material culture of the long eighteenth century.

Styles's discussion of design is preceded by useful summary discussions of manufacturing and consumption of the same period, and several other contributions to the book in which it appears are similarly informative including Amanda Vickery's 'Women and the World of Goods: a Lancashire consumer and her possessions, 1751–81' a detailed case study of what household goods meant to one eighteenth-century woman. See also Leora Auslander, in 'The Courtly Stylistic Regime: Representation and Power under Absolutism', in *Taste and Power: Furnishing Modern France* (1996), and Grant McCracken, '"Even Dearer in Our Thoughts": Patina and the Representation of Status Before and After the Eighteenth Century' in *Culture and Consumption: New Approaches to the Symbolic Character of Consumer Goods and Activities* (1988).

Andrew Ure's 'The Factory System' from *The Philosophy of Manufacturers* (1835), makes an instructive comparison with the Adam Smith text presented here. A design historical analysis of Ure's writing is provided by Steve Edwards in 'Factory and Fantasy in Andrew Ure' (2001). A much earlier primary text is Daniel Defoe's *The Complete English Tradesman* (1726), an engaging and opinionated discussion of various trades, styled as a 'collection of useful instructions for a young tradesman', which contains useful information about the organization and practice of craft and manufacturing in a watershed period for design.

Guyatt's analysis of Wedgwood complements existing studies by Neil McKendrick, including the introduction and Chapters 1 and 3 in *The Birth of a Consumer Society: The Commercialization of Eighteenth-Century England* (1983) and 'Josiah Wedgwood: An Eighteenth-Century Entrepreneur in Salesmanship and Marketing Techniques' (1960). McKendrick's later essay 'Josiah Wedgwood and Cost Accounting in the Industrial Revolution' (1970) also identifies Wedgwood's business acumen, rather than design or production expertise, as significant in his success.

All of the extracts presented here are interested in manufacture as much as design. Wider reading includes Maxine Berg, *The Age of Manufactures, 1700–1820* (1985), especially 'Industries', 'Adam Smith', and 'Domestic Manufacture and Women's Work'; and Adrian Forty, *Objects of Desire: Design and Society 1750–1980* (1986), 'The First Industrial Designers', and 'Neo-Classicism: an Antidote to

Progress'. Charles Saumerez Smith's *The Rise of Design: Design and the Domestic Interior in Eighteenth Century England* (2000) is pertinent; see particularly 'The Rise of the Designer'. Reed Benhamou's article 'Imitation in the Decorative Arts of the Eighteenth Century' (1991) also considers different perceptions of the designer's role, in relation to innovation and imitation. Studies of dress of the period include Daniel Roche, *The Culture of Clothing: Dress and Fashion in the Ancien Régime* (1994) and Aileen Ribeiro, *Dress in Eighteenth-Century Europe, 1715–1789* (2002).

SECTION 2

Design Reform, 1820–1910

INTRODUCTION

Rebecca Houze

Debates between designers, manufacturers and commentators on design, industry and economics continued and intensified into the nineteenth century as industrialization and its surrounding discourses grew. Of design historical relevance are the ideas of Andrew Ure (1778–1857), Karl Marx (1818–83) and A. W. N. Pugin (1812–52), the latter being notable among designers and writers to argue for a new understanding of quality and purpose of design. Public debates surrounding industrialization were stimulated by the many international exhibitions staged in the second half of the nineteenth century. London's Great Exhibition of 1851 was the first of these spectacular events held on a massive scale. It took place in architect Joseph Paxton's 'Crystal Palace', an enormous structure developed from his designs for glass houses. The public was invited to examine objects from around the globe. Factory-made furnishings were displayed alongside hand-made items from Britain's many colonies abroad, vividly marking the difference between a primitive past and technological future. Of the 100,000 exhibits, vast quantities of manufactured fabrics, glass, silver and other decorative objects seemed to reveal that the machine had not only conquered craft traditions but had even introduced new uses for media, such as industrial cast iron, papier-mâché, gutta-percha and celluloid, which could mimic traditional materials and forms in an endless variety of ways, fuelling the consumer's passion for novelty.

German architect and art historian Gottfried Semper was living in London as an exiled revolutionary when he was invited to design several installations at the Great Exhibition. Afterwards, Semper reflected on the aesthetic consequences of the promiscuous industrial manufacture that he had seen at the fair in his influential essay, 'Science, Industry and Art'. Now we could 'cut the hardest stone like cheese and bread', he observed, but what had we lost as a result? The wondrous vision of new technology was unsettling for Semper. In the many traditional crafts on display, such as hand-woven shawls from India, he discerned an intrinsically logical relationship between material, technique and aesthetic form that he believed was absent from industry all too ready to supply cheap, imitative goods to a hungry public.

The loss of meaningful aesthetic form was especially criticized by proponents of England's Gothic Revival, following A. W. N. Pugin. Prominent among them was John Ruskin, who found a deep spirituality in the architecture of late medieval churches. For Ruskin, the 'savage' decoration of these buildings signified 'truth' and mirrored the noble imperfection of nature and of the human soul. His meditative 1853 essay, 'The Nature of Gothic' was a source of inspiration for members of England's Arts and Crafts Movement, including William Morris, who advocated a return to pre-industrial craft traditions, in which both worker and consumer would be elevated spiritually by virtue of their close relationship to beautiful and lovingly made objects. In the passage reproduced here, Ruskin describes

'Savageness', one of the six key characteristics of the Gothic (the others being 'Changefulness', 'Naturalism', 'Grotesqueness', 'Rigidity' and 'Redundance'). Both Ruskin and Morris believed in design as a moral force for good, which could liberate humanity from their drudgery and enslavement to the capitalistic factory system of production.

Morris reprinted Ruskin's essay at his Kelmscott press in 1893 according to the design criteria outlined in his own article 'The Ideal Book', a manifesto for the organic relationship between typeface, illustration, ornament, and structure of a book. His theories, which countered the Victorian eclecticism and superficial historicism of objects on display at the Great Exhibition, led many of his followers and later design historians such as Nikolaus Pevsner to uphold Morris as a 'pioneer' of modern design.

Design historian John Heskett suggests that architects and designers in the USA may have been less critical of industrialism than their European counterparts. In his chapter 'The "American system" and Mass-Production', Heskett traces the emergence of new inventions, such as the mechanical McCormick reaper, the Singer sewing machine and the Remington typewriter, whose origins lay in the successful mechanization of firearms. These objects not only reflected the strength of industry to produce standardized, interchangeable, mechanical parts cheaply and efficiently; they also revolutionized processes of agriculture, clothes-making, and even writing. Advances made in the production of mechanical watches and revolvers led to the experiments in assembly-line production promoted by Frederick Taylor's theory of 'Scientific Management', which found its greatest expression in the automobile industry, with the exemplary success of Henry Ford's Model T.

Heskett also attributes the innovations of American architects Louis Sullivan and Frank Lloyd Wright to their enthusiasm for the machine. Sullivan's notion that 'form follows function', which he expressed in his analysis of contemporary skyscraper design, quickly became one of the central tenets of the modern movement. Indeed, both men grappled with industrialism in their invention of an entirely new form of architecture. But Heskett's assessment of American design as something that emerged from the purely utilitarian and commercial motivations of a young, audacious, and militaristic republic may obscure the complexity behind the work of Sullivan and Wright, whose ideas were rooted in a spiritualized organicism as well as in the American spirit of invention. Wright's utopian, visionary essay 'The Art and Craft of the Machine' demonstrates the architect's efforts to reform design by marrying William Morris's moral and aesthetic sensibility to the reality of modern mechanical production.

Theories of design at the turn-of-the-twentieth-century were rich, complex, idiosyncratic, and often contradictory. Historian Debora Silverman, in the concluding chapter to her book *Art Nouveau in Fin-de-siècle France: Politics, Psychology and Style*, describes the organic 'feminine' interiors designed by Georges de Feure and Eugène Gaillard for art dealer Siegfried Bing's installation of decorative arts at the 1900 Paris Exposition Universelle as a turning inward, having less to do with an outward enthusiasm for, or rejection of, the machine than with a nuanced effort to create a modern national and personal identity that looked both forward and back. De Feure's sinuous gilded settee with its tapestry of pale pink rosettes simultaneously recalled the long French aristocratic tradition of fine furniture craftsmanship, while also proclaiming its distinctly modern nature. Art Nouveau, or *Jugendstil*, as it was called in Germany, drew inspiration from the arts and crafts, studies of evolution, the symbolist movement in literature and the visual arts, with its love of the macabre and the femme-fatale. In a way similar to Ruskin's valorization of the 'savage' gothic, art nouveau designers found pleasure in the seemingly irrational forms of a fervent nature. Unlike those affiliated with the Arts and Crafts Movement, however, art nouveau designers did not reject industry or commerce. Rather they combined new attitudes towards fashion, shopping, luxury, and femininity, as well as erotic female sexuality, with a fine craft tradition, in which, nature, commerce and the 'new woman' were often conflated.

6

SCIENCE, INDUSTRY, AND ART

Gottfried Semper (1852)

I.

Scarcely four weeks have passed since the close of the Exhibition, some wares still stand unpacked in the deserted halls of the Hyde Park building, and already public attention has turned away from the "world-renowned event" toward other, perhaps more gripping events close at hand. None of the enthusiastic newspaper correspondents who on the opening day of the "world market" proclaimed the inauguration of a new era any longer voice their opinion on the subject. Yet the stimulation the event has left behind still ferments in the pensive minds and aspiring hearts of thousands. The far-reaching consequences of this impulse cannot be measured.

[...]

It is already evident that inventions are no longer, as before, a means for averting privation and for enjoyment. On the contrary, privation and enjoyment create the market for the inventions. The order of things has been reversed.

What is the inevitable result of this? The present has no time to become familiar with the half-imposed benefits and to master them. The situation resembles that of the Chinese, who should eat with a knife and fork. Speculation interposes itself there and lays out the benefits attractively before us; where there is none, speculation creates a thousand small and large advantages. Old, outdated comforts are called back into use when speculation cannot think of

anything new. It effortlessly accomplishes the most difficult and troublesome things with means borrowed from science. The hardest porphyry and granite are cut like chalk and polished like wax. Ivory is softened and pressed into forms. Rubber and gutta-percha are vulcanized and utilized in a thousand imitations of wood, metal, and stone carvings, exceeding by far the natural limitations of the material they purport to represent. Metal is no longer cast or wrought, but treated with the newest unknown forces of nature in a galvano-plastic way. The talbotype succeeds the daguerrotype and makes the latter already a thing forgotten. Machines sew, knit, embroider, paint, carve, and encroach deeply into the field of human art, putting to shame every human skill.

Are these not great and glorious achievements? By no means do I deplore the general conditions of which these are only the less important symptoms. On the contrary, I am confident that sooner or later everything will develop favorably for the well-being and honor of society. For now I refrain from proceeding to those larger and more difficult questions suggested by them. In the following pages I only wish to point out the confusion they now cause in those fields in which the talents of man take an active part in the recognition and presentation of beauty.

II.

If single incidents carried the force of conviction, then the recognized triumphs at the Exhibition of the half-barbaric nations, especially the Indians with their magnificent industries of art, would be sufficient to show us that we with our science have until now accomplished very little in these areas.

The same, shameful truth confronts us when we compare our products with those of our ancestors. Notwithstanding our many technical advances, we remain far behind them in formal beauty, and even in a feeling for the suitable and the appropriate. Our best things are more or less faithful reminiscences. Others show a praiseworthy effort to borrow forms directly from nature, yet how seldom we have been successful in this! Most of our attempts are a confused muddle of forms or childish triflings. As best, objects whose seriousness of purpose does not permit the superfluous, such as wagons, weapons, musical instruments, and similar things, we sometimes make appear healthier by the refined presentation of their strictly prescribed forms.

Although facts, as we said, are no argument and can even be disputed, it is easy to prove that present conditions are dangerous for the industrial arts, decidedly fatal for the traditional higher arts.

The *abundance of means* is the first great danger with which art has to struggle. This expression is illogical, I admit (there is no abundance of means but only an inability to master them); however, it is justified in that it correctly describes the inverted state of our conditions.

Practice wearies itself in vain in trying to master its material, especially intellectually. It receives it from science ready to process as it chooses, but before its style could have evolved through many centuries of popular usage. The founders of a flourishing art once had their material kneaded beforehand, as it were, by the beelike instinct of the people; they invested the indigenous motive with a higher meaning and treated it artistically, stamping their creations with a rigorous necessity and spiritual freedom. These works became universally understood expressions of a true idea that will survive historically as long as any trace or knowledge of them remains.

What a glorious discovery is the gaslight! [Figure 4] How its brilliance enhances our festivities, not to mention its enormous importance to everyday life! Yet in imitating candles or oil lamps in our salons, we hide the apertures of the gas pipes; in illumination, on the other hand, we pierce the pipes with innumerable small opening, so that all sorts of stars, firewheels, pyramids, escutcheons, inscription, and so on seem to float before the walls of our houses, as if supported by invisible hands.

This floating stillness of the most lively of all elements is effective to be sure (the sun, moon, and stars provide the most dazzling examples of it), but who can deny that this innovation has detracted from the popular custom of *illuminating* houses as a sign the occupants participate in the public joy? Formerly, oil lamps were placed on the cornice ledges and window sills, thereby lending a radiant prominence to the familiar masses and individual parts of the houses. Now our eyes are blinded by the blaze of those apparitions of fire and the facades behind are rendered invisible.

Whoever has witnessed the illuminations in London and remembers similar festivities in the old style in Rome will admit that the art of lighting has suffered a rude setback by these improvements.

This example demonstrates the two main dangers, the Scylla and Charybdis, between which we must steer to gain innovations for art.

The invention was excellent but it was sacrificed in the first case to traditional form, and in the second case its basic motive was completely obscured by its false application. Yet every means was available to make it more lustrous and to enrich it at the same time with a new idea (that of a fixed display of fireworks).

A clever helmsman, therefore, must be he who avoids these dangers, and his course is even more difficult because he finds himself in unknown waters without a chart or compass. For among the multitude of artistic and technical writings, there is sorely needed a practical guide to invention that maps out the cliffs and sandbars to be avoided

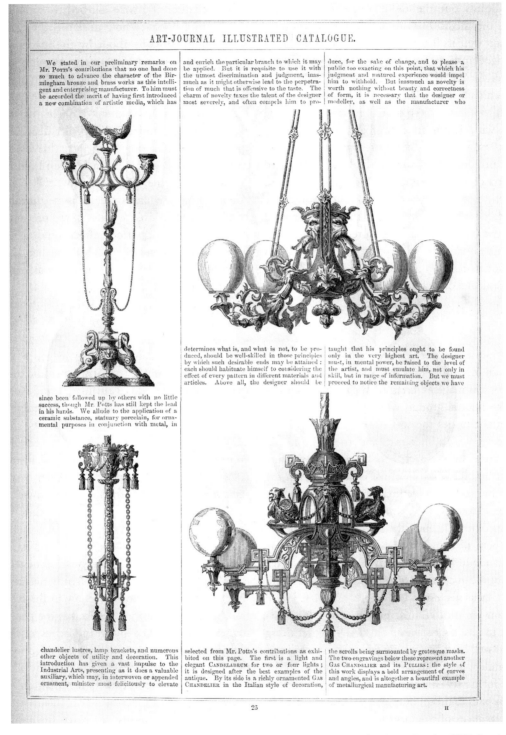

ART-JOURNAL ILLUSTRATED CATALOGUE.

We stated in our preliminary remarks on Mr. Potts's contributions that no one had done so much to advance the character of the Birmingham bronze and brass works as this intelligent and enterprising manufacturer. To him must be accorded the merit of having first introduced a new combination of artistic media, which has since been followed up by others with no little success, though Mr. Potts has still kept the lead in his hands. We allude to the application of a ceramic substance, statuary porcelain, for ornamental purposes in conjunction with metal, in

and enrich the particular branch to which it may be applied. But it is requisite to use it with the utmost discrimination and judgment, inasmuch as it might otherwise lead to the perpetration of much that is offensive to the taste. The charm of novelty taxes the talent of the designer most severely, and often compels him to produce, for the sake of change, and to please a public too exacting on this point, that which his judgment and matured experience would impel him to withhold. But inasmuch as novelty is worth nothing without beauty and correctness of form, it is necessary that the designer or modeller, as well as the manufacturer who determines what is, and what is not, to be produced, should be well-skilled in those principles by which such desirable ends may be attained : each should habituate himself to considering the effect of every pattern in different materials and articles. Above all, the designer should be taught that his principles ought to be found only in the very highest art. The designer must, in mental power, be raised to the level of the artist, and must emulate him, not only in skill, but in range of information. But we must proceed to notice the remaining objects we have

chandelier lustres, lamp brackets, and numerous other objects of utility and decoration. This introduction has given a vast impulse to the Industrial Arts, presenting as it does a valuable auxiliary, which may, in interwoven or appended ornament, minister most felicitously to elevate selected from Mr. Potts's contributions as exhibited on this page. The first is a light and elegant CANDELABRUM for two or four lights ; it is designed after the best examples of the antique. By its side is a richly ornamented GAS CHANDELIER in the Italian style of decoration, the scrolls being surmounted by grotesque masks. The two engravings below these represent another GAS CHANDELIER and its PULLIES : the style of this work displays a bold arrangement of curves and angles, and is altogether a beautiful example of metallurgical manufacturing art.

Figure 4. Candelabrum and Gas Chandeliers, *The Crystal Palace Exhibition Illustrated Catalogue, London 1851*, Special Issue of the *Art Journal*, p. 25. Rare Books and Special Collections, Northern Illinois University.

and points out the right course to be taken. Were the theory of taste (aesthetics) a complete science, were its incompleteness not compounded by vague and often erroneous ideas in need of a clearer formulation especially in its application to architecture and tectonics in general, then it would fill just this void. Yet in its present state it is with justification scarcely considered by gifted professionals. Its tottering precepts and basic principles find approval only with so-called experts of art, who measure the value of a work thereby because they have no inner, subjective standards for art. They believe they have grasped beauty's secret with a dozen precepts, while the infinite variation in the world of form assumes characteristic meaning and individual beauty just by the denial of any scheme.

[…]

The granite and porphryry monuments of Egypt exert an incredible sway over our feelings. In what resides this magic? Certainly in part because they are the neutral ground where the hard, resisting material engages the soft hand of man with his simple tools (the hammer and the chisel), and they enter into a pact: "So far and no further, in this manner and no other!" This has been the silent message for millennia. Their majestic repose and massiveness, the somewhat angular and flat elegance of their lines, the restraint shown in the treatment of the difficult material – their whole demeanor indicates a beauty of style that to us, who now can cut the hardest stone like cheese and bread, lacks necessity.

How should we treat granite now? It is difficult to give a satisfactory answer! The first thing might well be to use it only where its durability is demanded, and draw from this last condition the rules for its stylistic treatment. How little attention is paid to this in our time is shown by certain extravagances of the large granite and porphyry manufactures in Sweden and Russia.

This example leads to a more general question that by itself would provide sufficient material for a large chapter, if I were allowed to expand this essay into a book. Where does the depreciation of materials brought about by the machine, by their surrogates, and by so many new inventions lead us? What effect will the depreciation of labor, a result of the same causes, have on the painted, sculptured, and other kinds of decorative work? Naturally, I am not referring to the depreciation in fees, but in meaning, in the idea. Have not the new Houses of Parliament in London been made unbearable by the machine? How will time or science bring law and order to these thoroughly confused conditions? How do we prevent the general depreciation from also extending to all works executed in the old way by hand, how do we prevent them from being seen as antique, striking, or eccentric affectations?

[…]

We possess a wealth of knowledge, a never surpassed technical virtuosity, a profuse artistic tradition, recognized artistic images, and a proper view of nature, all of which we must certainly not abandon for half-barbaric ways. What we should learn from people of non-European culture is the art of catching those simple melodies in form and color – that instinct granted to human works in their most primitive formations, which we, with our more extensive means, always find more difficult to grasp and retain. We must therefore study the most primitive works of the hand of man and the history of their development with the same attentiveness that we study nature herself in her manifestations. We saw in the Exhibition, for instance, to what mistakes the generally praiseworthy effort of the art industries to imitate nature literally can lead, when it is guided neither by natural instinct nor by a prudent study of style. We saw so many childish, rather than childlike attempts at art.

While our art industries carry on aimlessly they unconsciously fulfill one noble task: the *disintegration of traditional types* by their ornamental treatment.

[…]

NOTE

Extracted from, Semper, G., 'Science, Industry, and Art: Proposals for the Development of a National Taste in Art at the Closing of the London Industrial Exhibition' (1852), in G. Semper, *The Four Elements of Architecture and Other Writings*, trans. Harry Francis Mallgrave and Wolfgang Herrmann, Cambridge: Cambridge University Press, 1989, pp. 130–67. Copyright Cambridge University Press 1989, reprinted with permission.

7

THE NATURE OF GOTHIC

John Ruskin (1853)

[...]

SAVAGENESS

I am not sure when the word 'Gothic' was first generically applied to the architecture of the North; but I presume that, whatever the date of its original usage, it was intended to imply reproach, and express the barbaric character of the nations among whom that architecture arose. It never implied that they were literally of Gothic lineage, far less that their architecture had been originally invented by the Goths themselves; but it did imply that they and their buildings together exhibited a degree of sternness and rudeness, which, in contradistinction to the character of Southern and Eastern nations, appeared like a perpetual reflection of the contrast between the Goth and the Roman in their first encounter. And when that fallen Roman, in the utmost impotence of his luxury, and insolence of his guilt, became the model for the imitation of civilized Europe, at the close of the so-called Dark Ages, the word Gothic became a term of unmitigated contempt, not unmixed with aversion. From that contempt, by the exertion of the antiquaries and architects of this century, Gothic architecture has been sufficiently vindicated; and perhaps some among us, in our admiration of the magnificent science of its structure, and sacredness of its expression, might desire that the term of ancient reproach should be withdrawn, and some other, of more apparent honourableness, adopted in its place. There is no chance, as there is no need, of such a substitution. As far as the epithet was used scornfully, it was used falsely; but there is no reproach in the word, rightly understood; on the contrary, there is a profound truth, which the instinct of mankind almost unconsciously recognizes. It is true, greatly and deeply true, that the architecture of the North is rude and wild; but it is not true, that, for this reason, we are to condemn it, or despise. Far otherwise: I believe it is in this very character that it deserves our profoundest reverence.

[...]

If, however, the savageness of Gothic architecture, merely as an expression of its origin among Northern nations, may be considered, in some sort, a noble character, it possesses a higher nobility still, when considered as an index, not of climate, but of religious principle.

In the 13th and 14th paragraphs of Chapter XXI. of the first volume of this work, it was noticed that the systems of architectural ornament, properly so called, might be divided into three: – 1. Servile ornament, in which the execution or power of the inferior workman is entirely subjected to the intellect of the higher; – 2. Constitutional ornament, in which the executive inferior power is, to a certain point, emancipated and independent, having a will of its own, yet confessing its inferiority and rendering obedience to higher powers; – and 3. Revolutionary ornament, in which no executive inferiority is admitted at all. I must here explain the nature of these divisions at somewhat greater length.

Of Servile ornament, the principal schools are the Greek, Ninevite and Egyptian; but their servility is of different kinds. The Greek master-workman was far advanced in knowledge and power above the Assyrian or Egyptian. Neither he nor those for whom he worked could endure the appearance of imperfection in anything; and, therefore, what ornament he appointed to be done by those beneath him was composed of mere geometrical forms, – balls, ridges, and perfectly symmetrical foliage, – which could be executed with absolute precision by line and rule, and were as perfect in their way, when completed, as his own figure sculpture. The Assyrian and Egyptian, on the contrary, less cognisant of accurate form in anything, were content to allow their figure sculpture to be executed by inferior workmen, but lowered the method of its treatment to a standard which every workman could reach, and then trained him by discipline so rigid, that there was no chance of his falling beneath the standard appointed. The Greek gave to the lower workman no subject which he could not perfectly execute. The Assyrian gave him subjects which he could only execute imperfectly, but fixed a legal standard for his imperfection. The workman was in both systems, a slave.[1]

But in the mediaeval, or especially Christian, system of ornament, this slavery is done away with altogether; Christianity having recognized, in small things as well as great, the individual value of every soul. But it not only recognizes its value; it confesses its imperfection, in only bestowing dignity upon the acknowledgment of unworthiness. That admission of lost power and fallen nature, which the Greek or Ninevite felt to be intensely painful, and, as far as might be, altogether refused, the Christian makes daily and hourly, contemplating the fact of it without fear, as tending, in the end, to God's greater glory. Therefore, to every spirit which Christianity summons to her service, her exhortation is: Do what

you can, and confess frankly what you are unable to do; neither let your effort be shortened for fear of failure, nor your confession silenced for fear of shame. And it is, perhaps, the principal admirableness of the Gothic schools of architecture, that they thus receive the results of the labour of inferior minds; and out of fragments full of imperfection, and betraying that imperfection in every touch, indulgently raise up a stately and unaccusable whole.

But the modern English mind has this much in common with that of the Greek, that it intensely desires, in all things, the utmost completion or perfection compatible with their nature. This is a noble character in the abstract, but becomes ignoble when it causes us to forget the relative dignities of that nature itself, and to prefer the perfectness of the lower nature to the imperfection of the higher; not considering that as judged by such a rule, all the brute animals would be preferable to man, because more perfect in their functions and kind, and yet are always held inferior to him, so also in the works of man, those which are more perfect in their kind are always inferior to those which are, in their nature, liable to more faults and shortcomings. For the finer the nature, the more flaws it will show through the clearness of it; and it is a law of this universe, that the best things shall be seldomest seen in their best form. […] Now, in the make and nature of every man, however rude or simple, whom we employ in manual labour, there are some powers for better things; some tardy imagination, torpid capacity of emotion, tottering steps of thought, there are, even at the worst; and in most cases it is all our own fault that they *are* tardy or torpid. But they cannot be strengthened, unless we are content to take them in their feebleness, and unless we prize and honour them in their imperfection above the best and most perfect manual skill. And this is what we have to do with all our labourers; to look for the *thoughtful* part of them, and get that out of them, whatever we lose for it, whatever faults and errors we are obliged to take with it. For the best that is in them cannot manifest itself, but in company with much error. Understand this clearly: You can teach a man to draw a straight line, and to cut one; to strike a curved line, and to carve it; and to copy and carve any number of given lines or forms, with admirable speed and perfect precision; and you find his work perfect of its kind: but if you ask him to think about any of those forms, to consider if he cannot find any better in his own head, he stops; his execution becomes hesitating; he thinks, and ten to one he thinks wrong; ten to one he makes a mistake in the first touch he gives to his work as a thinking being. But you have made a man of him for all that. He was only a machine before, an animated tool.

And observe, you are put to stern choice in this matter. You must either make a tool of the creature, or a man of him. You cannot make both. Men were not intended to work with the accuracy of tools, to be precise and perfect in all their actions. If you will have that precision out of them, and make their fingers measure degrees like cog-wheels, and their arms strike curves like compasses, you must unhumanize them. All the energy of their spirits must be given to make cogs and compasses of themselves. All their attention and strength must go to the accomplishment of the mean act. The eye of the soul must be bent upon the finger-point, and the soul's force must fill all the invisible nerves that guide it, ten hours a day, that it may not err from its steely precision, and so soul and sight be worn away, and the whole human being be lost at last – a heap of sawdust, so far as its intellectual work in this world is concerned: saved only by its Heart, which cannot go into the form of cogs and compasses, but expands, after the ten hours are over, into fireside humanity. On the other hand, if you will make a man of the working creature, you cannot make a tool. Let him but begin to imagine, to think, to try to do anything worth doing; and the engine-turned precision is lost at once. Out come all his roughness, all his dullness, all his incapability; shame upon shame, failure upon failure, pause after pause; but out comes the whole majesty

of him also; and we know the height of it only when we see the clouds settling upon him. And, whether the clouds be bright or dark, there will be transfiguration behind and within them.

And now, reader, look round this English room of yours, about which you have been proud so often, because the work of it was so good and strong, and the ornaments of it so finished. Examine again all those accurate mouldings and perfect polishings, and unerring adjustments of the seasoned wood and tempered steel. Many a time you have exulted over them, and thought how great England was, because her slightest work was done so thoroughly. Alas! If read rightly, these perfectnesses are signs of a slavery in our England a thousand times more bitter and more degrading than that of the scourged African, or helot Greek. Men may be beaten, chained, tormented, yoked like cattle, slaughtered like summer flies, and yet remain in one sense, and the best sense, free. But to smother their souls within them, to blight and hew into rotting pollards the suckling branches of their human intelligence, to make the flesh and skin which, after the worm's work on it, is to see God, into leathern thongs to yoke machinery with, – this it is to be slave-masters indeed; and there might be more freedom in England, though her feudal lords' lightest words were worth men's lives, and though the blood of the vexed husband-man dropped in the furrows of their fields, than there is while the animation of her multitudes is sent like fuel to feed the factory smoke, and the strength of them is given daily to be wasted into the fineness of a web, or racked into the exactness of a line.

And, on the other hand, go forth again to gaze upon the old cathedral front, where you have smiled so often at the fantastic ignorance of the old sculptors: examine once more those ugly goblins, and formless monsters, and stern statues, anatomiless and rigid; but do not mock at them, for they are signs of the life and liberty of every workman who struck the stone; a freedom of thought, and rank in scale of being, such as no laws, no charters, no charities can secure; but which it must be the first aim of all Europe at this day to regain for her children.

[…]

We have much studied and much perfected, of late, the great civilized invention of the division of labour; only we give it a false name. It is not, truly speaking, the labour that is divided; but the men: – Divided into mere segments of men – broken into small fragments and crumbs of life; so that all the little piece of intelligence that is left in a man is not enough to make a pin, or a nail, but exhausts itself in making the point of a pin or the head of a nail. Now it is a good and desirable thing, truly, to make many pins in a day; but if we could only see with what crystal sand their points were polished, – sand of human soul, much to be magnified before it can be discerned for what it is – we should think there might be some loss in it also. And the great cry that rises from all our manufacturing cities, louder than their furnace blast, is all in very deed for this, – that we manufacture everything there except men; we blanch cotton, and strengthen steel, and refine sugar, and shape pottery; but to brighten, to strengthen, to refine, or to form a single living spirit, never enters into our estimate of advantages. And all the evil to which that cry is urging our myriads can be met only in one way: not by teaching nor preaching, for to teach them is but to show them their misery, and to preach to them, if we do nothing more than preach, is to mock at it. It can be met only by a right understanding, on the part of all classes, of what kinds of labour are good for men, raising them, and making them happy; by a determined sacrifice of such convenience, or beauty, or cheapness as is to be got only by the degradation of the workman; and by equally determined demand for the products and results of healthy and ennobling labour.

And how, it will be asked, are these products to be recognized, and this demand to be regulated? Easily: by the observance of three broad and simple rules:

1. Never encourage the manufacture of any article not absolutely necessary, in the production of which *Invention* has no share.
2. Never demand an exact finish for its own sake, but only for some practical or noble end.
3. Never encourage imitation or copying of any kind, except for the sake of preserving records of great works.

[…]

For instance, glass beads are utterly unnecessary, and there is no design or thought employed in their manufacture. They are formed by first drawing out the glass into rods; these rods are chopped up into fragments of the size of beads by the human hand, and the fragments are then rounded in the furnace. The men who chop up the rods sit at their work all day, their hands vibrating with a perpetual and exquisitely timed palsy, and the beads dropping beneath their vibration like hail. Neither they, nor the men who draw out the rods or fuse the fragments, have the smallest occasion for the use of any single human faculty; and every young lady, therefore, who buys glass beads is engaged in the slave-trade, and in a much more cruel one than that which we have to long been endeavouring to put down. But glass cups and vessels may become the subjects of exquisite invention; and if in buying these we pay for the invention, that is to say, for the beautiful form, or colour, or engraving, and not for mere finish of execution, we are doing good to humanity.

[…] Imperfection is in some sort essential to all that we know of life. It is the sign of life in a mortal body, that is to say, of a state of progress and change. Nothing that lives is, or can be, rigidly perfect; part of it is decaying, part nascent. The foxglove blossom, – a third part bud, a third part past, a third part in full bloom, – is a type of the life of this world. And in all things that live there are certain irregularities and deficiencies which are not only signs of life, but sources of beauty. No human face is exactly the same in its lines on each side, no leaf perfect in its lobes, no branch in its symmetry. All admit irregularity as they imply change; and to banish imperfection is to destroy expression, to check exertion, to paralyze vitality. All things are literally better, lovelier, and more beloved for the imperfections which have been divinely appointed, that the law of human life may be Effort, and the law of human judgment, Mercy.

[…]

NOTES

Extracted from Ruskin, J., 'The Nature of Gothic' (1853), in *The Stones of Venice*, vol. 2, *The Sea Stories*, in E. T. Cook and A. Wedderburn (eds), *The Complete Works of John Ruskin*, vol. 10, London: George Allen, 1904, pp. 180–269.

1. The third kind of ornament, the Renaissance, is that in which the inferior detail becomes principal, the executor of every minor portion being required to exhibit skill and possess knowledge as great as that which is possessed by the master of the design; and in the endeavour to endow him with this skill and knowledge, his own original power is overwhelmed, and the whole building becomes a wearisome exhibition of well-educated imbecility. We must fully inquire into the nature of this form of error when we arrive at the examination of the Renaissance schools.

8

THE IDEAL BOOK

William Morris (1893)

Figure 5. John Ruskin, *The Nature of Gothic. A Chapter of the Stones of Venice*, Hammersmith: Printed by William Morris at the Kelmscott Press and published by George Allen, London, 1892, title page. © The British Library Board. BL Shelfmark C.43.3.4 General Reference Collection.

By the ideal book, I suppose we are to understand a book not limited by commercial exigencies of price: we can do what we like with it, according to what its nature, as a book, demands of Art. But we may conclude, I think, that its maker will limit us somewhat; a work on differential calculus, a medical work, a dictionary, a collection of statesmen's speeches, of a treatise on manures, such books, though they might be handsomely and well printed, would scarcely receive ornament with the same exuberance as a volume of lyrical poems, or a standard classic, or such like. A work *on* Art, I think, bears less of ornament than any other kind of book (*non bis in idem* is a good motto); again, a book that *must* have *illustrations*, more or less utilitarian, should, I think, have no actual *ornament* at all, because the ornament and the illustration must almost certainly fight. Still, whatever the subject-matter of the book may be, and however bare it may be of decoration, it can still be a work of art, if the type be good and attention be paid to its general arrangement. All here present, I should suppose, will agree in thinking an opening of Schoeffer's 1462 Bible beautiful, even when it has neither been illuminated nor rubricated; the same may be said of Schüssler, or Jenson, or, in short, of any of the *good* old printers; their works, without any further ornament than they derived from the design and arrangement of the letters were definite works of art. In fact a book, printed or written, has a tendency to be a beautiful object, and that we of this age should generally produce ugly books, shows, I fear, something like malice prepense – a *determination* to put our eyes in our pockets wherever we can.

Well, I lay it down, first, that a book quite un-ornamented can look actually and positively beautiful, and not merely un-ugly, if it be, so to say, architecturally good, which by the by, need not add much to its price, since it costs no more to pick up pretty stamps than ugly ones, and the taste and forethought that goes to the proper setting, position, and so on, will soon grow into a habit, if cultivated, and will not take up much of the master-printer's time when taken with his other necessary business.

Now, then, let us see what this architectural arrangement claims of us.

First, the pages must be clear and easy to read; which they can hardly be unless, *secondly*, the type is well designed; and *thirdly*, whether the margins be small or big, they must be in due proportion to the page of letters.

For clearness of reading, the things necessary to be heeded are, first, that the letters should be properly put on their bodies, and, I think, especially that there should be small whites between them. It is curious, but to me certain, that the irregularity of some early type, notably the Roman letter of the early printers of Rome, which is, of all Roman type, the rudest, does *not* tend towards illegibility: what does do so, is the lateral compression of the letter, which necessarily involves the over-thinning out of its shape. Of course I do not mean to say that the above-mentioned irregularity is other than a fault to be corrected. One thing should *never* be done in ideal printing, the spacing out of letters, that is, putting an extra white between them; except in such hurried and unimportant work as newspaper printing, it is inexcusable.

This leads us to the second matter on this head, the lateral spacing of words (the whites between them). To make a beautiful page great attention should be paid to this, which, I fear, is not often done. No more white should be used between the words than just clearly cuts them off from one another; if the whites are bigger than this it both tends to illegibility and makes the page ugly. I remember once buying a handsome fifteenth-century Venetian book, and I could not tell at first why some of its pages were so worrying to read, and so commonplace and vulgar to look at, for there was no fault to find with the type. But presently it was accounted for by the spacing; for the said pages were spaced like a modern book, i.e., the black and white nearly equal. Next, if you want a legible book, the white should be white and the black black. When that excellent journal the *Westminster Gazette*, first came out, there was a discussion on the advantages of its green paper, in which a good deal of nonsense was talked. My friend, Mr. Jacobi, being a practical printer, set these wise men right, if they noticed his letter, which I fear they did not, by pointing out that what they had done was to lower the tone (not the moral tone) of the paper, and that, therefore, in order to make it legible as ordinary black and white, they should make their black blacker – which of course they do not do. You may depend upon it that a grey page is very trying to the eyes.

As above said, legibility depends also much on the design of the letter; and again I take up the cudgels against compressed type, and that especially in Roman letters: the full-sized lower-case letters *a*, *b*, *c*, & *d*, should be designed on something like a square to get good results: otherwise one may fairly say that there is no room for the design. Furthermore, each letter should have its due characteristic drawing; e.g., the thickening out for a *b*, should not be of the same kind as that for a *d*; a *u* should not merely be an *n* turned upside down; the dot of the *i* should not be a circle drawn with compasses, but a delicately drawn diamond, and so on. To be short, the letters should be designed by an artist, and not an engineer. As to the forms of letters in England (I mean Great Britain), there has been much progress within the last forty years. The sweltering hideousness of the Bodoni letter, the most illegible type that was ever cut, with its preposterous thicks and thins, has been mostly relegated to works that do not profess anything but the baldest utilitarianism (though why even utilitarianism should use illegible types, I fail to see), and Caslon's letter, and the somewhat wiry, but in its way, elegant old-faced type cut in our own days, has largely taken its place. It is rather unlucky, however, that a somewhat low standard of excellence has been accepted for the design of modern Roman type at its best, the comparatively poor and wiry letter of Plantin, and the Elzeviers, having served for the model, rather than the generous and logical designs of the fifteenth-century Venetian printers, at

the head of whom stands Nicholas Jenson. When it is so obvious that this is the best and clearest Roman type yet struck, it seems a pity that we should make our starting point for a possible new departure at any period worse than the best. If any of you doubt the superiority of this type over that of the seventeenth century, the study of a specimen enlarged about five times will convince him, I should think. I must admit, however, that a commercial consideration comes in here, to wit, that the Jenson letters take up more room than the imitations of the seventeenth century; and that touches on another commercial difficulty; to wit, that you cannot have a book either handsome or clear to read which is printed in small characters. For my part, except where books smaller than an ordinary octavo are wanted, I would fight against anything smaller than pica; but at any rate small pica seems to me the smallest type that should be used in the body of any book. I might suggest to printers that if they want to get more in they can reduce the size of the leads, or leave them out altogether. Of course this is more desirable in some types than others; e.g., Caslon's letter, which has long ascenders and descenders, never needs leading, except for special purposes.

I have hitherto had a fine and generous Roman type in my mind, but after all, a certain amount of variety is desirable, and when you have once got your Roman letter as good as the best that has been, I do not think you will find much scope for development of it. I would, therefore, put in a word for some form of Gothic letter for use in our improved printed book. This may startle some of you, but you must remember that except for a very remarkable type used very seldom by Berthelette (I have only seen two books in this type, Bartholomew the Englishman, and the Gower of 1532), English black-letter, since the days of Wynkyn de Worde, has been always the letter which was introduced from Holland about that time (I except again, of course, the modern imitations of Caxton). Now this, though a handsome and stately letter, is not very easy reading, it is too much compressed, too spiky, and, so to say, too prepensely Gothic. But there are many types which are of a transitional character and of all degrees of transition; from those which do little more than take in just a little of the crisp floweriness of the Gothic, like some of the Mentelin or quasi-Mentelin ones (which, indeed, are models of beautiful simplicity), or, say, like the letter of the Ulm Ptolemy, of which it is difficult to say whether it is Gothic or Roman, to the splendid Mainz type, of which, I suppose, the finest example is the Schoeffer Bible of 1462, and which is almost wholly Gothic. This gives us a wide field for variety, I think, so I make the suggestion to you, and leave this part of the subject with two remarks: first, that a good deal of the difficulty of reading Gothic books is caused by the numerous contractions in them, which were a survival of the practice of the scribes; and in a lesser degree by the over abundance of tied letters, both of which drawbacks I take if for granted would be absent in modern types founded on these semi-Gothic letters. And, secondly, that in my opinion the capitals are the strong side of Roman, and the lower-case of Gothic letter, which is but natural, since the Roman was originally an alphabet of capitals, and the lower-case a deduction from them.

We now come to the position of the page of print on the paper, which is a most important point, and one that till quite lately has been wholly misunderstood by modern, and seldom done wrong by ancient printers, or indeed by producers of books of any kind. On this head, I must begin by reminding you that we only occasionally see one page of a book at a time; the two pages making an opening are really the unit of the book, and this was thoroughly understood by the old book producers. I think you will seldom find a book, produced before the eighteenth century, and which has not been cut down by that enemy of books (and of the human race), the binder, in which this rule is not adhered to: that the hinder edge (that which is bound in) must be the smallest member of the margins, the head margin must be larger than this, the fore larger still, and the tail

largest of all. I assert that, to the eye of any man who knows what proportion is, this looks satisfactory, and that no other does so look. But the modern printer, as a rule, dumps down his page in what he calls the middle of the paper, which is often not even really the middle, as he measures his page from the headline, if he has one, though it is not really part of the page, but a spray of type only faintly staining the head of the paper. Now I go so far as to say that any book in which the page is properly put on the paper, is tolerable to look at, however poor the type may be – always so long as there is no 'ornament' which may spoil the whole thing. Whereas any book in which the page is wrongly set on the paper is intolerable to look at, however good the type and ornaments may be. I have got on my shelves now a Jenson's Latin Pliny, which, in spite of its beautiful type and handsome painted ornaments, I dare scarcely look at, because the binder (adjectives fail me here) has chopped off two-thirds of the tail margin. Such stupidities are like a man with his coat buttoned up behind, or a lady with her bonnet put on hindside foremost.

Before I finish this section I should like to say a word concerning large paper copies. I am clean against them, though I have sinned a good deal in that way myself, but that was in the days of ignorance, and I petition for pardon on that ground only. If you want to publish a handsome edition of a book as well as a cheap one, do so; but let them be two books, and if you (or the public) cannot afford this, spend your ingenuity and your money in making the cheap book as sightly as you can. Your making a large paper copy out of the small one lands you in a dilemma even if you reimpose the pages for the larger paper, which is not often done I think. If the margins are right for the smaller book, they must be wrong for the larger, and you have to offer the public the worse book at the bigger price. If they are right for the large paper they are wrong for the small, and thus *spoil* it, as we have seen above that they must do; and that seems scarcely fair to the general public – from the point of view of artistic morality – who might have had a book that was sightly, though not high priced.

As to the paper of our ideal book we are at a great disadvantage compared with past times. Up to the end of the fifteenth, or, indeed, the first quarter of the sixteenth centuries, no bad paper was made, and the greater part was very good indeed. At present there is very little good paper made, and most of it is very bad. Our ideal book must, I think, be printed on hand-made paper as good as it can be made; penury here will make a poor book of it. Yet if machine-made paper must be used, it should not profess fineness or luxury; but should show itself for what it is. For my part I decidedly prefer the cheaper papers that are used for the journals, so far as appearance is concerned, to the thick, smooth, sham-fine papers on which respectable books are printed, and the worst of these are those which imitate the structure of hand-made papers.

But granted your hand-made paper, there is something to be said about its substance. A small book should not be printed on thick paper, however good it may be. You want a book to turn over easily, and to lie quiet while you are reading it, which is impossible, unless you keep heavy paper for big books.

And, by the way, I wish to make a protest against the superstition that only small books are comfortable to read. Some small books are tolerably comfortable, but the best of them are not so comfortable as a fairly big folio, the size, say, of an uncut *Polyphilus*, or somewhat bigger. The fact is, a small book seldom does lie quiet, and you have either to cramp your hand by holding it, or else to put it on the table with a paraphernalia of matters to keep it down, a table-spoon on one side, a knife on another, and so on, which things always tumble off at a critical moment, and fidget you out of the repose which is absolutely necessary to reading. Whereas, a big folio lies quiet and majestic on the table, waiting kindly till you please to come to it, with its leaves flat and peaceful, giving you no trouble of body, so that

your mind is free to enjoy the literature which its beauty enshrines.

So far, then, I have been speaking of books whose only ornament is the necessary and essential beauty which arises out of the fitness of a piece of craftsmanship for the use which it is made. But if we get as far as that, no doubt from such craftsmanship definite ornament will arise, and will be used, sometimes with wise forbearance, sometimes with prodigality equally wise. Meantime, if we really feel impelled to ornament our books, no doubt we ought to try what we can do; but in this attempt we must remember one thing, that if we think the ornament is ornamentally a part of the book merely because it is printed with it, and bound up with it, we shall be much mistaken. The ornament must form as much a part of the page as the type itself, or it will miss its mark, and in order to succeed, and to be ornament, it must submit to certain limitations, and become *architectural*; a mere black and white picture, however interesting it may be as a picture, may be far from an ornament in a book; while on the other hand, a book ornamented with pictures that are suitable for that, and that only, may become a work of art second to none, save a fine building duly decorated, or a fine piece of literature.

These two latter things are, indeed, the only absolutely necessary gift that we should claim of art. The picture-book is not, perhaps, absolutely necessary to man's life, but it gives us such endless pleasure, and is so intimately connected with the other absolutely necessary art of imaginative literature that it must remain one of the very worthiest things towards the production of which reasonable men should strive.

NOTE

Reproduced from Morris, W., 'The Ideal Book', an address given 19 June 1893 to the Bibliographical Society, London. *Transactions of the Bibliographical Society,* vol. 1 (1893).

9

THE 'AMERICAN SYSTEM' AND MASS-PRODUCTION, FROM *INDUSTRIAL DESIGN*

John Heskett (1980)

[…]

By the middle of the nineteenth century, […] largely as a result of the Great Exhibition of 1851, the rest of the world became aware of new methods of manufacture in the United States that established the fundamental patterns and processes of modern industrial mass-production. These were characterized by large-scale manufacture of standardized products, with interchangeable parts, using powered machine-tools in a sequence of simplified mechanical operations. The implications of this approach, which became widely known as the 'American system' of manufacture, were not confined to production methods, but also affected the whole organization and co-ordination of production, the nature of the work-process, the methods by which goods were marketed, and, not least, the type and form of the goods produced.

As with many developments in the United States, there were European precursors and influences. Around 1729, in Sweden, Christopher Pohlem had applied water-power to simple machine processes and precision measurement to produce interchangeable gears for clocks, at a factory in Stjärnsund. Later in the eighteenth century, a French armourer, known only as Le Blanc, applied similar methods to the production of muskets. After visiting Le Blanc's workshops in 1782, Thomas Jefferson, then American Minister to France, noted in a letter: 'An improvement

is here made in construction of muskets … It consists in making every part of them so exactly alike, that what belongs to any one, may be used for every other musket in the magazine … The advantages of this when arms need repair are evident.' Le Blanc's work met with considerable obstruction, however, from the official bureaucracy that administered government arsenals, and from craftsmen who saw their livelihood threatened.

French ideas were linked to English developments by one Marc Brunel, a Royalist refugee from the French Revolution, who designed machinery for the mass-production of pulley blocks for the Royal Navy, for Sir Samuel Bentham, then Inspector General of Naval Works and himself a pioneer inventor of many types of woodworking machinery. Once the exigencies of the Napoleonic Wars were past, however, the system was abandoned.

The basic approach was taken up in the United States around 1800, and was developed on a scale that thoroughly justifies its being called the 'American system'. Eli Whitney is often cited as its founder, largely on the basis of a proposal he made to the American government in 1798 for the manufacture of ten thousand muskets in two years (although in fact the contract was not completed until eleven years later). Research on surviving Whitney muskets indicates that the number of interchangeable parts was limited, and their precision, and thus the extent to which they were interchangeable, was variable. Other armourers in the United States, such as Simeon North and John Hancock Hall, were at least as advanced in their thinking, and probably more advanced in production methods. The truth would seem to be that, rather than any one person possessing a unique claim to having invented the system, it was an idea that had general currency at the time, emerging in a continuous series of improvements, each being eagerly seized on by competitors.

Hall, in particular, emphasized and developed the decisive elements permitting interchangeability, namely, precision measurements and accuracy in production. This work culminated in a simplified breechloading flintlock introduced in 1824 and produced for twenty years. His stated intention was to 'make every similar part of every gun so much alike that it will suit every gun, so that if a thousand guns were taken apart and the links thrown together promiscuously on a heap, they may be taken promiscuously from the heap and will come right'. In order to do this, Hall had to simplify each part as far as possible, and his products are a marked utilitarian contrast to the elegant, decorated products of master gunsmiths. His methods were later refined by firms that were to have international reputations in arms production, such as Sharp, Henry, Winchester and Remington.

The American system reached a high point of development by the mid-nineteenth century in another area of arms production – revolvers – with the establishment of Samuel Colt's armoury at Hartford, Connecticut. Colt was typical of this generation of American innovators, taking principles and inventions that were widely available, and combining them with a form that was distinctive and totally effective. Other contemporary armoureres produced excellent weapons, but it was Colt's throughgoing application of mass-production methods, and an exceptional flair for salesmanship and promotion, that made him so successful. His factory contained over fourteen hundred machine-tools, and under the leadership of Elisha K. Root, a technical genius, was a magnet

for anyone interested in the most advanced methods of manufacture. The United States Secretary for War referred to it as having 'the status of a national work'. Colt's Navy .36 Revolver of 1851 is typical of his products. Like Hall's flintlock, it was reduced to an essential simplicity, and the precision of its interchangeable parts defined standards for the form of hand-weapons for many years.

The fact that the American system developed in relation to the production of firearms is, in retrospect, hardly surprising. The supply of large quantities of reliable and inexpensive weapons was a corollary of the general expansion of the size of military forces, and the constant series of wars against neighbouring states and native inhabitants of the West in which the United States was involved. The only significant application of the American system abroad was also in armaments, the British government establishing the Enfield manufactory with American machine-tools in 1853, and American equipment also being supplied to Prussia and France. Government contracts were necessary in order to pay for the plant and equipment initially required to set up the new system.

What was unique to the United States, however, was the adaptation of the system to other areas of manufacture supported by government funds. In part, this was due to a lack of skilled labour and the absence of an entrenched craft tradition. Samuel Colt, in discussions with British engineers, stated that uneducated workers were best suited to the new mass-production methods since they had so little to unlearn. Innovation was not a challenge to established institutions and habits in the young Republic, and in an open, expanding society the commercial opportunities for wealth and advancement were a strong inducement. A British commission investigating the American system in 1853 noted 'the dissatisfaction frequently expressed in America with regard to present attainment in the manufacture and application of labour-saving machinery, and the avidity with which any new idea is laid hold of, and improved upon …'

[…]

The difference between Europe and America was not limited, however, to production systems, but applied in a much wider sense to general cultural and social values. This was remarked on in the Official Catalogue of the Great Exhibition [of 1851]: 'The expenditure of months or years of labour upon a single article, not to increase its intrinsic value, but solely to augment its cost or its estimation as an object of *virtu*, is not common in the United States. On the contrary, both manual and mechanical labour are applied with direct reference to increasing the number or the quantity of articles suited to the wants of a whole people, and adapted to promote the enjoyment of that moderate competency which prevails upon them.' The comparison was between European attitudes, based on crafts traditions, in which the value of a product, both economically and aesthetically, resided in the extent of skilled work it embodied, and the American approach, based on industrial methods, which emphasized quantity and utility for wider sections of the population. But was it true to say, as the catalogue asserted, that this difference gave 'the productions of American industry a character distinct from that of other countries'? […] the results of American ingenuity were beginning to be manifested in completely new products that did not fit comfortably into the European concept of decorative art, and these products were to proliferate to an extent that demanded attention. A crucial example was the sewing machine.

The process of sewing by hand requires a constant and subtle interplay of material, hand and eye. Many attempts had been made to replicate this manual dexterity by mechanical means, but it was not until 1844 when Elias Howe, a skilled mechanic from Boston, developed a needle with the eye placed at the point, using two to make an interlocking stitch below the surface of the material, that a mechanical sewing machine became feasible. After many vicissitudes, Howe finally managed to put his machine into production with considerable success. The idea was also taken up by Isaac Merrit Singer, who refined Howe's design, and by placing the sewing action on a vertical axis gave the machine its definitive form. Like Samuel Colt, Singer combined mechanical ingenuity with commercial flair. Realizing the potential of sewing machines, he marketed them with unflagging vigour, introducing what now seems an inevitable feature of modern life: hire purchase. The mass-production and sales generated by Singer also brought formal changes in his products. His first machine of 1851 was a very plain functional mechanism, but an appreciation of the importance of appearance led to the mechanism being shrouded in a pressed, japanned-metal casing, decorated with stenciled floral patterns. The stand and foot-treadle drive, produced as optional extras, also had patterns of scrolls and latticework, designed to make them more acceptable in a domestic setting. The basic form of Singer's machines was dictated by mechanical function, but presentation conformed to conceptions of what was aesthetically appropriate to the social context in which the machines were used.

[…]

Throughout most of the nineteenth century the progress of the American system had emphasized the analysis of objects and mechanisms, breaking them down into interchangeable constituent parts and designing them for mechanized mass-production. Between 1880 and 1900 an engineer, Frederick W. Taylor, began a series of studies of work-processes in which he sought to find 'the one best way' of performing tasks; in other words, to achieve a standardization of working methods in order to maximize production. By timing the most efficient workers by stop-watch and seeking to eliminate superfluous movements, he was in fact seeking to integrate human capacities into the sequence of machine operations. This marked a complete rejection of the craft concept of work, which depends upon the skill, judgment and responsibility of individuals. Taylor's methods became widely known in the early years of the present century under the title 'scientific management', and were widely adopted. The adverse reaction they frequently aroused among workers, however, was to lead to an important modification, discussed in the following chapter, to take account of the harm to efficiency caused by fatigue depending not only on physical but also on psychological factors.

Co-ordination of all work-processes in pursuit of improved efficiency and production was first fully developed in the production of motor cars. The United States came late in the field of automobile manufacture, most of the initial development taking place in Europe, but it was in America that the low-priced mass-produced car emerged with astonishing rapidity. Early vehicles were individually craft-built in limited quantities. In 1901, however, Ransome E. Olds began to produce a small, lightweight car on a mass-production basis in Detroit. The machine was very basic and designed for non-mechanically minded customers, with a curved dashboard and folding hood clearly derived from horse-drawn carriage forms, and tiller steering. Six hundred were sold in 1901, rising to 6,500 in 1905. It was a staggering achievement at the time, and opened up motoring to a broad public.

Olds' achievement was, however, to be dwarfed by Henry Ford's [Figure 6]. The 'Oldsmobile' was only suitable for urban conditions and good roads;

Figure 6. Workers Installing Engines on Ford Model T Assembly Line at Highland Park Plant, 1913. From the Collections of The Henry Ford.

Ford set out to design a car to cater specifically for a mass-market and the most rugged conditions. The outcome, in 1908, was the 'Model T'. From the first it was tremendously popular, and Ford and his team set out to produce it as cheaply as possible. As a result, in 1914 they brought together the constituent parts of the modern mass-production system: quantity production of a standard design with interchangeable parts, on a moving assembly line, to the pace and nature of which the workers were compelled to adapt.

The formula was decisive in increasing the volume of production and decreasing unit cost: in 1910 almost twenty thousand Model Ts were produced at a cost of $850 each; in 1916, nearly six hundred thousand at $360 each; before production ceased in 1917, nearly fifteen million had rolled off the production lines.

In design terms the Model T belonged to an interim stage: the influence of carriage design was still strong, for instance, in the spoked wheels and tonneau body with its folding hood; the body sat high on the chassis, in order to provide adequate clearance on poor rural roads; the bonnet was small, and the connecting panel to the body appeared ill-co-ordinated. But if the Model T was not the most beautiful car of its age, it was the most powerful symbol; the harbinger of a transformation in industrial work and industrial products that was to exceed anything previously experienced.

NOTE

Extracted from Heskett, J., *Industrial Design*, New York and Toronto: Oxford University Press, 1980, pp. 50–67. Copyright 1980 Thames & Hudson Ltd., London. Reprinted by kind permission of Thames & Hudson.

10

THE 1900 PARIS EXPOSITION, FROM
ART NOUVEAU IN FIN-DE-SIÈCLE FRANCE

Debora Silverman (1989)

The Paris Exhibition of 1889 had inaugurated a modern style of technological innovation and revealed the possibility of creating cultural monuments with the new materials of industrial production. The crafts, though by no means absent, were subordinated to the colossal presence of what was called the art nouveau of iron and glass.

A very different conception and configuration of the modern style emerged in 1900. The elaborately worked decorative arts, enclosed in their iron and glass frames in 1889, were externalized; they conquered the surface and substance of the exhibition. Now the new materials of iron and glass were shielded from view, overlaid with sculpted stone, ceramic, and plaster facades. The 1900 fair glorified an art nouveau of interior decoration, charged with contemporary organic, feminine, and psychological meanings, while evoking distinctively French design traditions.

This chapter analyzes the 1900 exhibition as the culmination of the modernist ideals of the official craft movement. These ideals, as they were defined by Victor Champier, Georges Berger, Louis de Fourcaud, and Roger Marx, were rococo inspiration, feminization, and psychological expression, unified by particularly French organic forms. At the Paris Exhibition of 1900, all of these elements crystallized not only in [Siegfried] Bing's Pavilion of Art Nouveau, but in a wide-ranging celebration of a new French modern style. Bing's pavilion was an essential part of that celebration, but not all of it. Art historians tend to isolate

Bing's contribution to the fair as they isolate his 1895 experiment from the broader official craft movement in France. But the model house Bing designed for the 1900 exhibition marked the reattachment of his project to the official movement for craft renewal in which he had already participated. Like the other constituents of craft modernism at the fair, it was a variation on the general theme: feminine, organic, nationalist, and psychological modernism in 1900.

Although the exhibition was an apotheosis of the craft modern style, it also recapitulated the essential tension within the craft movement. The two types of interiority that had surfaced in the arts of the reformed Salon and the Central Union exhibits of the 1890s reappeared at the 1900 fair. Modern comfort, intimacy, and organic integration marked one type; modern nervousness, indeterminacy, and psychological agitation marked the other. In 1900 both shaped the character of artistic modernism, glorified as the essence of France as the century turned.

BING'S 1900 PAVILION

In his pavilion for the 1900 fair, Bing reaffirmed, in a specifically national version, the principles that had guided his 1895 project: the integration of art and craft, the collaboration between artists and artisans, the creation of interior ensembles that unfolded as interdependent elements of a single design whole, composed from the vocabulary of nature. The 1900 exhibit was a model home with six fully decorated rooms. Each was marked by the artistic rendering of every surface, from walls and rugs to ceiling corners and bedposts.

Bing's model home of 1900 differed in two significant ways from his similar project of 1895. First, responding to the vehement nationalist criticism of the first Maison de l'Art Nouveau, Bing returned to the basic principles of the official French craft movement. He organized the 1900 pavilion as a project to be clearly in accordance with French traditions, especially the stylistic precedent of the eighteenth century. Second, Bing entered the 1900 fair in a new guise: although he continued his activities as an art dealer, after 1898 he concentrated on establishing and directing his own crafts workshops. Bing's 1900 exhibit represented the work of these luxury ateliers, which promoted a new design inspired by the French patrimony. Furniture and jewelry were the major crafts produced directly under his supervision, but Bing also contracted with other companies for tapestries, rugs, and wall coverings custom ordered to match the other components of the interiors.[1] In 1895 Bing had acted as an impresario and promoter, assembling objects from different countries to show the multiple possibilities for a new interior ensemble. In 1900 Bing, as artistic director, selected one of these possibilities for the public – only French designs were represented, and the interior style of the model modern home was conceived as distinctively French, derived from specifically French sources.

Bing commissioned three artists to design the model home, urging them to express their individual temperaments while seeking a graceful organic whole. Edward Colonna, an architect turned furniture maker and jeweler, designed a salon and music room, whose rich citrus wood furnishings were inlaid with colored marquetry; the walls were hung with pastel fabric, and the rugs repeated the floral shapes that had been incised into the wood furniture. Eugène Gaillard, a sculptor who had turned to furniture, designed

a dining room and a bedroom, with carpets, leaded glass, fabrics, and painted murals [Figure 7]. Finally Georges de Feure, a painter, engraver, and lithographer, tried his hand at the boudoir and a *cabinet de toilette* with silk tapestries and gilded screens. Each of the three artists was closely observed by Bing in the design stages; each subscribed to the principle of "a united effort, a collective will in which all are impelled to the same goal."[2] In some instances, this goal was realized by one artist adding to the room created by another, as when de Feure provided bedposts and silk embroidered curtains for Gaillard's bedroom.[3]

The critics celebrated Bing's Maison de l'Art Nouveau in 1900, identifying it as an embodiment of quintessentially French modern design. *Modern* was defined by critics as the evocation and transformation of the eighteenth century, the first French modern style of organic craft integration. One critic described the model rooms in Bing's dwelling:

> The minutely wrought metal follows almost voluptuously the moldings and panels of furniture of a solid elegance; their lines suggest, without actually imitating, the finest models of the eighteenth century … The furniture is soft to the touch, like silk, and has the shimmering hues of sumptuous damasks; the finish of the details, the preciosity of the chased copper, like so many jewels, make each item a collector's piece, a rare object, and – a delightful thing – it all blends into the whole … This return of gilding in the "New Art" … is a revelation … On the walls, in dream-like rosettes, the same dawn and twilight shades, of which de Feure seems to have discovered the secret, adorn the shimmering waters of a lake.[4]

Voluptuous elegance; soothing and soft slender shapes; dreamlike flora, and gilded settees – all evoke the eighteenth century while offering a nineteenth-century version of enveloping interior retreat.

Eugène GAILLARD

Chambre a coucher exposée au Pavillon de l''Art Nouveau''. Bing en 1900.

Figure 7. Bedroom by Eugène Gaillard for the Pavilion de l'Art Nouveau Bing in 1900, in Debora Silverman, *Art Nouveau in Fin-de-Siècle France: Politics, Psychology, and Style,* Berkeley, CA: University of California Press, 1989, p. 286. Courtesy of the Bibliothèque Nationale de France, Paris.

Another critic, echoing this one, glorified the feminine organic refuge of the truly French art nouveau. Gabriel Mourey, the writer and art critic, had been hostile to the Maison Bing of 1895 as a foreign invasion.[5] He had urged Bing then to "produce a work truly French which would be a genuine expression of the sensibility of our race and not an adaptation of foreign principles."[6] In 1900 Mourey was an absolute enthusiast of the Bing pavilion, seeing in it the "perfect example" of such a "truly French" work.[7] Mourey too identified the Maison Bing of 1900 as a contemporary transposition of the modernity of the eighteenth-century *goût nouveau* – organic, feminine and interiorizing. Mourey applauded Bing's purification of internationalism and the crystallization of quintessentially French design. "Rather than succumbing to international seduction," Mourey stated, "we are animated now by a lofty goal; we are wary of external influences and have reattached ourselves to the true sources of French national style."[8]

Mourey characterized the Bing pavilion as "a source of French inspiration," a resuscitation of the "treasures of grace, elegance and delicacy bequeathed to us by the eighteenth century." Bing's products had the merit and distinction of being "modern and original in our period in the same way that the furnishings for the Trianon were in theirs."[9]

Thus the critics complimented Bing for achieving a modern style inspired by, but not imitative of, the glorious phases of French design history. His pavilion, however, carried the "mark of the era" in ways that its critical champions did not explain. Paradoxically, the "quintessentially French" style that critics celebrated in Bing's art nouveau was the creation of artists who were not all native French. Colonna, for example, had been born in Cologne, had trained as an architect in Brussels, and had moved to the United States in 1882. He lived in Paris after 1897, when Bing hired him. Colonna's versatility enabled him to design furniture that clearly evoked the French eighteenth-century forms; Bing charged him "to eschew the bulky, box-like forms of British and Belgian furniture and instead to apply a modern decorative vocabulary to the light, graceful forms of Louis XV."[10] Georges de Feure had been born in Holland, though he had trained and lived in France for most of his life. He had been clearly integrated into the French craft movement when Bing commissioned him in 1898; de Feure had exhibited his work at the reformed Salon in 1893 and 1894. He was preoccupied with women and with the theme of the *femme-fleur* that was central to modern organic craftsmen.[11] Bing characterized him as Dutch by birth, though he noted how this origin was "hidden under a thick layer of French varnish."[12]

The "truly French" and "distinctively contemporary" character of the Bing pavilion was also carried in the new psychological themes of the intimate dwelling. Critics applauding it spoke generally of the "dream-like qualities" of the rooms;[13] Mourey called its foundations "stones of memories," "evocative motifs of thoughts and dreams."[14] Bing himself linked the interior to two psychological concepts. On the one hand,

"art in an enclosed space" was to supply "peace for the eye and the nerves," and the interior itself was "a refuge from the feverish haste of modern existence."[15] On the other hand, the interior refuge was a dynamic, vital place where the dream world was released. The "lavish interior," Bing noted is a site where the "mysterious gleam of a luminous wall emerges from the shadows, magical in its harmonies, whose appearance stimulates the imagination and transports it to enchanted dreams."[16] This idea that the interior could be at once a domain of tranquility for overwrought nerves and an arena for nervous stimulation surfaced in other places at the 1900 exhibition.

[…]

The feminine and psychological themes of crafts modernism in 1900 were brought together with their complex sources at the fair itself. The *femme nouvelle*, against whom, in part, union affiliates mobilized their ideal decorative craftswomen of the home, was represented in a second International Feminist Congress that met on the fairgrounds. The suggestible, imagistic consciousness of the *psychologie nouvelle* also made an appearance. A congress on the new psychology held at the 1900 fair partly resolved the decade-long debate between supporters of Bernheim's school in Nancy and the Salpêtrière in Paris in favor of Bernheim. By the time of Charcot's death in 1893, the core of his theories – the tripartite stages of hysteria and the belief that only psychopathological patients could be hypnotized – had been discredited. Charcot's own late work even acknowledged the role of unconscious *idées-forces* in human behavior, which he explored in his last book, *La Foi qui guérit* (Faith healing).[17] At the 1900 exhibition's Psychology Congress, Bernheim discussed the power of universal suggestibility, and he tried to defuse fears that the febrile, imagistic receptivity of the mind would entail the dethronement of rational discourse and rational behavior.[18] A disciple of Charcot's, the philosopher Théodule Ribot, provided the Parisian school with an explanation of how the new irrational tendencies could be accommodated by positivist intellection. Despite Charcot's having uncovered all the elements of volatile unreason, in 1900 many French psychic explorers remained bound to their Cartesian grid. Ribot's book *The Creative Imagination*, published in 1901, offered a potent variation on the Enlightenment theme of the melding of *raison* and *esprit* in a single mind. Ribot acknowledged the presence and power of the unconscious and of suggestibility, which he associated with the "creative imagination," characterizing it as visual, "diffluent," and fluid. Alongside this "diffluent" segment of the mind was a logical, sequential one of linear rationality. Rather than replace it or overturn it, Ribot affirmed that the diffluent and discursive arenas of mind coexisted in a dynamic complementarity.[19]

Despite the themes of containment and accommodation in the emergence of French modernism in 1900, the exhibition expressed the unstable, volatile compound of which the art nouveau was composed. Three artistic examples illustrate how an eruptive nonrational world exploded the boundaries of rococo precedent and physiological psychology. The characteristics of this nonrational world visible in 1900 – mobility, simultaneity, indeterminacy, and the metamorphic fluidity of the unconscious – are essential parts of twentieth-century modernity.

At first glance, the changes effected in the iron-and-glass Gallery of Machines between 1889 and 1900 seemed to signify the triumph of rococo ornamentalism over technological monumentalism. In 1889 the Gallery of Machines was the dramatic partner to the thousand-foot Eiffel Tower. Entering the fair through this "arch of triumph to science and industry,"[20] spectators were presented with a vast horizontal iron-and-glass shed, which displayed the industrial products and advanced machineries of all nations. The French contributions to this gallery – artisanal ware in elaborate wood and velvet cases – existed in spatial tension with the airy iron-and-glass frame surrounding them. This same tension between

public and private space reappeared in the Eiffel Tower itself, in the juxtaposition of Eiffel's wood and velvet private room at the top of the tower and the open and interlaced iron webbing of the whole structure enveloping it.[21]

[…]

Thus, the 1900 fair crystallized, in artistic expression and official celebration, a particularly French modernist form and meaning. The exhibition offered the culmination of a decade of searching for a French craft art nouveau, which resonated with eighteenth-century heritage and late nineteenth-century discoveries. Yet contained within this organic, psychological modern style were the seeds of a broader twentieth-century metamorphic consciousness.

NOTES

Extracted from Silverman, D., 'Conclusion: The 1900 Paris Exposition,' in D. Silverman, *Art Nouveau in Fin-de-Siècle France: Politics, Psychology, and Style*, Berkeley: University of California Press, 1989, pp. 284–314. © 1989 Regents of the University of California. Published by the University of California Press.

1. Gabriel P. Weisberg, "S. Bing's Craftsmen Workshops: A Location and Importance Revealed," *Source* 3, no. 1 (Fall 1983): 42–48; Gabriel P. Weisberg, *Art Nouveau Bing: Paris Style 1900* (New York: Abrams, 1986), pp. 142–157, 163–169.
2. G. M. Jacques, 1900, quoted in Franco Borsi and Ezio Godoli, *Paris 1900* (New York: Rizzoli, 1977), p. 39.
3. Philippe Julien, *The Triumph of Art Nouveau: Paris Exhibition of 1900* (New York: Larousse, 1978), p. 117.
4. Jean Lorrain, 1900, quoted in Julien, *The Triumph of Art Nouveau*, pp. 116–117.
5. Martin Eidelberg, "The Life and Work of E. Colonna," pt. 2: "Paris and L'Art Nouveau,"

Decorative Arts Society Newsletter 7, no. 2 (June 1981): 3.

6. Mourey, quoted in Borsi and Godoli, *Paris 1900*, p. 39.

7. Mourey, quoted in Eidelberg, "Colonna," p. 3.

8. Mourey, "L'Art nouveau à l'Exposition universelle," *Revue des arts décoratifs* 20 (1900): 265.

9. Gabriel Mourey, "L'Art nouveau de M. Bing à l'Exposition universelle," deuxième article, *Revue des arts décoratifs* 20 (1900): 280, 283. Weisberg, in *Art Nouveau Bing* (179, 191, 210) quotes other critics who echoed precisely this theme of Bing's 1900 art nouveau as, in the words of one, "a compromise between the 'new style'... on the one side and the favorite French style, rococo, on the other." The critic continued:

> No one can but admire the nimbleness with which these, Bing's new artists, have understood how to combine the new style elements with the thread of a rediscovered tradition. Some of the charm which used to surround noblemen's radicalism is to be found in their art. The art in l'Art Nouveau has, for the most part, a radical character; but it has found its ancestry. It clearly bears rococo's family character, and no heritage can be more advantageous for art in the eyes of a Frenchman. (p. 201)

10. Eidelberg, "Colonna," p. 3.

11. De Feure's many lithographs and paintings centered on the femme-fleur and the women as decorative object, that is, as an integral aesthetic part of an interior decorative world. In 1895, de Feure was preparing a series of illustrations called Féminiflores, a series of women's figures symbolizing certain flowers. See Octove Uzanne, "On the Drawings of Georges de Feure," *The Craftsman* 1 (1899): 95–102.

12. Quoted in Weisberg, *Art Nouveau Bing*, p. 241.

13. Lorrain, 1900, quoted in Julien, *The Triumph of Art Nouveau*, p. 117.

14. Mourey, "L'Art nouveau à l'Exposition universelle," p. 257.

15. Quoted in Weisberg, *Art Nouveau Bing*, p. 148.

16. S. Bing, *Artistic America, Tiffany Glass, and Art Nouveau*, trans. Benita Eisler, with an introduction by Robert Koch (Cambridge, Mass.: MIT Press, 1970), p. 183. There is other evidence that Bing absorbed theories of suggestion and dreams triggered by images in rooms. In his catalogue to the collection of Philippe Burty, Bing describes the power of "*objets enchantés*," which, in the "refuge" of the interior space, project a "*fluide magnétique*" into the mind of the collector (introduction to Collection Philippe Burty: *Objets d'art japonais et chinois quie seront vendus à Paris dans les Galeries Durand-Ruel* [Paris: Chamerot, 1891] pp. vi–ix.)

17. Georges Guillain, *J.-M. Charcot: His Life, His Work*, trans. Pearse Bailey (New York: Paul Hoeber, 1959), pp. 177–179; George Frederick Drinka, *The Birth of Neurosis: Myth, Malady, and the Victorians* (New York: Simon & Schuster, 1984), pp. 276–278.

18. Hippolyte Bernheim, "La Doctrine de la suggestibilité et ses sonséquences: Discours prononcé à l'ouverture des travaux de la Ve section du IXe Congrès international de psychologie," *La Revue* 34 (1900): 532–535.

19. Théodule Ribot, *Essai sur l'imagination créatrice* (Paris: Alcan, 1901).

20. Eiffel's words, quoted in Joseph Harriss, *The Tallest Tower: Eiffel and the Belle Epoque* (Boston: Houghton Mifflin, 1975), p. 19.

21. Debora L. Silverman, "The Paris Exhibition of 1889: Architecture and the Crisis of Individualism," *Oppositions* 8 (Spring 1977): 71–91.

11

THE ART AND CRAFT OF THE MACHINE

Frank Lloyd Wright (1901)

As we work along our various ways, there takes shape within us, in some sort, an ideal – something we are to become – some work to be done. This, I think, is denied to very few, and we begin really to live only when the thrill of this ideality moves us in what we will to accomplish. In the years which have been devoted in my own life to working out in stubborn materials a feeling for the beautiful, in the vortex of distorted complex conditions, a hope has grown stronger with the experience of each year, amounting now to a gradually deepening conviction that in the Machine lies the only future of art and craft – as I believe, a glorious future; that the Machine is, in fact, the metamorphosis of ancient art and craft; that we are at last face to face with the machine – the modern Sphinx – whose riddle the artist must solve if he would that art live – for his nature holds the key. For one, I promise "whatever gods may be" to lend such energy and purpose as I may possess to help make that meaning plain; to return again and again to the task whenever and wherever need be; for this plain duty is thus relentlessly marked out for the artist in this, the Machine Age, although there is involved an adjustment to cherished gods, perplexing and painful in the extreme; the fire of many long-honored ideals shall go down to ashes to reappear, phoenix like, with new purposes.

The great ethics of the Machine are as yet, in the main, beyond the ken of the artist or student of sociology; but the artist mind may now approach the nature of this thing from experience, which has become the commonplace of his field, to suggest, in time, I hope, to prove, that the machine is capable of carrying to fruition high ideals in art – higher than the world has yet seen!

Disciples of William Morris cling to an opposite view. Yet William Morris himself deeply sensed the danger to art of the transforming force whose sign and symbol is the machine, and though of the new art we eagerly seek he sometimes despaired, he quickly renewed his hope.

He plainly foresaw that a blank in the fine arts would follow the inevitable abuse of new-found power, and threw himself body and soul into the work of bridging it over by bringing into our lives afresh the beauty of art as she had been, that the new art to come might not have dropped too many stitches nor have unraveled what would still be useful to her.

That he had abundant faith in the new art his every essay will testify.

That he miscalculated the machine does not matter. He did sublime work for it when he pleaded so well for the process of elimination its abuse had made necessary; when he fought the innate vulgarity of theocratic impulse in art as opposed to democratic; and when he preached the gospel of simplicity.

All artists love and honor William Morris.

He did the best in his time for art and will live in history as the great socialist, together with Ruskin, the great moralist: a significant fact worth thinking about, that the two great reformers of modern times professed the artist.

The machine these reformers protested, because the sort of luxury which is born of greed had usurped it and made of it a terrible engine of enslavement, deluging the civilized world with a murderous ubiquity, which plainly enough was the damnation of their art and craft.

It had not then advanced to the point which now so plainly indicates that it will surely and swiftly, by its own momentum, undo the mischief it has made, and the usurping vulgarians as well.

Nor was it so grown as to become apparent to William Morris, the grand democrat, that the machine was the great forerunner of democracy.

The ground plan of this thing is now grown to the point where the artist must take it up no longer as a protest: genius must progressively dominate the work of the contrivance it has created; to lend a useful hand in building afresh the "Fairness of the Earth."

That the Machine has dealt Art in the grand old sense a death-blow, none will deny.

The evidence is too substantial.

Art in the grand old sense – meaning Art in the sense of structural tradition, whose craft is fashioned upon the handicraft ideal, ancient or modern; an art wherein this form and that form as structural parts were laboriously joined in such a way as to beautifully emphasize the manner of the joining: the million and one ways of beautifully satisfying bare structural necessities, which have come down to us chiefly through the books as "Art."

[…]

The steel frame has been recognized as a legitimate basis for a simple, sincere clothing of plastic material that idealizes its purpose without structural pretense.

This principle has at last been recognized in architecture, and though the masters refuse to accept it as architecture at all, it is a glimmer in a darkened field – the first sane word that has been said in Art for the Machine.

The Art of old idealized a Structural Necessity – now rendered obsolete and unnatural by the Machine – and accomplished it through man's joy in the labor of his hands.

The new will weave for the necessities of mankind, which his Machine will have mastered, a robe of ideality no less truthful, but more poetical, with a rational freedom made possible by the machine, beside which the art of old will be as the sweet, plaintive wail of the pipe to the outpouring of full orchestra.

It will clothe Necessity with the living flesh of virile imagination, as the living flesh lends living grace to the hard and bony human skeleton.

The new will pass from the possession of kings and classes to the every-day lives of all – from duration in point of time to immorality.

This distinction is one to be felt now rather than clearly defined.

The definition is the poetry of this Machine Age, and will be written large in time; but the more we, as artists, examine into this premonition, the more we will find the utter helplessness of old forms to satisfy new conditions, and the crying need of the machine for plastic treatment – a pliant, sympathetic treatment of its needs that the body of structural precedent cannot yield.

To gain further suggestive evidence of this, let us turn to the Decorative Arts – the immense middle-ground of all art now mortally sickened by the Machine – sickened that it may slough the art ideal of the constructural art for the plasticity of the new art – the Art of Democracy.

Here we find the most deadly perversion of all – the magnificent prowess of the machine bombarding the civilized world with the mangled corpses of strenuous horrors that once stood for cultivated luxury – standing now for a species of fatty degeneration simply vulgar.

Without regard to first principles or common decency, the whole letter of tradition – that is, ways of doing things rendered wholly obsolete and unnatural by the machine – is recklessly fed into its rapacious maw until you may buy reproductions for ninety-nine cents at "The Fair" that originally cost ages of toil and cultivation, worth now intrinsically nothing – that are harmful parasites befogging the sensibilities of our natures, belittling and falsifying any true perception of normal beauty the Creator may have seen fit to implant in us.

[...]

If the artist will only open his eyes he will see that the machine he dreads has made it possible to wipe out the mass of meaningless torture to which mankind, in the name of the artistic, has been more or less subjected since time began; for that matter, has made possible a cleanly strength, an ideality and a poetic fire that the art of the world has not yet seen; for the machine, the process now smoothes away the necessity for petty structural deceits, soothes this wearisome struggle to make things seem what they are not, and can never be; satisfies the simple term of the modern art equation as the ball of clay in the sculptor's hand yields to his desire – comforting forever this realistic, brain-sick masquerade we are wont to suppose art.

William Morris pleaded well for simplicity as the basis of all true art. Let us understand the significance to art of that word – SIMPLICITY – for it is vital to the Art of the Machine.

[...]

Simplicity in art, rightly understood, is a synthetic, positive quality, in which we may see evidence of mind, breadth of scheme, wealth of detail, and withal a sense of completeness found in a tree or a flower. A work may have the delicacies of a rare orchid or the stanch fortitude of the oak, and still be simple. A thing to be simple needs only to be true to itself in organic sense.

With this ideal of simplicity, let us glance hastily at a few instances of the machine and see how it has been forced by false ideals to do violence to this simplicity; how it has made possible the highest simplicity, rightly understood and so used. As perhaps wood is most available of all homely materials and therefore, naturally, the most abused – let us glance at wood.

Machinery has been invented for no other purpose than to imitate, as closely as possible, the wood-carving of the early ideal – with the immediate result that no ninety-nine cent piece of furniture is salable without some horrible botchwork meaning nothing unless it means that art and craft have combined to fix in the mind of the masses the old hand-carved chair as the *ne plus ultra* of the ideal.

The miserable, lumpy tribute to this perversion which Grand Rapids alone yields would mar the face of Art beyond repair; to say nothing of the elaborate and fussy joinery of posts, spindles, jig sawed beams and braces, butted and strutted, to outdo the sentimentality of the already overwrought antique product.

Thus is the wood-working industry glutted, except in rarest instances. The whole sentiment of early craft degenerated to a sentimentality having no longer decent significance nor commercial integrity; in fact all that is fussy, maudlin, and animal, basing its existence chiefly on vanity and ignorance.

Now let us learn from the Machine.

It teaches us that the beauty of wood lies first in its qualities as wood; no treatment that did not bring out these qualities all the time could be plastic, and therefore not appropriate – so not beautiful, the machine teaches us, if we have left it to the machine that certain simple forms and handling are suitable to bring out the beauty of wood and certain forms are not; that all wood-carving is apt to be a forcing of the material, an insult to its finer possibilities as a material having in itself intrinsically artistic properties, of which its beautiful markings is one, it texture another, its color a third.

The machine, by its wonderful cutting, shaping, smoothing, and repetitive capacity, has made it possible to so use it without waste that the poor as well as the rich may enjoy to-day beautiful surface treatments of clean, strong forms that the branch veneers of Sheraton and Chippendale only hinted at, with dire extravagance, and which the middle ages utterly ignored.

The machine has emancipated these beauties of nature in wood; made it possible to wipe out the mass of meaningless torture to which wood has been subjected since the world began, for it has been universally abused and maltreated by all peoples but the Japanese.

Rightly appreciated, is not this the very process of elimination for which Morris pleaded?

[...]

And the texture of the tissue of this great thing, this Forerunner of Democracy, the Machine, has been deposited particle by particle, in blind obedience to organic law, the law to which the great solar universe is but an obedient machine.

Thus is the thing into which the forces of Art are to breath the thrill of ideality! A SOUL!

NOTE

Extracted from Lloyd Wright, F., 'The Art and Craft of the Machine,' in E. Kaufmann and B. Raeburn (eds), *Frank Lloyd Wright: Writings and Buildings*, New York: Penguin, 1960, pp. 55–73. From an address to the Chicago Arts and Crafts Society, at Hull House, 6 March and to the Western Society of Engineers, 20 March 1901. © 2009 Frank Lloyd Wright Foundation, Scottsdale, AZ/Artists Rights Society (ARS), NY.

GUIDE TO FURTHER READING

Paul Greenhalgh, in his book *Ephemeral Vistas: The Expositions Universelles, Great Exhibitions, and World's Fairs, 1851–1939* (1988), discusses the World's Fair of the late nineteenth and early twentieth centuries as a visual medium that not only introduced new technologies and promoted the economic strength of the host country, but which also initiated new modes of display and advertising that asserted commercial and national identity. See also Sabine Clemm, '"Amidst the Heterogeneous Masses": Charles Dicken's *Household Words* and the Great Exhibition of 1851' (2005).

Whereas Ruskin and Morris espoused a moral reform of design through their return to the spiritualized aesthetic of the Gothic period, outlined in Pugin's *True Principles of Pointed or Christian Architecture* (1841), others, including Owen Jones and Christopher Dresser, sought to understand better the capability of the machine and to improve the artistic possibilities of industrial manufacture through careful education, rather than do away with it altogether. Jones's reference book *The Grammar of Ornament* (1856) provided hundreds of examples of decorative patterns to be applied by designers to all different media. See Elizabeth Kramer, 'Master or Market? The Anglo-Japanese Textile Designs of Christopher Dresser' (2006). Tracey Avery explores the Victorian design debate from the perspective of Australia in her article 'Furniture Design and Colonialism (2007), which is reproduced in Section 12 of the *Reader*.

Semper's theories influenced design education throughout Europe, including at London's South Kensington Museum, established by Henry Cole following the 1851 exhibition. See Louise Purbrick, 'South Kensington Museum: The Building of the House of Henry Cole' (1994). The arguably more enthusiastic industrialization of manufacture in the US during this period is further examined by David A. Hounshell in his book *From the American System to Mass Production, 1800–1932: The Development of Manufacturing Technology in the United States* (1984), which elaborates on Heskett's discussion. Journals devoted to the decorative arts, such as *The Studio, L'Art Décoratif, Deutsche Kunst und Dekoration* and *The Craftsman*, disseminated reform ideas, largely rooted in the theories of William Morris, to a wide audience. Two insightful studies of Morris are Fiona MacCarthy, *William Morris: A Life for Our Time* (1994) and Charles Harvey and Jon Press, *William Morris: Design and Enterprise in Victorian Britain* (1991). The exhibition 'The Arts and Crafts in Europe and America: Design for the Modern World' (Los Angeles, Los Angeles County Museum of Art, 2004), with catalogue edited by Wendy Kaplan, examines the overlapping philosophies among designers on both sides of the Atlantic.

The area of most fraught design reform debate in the late nineteenth century was women's clothing. The 'reform dress', with its loose and comfortable cut, resisted the confining wasp-waisted shapes of contemporary ladies' fashions. See Patricia A. Cunningham, *Reforming Women's Fashion, 1850–1920: Politics, Health, and Art* (2003). The struggle to reform design, and to come to terms with the relationship between industry and craft at the end of the nineteenth-century was also poignantly expressed in art nouveau meditations such as Siegfried Bing's essay 'Where Are we Going?' (1897), as well as in

Louis Sullivan's canonical essay 'The Tall Office Building Artistically Considered' (1896), in which the architect unites the technological progress of the steel-framed building with the organic model of a vibrant nature, in his assertion that 'form follows function'. Paul Greenhalgh, in his article 'The Style and the Age' (2000), demonstrates that the reform efforts of Semper, Ruskin and Morris ushered in a complex and contradictory design sensibility, which was at once urban and rustic, national and international, and which saw the exciting potential of the machine expressed in the vital forms of nature, as well as the integrity of materials, as its innovators forged a new path into the twentieth century.

SECTION 3

Modernisms, 1908–50

INTRODUCTION

Rebecca Houze

The intense debate in the second half of the nineteenth century concerning the relationship between craft and industrial production continued unabated into the twentieth century. In the years leading up to the First World War, designers continued the search for a new language of form that had been initiated with the Art Nouveau movement of the 1890s, and increasingly began to question the meaning of ornament, as well as the role of national identity, in the style of manufactured objects.

Expanding on the *Jugendstil* notion of the *Gesamtkunstwerk,* the 'total work of art', progressive painters, illustrators and craftsmen, such as Hermann Obrist and Henry van de Velde, associated with the Munich Vereinigten Werkstätten für Kunst im Handwerk, and Josef Hoffmann and Koloman Moser, members of the Vienna Secession and Wiener Werkstätte, engaged in practice that spanned the fine and applied arts, creating organic spaces guided by an overarching aesthetic, in which buildings, interiors, furnishings, art objects, utensils, and even their inhabitants' dress were united.

In his famous 1908 diatribe 'Ornament and Crime', Viennese architect and adversary of the Secession movement, Adolf Loos, attacked the decorative craft-based style of van de Velde, Obrist and others as antithetical to modern life, which in his opinion was better represented by well-tailored English men's clothing and the industrial buildings and products of America. Loos's views were outside the mainstream when they were written but, during the course of the first half of the twentieth century, they came to dominate the understanding of modernist as ascetic, utilitarian, masculine and industrial, as opposed to decorative, feminine or primitive – an interpretation that we can find repeated in the writings of Le Corbusier, as well as in the objects produced by designers at the Bauhaus in the 1920s.

Paul Greenhalgh, writing from the postmodern vantage point of the 1980s, defined the 'Modern Movement' in the first half of the twentieth century as a set of ideas and visionary goals, which by the 1930s devolved into the pervasive look and technology of the 'International Style'. Although the imaginative designs of the Italian Futurists, Russian Constructivists, De Stijl, Purists and early Bauhaus workshops did not set out to describe a particular look, these avant-garde movements' valorization of industrial production, emphasis on abstract forms and international collaboration inevitably led them, he writes, to explore the spare rectilinear forms that we see expressed in architecture, furnishings, fashions, and typography, which were indeed employed around the globe, and which persisted in some places even into the 1970s. Due to the influence of modernist institutions and scholarship, including the 1932 'International Exhibition of Modern Architecture' at the New York Museum of Modern Art, organized by Henry Russell Hitchcock and Philip Johnson, as well as architectural historian Nikolaus Pevsner's canonical 1936 book *Pioneers of the Modern Movement*, the International Style and the functionalist theories that were believed to precede it have overshadowed the fact that a plurality of paradoxical design aesthetics co-existed in the first half of the twentieth century, all of which understood themselves as 'modern'.

The Deutscher Werkbund, founded in 1907, was an outgrowth of the German crafts workshops with a new goal of forging an alliance between art and industry. The 1914 Werkbund exhibition in Cologne showcased a diverse array of designs, including decorative Wiener Werkstätte furnishings, expressionistic coloured glass buildings designed by Bruno Taut and the industrial factory architecture of Walter Gropius. As the debate between Henry van de Velde and Hermann Muthesius reveals, it was not at all clear, on the eve of the First World War, which goals, ideology, and aesthetic direction would be most appropriate for twentieth-century designers to pursue. Whereas van de Velde argued for the necessity of individual artistic integrity, Muthesius prophesied a new architecture, like that seen in Gropius's model factory, which would be based on standardized forms and which promised to erase class boundaries while bolstering German industry and economy through international export.

The chapter 'From Workshop to Laboratory', taken from Gillian Naylor's book *The Bauhaus Reassessed*, examines this dynamic between craft and industry, standardization and individuality, within the programme of the German design school, which in many ways came to be seen as the face of modern design. Unlike Pevsner's didactic canonization of monumental buildings, objects and 'pioneers', however, Naylor's case study of the institution and personalities within, based on archival research, is a nuanced and subtle examination of this pivotal moment in the history of design.

Nancy Troy's insightful reading of Le Corbusier's early career and his deep involvement with the decorative arts in France further complicate the notion of the 'International Style' as a tendency that entirely rejected ornament or that was dominated by the successes of German industry. On the eve of the First World War, when he was still Charles Edouard Jeanneret, the Swiss architect later known for his radical city planning and buildings of reinforced concrete consciously crafted his career within a community of fashionable French furnishing and dress designers, the *coloristes*. Inspired by the colourful neoclassical products of André Groult and Paul Poiret, Jeanneret shaped his own vision of modern design, which was built on the new materials and technologies of the industrial age, while still remaining rooted in the historical forms of a national French tradition.

The 1925 Paris Exposition des Arts Décoratifs et Industriels Modernes furthered the program of the *coloristes* and popularized the eclectic art deco style throughout Europe and North America. But the reception of Art Deco in the United States was mixed in the late 1920s and early 1930s. Whereas many architects incorporated art deco ornament into their design of skyscrapers, resorts, and movie theaters, much of the general public was wary of the foreign abstract style. Nicolas P. Maffei traces the efforts of American industrial designers in the 1930s, such as Norman Bel Geddes and Walter Dorwin Teague, to develop a distinctly American style, which would reflect the industrial technology of the modern age, while also expressing the necessary charm of domestic comforts. Their transformation of European Art Deco into native 'streamlined' designs of automobiles, trains and domestic appliances culminated with the sensational exhibits at the 1939 New York World's Fair, where Bel Geddes's 'Futurama' installation for General Motors offered a new vision to the public – the world of tomorrow.

12

INTRODUCTION TO *MODERNISM IN DESIGN*

Paul Greenhalgh (1990)

[...]

Viewed from the safe distance of the 1990s, we can perceive a chronology within the Modern Movement in design; it had two phases. The first I will fashion the Pioneer phase, this opening amid the deafening thunder of the guns of the First World War and closing with the demise of the key movements between 1929 and 1933. The second, opening in the early 1930s, I will label the International Style.

[...]

Pioneer Modernism consisted of a series of movements and individuals who addressed themselves to the problem of an appropriate design for the twentieth century. They were very much concerned with three spheres of activity: architecture, furniture and graphics, the former of which undoubtedly held sway.[1] They were not the first to ponder the idea of an appropriate 'modern' style, neither did they invent all of their own ideas, technologies and stylistic mannerisms. Indeed, they invented few of them. Rather, what made them different from anything which had gone before was the holistic world-view they constructed from earlier, disparate ideas, and the absolutist nature of their vision.

[...]

Between 1920 and 1930 Modernists throughout Europe argued violently through letters, articles and personal confrontations and by 1935 they had drifted apart in terms of their actual design work. Accepting this, it is still possible to discern a core of common ideas. I have identified twelve, of which some are closely based on the published manifestos, some are distillations from broadly held (and voiced) ideas of the time and some are observations made from the safe haven of 1990. My aim, therefore, is not to define in specific detail the nature of the Modern Movement (even if this were possible) but to identify the theoretical features which characterized the broad sweep of its activity before the advent proper of the International Style. I shall list the features and then I will go on to discuss them at some length:

[...]

1. Decompartmentalisation
2. Social morality
3. Truth
4. The total work of art
5. Technology
6. Function
7. Progress
8. Anti-historicism
9. Abstraction
10. Internationalism/universality
11. Transformation
12. Theology

The over-arching concern of the Modern Movement was to break down barriers between aesthetics, technics and society, in order that an appropriate design of the highest visual and practical quality could be produced for the mass of the population. Perhaps, this idea, of the *decompartmentalisation* of human experience, was the single most important ideal.[2] Most of the points that follow relate back to this initial promise.

Design was to be forged into a weapon with which to combat the alienation apparent in modern, urban society. It was therefore construed to be fundamentally a political activity, concerned with the achievement of a proper level of *social morality*. It was meant to improve the conditions of the population who consumed it: 'I have the unfashionable conviction that the proper concern of architecture is more than self-display. It is a thesis, a declaration, a statement of the social aims of the age.'[3]

By 1920, it was widely accepted by intellectuals on the left that the masses had been brutalized by the economic and political processes which shaped their lives: 'Owing to the extensive use of machinery and to [the] division of labour, the work of the proletarians has lost all individual character, and, consequently, all charm for the workman. He becomes an appendage of the machine ... Hence, the cost of production of a workman is restricted, almost entirely, to the means of subsistence that he requires for his maintenance, and for the propagation of his race.'[4] For Marxists, the combination of capital and industry had led to the alienation of the worker from the processes and objects of production, with far-reaching effects: 'Thus alienated labour turns [Man] ... into an alien being and into a *means* for his *individual existence*. It alienated from Man his own body, external nature, his mental life and his human life. A direct consequence of the alienation of Man from the product of his labour ... is that *Man* is *alienated* from other *Men*.'[5] Alienation thus became an intense psychological impoverishment, characterized as the negation of the spiritual essence of humankind: 'We arrive at the result that Man (the worker) feels himself to be freely active only in his animal functions – eating, drinking and procreating, or at most also in

his dwelling and personal adornment – while in his human functions he is reduced to an animal.'[6] The subject was prevented from taking control of, and transforming, the circumstances he or she found themselves in. Because of this, the alienated masses were understood to have been perpetual victims of capitalism, spectacularly so in the form of the First World War.

Design was inextricably bound up with commodity production, which in turn was the driving force behind the creation of wealth. It was reasoned, therefore, that it had the potential to transform the economic and social conditions of the masses. By doing so, the spectre of alienation could be vanquished.

'A question of Morality; a lack of Truth is intolerable, we perish in untruth.'[7] Truth as a moral value was transposed into being simultaneously an aesthetic quality. Within the terms of the construction and appearance of objects, truth meant the avoidance of contrivances which created an illusion or false impression. The designer had to avoid 'formalistic imitation and snobbery' which often 'distorted the fundamental truth.'[8] The way an object was made had to be apparent and its visual attractiveness had to come directly out of those processes of construction. Truth as an ideal led, therefore, to a wholesale rejection of decoration, especially when it was perceived to be an element added after the major constructional work had taken place. Decoration could only mask the structural and spatial honesty of the object. In the Fine Arts arena, with the rejection of the use of modeling, perspective and other devices for the creation of illusionary space, illusion or disguise of any kind in any of the visual arts was synonymous with a lie.

Following this idea to its logical conclusion, objects had to be self-consciously proud of what they were and how they had arrived in the world, much in the way that the democratized masses were encouraged to be proud of their origins and their status as workers. Indeed, an object had to reveal its mode of work and its ability to perform it in order to be fully Modern.

With themselves, the various arts had to work in conjunction in order that they created a *total work of art* (Gesamtkunstwerk).[9] The fine, applied, decorative and design arts should be a single continuum, allowing for their different practical functions and production techniques. All Modernists, particularly those at the Bauhaus, resented the privileged status enjoyed by some arts over others. Such privileging was perceived to mirror the class system at work in society. The Fine Arts, in a Modernist world, would integrate completely with other disciplines. It would be wrong to assume, however, that the Pioneer Moderns successfully addressed the design issue in every medium.

Technology had to be used in its most advanced forms in order to facilitate economy and, from this, availability. Mass production and prefabrication were embraced as being the means through which Modernism would arrive on the streets. Beyond this, the standardization of components would allow for the rapid erection and repair of objects. 'Mass production, the inevitable purpose for which the first power-driven machine, the modern tool, was invented, today can be utilized for the production of essential elements for the millions who at the moment lack them ... Mass production and prefabrication of all essential structural parts of the simplest dwelling could contribute some form of standardized architecture.'[10] It must be stressed, however, that amongst the Pioneers at least, mass production remained an idea. Virtually nothing that was designed in the first phase of Modernism went into mass production, or, indeed, was designed so as to be capable of adaptation to genuine standardization. It was an ideal the likes of Henry Ford being an exemplar of a designer they talked about but could not, at that stage, emulate. Mass-produced Modernism only became a reality when the International Style achieved legitimacy.

There was also a strong sense in some schools of thought that the application of new technology to objects gave them an appearance which the masses could understand. Technology functioned not only in a practical way then, but in a symbolic one also.

The successful *functioning* of all designed produce was deemed of great importance. Connected to the desire for technology expressed above, therefore, was a pronounced rationalism. 'In the conviction that household appliances and furnishings must be rationally related to each other, the Bauhaus is seeking – by systematic, practical and theoretical research in the formal, technical and economic fields – to derive the design of an object from its natural functions and relationships.'[11] Objects had to be planned in order to work effectively and when things were planned effectively, it was suggested, they tended to be beautiful. The proof of this aesthetic was in the machine, which was beautiful because its form had been largely determined by the way it worked: 'A good modern machine is ... an object of the highest aesthetic value – we are aware of that.'[12] 'Civilizations advance. They pass through the age of the peasant, the soldier and the priest and attain what is rightly called culture.'[13] The concept of *progress* was a central driving force. The world was perceived to have been in a chaotic, if not overtly evil, condition; every aspect of humanity had to be advanced towards a higher form, away from this previous state. The advent of democracy and the anticipation of socialism appeared, for many, to indicate social progress; indeed, it was a precondition for all Marxists that such progress was an historical phenomenon. Equally, social-Darwinism was a potent influence. Belief in the biological advance of humankind along Darwinian lines suited Modernists, despite its heinous implications for non-industrial societies.[14] New technologies demonstrated a virtual model of linear advance in the sciences. Design could do the same. Modernists believed in the idea of aesthetic advance, rather than simply of aesthetic change.

Following from this, historical styles and technologies had to be eliminated wherever possible. If the human race was in a process of advance and if the past represented the unsatisfactory condition society was striving to move away from then past styles were both aesthetically and morally undesirable. As the majority of ornament was historical, *anti-historicism* was therefore synonymous with anti-decoration: 'The evolution of culture is synonymous with the removal of ornament from utilitarian objects.'[15] Compounded with the idea of aesthetic truth, this principle effectively eliminated the possibility of a Modern Movement decoration. Having said this, it would be wrong to assume that the Pioneers didn't use the ideas of the great designers and artists of the past. Rather, they were against the use of previous styles when these were intended simply to evoke memory of the past: 'Modern architecture has nothing but the healthiest lessons to learn from the art of the … past, if that art be studied scientifically and not in a spirit of imitation.'[16]

Anti-historicism also led to a redefinition of the meaning of the word 'style.' Prior to the twentieth century, styles were associated with particular periods or cultural groups and used in order to reflect their meaning in the object. It had been previously inconceivable that a designer could have his own style, or that an object of aesthetic value could have no style.

Abstraction was the key aesthetic device employed by the majority of designers. The first pure, non-objective art was produced by painters in the wake of Cubism: Frantisek Kupka, Vasili Kandinsky, Sonia and Robert Delaunay all abandoned figuration during the course of 1911–12. Between 1914 and 1919, Piet Mondrian, Kasimir Malevich and many others took it to its logical conclusion.[17] Essentially, abstract art was understood to be that which eliminated figurative or symbolic elements in favour of the manipulation of 'pure' form. The search for purity was closely related to the idea of truth: 'Although one has always to operate more or less speculatively in the domain of abstraction, there is good reason to accept this latter manner of visionary thinking about plastic art as true.'[18]

Obviously abstraction implied an outright rejection of figurative elements in design and,

consequently, a severe reduction in the potential of the object as a conveyor of narrative or symbol. In European design, much of the narrative conveyed by an object had been via its ornament; the embracing of abstraction led therefore to a yet further assault on the viability of ornamentation. The abstract form of an object was normally developed within the parameters of the structure, rather than as an addition to it.

Internationalism and universality are two ideas which to all intents and purposes came to mean virtually the same thing for Pioneer Moderns. If barriers between disciplines and classes of consumer were to be eliminated, and if historical styles as indicators of chronological divides were to be proscribed, then inevitably national differences had to go. The Modern Movement was therefore unavoidably internationalist in outlook, this being part of the quest for a universal human consciousness; 'The International of the Mind is an inner experience which cannot be translated into words. It does not consist of vocables but of plastic creative acts and inner intellectual force, which thus creates a newly shaped world.'[19]

The two ideas had both a political and an aesthetic rationale. The former is easily explicable in terms of the historical context. The First World Ward, fuelled by nationalism, raged while the various Modernist schools were forming. The humanitarian way of explaining the success of nationalism (which was largely irrational both historiographically and demographically)[20] was that it could only be successful in a climate of alienation. By offering the masses a sense of belonging, ancestry and identity, nationalism was the ultimate false religion. Since nationalism was the spawn of, and a parasite on, alienated peoples, it was inevitable that Modernists would be internationalist in outlook. It was reasoned that if in its very appearance the new design was international, this would facilitate cultural exchange and reduce the sense of Difference which often led to war. It would also encourage creativity in design outside of the hegemony of local politics.

The quest for a self-conscious internationalism was not new. Practitioners associated with Art Nouveau were the first to suggest it as an aesthetic solution to a moral discourse. They used nature as a common language. The substitution of nature with abstraction was the key to internationalism for the Pioneer Moderns, as it bypassed the need for the commonly held symbology and language which nature demanded. Abstraction would enable the various national schools to work intuitively and still arrive at design solutions parallel with those of their colleagues broad. In its exclusion per se of language, abstraction was the aesthetic which enabled the ethic, internationalism, to be realised.

The aesthetic rationale also pertained to the idea of universality. Many Modernists believed that beauty was a timeless, immutable value and that it could be exposed and utilized to produce a single, universal aesthetic. This could be (potentially) perceived by all. Geometric abstraction was the key device for the achievement of this universality, as it escaped immediate social contexts and contained the immutable truths of mathematics. Ancient sources were frequently cited to support the argument, giving weight to the idea of timelessness. For example, the catalogue of the exhibition, 'Machine Art,' held at the Museum of Modern Art, New York, in 1934, opened with a quotation from Plato: 'By beauty of shapes I do not mean, as most people would suppose, the beauty of living figures or pictures, but, to make my point clear, I mean straight lines and circles, and shapes, plane or solid, made from them by lathe, ruler and square. These are not, like many things, beautiful relatively, but always and absolutely.'[21]

Design was perceived to have the ability to *transform the consciousness* of those who were brought into contact with it. For example, if one were to redesign a city, this would not simply improve the environmental conditions of those who lived in it, it would have the potential to shift their psychological outlook. This attitude to visual stimuli was undoubtedly given additional credence by the ascendancy of Gestalt psychology in the first two decades of the new century. After this, Behaviourists produced evidence which seemed to support determinist ideas of design.[22]

Design therefore could function as a 'great improver,' a sophisticated kind of mental therapy which could change the mood and outlook of a population. It followed, then, that once introduced to the right kind of design in the right conditions, the masses would come to accept it as being the only viable way of making things. One would not need many styles or methodologies if one had a single correct one.

The logic of this argument was first clearly articulated in the nineteenth century by the more liberal of the unitarian philosophers, particularly John Stuart Mill, as a corrective to their otherwise stark Populism.[23] Perhaps its greatest consequence was to naturalise the idea amongst all followers of Modernism that the role of the designer was central to the enhancement of the human potential of the masses. The Modern Movement was concerned almost wholly with means of production rather than with consumption; the perfection of production would lead to a higher form of society. Designers were in effect to be the equivalent of Plato's 'Philosopher Kings.'

There was an atmosphere of a crusade amongst all Moderns. Their programme went well beyond that of making functional goods to economic ends and was deeply concerned with 'the aesthetic satisfaction of the human soul.'[24] The Pioneer phase had a theological intensity about it: 'A great epoch has begun, / There exists a new spirit.'[25] Indeed, in their intellectual and emotional allegiances, some of the Pioneers pushed their commitment into a realm analogous to a religion. Numerous members of the De Stijl and Bauhaus communities actually practiced theosophy and the Purists were infected with a Platonism which bordered on the mystical. This simply reinforced the idea that design was not to do with styles, but was a way of seeing the world. That worldview demanded singular allegiance and active commitment.

NOTES

Extracted from Greenhalgh, P., 'Introduction', in Paul Greenhalgh (ed.), *Modernism in Design*, London: Reaktion Books, 1990, pp. 1–24. Copyright © Reaktion Books 1990. Reprinted with permission.

1. This was more than partly due to the more advanced condition of architectural training. In the early years of this century architecture became a more singularly identifiable profession, enabling an intellectual forum to evolve and to forge links with other disciples. Moreover, architects not infrequently became furniture and product designers. Throughout most of this text, then, the use of the term design implies architecture as well as other forms.
2. I believe I first used this term after seeing it in an essay by Irwin Panofsky, in which he attributes the flowering of cultural activity during the Renaissance to a process of decompartmentalisation. I apologise to the reader for my inability to find this reference. The idea of decompartmentalisation in the present context is exemplified in Lewis Mumford, *Technics and Civilization* (New York, 1963) and Jurgen Habermas, 'Modernity – An Incomplete Project' (1980) in Hal Foster (ed.), *Post-modern Culture* (London, 1985).
3. Berthold Lubetkin, quoted from a letter written to Dr. Monica Felton in 1947, reproduced in Peter Coe and Malcolm Reading, *Lubetkin and Tecton: Architecture and Social Commitment* (Bristol, 1981).
4. Karl Marx and Friedrich Engles, *The Communist Manifesto* (1872; English trans. 1888, this edn. Harmondworth, 1967, with introduction by A.J. P. Taylor).
5. Karl Marx, 'Alienated Labour,' from *Economic-Philosophical Manuscripts* (1844). Quoted from Alaistair Clayre (ed.), *Industrialization and Cuture* (Milton Keynes, 1977), pp. 245–50.
6. Ibid.
7. Le Corbusier, *Towards a New Architecture*, originally published in French 1924, English translation Frederick Etchells (London, 1927). p. 17.
8. Walter Gropius, *The New Architecture and the Bauhaus* (London, 1935), p. 20.
9. The term emerged with Wagner, who believed the opera capable of using every art towards a single end. It then became part of the common parlance of Art Nouveau designers, before filtering through into Modern Movement thinking.
10. Serge Chermayeff, 'The Architect and the World Today' (1935) in *Design and the Public Good*, ed. S. Chermayeff and R. Plunz (Cambridge, Mass., 1982), p. 117.
11. Walter Gropius, *Principles of Bauhaus Production* (Dessau, 1926), quoted from Ulrich Conrads (ed.), *Programmes and Manifestos on Twentieth Century Architecture* (London, 1970).
12. Kurt Ewald, 'The Beauty of Machines' (1925–6), quoted from Charlotte Benton, Tim Benton and Aaron Scarf, *Form and Function* (Milton Keynes, 1975).
13. Le Corbusier, *Towards a New Architecture*.
14. See Charles Darwin, *The Descent of Man* (London, 1871); Raymond Williams, 'Social Darwinism,' in his *Problems in Materialism and Culture* (London, 1980); John MacKenzie, *Propaganda and Empire: The Manipulation of British Public Opinion 1880–1960* (Manchester, 1984); Paul Greenhalgh, 'Human Showcases,' in *Ephemeral Vistas: Expositions Universelles, Great Exhibitions and World Fairs, 1851–1939*.
15. Adolf Loos, 'Ornament and Crime,' 1908, quoted from Nuenz and Pevsner, *Adolf Loos* (London, 1966).
16. P. Johnson and H.R. Hitchcock, *The International Style* (New York, 1966), p. 19.
17. There is a vast literature on this period of European painting. Recommended reading: Werner Haftmann, *Painting in the Twentieth Century* (London, 1965), 2 vols.; John Golding, *Cubism: A History and an Analysis 1907–14* (London, 1968); Alfred H. Barr, *Cubism and Abstract Art* (New York, 1936);

Virginia Spate, *Orphism: The Evolution of Non-figurative Art in Paris 1910–1914* (Oxford, 1979); Tate Gallery, *Towards a New Art: Essays on the Background to Abstract Art 1910–1920* (London, 1980).

18. Theo Van Doesburg, 'Thought Vision Creation,' *De Stijl Magazine*, December 1918, pp. 23–4, quoted from Joost Baljeu, *Theo Van Doesburg* (New York, 1974).

19. De Stijl, 'Manifesto III, Towards a Newly Shaped World,' *De Stijl Magazine*, August 1921, pp. 125–6, quoted from Baljeu, *Theo Van Doesburg*.

20. See W. Ray Crozier and Antony J. Chapman, 'The Perception of Art: The Cognitive Approach and Its Context,' in Crozier and Chapman (eds.), *Cognitive Processes in the Perception of Art* (Oxford, 1984).

21. A good introductory discussion of this topic can be found in Eric Hobsbawn, 'Waving Flags: Nations and Nationalism,' in his *The Age of Empire*, 1870–1914 (London, 1987).

22. Museum of Modern Art, New York, 'Machine Art,' exhibition held 6 March – 30 April 1934, organized in part by Philip Johnson. Catalogue reprinted by Arno press (New York, 1966).

23. See, for example, Mary Warnock (ed.), *Utilitarianism by John Stuart Mill* (London, 1962). The logic of the argument was that the 'greatest number' would decide the 'greatest good' if they were in a position to choose properly. This meant that they had to have prior access to knowledge before they decided. In other words, they had to be allowed to choose for themselves. Thus populism became paternalism.

24. Gropius, *New Architecture and the Bauhaus*.

25. Le Corbusier, *Towards a New Architecture*.

13

ORNAMENT AND CRIME

Adolf Loos (1908)

In the womb the human embryo goes through all phases of development the animal kingdom has passed through. And when a human being is born, his sense impressions are like a new-born dog's. In childhood he goes through all changes corresponding to the stages in the development of humanity. At two he sees with the eyes of a Papuan, at four with those of a Germanic tribesman, at six of Socrates, at eight of Voltaire. At eight he becomes aware of violet the color discovered by the eighteenth century; before that, violets were blue and the purple snail was red. Even today physicists can point to colors in the solar spectrum which have been given a name, but which it will be left to future generations to discern.

A child is amoral. A Papuan too, for us. The Papuan slaughters his enemies and devours them. He is not a criminal. But if a modern person slaughters someone and devours him, he is a criminal or a degenerate. The Papuan covers his skin with tattoos, his boat, his oars, in short everything he can lay his hands on. He is no criminal. The modern person who tattoos himself is either a criminal or a degenerate. There are prisons in which eighty percent of the inmates have tattoos. People with tattoos not in prison are either latent criminals or degenerate aristocrats.

The urge to decorate one's face and anything else within reach is the origin of fine arts. It is the childish babble of painting. But all art is erotic.

A person of our times who gives way to the urge to daub the walls with erotic symbols is a criminal or a degenerate. What is natural in the Papuan or the child is a sign of degeneracy in a modern adult. I made the following discovery, which I passed on to the world: *the evolution of culture is synonymous with the removal of ornamentation from objects of everyday use*. I thought by doing so I would bring joy to the world: it has not thanked me for it. People were sad and downcast. What? We alone, the people of the nineteenth century, were not capable of doing something every negro tribesman could do, something every age and nation before us had done!?

The objects mankind created in earlier millennia without ornament have been casually tossed aside and allowed to go to wrack and ruin. We do not possess a single workbench from the Carolingian period, but any piece of trash having even the slightest decoration was collected, cleaned up, and put in an ostentatious palace built specially to house it. And we made our way sadly around the showcases, ashamed of our impotence. Every epoch had its own style, and ours alone should be denied one? By style people meant ornamentation. But I said, "Do not weep. Do you not see the greatness of our age resides in our very inability to create new ornament? We have gone beyond ornament, we have achieved plain, undecorated simplicity. Behold, the time is at hand, fulfillment awaits us. Soon the streets of the cities will shine like white walls! Like Zion, the Holy City, Heaven's Capital. The fulfillment will be ours."

[…]

The harm done by ornament to the ranks of the producers is even greater. Since ornament is no longer a natural product of our culture, but a symptom of backwardness or degeneracy, the craftsman producing the ornament is not fairly rewarded for his labor. The conditions among wood carvers and turners, the criminally low rates paid to embroiderers and lace makers are well-known. An ornamental craftsman has to work for twenty hours to reach the pay a modern worker earns in eight. In general, decoration makes objects more expensive, but despite that it does happen that a decorated object, with materials costing the same and demonstrably taking three times as long to produce, is put on sale at half the price of a plain object. The result of omitting decoration is a reduction in working hours and an increase in wages. A Chinese wood carver works for sixteen hours, an American laborer for eight. If I pay as much for a plain box as for one with ornamentation, the difference in labor time belongs to the worker. And if there were no ornaments at all – a state that will perhaps come about after thousands of years – we would need to work for only four hours instead of eight, since at the moment half of our labor is accounted for by ornamentation.

Ornament means wasted labor and therefore wasted health. That was always the case. Today, however, it also means wasted material, and both mean wasted capital.

As there is no longer any organic connection between ornament and our culture, ornament is no longer an expression of our culture. The ornament being created now bears no relationship to us, nor to any human being, or to the system governing the world today. It has no potential for development. Where is Otto Eckmann's ornamentation now, or that of van de Velde? In the past the artist was a healthy, vigorous figure, always at the head of humanity. The modern ornamental artist, however, lags behind or is a pathological case. After three years even he himself disowns his own products. Cultured people find them intolerable straight away, others become aware of it only after a number of years. Where are Otto Eckmann's works today? Where will Olbrich's be in ten years' time. Modern ornament has no parents and no

offspring, no past and no future. Uncultivated people, for whom the greatness of our age is a closed book, greet it rapturously and then disown it after a short time.

Humanity as a whole is healthy, only a few are sick. But these few tyrannize the worker, who is so healthy he is incapable of inventing ornaments. They compel him to execute the ornaments they have invented, in a wide variety of different materials. The changing fashion in ornament results in a premature devaluation of the product of the worker's labor; his time and the materials used are wasted capital. I have formulated the following principle: *The form of an object should last, that is, we should find it tolerable as long as the object itself lasts.* I will explain: A suit will change its style more often than a valuable fur. A woman's ball outfit, intended for one night alone, will change its style more quickly than a desk. Woe betide us, however, if we have to change a desk as quickly as a ball outfit because we can no longer stand the old style. Then we will have wasted the money we paid for the desk.

[…]

My shoes are covered with decoration formed by sawtooth patterns and holes. Work done by the shoemaker, work he has not been paid for. Imagine I go to the shoemaker and say, "You charge thirty crowns for a pair of shoes. I will pay you forty-eight." It will raise the man to such a transport of delight he will thank me through his workmanship and the material used, making them of a quality that will far outweigh my extra payment. He is happy, and happiness is a rare commodity in his house. He has found someone who understands him, who respects his work, and does not doubt his honesty. He can already see the finished shoes in his mind's eye. He knows where the best leather is to be found at the moment, he knows which of his workers he will entrust with the task, and the shoes will have all the sawtooth patterns and holes an elegant pair of shoes can take. And then I say, "But there is one condition.

The shoes must be completely plain." I will drag him down from the heights of bliss to the depths of hell. He will have less work, and I have taken away all his pleasure in it.

The ideal I preach is the aristocrat. I can accept decoration on my own person if it brings pleasure to my fellow men. It brings pleasure to me, too. I can accept the African's ornament, the Persian's, the Slovak peasant woman's, my shoemaker's, for it provides the high point of their existence, which they have no other means of achieving. *We* have the art that has superseded ornament. After all the toil and tribulations of the day, we can go to hear Beethoven or *Tristan.* My shoemaker cannot. I must not take his religion away from him, for I have nothing to put in its place. But anyone who goes to the *Ninth* and then sits down to design a wallpaper pattern is either a fraud or a degenerate.

The disappearance of ornament has brought about an undreamed-of blossoming in the other arts. Beethoven's symphonies would never have been written by a man who had to dress in silk, velvet, and lace. Those who go around in velvet jackets today are not artists, but clowns or house painters. We have become more refined, more subtle. When men followed the herd they had to differentiate themselves through color, modern man uses his dress as a disguise. His sense of his own individuality is so immensely strong it can no longer be expressed in dress. Lack of ornamentation is a sign of intellectual strength. Modern man uses the ornaments of earlier or foreign cultures as he likes and as he sees fit. He concentrates his own inventive power on other things.

NOTE

Extracted from Loos, A., 'Ornament and Crime' (1908), in A. Loos, *Ornament and Crime: Selected Essays*, trans. Michael Mitchell, Riverside, CA: Ariadne Press, 1998, pp. 167–76. Reprinted with permission of Ariadne Press.

14

WERKBUND THESES AND ANTITHESES

Hermann Muthesius and Henry van de Velde (1914)

1. Architecture, and with it the whole area of the Werkbund's activities, is pressing towards standardization, and only through standardization can it recover that universal significance which was characteristic of it in times of harmonious culture.

2. Standardization, to be understood as the result of a beneficial concentration, will alone make possible the development of a universally valid, unfailing good taste.

3. As long as a universal high level of taste has not been achieved we cannot count on German arts and crafts making their influence effectively felt abroad.

4. The world will demand our products only when they are the vehicles of a convincing stylistic expression. The foundations for this have not been laid by the German movement.

5. The creative development of what has already been achieved is the most urgent task of the age. Upon it the movement's ultimate success will depend. Any relapse and deterioration into imitation would today mean the squandering of a valuable possession.

6. Starting from the conviction that it is a matter of life and death for Germany constantly to ennoble its production, the Deutscher Werkbund, as an association of artists, industrialists, and merchants, must concentrate its attention upon creating the preconditions for the export of its industrial arts.

7. Germany's advances in applied art and architecture must be brought to the attention of foreign countries by effective publicity. Next to

exhibitions the most obvious means of doing this is by periodical illustrated publications.

8. Exhibitions by the Deutscher Werkbund are only meaningful when they are restricted radically to the best and most exemplary. Exhibitions of arts and crafts abroad must be looked upon as a national matter and hence require public subsidy.

9. The existence of efficient large-scale business concerns with reliable good taste is a prerequisite of any export. It would be impossible to meet even internal demands with an object designed by the artist for individual requirements.

10. For national reasons large distributive and transport undertakings whose activities are directed abroad ought to link up with the new movement, now that it has shown what it can do, and consciously represent German art in the world.

Hermann Muthesius

1. So long as there are still artists in the Werkbund and so long as they exercise some influence on its destiny, they will protest against every suggestion for the establishment of a canon and for standardization. By his innermost essence the artist is a burning idealist, a free spontaneous creator. Of his own free will he will never subordinate himself to a discipline that imposes upon him a type, a canon. Instinctively he distrusts everything that might sterilize his actions, and everyone who preaches a rule that might prevent him from thinking his thoughts through to their

own free end, or that attempts to drive him into a universally valid form, in which he sees only a mask that seeks to make a virtue out of incapacity.

2. Certainly, the artist who practices a 'beneficial concentration' has always recognized that currents which are stronger than his own will and thought demand of him that he should acknowledge what is in essential correspondence to the spirit of his age. These currents may be very manifold; he absorbs them unconsciously and consciously as general influences; there is something materially and morally compelling about them for him. He willingly subordinates himself to them and is full of enthusiasm for the idea of a new style *per se*. And for twenty years many of us have been seeking forms and decorations entirely in keeping with our epoch.

3. Nevertheless it has not occurred to any of us that henceforth we ought to try to impose these forms and decoration, which we have sought or found, upon others as standards. We know that several generations will have to work upon what we have started before the physiognomy of the new style is established, and that we can talk of standards and standardization only after the passage of a whole period of endeavors.

4. But we also know that as long as this goal has not been reached our endeavors will still have the charm of creative impetus. Gradually the energies, the gifts of all, begin to combine together, antitheses become neutralized, and at precisely that moment when individual strivings begin to slacken, the physiognomy will be established. The era of imitation will begin and forms and decorations will be used, the production of which no longer calls for any creative impulse: the age of infertility will then have commenced.

5. The desire to see a standard type come into being before the establishment of a style is exactly like wanting to see the effect before the cause. It would be to destroy the embryo in the egg. Is anyone really going to let themselves be dazzled by the apparent possibility of thereby achieving quick results? These premature effects have all the less prospect of enabling German arts and crafts

to exercise an effective influence abroad, because foreign countries are a jump ahead of us in the old tradition and the old culture of good taste.

6. Germany, on the other hand, has the great advantage of still possessing gifts which other, older, wearier peoples are losing: the gifts of invention, of brilliant personal brainwaves. And it would be nothing short of castration to tie down this rich, many-sided, creative élan so soon.

7. The efforts of the Werkbund should be directed toward cultivating precisely these gifts, as well as the gifts of individual manual skill, joy, and belief in the beauty of highly differentiated execution, not toward inhibiting them by standardization at the very moment when foreign countries are beginning to take an interest in German work. As far as fostering these gifts is concerned, almost everything still remains to be done.

8. We do not deny anyone's good will and we are very well aware of the difficulties that have to be overcome in carrying this out. We know that the workers' organization has done a very great deal for the workers' material welfare, but it can hardly find an excuse for having done so little towards arousing enthusiasm for consummately fine workmanship in those who ought to be our most joyful collaborators. On the other hand, we are well aware of the need to export that lies like a curse upon our industry.

9. And yet nothing, nothing good and splendid, was ever created out of mere consideration for exports. Quality will not be created out of the spirit of export. Quality is always first created exclusively for a quite limited circle of connoisseurs and those who commission the work. These gradually gain confidence in their artists; slowly there develops first a narrower, then a national clientele, and only then do foreign countries, does the world slowly take notice of this quality. It is a complete misunderstanding of the situation to make the industrialists believe that they would increase their chances in the world market if they produced *a priori* standardized types for this world market before these types had become well tried common property at home. The wonderful

works being exported to us now were none of them originally created for export: think of Tiffany glasses, Copenhagen porcelain, jewellery by Jensen, the books of Cobden-Sanderson, and so on.

10. Every exhibition must have as its purpose to show the world this native quality, and it is quite true that the Werkbund's exhibitions will have meaning only when, as Herr Muthesius so rightly says, they restrict themselves radically to the best and most exemplary.

Henry van de Velde

NOTE

Reproduced from Muthesius, H. and van de Velde, H., 'Werkbund Theses and Antitheses' (1914), in U. Conrads (ed.), *Programs and Manifestoes on 20th-century Architecture*, Cambridge, MA: MIT Press, 2001, pp. 28–31, © 1971 Massachusetts Institute of Technology, by permission of The MIT Press.

15

THE MODERN MOVEMENT BEFORE NINETEEN-FOURTEEN, FROM *PIONEERS OF MODERN DESIGN*

Nikolaus Pevsner (1936, 1949)

[...]

While the transition to the new simplicity and severity was facilitated in England by the absence of Art Nouveau and by an inborn English reasonableness, in America by the technical requirements of the huge office building, and in France by the splendid traditions of nineteenth-century engineering, Germany was, in 1900, almost completely under the spell of Art Nouveau, enjoying wild ornamentation, as she had done so often in past centuries. Only a few among those who had played a leading part in the Jugendstil found a way out of its entanglement.

[...]

In Germany the most important architect during those years was Peter Behrens[1] (1866–1940). Characteristically of the situation about 1900, he began as a painter and underwent the 'moral' reformation towards the applied arts, before he trained as an architect. The applied arts, when Behrens started, meant Art Nouveau. He soon escaped from its enervating atmosphere. His first building, his own house in Darmstadt (1901), already shows a hardening of the tender curves of Art Nouveau.[2] In the same year, Behrens designed a type face in which the change is complete. The curves are straightened, and ornamental initials

are decorated with squares and circles only. A comparison between Behren's first type face and Eckmann's (1900) is historically very instructive.[3] Again this new simplicity was brought about under English influence. The Doves Press stands at the beginning of German twentieth-century printing. Honesty and saneness became the ideals that replaced the sultry dreams of Art Nouveau aesthetics.

Behrens was not alone in this revulsion from Art Nouveau. Its earliest witness in Germany seems to be the flat designed by R. A. Schröder (1878–1962), a poet and decorator and a founder of the Insel Verlag, for his cousin Alfred Walter von Heymel (1878–1914), also a poet and also a founder of the Insel Verlag. The flat was in Berlin and dates from 1899.[4] Here for the first time – even if perhaps not without some inspiration from the hieratic stiffness of some Mackintosh furniture – are chairs without curves, and walls, ceilings, and fireplaces divided into simple rectangular geometric patterns.

In Behrens's buildings from 1904 onwards the same new somewhat classicist spirit is expressed in the exteriors. Take for instance the Art Building at an exhibition held at Oldenburg in 1905 and compare it with Olbrich's Sezession. In Behrens's design the florid cupola and the curved cornice have disappeared. The centerpiece and the outer pavilions have roofs of pyramidal form – a motif incidentally taken over by Olbrich in his exhibition buildings at Darmstadt in 1907–8 – the rest of the building has flat roofs. Walls without windows are decorated with delicate lines forming oblong panels and squares. The porch has been left completely bare, just two square posts and a square lintel.[5]

This indicates the direction in which Behrens was to develop during the years that followed. His principal buildings before the war he designed for the AEG [Allgemeine Elektrizitäts-Gesellschaft], one of the big German electrical combines, of which the managing director, P. Jordan, had appointed him architect and adviser. In 1909 the turbine factory was built, perhaps the most beautiful industrial building ever erected up to that time [Figure 8]. The steel frame is clearly exhibited; wide, perfectly spaced glass panes replace the walls on the side and in the middle of the ends; and if the corners are still expressed by heavy stone with banded rustication and rounded at the angles, the metal frame projecting its sharp corners above these stones pylons redresses the balance boldly and effectively. This design has nothing in common with the ordinary factories of that time, not even the most functional American ones of Albert Kahn with their exposed steel frames. Here for the first time the imaginative possibilities of industrial architecture were visualized. The result is a pure work of architecture, so finely balanced that the huge dimensions are scarcely realized, unless one looks at the people in the street for comparison. The two-storeyed aisle on the left has the flat roof and the row of windows which we find in all the most advanced works of that time.

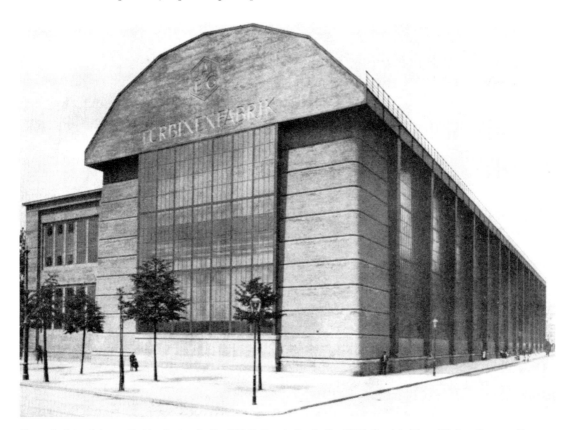

Figure 8. Peter Behrens, Turbine factory for the AEG, Huttenstraße, Berlin, 1909. Reprinted from Nikolaus Pevsner, *Pioneers of Modern Design from William Morris to Walter Gropius*, Harmondsworth: Penguin, 1969, p. 205, by permission of the Estate of Nikolaus Pevsner. Photo © 2009 Artists Rights Society (ARS), New York/VG Bild-Kunst, Bonn.

The factory for the production of small electric motors was built in 1911. The proportions of that part of the building which is to be seen on the left, its rows of rather narrow high windows without any mouldings, are reminiscent of the factory of 1909 and more reminiscent of Schinkel's, than of Hoffmann's or Loos's favourite proportions. The same strength and noble vigour are expressed in the composition of the main block with its round-fronted pillars and recessed windows.

And while Behrens was employed on such monumental tasks, he managed to spend the same amount of care and thought on improvements in the design of small things for everyday use and larger things of so utilitarian a kind that they had never before been regarded as works of art at all. An example of the first is the excellent tea-kettle brought out in 1910 [Figure 9], an example of the second the street lamps of 1907–8. They show the same purity of form, the same sobriety in limiting the design to simple geometrical forms, and the same beauty of proportion which delight us in Behrens's buildings.

The solidarity of the Deutscher Werkbund with this attitude of Behrens's is a matter of course. It has already been reported that the Werkbund was founded in 1907. Behrens had become adviser to the AEG in the same year. One year earlier the Deutscher Werkstätten, as we have also seen before, had shown their first machine-made furniture at an exhibition in Dresden. By the time the Werkbund brought out its first Annual, that is by 1912, they could without effort show well over a hundred illustrations of works of industrial

Figure 9. Peter Behrens, Electric tea-kettle for the AEG, 1910. Reprinted from Nikolaus Pevsner, *Pioneers of Modern Design from William Morris to Walter Gropius*, Harmondsworth: Penguin, 1969, p. 207, by permission of the Estate of Nikolaus Pevsner. Photo © 2009 Artists Rights Society (ARS), New York/VG Bild-Kunst, Bonn.

design as well as architecture in the style of which they approved. Both the Deutsche Werkstätten and the AEG appeared in its pages, and Riemerschmid, and Josef Hoffmann, and also Gropius.

[...]

The Modern Movement in architecture, in order to be fully expressive of the twentieth century, had to possess both qualities, the faith in science and technology, in social science and rational planning, and the romantic faith in speed and the roar of machines. We have seen in Chapter I how the one set of values was appreciated by Muthesius, the Werkbund, and finally Gropius's Bauhaus, the other by the Italian Futurists and by Sant'Elia, their architectural precursor rather than representative. It is the same in architecture. Sant'Elia's drawings and Gropius's first building stand for the two interpretations of the new metropolitan, technological civilization of the twentieth century. A decision had to be taken between the two, as soon as the First World War was over, and a decision has still or again to be taken now.

[...]

The real solid achievement had its source not in Sant'Elia, not in Poelzig and Mendelsohn, but in Behrens and his great pupil Walter Gropius (born in 1883). Almost immediately after he had left Behren's office, in 1911, he was commissioned to build a factory at Alfeld on the Leine (Fagus-Fabrik). His designs go distinctly beyond those by Behrens for the AEG. Only small details such as the windows on the right of the main block show Behrens's influence. As for the main block itself, everything is new and full of stimulating ideas. For the first time a complete façade is conceived in glass. The supporting piers are reduced to narrow mullions of brick. The corners are left without any support, a treatment which has since been imitated over and over again. The expression of the flat roof has also changed. Only in the building by Loos which was done one year before

the Fagus Factory, have we seen the same feeling for the pure cube. Another exceedingly important quality of Gropius's building is that, thanks to the large expanses of clear glass, the usual hard separation of exterior and interior is annihilated. Light and air can pass freely through the walls so that the closed-in space is no longer different in essence from the great universe of space outside. This 'etherealization' of architecture, as Frank Lloyd Wright had called it in 1901,[6] is one of the most characteristic features of the new style. We have seen it develop in the usual ground plan of late-nineteenth-century office buildings, where the supporting steel girders made all the partition walls easily removable, and then in Wright's ground plans of private houses, in the arrangement of the rooms in Perret's house of 1903, and in Mackintosh's entrancing vistas; and we may recognize its counterpart in the field of planning in the move from the town to a whole province, which was made in Germany immediately after the First World War (*Landesplanung*, Ruhr District, 1920). Here too it is the conquest of space, the spanning of great distances, the rational co-ordination of heterogeneous functions that fascinates architects. The profound affinity of this passion for planning with the characteristics of the twentieth-century style in architecture and with the eternal concern of Western architecture with the conquest of space is evident. The new style in the form Gropius gave it takes its place in the procession which leads from the Romanesque and the Gothic to the Renaissance of Brunelleschi and Alberti and the Baroque of Borromini and Neumann. The warmth and directness with which ages of craft and a more personal relation between architect and client endowed buildings of the past may have gone for good. The architect, to represent this century of ours, must be colder, cold to keep in command of mechanized production, cold to design for the satisfaction of anonymous clients.

However, genius will find its own way even in times of overpowering collective energy, even within the medium of this new style of the twentieth century which, because it is a genuine style as opposed to a passing fashion, is universal. For the Werkbund Exhibition of 1914, Gropius built a small model factory. The north side is his comment on his master's turbine factory of five years before. The reduction of motifs to an absolute minimum and the sweeping simplification of outline are patent. The replacement of Behrens's heavy corner piers by thin metallic lines is specially impressive. Bolder still is the south front with the superb contrast between the decidedly Wrightian brick centre and the completely glazed corners. In the middle there are only the narrowest slits for the windows and the lowest entrance; at the corner, where according to all standards of the past, a sufficient-looking supporting force should show itself, there is nothing but glass encasing transparently two spiral staircases.

The motif has since been imitated as often as the girderless corner of the Fagus Factory; and it shows that Gropius's personal expression by no means lacks grace. There is something sublime in this effortless mastery of material and weight. Never since the Sainte-Chapelle and the choir of Beauvais had the human art of building been so triumphant over matter. Yet the character of the new buildings is entirely un-Gothic, anti-Gothic. While in the thirteenth century all lines, functional though they were, served the one artistic purpose of pointing heavenwards to a goal beyond this world, and walls were made translucent to carry the transcendental magic of saintly figures rendered in coloured glass, the glass walls are now clear and without mystery, the steel frame is hard, and its expression discourages all other-worldly speculation. It is the creative energy of this world in which we live and work and which we want to master, a world of science and technology, of speed and danger, of hard struggles and no personal security, that is glorified in Gropius's architecture, and as long as this is the world and these are its ambitions and problems, the style of Gropius and the other pioneers will be valid.

NOTES

Extracted from Pevsner, N., *Pioneers of Modern Design: From William Morris to Walter Gropius*, London: Penguin, 1975. (First published as *Pioneers of the Modern Movement*, London: Faber, 1936; second edition New York: Museum of Modern Art, 1949; third revised edition, London: Pelican Books, Penguin), pp. 179–217. Copyright © the Estate of Nikolaus Pevsner, 1936, 1960, 1976. Reprinted with permission.

1. Hoeber, Fritz. *Peter Behrens*, Munich, 1913; Cremers, Paul Joseph. *Peter Behrens, sein Werk von 1909 bis zur Gegenwart*, Essen, 1928.
2. Illustrated in the *Architectural Review*, lxxvi, 1934, p. 40.
3. Cf. Schmalenbach, Fritz, *Jugendstil*, Wurzburg, 1935, pp. 28–9, 85; Rodenberg, J. 'Karl Klingspor.' *Fleuron*, v, 1926; Baurmann, Roswitha, 'Schrift', in *Jugendstil*, edited by Seling, H., Heidelberg and Munich, 1959.
4. On this see Ahlers-Hestermann, Friedrich, *Stilwende*, Berlin, 1941, p. 109. He dates the room 1901, but Dr. Schröder himself told me in a letter that the date is 1899.
5. Linear decoration in square and oblongs is as typical of Behrens at this stage as of Schröder, of Mackintosh, and of course of Josef Hoffmann whose nickname was 'Quadratl-Hoffmann.'
6. And as Octave Mirbeau had visualized it as early as 1889. His term is '*combinaisons aériennes*' (Siegfried Giedion, *Bauen in Frankreich, Eisen, Eisenbeton*, Leipzig, 1928, p. 18).

16

THE *COLORISTES* AND CHARLES-EDOUARD JEANNERET, FROM *MODERNISM AND THE DECORATIVE ARTS IN FRANCE*

Nancy Troy (1991)

[...]

The interaction between Jeanneret and the French design world was complex, cumulative, and at times expressed in contradictory ways. It is, however, crucial for understanding that his Purist design work of the late teens and twenties was fashioned in response to French debates about the decorative arts in which Jeanneret had already been engaged before the First World War.

Jeanneret's pre-1907 training in the Ruskinian decorative arts tradition, his student work as an Art Nouveau designer of decorative motifs for watchcases as well as architectural surfaces, and his involvement with the Swiss Romande decorative arts movement following his return to La Chaux-de-Fonds [Switzerland] in 1911 after several years of travel abroad, have received considerable attention. Less familiar is the fact that during the next few years, when Jeanneret was reformulating and refining his approach to design, he paid a great deal of attention to the contemporary practice of the decorative arts in France.[1] French developments in that arena are, in turn, greatly illuminated by a consideration of both Jeanneret's writings and his activities as a designer in the period just before and during the war.

[...]

He [Jeanneret] wrote to a friend in 1913, "It is very, very odd: all my studies have been on the subject of reinforced concrete and yet I have barely cast 20 cubic metres of it! And while I have never studied interior architecture, preferring merely to look at it, lo and behold it has constituted *all* my work in 1913!"[2]

Between 1912 and 1917, when Jeanneret built only three houses and a movie theater, he was employed as an interior designer by members of several wealthy families prominent in the watch-making industry of La Chaux-de-Fonds. The clients called upon him to redesign and decorate one or more rooms in their homes; in such commissions Jeanneret was responsible for virtually every aspect of the interiors, including the choice of colors and fabrics, the light fixtures, and the furniture to be used.

[...]

[H]is notation [in travel sketchbooks from his trips to Paris] of the names André Groult, Paul Iribe, and La Maison Martine – established in 1911 by Paul Poiret – is much more suggestive of the direction Jeanneret was pursuing around this time, and it is therefore important to consider who these Parisian decorators were and what their designs would have represented to Jeanneret.

Of the three, Poiret was certainly the most inventive and influential figure.[3] Having started his career as a couturier in 1898 under Jacques Doucet, he established his own business in 1903 and began to develop a substantial following among the *haute monde*, which was attracted no doubt as much by Poiret's flair for publicity as by the graceful elegance of his fashion design, the controversial hallmark of which was a relatively loosely fitted, straight gown that allowed for expression of the natural contours of the female form unencumbered by a corset.

[…]

Jeanneret visited La Maison Martine's shop at 83, rue du Faubourg Saint-Honore not only in October 1913, but again in December of that year, when he made another trip to Paris, this time with the intention of studying the interiors displayed in the Salon d'Automne. The copious notes he took at the exhibition reveal a design sensibility that is strikingly different from the one he identified with some ten years later, as Le Corbusier. In 1913, Jeanneret paid particular attention to designers in the Poiret orbit; in his notes he recorded, often in minute detail, isolated elements as well as more general aspects of the ensembles displayed by seven individuals and one pair of designers.[4] The pair, Maurice Lucet and Pierre Lahalle, are not well know today, but their work was comparable to that of the others, all of whom could be counted among the most prominent young designers of the period before the First World War: Andre Groult, Paul Huillard, Leon Jallot, Gustave-Louis Jaulmes, Robert Mallet-Stevens, Andre Mare, and Louis Sue. […] Apart from Jallot, whose relatively conservative designs reflected his earlier participation in the craft workshops of Siegfried Bing's gallery, all these designers were recognized for their adherence to the *coloriste* approach to interior decoration. Thus the work to which Jeanneret was most attracted in late 1913 was the product of a closely knit group of fashionable and controversial artists who occupied a well-defined position on the Parisian decorative arts scene. Yet it is important to consider not only links but also the differences between the *coloristes*; although intimately related, they did not form a monolithic group. The choices Jeanneret made from among their designs can therefore shed light on the nuances of his own attitude toward design around this time when his ideas on the subject were open to a variety of influences.

[…]

Jeanneret's notes from the Salon d'Automne of 1913 suggest that, like many others at the time, he recognized features that distinguished the work of each *coloriste* but was attracted as well by qualities that they all shared. He must have been familiar with the opinions of numerous critics who sensed that these designers were not particularly anxious to "discover a cohesive style."[5] Theirs was a heterodox spirit fundamentally opposed to the totally unified design aesthetic that the *constructeurs* [French designers known for their technical proficiency and sobriety of approach] inherited from Art Nouveau. The *coloristes* favored collaborative endeavors in which each contributor would expose "his sensibility, his personal manner," while nonetheless subscribing to a common "affinity of taste and – to use a popular term – of tendencies."[6]

These words were written by the poet Roger Allard in the preface to a privately printed catalogue that Groult, Jaulmes, Mare, Sue, and several other designers produced to accompany their entries in the Salon d'Automne of 1913. Allard sought in particular to explain their commonly held conception of French tradition, which, like Gustave Kahn, Allard saw as central to their approach to decorative art. These designers appealed to the past, Allard suggested, not simply for the purpose of copying old styles, but because there they found a storehouse of history into which they hoped to insert their work without negating the heritage they had received. He asserted that they were "innovators and traditionalists" at one and the same time. Their designs corresponded to a collection of furniture accumulated by successive generations of a single family and ought therefore to appeal to those who customarily rejected any new style on the grounds that it could not be assimilated along with the style of the past. "Of all the artisans," Allard wrote, "memory is the most skillful. It possesses the secret of precious sheens, rare patinas, and beautiful gold ornaments. Time, which harmonizes and reconciles everything, is the prince of *ensembliers*."[7]

This attitude must have been very attractive to Jeanneret, for his own interior design work was characterized by the same electric spirit.

Indeed, he was bringing together actual antique pieces, mostly from the Louis XVI and Directoire periods, and juxtaposing them with furniture he designed himself, inspired by these same historical styles. Scattered throughout his sketchbooks from the early- and mid-teens are rapidly executed drawings of such objects as chairs, settees, desks, armoires, and lamps that he came across either in Paris or in Swiss cities such as Geneva and Lausanne [Figure 10]. Many of them are annotated with brief remarks concerning the dimensions, condition, and price of the pieces involved.[8] One shows an armchair with a rush seat and a simple wood frame whose squared-off back is articulated by plain, rectilinear splats. Jeanneret

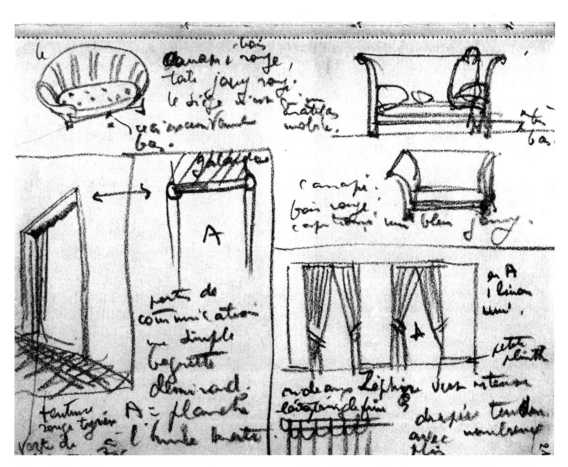

Figure 10. Charles-Edouard Jeanneret, page from *carnet bleu*, c.1912–14, in Nancy Troy, *Modernism and the Decorative Arts in France: Art Nouveau to Le Corbusier,* New Haven, CT: Yale University Press, 1991, pp. 103–58, p. 115. Photo © 2009 Artists Rights Society (ARS), New York/ADAGP, Paris/FLG.

bought this chair, or one very much like it, for the salon of the house he built for his parents in 1912. There he placed it in a corner and alongside an upholstered settee of his own design – inspired by the geometry of the Empire style – which was remarkable for its bold juxtaposition of similarly simple, rectangular forms. In subsequent years Jeanneret also conceived a number of interior ensembles for members of the Ditisheim family in La Chaux-de-Fonds in which he integrated antiques that they already owned or that he found on the market with original pieces that evoke late eighteenth- and early nineteenth-century French styles.[9]

Jeanneret's activity as a designer should also be considered in the context of his professional circumstances during this early period, for it was as a designer of furniture and interior ensembles (rather than as an architect) that he managed to become involved at this time in the Parisian artistic community. On most of his trips to Paris – and those of 1913 were no exception – Jeanneret made a point of visiting Auguste Perret, for whom, as has been mentioned, he had worked in 1908–09. During those years, Perret had introduced him to the technical problems involved in building with reinforced concrete and exposed him to an approach to architecture based on the use of modern materials and standardized parts. In 1913, however, Perret was important to Jeanneret less as a teacher than as a conduit to the Parisian cultural circles in which Perret had become prominent as a result, in part, of his work on the Theatre des Champs-Elysees.[10] Jeanneret had recognized the importance of the theater as early as the summer of 1911 when he had been tempted by Perret's offer of a position in his office, where work on the project was under way. At the time, for Jeanneret, Perret already virtually symbolized "all Paris, with his modern poets, musicians and painters."[11] Moreover, in 1912 Perret had become involved with the Artistes de Passy and was therefore in touch with representatives of the most advanced tendencies in French literature and the arts. No wonder Jeanneret wrote with such ardor about his encounter with Perret in the autumn of 1913! For in his brief visit of only two hours, he had been able to breathe in "the enchantment of an avant-garde atmosphere and a beautiful *force sirene*."[12]

NOTES

Extracted from Troy, N., *Modernism and the Decorative Arts in France: Art Nouveau to Le Corbusier*, New Haven: Yale University Press, 1991, pp. 103–58. Copyright © Yale University Press, 1991. Reprinted with permission.

1. Scholarly interest in Jeanneret's early career has been fostered not only by major retrospective exhibits and publications designed to coincide with the celebration of the hundredth anniversary of his birth in 1987, but also by a widespread effort to re-examine the roots of twentieth-century modernism in general. In Le Corbusier studies this trend is demonstrated, for example, in La Chaux-de-Fonds, Musee des Beaux-Arts and Musee d'Histoire, *La Chaux-de-Fonds et Jeanneret (avant Le Corbusier)*, exh. cat. (May 19–July 31, 1983) (this publication is an enlarged, special edition of *Archithese* 13 [March–April 1983]); Luisa Martina Colli, *Arte artigianato e tecnica nella poetica di Le Corbusier*, Biblioteca di Cultura Moderna Laterza (Rome and Bari: Laterza, 1982); Eleanor Gregh, "The Dom-ino Idea," *Oppositions*, no. 15–16 (Winter-Spring 1979): 61–87; Mary Patricia May Sekler, *The Early Drawings of Charles-Edouard Jeanneret* (*Le Corbusier*) *1902–1908* (New York and London: Garland, 1977).

It has been shown that Jeanneret's advocacy of internationalism during the 1920s was in part determined by his earlier rejection of the regionalist implications of the Swiss Romande movement in which he had participated as a youth. However, the important role that French decorative artists played in Jeanneret's maturation process has not been appreciated, and the same is also true of the influence that French decorative art in general exercised on Jeanneret in the teens. Justice has, on the other hand, been done to the French as well as the German roots of Jeanneret's architectural ideas, but in that arena too the significance of his interests in design and his work as a designer during the teens – both of which fostered his involvement with contemporary developments in France at that time – have not often been acknowledged. Greater recognition of Jeanneret's activities in the field of design and the decorative arts will enhance the understanding of him as an artist, architect, and thinker who, during the teens, pursued many avenues in order to insure his entry into the French design scene (where, as Le Corbusier, he would have a profound impact after the First World War).

2. Quoted in Joyce Lowman, "Corb as Structural Rationalist," *Architectural Review* 160 (October 1976): 230.

3. See Paul Poiret, *En habillant l'époque* (1930; repr. Paris: Bernard Grasset, 1986); Palmer White, *Poiret* (New York: Clarkson N. Potter, 1973).

4. See Charles-Edouard Jeanneret, "Carnet I, Paris Automne 1913," Bibliothèque de la Ville, La Chaux-de-Fonds [hereafter cited as BV/LCdF] LCms88.

5. Maurice Maignan, "A propos du XVIIIe Salson de la Societe des Artistes Decorateurs," *L'Art Decoratif* 29 (May 1913): 231.

6. Roger Allard, pref., *Salon d'Automne 1913. Art decoratif. Groupe Dresa, Jean-Louis Gampert, Andre Mare, Louis-Gustave Jaulmes, Andre Groult, Louis Sue, Jacques Palyart, Paul Vallois & Paul Vera* [Paris: 1913].

7. Several months later Claude Roger-Marx made a closely related point: "it is necessary – this is the essential condition of their success and of their diffusion – that modern pieces of furniture be able to relate to antique furniture without either suffering from this association. Wouldn't this be this best proof that our modern furniture ties in again with our tradition, by renewing it, and perpetuates its gifts of equilibrium and grace that, of all races, ours has received a share?" Roger Marx, "Interieurs modernes," *Gazette de Bon Ton* 2 (May 1914): 179.

8. See Charles-Edouard Jeanneret, "Carnet I, Paris Automne 1913," BV/LCdF, LCms88; *Le Corbusier Sketchbooks*, vol. 1: 1914–1948, pref. Andre Wogenscky, intro. Maurice Besset, notes Francoise de Franclieu, trans. Agnes Serenyi et al. (New York: The Architectural History Foundation; Cambridge, Mass.: MIT Press, in collaboration with the Fondation Le Corbusier, Paris, 1981), Sketchbook A1.

9. Jeanneret's correspondence with Ernest Albert Ditisheim and Hermann Ditisheim (mostly from December 1914 through October 1915) is preserved in BV/LCdF, Nd-63. In addition to the sketchbooks mentioned above, see also Jeaneret's *Carnet bleu* of ca. 1912–14 (Fondation Le Corbusier, Paris [hereafter cited as FLC], T.71), which contains sketches of furniture from a variety of periods, including examples Jeanneret saw in the Musee des Arts Decoratifs. The first page of the *Carnet bleu* lists the names and addresses of five contacts in Paris, including Rupert Carabin and Andre Groult. On page 10 is a sketch of a chair by Groult, the back of which is carved with a stylized basket containing three flowers (fig. 114). Other designs by Groult, including lamps, chairs, and settes, are depicted elsewhere in the sketchbook. Jeanneret's copies of his letters to Jules and Georges Ditisheim are in BV/LCdF, LCms89. On June 12, 1915, Jeanneret mentioned Groult's name to Georges Ditisheim with regard to designs for lighting fixtures in the vestibule of Ditisheim's home; see BV/LCdF, LCms89, 217. Earlier, on December 10, 1913, Jeanneret had written to the Maison Bagues in Paris to announce the impending visit of Georges Ditisheim, "whom I strongly advised to purchase for his vestibule, which I have just installed, a lighting fixture that I noticed in your shop during my visit in November. It is a Pompeian tripod with a bronze basket filled with crystal fruits." Bagues's products, he continued, "made such a good impression on me that I would be pleased, I

repeat, to make use of your creations, which are in perfect taste, very unusual." See BV/LCdF, LCms89, 10.

It is unclear whether the November visit mentioned by Jeanneret occurred on the same trip to Paris he made with Salomon Schwob in late October or involved a separate trip the following month (which seems unlikely).

Jeanneret's "style" furniture has been discussed in detail by Arthur Ruegg, who notes that Jeanneret also selected Louis XIII furniture, but in that case rush-seated chairs intended for more informal settings, and not for the interiors of Directoire-inspired furniture, would have been considered more appropriate. In this distinction Ruegg discerns a developing interest on Jeanneret's part in the notion of types adapted to specific functions, and in general he describes Jeanneret's "style" furniture with a view toward his later, mature work of the 1920s. See Ruegg, "Anmerkungen zum *Equipement de l'habitation* und zur *Polychromie interieur* bei Le Corbusier," in *Le Corbusier: la ricerca paziente*, exh. Cat. (Lugano: Villa Malpensata, 1980),

152–62; Ruegg, "Charles-Edouard Jeanneret, architecte-conseil pour toutes les questions de decoration interieure …," in *La Chaux-de-Fonds et Jeanneret*, 39–43; Ruegg, "Les Contributions de Le Corbusier a l'art d'habiter, 1912–1937: de le decoration a l'equipement," in *Le Corbusier: une encyclopedie*, ed. Jacques Lucan (Paris: Centre Georges Pompidou, 1987), 124–35.

10. See the discussion of the Theatre des Champs-Elysees in chap. 2, above. According to an article in *Gil Blas*, the gala opening of the theater was attended by "the elite of the Parisian worlds of high society, politics, finance, theater, literature and the arts." Jodelet, "L'inauguration du Theatre des Champs-Elysess," *Gil Blas* (April 1, 1913): 1. See also the report in *Comoedia* (April 1, 1913): 2.

11. Charles-Edouard Jeanneret, Letter to William Ritter, [Summer 1911], quoted in Gregh, "The Dom-ino Idea," 76.

12. Charles-Edouard Jeaneret, Letter to William Ritter, [postmarked November 3, 1913], photocopy FLC, Box R3 (18), 217.

17

FROM WORKSHOP TO LABORATORY, FROM *THE BAUHAUS REASSESSED*

Gillian Naylor (1985)

The move from Weimar to Dessau in 1925 was symbolic as well as expedient. The school had left an 'art town' for an industrial city, so that the potential for collaboration in industrial production could, in theory, be exploited, and in an attempt to consolidate the school's finances, as well as its professional intentions, a Bauhaus Corporation was formed to deal with the marketing of Bauhaus products. (In 1926–27 the business manager was the second-highest paid member of the school's staff; he was paid RM 10,000 a year, while Gropius received RM 11,000.)

In spite of these practical measures, however, the fundamental problem remained: how was the school to identify, test and establish the 'norms' or prototypes for industrial production [see Figure 11]? The theories of standard and standardization on which the Dessau programme was based implied both an ideal and achievable concept of form: the need for standardization at various levels of production had been acknowledged throughout German industry, but the identification and definition of 'standards' remained elusive. The belief in 'art' as a determining force in establishing standards for industry, which was fundamental to Gropius's declared philosophy at this time, was not necessarily a viable one, as Georg Muche was to point out. [Lyonel] Feininger, one of the 'old masters' who was persuaded to move to Dessau because of his conciliatory personality and his long association with the school, identified the problem at its most basic level. Describing [Laszlo Moholy-Nagy's] enthusiasm for 'movies, optics, mechanics, projections and movement' in [a] letter to his wife […] he wrote: 'We can say to ourselves that this is terrifying and the end of all art – but actually it is a question of mass-production, technically very interesting – but why attach the name of art to this mechanization of all visual things, why call it the only art of our age and, moreover, of the future?' These were, of course, personal preoccupations, and not, like Muche's essay, polemical in intention. Nevertheless, the Constructivist vision of the 'systemization of the means of expression to produce results that are universally comprehensible'[1] remained the goal of the Bauhaus. The role played by 'art' in the expression of this ideal was difficult to define, for art, as both Feininger and Muche realized, could no longer be autonomous if its methods as well as its values were related to objects – objects which, as far as the Bauhaus was concerned, were for the most part designed according to expectations that had been established in Weimar, and which therefore bore little or no relationship to industrial production. But as Kandinsky confidently put it, 'the obsolete word Art has been positively resurrected at the Bauhaus. And linked to the word, The Deed.'[2]

The form and nature of the 'deed', however, was determined by the Weimar-trained designer in the early years at Dessau, and work there demonstrated the personal pre-occupations and convictions of the new 'Masters of Form' rather than any objective ideal of design for industry.

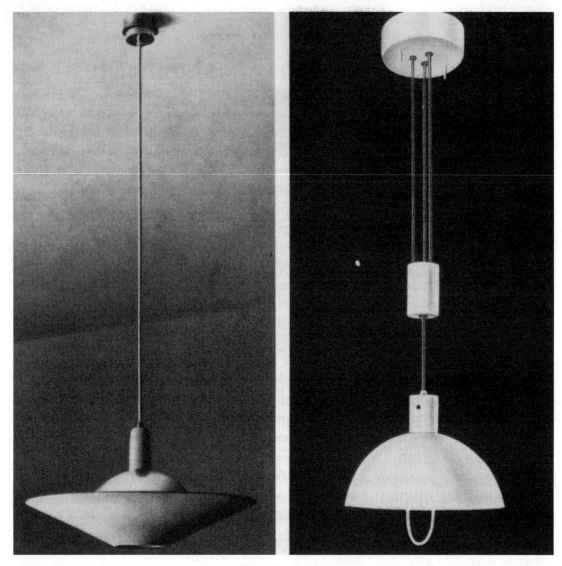

Figure 11. (Left) Ceiling light by Wilhelm Wagenfeld, 1912. (Right) Adjustable ceiling light by Marianne Brandt, 1927, in Gillian Naylor, *The Bauhaus Reassessed: Sources and Design Theory*, London: The Herbert Press, 1985, p. 147. Reprinted by permission of The Herbert Press, an imprint of A&C Black Publishers.

MOHOLY-NAGY AND THE NEW VISION

The most exuberant and perhaps the most dominant personality in the school after the move to Dessau was Moholy-Nagy – 'Gropius's faithful drummer-boy and teeth-chatterer', as Schlemmer uncharitably described him.[3] In spite of his Constructivist allegiances, however, Moholy's approach was pragmatic: he wrote copiously and enthusiastically about his discoveries and convictions, but his writing is too mercurial and derivative to constitute a consistent theory. Magpie-like, he picked up current ideas and added them to his stockpile, but two themes persist in his writing: first that design is a social process, and second that intuition has a major role to play in this process. Whether the end-product was called 'art' or 'design' was immaterial to him: 'The criterion should never be "art" or "not art", but whether the right form was given to the stated function,' he wrote in *The New Vision*, 'whether this ever will be called "art" is of secondary importance.'[4] Establishing the 'right form for the stated function' could never be predetermined. In *The New Vision* Moholy considers what he describes as 'biotechnics as a method of creativity', quoting Raoul H. France's *Die Pflanze als Erfinder (Plants as Inventors)*: 'All technical forms can be deduced from forms in nature. The laws of least resistance and of economy of effort make it inevitable that similar activities shall always lead to similar forms ... Every bush, every tree, can instruct him, advise him, and show him inventions, apparatuses, technical appliances without number.' Biological and botanical analogies alone, however, are not a sufficient basis for design since, according to Moholy, 'psychological, social and economical conditions' must be taken into account, and the results might 'even serve functions which could not be foreseen during the process of designing'.[5] Moholy's ideal was 'an organic system of production whose focal point is man; not profit', and he was, significantly, one of the few Bauhaus designers to discuss the role of the worker in the process of production. In *The New Vision* he considers that 'the Taylor system, the conveyor belt, and the like remain misinterpreted as long as they turn man into a machine'. When he wrote *Vision in Motion*, however (the book was published in Chicago in 1947), Moholy's holistic attitude to design was reinforced by his experience of the United States – a country 'rich in resources, raw materials and human ingenuity', which could 'afford to be wasteful', and where the design profession had been established to satisfy the salesman's 'desire for the sensationally new'. Such a society, according to Moholy, demanded more than skill, knowledge, and an understanding of techniques and production processes from the designer: it forced him to recognize his social obligations. 'He should make his design with the aim of eliminating fatigue from the worker's life. He must see his design through, not only in the technical but in its human effects as well. This quality of design is dependent not alone on function, science and technological processes, but also on social consciousness.'[6] Again, it is significant that Moholy predicted 'the coming of an "electronic age"', with 'the reduction of manpower and labour hours' as an 'inevitable consequence'; the dilemma of 'technological unemployment', he wrote, although essentially political, also involved 'the social obligations of the designer'.

Moholy's awareness of the social implications of design had, like that of his colleagues, been reinforced by his experiences in Germany in the 1920s and '30s, when design, as well as art and architecture, were subject to political interpretation. His aim then was to 'translate revolution into material reality', and he attempted to do this at the Bauhaus 'through form and word'.[7] Underlying these activities was the assumption that the worker would participate in this revolution through design: the tragic ideal of William Morris as well as Moholy-Nagy. The ambiguity of this idealism did not strike Moholy until Hannes Meyer took over the school, so that Moholy had three years at Dessau in which to attempt to translate his philosophies into action.

Gropius has described how Moholy approached his work with the 'attitude of an unprejudiced, happy child at play';[8] the 'play' element in his teaching, however, owed nothing to Froebel or Montessori and had more to do with his enthusiasm for the integrative ideals of the school, and the release they represented from 'the terrible great quietness of his childhood' as well as the trauma of the war.[9] 'Many of us used him for our own advantage,' wrote Paul Citroen, 'and burdened him with tasks we ourselves should have solved. But, with the smiling enthusiasm of a child, Moholy accepted all demands, and his vitality seemed unlimited.'[10]

At Dessau, Moholy continued to accept demands: he contributed to the Preliminary Course, he was also in charge of the metal workshop, and he became more involved in typography, photography and film. His work on the Preliminary Course, which, as in Weimar, complemented that of Albers and Kandinsky, extended the preoccupations he had established in Weimar. His main concern was with what he described as 'spatial design', and the demonstration of concepts of space in three- rather than two-dimensional form. The exercises – abstract constructions in wire, metal, glass and wood – were intended to demonstrate the 'interweaving of shapes' and 'the fluctuating play of tensions and forces', and to serve as an introduction to concepts of architectural space, light and shadow and transparency.[11] In the metal workshop, on the other hand, Moholy was in theory more concerned with practicality than with abstract concepts. 'Goods intended for common use', he wrote, 'are neither sacramental vessels nor objects of contemplation'[12] and it is significant that his 'statement' about the Metal Workshop in *Bauhaus 1919–1928* is called 'From Wine Jugs to Lighting Fixtures'. The transition from the concentration on craft-based objects in precious metals to the design of 'lighting-fixtures' for mass-production was due more to developments within the German lighting industry, however, than to efforts on the part of the school to establish 'norms' or prototypes [see Figure 11]. Korting and Matthiesen, the Leipzig firm that produced the Kandem range of light-fittings, worked with Christian Dell, as well as with the Bauhaus. But as John Heskett points out in *Industrial Design*, the German lighting industry in the 1920s was involved in advanced research into lighting in factories and offices, and Korting and Matthiesen produced a wide range of equipment for industrial use.[13] The introduction of commercial techniques and forms into ranges for the domestic market, therefore, was not difficult, although it may have needed designers of the calibre of Marianne Brandt and Christian Dell to demonstrate that the factory 'aesthetic' could also relate to the domestic market. Marianne Brandt, by that time well-established in the metal workshop (so much so that the Dessau

metalwork designs illustrated in both Wingler and *Bauhaus* 1919–28 are almost exclusively hers) has described the designers' interaction with the industry. 'Gradually, through visits to the industry and inspections and interviews on the spot, we came to our main concern – industrial design. Moholy-Nagy fostered this with stubborn energy. Two lighting firms seemed particularly interested in our aims. Korting and Matthiesen (Kandem) and Leipzig Leutzsch helped us enormously with a practical introduction into the laws of lighting technique and the production methods, which not only helped us with designing, but also helped the firms.'[14] 'We also', she continues, 'tried to create a functional but aesthetic assembly line, small facilities for garbage disposal, and so forth, considerations which in retrospect seem to me no longer prerequisite for a first-class lamp.' The preoccupation with 'a functional but aesthetic assembly-line', whatever that may mean, indicates the attempts on Moholy's part to create or ape the conditions of industrial production within the laboratory/workshop. In Dessau, of course, up-to-date equipment was provided – 'presses and lathes, drills and large shears, etc.' – according to Marianne Brandt, and although the production of silverware and hollow-ware within the tradition established by Dell in Weimar did continue, there was obviously not a substantial market for avant-garde designs in this area. Lighting fittings, however, did produce royalties for the school, and between 1926 and 1928 the Bauhaus designed adjustable ceiling lamps, jointed wall-mounted fittings, and of course, the ubiquitous 'Kandem' table lamp, designed by Marianne Brandt in 1928. 'We furnished whole buildings with our industrially-produced lamps and only rarely designed and produced special pieces in our workshops for particular rooms or showrooms. At the time I was convinced that an object had to be functional and beautiful because of its material. But I later came to the conclusion that the artist provides the final effect.'[15] Such reflections highlight the dilemma of students in interpreting the philosophy of the school.

Certainly in Marianne Brandt's case, there was a loss of 'artistry' in her work in the transition from Weimar to Dessau. None of her designs for lighting fittings, however commercially successful, can match the formal and iconic qualities of her work in Weimar. In this case the 'aura' of craft-based designs was replaced by the anonymity implicit in the Bauhaus ideal for mass production. It is significant, however, that in the presentation of the workshop's production in sales material and catalogues, etc., the consistency and order implicit in standardization is stressed. There is unity in the variety of the designs offered, but the light fittings are rarely presented in their 'natural' or domestic surroundings. The materials are those associated with industrial production – chrome and aluminum with combinations of clear and opaque glass, and the factory aesthetic is modified by the attention to proportion, scale and detail. They are in Marianne Brandt's terms 'functional and beautiful' in their consistency of form and their use of material, and they were no doubt commercially successful, partly because a technology existed to produce them, partly because their aesthetic was already established by commercial use, and partly because they related to national concepts of standardization.

NOTES

Reproduced from Naylor, G., *The Bauhaus Reassessed: Sources and Design Theory*, London: The Herbert Press, 1985, pp. 144–64. Reprinted by permission of The Herbert Press, an imprint of A&C Black Publishers.

1. Statement by the International Faction of Constructivists, Congress of International Progressive Artists *1922; The Tradition of Constructivism*, ed. Stephen Bann, Thames and Hudson, 1974, p. 68
2. *Kandinsky: Complete Writings on Art*, eds Kenneth C. Lindsay and Peter Vergo, Faber and Faber, 1982, p. 734. Article 'Bare Wall', published in *Das Kunstnarr, 1929*
3. *The Letters and Diaries of Oskar Schlemmer*, selected and edited by Tut Schlemmer, Wesleyan University Press, 1972, p. 228
4. Laszlo Moholy-Nagy *The New Vision and Abstract of an Artist*, George Wittenborn Inc., 1947, p. 31
5. Ibid. p. 29 (Raoul France's book was published in Stuttgart in 1920)
6. Laszlo Moholy-Nagy *Vision* in *Motion*, Paul Theobald and Co., 1947, pp. 33, 34, 55
7. Sibyl Moholy-Nagy *Moholy-Nagy: Experiment in Totality*, MIT Press, 1969, pp. 43, 44
8. Laszlo Moholy-Nagy *The New Vision*, op. cit., p. 89
9. Sibyl Moholy-Nagy op. cit., p. 44
10. Ibid. p. 41
11. *Bauhaus 1919–1928,* eds. Herbert Bayer, Walter Gropius, Ise Gropius, Museum of Modern Art, New York, 1938. English edition Secker and Warburg, 1975, pp. 122–3
12. Laszlo Moholy-Nagy, *The New Vision*, op. cit., p. 30
13. John Heskett, *Industrial Design,* Thames and Hudson, 1980, pp. 78–9
14. *Bauhaus and Bauhaus People.* ed. Eckhard Neumann, Van Nostrand Reinhold, 1970, p. 98
15. Ibid. p. 98

18

THE SEARCH FOR AN AMERICAN DESIGN AESTHETIC: FROM ART DECO TO STREAMLINING

Nicolas P. Maffei (2003)

Streamlining was not an American invention, but its widespread application in the 1930s to the design of vehicles and stationary consumer goods was America's distinctive contribution to the development of Art Deco. It emerged in the context of serious and often contentious discussions – which raged among American cultural commentators, museum curators, designers and others – concerning the need for an authentic national aesthetic to replace the United States' artistic dependence upon Europe. [...]

[...] By 1929, the exhibitions of European applied art in American department stores and museums had prompted the question 'who are our designers?' This became the central concern of an editorial in *Good Furniture Magazine* that year.[1] Its author wrote that the great department store exhibits had 'ruffle[d] the placid surface of our industrial art'; it was only then that we 'started the search for talent in our own country to compete with the very evident European talent seen in the exhibits'. [...] Referring to the exhibits of modern decorative arts recently shown at department stores and elsewhere, he noted that there:

we have the chance not only to see what American designers have done, but to compare with similar work by European designers. When Eugene Schoen, Joseph Urban, Paul Frankl, Lucian Bernhard, Winold Reiss and Pola Hoffmann appear in these showings of American designers, it should be remembered that,

by years of training, practice and experience, this group is 'American' only in the matter of citizenship.[2]

This view was not unusual in the climate of nativism that existed in America in the 1920s and favoured the interests of the established inhabitants over those of immigrants. Created by a mixture of First World War propaganda, post-war immigration, labour unrest, political radicalism and the growth of the Ku Klux Klan, this climate resulted in immigration restrictions, 'Americanization' initiatives and deportation drives.

[...]

Whereas writers in *Good Furniture Magazine* in the late 1920s had cautioned their readers against the work of Europeans and European émigrés, [Austrian-American designer] Paul Frankl proclaimed, in his book *Form and Re-Form* (1930), that both European émigré and native-born American designers had contributed to a vigorous modern American design movement. He wrote that 'our country assimilates artists of many countries – Hungarians, Russians, Germans, Viennese, Frenchmen, Japanese. *Je prends mon bien ou je le trouve.*'[3] And he presented the work of a number of émigrés alongside that of native-born American designers.[4] [...] And, in contrast to conservative critics, Frankl claimed that 'extreme ideas in modernism are not all imported from Europe;

artists of American stock are often the most daring radicals of the "left wing".' He offered a list of American extremists, including the ceramicist Henry Varnum Poor and the textile designer Ruth Reeves – 'who dares to be "profoundly passionately" herself'.[5] [...]

[...]

Ruth Reeves – singled out by Frankl for her individuality – is best known today for 'Manhattan', her cubistic textile design depicting an American cityscape. By the early Thirties, however, Reeves's work was increasingly presented as an example of the more moderate approach and referred to as 'agreeable', 'elegant' and 'individual'. Frankl, too, came to recognize the need for a more restful attitude, writing that 'Simple lines are modern. They are restful to the eye and dignified and tend to cover up the complexity of the machine age.'[6] His designs and those of Kem Weber of the early 1930s for simple, horizontal furniture reflected this belief. A stress on 'charm' became a means of claiming equal status for American design with that of Europe and of countering notions that the former was naturally brash. Thus, in 1932 Walter Dorwin Teague's designs for glass for Steuben were presented as 'casual', 'charming', 'subtle', 'poised and graceful', and of 'equal distinction' to those of Europe. They were described as 'modern' but 'not bizarre', as 'decidedly American as Orrefors is Swedish'.[7] Increasingly, American decorative arts journals showcased the work of American designers, presenting their work as equal in quality to that of European designers, as well as more appropriate to American tastes.

Not everyone accepted 'charm' as an essential element in modern American design, however. In an effort to put an end to being 'deceived by the external charms of decoration', an article in the *American Magazine of Art* recommended the elimination of ornament and the reduction of an object to its 'primary form'.[8] In the following years the promoters of Modernist design would become even more vocal. Yet the notion of charm was not altogether lost; instead, it was transformed, with the rise of notions of styling. As Norman Bel Geddes, one of the leading stylists, observed, styling addressed the 'psychological' dimension of design to 'appeal to the consumer's vanity and play upon his imagination'.[9] One of the devices frequently deployed by stylists was streamlining; while offering a symbol of science and rationality, it was also used to appeal to irrational desires and thereby seduce potential customers.

After the 1929 stock market crash the need for mass production and for ways to appeal to the consumer by active salesmanship meant that new approaches to design were vigorously promoted. The example of annual fashion changes in Parisian couture intensified American manufacturers' and retailers' interest in the economic value of stylistic obsolescence. Towards the end of 1930 the *American Magazine of Art* published Earnest Elmo Calkins' plan for jumpstarting the economy. Calkins had founded the Calkins & Holden advertising agency in 1901 with Ralph Holden and had long been an ardent promoter of the cash value of art in industry. His article explained how consumer dissatisfaction could be generated through the styling of products – the 'new merchandising device' known as 'styling the goods'. Goods were to be 'redesigned in the modern spirit … to make them markedly new, and encourage new buying'. This would result in the displacement of 'still useful' things which are now 'outdated, old-fashioned, obsolete'. The application of 'modern' design allowed products to express abstract qualities that consumers found irresistible and a 'new field', that of the industrial designer, was emerging to facilitate this method of stylistic obsolescence.[10] In 1932 Calkins reiterated his views in Roy Sheldon and Egmont Arens' book, *Consumer Engineering*, stressing the need to manipulate psychologically consumers' 'latent and unsuspected demands and desires' by using styling to raise goods 'from the commonplace to the distinctive'. The book also recommended the use of psychology to reduce friction at the point of sale and thus 'streamline' consumption.[11]

The adoption of such views by American manufacturers in the early 1930s aided the success of the emergent genre of the 'industrial designer' or 'stylist'. Often decorative, theatrical and advertising artists by background, they included Walter Dorwin Teague, Norman Bel Geddes, Henry Dreyfuss, Harold Van Doren and the French-born Raymond Loewy. This first generation of American industrial designers opened their offices in the late 1920s, often finding clients through advertising agencies and self-promotion. They came to be seen as the logical and mature leaders of the country's indigenous design movement, who had 'grown up' past the need for 'childish effort' in decoration.[12] It was with the promotion and development of their work, spurred on by the increased commercial competition during the Depression, that the self-conscious comparisons of American and European design began to wane. An emphasis on styling to promote mass consumption and mass production came to be seen as the hallmark of American design.

Harold Van Doren, a leading first generation industrial designer, wrote that the term 'streamline' first appeared in print in 1873 in reference to hydrodynamics, and that by 1909 automobile manufacturers were using the term to refer to the 'sweeping lines' of their products.[13] Although streamlining was eventually widely adopted for the design of consumer goods and services, it made its greatest impact on the public imagination in the area of transportation. By the early 1930s American railroad companies had lost many of their passengers as a result of the Depression and increased competition from automobiles, buses and aeroplanes. Several companies introduced streamlined locomotives and rolling stock to modernize and make more glamorous the image of their services. Streamlined trains, such as the Union Pacific's M-10,000 and the Burlington *Zephyr*, were exhibited at the Chicago World Fair of 1933–4 and helped to popularize both rail travel and the new style. During the second year of the fair these streamliners made extensive tours of American cities where millions clamoured to

see them, further popularizing the style across the nation. The application of contoured lines, smooth surfaces and horizontality was intended not only to decrease the vehicles' air resistance but also to provide a style expressive of modernity, while at the same time suggesting comfort and restfulness. Streamliners proved highly successful during the Depression, sometimes having to turn passengers away – though railroads as a whole were then underused.[14] Streamlining was often applied to the total 'package': exteriors, interiors and accessories. Among product engineers the term 'package' engineering was synonymous with industrial design as early as 1931.[15] Significantly many American industrial designers, including Teague, Van Doren and Dreyfuss, had backgrounds in packaging design, a practice that was particularly applicable to the styling of vehicles.

Although streamlining had been actively explored by product and vehicle designers for some years, Norman Bel Geddes's book *Horizons* (1932), with its spectacular visionary designs of streamlined trains, planes and cars, did much to popularize the style. *Horizons* was widely reviewed, and its striking images of streamlined vehicles were reprinted in the Sunday supplements. Like many other first generation American industrial designers, Bel Geddes had been to Europe in the 1920s; the horizontal lines and rounded corners in his designs for streamlined vehicles have precedents in the expressive architectural sketches made during the First World War by the German architect Erich Mendelsohn.[16] But Bel Geddes's visionary book strikingly encapsulated contemporary American aspirations. Significantly, *Horizons* found its way onto the desks of automotive engineers at Chrysler and General Motors. In 1933 Chrysler's head of engineering, Fred M. Zeder, claimed the book was an inspiration to him and his associates. He made his senior engineers read it and said that *Horizons* gave him the courage to go forward with the first streamlined production car, the Airflow.[17]

1934 was a watershed year for streamlining. In addition to the excitement surrounding

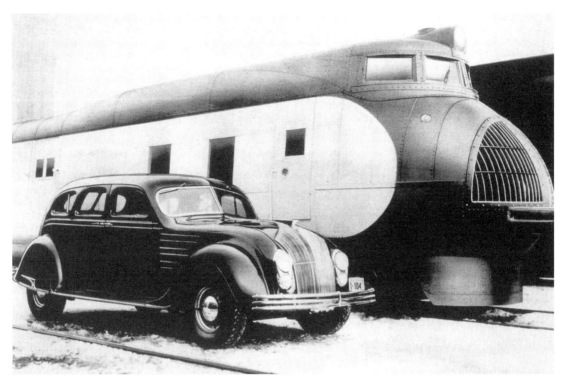

Figure 12. The Chrysler Airflow next to a Union Pacific 'Streamline Express' train. American, 1934. Photo: DaimlerChrysler Corporation.

the streamliners, the 1934 annual meeting of the Society of Automotive Engineers adopted streamlining as a major conference theme. The same year saw the production of the Chrysler Airflow, which was visually, aerodynamically and structurally streamlined [Figure 12]. Its exterior was integrated into a visible whole in order to direct air currents and reduce turbulence, and its chassis and framework were fused to add body strength. In an advertisement for the car Bel Geddes was shown sitting in it, holding an open copy of *Horizons*. The text read: 'Norman Bel Geddes [sic] famous book "Horizons", in which he forecast the Airflow motor cars'.[18] [...]

[...] In 1934, as streamlining developed into a full-blown craze, MOMA's *Machine Art* exhibition presented a display of American machine parts and industrial design whose elementary geometric forms resembled those of Bauhaus Modernism. [...] In his catalogue essay

Philip Johnson, one of the exhibition's organizers, rejected both the '"modernistic" French machine-age aesthetic' and American 'principles such as "streamlining"'.[19] [...]

In the wake of MOMA's critique of streamlining, proponents of the style more vigorously defended it, both as *the* expression of the age – representing speed, efficiency and science – and on aesthetic grounds. In their overview of American industrial design, *Art and the Machine* (1936), the historians Sheldon and Martha Cheney defended streamlining in the design of vehicles and stationary products. They wrote, 'we subjectively accept the streamline as valid symbol for the contemporary life flow, and as a badge of design integrity in even smaller mechanisms, when it emerges as form expressiveness'. For them, the essential task of the industrial designer was to express in everyday objects the most vital of contemporary values: 'In its own smaller and often more menial form' an

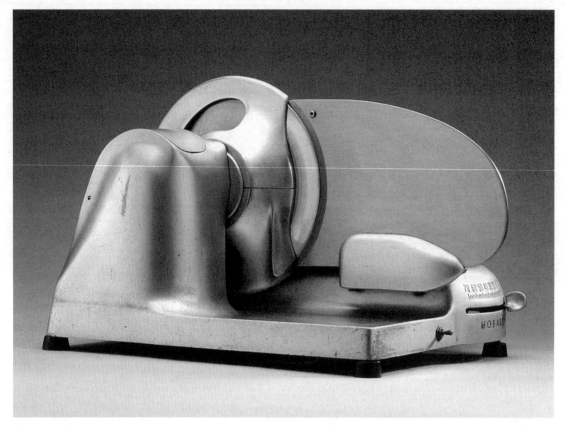

Figure 13. Egmont Arens and Theodore C. Brookhart, 'Streamliner', meat slicer. Aluminium, steel and rubber. American, designed in 1940. Made from 1944 by Hobart Manufacturing Company. Gift of John C. Waddell, 2002. The Metropolitan Museum of Art, New York. The Metropolitan Museum of Art, John C. Waddell Collection. Gift of John C. Waddell, 2000 (2000.600.1). Image © The Metropolitan Museum of Art.

ordinary streamlined product was as 'conspicuous a symbol … of the age' as the 'symbol of the cross' was to the 'medieval mind' [Figure 13].[20]

[…]

Harold Van Doren also defended streamlining, claiming that what 'many attacked as a 'faddish style' was actually the 'technological result of high-speed mass production'. He explained that in plastic-moulded and pressed sheet-steel products it was more efficient to employ designs with gentle curves and rounded corners, writing that 'what may thus appear to be a captious preference for voluptuous curves and bulging forms in place of a more athletic spareness proves to be

one result of the evolution of fabricating methods and assembly-line techniques'. Additionally, Van Doren defended the style on aesthetic grounds, seeing streamlined form as a visual metaphor for progress, and the egg-shape it often depended on as a more 'dynamic' shape than the 'static' circle and sphere found in classical design.[21]

[…]

By the end of the decade streamlining and geometry shared the same stage at the New York World's Fair of 1939. The show significantly increased the profile of industrial design by associating the new profession with the vision of the future. This was the theme of the fair, developed by Teague, who served on the Board of Design alongside six architects. 'Focal exhibits' within the major buildings were provided by Teague and other leading industrial designers, including Dreyfuss, Rohde, Russel Wright, Egmont Arens, Donald Deskey, George Sakier and Raymond Loewy. The fair's architecture reflected the popularity of streamlining as well as Teague's own preference for geometric forms. Exemplifying the streamlined style was the hook-shaped General Motors building, designed in association with Norman Bel Geddes and containing his 'Futurama' exhibit, a vast diorama of the world of tomorrow dominated by superhighways, teardrop-shaped automobiles and tower cities.[22] [...]

The New York World's Fair is usually seen to mark the end of streamlining. In the years after the Second World War, however, aerodynamic automotive design continued to develop, eventually leading to an orgy of non-functional styling. The 1948 Cadillac Coupe was the first post-war car to show tailfins. Designed by Harley Earl's team at General Motors, it initiated a mad rush among Detroit manufacturers exuberantly to express speed and flight in automobiles. Such design was often derided by critics and designers. Already in 1948 the historian Siegfried Giedion considered streamlining and the Detroit look retrogressive. Since its inception the streamlined style had been presented as alternately restful and an expression of speed, as well as the natural outcome of science. But Giedion noted that all styles, even streamlining, had a history. Rejecting the popular assumption that streamlining was based solely on the image of speed, he suggested instead that it derived from Art Deco products shown at the Paris 1925 Exhibition. [...]

In 1959 Henry Dreyfuss, an innovator of streamlining in the 1930s, was asked if America had a 'heritage of good design'. He answered in the affirmative, claiming that it was rooted in the 'pioneer tradition' of America's European settlers which resulted in designs of great 'simplicity, toughness, efficiency and good workmanship'. Ignoring his previous forays into streamlined

design, he added that American design had devolved into the 'Detroit' look of 'motorized jewellery', which had begun to 'infect other types of products ... [including] refrigerators and washing machines'. Other 'deviations' included 'the many attempts to introduce European styles of lush decoration'.[23] Streamlining was now effectively defined in opposition to 'good design'. But Dreyfuss also emphasized the importance of drama and power, adding that American design expressed 'cleanliness, dramatic shapes, and powerful forms', echoing the expressive values of American design which the Cheneys had appreciated in the streamlined style.

As early as 1935 [the cultural historian] Constance Rourke had argued that early Americans, though restricted by the need for economy, had practised a 'free sense of personal decoration' and valued material goods, such as 'portraits or clocks with glass paintings or delicate china', for the emotional and symbolic meanings they evoked and the 'pleasure' they provided.[24] In other words, they enjoyed goods with charm and personality. Rourke's perspective helped to define an American art that was diverse and expressive without denying non-native influences. In this expansive view we can recognize American streamlining, not as a purely American style without a history, but as a complex product of twentieth-century modernity – a product of a transatlantic collaboration that embodied the contradictions of modernity. Both restful and dynamic, streamlining reflected and responded to the fluid changes of a modern world.

NOTES

Extracted from Maffei, N., 'The Search for an American Design Aesthetic: From Art Deco to Streamlining,' in Charlotte Benton, Tim Benton, and Ghislaine Wood (eds), *Art Deco 1910–1939*, London: V&A Publications, 2003, pp. 361–9. Copyright © V & A Publications, 2003. Reprinted with permission.

1. 'Editorial: Designers – European and American', *Good Furniture Magazine*, vol. xxxii, no.4 (April 1929), pp. 167, 172; quote from p. 167.

2. As note 1.

3. Paul Frankl, *Form and Re-Form: A Practical Handbook for Modern Interiors* (New York, 1930), p. 13.

4. The former including Frederick Kiesler, Kem Weber, Winold Reiss, Ilonka Karasz, Joseph Urban, William Lescaze and Walter Von Nessen; the latter including Frank Lloyd Wright, Donald Deskey, Ruth Reeves, Gilbert Rohde and Eugene Schoen.

5. Frankl (1930), pp. 18–19.

6. See 'Are We Different?', *Arts & Decoration*, vol. xl, no. 11 (December 1933), p.18. For Frankl's evolving views, see Paul Frankl, *New Dimensions: The Decorative Arts of Today in Words and Pictures* (New York, 1928), pp. 16–17.

7. Elizabeth M. Boykin, 'The Grace of Modern Glass Design', *Arts & Decoration*, vol. xxxvii, no. 5 (September 1932), pp. 15, 59; quotes from pp. 15, 59.

8. Wilhelm Lotz, 'Industrial Art in Germany', *American Magazine of Art*, vol. xxii, no. 2 (February 1931), p. 103–8.

9. Norman Bel Geddes, *Horizons* (Boston, 1932), p. 222.

10. Earnest Elmo Calkins, 'Advertising, Builder of Taste', *American Magazine of Art*, vol. xxi, no. 9 (September 1930), pp. 497–502 (quote from p. 499.)

11. Roy Sheldon and Egmont Arens, *Consumer Engineering: A New Technique for Prosperity* (New York, 1932), p. 2.

12. 'Modern Growing Up?', *Arts & Decoration*, vol. xlii, no. 2 (December 1934), p. 2.

13. Harold Van Doren, *Industrial Design: A Practical Guide to Product Design and Development* (New York, 1940; reprinted New York, 1954), p. 180.

14. This success helped to secure a role for the industrial design profession.

15. 'Consumer Engineering', *Product Engineering*, vol. 2, no. 5 (May 1931), p.221.

16. Jeffrey L. Meikle, *Twentieth Century Limited: Industrial Design in America, 1925–1939* (Philadelphia, 1979), pp. 48, 36, 49. Bel Geddes had befriended Mendelsohn in 1924.

17. 'AE-79, Chapter 75', autobiography, stamped 1955; memorandum, 26 October 1933, from Norman Bel Geddes to Earl Newsom regarding Chrysler 'Secret Account'; NBG Archive, Harry Ransom Humanities Research Center, University of Texas, Austin. See also Nicolas P. Maffei, 'Designing the Image of the Practical Visionary: Norman Bel Geddes, 1893–1958', unpublished PhD thesis, Royal College of Art, London, 2001.

18. 'I salute Walter P. Chrysler and Fred Zeder FOR BUILDING THIS AUTHENTIC AIRFLOW CAR'; advertisement, *Saturday Evening Post*, 16 December 1933. Chrysler Corporation, Q account, 271, O/S7, advertisement announcing arrival of Airflow. NBG Archive, Harry Ransom Humanities Research Center, University of Texas, Austin.

19. Philip Johnson 'History of Machine Art: Machine Art and Handicraft', Museum of Modern Art, *Machine Art* (New York, 1934; reprints 1969, 1994), n.p.

20. Sheldon Cheney and Martha Candler Cheney, *Art and the Machine: An Account of Industrial Design in 20th-Century America* (New York, 1936), pp. 98, 102.

21. Van Doren (1940/1954), pp. 179, 189, 196, 187.

22. The Futurama emphasized streamlined living, where science, technology and urban planning would make for more efficient travel, increased health and a superior standard of living. In a simulated aeroplane flight the miniature world was viewed from moving seats by 27,500 people a day for nearly two years.

23. 'Does America Have a Design Heritage?', *Product Engineering*, vol. 30, no. 20 (18 May 1959), pp. 36–43; Dreyfuss quotes from pp. 36, 37.

24. Rourke (1935), pp. 390–404; quotes from p. 392.

GUIDE TO FURTHER READING

For more on Pugin and Ruskin's influence on modernists see Clive Wainwright, 'The Legacy of the Nineteenth Century' (1900). Henry Russell Hitchcock and Philip Johnson's 1932 New York Museum of Modern Art exhibition and catalogue *The International Style*, like Pevsner's *Pioneers*, celebrated modern architecture that exalted the machine and repudiated ornament. Loos had argued strongly for this ascetic modernism, as had Le Corbusier in *The Decorative Art of Today* (1925) and *Towards a New Architecture* (1927). Walter Gropius expressed his evolving theories of design in his 'Programme of the Staatliches Bauhaus in Wiemar' (1919) and 'Principles of Bauhaus Production' (1926).

The narrow focus by Pevsner and others on innovations in concrete and steel, advanced by science and technology for a clean, orderly, and efficient world exaggerates the role of the Bauhaus, however, and overlooks the dynamic experimentation of the Futurists, Dadaists and Constructivists. Johanna Drucker corrects this bias in her book *The Visible Word: Experimental Typography and Modern Art, 1909–1923* (1994), as does Victor Margolin in *The Struggle for Utopia: Rodchenko, Lissitzky, Moholy-Nagy, 1917–1946* (1997). Terry Smith, *Making the Modern: Industry, Art and Design in America* (1993) and Jeffrey L Meikle, *Design in the USA* (2005), offer engaging readings of the theories and questions first proposed by industrial designers in the first half of the twentieth century, such as Norman Bel Geddes, *Horizons* (1932), Harold van Doren, 'Streamlining: Fad or Function?' (1949), and Raymond Loewy, *Never Leave Well Enough Alone* (1951).

As applied arts institutions began to admit more women to their programmes, new issues surrounding women's professionalization arose. Christine Frederick's scientific analysis of modern kitchen designs, in *The New Housekeeping: Efficiency Studies in Home Management* (1913), applied scientific theory to common-sense principles that would help women save time and labour in more sanitary and efficient work spaces. Like Margarete Schutte-Lihotzky, who introduced the 'Frankfurt kitchen' in Germany, Frederick articulated practical ways to adapt industrial methods and technology to the home. The masculinized concept of industry upheld in some of the most influential histories of design, including Siegfried Giedion's *Mechanization Takes Command* (1948) and Reyner Banham's *Theory and Design in the First Machine Age* (1960), has obscured the complex gender dynamics of the modern movement. Sigrid Wortman Weltge explores the marginalization of female students at the Bauhaus in her book *Bauhaus Textiles: Women Artists and the Weaving Workshops* (1993). See also Nicholas Bullock, 'First the Kitchen, then the Façade', (1988), and Rebecca Houze, 'From "Wiener Kunst im Hause" to the Wiener Werkstätte: Marketing Domesticity with Fashionable Interior Design' (2002). Frederic J. Schwartz, in his book *The Werkbund: Design Theory and Mass Culture before the First World War* (1996), considers the emergence of standardized type-forms as well as corporate trademarks from within a cultural discourse of 'fashion' and 'style', revealing that masculine philosophies of commerce and design were intimately tied to ideas surrounding dress.

The emphasis on industrial manufacture in much of the earlier design history makes it difficult to reconcile varying aesthetic strains and modes within the modern movement, such as the organic shapes of Scandinavian designs by Alvar Aalto and Eliel Saarinen, the eclectic and surrealist interiors of the 1920s and 1930s, or the futuristic shapes of Art Deco in America. More recent studies that draw attention to these alternate and competing modernisms include Christopher Reed, *Bloomsbury Rooms: Modernism, Subculture, and Domesticity* (2004), and Penny Sparke, *Elsie de Wolfe: The Birth of Modern Interior Decoration* (2005). None of these modernisms of the first half of the twentieth century, however, can be understood without also looking closely issues of national identity and design – see Wendy Kaplan, ed., *Designing Modernity: the Arts of Reform and Persuasion, 1885–1945* (1995) and the political, economic and psychological repercussions of two continents twice traumatized by violent nationalism and world war.

SECTION 4

War/Post-War/Cold War, 1943–70

INTRODUCTION

Grace Lees-Maffei

This section continues from the previous section in tracing various modernisms. The extracts here show how versions of modernism were promoted and modified in response to specific political and economic contexts, specifically Second World War Utility furniture (Denney), the post-war 'Populuxe' consumer society (Hine) and Festival of Britain (Conekin), the Soviet kitchen (Reid) and the ways in which, for Banham, speaking in 1966, materials embodied design ethics. During the period examined in this section, attempts were made to promote competing ideologies through claims to improved standards of life epitomized by new developments in the domestic interior and its contents. During the mid-twentieth century, the domestic interior became explicitly politicized through government and state intervention.

As the preceding section suggests, there is scope for more comparative work exploring the relationships between the 'International Style' as it emerged in Germany, the Netherlands and elsewhere, and was promoted in the US by retailers and organizations such as MoMA, and modernism as it appeared in the UK. It has been argued that, prior to 1940, British approaches to modernism represented a compromise. State-sponsored design, made compulsory through special measures such as materials rationing and the Utility scheme, and the concerted government-led campaign of design promotion following the war, had the effect of promulgating modernism more widely within the UK, but the extent to which it was genuinely popular with consumers has yet to be fully examined.

Design historians have recognized the fact that products originally developed for military applications have found success in the mass market. Examples include the Jeep (see Porter, W., 'Toledo Wheels: The Design Story of Willys-Overland, the Jeep, and the Rise of the SUV', in *The Alliance of Art and Industry: Toledo Designs for a Modern America*, Toledo, Ohio: The Toledo Museum of Art, 2002, pp. 109–28) and Rayban Aviator sunglasses (Sudjic, D., *Cult Objects*, London: Paladin, 1985). However, British Utility design of the Second World War involved a different situation: designing for the wartime mass market within the constraints of manufacturing and materials shortages. Purchased with rationing coupons, also issued for food, Utility design encompassed not only garments, which wear out relatively quickly or are grown out of, but also the ostensibly more permanent category of furniture, which was destroyed as people's homes were routinely bombed. While Norman Hartnell's Utility clothing enabled the whole country to be dressed in patriotic quasi-militaristic styles by the Queen's dressmaker, Utility furniture has been seen as a route through which a British public notoriously resistant to continental modernism was persuaded to accept a pared-down practical aesthetic. Utility design was informed by the more extreme manifestations of modernist design and, indirectly, by the design reformers of the nineteenth century and was offered to consumers who had little alternative. Matthew Denney challenges several misconceptions about Utility design, in the extract presented here, from a book edited by the late Judy Attfield, who saw Utility as a precursor to today's concerns for ethical design in terms of ecological sustainability.

To say that the post-war period, beginning with the end of the Second World War in 1945, was one of optimism is both a cliché and a truism. In the UK, national pride was harnessed and engendered through social programmes such as the introduction of free universal healthcare through the National Health Service in 1948, just as it was through a government programme of countrywide celebrations including the Festival of Britain of 1951 and its precursor, the Britain Can Make It exhibition of 1946. Conceived in part as a reprise of the Great Exhibition of 1851, the organizers of the Festival of Britain were interested in promoting ideas about the future as much as the past, as Becky Conekin shows in her analysis, extracted here. However, the extent to which post-war prosperity was actually enjoyed by consumers outside the US needs qualification. Rationing continued until 1954 and while young people had the opportunity to earn more than their parents for the first time, the post-war period was not one of unalloyed prosperity; rather, the end of the war left the UK both culturally energized and materially impoverished.

Post-war culture across the 'Western' world has typically been characterized as having undergone a process of Americanization, in which the international influence of the US increased both politically and culturally. Hine's writing on what he has termed 'Populuxe' shows how consumerist practices and values were supported by a sense of material abundance communicated in rapidly developing popular culture media channels, such as television and advertising, which seemed an appropriate response to increased prosperity. Consumerism permeated post-war daily life, from the development of convenience food, which relied on new technologies in food distribution and storage enabled by applications of freezer technology, to the introduction of mass air travel, expanding the horizons of middle-class holidaymakers as well as the jet set. Commentators have tried variously to articulate this broad cultural process with phrases such as J. B. Priestley's 'Admass society', Bevis Hillier's 'austerity/binge', Thomas Hine's 'Populuxe' – extracted here – and Reyner Banham's 'throwaway aesthetic'. Within the context of the other texts extracted here, Hine's Populuxe is shown to be as ideologically laden as the other examples examined in this section. Populuxe was not mandated by government decree, as was Utility and the Khrushchev kitchen, but the market-led design by which it is characterized was the result of a political decision to allow a free-market economy to spread relatively unchecked in a capitalist, consumerist society.

The 'Cold War', from 1945, was one in which newly developed nuclear weapons were largely kept on standby rather than being detonated – their symbolic force being so great as to constitute a war of threats and menace distinct from the carnage of trench warfare and air raids in the First and Second World Wars. It was a war of competing ideologies in which socialism and capitalism, as represented by their respective leaders, the USSR and the US, sought to assert primacy over one another and thereby gain global dominance. Within the Cold War context, the quality of life enjoyed by ordinary people became highly politicized, with each superpower seeking to show that it offered superior living standards. As Susan Reid shows here, in her analysis of the Khrushchev kitchen, the Cold War was fought as much through public debate about the domestic interior as it was through the space race: 'Scientific communism', she writes, was embedded in 'household advice, domestic science education, rational planning of the kitchen or "scientific management" and the domestication of the scientific-technological revolution through the mechanization of housework'. Design was a crucial tool in the armoury of ideology and iconography, whether directly – for example in the flexible and space-saving furnishings developed to meet the needs of citizens of the new apartment blocks showcased by Soviet city planners – or indirectly – from the space-inspired fashion of Frenchman Pierre Cardin to the application of new materials to furniture and interior design, exemplified by the fibre-glass chairs of Charles and Ray Eames and the anonymous pattern designers at Formica.

Both within and outside the US, many people's lives remained unrelieved by an Americanization that was, in practice, largely confined to the cultural realm of aspiration, in movies, magazines and television programmes. It was the America of dreams and cultural artefacts that the Independent Group, Banham prominent among them, invoked in its debates about high culture and mass culture. The talk by Banham presented here explains something of the moral weight attached by designers and design commentators to materials and their use. Banham presents a war of design philosophies attendant upon the use of materials, which engaged modernist notions of honesty and dishonesty. His analysis of the opposition of materials is set, in this section, between the larger opposition of Utility, the Festival of Britain, the Khrushchev kitchen and Populuxe. In retrospect, Banham's talk can be seen as a watershed between modernist and postmodernist sensibilities.

19

UTILITY FURNITURE AND THE MYTH OF UTILITY 1943–1948

Matthew Denney (1999)

The period between 1943 and 1948 represents a unique moment in English furniture history when the government took complete control of the furniture industry. Only a limited number of authorised firms could obtain timber for furniture production, and of those, each firm was authorised to manufacture a small range of furniture types, the designs for which were clearly laid down by the Board of Trade. For the potential purchaser of furniture, supply was strictly rationed between February 1943 and June 1948. Furniture could only be purchased by those in possession of 'units' issued by the government. Initially units were only available to newly-weds setting up home for the first time, or to those replacing essential furniture damaged by bombing. Towards the end of 1944 rationing expanded to include expectant mothers and families requiring furniture for growing children.

The experience of severe shortages during the First World War had prompted the Government to prepare for the inevitable supply problems in advance, and it was therefore ready with the legislation to take control of timber prior to the declaration of war. The Ministry of Supply intervened in the furniture industry within days of war being declared by introducing strict controls of all timber supplies.[1] To prevent exploitation of the public, price control was enforced through the Central Price Regulation Committee. Intervention in the furniture industry was introduced with the control of prices for both new and second-hand furniture from 10 June 1940.[2] Because of the highly diverse nature of the furniture industry, the government found that the control of furniture was difficult to achieve. It was forced to take responsibility for the supply of furniture to those whose need was considered urgent. 'Bombees', as they became known, were the major catalyst for an increase in urgent demand when the London blitz began in September 1940.

From December 1940 only very limited supplies of timber were made available for domestic furniture production.[3] In an attempt to continue to supply those in need, the government introduced Standard Emergency Furniture in February 1941.[4] The furniture for this precursor of the Utility Scheme proper was produced under government contract and was administered by the Ministry of Health, which was responsible for bombees. It was intended that this furniture would be loaned to claimants who could then either return the furniture or purchase it at a reasonable price.

A further attempt to control production was made by the Ministry of Supply in November 1941. The Ministry would only allow the supply of timber to firms who were making furniture which conformed to a Ministry of Supply list of items. This list included twenty-two items of furniture, the only limitation on the manufacturer being the quantity of timber allowed for each item: for example, a 3 foot wardrobe was allowed to include 1.614 cubic feet of wood or material resembling wood and 83.45 square feet of ⅛ inch thick plywood or material resembling plywood.[5]

Prior to the production of Standard Emergency Furniture the Assistance Board had been responsible for allocating compensation to those who had lost furniture because of enemy action. But claims for compensation only fuelled the demand for furniture from a trade that was finding it increasingly difficult to obtain timber. The problem of supplying essential goods at a reasonable price is clearly illustrated by an item that appeared in the *Manchester Daily Despatch* of 15 October 1941, which reported:

> Councillor J.D.L. Nicholson quoted the case of a person who, receiving £45 from the Assistance Board for replacements, found the amount inadequate when she had to pay £18 for a bedstead and things like that, sooner or later some Government steps will have to be taken, because it is amounting to racketeering.[6]

The Board of Trade became involved with consumer needs and supply through necessity. As late as November 1940 the President of the Board of Trade was still hoping that with the co-operation of all those concerned in distribution it would be possible to avoid the rationing of consumer goods.[7] However, the increasingly difficult receding supply situation, causing inflation and a certain amount of exploitation of the public by some sectors of the furniture trade, forced the Board of Trade to intervene. The initial involvement of so many government departments trying to control the supply of furniture had only confused the situation. A major concern in transferring responsibility to one department was to ensure that domestic furniture should remain available to those in genuine need throughout the war.

By April 1942 the Ministry of Supply warned the Board of Trade that it could no longer guarantee the supply of timber for any domestic furniture production.[8] This was not acceptable to

the government, and there were questions in the House of Commons on 5 May 1942, including Watkins's question: 'Are any arrangements afoot by which good substantial furniture at a reasonable price will be provided for the public under Government control?'[9]

In reply Hugh Dalton confirmed that Utility schemes were being considered for a number of different articles, but that furniture was not yet one of these. However, it was not long before plans for a Utility Furniture Scheme were under way, although it took some time for it to take shape and the announcement of its introduction was finally made at a press conference on 3 July 1942.[10] The introduction of the scheme was to be overseen by a Utility Furniture Advisory Committee, which met for the first time on 14 July 1942 under the chairmanship of Charles Tennyson, to 'produce specifications for furniture of good sound construction in simple but agreeable designs for sale at reasonable prices and ensuring the maximum economy of raw materials and labour.'[11] The designs selected by the Advisory Committee for the first range of furniture from drawings submitted by a number of different designers were those of two trade designers from High Wycombe, Edwin Clinch of Goodearl Brothers and Herbert Cutler, who at that time was deputy head of the Wycombe Technical Institute. The chosen designs were for ten standard items comprising two bedroom suites, two dining-room sets and two easy chairs. Although additions were made to the first batch of Utility designs during the various stages of the Utility Furniture Scheme, the originals remained unchanged throughout the duration of the Scheme.

From November 1942 it was decreed that all non-Utility furniture was to be completed by the end of the year and sold by the end of February 1943.[12] All manufacturers had to register with the Board of Trade, abide by its legislation, and all Utility furniture was to be marked as such. With this action the Board of Trade had taken complete control of furniture production and brought all non-Utility production to an end.

The first range of Utility furniture, introduced at the beginning of 1943,[13] consisted of 22 items available in a number of different finishes, bringing the total available choice to 66 items, including five different designs of oak dining-chairs, costing between £1 3s and £1 10s, each requiring a single furniture unit.

The regulations governing the Utility Furniture Scheme underwent constant changes. When materials became available the schedules of furniture would be increased, and as demand and supply varied, the number of units made available to qualifying purchasers by the Board of Trade were adjusted accordingly. The first changes to the furniture schedules were made as early as March 1943, when a new 'cot (with mesh) model No. 1A' was added.[14] This small alteration was the first of very many changes made to the schedules of furniture between 1943 and 1948. The most important change to the schedules took place after the end of the war in September 1946, when a further 112 items of furniture were added, bringing the total number of different items available to 266.[15]

As the supply and demand situation began to stabilise after the war, the government was eager to relax the Utility Scheme as soon as possible. The rationing of furniture was brought to an end in June 1948, and in November of the same year the 'Freedom of Design' legislation was introduced.[16] The Utility Scheme was finally abolished in 1952, by which time the scheme had become more one of tax control than of design enforcement.

The history of the Utility designs that were first produced in 1943 needs to be reassessed in the light of the myth which has built up around the Utility Scheme through the ways in which it has been represented. As Judy Attfield has written, 'most accounts of the history of design which deal with the Utility scheme (1942–1952) present it in a heroic light from the Good Design establishment's point of view.'[17] The majority of general furniture histories tend to deal very briefly with the Second World War and the Reconstruction period. This is perhaps not surprising, as there was so little decorative design produced then.

Many of the texts are more concerned with issues of style rather than design history, and therefore ignore the Utility scheme, like the trade designers who didn't consider the Utility designs to be 'design'. When it is mentioned in books on the history of the decorative arts, it is usually fitted in between the 'Art Deco' of the inter-war period and the 'contemporary' of the Festival of Britain and dealt with summarily in a few paragraphs or relegated to a footnote.

Much of the literature which considers Utility furniture in more detail characterises it in an over-simplified manner, concentrating on the period from 1943 to 1946 before the Freedom of Design and overemphasising the role of Gordon Russell.[18] […] Jonathan Woodham has traced the traditional view of 'good design' and its Arts and Crafts roots from the Design and Industries Association (DIA) onwards as a 'continuity in aesthetic hegemony from the pre- to the post-Second World War period via the Utility Design Scheme', recognising the limitations of the small circle of cultural elite from which the principal players were drawn.[19]

Two key works on Utility furniture design that have contributed to the personality-cult of the designer as 'hero' are Gordon Russell's own memoirs, *Designer's Trade*, published in 1968 and the Geffrye Museum's 1974 exhibition *Utility Furniture and Fashion 1941–1951*.[20] In *Designer's Trade* the […] assertion that 'the basic rightness of contemporary design won the day'[21] was reiterated in the often-quoted claim: 'I felt that to raise the whole standard of furniture for the mass of the people was not a bad war job'[22] explained as 'attempting to interpret to the trade and to the public what was in effect a nation-wide drive for better design'[23] and suggesting much more control than was actually the case. Russell's belief that the Utility Scheme would have a far-reaching beneficial effect on the British public's taste was never more than an aspiration, described by Sparke as a 'rash prediction'.[24] […]

The Geffrye Museum catalogue for the exhibition *Utility Furniture and Fashion 1941–1951*, mounted in 1974, still represents an important document providing a chronological outline of the development of the Utility Scheme. Nevertheless, [...] the featuring of the Russell-inspired Cotswold and Diversified ranges reflected the interests of the design reformers and the heroic role they conferred on Utility design to lead the way in design reform, with little reference to the perspective on the Scheme of either the trade or the general public at the time.

[...]

The interpretation of the Utility furniture designs by the Geffrye Museum catalogue, upholding the myth of Utility as producing 'new' design, is not uncharacteristic of the period when 'Good Design' was synonymous with Modernism. Its insistence on treating the Utility Scheme as innovative is apparent even while overriding the designers' own claims. [...] For Edwin Clinch and Herbert Cutler, two experienced trade designers, to approach the designing without 'any preconceived ideas' is not only highly unlikely but apparently not true, according to the interviews reported in *Design* magazine of September 1974.[25] [...] [T]he designs were clearly on very similar lines to types which not only already formed part of the furniture industry's repertoire, but also were almost identical to recommended pre-war models of 'Good Design'. In 'Good Design By Law: Adapting Utility Furniture to Peace-time Production – Domestic Furniture in the Reconstruction Period 1946–1956' Judy Attfield writes:

> [The] No. 3 Utility ladder-back dining chair, apart from slimmer members, is exactly the same as an unidentified model illustrated among the recommended items in The Council for Art and Industry Report – The Working Class Home published in 1937. While the No. 3a Utility dining chair appears to be a slimmed down version of a model illustrated in Anthony Bertram's *Design in Everyday Things* produced to accompany a series of lectures broadcast by the BBC in the same year.[26]

Another usual misrepresentation of the Utility Scheme portrays the furniture designs as completely standardised. In *Designer's Trade* Russell's description of the range – 'Nothing less than standard design and rigid specification would meet this exceptional case'[27] – never became a reality. It is true that in 1943, when Utility was first introduced, the scheme only included 66 items, but by 1946 the number had grown to 266 pieces, including 99 different types of beds.[28] The principle of standardisation that depended on arriving at a single best type for each set of requirements was incompatible with the concept of consumer choice that depended on variety allowed by the 'Freedom of Design' legislation introduction in November 1948, which remained in force until 1952.

A full study of the public reaction to Utility furniture has not yet been made, but there is sufficient material to suggest that it was not widely popular with the consumer, nor with the furniture trade.[29] Government files indicate that once the choice of Utility furniture was extended, the Cotswold range proved unpopular.[30] [...]

The link between Utility furniture and the Arts and Crafts Movement was explained in an article that appeared in the *Architectural Review* in 1943, attributing the limitations of the design of the first range to '[hardboard], a comparatively new and not yet fully tried-out material' that 'limited the design to the Arts and Crafts technique of frame and panel construction and to small panels at that'.[31] The reason for the limitation to small panels was the fear that hardboard would warp if not firmly held in place. It was also difficult to cut hardboard without leaving a ragged edge, thus eliminating the possibility of flush panelling. Had it been available, plywood would have been used, but all supplies were required for more urgent war needs. In the wider context of furniture history, the technique of frame and panel construction can be traced much further back than the nineteenth-century Arts and Crafts Movement, since it was part of a traditional constructional practice in furniture-making that was already in general use by the seventeenth century.

Alongside frame and panel construction there were certain other stylistic features present in the first range of Utility furniture which may have led some authors to describe it as being 'Arts and Crafts'-inspired. The predominant use of an oak finish, the linear nature of the designs, the lack of ornamentation and decorative carving and the choice of [wooden] handles used for the first range of Utility furniture are all important features. [...]

The association between Utility furniture and the Arts and Crafts Movement has also been encouraged by the similarities between the theories of William Morris and other Arts and Crafts supporters and the information provided by the Board of Trade regarding the principles of Utility furniture. The Advisory Committee's brief for 'furniture of good sound construction in simple but agreeable designs' finds a parallel in William

Figure 14. Four dressing-tables from the second Utility Furniture Catalogue published in June 1947: (top left) Cotswold Range; (top right) Cotswold Range; (bottom left) Chiltern Range; (bottom right) Chiltern Range. Catalogue published in June 1947. Public Record Office, in Matthew Denney 'Utility Furniture and the Myth of Utility 1943–1948' in *Utility Reassessed: the Role of Ethics in the Practice of Design*, ed. Judy Attfield, Manchester: Manchester University Press, 1999, pp. 110–24, p. 119. Reprinted by permission of the National Archives, London.

Morris's often-quoted maxim that furniture should be 'solid and well made in workmanship, and in design should have nothing about it that is not easily defensible, no monstrosities or extravagances'.[32] [...]

The alternative view that there are links between Utility furniture and Modernism can be argued by suggesting that the reforming and improving ideas contained within the 1937 Working Class Home report[33] were put into practice through the Utility furniture scheme. There is a general perception that many of the wartime controls were part of a wider socialist economic policy. This has been argued on the grounds that the agenda of the Utility Scheme was to democratise 'Good Design' and make it available to all levels of society. [...] Had the Utility Furniture Scheme continued to dictate design after 1948, when the supply situation began to improve, then it could have been accused of upholding a socialist ideology. However, the 1948 relaxation of control, when Utility was limited only by 'Freedom of Design' legislation suggests that any such latent plans for the Utility Scheme were dropped by the government as soon as the supply and demand restrictions allowed.

Perhaps the main problem with the use of terms like 'Modernism' and 'Arts and Crafts' lies in the use of such terms as stylistic historical pigeon-holes, suggesting that a particular style such as 'Modernism' was confined to a particular political ideological denomination. Furniture produced under the aegis of Utility is far too diverse to be categorised so narrowly. In relation to the history of the Utility Furniture Scheme, neither description is particularly helpful. Such attempts to theorise the designs of Utility furniture produced between 1943 and 1948 ignore the overriding factors which brought about the scheme in the first place.

The factors which led to the introduction of Utility furniture and the designs supplied by the Board of Trade between 1943 and 1948 are many, but they can be briefly summarised under six headings – (1) the shortage of furniture due to lack of timber supply to the furniture trade; (2) the demand for new furniture created by damage from bombing, new households and a degree of disposable income; (3) general shortages resulting in rapid inflation and the threat of racketeering if there were no supervision; (4) the introduction of rationing; (5) the established trade practices and traditional forms built into the Utility designs by its two trade designers, Edwin Clinch and Herbert Cutler, ensuring that the rump of the furniture industry not recruited to essential war production could cope with the production of civilian furniture; (6) the paramount importance of the need for economy, simplicity of manufacturing techniques and the limitations of available materials, for example, substituting hardboard for plywood.

So it is more accurate to conclude that the designs for Utility furniture were not the result of any one particular design ideology, but the result of a complex scheme of rationing which was attempting to meet the constantly changing economic and supply problems under wartime conditions.

NOTES

Extracted from Denney, M., 'Utility Furniture and the Myth of Utility 1943–1948' in Judy Attfield (ed.), *Utility Reassessed: the Role of Ethics in the Practice of Design*, Manchester: Manchester University Press, 1999, pp. 110–24. Reprinted by permission of the author and Manchester University Press.

1. The Ministry of Supply issued the Control of Timber (No. 1) Order on 5 September 1939, two days after war was declared. This Order established the Ministry of Control of Timber. The Utility Furniture Scheme was controlled by many different laws issued by the government. These laws provide the historian with a precise historical chronology of the scheme. However, due to the continual changes in the supplies of raw materials, many of the laws enacted

were revoked or re-enacted with amendments within weeks of being issued. The large number of different laws which were issued to control the production, marking, supply and price of furniture make the scheme's history a complex one.

2. Public Record Office Assistance Board documents (AST) 11/214. Although price control was extended to furniture at this date, the control was difficult to enforce, and full control of the industry was not brought about until the Utility furniture scheme was introduced.

3. The almost total withdrawal of timber to the furniture trade from July 1940 (Public Record Office Board of Trade documents (BT) 64/1835), linked with the increase in disposable income among certain sections of the public, was to lead to racketeering by certain sectors of the furniture trade.

4. Standard Emergency furniture was featured in *The Cabinet Maker and Complete House Furnisher* in February 1941.

5. BT 64/1730. The list of furniture was introduced by the Ministry of Supply in November 1941, but it was not until 1942 that the list was adopted by the Board of Trade which, by the publication of an Interim Order, prohibited the production of furniture which did not comply with the list from 1 August.

6. Press cutting filed with AST 11/196.

7. BT 131/41. The Board of Trade took an interest in consumer goods from the summer of 1940, although traditionally it had been a non-interventionist department concerned with the promotion of trade abroad, rather than the affairs of individual home industries.

8. This warning was given in a letter from the Ministry of Supply to the Board of Trade (BT 64/1835).

9. BT 64/1835 contains notes for and reports of parliamentary questions from 5 May 1942.

10. BT 64/1835.

11. BT 64/1897.

12. These regulations were introduced in the Domestic Furniture (Control of Manufacture and Supply) (No. 2) Order 1942.

13. The first Utility catalogue was published on 1 January 1943, but it was a number of weeks later before the furniture was available for sale.

14. The cot was introduced in the Domestic Furniture (Control of Manufacture and Supply) (No. 4) Order issued on 22 March 1943.

15. The additional items were added to the schedules through the Furniture (Control of Manufacture and Supply) (Amendment) (No. 5) Order. The new designs were published in a second catalogue published in June 1947.

16. See Chapter 13, 'Freedom of Design', in *Utility Reassessed: the Role of Ethics in the Practice of Design*, ed. Judy Attfield, Manchester: Manchester University Press, 1999, pp. 203–20.

17. J. Attfield, '"Then we were making furniture, and not money": a Case Study of J. Clarke, Wycombe Furniture Makers', *Oral History*, Vol. 18, No. 2, Autumn 1990, p. 54.

18. For example, in his *Fifties Source Book* (Virgin, 1990, p. 14) C. Pearce states 'The functional well made Utility furniture was produced by designer Gordon Russell', while C. and P. Fiell's *Modern Furniture Classics Since 1945* (Thames and Hudson, 1991) attributes to Russell 'the chairmanship of the Board of Trade' (an office he never held), when he is supposed to have 'designed a range of Utility furniture' (p. 14).

19. J.M. Woodham, 'Managing British Design Reform I: Fresh Perspectives on the Early Years of the Council of Industrial Design', *Journal of Design History*, Vol. 9, No. 1, 1996, p. 55.

20. G. Russell, *Designer's Trade*, Allen and Unwin, 1968; Geffrye Museum, *Utility Furniture and Fashion 1941–1951*, ILEA, 1974.

21. Russell, *Designer's Trade*, p. 199.

22. Ibid., p. 200.

23. Ibid., p. 205.

24. P. Sparke, *Furniture*, Bell and Hyman, 1986, p. 75.

25. M. Bretton, 'Utility: Strengths and Weaknesses of Government Controlled Crisis Design', *Design*, No. 309, September 1974, pp. 66–9.

26. Attfield, 'Good Design By Law: Adapting Utility Furniture to Peace-time Production

– Domestic Furniture in the Reconstruction Period 1946–1956', in J.M. Woodham and P. Maguire (eds), *Design and Cultural Politics in Post-war Britain*, Leicester University Press, 1997.

27. Russell, *Designer's Trade*, p. 198.
28. The list of 266 different pieces can be found in the Schedule of Furniture No. 1530 (Control of Manufacture and Supply) (Amendment) (No. 5) Order, 1946, dated 16 September 1946.
29. See, for example, *The Cabinet Maker and Complete House Furnisher* and similar publications of the period.
30. BT 64/2091. An internal Board of Trade report dating from the end of 1947 documents that since the increase in choice, certain items of Utility furniture were becoming difficult to sell.
31. 'Utility and Austerity', *Architectural Review*, Vol. 93, January 1943, p. 3.
32. W. Morris, 'The Lesser Arts of Life', *The Collected Works of William Morris*, ed. M. Morris, Longmans, Green and Co., 1914, p. 261.
33. The Council for Art and Industry, *The Working Class Home: Its Furnishing and Equipment*, HMSO, 1937.

20

'HERE IS THE MODERN WORLD ITSELF', THE FESTIVAL OF BRITAIN'S REPRESENTATIONS OF THE FUTURE

Becky Conekin (1999)

The 1951 Festival of Britain was conceived in the immediate post-war period, a period characterised by housing shortages, the continuation and even extension of wartime restrictions and rationing, as well as the initial stages of the dissolution of the British Empire. It was to be both a celebration of Britain's victory in the Second World War and a proclamation of its national recovery. There were eight official, government-funded exhibitions in England, Scotland, Northern Ireland and Wales, twenty-two designated arts festivals and a pleasure garden in Battersea. Eight and a half million people visited the London South Bank exhibition and the BBC aired 2700 festival-related broadcasts. On the local level 2000 cities, towns and villages across the United Kingdom organised and funded a festival event of some kind.

Robert Hewison has recently written that 'the lasting imagery' of much of the South Bank exhibition 'suggests that the Festival of Britain was more forward-looking than it really was … The modernist architecture was a lightweight framework for yet another exploration of Deep England.'[1] In contrast with Hewison's judgment, this chapter argues that the festival betrayed surprisingly little nostalgia. […] As well as acting as 'a tonic to the nation', the festival's stated intention was to project 'the belief that Britain will have contributions to make in the future.'[2] […] The goals of redistributing knowledge and

constructing a modern, cultured citizenry were ones which the festival planners shared with many within the post-war Labour Party. As such, the festival can be read simultaneously as a public celebration and a government-sponsored educational event.

When the government approved the final, scaled-down version of the festival in 1947 (the original conception had been an international exhibition to mark the centenary of the Great Exhibition of 1851) the Lord President of the Council, Herbert Morrison […] and his Under-Secretary, Max Nicholson, selected most of the festival committee. […] The planners were overwhelmingly middle-class men of the sort Michael Frayn has described as 'do-gooders; the readers of the *News Chronicle*, the *Guardian*, and the *Observer*, the signers of petitions; the backbone of the BBC'.[3] These philanthropic experts were characteristically entering early middle-age in 1951; many of them had been students in the 1930s. Architectural critic, John Summerson, wrote in October 1951 that the festival architects, for example, were 'the troublesome students of around 1935 … who at that date, discovered Lloyd Wright, Gropius and Le Corbusier for themselves'.[4] Some of the planners, like the landscape architect, Peter Shepheard, saw the war as an interruption to their careers, whilst others acknowledged that they had actually acquired their expertise in the war, on finding themselves working in the Ministry of Information, often designing camouflage or educational exhibitions.[5] Whatever their perspective, war service followed by austerity meant that most of the festival's architects and planners saw the 1951 Festival as their first real chance to design and build modern structures in Britain.

SCANDINAVIAN MODERNISM AND THE FESTIVAL

Most of the festival's planners were influenced by the Stockholm Exhibition of 1930 and it is hardly surprising to find amongst the 1951 festival's official records a report on the Stockholm project.[6] Stockholm's modernist, social democratic

Figure 15. The view of the Festival of Britain's South Bank from the entrances. Photograph by de Burgh Gallery, reproduced courtesy of the *Architectural Review*, vol. 109 (1951).

exhibition was clearly a model. Architectural critic, Reyner Banham, has stated that the semi-official line was that the Festival of Britain was indebted to its Scandinavian predecessor.[7] Both exhibitions marked a departure from the nineteenth-century model of international exhibitions and in many respects the 1951 festival greatly resembled the 1930 Stockholm Exhibition.[8] This was especially true in terms of the way national imagery was married to international pretensions. The organisational structure of both exhibitions was similar, consisting of a small executive committee, a tight-knit staff of experts, and a panel who selected the products to be exhibited.[9] Furthermore, the narrative structure of the 1951 festival seems to have been borrowed from the Scandinavian exhibition. The Swedish project was described by Ludvig Nordstrom, one of its key planners, as laid out to be an 'amusing and interesting picture-book' with a 'pedagogic purpose'.[10] Likewise, the Festival of Britain was called 'the autobiography of a nation', and visitors were instructed how to go round the South Bank displays, reading them as 'one continuous, interwoven story'.[11] The festival brochures proudly boasted of the originality of this method of display, calling it 'something new in exhibitions'.[12] [...] Finally, the Stockholm exhibition shared with its 1951 counterpart the goal of raising 'the taste and cultivation of our entire population'.[13] [...]

THE LABOUR PARTY AND THE FESTIVAL

Herbert Morrison appeared sincere when he asserted that 'the last thing in the world I would wish would be that this should turn into or was ever contemplated as a political venture'.[14] However, Hugh Casson, the South Bank exhibition's chief architect, stated that: 'Churchill, like the rest of the Tory Party, was against the Festival which they (quite rightly) believed was the advanced guard of socialism'.[15] In addition, a number of prominent members of the Labour government

considered the festival to be an overtly Labour undertaking, which would contribute to future election success. When Attlee wrote to Morrison to say that the autumn of 1951 was the best time to call an election, he explained that this would allow the festival as much time as possible to amass support for the Labour Party.[16] To this end, Labour published a special festival magazine, simply called *Festival,* in which the party was accredited both with the success of the festival and with the higher post-war standard of living. In page after page, life under Labour was proclaimed far better than it had been under the Conservatives, especially for ordinary British people.[17] [...] Diffusing knowledge through popular education, encouraging people to partake in 'culture' in their leisure time, improving their material surroundings, stimulating the arts, broadly fostering an enlightened citizenry 'rich in culture', these were all goals shared by the 1951 festival and the post-war Labour Party.

AGENDA FOR TASTE

Many of the London festival planners, especially those who were members of the Council of Industrial Design or young architects, had as one of their objectives a large-scale change in the tastes of the British public. Their aim was to dispel the fussy, old-fashioned, even 'repellent extravagances of the 1930s', replacing them with simple, clean lines for interior and exterior design and for household objects.[18] These middle-class arbiters of taste hoped that a newly constituted British citizenry would become educated in and eventually embrace 'good design', as defined by the COID and magazines such as *House and Garden.*[19]

The COID was established by the Board of Trade in 1944. The 'upper-class socialists' at the Board of Trade, Hugh Dalton and his successor, Stafford Cripps, were motivated by their commitment to the democratisation of design, as well as by their desire to rejuvenate British manufacturing after the war.[20] The COID stimulated media interest with the 1946 'Britain Can Make It' exhibition, which occupied the entire ground floor of the Victoria and Albert Museum. This exhibition, attended by well over a million people, sought to generate interest among manufacturers and the public in good design, while showing the rest of the world that British industries were producing goods of high quality which could be ordered, even after the exigencies of war.[21] Ironically, 'Britain Can Make It' was renamed 'Britain Can't Have It' by the press, thanks to the fact that most of the articles on display were merely prototypes or for export only.[22] The products were labelled 'now', 'soon' and 'later' – the 'later' label dominated. During the Festival of Britain itself, the COID took overall responsibility for selecting every product in the South Bank exhibition – a total of 10,000 objects in all, used not only in the official displays, but in all aspects of the exhibition, down to the public toilets![23]

The COID's meticulous commitment to good design was shared by another post-war arbiter of taste, the BBC. Programmes such as the *Looking at Things* series, transmitted as part of the BBC schools' broadcasts, worked to a similar cultural agenda. An early instalment aired in September of 1951, asked school listeners *Have You a Seeing Eye?* explaining that:

> Designing something means more than just drawing a picture of what it is to look like; it also means thinking about how it is to be made and making sure that it will do its job properly. Not everything you see in the shops has been carefully designed, and the most expensive things are not necessarily the best, nor are the cheapest always the worst … A 'seeing eye' will help you to distinguish good design from bad, to choose wisely when you go shopping, and to make the best of what you have already … You can start straight away by looking critically at the things around you – the things you use every day. Look at things in shop windows, although you may not yet be able to buy them.[24]

Such wide-ranging training in 'good design' aimed to educate young people in more aesthetically orientated consumption. The explicit intention was to encourage modernist tastes through the prioritisation of functionality and of high-quality materials.[25]

The Festival of Britain's modernist agenda in design, art and architecture aimed to encourage people of all ages to learn about and, when available, consume well-designed modern artefacts. An official festival brochure entitled *Design in the Festival* (1951), produced by the COID, stated:

> There is now no logical reason why well-designed things should not be available to all of us … They affect our whole outlook, whether we admit it or not; and if we are critical we have to confess that many of them are downright ugly … one can hardly expect to get a high standard of design unless there is a critical and appreciative public.[26]

The COID's strategy rested on a type of educational populism which appealed to the rational and cultured citizen. The brochure concluded with the assertion that: 'When consumer knowledge increases still further, the minority of less satisfactory appliances will be reduced to a negligible quantity'.[27] […]

There can be little doubt that the festival helped to shape popular definitions of good and modern design. The term 'Festival style' came to be applied to buildings utilising concrete, aluminium and plate glass, as well as to household furnishings. According to William Feaver, 'the South Bank remained the popularly accepted idea of "modern" for a whole generation'. Other examples of modern design which first appeared at the festival were canework for indoor furniture, blond wood, 'lily-of-the-valley splays' for light bulbs, 'flying staircases' and textiles sporting thorns, spikes and molecular patterns.[28]

In the words of Raphael Samuel, the festival 'was determinedly modernist in bias, substituting, for the moth-eaten and the traditional, vistas of progressive advance: a great looking forward after years of rationing and greyness'.[29] This agenda stretched beyond domestic artefacts to the field of public architecture. Morrison himself described the South Bank site as 'new Britain springing from the battered fabric of the old'.[30] In a London guide, produced in association with the *Architects' Journal* and published in May 1951, the editors asserted that the exhibition was:

> the first full-scale example of modern architecture doing a popular job ... for the very first time in history it is trying to create a still greater thing than architecture, a modern *background,* a twentieth century urban environment.[31]

The South Bank's architects and planners were indeed endeavouring to construct more than just an exhibition, they were attempting to build a vision of a brighter future for Britain – a future that was clean, orderly and modern after the dirt and chaos of the war. In this context, the best-remembered symbol of the festival's modernity was the award-winning vertical feature, the Skylon. Modern engineering meant that the Skylon's almost 300 feet of steel frame clad in louvred aluminium created the illusion that it was floating forty feet above the ground, especially at night when it was lit from the inside. Not only was it modern, it was futuristic and found itself gracing the cover of more than one science fiction magazine. Science fiction author Brian Aldiss wrote, twenty-five years after the event, that 'the South Bank Exhibition was a memorial to the future', and the Skylon was its centrepiece.[32]

A FUSION OF ART AND SCIENCE

The festival's executive committee asserted that Britain was uniquely placed in the constellation of post-war powers to mark out a new course for the integration of science and the arts. [...] Neither Russia nor the United States was capable of such coordination. However, Britain could and

should coordinate the fine arts with the sciences because a proper balance was essential for the survival of Western Civilisation.[33] Written as it was in the immediate aftermath of the war, this rhetoric reflected a commonly held anxiety about the excesses of science manifested in the recent global conflict and especially about the role of the atomic Bomb. [...]

The festival pattern group was the quintessential expression of this desire for bridge-building between the arts and science. The group aimed to create a new modernist aesthetic which combined the two fields. [...] Mark Hartland Thomas, a member of the COID and a distinguished architect who later founded the Modular Society, was the originator of the festival pattern group. Professor Kathleen Lonsdale suggested that some crystal-structure diagrams could provide the bases for original textile designs [Figure 16]. At the same time, a junior colleague of Lonsdale's, Dr Helen Megaw, had produced diagrams which would serve well as patterns for fabric decoration. Hartland Thomas convinced twenty-eight manufacturers to join the scheme and use these patterns. From the point of view of the festival organisers, crystallography was the perfect science. It was futuristic, yet had its aesthetic origins in the natural world. As such it was perceived as quintessentially British. [...]

Yet, science was not only aestheticised in the festival. The exhibitions combined a somewhat fanciful vision of a modernist future with a more or less realistic appreciation of the potential of science to transform everyday life. The official exhibition in Scotland, the exhibition of industrial power in Glasgow, aimed to tell 'the story of man's conquest of "Power" and the part played by Britain in that conquest'.[34] [...] The narrative was divided into eleven essential chapters on topics such as coal, steel, steam, electricity, civil engineering and atomic energy. [...] In the hall of the future, according to the guide-catalogue: 'the visitor walks in the present, looks down on the past, and looks up to the future.'[35] The end point of the display focused on atomic power,

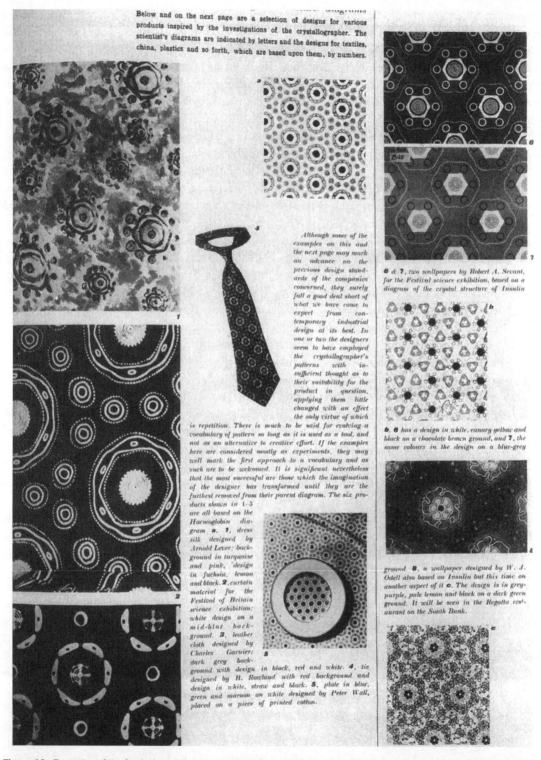

Below and on the next page are a selection of designs for various products inspired by the investigations of the crystallographer. The scientist's diagrams are indicated by letters and the designs for textiles, china, plastics and so forth, which are based upon them, by numbers.

6 & 7, two wallpapers by Robert A. Sevant, for the Festival science exhibition, based on a diagram of the crystal structure of Insulin

6, 6 has a design in white, canary yellow and black on a chocolate brown ground, and 7, the same colours in the design on a blue-grey

Although some of the examples on this and the next page may mark an advance on the previous design standards of the companies concerned, they surely fall a good deal short of what we have come to expect from contemporary industrial design at its best. In one or two the designers seem to have employed the crystallographer's patterns with insufficient thought as to their suitability for the product in question, applying them little changed with an effect the only virtue of which is repetition. There is much to be said for evolving a vocabulary of pattern so long as it is used as a tool, and not as an alternative to creative effort. If the examples here are considered mostly as experiments, they may well mark the first approach to a vocabulary and as such are to be welcomed. It is significant nevertheless that the most successful are those which the imagination of the designer has transformed until they are the furthest removed from their parent diagram. The six products shown in 1–5 are all based on the Haemoglobin diagram a. 1, dress silk designed by Arnold Lever; background in turquoise and pink, design in fuchsia, lemon and black. 2, curtain material for the Festival of Britain science exhibition; white design on a mid-blue background. 3, leather cloth designed by Charles Garnier; dark grey background with design in black, red and white. 4, tie designed by B. Rowland with red background and design in white, straw and black. 5, plate in blue, green and maroon on white designed by Peter Wall, placed on a piece of printed cotton.

ground, 8, a wallpaper designed by W. J. Odell also based on Insulin but this time on another aspect of it c. The design is in grey-purple, pale lemon and black on a dark green ground. It will be seen in the Regatta restaurant on the South Bank.

Figure 16. Examples of the festival pattern group's crystal designs. Photograph reproduced courtesy of the *Architectural Review* 109 (1951).

claimed as a partly British achievement, thanks to Rutherford's discoveries. The more recent work of British scientists on the atomic bomb was omitted. However, the problematic nature of the new source of power was not entirely glossed over. The catalogue pointed out that the atomic future held out both the possibility of unfathomable positive opportunities and the prospect of utter annihilation, stating:

> The use which has been made of these discoveries and the work which is being based on them today will determine whether we are entering an age of undreamed-of plenty and comfort, or whether we are working out our complete extinction.[36]

Such a double-edged appraisal is noteworthy when compared to more popular celebrations of atomic energy in early 1950s Britain. The tone in the festival literature was level and considered, whereas the more prevalent, popular thinking on atomic energy was far less reasoned, presenting it simply as the solution to every kind of modern-day problem.[37] [...]

'Building science' was the key to the better-known 'live architecture exhibition' built in Poplar in the East End of London. A badly bombed working-class neighbourhood was chosen as the home of a new, modern estate named after local Labour politician, George Lansbury, the architect of early twentieth-century municipal socialism. The Lansbury estate consisted of 'scientifically' built flats and houses, as well as a school, a church and a pedestrianised shopping zone.[38] [...] Evocations of the frightful history of this 'slum area', as well as a version of the present, littered with Jerry-built and pokey dwellings', were on display. These miserable environments were counterposed by the exhibition's well-planned, 'new urban landscape in which the buildings are growing together as a community'.[39] In short, the problems of the past and present were solved through modern science and planning; the future would be brighter: [...] 'Here at Poplar then you may catch a glimpse of that future London which is to arise from blitzed ruins and from the slums and chaotic planning of the past'.[40]

[...]

Clearly, the festival exhibitions represented only one of many possible ways the post-war British nation could have been imagined. Emphasising an improving, modern future underscored the recovery and renewal of a badly shaken but victorious country – a country which could make a distinctive contribution alongside the superpowers. This collective project of imagining also created a space for an unuttered, yet unmistakable message that the Labour Party, in office since 1945, was the force behind Britain's recovery, as well as its guiding light for the future. A rational and cultured citizenry with greater access to knowledge would be able to evaluate Labour's contribution. Unfortunately for Labour, the general election results in the autumn after the festival revealed that not everyone had heeded the message. For whatever reason, it seems that many found in the Coronation Day celebrations two years later a more reassuring balance of the modern and the quintessentially British.

NOTES

Extracted from Conekin, B., '"Here Is the Modern World Itself", the Festival of Britain's Representations of the Future', in B. Conekin, F. Mort and C. Waters (eds), *Moments of Modernity: Reconstructing Britain 1945–1964*, London and New York: Rivers Oram Press, 1999, pp. 228–46. Reproduced by permission of Rivers Oram Press.

1. R. Hewison, *Culture and Consensus: England, Art and Politics Since 1940*, London, Methuen, 1995, p. 59.
2. I. Cox, 'The Story the Exhibition Tells: F.S. Campania, Festival of Britain 1951', n.d., *PRO WORK* 25/21, p. 4.

3. M. Frayn, 'Festival', in M. Sissons and R. French (eds.), *Age of Austerity, 1945–1951*, Harmondsworth, Penguin, 1964, p. 331.

4. J. Summerson, *New Statesman,* October, 1951, quoted in R. Hewison, *In Anger: British Culture in the Cold War 1945–60*, New York, Oxford University Press, 1981, p. 49.

5. See for example M. Girouard, 'It's Another World', *Architectural Review*, August 1974, reprinted in *Architects' Journal*, vol. 179, 27 June 1984, p. 108.

6. Report by G. Bowyer and E.W. Swaine on their visit to the Stockholm Exhibitions. Report filed on 16th September, 1949, PRO WORK 25/19.

7. R. Banham, 'The Style: "Flimsy … Effeminate?"', in M. Banham and B. Hillier (eds.), *A Tonic to the Nation: the Festival of Britain, 1951*, London, Thames and Hudson, with the co-operation of the Victoria and Albert Museum, 1976, p.193. See also H. Hopkins, *The New Look: A Social History of the Forties and Fifties in Britain*, London, Readers Union/Secker and Warburg, 1964, p.271.

8. A. Pred, *Recognizing European Modernities: a Montage of the Present*, London and New York, Routledge, 1995, p.100.

9. Ibid., p.101.

10. L. Nordström, 1930, quoted in Pred, *Recognizing European Modernities*, p. 134.

11. I. Cox, *Festival of Britain Guide, South Bank*, London, HMSO, 1951, p. 4. See also Barry Curtis, 'One Continuous Interwoven Story (The Festival of Britain)', *Block*, 11, 1985–6, pp. 48–52.

12. Ibid. See also 'F.O.B./Press/14/49 16th November, 1949, The 1951 Exhibition, South Bank, London', Information Office File, AAD 5/1-1979-5/44-1979, Victoria and Albert Archive of Art and Design, Blythe Road, London.

13. Archbishop of Canterbury quoted in *The Festival of Britain: The Official Book of the Festival of Britain, 1951*, London, HMSO, 1951.

14. H. Morrison, quoted in Forty, 'Festival Politics', in Banham and Hillier (eds.), *A Tonic to the Nation*, p. 36.

15. Sir H. Casson, quoted in Hewison, *Culture and Consensus*, p. 58.

16. Forty, 'Festival Politics', p. 37.

17. Labour Party, *Festival*, London, Labour Party, 1951, pp. 8–9, in Labour Party Archives, Manchester.

18. J. Gloag, 'Furniture Design in Britain' in Council of Industrial Design, *Design in the Festival: Illustrated Review of British Goods*, London: HMSO, 1951, p. 14.

19. For discussions of this controversial agenda see: S. MacDonald and J. Porter, 'Mid-Century Modern: The Campaign for Good Design', in *Putting on the Style: Setting up Home in the 1950s*, London, The Geffrye Museum, 1990, n.p.; A. Partington, 'Popular Fashion and Working-Class Affluence', in J. Ash and E. Wilson (eds), *Chic Thrills,* London, Pandora Press, 1992, pp. 145–61; P. Sparke, *As Long As It's Pink: The Sexual Politics of Taste*, London, Pandora Press, 1995, pp. 219–21.

20. MacDonald and Porter, 'Mid-Century Modern', n.p.

21. Ibid.

22. Ibid.

23. MacDonald and Porter, 'The Festival Spirit', in *Putting on the Style*, n.p.

24. *Have You A Seeing Eye?* 'Looking at Things' series, BBC Broadcasts to Schools, aired 21 September 1951, quoted in *Brochures from the BBC for the School Broadcasting Council for the United Kingdom*, London, BBC, 1951, p. 3.

25. See Sparke, *As Long As It's Pink*, p. 215.

26. G. Russell, 'Design in Industry: Today and Tomorrow', in *Design in the Festival*, p. 11.

27. P. Garbutt, 'Domestic Appliances', in Council of Industrial Design, *Design in the Festival: Illustrated Review of British Goods,* London, HMSO, 1951, p. 31.

28. W. Feaver, 'Festival Star', in Banham and Hillier (eds), *A Tonic to the Nation*, p. 54.

29. R. Samuel, *Theatres of Memory, vol. 1: Past and Present in Contemporary Culture*, London, Verso, 1994, p. 55.

30. B. Donoghue and G.W. Jones, *Herbert Morrison: Portrait of a Politician,* Weidenfeld & Nicolson, 1973, p. 492.
31. S. Lambert, *Architects' Journal*, May, 1951, quoted in 'Everything from Townscape', *Architects' Journal*, vol. 179, 27 June 1984, p. 92.
32. B. Aldiss, A Monument to the Future', in Banham and Hillier (eds.), *A Tonic to the Nation*, p.176.
33. 'Festival of Britain, 1951', 1 April, 1948, *PRO WORK* 25/21, p. 2.
34. 'Industrial Power at Glasgow', in *The Story of the Festival of Britain, 1951*, London: HMSO, 1952, p. 27.
35. 'Exhibition of Industrial Power, Glasgow, Festival of Britain, 1951', in Banham and Hilliers (eds.), *A Tonic to the Nation*, p. 154.
36. Ibid.
37. K. Willis, 'The Promotion of Nuclear Power in Britain 1945–1960', unpublished paper presented at the North American Conference on British Studies, Vancouver, October 1994.
38. See Labour Party, *Festival*, pp. 6–7; 'Exhibition of Architecture, Lansbury at Poplar', BBC Radio Broadcast, Summer, 1951, BBC Radio Broadcast 16931, National Sound Archives; *The Festival of Britain, The Official Book*, p. 13.
39. *The Festival of Britain, The Official Book*, p. 13.
40. Ibid.

21

POPULUXE

Thomas Hine (1987)

TAKING OFF

Populuxe is a synthetic word, created in the spirit of the many coined words of the time. Madison Avenue kept inventing words like 'autodynamic,' which described a shape of car which made no sense aerodynamically. [...] Like these synthetic words, Populuxe has readily identifiable roots, and it reaches toward an ineffable emotion. It derives, of course, from populism and popularity, with just a fleeting allusion to pop art, which took Populuxe imagery and attitudes as subject matter. And it has luxury, popular luxury, luxury for all. This may be a contradiction in terms, but it is an expression of the spirit of the time and the rationale for many of the products that were produced. And, finally, Populuxe contains a thoroughly unnecessary 'e,' to give it class. That final embellishment of a practical and straightforward invention is what makes the word Populuxe, well, Populuxe. [...]

The decade's description of the average American probably fit very few of its citizens. It excluded not only blacks but residents of ethnic urban neighborhoods, the single, widowed and divorced and their children and a great many others who did not often show their faces in advertisements. Yet what was remarkable was not that many were excluded from the bounty of a prosperous time, but that a vast majority got a share of the wealth and were able to take large steps up the economic ladder. [...] In this time of great change people chose most often to celebrate change itself. 'We are moving ahead,' John Kennedy said repeatedly during his 1960 presidential campaign. 'But we are not moving ahead rapidly enough.' Forward motion at ever-increasing speed was what Americans expected from their nation, their cars and their careers. [...]

Populuxe arose well after World War II, despite the orgy of consumption that characterized the immediate postwar years. The initial postwar period, from about 1946 to 1954, produced a lot of cars, a lot of babies, a lot of appliances, a lot of suburbs. Americans were catching up on the consumption they had put off during World War II and the Depression. [...] The turning point came in 1954, an eventful year by any standard. It brought not only the downfall of McCarthy and the momentous Supreme Court decision outlawing segregated schools but also the introduction of sleek, powerful and finny low-priced cars and the emergence of a sexy, urgent new kind of popular music – rock and roll. Some 1.5 million new homes were built that year, the great majority of them outside the central cities; 1.4 million power lawn mowers were sold and 4 million babies were born. It was a year in which Americans began to feel less threatened by Communism, and more anxious to enjoy the fruits of American affluence. And it was also a year in which major corporations changed their marketing strategies in order to induce people to spend their increasing incomes. [...]

Populuxe is vulgar by definition. It is the result of an unprecedented ability to acquire, reaching well down into the working class, to the sort of people who had historically been able to have only a few mean objects. These people did not acquire the good simple objects many tastemakers advocated. They had had it with simple, and now they wanted more. […]

Although Populuxe objects had a broad popular appeal, and could be found nearly everywhere, their overwrought design was primarily reserved for private indulgence, not public gestures. During the entire Populuxe era, the 'official' style was European modernism, interpreted in a strict, rather ascetic way. While much of what Americans were buying was termed 'modernistic,' it was hardly modern in the way that tastemakers used that term. This led to a reversal of the age-old pattern in which seats of government and houses of worship received the highest craftsmanship and ornamentation a society could produce, while the individual house was relatively bare. During the Populuxe era, the town hall and even the church or synagogue might be a featureless glass-and-steel crate, while the individual home would be carefully landscaped and lavishly furnished with things that evoked different historical periods and the future besides. A few architects, notably Eero Saarinen and Edward Durrell Stone, caught the public imagination and contributed to the development of Populuxe design. But for most design professionals, the Populuxe attitude bordered on the immoral. The Museum of Modern Art, for example, was an aggressive propagandist for European modernism and simplicity, and even some of the home and design magazines and mass magazines such as *Life* offered forums for those who warned Americans against ornamental overindulgence. They listened politely, then, like adolescents who have come into a windfall, went on a binge.

THE LUCKIEST GENERATION

America had been able to turn its war machine into a consumer economy almost overnight. Productivity rose at a rate of better than 2 percent a year for most of the decade after World War II. American industry was using half the world's steel and oil. American consumers were able to buy three-quarters of the cars and appliances on earth. Real income, after very modest inflation, was on the rise. Indeed, by 1953, the average income per person was half again the figure in 1929, and although the special conditions of the war made comparisons difficult, it is clear that nearly all this growth occurred after 1945. […]

Better-paid jobs running or maintaining the machinery of automation increased much faster than the low-paid jobs were declining. People in factories, the very heart of the working class, were rapidly ascending to middle-class incomes. The average industrial wage rate had doubled from pre-Depression levels, and there were a lot more jobs available. […] The postwar period brought a much more equitable distribution of income than ever before. The increase in real income went almost entirely to the middle class. The absolute number of high-income people, which *Fortune* defined as those making more than $7,500 annually in 1953 dollars, more than doubled from 1929, but their share of the nation's total income declined sharply. The biggest increase came in the number of families in the $4,000–$7,000 salary range, which was understood to be solidly middle class. There were 5.5 million families in this category in 1929, 17.9 million in 1953. They accounted for 35 percent of the nation's population; they earned 42 percent of its income. These were the candidates for suburbia, the cream of the American market.

Unlike the classic definition of the middle class as a collection of small proprietors, this newly minted middle class was made up almost entirely of employees of corporations, and their income came almost entirely from salaries. Moreover, there was a decline in the number of families in the lowest income class, from 15.6 million to 11.7 million. The nation's total income was rising twice as rapidly as the population, so there was a lot more wealth per person. And the distribution of this new wealth was very fair, with average working people as the chief beneficiaries. By the beginning of the Populuxe era, America was materially more democratic than it had been at any time in its history. [...]

Those just starting households and having families constitute the group most desirable to home builders and manufacturers because they must make many large expenditures quickly. During the late 1940s and early 1950s, those doing so at a 'normal' age were augmented by an enormous number of people who had delayed doing so because of the Depression and World War II. [...] The number of automobile registrations in the United States more than doubled during the decade after World War II. [...]

It had long been obvious that this great spending spree could not continue indefinitely, and by 1952 businessmen began to worry. Not only were Americans finally catching up with their consumption, but the new prime generation of consumers that was about to come on line was the smallest ever. [...] The one good thing about this smaller generation was that it had more money to spend, and it wanted to spend it. [For example] the addition of styling, decoration and fantasy to the car [encouraged] the frequent replacement of automobiles. By giving a car the same lifespan as a stylish dress, the Big Three [motor manufacturers] could sell nearly as many cars as they had during periods when there were more potential buyers. [...]

Nearly every industry followed the lead of the automobile companies, with more or less success. Home builders phased out the basic house and started coming up with new and elaborate models which could be fitted and personalized with a series of options and upgrades. Furniture makers tried to follow this trend toward increasing fantasy and stylization, and certainly the artifacts that survive bear witness to the energy, creativity and sense of the outrageous that they brought to their task. The arrival of new materials, particularly new kinds of floor and wall coverings, brought distinctly new looks. From both automobiles and clothing fashions came new colors and color combinations that rendered old rooms stodgy. [...]

Appliance manufacturers, some of which were owned by automobile companies, followed the same philosophy of bringing new looks and new features to familiar machines, while introducing many new products along the way. Appliances, which had taken on a streamlined form during preceding decades, became flatter and boxier, and they often sported decorative appliqués. They also were manufactured in color for the first time, something that introduced a new fashion element that was able to make kitchens and their appliances appear dated in a shorter time. [...] The television set, a less practical and relatively new machine, went two-toned, modern, Early American, space age and every other trend that came along. Television, the most pervasive and influential novelty of the era, was widespread by 1954, and manufacturers were already starting to sell people on the idea of a second set for the kids, or for the bedroom, and also to gear up for the arrival of color. Not even the magic box could escape the implications of the demographic trough. [...]

Vance Packard's best-selling book on the psychological dimensions of advertising, *The Hidden Persuaders*, came as a shock to many consumers when it appeared in 1957, although the methods discussed seem fairly blatant today. The book was strident in its condemnation of the way in which advertising experts manipulate consumers, and it almost certainly overstated the power of advertising to change people's behavior. At the same time, it couldn't help but evoke admiration for the cleverness of the industry, how much it had learned about people and the wit with which it used the information. People enjoy being fooled creatively, never more so than during the Populuxe era. Was convincing people that a detergent is mild by putting it in a blue box and that it is powerful by using an orange box any more fraudulent than a car that copies the look of an airplane or an apple pie made out of crackers? All were more often admired than condemned.

DESIGN AND STYLING

Material democracy had been achieved not through any arts-and-crafts utopia, or through a socialist forced redistribution of wealth, but rather through the workings of big business and its expertise in making people feel good about its products. Progress was not merely an abstraction, but an array of goods that could be touched, switched on, photographed, improved and fantasized about. [...] Some who cared about fine design and well-made products felt that democracy was on trial during this period and that it was failing miserably. They looked at the landscape of subdivision houses, the gaudy cars in the showrooms, the profusion of overweight furniture standing on tiny legs, and despaired that aristocracy had done things so much better. 'We have yet to prove that a democracy can produce a beautiful environment,' wrote the architect Edward Durrell Stone in a 1959 article, 'The Case against the Tailfin Age.' [...]

The standard was, of course, that of the marketplace. Products were judged not by how well they were made, or how well they did their jobs, but by how well they sold. Indeed, the American tradition of industrial design is based on just this premise. In contrast with the tradition of craftsmanship exemplified by William Morris and his followers, and with the ideology of technical expression that arose with the Bauhaus and European modernism, American industrial design has been concerned most of all with inducing consumers to accept, understand and use a product. [...]

It is possible to trace the evolution of this approach in the changing image of the ideal kitchen. During the early 1950s, when families were still catching up after the war, a modern kitchen was simply an old-fashioned kitchen to which many

Figure 17. Appliances evolved from big boxes in the kitchen to efficient square-edged, laboratory-like objects to assertive built-ins, before disappearing into an overall decorating scheme. Reprinted from Thomas Hine, *Populuxe*, New York, Alfred A. Knopf, 1987, p. 67.

new appliances had been added. Each of the appliances was slightly streamlined. Each stood on its own, a separate piece of machinery. […] At the dawn of the Populuxe era […] appliances were no longer seen as objects in the kitchen. Rather, they were the kitchen. Modern life was close to inconceivable without them. Thus, appliances were increasingly built into kitchens […] as part of an overall decorating scheme. Appliances no longer had to be dramatized; they were thoroughly domesticated. […]

This new perception of objects as part of a way of life rather than as tools for carrying out a particular task required that design be thought about in a whole new way. The individual object became less important. Design for mass production involved more sociological insight than technical expertise or aesthetic intention. It is likely that even the famous Good Design shows at the Museum of Modern Art, which were trying to fight this trend, ended up being a part of it. They were intended to spotlight well-made, visually graceful objects for everyday use. Their effect was to let a small group of consumers signal that their households had the approval of the Museum of Modern Art. […]

By traditional standards, this approach to making and using things was enormously wasteful. It did not merely encourage but depended on the discarding of valuable materials, the scrapping of things that still worked. Throughout the first half of the 1950s, intellectuals condemned American behavior as wasteful […
but …] by the latter half of the decade, the argument had swung in the other direction. The economic commentator Peter Drucker argued, for example, that the apparent wastefulness was actually a form of subsidy which allowed those at the lower end of the economic ladder to partake of the same pleasures as everyone else. Thus, a person who wanted a stylish and exciting new car would usually discard an old car that still ran well but was no longer in style. A poorer person could then buy it used for less than it was really worth. […]

The celebration of the production and sales process at the expense of the products proved doubly painful to many who were, like George Nelson, design director of Herman Miller furniture, advocates of modern furniture design. The postwar period was a kind of golden age of American design. Charles and Ray Eames produced a series of designs that proved to be classics, as did Charles Eames's sometime collaborator Eero Saarinen. Harry Bertoia's wire chairs and Nelson's 'coconut' chair and storage walls were also familiar parts of the American landscape. Between them, Knoll and Herman Miller seemed to be making possible the creation of a distinctly American modernism in furniture. Like Bauhaus and most other prewar European modernist designs, these pieces sought to reflect a machine-based society. But the European pieces were primarily formal experiments, handcrafted objects which sought to question the familiar images of particular pieces, and they were concerned most of all with structure. […] Of the Europeans, only Alvar Aalto had designed pieces in terms of the processes by which they would be made. And Aalto worked only in laminated wood.

The postwar American designs, by contrast, followed the native method of close integration of design, marketing and production. And they were designed to take advantage of new materials and new technologies. Perhaps the definitive example was the foam and molded fiberglass 'womb' chair, designed by Eero Saarinen and introduced by Knoll in 1948. This bucket seat proved to be the prototype for a great many variations on the theme of a molded sculptural seat standing on frail metal legs. 'Ass trays,' Frank Lloyd Wright called them, but they started turning up everywhere. […]

The designs of Eames, Saarinen, Nelson, Bertoia and others were generally informal. They sought to be light and comfortable. They were realistic about the body and did not make it conform to a particular sculptural form, but rather let the furniture mirror the shapes and motions of the body on the surfaces where contact would be made. This furniture was, therefore, a bit more ungainly than the canonical 1920s modernist forms, but it was closer to modernist ideals of practical, affordable, machine-made furniture. It was extremely influential, and it did turn up in people's lives, if not necessarily in their houses. Moreover, it conveyed a sense of the new and the dynamic.

But the work of the innovative American designers did not ultimately add up to the kind of environment in which people actually lived. This had something to do with the nature of the furniture industry itself, which was divided into many small companies, most of them making only chests or upholstered goods or metal furniture. The new furniture used combinations of materials and technologies that most manufacturers defined as being outside of their particular business. And while Knoll and Herman Miller did pursue the residential market in their early years, their standards of construction and the prices they had to charge made their products much more attractive to the corporate and institutional market, where the durability they offered was more in demand. And the immediate and widespread acceptance of modern American furniture for institutional uses probably worked against its use in the home. The Populuxe house was viewed as being an island of individuality, a refuge from the world at large. If a chair could be found at the school library, it probably would not be found in the home.

Nevertheless, a lot of modern and contemporary furniture was sold for the home. Much of this had a superficial similarity to the sort of thing Eames was doing, but it generally left out the technological innovation. The commercial-grade furniture, called 'borax' and 'waterfall' in the trade, was made essentially the same way whether it was labeled 'contemporary,' 'traditional' or 'Early American.' Today, one can look at the advertising of a big company like Kroehler and not be able to tell the traditional from the modern without a label. [...] The word 'modern' was often used for furniture that was a bit more daring in design, a bit more fashionable, than the furniture designated as 'contemporary.' Confusingly, the terms were often used in a different way, with 'modern' used as an antonym for 'formal,' describing an attitude toward living and room arrangement that could embrace traditional pieces as well as those that were consciously contemporary. But both definitions of 'modern' implied an aspiration to lightness, both in color and in line. [...] Contemporary tables and small decorative objects such as ashtrays took on dynamic asymmetrical forms, such as boomerang or palette shapes, while larger contemporary objects tended to be boxy. There were no moldings, and thin, slightly splayed, round metal or metal-footed wooden legs were almost universal. [...]

The other feature of contemporary design which was found in both high-style and mainstream homes was wall-mounted shelving, either attached to the wall or featuring thin metal stanchions. Several decorating books published at the time identified such shelving, along with what was termed 'the color revolution,' as the decorative touch by which the era would be known. Like the pole lamp, this shelving appeared serviceable and almost weightless, with an industrial quality that was not particularly overbearing. The shelves defined a grid on which all sorts of objects, from books to record players to clusters of African sculpture, family pictures or souvenir bric-a-brac, could be placed. The grid was an important motif, one that was identified both with the walls of new downtown office buildings and with the paintings of Mondrian, whose influence had trickled down to cigarette advertisements and the decoration of kitchen cabinets.

NOTE

Extracted from Hine, T., *Populuxe*, New York: Alfred A. Knopf, 1987, 'Taking Off', pp. 3–14, 'The Luckiest Generation,' pp. 15–36, and 'Design and Styling', pp. 59–81. Copyright © 1987, 2007 by Thomas Hine, published by The Overlook Press, New York, NY. All rights reserved. www.overlookpress.com.

22

THE KHRUSHCHEV KITCHEN: DOMESTICATING THE SCIENTIFIC-TECHNOLOGICAL REVOLUTION

Susan E. Reid (2005)

In the cosmos, socialist science had proved its superiority with the launch of the first Sputnik in October 1957. The kitchen, meanwhile – and the conditions of women's work in general – remained the site of the Soviet system's humiliation and a symbol of its backwardness.[1] In the notorious confrontation between the superpowers at the American National Exhibition in Moscow 1959, it was the state-of-the-art kitchen of the model American home that served Vice-President Richard Nixon as the ideal platform from which to challenge Soviet state socialism. For if US superiority in the space race and arms race was in doubt, capitalism's victory in the standard-of-living race seemed assured.[2]

These were far from trivial matters to the Soviet regime. As it held, the ultimate global victory of socialism was to be achieved through superior living standards rather than military might. It was an article of faith – and not only of Cold War polemics – that socialism would guarantee the best possible conditions of life for the largest number of people.[3] The Khrushchev regime repeatedly indexed the imminent transition to communism to the achievement of superabundance and unprecedented prosperity, and devoted an extraordinary degree of attention to consumption and everyday, domestic life.[4]

The promised abundance that would win the Cold War for socialism was to be attained by harnessing the achievements of modern science and technology. 'We stand on the threshold of a new scientific-technological and industrial revolution', declared Premier Nikolai Bulganin at the July 1956 Central Committee plenum.[5] The Scientific-Technological Revolution or 'STR' was a central term in official pronouncements of the Khrushchev era, which made it a defining characteristic of socialist modernity. In the postwar world, advanced science and technology were fundamental to the arms and space race as well as for international prestige. But only the socialist system, founded on scientific principles, it was argued, was capable of fully applying the technological revolution to benefit human life. The Third Party Programme adopted in 1961 – the definitive ideological statement of the Khrushchev period – identified social progress with scientific and technological progress. It was to be achieved through electrification of the whole country, comprehensive mechanization of production, and civilian applications of atomic energy and chemistry.[6] […]

In the Marxist tradition, the source of woman's backwardness was her confinement to the home and imprisonment by domestic labour. As Lenin wrote, woman would 'remain a domestic slave in spite of all liberating laws' as long as housework remained isolated labour conducted in the home.[7] The solution, for Lenin and Aleksandra Kollontai – as for a series of socialists and feminists before them, from the German Social Democrat August Bebel to the American feminist Charlotte Perkins Gilman – lay in the abolition of the individual kitchen.[8] It was to be replaced by public dining, socialized housework and collective childcare. Only the development of services and new, collective forms of everyday living, would, according to Lenin, 'in practice be able to liberate woman, and reduce and eventually annihilate her inequality with man'.[9]

In the late 1920s and early 1930s, some experiments were made with the restructuring of domestic life through the establishment of communal and kitchen-less dwellings. Ernst May designed housing of this sort for the new 'socialist city', Magnitogorsk, while Moisei Ginzburg and the Constructivist architectural group OSA (Union of Contemporary Architects) developed minimal kitchen niches for the Narkomfin communal house, Moscow, in 1930.[10] However, the priorities of rapid industrialization in the early 1930s were in conflict with the investment required to transform cooking and childcare from isolated homecrafts into scientifically-organized, socialist service industries. Moreover, beginning with the dissolution of the Zhenotdel (the women's section of the party) in 1930, the Stalinist state retreated from the commitment to the restructuring of gender roles, the withering away of the family and the emancipation of women. To promote social stability and increase the birth rate, new legislation in 1936 and 1944 reinstated the family as the pillar of society and asserted women's social obligation to reproduction as well as production.[11] [...]

The retrenchment of the Stalin years and the image of the woman-centred home as a dream of normality left a legacy to the Khrushchev era that was only partly addressed. [...] On the one hand, the project of the 1920s to build a 'new way of life' was resumed, including the aim to emancipate women from kitchen slavery. On the other, as will be shown, both the discourse of modern Soviet living and the actual, built form of housing in the Khrushchev era, reconfirmed the individual family home as the site of reproductive labour, and the housewife as its isolated and unpaid workforce. [...]

Only by active participation in the sphere of production and public life could a person fully realize herself as the integrated, all-round individual who would be a citizen of communism. But, as [Khrushchev] recognized, the combined burden of job, childcare and housework prevented many women from fully engaging in social and political life.[12] His preferred approach to the dual task of raising living standards and liberating women lay (in accordance with the declared 'return to Leninist norms') in the expansion of communal services and public institutions such as mass housing, schools, healthcare, and public dining facilities. These were promoted under the seven-year economic plan adopted in 1959.[13] The need for service establishments would be fully met within years, promised the new Party Programme, and free public dining would be provided at workplaces by the 1970s.[14] [...]

But the intensive housing campaign of the late 1950s was based not on the model of the communal houses and social condensers of the 1920s, intended radically to restructure everyday life, but on small-scale apartments designed for a single nuclear family.[15] Far from rendering the kitchen obsolete, they provided families with their own dedicated kitchen space, often for the first time in their lives. As an astute Western commentator Alexander Werth, noted in 1962, 'All this business about "communal feeding" and "boarding schools for children" seemed in contradiction with the present tendency to cultivate the family, to give individual flats to every family'.[16] [...]

Women's labour in the home seemed particularly resistant to reform because it consisted of traditional practices passed down the generations from mother to daughter and unconsciously perpetuated. By the postwar period, however, the continual social and demographic upheavals of the twentieth century – urbanization and industrialization, revolutions and war – had done much to loosen the hold of traditional patterns of domesticity.[17] Khrushchev's intensive housing drive accelerated the process of urbanization so that some had to adapt to apartment living.

Furthermore, the explicit commitment to providing one-family flats 'even for newly-weds' meant that many, for the first time, set up house on their own, instead of slotting into an established household run by mother or mother-in-law, or working alongside other women in a communal kitchen.[18] These developments created opportunities for specialists and professionals to step in with advice and reshape this tradition-bound domain. The period saw a flood of household advice addressed

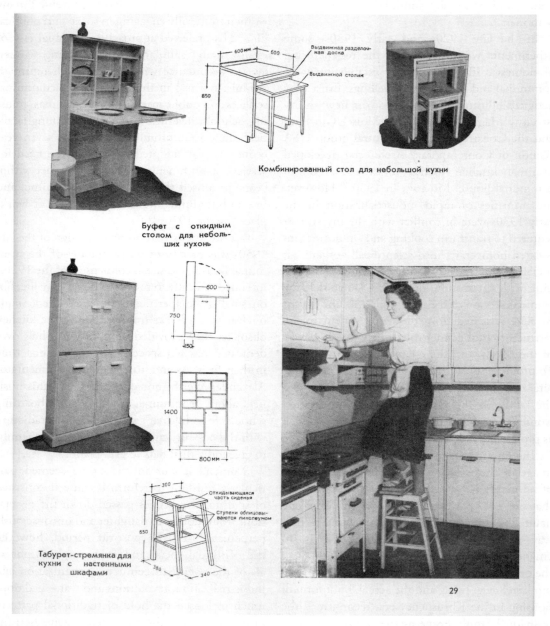

Figure 18. Space-saving kitchen units. Reprinted from O. Baiar and R. Blashkevich, *Kvartira i ee ubranstvo* (Moscow, 1962), p. 29, in Susan E. Reid, 'The Khrushchev Kitchen: Domesticating the Scientific-Technological Revolution', *Journal of Contemporary History* 40(2) (2005), pp. 289–316, p. 307.

to the khoziaika (housewife), which attempted to inculcate modernized household management practice in a generation of women struggling under their 'double burden'. [...]

In the ideal world of planners and advice-givers, the rational plan of the kitchen, designed to facilitate woman's labour, became a regulator of her movement within it and directed and disciplined her body. [...] Compactness was the key to efficiency. It was also hard to avoid in the 'economical' kitchen of the new, one-family apartments, measuring between 4.5 and 6 square metres. In the interest of both 'labour saving' and 'space saving', free-standing equipment was to be replaced by compact blocks of units along the wall, with suspended cabinets above.[19] Wall-mounted cupboards had the added advantages that they did not take up precious floor space, and that they saved the housewife from having to bend down to reach dishes or ingredients.[20] A rack for drying dishes hung over the sink saved time in one of the most wearing domestic tasks – dishwashing.[21] At the same time, the compact arrangement of equipment also saved on plumbing and wiring.[22] Thus, labour saving, space saving and economy of connecting to utilities were identified. The small dimensions of the kitchen, imposed by require-ments of economy and as a pledge to its future elimination, became a virtue, the source of its efficiency. [...]

Compactness, it should be noted, was also the founding principle of rational kitchens developed for social housing in many parts of Europe in the 1920s and again in the postwar period. The synergy of 'labour saving' and 'space saving' underpinned what is widely regarded as the historical proto-type of the modern fitted kitchen, the small-scale 'Frankfurt Kitchen', designed in 1926 by Austrian communist architect Grete Schütte-Lihotzky for Ernst May's public housing programme in Frankfurt-am-Main. Schütte-Lihotzky conceived the kitchen as a quasi-industrial site of food production, looking to the most up-to-date trans-portation of the day, the tiny kitchen galley on express trains, for a model of modern efficiency.

'The amount of work that is done in restaurant-car kitchens only gets done because the kitchen is so small', she observed. 'Time-wasting walks are impossible.'[23] [...]

The roots of the efficiency ideology at work in the Soviet discourse of the Khrushchev kitchen can be traced ultimately to American capitalism, whether directly or mediated through earlier and recent European assimilations, including Rus-sian ones. Soviet design and advice literature of the late 1950s–60s has clear echoes of Christine Frederick's 'scientific management' which applied to 'household engineering' Taylorist management principles appropriated from industry. In the 1920s and 1930s Frederick's book *Household Engineering: Scientific Management in the Home* (1915) was translated into a number of European languages and interpreted through European household efficiency ideologues such as Paulette Bernège and Erna Meyer.[24] It was highly influen-tial on the conception of 'labour-saving' kitchens in Europe (including the Baltic States) as well as America in the 1920s.[25] The ideology of labour efficiency and of industrial-style rationalization in the home also entered Russian and Soviet discourse and design practice at that time, as part of the campaign for the new way of life. It was one aspect of broader enthusiasm for Taylorism and Fordism, which was shared by Lenin and capitalists alike, seeming to transcend differences of political ideology.[26]

The Khrushchev kitchen was founded, then, on common principles of modern industrial plan-ning such as also underpinned the development of the American fitted kitchen, promoted at the American National Exhibition in 1959 as the em-bodiment of the American dream. This conver-gence belies assertions that 'ideological irreconcil-ability' with the capitalist camp would continue in spite of peaceful co-existence and economic competition. Indeed, American models were closely studied by Soviet designers and planners. Nevertheless, the American dream kitchen was far from compact and had too many appliances to be affordable on a mass scale in Soviet conditions.

Moreover, it was ideologically inappropriate, designed not for the working woman, but to frame the middle-class 'professional housewife'. It was her surrogate domain to compensate for her lack of a place in the public arena.[27] Contradicting the officially-espoused commitment to equality and emancipation of women, this opened an angle from which to dismiss the unaffordable model as one with which the Soviet Union would not even try to 'catch up and overtake'. As a construction engineer wrote in the comments book at the American exhibition in Moscow, referring to the fully-automated Whirlpool 'Miracle Kitchen' shown there: 'In the "miracle kitchen" a woman is just as free as a bird in a miracle cage. The "miracle kitchen" shown at the exhibition demonstrates America's last word in the field of perfecting obsolete forms of everyday living which stultify women.'[28]

While the American housewife was represented in the thrall of her many possessions, the most radical advocates of the scientific kitchen in the Soviet Union claimed its austere, standard form as a liberation. One such, G. Liubimova (in an article that makes a rare and telling reference to Schütte-Lihotzky as well as to the Russian Constructivists), justified proposals to equip new flats with standard, fully-fitted kitchens in spite of the added cost to the state, because 'a rationally-organized interior enables a certain … "automation" of domestic processes … the person is not distracted and gets less exhausted'. Furthermore, 'in an apartment equipped according to scientifically worked-out norms, when using the objects a person does not fix attention on them, does not fetishize things, and this has an educational significance'.[29] Standardization of utilitarian routines and domestic fittings would thus have the added advantage of combating the regressive influence of the nuclear household and of the increased availability of consumer goods.[30] This concern to forestall fetishism marks a key difference in principle between the ideal Khrushchev kitchen and its better-known American counterpart. […]

The story remains to be told of how Soviet people in practice arranged and used their kitchens, obeyed, negotiated or ignored the norms that were so insistently promulgated. Numerous obstacles lay in the path of even the most zealous convert. The Scientific-Technological Revolution failed to march triumphant into people's homes, not – or not necessarily – because people resisted it, but because of Soviet economic realities. […] Fully-fitted kitchens were rarely installed in the new flats built under Khrushchev; for reasons of economy and speed, only minimal equipment was provided. The Khrushchev kitchen was not a factory-made unit in the way that the Frankfurt kitchen was, but required a large element of reciprocal effort from its occupants, depending on their readiness to follow the ubiquitous advice, and on their resourcefulness and skills to find, build and install the equipment themselves. Acknowledging the failings of the system, domestic advice often reflected this situation, being of a directly practical nature: to help the occupant construct or adapt cabinets, and install the recommended devices themselves.[31]

The compact and standardized kitchen, equipped with electric devices and hygienic surfaces, should be understood as one of the key symbols of Khrushchevism and a demonstration of the will to extend the Scientific-Technological Revolution into the 'private' domain of domestic everyday life. Its failure to materialize, however, marked the limits of the Soviet order's ability to impose its version of modern living on its citizens.

NOTES

Extracted from Reid, S. E., 'The Khrushchev Kitchen: Domesticating the Scientific-Technological Revolution', *Journal of Contemporary History*, 40(2) (2005), pp. 289–316. Copyright © 2005 by Sage Publications. Reprinted by permission of SAGE.

1. Khrushchev publicly admitted embarrassment that Western perceptions of Soviet life were

dominated by the image of downtrodden women engaged in manual labour, and that visitors took home the impression of a backward and uncivilized country. 'Rech' tovarishcha N.S. Khrushcheva', *Pravda*, 15 March 1958.

2. See Elaine Tyler May, *Homeward Bound: American Families in the Cold War Era* (New York 1988); Cynthia Lee Henthorn, 'The Emblematic Kitchen. Labor-Saving Technology as National Propaganda, the United States, 1939–1959', *Knowledge and Society*, 12 (2000), 153–87; idem, 'Commercial Fallout: The Image of Progress and the Feminine Consumer from World War II to the Atomic Age, 1942–1962' in A. Scott and C. Geist (eds), *The Writing on the Cloud: American Culture Confronts the Atomic Bomb* (Lanham, MD 1997), 24–44.

3. W. Tompson, *Khrushchev, A Political Life* (Basingstoke 1995), 266; W. Turpin, 'Outlook for the Soviet Consumer', *Problems of Communism*, 9, 6 (1960), 36; and J.K. Gilison, *The Soviet Image of Utopia* (Baltimore, MD 1975), 7.

4. See S. Reid, 'Cold War in the Kitchen. Gender and the De-Stalinization of Consumer Taste in the Soviet Union under Khrushchev', *Slavic Review*, 61, 2 (2002), 212–52.

5. N. Sokolova, 'Masterstvo populiarizatsii', *Literaturnaia gazeta*, 24 January 1957.

6. Grey Hodnett (ed.), *Resolutions and Decisions of the Communist Party of the Soviet Union*, vol. 4, *The Khrushchev Years 1953–1964* (Toronto 1974), 252.

7. V.I. Lenin, 'Velikii pochin. (O geroizme rabochikh v tylu)', *Polnoe sobranie sochinenii*, 5th edn (Moscow 1970), vol. 39, 24 (emphasis in the original).

8. Such ideas are surveyed by Dolores Hayden, *The Grand Domestic Revolution. A History of Feminist Designs for American Homes, Neighborhoods and Cities* (Cambridge, MA 1981).

9. Lenin, 'Velikii pochin', op. cit., 23–4.

10. See Stephen Kotkin, *Magnetic Mountain. Stalinism as a Civilization* (Berkeley, CA 1995), 109–20; Victor Buchli, *An Archaeology of Socialism* (Oxford 1999).

11. Gail Warshofsky Lapidus, *Women in Soviet Society. Equality, Development, and Social Change* (Berkeley, CA 1979); Robert Thurston, 'The Soviet Family during the Great Terror, 1935–1941', *Soviet Studies*, 43, 3 (1991), 553–74; M. Ilič (ed.), *Women in the Stalin Era* (Basingstoke 2001).

12. Robert A. Feldmesser in discussion with Mark G. Field, 'Workers (and Mothers). Soviet Women Today' in D. Brown, (ed.), *The Role and Status of Women in the Soviet Union* (New York, 1968), 8.

13. CPSU Central Committee and Council of Ministers Resolution, 'O merakh po uluchsheniiu bytovogo obsluzhivaniia naseleniia', *Sobranie postanovlenii pravitel'stva SSSR* (Moscow 1959), article 30, 86–91; Tompson, *Khrushchev*, op. cit., 200–1.

14. Hodnett, *Resolutions*, op. cit., 232.

15. On the problems of houses with services, see I. Zhuchok and E. Zuikova, 'Dom s privilegiami', *Literaturnaia gazeta*, 8 January 1969; on their incompatibility with contemporary social trends, see D. Platonov, 'Sovremennye tendentsii i puti razvitiia perspektivnykh tipov zhilikh zdanii' in A. G. Kharchev et al. (eds), *Sotsial'nye problem zhilishcha*, (Leningrad 1967) 23, 167.

16. Alexander Werth, *Russia Under Khrushchev* (New York 1962; reprint Westport, CT 1975), 125.

17. See Catriona Kelly, *Refining Russia* (Oxford 2001), 320; David Hoffmann, *Peasant Metropolis. Social Identities in Moscow 1929–1941* (Ithaca, NY 1994).

18. S. Pogodinskii, 'Vertolet na kukhne', *Sem'ia i shkola*, no. 3 (1962), 26–7; I. Abramenko and L. Tormozova (eds), *Besedy o domashnem khoziaistve* (Moscow 1959) 4. In recent interviews conducted by Iuliia Gradskova, women of this generation recalled that as young women they knew nothing, for example, about pregnancy or infant care. They had learned nothing from their mothers, while the traditional profession of midwife, outside the

formal medical system, had disappeared. Iuliia Gradskova, personal communication, August 2003. Similarly, in early twentieth-century America, the increasing isolation of women in the home was one factor that rendered them particularly susceptible to 'expert' advice. Susan Strasser, *Never Done. A History of American Housework* (New York 1982), 237.

19. R. Blashkevich, 'Novaia mebel' dlia kukhni', *DI SSSR*, no. 8 (1962), 25–7; N. Svetlova, 'Tvoi dom', *Ogonek*, no. 3 (11 January 1959) 16; A. Cherepakhina, 'Vasha domashniaia masterskaia', *Rabonitsa*, no. 10 (1959), 32.

20. I. Luchkova and A. Sikachev, 'Sushchestvuet li nauka o zhil'e?', *Nauka i zhizn*', no. 10 (1964), 25; Svetlova, 'Tvoi dom', op. cit., 16.

21. Cherepakhina, 'Vasha domashniaia masterskaia', op. cit., 32.

22. O. Baiar and R. Blashkevich, *Kvartira i ee ubranstvo* (Moscow 1962), 14.

23. Grete Schütte-Lihotzky, 1927, cited by Karin Kirsch, *The Weissenhofsiedlung* (New York 1989), 26; Peter Noever (ed.), *Die Frankfurter Küche von Margarete Schütte-Lihotzky* (Vienna 1999); Susan R. Henderson, 'A Revolution in the Woman's Sphere. Grete Lihotzky and the Frankfurt Kitchen' in D. Coleman, E . Danze and C. Henderson (eds), *Architecture and Feminism* (Princeton, NJ 1996), 221–53.

24. Cieraad, '"Out of My Kitchen!" Architecture, Gender and Domestic Efficiency', *The Journal of Architecture*, 7 (Autumn 2002), 264.

25. Ibid.; Mary Nolan, *Visions of Modernity. American Business and the Modernization of Germany* (Oxford 1994), chap. 6. A British publication which seems to be the source of a number of the Khrushchev-era prescriptions cited above (and even of their precise formulation), acknowledged America as the source of 'many of the good ideas in the modern kitchen'. George Mansell, 'Kitchen Commentary', *Daily Mail Ideal Home Book, 1957* (London 1957), 131–5.

26. Charles S. Maier, 'Between Taylorism and Technocracy. European Ideologies and the Vision of Industrial Productivity in the 1920s', *Journal of Contemporary History*, 5, 2

(April 1970), 27–63; James C. Scott, *Seeing Like a State. How Certain Schemes to Improve the Human Condition Have Failed* (New Haven, CT 1998), 99; Rainer Traub, trans. Judy Joseph, 'Lenin and Taylor. The Fate of "Scientific Management" in the (Early) Soviet Union', *Telos*, 34 (Fall 1978), 82–92; Nolan, *Visions*, op. cit.

27. Marietta Shaginian, 'Razmyshleniia na amerikanskoi vystavke', *Izvestiia*, 23 August 1959. Christine Frederick's spacious kitchen schemes were not determined by shortage and economies of space but only of labour. See Tag Gronberg, 'Siting the Modern', review article, *Journal of Contemporary History*, 36, 4 (October 2001), 685, n. 10; Ruth Oldenziel, 'The "Idea" of America and the Making of "Europe" in the Twentieth Century', discussion paper, European Science Foundation Workshop, Stockholm, April 2002.

28. S. Iatsenko, construction engineer, 19 August 1959. National Archives, Washington DC (NARA), RG 306 1043, box 11 (viewers' comments on American National Exhibition, Moscow 1959). Translation modified.

29. G. Liubimova, 'Ratsional'noe oborudovanie kvartir', DI SSSR, no. 6 (1964), 15. Note that this is published 'for discussion' and is more radical than most. It takes the Marxist, neo-Productivist line that would be institutionalized in the All-Union Research Institute of Technical Aesthetics, VNIITE, of which the author became a member after it was founded in 1962.

30. The author saw off possible objections that it would prevent the manifestation of individuality, protesting that this would find full expression in the aesthetics of the interior decoration. Liubimova, 'Ratsional'noe oborudovanie kvartir', op. cit., 16.

31. E.g. Irina Voeikova, 'Vasha kvartira', *Rabotnitsa*, no. 9 (1962), 30. Some specialists (notably the more radical neo-Constructivist ones around VNIITE) regretted that so much was left to the tenant and pressed for a more thoroughgoing standardization of the government-issue domestic interior.

23

ALL THAT GLITTERS IS NOT STAINLESS

Reyner Banham (1966)

Two of the most important resources of modern design are about a hundred and twenty years old now; one is the plastics industry, the other is the tradition of worry about the state of the art. As far as plastics are concerned, celluloid molding dates from the work of my countryman, Alexander Parkes, in the middle 1850s, and the vulcanizing of rubber dates from the work of the brilliant American, Charles Goodyear, a decade earlier.

In the divided culture in which we live and work, we have to remind ourselves who founded plastics, but I don't have to remind you that design worry was founded by old John Ruskin and young William Morris, not to mention stylish Gottfried Semper in Germany and functional Horatio Greenough in the United States, in those same middle years of the last century. Yet, if you cast eyes on the visible scene or lay hands on the tangible environment, you will know that the effect of the plastics industry has been vast and all-pervasive.

But what has the tradition of worry about the state of the art done for design that can be compared to the avalanche of new materials and products that the plastics industry has emptied over the face of the earth?

One thing it has done is to worry about new materials like plastics, new materials that drive out old familiar ones because their performance can be more accurately specified than any ancient craftsman could select wood. Such materials can be more accurately specified by the designer, but remain totally inscrutable to the ultimate consumer.

So, John Q. Public, the well-known car buff, looks at the badge on the front of the 1967 GT Supremo Saddlestitched Hodad Fastback and can't tell by looking whether it is an exquisite specimen of the goldsmith's art sealed under crystal glass or just crafty vapor gilding on the back of one-shot styrene molding – though he has his suspicions! Or another instance: The red minicar in which the Banham family used to thread its way deftly through the wild, swinging, miniskirted London scene was protected all around its lower perimeter by a strip of what was implied to be stainless steel but proved to be metal foil sealed under clear plastic. It glittered like stainless, but it wasn't. What is more, it did a better job than stainless could have done by not introducing certain risks of snagging, tearing and spearing that make steel dangerous in an accident. Yet the classic tradition of design worry would insist on genuine stainless and denounce the plastic trim as a cheap substitute or a trick. To satisfy the conscience of design (a monster on which I shall have much more to say), we have to be impaled by genuine stainless steel.

Fortunately, design worry offers other precepts to guide us: For instance, the plastic trim would be OK if it didn't pretend to be something it isn't. But that would deprive us of some things we all clearly love: Glitter, high finish, and shine. These are visual qualities that plastics have democratized, so that the average parking lot or appliance showroom bounces back the light in a way previous ages probably saw only on the serf-polished armor at aristocratic jousts and tourneys.

And this love of glitter is not just a vulgar dream of the silly and underprivileged. The greatest generation of design theorists, who flourished from 1910 to 1930, all loved glitter and taught us to love it too. Frank Lloyd Wright rejoiced in the lights of Chicago by night; Marinetti saw the new age reflected in the light bouncing back from control-consoles and electrical plants; Gropius called for buildings like crystal symbols, and Mies van der Rohe built them; Fernand Leger was struck by the magic of light on metal on a field gun; Le Corbusier and Marcel Breuer put that magic into production on furniture; Sir Herbert Read invited us to admire instruments and vessels of stainless steel.

Industrial design rides upon the back of an industrial complex that exists primarily to satisfy such desires of man as universal glitter. But why does the heart of man desire it? Why did the great masters of modern design teach us to echo, in life, Goethe's dying demand, "Mehr Licht"? What is the source of this modern desire that plastics above all can supply?

Philosophers, semanticists, psychologists, historians (and *there's* a bundle of resources every progressive design office and school increasingly employ) can all shed some light on this. The hypnotic effect of glitter and brightness caught up even Saint Thomas Aquinas, perhaps because "shining" is a word that rings with virtue throughout Holy Writ; the face of Moses shone, and the house of a latterday patriarch was called "Taliesin" – Shining Brow. That old magic still works today for copywriters pushing toothpaste and for poets pushing the millennium, asking the Almighty to "look shining at new styles of architecture, a change of heart!" And that stunning phrase from W. H. Auden sums up exactly what modern design has done for the ancient magic of glitter. The great source of our preoccupation with the shininess of modern design is that it symbolizes the fresh start, the clean new way of life that was, and is, to replace the miseries of those dark satanic mills in which industry and its arts of design were born.

The generation of great gray eminences who presided over the birth of modern design as a responsible profession grew up in the grubby, coarse-textured world of late-Victorian industry. They saw that industry's main product – soot – irremediably caking the unpolished and unwashable surfaces of its main structural materials, brick and cast iron, and they complained, in the words of a great visionary of light, Paul Scheerbart: "Backstein-Kultur tut uns nur Leid (brick brings us only hurt)." No wonder that Adolf Loos wanted the walls of the heavenly city to be flush and smooth from top to bottom and that his generation saw the task of design in Augean terms; a total, global cleanup. And not just a physical cleanup. In the writings of Le Corbusier, for instance, words like "health" and "morality" frequently turn up in adjacent phrases of the same sentence as twin attributes of modern design. One of the great intellectual resources of our times, the concept of moral improvement through design, is also one of its most powerful sources of intellectual confusion. I suppose it goes back to that lovable Victorian nut, A. W. N. Pugin, and his implied proposition that the revival of truly Christian, or pointed architecture would bring back the Age of Faith he supposed to have been in full swing when pointed, or Gothic, architecture appeared for the first time round.

Ever since, the design theorists and worriers over the state of the art have insisted that style betrays the moral intention of the designers: Art Nouveau equals decadence; Expressionism equals selfishness; white walls and flat roof equal care for functional performance; redwood and roof overhangs equal care for human values; glass boxes equal inhuman disregard for people; chromium brightwork equals commercial swindle; and so forth.

Not one of these propositions is demonstrably true, yet each has been (and many still are) passionately believed in or persists as unrevised prejudice. Yet we know that many flat-roofed and white-walled modern buildings were indifferently designed for functional performance.

Or again, when General Motors came up with the neat, sweet, almost chrome-free body shell of the first Corvair, moralizing design critics congratulated Detroit on mending its wicked ways. Yet this is the model that Ralph Nader and all the litigants assert is a deathtrap sold by General Motors with full knowledge of its instability. It seems that the glitter of a morally sound style does not guarantee a stainless reputation to the product in use.

Yet the moral reassurance seems to be remarkably necessary in all branches of design, and professional designers go to camp meetings in the mountains to be told what's right and what's wrong. No other profession, not even those bound by massive oaths of probity like the Hippocratic oath of the medicals, has this rage to keep itself morally pure by public self-examination. A man sitting next to me at a particularly bitter session of an architectural conference in England some time ago said incredulously, "Do dentists have meetings like this?"

This moral preoccupation is one of the principal driving forces of modern design and could be a great guarantee to the general public were it not so self-regarding. That line of W. H. Auden I quoted earlier reminded me of something contemporary from Louis MacNeice:

Our freedom as free-lances
Advances towards its end;
The earth compels, upon it
Sonnets and Birds descend;
And soon, my friend,
We shall have no time for dances.

The concept of the freedom of free-lances coming to an end is sure to strike a familiar note, if only because it has been said so often at places like Aspen. Year after year, men have stood at the microphone and preached hellfire, the population explosion, and the sands of time running out. We love it, gladly agree that our time for dancing has come to an end, and resolve to go out and do better by taking the situation more seriously.

Better? What's so good about a world where the designers have salved their consciences by taking everything so seriously that poetry falls flat, the birds are all grounded, and nobody dances. One of humanity's main motives for surviving the bomb, the baby boom, and the final solidification of the freeway system into a coast-to-coast parking lot will be to get the birds and the poets back into orbit, revive the watusi and the pavane, and clip on the optional equipment generally. Humanity is not going to survive just so designers can work up a high polish on their consciences, nor will it thank them for being less autarchic and more systematic in their thinking if the products don't get any better.

Any person in his right mind will know that conscience divorced from function helps nobody, yet the design profession at large is chronically prone to elevate the demands of private conscience. Why? The answer again lies in the source from which modern design has sprung: the concept of the designer as some kind of artist. On the one hand, this idea descends from the traditional view of the architect as one who imposes cultural values on the mere construction of buildings; on the other hand, from the William Morris fiction of the designer-craftsman as an artist in the sense in which the nineteenth century understood the artist, that is, as a free spirit answerable only to himself. If the public didn't understand the artist's work, so much the worse for the public, especially as they still owed him a living.

Morris himself took a more socially responsible view than this, but my reading of many of his professed followers is that they believed the only good product was one that brought pleasure to its producer. You will hear this proposition usually in the guarded and inverted form that mass production is evil because it brings no pleasure to the worker, but which ever way you phrase it, the whole conception is antisocial and perverse. No more in design than in dentistry can society accept that the first responsibility of its servants is to please themselves. And so to the big crossup: The public conscience of the design profession tells it that it cannot give absolute allegiance to the promptings of its private conscience. The designer as a social being confronts the designer as a creative individual in an unresolvable dilemma, and he is glad to have any hellfire demographer or revivalist cybernetician come and hand him a ready-made answer to this problem or any of the others.

For the conscience problem is no more than typical, in its inner contradictions, of the situation that modern design has inherited from its historical sources. Whereas most of its physical resources have unequivocal value – new materials, new production methods, etc. – many of its psychological sources bear signs of the confusions and misdirections that have resulted from trying to keep up with the physical resources and failing.

Take the concept of the basic design course, the *Vorkurs*, or what have you. There is a great primary source if you like! As a concept, it has a noble simplicity to it; the student is to be returned to zero and made to begin again with the elementary materials and primary relationships of his craft. The sophisticated shall be brought low, the honest and humble shall be lifted up.

Yet all over the world the "Bauhaus system," as this kind of teaching is often called, is in disarray and contention. Most design educators seem not to know where else to start, even while admitting that the system doesn't work. What has gone wrong? Firstly, and obviously, it never was a system, it was a body of teaching methods under constant revision from 1919 to 1933 by a body of remarkable men. And it was the men who mattered – the system never went wrong while it was administered by men who had been through the Bauhaus mill. It never went wrong on Joseph Albers, for instance.

But the other thing to note is that these old *Bauhausler* kept the methods under revision. There is startlingly little resemblance between what Moholy-Nagy was doing in his last years at the Institute of Design in Chicago and what he and Albers had been doing in Weimar in 1923. And I suspect the driving motivation to change

everything was that one of the chief justifications of the original Weimar course invented by Hannes Itten had disappeared – it was no longer necessary to disabuse students of ingrained visual prejudices, and it is even less necessary today.

A lot of things have happened to people since the Bauhaus was young, things like junk sculpture, hand-held movies, Batman, action painting, Hell's Angels, surrealism, custom-car shows, Op art, Henry Moore, Cinerama, and so on. As a result, people have become sophisticated – remarkably so – and far less visually prejudiced. Beady little eyes that can tell stainless from spray chrome at fifty paces and prefer the latter because it is more jokey clearly need a very different type of education from what suited the mystical peasants who crawled out of the Biedermier woodwork to join Gropius at Weimar.

Something else that has happened to people since the Bauhaus is, of course, the Bauhaus – and industrial design generally. It has not gone unnoticed, either; the public has picked up some famous names and even a few fairly far-out tastes. A top New York design pundit told me how he observed suburban housewives admiring some Barcelona chairs in Macy's. His comment: "God, it was horrible!"

My own comment on that comment would be: "When they stop throwing rocks at your head and throw a lifebelt instead, have the decency to say 'thank you' as you drown." But plenty of other design people would have responded in the same way. After a hundred years or more of regarding the bad taste of the public as one of design's major problems, it can be difficult to adjust to the idea that they may now be on your side and may have stopped throwing rocks.

Furthermore, a lot of design people seem not to want to adjust. The belief that design is a thankless task definitely appeals to the martyr complex that design has inherited from the artistic forebears. And furthermore yet, being out of step was a guarantee to their consciences that they were in the right, for design is also part of the great progressive do-gooder complex of ideas based upon the proposition that the majority is always wrong, that the public must be led, cajoled, sticked, and garroted onward and upward.

This evil backside on the face of public concern is one of the nastier aspects of worrying about the state of the art. It leaves behind some unpleasant questions, such as: Is the shine on the brow of the designer as he hands out the tablets of his lore the true stainless glitter of Messianic inspiration, or is it just the spray chrome of self-righteousness? Too many of the great unquestioned assumptions on which modern design is based have begun to peel and flake of late; neither they nor their advocates appear to be quite such stainless representatives of the shining new world as once we thought. It is high time we checked to see which ones have rusted through and must be junked, which need to go back in the plating tank, and which only need a wipe over with the silvercloth.

NOTE

Reproduced from Banham, R., 'All that Glitters Is not Stainless', in R. Banham (ed.) *The Aspen Papers: Twenty Years of Design Theory from the International Design Conference in Aspen*, London: Pall Mall Press, 1974, pp. 155–60. Copyright 1974 by the Pall Mall Press. Reprinted by kind permission of Mrs. Mary Banham and the Shelley Power Literary Agency and by arrangement with Henry Holt and Company, LLC.

GUIDE TO FURTHER READING

On the development of British modernism prior to the Utility scheme, see Paul Greenhalgh's 1995 essay 'The English Compromise: Modern Design and National Consciousness, 1870–1940'. In addition to Utility, the British response to the Second World War was also notable in design terms for a particularly effective body of print propaganda; see *Abram Games, Graphic Designer: Maximum Meaning, Minimum Means* (2003). On exhibiting post-war British design, see Lucy Bullivant's '"Design for Better Living" Public Response to Britain Can Make It', in *Did Britain Make It? British Design in Context 1946–86* (1986); also *Design and Cultural Politics in Postwar Britain: the Britain Can Make It Exhibition of 1946* (1997). On the Festival of Britain, see Adrian Forty, 'Festival Politics' in *A Tonic to the Nation: The Festival of Britain 1951* (1976) and on the Festival Pattern Group, 'New Imagery', in Leslie Jackson, *The New Look: Design in the Fifties*, (1998). A characterization of the period is provided in Bevis Hillier, *Austerity/Binge: the Decorative Arts of the Forties and Fifties* (1975). Case studies of post-war British design and culture include: Frank Jackson, 'The New Air Age: BOAC and Design Policy 1945–60', (1991); Andrew Jackson, 'Labour as Leisure: The Mirror Dinghy and DIY Sailors', (2006) and John Hewitt, 'Good Design in the Market Place: The Rise of Habitat Man' (1987).

For more by the Independent Group, see Banham's 'A Throw-Away Aesthetic' and Richard Hamilton's article 'The Persuasive Image', both from 1960. Reflective analyses include Anne Massey's 'The Independent Group as Design Theorists', (1985) and 'The Independent Group: Towards a Redefinition' (1987) and her book *The Independent Group: Modernism and Mass Culture, 1945–59* (1995). Also, Nigel Whiteley's 'Pop, Consumerism, and the Design Shift' (1985) and 'Toward a Throw-Away Culture: Consumerism, "Style Obsolescence" and Cultural Theory in the 1950s and 1960s' (1987) and Ben Highmore's complex analysis 'Richard Hamilton at the *Ideal Home Exhibition* of 1958: Gallery for a Collector of Brutalist and Taschist Art' (2007).

As a comparative example of the politicization of design in national context see the studies of Germany by Eli Rubin, *Synthetic Socialism: Plastics and Dictatorship in the German Democratic Republic* (2008), and Paul Betts, *The Authority of Everyday Objects: A Cultural History of West German Industrial Design* (2004). By the same author, see 'The Politics of Post-Fascist Aesthetics: West and East German Design in the 1950s' (2003) and 'Building Socialism at Home: The Case of East German Interiors' (2008).

Banham's discussion of plastics may be further explored from a wide range of approaches, including Wiebe E. Bijker's 'The Social Construction of Bakelite: Toward a Theory of Invention' (1987); Penny Sparke's 'Plastics and Pop Culture' and Ezio Manzini's 'Objects and Their Skin', in *The Plastics Age: From Modernity to Post-Modernity* (1990). Jeffrey L. Meikle reviews sceptical opinions in 'Material Doubts and Plastic Fallout', from his book *American Plastics: A Cultural History* (1995), which is extracted in this *Reader*, as is Alison J. Clarke's *Tupperware: The Promise of Plastic in 1950s America* (1999). Also on Tupperware in social context, see Anath De Vidas's 'Containing Modernity: The Social Life of Tupperware in a Mexican Indigenous Village' (2008).

A contemporary account of the Khrushchev Kitchen is given in Harrison E. Salisbury, 'Nixon and Khrushchev Argue in Public as US Exhibit Opens; Accuse Each Other of Threats' (1959). Wider reading on Cold War design includes David Crowley and Jane Pavitt's *Cold War Modern* (2008). Also helpful are Sarah A. Lichtman's 'Do-It-Yourself Security: Safety, Gender, and the Home Fallout Shelter in Cold War America' (2006); Eli Rubin's 'The Form of Socialism without Ornament: Consumption, Ideology, and the Fall and Rise of Modernist Design in the German Democratic Republic'; and Milena Veenis's 'Consumption in East Germany: the Seduction and Betrayal of Things' (1999). East Germany receives further consideration in Raymond G. Stokes's 'Plastics and the New Society: the German Democratic Republic in the 1950s and 1960s', in *Style and Socialism: Modernity and Material Culture in PostWar Eastern Europe* (2000).

SECTION 5

Postmodernisms, 1967–2006

INTRODUCTION

Rebecca Houze

Following the significant social and political changes of the Cold War period, which included struggles for civil rights, protests in both Europe and the United States against the war in Vietnam, and independence movements in the former European colonies of Asia, Africa and Latin America, many thinkers, artists and writers sought to describe a new cultural and psychological state of being – a condition of 'postmodernity', confusing and unstable, in which our sense of self had become fragmented. Fredric Jameson described the 1970s and 1980s as a simultaneously seductive and alienating period of late capitalism in which global commerce enabled the fluid distribution of an enormous range of manufactured objects. For Jean Baudrillard, these objects are 'simulacra', or multiple copies for which there is no original. But we can't view postmodernism simply as a break from modernism; rather, as its name implies, it is in some senses a continuation. In *All that Is Solid Melts into Air: The Experience of Modernity* (1982), Marshall Berman described the instability of the contemporary world as a feeling that was also expressed in the work of some artists and thinkers of the late nineteenth and early twentieth centuries.

The five texts in this section reflect ways in which designers, critics and historians, beginning in the late 1960s, started to reinterpret design aesthetically, socially and philosophically. Many, influenced by French post-structuralist literary theory, sought to reveal the political and economic forces behind design, while others gained a greater appreciation for the consumer's role in the design process, shaping an object's meaning in unforeseen ways. We begin with 'A Significance for A&P Parking Lots or Learning from Las Vegas', by architects Robert Venturi, Denise Scott Brown and Steven Izenour, first published in 1967. The Las Vegas strip of the 1960s was a vast decorated landscape oriented to a popular culture of consumption. Disconnected from the buildings themselves, oversized signs along the highway advertised hotels, gas stations and casinos with sculptural forms and neon lights that seemed both magical and banal. Was this the world of tomorrow that had been promised at the 1939 World's Fair? For Venturi, Scott Brown and Izenour, the vivid asphalt world of Las Vegas, so different from the spare and colourless modernist utopias of the early twentieth century, was a spiritualized realm of the everyday whose forms, they believed, should be celebrated. This attitude had been shared as well by Reyner Banham and the Independent Group, whose work in the previous decade oriented architectural discourse towards design history. Baudrillard, by contrast, found the excessive signage and visual stimuli of the late twentieth century to be oppressive and obscene, even 'pornographic', as he describes our experience of new media – especially film, television, and the emerging digital technologies – in his essay 'The Ecstasy of Communication'. The contradictory views expressed in these two essays, joyful and embracing of the fruits of capitalism on the one hand, and skeptical, pessimistic, even paranoid, in the face of its processes on the other, represent the diverse attitudes that contributed to design historical readings of this period.

German design historian Gert Selle, in his essay 'There is No Kitsch, There is Only Design!', which was written on the occasion of the 1983 exhibition 'Genial Design of the '80s' at the IDZ (Internationales Design Zentrum) in Berlin, argues in the spirit of Venturi, Scott Brown and Izenour that, 'A democratization of design has occurred … A product culture – opulent, hedonistic, valid for all, and open to interpretation by all – has prevailed …' Echoing the 'Populuxe' aesthetic described by Thomas Hine in a text extracted in section 4 of this *Reader*, Selle emphasizes the sensuous nature of this product culture and the psychological meanings that objects take on as they are adopted by consumers. His valorization of material goods was especially relevant in a politically divided Berlin, where capitalism was upheld by some as the arbiter of freedom and individuality, while demonized by others for fostering excess and greed, and where Baudrillard's postmodern critique of the 'hyperreality' of mass culture was perhaps less resonant.

Whereas Selle embraced the anonymity of mass-produced goods, the Italian decorative household goods manufacturer Alessi attempted to circumvent the popular realm by insisting upon the primacy of well-known designers, such as Philippe Starck and Michael Graves. Peter A. Lloyd and Dirk Snelders question the idea of the 'omnipotent designer' in their lively and critical examination of Starck's own account of the origins of his 'Juicy Salif Lemon Squeezer', designed for Alessi in the late 1980s. In his 1968 essay 'Death of the Author', Roland Barthes argued that one ought not to bring the biography or supposed intentions of a work's maker into one's interpretation of it. Michel Foucault challenged Barthes's theory the following year in his 1969 essay 'What is an Author?' Building on the work of both Barthes and Foucault, as well as Adrian Forty's influential book *Objects of Desire: Design and Society Since 1750* (1986), Lloyd and Snelders demythologize Starck's exclusive role and attribute further credit to the object's users in determining the meaning of the lemon squeezer.

Ellen Lupton and J. Abbott Miller examine the evolution of graphic design practices in the 1980s and 1990s under the influence of deconstruction, a school of thought based on the ideas of French philosopher Jacques Derrida, who argued in his book *Of Grammatology* – first published in French in 1967, expanding on the theories of linguist Ferdinand de Saussure – that the meaning conveyed through language is culturally constructed, and that writing disrupts and activates meaning, inserting itself into its production. Many artists, architects, writers and designers, from Barbara Kruger and Victor Burgin to Katherine McCoy and Daniel Libeskind, often aided by the possibilities of digital technology, explored new ways of revealing the arbitrariness and discontinuity of language and conceptual frames of reference.

Postmodernism is a complex and heterogeneous cultural tendency rather than a period style and it emerged at different times in different geographical locations and within diverse media. Indeed, the very nature of postmodernist thought argued against homogeneity, unity or the completeness of the 'grand narrative', imposing instead a constant questioning, criticism and self-consciousness. While French literary critics such as Derrida, Barthes, Foucault and Baudrillard questioned the authority of myriad institutions from Western art and literature to prison systems, others, from Edward Said and Frantz Fanon to Gayatri Chakravorty Spivak and Homi K. Bhabha, applied this critical framework to problematize cultural identity in the postcolonial worlds of India, Africa and the Middle East. Fashion, a medium that has long traversed national boundaries in its globalized production and consumption, offers a particularly fruitful avenue for postcolonial design history. In 'Fabricating Identities: Survival and the Imagination in Jamaican Dancehall Culture', first published in *Fashion Theory* in 2006, Bibi Bakare-Yusuf examines the idiosyncratic costumes created and worn by young women in Jamaica's 'dancehall' culture, drawing from an array of scholarship on subculture, feminist theory and racial politics, and shows how sartorial expression can mobilize concepts of irony, history, parody and resistance. Like the sampling and recycling of 'ragga' music, Jamaican dancehall costumes are a bricolage of clashing and contradictory elements – ripped jeans, bondage tops and sparkling gold jewelry – revealing a bawdy and baroque love of excess and artificiality that references carnivalesque forms and traditions of African and Caribbean folk culture while also resisting hegemonic narratives of class, sex and race.

24

A SIGNIFICANCE FOR A&P PARKING LOTS, OR LEARNING FROM LAS VEGAS

Robert Venturi, Denise Scott Brown and Steven Izenour (1972)

Substance for a writer consists not merely of those realities he thinks he discovers; it consists even more of those realities which have been made available to him by the literature and idioms of his own day and by the images that still have vitality in the literature of the past. Stylistically, a writer can express his feelings about this substance either by imitation, if it sits well with him, or by parody, if it doesn't.[1]

Learning from the existing landscape is a way of being revolutionary for an architect. Not the obvious way, which is to tear down Paris and begin again, as Le Corbusier suggested in the 1920s, but another more tolerant way; that is, to question how we look at things.

The commercial strip, the Las Vegas Strip in particular – the example par excellence – challenges the architect to take a positive, non-chip-on-the-shoulder view. Architects are out of the habit of looking nonjudgmentally at the environment, because orthodox Modern architecture is progressive, if not revolutionary, utopian, and puristic; it is dissatisfied with *existing* conditions. Modern architecture has been anything but permissive: Architects have preferred to change the existing environment rather than enhance what is there.

But to gain insight from the commonplace is nothing new: Fine art often follows folk art. Romantic architects of the eighteenth century discovered an existing and conventional rustic architecture. Early Modern architects appropriated an existing and conventional industrial vocabulary without much adaptation. Le Corbusier loved grain elevators and steamships; the Bauhaus looked like a factory; Mies refined the details of American steel factories for concrete buildings. Modern architects work through analogy, symbol, and image – although they have gone to lengths to disclaim almost all determinants of their forms except structural necessity and the program – and they derive insights, analogies, and stimulation from unexpected images. There is a perversity in the learning process: We look backward at history and tradition to go forward; we can also look downward to go upward. And withholding judgment may be used as a tool to make later judgment more sensitive. This is a way of learning from everything.

[…]

VAST SPACES IN THE HISTORICAL TRADITION AND AT THE A&P

The A&P parking lot is a current phase in the evolution of vast space since Versailles. The space that divides high-speed highway and low, sparse buildings produces no enclosure and little

Figure 19. View of the Las Vegas strip, c.1970. Reprinted from Robert Venturi, Denise Scott Brown and Steven Izenour, *Learning From Las Vegas: The Forgotten Symbolism of Architectural Form*, revised edition, photograph on page 36. © 1977 Massachusetts Institute of Technology, by permission of The MIT Press.

direction. To move through a piazza is to move between high enclosing forms. To move through this landscape is to move over vast expansive texture: the megatexture of the commercial landscape. The parking lot is the *parterre* of the asphalt landscape. The patterns of parking lines give direction much as the paving patterns, curbs, borders and *tapis vert* give direction in Versailles; grids of lamp posts substitute for obelisks, rows of urns and statues as points of identity and continuity in the vast space. But it is the highway signs, through their sculptural forms or pictorial silhouettes, their particular positions in space, their inflected shapes, and their graphic meanings, that identify and unify the megatexture. They make verbal and symbolic connections through space, communicating a complexity of meanings through hundreds of associations in few sections from far away. Symbol dominates space. Architecture is not enough. Because the spatial relationships are made by symbols more than by forms, architecture in this landscape becomes symbol in space rather than form in space. Architecture defines very little: The big sign and the little building is the rule of Route 66.

The sign is more important than the architecture. This is reflected in the proprietor's budget. The sign at the front is a vulgar extravaganza, the building at the back, a modest necessity. The architecture is what is cheap. Sometimes the building is the sign: The duck store in the shape of a duck called "The Long Island Ducklings," sculptural symbol and architectural shelter. Contradiction between outside and inside was common in architecture before the Modern Movement, particularly in urban and monumental architecture. Baroque domes were symbols as well as spatial constructions, and they are bigger in scale and higher outside than inside in order to dominate their urban setting and communicate their symbolic message. The false fronts of Western stores did the same thing: They were bigger and taller than the interiors they fronted to communicate the store's importance and to enhance the quality and unity of the street. But false fronts are of the order and scale of Main Street. From the desert town on the highway in the West of today, we can learn new and vivid lessons about an impure architecture of communication. The little low buildings, gray-brown like the desert, separate and recede from the street that is now the highway, their false fronts disengaged and turned perpendicular to the highway as big, high signs. If you take the signs away, there is no place. The desert town is intensified communication along the highway.

[…]

LAS VEGAS SIGNS

Signs inflect toward the highway even more than buildings. The big sign – independent of the building and more or less sculptural or pictorial – inflects by its position, perpendicular to and at the edge of the highway, by its scale, and sometimes by its shape. The sign of the Aladdin Hotel and Casino seems to bow toward the highway through the inflection in its shape. It also is three dimensional, and parts of it revolve. The sign at the Dunes Hotel is more chaste: it is only two dimensional, and its back echoes its front, but it is an erection 22 stories high that pulsates at night. The sign for The Mint Hotel on Route 91 at Fremont Street inflects toward the Casino several blocks away. Signs in Las Vegas use mixed media – words, pictures, and sculpture – to persuade and inform. A sign is, contradictorily, for day and night. The same sign works as polychrome sculpture in the sun and as black silhouette against the sun; at night it is a source of light. It revolves by day and becomes a play of lights at night. It contains scales for close-up and for distance. Las Vegas has the longest sign in the world, the Thunderbird, and the highest, the Dunes. Some signs are hardly distinguishable at a distance from the occasional high-rise hotels along the Strip. The sign of the Pioneer Club on Fremont Street talks. Its cowboy, 60 feet high, says "Howdy Pardner" every 30 seconds. The big sign at the Aladdin Hotel has spawned a little sign with similar proportions to make the entrance to the parking. "But such signs!" says Tom Wolfe. "They soar in shapes before which the existing vocabulary of art history is helpless. I can only attempt to supply name – Boomerang Modern, Paletter Curvilinear, Flash Gordon Ming-Alert Spiral, McDonald's Hamburger Parabola, Mint Casino Elliptical, Miami Beach Kidney."[2] Buildings are also signs. At night on Fremont Street, whole buildings are illuminated but not through reflection from spotlights; they are made into sources of light by closely spaced neon tubes. Amid the diversity, the familiar Shell and Gulf signs stand out like friendly beacons in a foreign land. But in Las Vegas they reach three times higher into the air than at your local service station to meet the competition of the casinos.

[...]

NOTES

Extracted from Venturi, R., Scott Brown, D. and Izenour, S., *Learning from Las Vegas: The Forgotten Symbolism of Architectural Form*, Cambridge, MA: MIT Press (1972) 1977, pp. 3, 13, 18, 51, 52. Copyright 1977 Massachusetts Institute of Technology, by permission of The MIT Press.

1. Richard Poirier, "T.S. Eliot and the Literature of Waste," *The New Republic* (May 20, 1967), p. 21.
2. Tom Wolfe, *The Kandy-Colored Tangerine-Flake Streamline Baby* (New York: Noonday Press, 1966).

25

THE ECSTASY OF COMMUNICATION

Jean Baudrillard (1987)

[…] Advertising in its new version – which is no longer a more or less baroque, utopian or ecstatic scenario of objects and consumption, but the effect of an omnipresent visibility of enterprises, brands, social interlocuters and the social virtues of communication – advertising in its new dimension invades everything, as public space (the street, monument, market, scene) disappears. It realizes, or, if one prefers, it materializes in all its obscenity; it monopolizes public life in its exhibition. No longer limited to its traditional language, advertising organizes the architecture and realization of superobjects like Beaubourg and the Forum des Halles, and of future projects (e.g., Parc de la Villette) which are monuments (or anti-monuments) to advertising, not because they will be geared to consumption but because they are immediately proposed as an anticipated demonstration of the operation of culture, commodities, mass movement and social flux. It is our only architecture today: great screens on which are reflected atoms, particles, molecules in motion. Not a public scene or true public space but gigantic spaces of circulation, ventilation and ephemeral connections.

It is the same for private space. In a subtle way, this loss of public space occurs contemporaneously with the loss of private space. The one is no longer a spectacle, the other no longer a secret. Their distinctive opposition, the clear difference of an exterior and an interior exactly described the domestic *scene* of objects, with its rules of play and limits, and the sovereignty of a symbolic space which was also that of the subject. Now this opposition is effaced in a sort of obscenity where the most intimate processes of our life become the virtual feeding ground of the media (the Loud family in the United States, the innumerable slices of peasant or patriarchal life on French television). Inversely, the entire universe comes to unfold arbitrarily on your domestic screen (all the useless information that comes to you from the entire world, like a microscopic pornography of the universe, useless, excessive, just like the sexual close-up in a porno film): all this explodes the scene formerly preserved by the minimal separation of public and private, the scene that was played out in a restricted space, according to a secret ritual known only by the actors.

Certainly, this private universe was alienating to the extent that it separated you from others – or from the world, where it was invested as a protective enclosure, an imaginary protector, a defense system. But it also reaped the symbolic benefits of alienation, which is that the Other exists, and that otherness can fool you for the better or the worse. Thus consumer society lived also under the sign of alienation, as a society of the spectacle.[1] But just so: as long as there is alienation, there is spectacle, action, scene. It is not obscenity – the spectacle is never obscene. Obscenity begins precisely when there is no more spectacle, no more scene, when all becomes transparence and immediate visibility, when everything is exposed to the harsh and inexorable light of information and communication.

We are no longer a part of the drama of alienation; we live in the ecstasy of communication. And this ecstasy is obscene. [...]

In any case, we will have to suffer this new state of things, this forced extroversion of all interiority, this forced injection of all exteriority that the categorical imperative of communication literally signifies. There also, one can perhaps make use of the old metaphors of pathology. If hysteria was the pathology of the exacerbated staging of the subject, a pathology of expression, of the body's theatrical and operatic conversion; and if paranoia was the pathology of organization, of the structuration of a rigid and jealous world; then with communication and information, with the immanent promiscuity of all these networks, with their continual connections, we are now in a new form of schizophrenia. No more hysteria, no more projective paranoia, properly speaking, but this state of terror proper to the schizophrenic: too great a proximity of everything, the unclean promiscuity of everything which touches, invests and penetrates without resistance, with no halo of private protection, not even his own body, to protect him anymore.

The schizo is bereft of every scene, open to everything in spite of himself, living in the greatest confusion. He is himself obscene, the obscene prey of the world's obscenity. What characterizes him is less the loss of the real, the light years of estrangement from the real, the pathos of distance and radical separation, as is commonly said: but, very much to the contrary, the absolute proximity, the total instantaneity of things, the feeling of no defense, no retreat. It is the end of interiority and in intimacy, the overexposure and transparence of the world which traverses him without obstacle. He can no longer produce the limits of his own being, can no longer play nor stage himself, can no longer produce himself as mirror. He is now only a pure screen, a switching center for all the networks of influence.

NOTES

Extracted from Baudrillard, J., 'The Ecstasy of Communication', in Foster, H. (ed.) *The Anti-Aesthetic: Essays on Postmodern Culture*, translated by John Johnston, New York: The New Press, 1998, pp. 126–34. Reprinted by permission of The New Press. Originally published as *L'Autre par Lui-même*, Paris, 1987.

1. A reference to Guy Debord's *La société du spectacle* (Paris: Buchet-Chastel, 1968). [Tr.]

26

THERE IS NO KITSCH, THERE IS ONLY DESIGN!

Gert Selle (1984)

Figure 20. Leopard from the "Genial Design of the '80s" exhibition at the IDZ Berlin in 1983. Photo © IDZ/International Design Center Berlin.

THEME AND BACKGROUND

The exhibition "Genial Design of the '80s: Objects of Desire and Daily Use" has aroused controversy. It did not hold to the usual criteria of design. It dealt with design for all. It showed beautiful everyday objects without condemning their consumption and without denouncing or indoctrinating their users. It stressed what design means today to the majority of the population in the Federal Republic (West Germany) and West Berlin and in other industrial countries: realization of a dream of luxury, beauty, belongingness, shelter, adventure, individuality, and cultural identity.

The exhibition thus intentionally remained as open to controversy as the facts to which it pointed. However, if one only criticizes this dream or ignores what, besides thoughtlessness and alienation, is still tucked in it, one not only strides heedlessly and arrogantly over the many who need this dream, one forgets one's own involvement in this product culture. The discovery that it has a history and a continuity is not made. This real product culture of the "mass-everyday" is not founded merely on deceit; it is not an "as if" culture, it is "lived" culture, and whoever calls it kitschy is making an absolute of a position based on educational tradition and normative interest, which would first have to be exposed to a critique of its ideology.

The exhibition was a provocation, because it violated the rule that the guidelines for dealing with objects, the nature of their beauty and their understanding, be prescribed by "progressive" designers. It is a professional tradition to think that the proper and moral use of things must never be left to the users. For more than 80 years, every designer with self-respect has considered himself a cultural guardian of any user whatsoever. He thinks that the users have to be led out of kitsch into the freedom of a rational use of goods specially designed for that purpose. In truth, however, the relations have been reversed; the mass user has mutely but consistently developed and implemented his own concepts and competencies, a process with still unforeseeable consequences that is stamped with confusion today by the theory and practice of design.

The fact is: the ordinary beautiful design of the world at large *is* design, while all schemes of high design laden with hopes of cultural pedagogy have run into a void or have been absorbed by everyday-beautiful design. The leadership claim of an exemplary design has become extremely questionable. And it is surely wrong to look down sneeringly on the anonymous creators of everyday beauties as if they were not designers at all. They are. It is necessary to learn from them. This is already being done, shamefacedly or shamelessly as, for example, in the recent exhibition of competition projects "Fashioning between 'Good Design' and 'Kitsch'" at the IDZ, Berlin, 1983.

It is high time, therefore, to point out in an exemplary survey the fantastically beautiful design for all and to pose old questions a new. Violating the prevailing "official" standards of taste cannot be avoided here anymore than can challenging institutions all concerned with design questions and, of course, every designer who considers himself a pedagogue and an innovator. The IDZ exhibition showed nothing out of the ordinary, unless the intensity of wishing, the stubbornness, and the sense of beauty with which masses of ordinary users cling to their concepts and force designers go along with them is considered extraordinary. The anonymous design for all has reached such a degree of esthetic perfection that attempts of avant-garde designers to create a postfunctionalist

decorative product culture for connoisseurs and rich snobs recalls the folk tale in which the tortoise always gets there before the hare. The real avant-garde was already long on the warehouse shelves before "Memphis" and others acted as if our product environment had for once to be brought to life and made playful, colorful, and all new. A self-appointed designer avant-garde picking up charms from the motley creations of the world at large is not the same thing that the protagonists of Pop Art did when they turned soup cans and comic strip heroes into artistic material. Design for the everyday masses is something different from art production, which reflects this daily life. If designers today are playing around with bizarre everyday-esthetic motifs, then this is the belated "same concept" only insofar as they behave like artists. In reality, they concede that their earlier pedagogical intentions have been wrecked (the artists never had such intentions). And what they create that is new and colorful and what they want to decree for use has already been created before them and is in regular use. They expropriate, as it were, from their anonymous colleagues and the mass users that quantum of imagination that has always distinguished every universally beautiful design from esthetically and morally pretentious production.

Alessandro Mendini says this in plain words: "Why should one not make use of the intimate and mythical relation that exists in every mass society between human beings and the so-called 'ugly' object?"[1] The Italians and their German imitators lionize the everyday beauties and elevate them to new forms of individual artistic creation.[2] They forget that the consumer masses never deal with their beautiful things ironically, but use them seriously. From the concepts of the avant-garde that designs these beauties afterward, hardly anything can be reflected back to the everyday-beautiful and fantastically rich design; for this, after all, is the original, the socially lived and vitalized, serious form of design.

It is to this that the exhibition wanted to invite attention. The aim was to make visible the richness of ideas, the variety of forms, and the openness of meaning of such designs. These designs can compete very well with the most far-out avant-garde products, because, after all, they were their model and because, by reason of their mass presence in social use, they have a substantially more intense record of functioning behind them and promise ahead of them than any artistic high-class design.

The design of the world at large is mass-sensuous and concrete in use. It impresses all and is used in different life situations for different purposes by different people; for example, by the specialist, by the professor, by the cleaning woman, as well as by the wife of the chief physician, moreover by children and youth of all strata. If one pushes aside all prejudices, one must grant to this design offering that it combines high esthetic fantasy with social competence in its purpose. At the exhibition, the fascination of a very heterogeneous street public was observed as people turned to the objects of their desire and use through the show windows of the IDZ.

[…]

Is over-esthetization a trick of survival? An attempt to bridge over the desensualization of life? The Bauhaus once considered technical progress and the nature of man to be reconcilable. It created a humanly meant functionalism and a clear system of esthetics, which for then-unforeseeable reasons was unable to prevail or prevailed only in a distorted form.

At present, design for everyone encompasses highly functional ensembles in altogether anachronistic esthetic costumes or costumes that seem to have been borrowed from the wardrobe of science fiction films. The unsuitable is trump. Perhaps the unsuitable is, on one hand, an expression of supercharging the project. In the age of microchips, it is no longer possible to express highly complex technical structures plastically. The telephone made of Plexiglas was a decorative expedient solution; the interior of a super-flat electronic pocket calculator remains just as

boring as it is unintelligible. On the other hand, the contradiction between high technology and antiquated esthetics of use could point to a path of affirmation. It is not the first time in the history of design that this contradiction gapes open at moments when technology is being revolutionized. Neither the gas lamp nor any electric light has ever – before Peter Behrens – managed to make do without references to the past; even the automobile was only slowly able to free itself from the coach form. Is there an esthetic of delay?

The "Genial Design of the '80s" exhibition raises such questions anew. Designers and their theoreticians can hardly answer them, but they will become research fields for anthropology, social philosophy, and the history of technology. For example, a connection is cropping up between the material demonstrated by Giedion for progressive abstraction of work and life through mechanization and Rudolf zur Lippe's studies on the "Geometrization of Man."[3] Electronic apparatuses and programs are pushing their way into the game room and forcing hand and eye into new patterns of covariant perception and manipulation skills. The exhibition contains an example of suggestive attraction. No one yet knows what forms these new "technologies of sense perception" in everyday life will have for the nature of human beings. The designer knows it last of all. Is he also providing for an esthetic of acceleration?

THE UNSUITABILITY OF THE KITSCH CONCEPT

At present, the final shedding of the kitsch concept suggests itself. It has become superfluous, a leftover from earlier periods of cultural delimitation. To be sure, it is necessary to face this imaginatively beautiful genial design of the 1980s critically, but not with the kitsch concept. A basic trait of unreality and escapism clings to this highly artificial environment. Certainly this product culture bears witness to everything but ecological sensitivity and economic logic. It not only makes experience and history possible, but also destroys them. Certainly it awakens needs and suffocates them at the same time. But it is the sole existing mass product culture of significance. It makes available a material with which the everyday can be organized esthetically as a social and personal ensemble in space and time. The everyday turns over much more slowly than it ought to according to the laws of commodity esthetics – therefore in the proper order of things. The attempts, repeated again and again in history, of righteous pedagogues, mission-conscious designers, and cultural institutions to habituate people to better taste have been brilliantly withstood by the beautiful design of the world at large. So-called "good form" has entered into countless associations with this design and very nearly vanished in it. Only incorrigible cultural pedagogues are still preaching against kitsch.

The kitsch concept is an invention of the nineteenth century – taken into use at a time when bourgeois culture was already going downhill and positions had to be firmly established.[4] However, this bourgeois high culture has vanished today, except for remnants. Therewith ends at least the old necessity of culture delimitation. The parvenus know themselves what is suitable, and their measure of suitability has, as a new standard, taken the place of temperate restraint. To this extent the kitsch concept is obsolete; it no longer holds, despite the fact that many educated persons have at their disposal a learning history that is laden with this antiquated value concept and that permits them in their own life context to classify their personal environment according to such criteria.

However, it seems extremely doubtful whether a classification of the esthetic manifestations of contemporary product culture into *kitschy* or *non-kitschy* is a performance of insight. Taste judgments are standpoint judgments. It is from a value awareness that one observes and judges. Where a fixed coordinate system for social and individual value decisions is lacking, however, this judgment is irrelevant and noncommittal.

One should at least first try to determine for oneself the position one objectively occupies: "To follow one's taste means to sight the goods that are objectively allocated to one's own social position and which harmonize with one another because they are approximately of equal rank," writes Bourdieu.[5]

Such an attempt would also make it possible to understand other people's positions and values. A sort of social-esthetic empathy would be needed in situations in which old, internalized value systems again and again play tricks on us. There simply is no absolute "good taste." It exists only in relation to a basis of social points of departure, that is, everyone who lives according to his taste has a "good taste," which, of course, can be distinguished from another "good taste." In the pluralistic permissive esthetic of our everyday, this is already experienced by countless individuals, while the guardians of the once-leading good taste do not trust their eyes.

Thus, "Genial Design of the '80s" is not a collection of kitsch examples, but a cool factual reference to esthetic orientations of large majorities who rightly protest against the thesis that all these beautiful objects laden with desire, memory, and experience are kitsch and, therefore, something inferior.

Failing to recognize that esthetic value awareness is based on a specific orientation, we may still, however, slip into another false appraisal, namely, the Camp esthetic described by Susan Sontag. The Camp esthetic is the allocation of the exaggerated and fantastic to an intellectual "manner of experience" that grasps and seizes certain phenomena from the province of the old kitsch concept as a special possibility of one's own identity formation. "The old-style dandy hated vulgarity. The new-style dandy, the lover of Camp, appreciates vulgarity."[6]

The adaptation of the exaggerated or the enjoyment of the apparent parody of seriousness by a certain stratum – I would like to say of parasitic users of imaginative design for everyone – only relates, however, to a small subculture in that great, immeasurable subculture of the earnest use of exaggeratedly beautiful goods. "Here Camp taste supervenes upon good taste as a daring and witty hedonism."[7] The terrible, beautiful design of the world at large, therefore, produces a tricky enlivening of feelings and becomes an ironic manner of experiencing the self.

Undoubtedly some educated visitors to the exhibition "Genial Design of the '80s" must have sensed such spasms with a certain horror, but also with secret fascination. (It was necessary for the exhibition to reckon with this misunderstanding.) At the same time, however, many "naive" visitors showed a direct, non-ironic interest in the things – which is evidenced, incidentally, by the pilfering statistics.

A distinction must be made between two cultural spheres of interest. The one points to dimensions of the game and remains a variant of the traditional bourgeois one-culture standpoint, from which one inclines hedonistically, noncommittally, and voyeuristically toward the alien fantastic and beautiful. The other is that of the immediacy and earnestness of mass use. The mass users do not play; they are serious with their imagination. They have only this one rich product culture. Thus, "Memphis" will perhaps lead to the manner of experience of Camp, but never to substitution for the naive models.

This means that the observer seriously concerned with cultural empathy must detach himself from the old kitsch concept *and* must avoid personal entanglement in the Camp esthetic, because anchorings hamper perception of the socioesthetic facts. Comprehension of mass-effective design of the world at large will be acquired only by asking without reservation (which does not mean without criticism) what this design replaces, what it redeems, what sensuality it curtails, what sensuality it promotes, and where it dissolves norms, where it sets up new ones, whether and where in the alienation familiarity flashes up (and thereby history in the seemingly historyless), what it means in the hands of different users, and what it does not mean.

The much-disdained design for all is highly complex and springy in its nasty imaginativeness, warped absurdity, and apparent solidification. It deserves the close attention of those interested in esthetic perception, as it has outstripped all cultural competition and strivings for something better.

CONCLUSION

Never before has such a broad offering of everyday beauties been available to such large masses of users. The build-up, acquisition, and implementation of industrial product culture has taken place socially (and in part biohistorically) in long waves, interrupted by two world wars and long phases of shortage economy. The culture of beauty for all, today so obvious, has its history, is making history at the moment, and will continue to do so. To take design for all seriously, therefore, means to open our awareness to individual phenomena and to the totality of manifestations of this mass product culture from an historical viewpoint to consider what sociological and historical structural changes society is undergoing. Design problems are then suddenly no longer so important; at least they are relativized.

The old Köhler belief that design can change the world or even produce good human beings is then spoiled for us. Cultural pedagogic work can be performed only in this cultural reality, not against it, be it by teachers, designers, or institutions. Theoretical constructs based on exclusivity, such as the critique of commodity esthetics or more or less relativized postulates of a Socio-Design, must in the future be subjected to the test of experimental science. The revaluation process of design, which is mirrored in the universal presence of the everyday – beautiful design for everyone, can no longer be checked by strengthened design measures, counter-propaganda or counter-education. This, after all, has long been attempted to no avail. Such activities would only be directed against the majorities who shape their lives with this design and who perhaps already use it much more freely and much less excitedly than many critics think.

The swing of the designer avant-garde to the fantastic of the everyday (or its flight into a new artificiality) is a forced act of adaptation, not a new departure. The entry into the postmodern could also mean that the age of the once irreconcilable two cultures, the lower and the upper, is over. The might of esthetic guardianship is thereby broken, even if the ward seems immature to many. A product culture – opulent, hedonistic, valid for all, and open to interpretation by all – has prevailed with the normative power of the factual, even if the dubious aspect of this culture is ever so patently evident.

As for the morality of this fantastic world of phenomena in which everything is allowed that pleases and obtains its meaning in the plaiting of social relations and manners of expression, it must be emphasized that this mass-product culture so often represented as bad is, all in all, far more peaceful, more humane, more economical, and more rational than the weapons design that threatens us all. The beautiful design of the world at large probably acquires its special density of meaning in the awareness of crises, of political helplessness, and under the sense of anxiety. This peaceable withdrawal culture prevails among the working masses in West and East. A comparison between West German allotment garden colonies and the extended Datschen zones on the edge of East Berlin conveys – with all difference that one must furthermore still perceive – an image of high community in the push toward normality, in the esthetic language of privacy, in the quest for meaningful activity, in the placidity of enjoyment, and the forms of *petit bourgeois* joy of life. The Hollywood merry-go-round, gaudy and florid, here as well as there, is a culture symbol.

It is not so wrong, after all. On the far side of commodity character, squandering and artificiality, no general new high culture has ever arisen; the culture, namely, of which all social planners of the beautiful have always dreamed. Wherever we look around us, subculture reigns, the lower is turned up, the "wrong" is preferred to the "correct." Permeability prevails.

The masses are realizing long-cherished dreams. How they are doing this, what accrues to them in the use of the things, what consequence this cultural development has in detail these questions must be posed anew, even if they seem to have been already answered long, long ago. Acknowledgement of cultural facts must finally take the place of shamefaced blocking out or unjustified discrimination.

The thematization of the everyday is not merely a fashion, as someone said at the opening of the exhibition. On the contrary, the everyday, based on historical insight into the contemporary culture experience, is to be regarded as a richly instructive field for future social action. Agnes Heller regards everyday life as the "secret leaven of history." In its development, she says, it often expresses "the changes that have arisen in the manner of production ... before the due social revolution."[8] Now the fantastically beautiful "genial" design of the 1980s is part of everyday life. Therefore, paths of perception should be sought that open up presentient understanding and new accesses beyond hard and fast positions. Hitherto, one has found oneself as a design critic in the remarkable situation of knowing better one's head and proposing something other than what body and senses experience, while we are ourselves living in the midst of the real product culture.

NOTES

Extracted from Selle, G., 'There Is No Kitsch, There Is Only Design!', translated by Peter Nelles, *Design Issues* 1(1) (1984), pp. 41–52. Reprinted by permission of the author.

1. Alessandro Mendini, "Fur ein Banales Design," in *Design aus Italien* (Hannover: Deutsche Werkbund, 1982), 279.
2. See "Möbel perdu," *Der Spiegel* 51 (1982).

3. See Rudolf zur Lippe, *Die Geometrisierung des Menschen in der Europaischen Neuzeit: Eine Ausstellung des Instituts fur Praktische Anthropologie* (Oldenburg: Bibliotheks- und Informationssystem der Universitat Oldenburg, 1982).

4. See Abraham Moles, *Psychologie des Kitsches* (München: Hanser, 1972).

5. Pierre Bourdieu, *Die Feinen in Unterschiede: Kritik der Gesellschaftlichen Urteilskraft* (Frankfurt: Suhrkamp, 1982), 366.

6. Susan Sontag, "Anmerkungen zu 'Camp,'" in Susan Sontag, *Kunst und Anti-Kunst: Essays* (München: Hanser, 1980), 282.

7. Sontag, "Anmerkungen zu 'Camp,'" 284.

8. Agnes Heller, *Das Alltagsleben: Versuch einer Erklarung der Individuellen Reproduktion* (Frankfurt: Suhrkamp, 1978), 25.

27

DECONSTRUCTION AND GRAPHIC DESIGN: HISTORY MEETS THEORY

Ellen Lupton and J. Abbott Miller (1994)

Since the surfacing of the term "deconstruction" in design journalism in the mid-1980s, the word has served to label architecture, graphic design, products, and fashion featuring chopped up, layered, and fragmented forms imbued with ambiguous futuristic overtones. This essay looks at the reception and use of deconstruction in the recent history of graphic design, where it has become the tag for yet another period style.

We then consider the place of graphics within the theory of deconstruction, initiated in the work of philosopher Jacques Derrida. We argue that deconstruction is not a style or "attitude" but rather a mode of questioning through and about the technologies, formal devices, social institutions, and founding metaphors of representation. Deconstruction belongs to both history and theory. It is embedded in recent visual and academic culture, but it describes a strategy of critical form-making which is performed across a range of artifacts and practices, both historical and contemporary.

Jacques Derrida introduced the concept of "deconstruction" in his book *Of Grammatology*, published in France in 1967 and translated into English in 1976.[1] "Deconstruction" became a banner for the advance guard in American literary studies in the 1970s and 80s, scandalizing departments of English, French, and comparative literature. Deconstruction rejected the project of modern criticism: to uncover the meaning of a literary work by studying the way its form

and content communicate essential humanistic messages. Deconstruction, like critical strategies based on Marxism, feminism, semiotics, and anthropology, focuses not on the themes and imagery of its objects but rather on the linguistic and institutional systems that frame the production of texts.[2]

In Derrida's theory, deconstruction asks how representation inhabits reality. How does the external image of things get inside their internal essence? How does the surface get under the skin? Western culture since Plato, Derrida argues, has been governed by such oppositions as reality/representation, inside/outside, original/copy, and mind/body. The intellectual achievements of the West – its science, art, philosophy, literature – have valued one side of these pairs over the other, allying one side with truth and the other with falsehood. For example, the Judeo-Christian tradition has conceived the body as an external shell for the inner soul, elevating the mind as the sacred source of thought and spirit, while denigrating the body as mere mechanics. In the realm of aesthetics, the original work of art traditionally has carried an aura of authenticity that its copy lacks, and the telling of a story or the taking of a photograph is viewed as a passive record of events.

"Deconstruction" takes apart such oppositions by showing how the devalued, empty concept lives inside the valued, positive one. The outside inhabits the inside. Consider, for example, the opposition between nature and culture. The idea of "nature" depends on the idea of "culture," and yet culture is part of nature. It's a fantasy to conceive of the non-human environment as a pristine, innocent setting fenced off and protected from the products of human endeavor – cities, roads, farms, landfills. The fact that we have produced a concept of "nature" in opposition to "culture" is a symptom of our alienation from the ecological systems that civilization depletes and transforms.

A crucial opposition for deconstruction is speech/writing. The Western philosophical tradition has denigrated writing as an inferior copy of the spoken word. Speech draws on interior consciousness, but writing is dead and abstract. The written word loses its connection to the inner self. Language is set adrift, untethered from the speaking subject. In the process of embodying language, writing steals its soul. Deconstruction views writing as an active rather than passive form of representation. Writing is not merely a bad copy, a faulty transcription, of the spoken word; writing, in fact, invades thought and speech, transforming the sacred realms of memory, knowledge, and spirit. Any memory system, in fact, is a form of writing, since it records thought for the purpose of future transmissions.

The speech/writing opposition can be mapped onto a series of ideologically loaded pairs that are constitutive of modern Western culture:

Speech/Writing
Natural/artificial
Spontaneous/constructed
Original/copy
interior to the mind/exterior to the mind
requires no equipment/requires equipment
intuitive/learned
present subject/absent subject

Derrida's critique of the speech/writing opposition locates the concerns of deconstruction in the field of graphic design. We will return to the speech/writing problem in more detail later, but first, we will look at the life of deconstruction in recent design culture.

THE DESIGN HISTORY OF DECONSTRUCTION

Deconstruction belongs to the broader critical field known as "post-structuralism," whose key figures include Roland Barthes, Michel Foucault, Jean Baudrillard, and others. Each of these writers has looked at modes of representation – from literature and photography to the design of schools and prisons – as powerful technologies which build and remake the social world. Deconstruction's attack on the neutrality of signs is also at work in the consumer mythologies of Barthes, the institutional archaeologies of Foucault, and the simulationist aesthetics of Baudrillard.[3]

The idea that cultural forms help to fabricate such seemingly "natural" categories as race, sexuality, poetic genius, and aesthetic value had profound relevance to visual artists in the 1980s. Post-structuralism provided a critical avenue into "post-modernism," posing a left-leaning alternative to the period's nostalgic returns to figurative painting and neo-classical architecture. While Barbara Kruger, Cindy Sherman, and Victor Burgin attacked media myths through their visual work, books such as Hal Foster's *The Anti-Aesthetic* and Terry Eagleton's *Literary Theory* delivered post-structuralist theory to students in an accessible form.[4]

Graphic designers in many U.S. art programs were exposed to critical theory through the fields of photography, performance and installation art during the early 1980s. The most widely publicized intersection of post-structuralism and graphic design occurred at the Cranbrook Academy of Art, under the leadership of co-chair Katherine McCoy.[5] Designers at Cranbrook had first confronted literary criticism when they designed a special issue of *Visible Language* on contemporary French literary aesthetics, published in the summer of 1978.[6] Daniel Libeskind, head of Cranbrook's architecture program, provided the graphic designers with a seminar in literary theory, which prepared them to develop their strategy: to systematically disintegrate the series of essays by expanding the spaces between lines and words and pushing the footnotes into the space normally reserved for the main text. "French Currents of the Letter," which outraged designers committed to the established ideologies of problem-solving and direct communication, remains a controversial landmark in experimental graphic design.

According to Katherine McCoy, post-structuralist texts entered more general discussions at Cranbrook around 1983. She has credited Jeffery Keedy, a student at the school from 1983–85, with introducing fellow course members to books by Barthes and others.[7] The classes of 1985/87 and 1986/88 also took an active interest in critical theory; students at this time included Andrew Blauvelt, Brad Collins, Edward Fella, David Frej, and Allen Hori [Figure 21]. Close interaction with the photography department, under the leadership of Carl Toth, further promoted dialogue about post-structuralism and visual practice.[8]

Post-structuralism did not serve as a unified methodology at the school, however, even in the period of its strongest currency, but was part of an eclectic gathering of ideas. According to Keedy, students at Cranbrook when he was there were looking at everything from alchemical mysticism to the "proportion voodoo" of the golden section.[9] McCoy recalled in a 1991 interview: "Theory had become part of the intellectual culture in art and photography. We were never trying to apply specific texts – it was more of a general filtration process. The term 'deconstructivist' drives me crazy. Post-structuralism is an attitude, not a style."[10] But what is the difference between "style" and "attitude"? If "style" is a grammar of form-making associated with a particular historical and cultural situation, then perhaps "attitude" is the unarticulated, just out-of-focus background for the specificities of style.

The response to post-structuralism at Cranbrook was largely optimistic, side-stepping the profound pessimism and political critique that permeates these writers' major works. McCoy used the architectural theory of Robert Venturi

and Denise Scott Brown as a "stepping stone" to post-structuralism, enabling her to merge the Pop aestheticization of the American commercial vernacular with post-structuralism's critique of "fixed meaning."[11] McCoy's preference for celebration over criticism is echoed in Keedy's comment, "It was the poetic aspect of Barthes which attracted me, not the Marxist analysis. After all, we're designers working in a consumer society, and while Marxism is interesting as an idea, I wouldn't want to put it into practice."[12]

Post-structuralism's emphasis on the openness of meaning has been incorporated by many designers into a romantic theory of self-expression: as the argument goes, because signification is not fixed in material forms, designers and readers share in the spontaneous creation of meaning. This approach represents a rather cheerful response to the post-structuralist theme of the "death of the author" and the assertion that the interior self is constructed by external technologies of representation. According to the writings of Barthes and Foucault, for example, the citizen/artist/producer is not the imperious master of systems of language, media, education, custom, and so forth; instead, the individual operates within the limited grid of possibilities these codes make available. Rather than view meaning as a matter of private interpretation, post-structuralist theory tends to see the realm of the "personal" as structured by external signs. Invention and revolution come from tactical aggressions against this grid of possibilities.

"Deconstructivism" catapulted into the mainstream design press with MoMA's 1988 exhibition *Deconstructivist Architecture*, curated by Philip Johnson and Mark Wigley.[13] The curators used the term "deconstructivism" to link certain contemporary architectural practices to Russian Constructivism, whose early years were marked by an imperfect vision of form and technology. The MoMA exhibition located a similarly skewed interpretation of modernism in the work of Frank Gehry, Daniel Libeskind, Peter Eisenman, and others. Wigley wrote in his catalogue

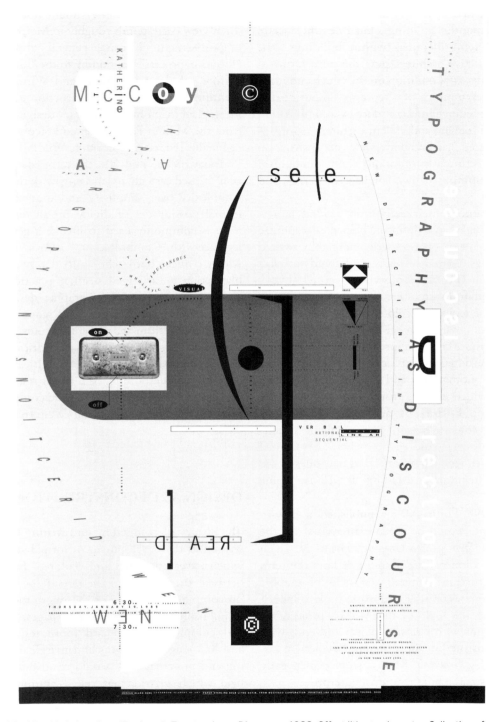

Figure 21. Allen Hori, American (Designer), *Typography as Discourse*, 1988. Offset lithograph poster. Collection of Cranbrook Art Museum, Bloomfield Hills, MI. Gift of Katherine and Michael McCoy (CAM 2008.131). Photographer: R. H. Hensleigh. Photo courtesy of Cranbrook Art Museum. Reprinted by permission of Allen Hori.

essay: "A deconstructive architect is … not one who dismantles buildings, but one who locates the inherent dilemmas within buildings. The deconstructive architect puts the pure forms of the architectural tradition on the couch and identifies the symptoms of a repressed impurity. The impurity is drawn to the surface by a combination of gentle coaxing and violent torture: the form is interrogated." In Wigley's view, deconstruction in architecture asks questions about modernism by re-examining its own language, materials, and processes.

By framing their exhibition around a new "ism," Wigley and Johnson helped to canonize the elements of a period style, marked by twisted geometries, centerless plans, and shards of glass and metal. This cluster of stylistic features quickly emigrated from architecture to graphic design, just as the icons and colors of neo-classical post-modernism had traveled there shortly before. While a more critical approach to deconstruction had been routed to graphic designers through the fields of photography and the fine arts, architecture provided a ready-to-use formal vocabulary that could be broadly adopted. "Deconstruction," "deconstructivism," and just plain "decon" became design-world clichés, where they named existing tendencies and catalyzed new ones in the fields of furniture and fashion as well as graphic design.[14]

In 1990 Philip Meggs published a how-to guide for would-be deconstructivists in the magazine *Step-by-Step Graphics*. His essay, which includes a journalistic account of how the term "deconstruction" entered the field of graphic design, focuses on style and works back to theory. Following the logic of the MoMA project, his story begins with Constructivism and ends with its "deconstruction" in contemporary design; unlike Wigley, however, Meggs's story depicts early modernism as a purely rational enterprise.[15]

Chuck Byrne and Martha Witte's more analytical piece for *Print* (1990) describes deconstruction as a "zeitgeist," a philosophical germ circulating in contemporary culture that influences graphic designers even though they might not know it. Their view corresponds roughly to McCoy's sense of post-structuralism as a general "attitude" or "filtration process" responding to the "intellectual culture" of the time. Byrne and Witte's article identifies examples of deconstruction across the ideological map of contemporary design, ranging from the work of Paula Scher and Stephen Doyle to Lucille Tenazas and Lorraine Wild.

Today, in the mid-90s, the term "deconstruction" is used casually to label any work that favors complexity over simplicity and dramatizes the formal possibilities of digital production – the term is commonly used to invoke a generic allegiance with "Cranbrook" or "CalArts," a gesture which reduces both schools to flat symbols by blanketing a variety of distinct practices. Our view of deconstruction in graphic design is at once narrower and broader in its scope than the view evolving from the current discourse. Rather than look at deconstruction as a historical style or period, we see deconstruction as a critical activity – an act of questioning. The visual resources of typography help demarcate Derrida's ideological map of the biases governing Western art and philosophy.

[…]

DESIGN AS DECONSTRUCTION

The history of typography and writing could be written as the development of formal structures which have articulated and explored the border between the inside and the outside of the text. To compile a catalogue of the micro-mechanics of publishing – indexes and title pages, captions and colophons, folios and footnotes, leading and line lengths, margins and marginalia, spacing and punctuation – would contribute to the field which Derrida has called grammatology, or the study of writing as a distinctive mode of representation. This word, grammatology, serves to title the book whose more infamous legacy is deconstruction.

[…]

[…] A history of typography informed by deconstruction would show how graphic design has revealed, challenged, or transformed the accepted rules of communication. Such interventions can represent either deliberate confrontations or haphazard encounters with the social, technological, and aesthetic pressures that shape the making of texts.

In a 1994 interview in *The New York Times Magazine*, Derrida was asked about the purported "death" of deconstruction on North American campuses; he answered, "I think there is some element in deconstruction that belongs to the structure of history or events. It started before the academic phenomenon of deconstruction, and it will continue with other names."[16] In the spirit of this statement, we are interested in de-periodizing the relevance of deconstruction: instead of viewing it as an "ism" of the late-80s and early-90s, we see it as part of the ongoing development of design and typography as distinctive modes of representation. But deconstruction also belongs to culture: it is an operation that has taken a name and has spun a web of influence in particular social contexts. Deconstruction has lived in a variety of institutional worlds, from university literature departments to schools of art and design to the discourse of popular journalism, where it has functioned both as a critical activity and as a banner for a range of styles and attitudes. […]

Vincent Gagliostro's cover for *NYQ* [Figure 22], a gay and lesbian news magazine, was designed in November, 1991, in response to Magic Johnson's announcement that he is HIV+. Gagliostro imposed *NYQ*'s own logo and headline over a *Newsweek* cover featuring Magic Johnson proclaiming "Even me," his upheld arms invoking saintly sacrifice and athletic vigor. "He is not our hero," wrote *NYQ* over the existing cover. While Gagliostro's layering and splicing of type and image are shared with more aestheticized, individualized gestures found elsewhere in contemporary design, this cover does not aim to trigger an infinite variety of "personal" interpretations but instead explicitly manipulates an ideologically loaded artifact. Gagliostro's act of cultural rewriting is a powerful response to the ubiquity of normative sign systems, showing that the structures of mass media can be reshuffled and reinhabited. The *NYQ* cover reveals and exploits the function of framing as a transformative process that refuses to remain outside the editorial content it encloses.

The manipulation of existing media imagery is one activity in contemporary design that can be described as deconstruction; another is the exploration of the visual grammar of communication, from print to the electronic interface. Designers working in hypermedia are developing new ways to generate, distribute, and use information – they are reinventing the language of graphic design today, just as typographers reacted to the changing technologies and social functions of printed media in the past. […]

Spacing, framing, punctuation, type style, layout, and other nonphonetic marks of difference constitute the material interface of writing. Traditional literary and linguistic research overlook such graphic structures, focusing instead on the Word as the center of communication. According to Derrida, the functions of repetition, quotation, and fragmentation that characterize writing are conditions endemic to all human expression – even the seemingly spontaneous, self-present utterances of speech or the smooth, naturalistic surfaces of painting and photography.[17] Design can critically engage the mechanics of representation, exposing and revising its ideological biases; design also can remake the grammar of communication by discovering structures and patterns within the material media of visual and verbal writing.

NOTES

Extracted from Lupton, E. and Abbott Miller, J., 'Deconstruction and Graphic Design: History Meets Theory', *Visible Language* 28(4) (Fall 1994), special issue edited by Andrew Blauvelt, pp. 346–66. Reprinted by permission of the authors.

Figure 22. Magazine cover, *NYQ*, designed by Vincent Gagliostro, New York, 1991, from Ellen Lupton and J. Abbott Miller, 'Deconstruction and Graphic Design: History Meets Theory,' *Visible Language* 28(4) (Fall 1994), special issue edited by Andrew Blauvelt, pp. 346–66, p. 365. Reprinted with permission of the designer.

1. Jacques Derrida introduced the theory of deconstruction in *Of Grammatology*, trans Gayatri Chakravorty Spivak, 1976, Baltimore: Johns Hopkins University Press. See especially Chapter 2, "Linguistics and Grammatology," 27–73.

2. Jonathan Culler explores the impact of deconstruction on literary criticism in his book, *On Deconstruction: Theory and Criticism after Structuralism*, 1982, Ithaca: Cornell University Press.

3. Post-structuralist texts widely read by students of art and design include: Roland Barthes, *Mythologies*, trans. Annette Lavers, 1972, New York: Farrar, Straus & Giroux; Michel Foucault, *Discipline and Punish: The Birth of the Prison*, trans. Alan Sheridan, 1979, New York: Random House; and Jean Baudrillard, *For a Critique of the Political Economy of the Sign*, trans. Charles Levin, 1981, St. Louis: Telos Press.

4. Books which helped popularize post-structuralism in schools of art and design include Hal Foster, editor, 1983, *The Anti-Aesthetic: Essays on Postmodern Culture*. Port Townsend, WA: Bay Press, and Terry Eagleton, 1983, *Literary Theory: An Introduction*, Minneapolis: University of Minnesota Press.

5. Graphic design produced at Cranbrook between 1980 and 1989 is documented in *Cranbrook Design: The New Discourse*, 1990, New York: Rizzoli, with essays by Katherine McCoy, Lorraine Wild and others. Wild discusses the *French Currents of the Letter* project in her essay. See also Katherine McCoy, 'American Graphic Design Expression,' in *The Evolution of American Typography*, Mildred Friedman, ed., *Design Quarterly* 148, 4–22.

6. *French Currents of the Letter* includes essays on the use of typography in the theory of deconstruction and in other post-structuralist writings. See Andrew J. McKenna, "Biblioclasm: Derrida and his Precursors," *Visible Language* 12: 3, 289–304.

7. Katherine McCoy, interview with Ellen Lupton, February 1991.

8. Communication with Andrew Blauvelt, June 1994.

9. Jeffery Keedy, interview with Ellen Lupton, February 1991.

10. Interview with Ellen Lupton, February 1991.

11. *Learning from Las Vegas*, by Robert Venturi, Denise Scott Brown and Steven Izenour. 1972. Cambridge: MIT Press, had been an important text at Cranbrook since the mid-1970s.

12. Interview with Ellen Lupton, February 1991; quoted in Ellen Lupton, "The Academy of Deconstructed Design," *Eye* 3, 44–52.

13. Philip Johnson and Mark Wigley brought deconstruction into the mainstream of design journalism with their exhibition and catalogue *Deconstructivist Architecture*, 1988, New York: Museum of Modern Art.

14. Michael Collins and Andreas Papadakis include a chapter on "Deconstruction, Deconstructivism, and Late-Modernism" in their book, *Post-Modern Design*, 1989, New York: Rizzoli, 179–95, a survey of furniture, jewelry, and other decorative arts.

15. Essays on deconstruction and graphic design include Philip Meggs, "De-constructing Typography," *Step-by-Step Graphics* 6, 178–181; and Chuck Byrne and Martha Witte, "A Brave New World: Understanding Deconstruction," *Print* XLIV, 80–87.

16. Mitchell Stevens, "Jacques Derrida," *The New York Times Sunday Magazine*, January 23, 1994, 22–5.

17. Several recent writers have extended Derrida's theory of writing by addressing the technological conditions of texts. Friedrich Kittler has studied modern and romantic literature in terms of "discourse networks," defined by the systemic conditions of writing, from methods of pedagogy to the technologies of printing and the typewriter. See *Discourse Networks 1800/1900*, trans. Michael Meteer with Chris Cullens, 1990, Stanford: Stanford University Press. George Landow's book, *Hypertext: The Convergence of Contemporary Critical Theory and Technology*, 1992, Baltimore: Johns Hopkins University Press, describes electronic media as an embodiment of post-structuralist literary theory.

28

WHAT WAS PHILIPPE STARCK THINKING OF?

Peter Lloyd and Dirk Snelders (2003)

Adrian Forty, in the last chapter of his book *Objects of Desire*[1] and after sustained commentary on how design necessarily reflects wider concerns within society, presents an argument about the process of designing in which he seeks to de-emphasize the 'creativity' of the designer, and emphasize the

Figure 23. Original photograph for Juicy Salif packaging. Reproduced by permission of Alessi.

'material constraints over which [the designers] had no control'. According to Forty our (mis) conception of what designers do arises from two directions. First, from experiments 'studying the empirically verifiable connections between what designers think and what they do'. Secondly, in the 'tendency of designers, when asked about design, to describe [...] the creative steps *they* have taken, *their* ideas about form, the constraints under which *they* have operated and *their* methods of working.' (italics ours). Here, Forty has in mind not only monographs written by well-known designers, but also case studies reporting what designers have said about their design process. 'Design has come to be regarded as belonging entirely within the realm of the designer' Forty writes, and this has had pernicious consequences, particularly in design schools where students learn to indulge what Forty refers to as 'the myth of their own omnipotence'. Designers describe their work as if they had overall power, at the expense of neglecting ideology as a determinant of design. Forty concludes that: 'no design works unless it embodies ideas that are held in common by the people for whom the object is intended'. It is these ideas that, although to some degree harnessed by designers, ultimately lie outside their control.

This raises a question that could do with resolving: does personal creativity provide either a necessary or sufficient condition for attributing success to a design object? Following from this is a question about the relationship between the intentions of the designer for a particular design and the ideas embedded in the public consciousness.

There are, then, two strands to Forty's reasoning, the first is the idea that another designer could conceivably come up with similar results. The second is the attribution of the design's success; is it to the intentions of the designer (in which case there is a good argument for omnipotence) or to cultural or ideological factors in the consuming public (in which case there is a good argument for impotence).

These issues will be taken up in the present paper by using a 'hard' case study having four key characteristics. First, it concerns an original design with no obvious precedent. Secondly, it is a design simple enough to have been created by one person autonomously (and is not, at least in principle, the product of combined social effort). Thirdly, it is a design considered successful in terms of number of units sold. Finally, it is a design having a distinctive three dimensional form together with a specific and singular purpose.

The case that we have chosen to deconstruct is Philippe Starck's *Juicy Salif* lemon squeezer, a product that has so-far sold over 550,000 units, at a steady rate of 50,000 a year since its launch in 1990. We shall discuss, using this case, whether personal creativity forms either a necessary and perhaps even a sufficient condition for the design being considered successful. We also discuss whether ideological factors – what Forty refers to as ideas embodied in the product and held in common by the people for whom the product was intended – could provide a sufficient condition for a product's success. Before we look at our case study we first consider the idea of an 'omnipotent' designer.

[…]

WHAT PHILIPPE STARCK COULD HAVE BEEN THINKING OF

Let us for one moment take the risky step of believing Philippe Starck. According to his own account of how the design for his lemon squeezer

Juicy Salif came about, what happened was that: 'once in a restaurant, this vision of a squid like lemon came upon me, so I started sketching it … and four years later it became quite famous'.[2] After a bit of historical delving into the life of Starck, we can begin to build up quite a plausible account of why this 'squid-like lemon' was significant to Starck, and not to the other people who were eating the squid in the restaurant that night:

In the mid-1950s the little Philippe often likes to fall asleep under his father's drawing board as he works at the job that will occupy his whole life: aircraft design.[3] When his father is out of the room the little Philippe often sneaks a peek at his work and he dreams about flying away in his own little aeroplane. In his teenage years – his father now gone – he continues to like modern things; flight was (after all) a modern thing in the 1960s. He likes looking forwards too; to the future, and to science fiction. His favourite films of the time include *Forbidden Planet* and *Godzilla*. He reads nearly every book of his favourite author Phillip K. Dick[4] and every now and then passages stick in his mind:

> Studying the pin, Paul went on: 'one can easily understand this reaction. Here is a piece of metal which has been melted until it has become shapeless. It represents nothing. Nor does it have any design, of any intentional sort. It is merely amorphous. One might say, it is mere content, deprived of form.'[5]

Philippe likes looking at Sci-Fi cartoons,[6] and he spends much of his time re-drawing characters and objects from comic strips, particularly the spaceships, which remind him of his father. He likes looking backwards too, but always with an eye on the future of history. The idea of organic evolution fascinates him.[7]

Now in his mid-thirties, early-middle-age Philippe has found success as a designer. Not without controversy it must be said, but this has helped to define his 'star' personality. The top companies want to work with him. He gets a commission to design a range of kitchenware from Italian household goods manufacturer Alessi. After meeting Alessi he takes a quick break on the Italian island of Capraia. In the evening he ambles along to a local restaurant – a pizzeria called Il Corsaro.[8] As he sits waiting for his food to arrive he turns the problem of the lemon squeezer over in his head. He thinks about a conventional squeezer and sketches the form on the restaurant place mat. He puts his pencil down, the food has arrived – baby squid. He skewers one with a fork and just as he is about to put it into his mouth he stops, looks at it, and realizes that this is the solution to his lemon squeezer problem.

He starts to sketch, there and then. 'If I'm quick', he thinks, 'I can design this before the primi piatti.'[9] First he tries to make a conventional lemon squeezer out of a squid, but then he realizes that won't really work. The squid begins to evolve – Philippe has always been interested in evolution – into something with legs, but he doesn't like it. It seems to be dragging, injured almost. He keeps going, eating while he sketches. His sketches abstractly remind him of the old comics he used to read. He recalls the words 'merely amorphous' from some book he read, he can't remember where. Things begin to gel in his mind, and from the dragging creature emerges a lighter, three-legged form. Like one of the space-ships he used to think about jetting up to space in. He likes the form, it's 'working'. He puts down his pencil, makes an approving noise, and starts his tiramisu. The next morning he phones Alessi 'I've got a lemon squeezer for you' he teases. Of course there are a few details to work out, exact dimensions, what material to use, how to get the juice out of the lemon efficiently. But these are all sub-problems; someone else can solve them. The main problem is solved.

The design is made. Philippe likes it, it's what he intended. But people begin to criticize it. They say that it doesn't work. It doesn't fulfil the function of the lemon squeezer, they argue. 'Look! the pips get squeezed out along with their juice, who wants to chew on a lemon pip when you're

enjoying a paella?' Philippe is used to criticism, he thinks for a while, straightens his story, and then says:

> Sometimes you must choose why you design – in this case not to squeeze lemons, even though as a lemon squeezer it works. Sometimes you need some more humble service: on a certain night, the young couple, just married, invites the parents of the groom to dinner, and the groom and his father go to watch football on the TV. And for the first time the mother of the groom and the young bride are in the kitchen and there is a sort of malaise – this squeezer is made to start the conversation.[10]

This description of designing puts Starck firmly centre-stage, as do many other descriptions of design processes. It is couched in terms of the genius narrative: a memorable solution occurring very quickly; almost a gift from God. With very little apparent effort an exquisite artifact is produced. It is a plausible account rather than an actual account, but what if it were true? Would it explain anything? It certainly doesn't tell us why the design has been successful. Perhaps all it does tell us is that designers draw on their experiences, that they play with form, that they then have to interpret the form for us in telling us how it realizes a certain function. What such an account does do is explain the significance of this object to this one person, the designer. It doesn't, indeed cannot, explain the significance of this object to all the other people that 'consume' it in some or other way. Although, of course, not impossible, it is highly unlikely that another designer could have come up with a design similar to Starck's. Not in terms of form, of course, for it is relatively easy to find precedents for Starck's *Juicy Salif*. The difficult step is to imagine this basic raw material – science fiction, cartoons, evolutionary theorizing – expressly being applied to the particular problem of squeezing lemons (or, if we are to believe Starck, creating conversation). Clearly the form itself is not original, but the form realized as a lemon squeezer could be. Maybe this much alone might allow us to attribute Starck's personal creativity as a necessary condition for the design's success. The question then is whether it could also form a sufficient condition.

[...]

There are a number of aspects to consider about the lemon squeezer. The first is the material it is made from: aluminum. Compared with steel, aluminum is a modern metal, one that has associations with aircraft, with lightness, and with anti-corrosion. The lemon squeezer won't rust away, it has a feeling of permanence about it. This permanence is emphasized by the temporariness of its rubber feet. The user instructions rather apologize for the fact that the rubber feet will wear out, noting that new ones can be bought should they do so. The feeling of the object's permanence also comes from the method of making the squeezer: casting. It is a simple, traditional technique, that sometimes produces imperfections, but generally works well. Strong things are usually cast. Industrial revolutions were founded on cast iron as an industrial material. The modern material is, then, underpinned by a traditional technique. The result is a monument, standing with the 'power' graphic perspective of socialist realism. This is also how it is presented on the packaging: a photo taken from a low angle. One could easily imagine it as a huge object, out of all proportion with human scale.

Aluminium as a material has been said to give a feeling of 'nostalgia for the future',[11] and there are other features of the lemon squeezer that one can associate with a future imagined from the past. Chief among these is its rocket or spaceship associations. Not with rockets of the present, but with old-style rockets, like those of Soviet inventors. At the time rockets promised an exciting, high-tech future of space exploration, a long way from war-torn planet Earth. This 'future of the past' feeling is maintained by the streamlining of the squeezer's body (a teardrop being a good

aerodynamic shape). Starting in the thirties and continuing into the fifties streamlining made everything look modern, and the metaphor of streamlining, speeding unhindered towards the future, became a metaphor of social and technological progress.[12] In the late 1980s streamlining might just be thought of as retro, but it could also be taken as ironic, especially as there *is* actually a fluid moving over the surface of the lemon squeezer, albeit not at a speed that streamlining would help at all.

What could a monument in a progressive, social realist style mean? An ode to the socialist ideals of the then crumbling Soviet Union? It's certainly plausible though there are also less monumental aspects to the lemon squeezer. Its tripod configuration combined with the long legs and the top heavy form gives a feeling that the squeezer might easily tip over, and indeed it takes only an angle of around 10 degrees for the squeezer to become unstable. Could we find here the embodiment of a monument just about to topple? The Soviet Union perhaps, which did finally topple in 1991, or the eighties commitment to rampant capitalism, that didn't.

One might also read a certain sexiness into the object, the raised legs suggesting can-can images of the Follies Bergere, and the exaggerated length of the lower legs recalling the portraits of Vargas. Additionally the lemon juice dripping off the body is reminiscent of micturation.[13] Why have this suggestion of sex in the kitchen? It could be argued that by the late eighties, cooking had come to stand for a traditional, restrained sense of pleasure, whereas sex had come to stand for more liberal, and less restrained values towards pleasure.

[...]

We have, then, a number of possible ways to construe the lemon squeezer as an object that expresses or embodies ideas. We have the idea of permanence, the idea of 'a past future', the possibility of irony, the idea of instability, and of sex. A sexy, Soviet, statue; a morality tale for the overspending consumer: beware of fixed, top-heavy systems, for they may be toppled. And these, we have tried to show, might have been ideas running around people's heads during the social and political situation of the late eighties (when the lemon squeezer was produced) and the early nineties (when it was introduced into the market).

This is a potted historical sketch, certainly, but a sketch that puts the lemon squeezer in some sort of historical and political context able to suggest why the 'ideas' of certain groups of people might chime with the expressive possibilities of the lemon squeezer and go some way in explaining its success. It is a suggestion that makes no attempt at all to take into account Philippe Starck's professed intention for the lemon squeezer, instead trying to work from the 'facts' of it's form, construction, and function towards the values and ideas prevalent in the society of the time. Unfortunately it is rather unconvincing. This is because as a historical and situated account it provides a 'reading' of history with little explanatory power across large differences at the cultural, or even individual, level. One could say that such a reading is almost as 'creative' as the design itself.

THE FATE OF THE DESIGNER: OMNIPOTENCE, LIFE OR DEATH?

We started this paper with two contentions of Adrian Forty. The first was that the success of a design could not be entirely due to the personal creativity of the designer. The second was that 'no design works unless it embodies ideas that are held in common by the people for whom the object is intended'. Taking the two hypotheses together we set out to find out whether personal creativity could be considered a necessary or sufficient condition for a design's success. To this end we took Philippe Starck's lemon squeezer *Juicy Salif* as a case study. First looking at it from the viewpoint of Starck's creativity, then from the viewpoint of what the lemon squeezer might

embody or express in wider terms. We concluded first that it was unlikely that any other designer could have come up with the particular form that Starck did *as* a lemon squeezer; good evidence for us attributing Starck's creativity, or at least his personal background, as a necessary condition for its success. Secondly, we suggested that the argument for the lemon squeezer embodying the zeitgeist in some way – and its success being attributable to consumers sensing (and wanting) this embodiment – was a little shaky.

So does it matter at all what Philippe Starck thought when he sat in that Italian restaurant just off the coast of Tuscany and started to sketch? The evidence would suggest that he sat down with the intention of designing a lemon squeezer – an object to squeeze lemons that is – and probably do it provocatively and with some style. The lemon squeezer clearly does squeeze lemons, however badly some people may think it achieves this. It does also start conversations, Starck's professed intention for the design; this paper is testament to that function. Could these simple intentions be a sufficient condition in accounting for the product's success?

We argued earlier that the actual intentions about a design must logically exist prior to the existence of any particular design. The intention to design an object to squeeze lemons must certainly precede the design of any lemon squeezer, but the intention to design a 'conversational object' doesn't necessarily have to (otherwise the object would be called a 'conversation starter' and not a 'lemon squeezer'). It would seem that 'starting a conversation' is more of a description of the product's *actual* functioning than its intended functioning. Yet this kind of description used to justify a design might go a long way in accounting for the success of a design. This is because it is a description that can encompass the idiosyncratic use, systematic mis-use, or multiple uses of a product. These are the stories that emerge about a product once a consumer lives and engages with it. All Starck has done, we suggest, is observed how his product is *actually* used, and turned that into his realized intention as the reason for its success. But such a description is never something he could intend to produce in the design object since not every consumer will experience the lemon squeezer in its 'social lubricant' function. If a lemon squeezer does start a conversation it is because of the manifold associations, symbolisations, ideas, and evaluations it produces, and how these reveal themselves during the ongoing interaction with the product, not by the design of a single individual.

This conclusion is also that of Stanley Fish[14] and Roger Scruton.[15] Both argue, rather differently we might add, that consumers choose a product with the abstract aim of that product fitting their way of living (Fish), or goals in life (Scruton). And this abstract aim cannot be given in advance since the product initiates the process of realizing those aims. The success of the product, then, only comes about through the consumer's engagement with that product. The idea of the omnipotent designer may actually turn out to be useful for the consumer in realizing those aims – in shaping the engagement with the product – but this omnipotence derives from a different source than 'merely' solving a demonstrable problem through design.

The irony of all this of course is that, in questioning the omnipotence of the designer, the name of Philippe Starck has appeared in this paper 27 times. If we wanted to kill off the idea of the omnipotent designer, we've certainly been going about it a funny way. This contradiction alone should make us alive to the possibility of a design's success in some way encompassing the idea of the omnipotent designer. The main conclusions of our analysis suggest that we should conduct our search for the reasons of a particular design's success by looking for descriptions of engaged use that contradict, ignore, but sometimes support the original intentions of the designer.[16] And of course these descriptions can come from the designers themselves, it is just that they shouldn't be misconstrued as evidence for omnipotence, only as another drop in the ocean of consumer experience.

In summary it could be argued that a designer's personal creativity does form a necessary condition for a design's success, but it will never be a sufficient condition. For that we would need to take into account, not the ideas present in a particular society as Forty has suggested, but the personal creativity of the consumer to use or misuse the products that they buy. There is certainly skill in designing, it is just not a magical skill, and not a skill that extends past the completion of the design into its consumption.

[…]

NOTES

Reprinted from Lloyd, P. and Snelders, D., 'What Was Philippe Starck Thinking of?' *Design Studies* 24(3) (2003), pp. 237–53. Copyright © 2003, with permission from Elsevier.

1. Forty, A *Objects of Desire* Moffat, London (1986)
2. Carmel-Arthur, J *Philippe Starck* Carlton, London (1999)
3. Aldersey-Williams, H 'ID' *Starck and stardom* Vol May/June (1987) 46–51
4. Nobel, P 'Starck realities' *Metropolis* October (1998) www.metropolismag.com
5. Dick, P K *The man in the high castle* Vintage, New York (1962)
6. Morgan, C L *Philippe Starck* Universe, New York
7. Nobel, P 'Starck realities'
8. Starck, P *Starck* Taschen, Cologne, Germany (2000)
9. Cooper, M 'Philippe le roi' *Blueprint* November (1985) p. 48
10. Starck, P 'Starck speaks: politics pleasure play' *Harvard Design Magazine* Summer (1998) www.gsd.harvard.edu/desarts/
11. Nicols, S *Aluminium by design* Harold Abrams, New York (2000)
12. Giedion, S *Mechanization takes command: a contribution to anonymous history* Norton, New York (1948)

13. The name of the lemon squeezer, *Juicy Salif*, would appear to derive not from the name of a character in a Phillip K. Dick novel, as many of Starck's other designs have, but from the French word for saliva, salive.

14. Fish, S 'The unbearable ugliness of Volvos' in S Fish (ed.) *There's No Such Thing as Free Speech And it's a Good Thing Too*, Oxford University Press, Oxford UK (1994) pp 273–279

15. Scruton, R *The aesthetics of architecture* Methuen, London UK (1979)

16. See also J. L. Meikle, 'Material virtues: on the ideal and the real in design history' *Journal of Design History* Vol. 11 (1998) 191–199, for similar arguments.

29

FABRICATING IDENTITIES: SURVIVAL AND THE IMAGINATION IN JAMAICAN DANCEHALL CULTURE

Bibi Bakare-Yusuf (2006)

INTRODUCTION

An assessment of recent work on Jamaican dancehall culture reveals the absence of any systematic analysis of the role that fashion and adornment play in the culture. This is surprising given that fashion is a prominent and constitutive part of the culture *and* the site for vigorous debate about lower-class women's morality and sexuality in Jamaica. This failure can only be attributed to the fact that analyses of dancehall culture have generally focused on lyrical content, the sound system and the economic production of music.[1] I suggest that underlying this focus is the implicit assumption that music equates with interiority, language and "deep" meaning. In contrast, adornment and fashion are considered to elude or even destroy meaning. Therefore, to invest energy on adornment conjures up images of superficial, transient and frivolous activities undertaken only by women,[2] in contrast to the serious male world of ideas connoted by music production. While undeniably significant for a critical analysis of dancehall culture, a continued over-emphasis on music and lyrical content, to the neglect of other aspects of the culture, unwittingly privileges the activities of men and their interpretation of the culture to the exclusion of women.[3]

In this article, I want to shift attention away from lyrical content and to examine the embodied practices that emerged in the late 1980s to the end of the 1990s in Jamaica. I argue that working-class Black women in Jamaica use fashion to fabricate a space for the presentation of self-identity and assertion of agency. Through adornment, dancehall women have been able to address creatively the anxiety, violence and joy of daily life. At the same time, they have been able to register historical, cultural, economic and technological changes through their bodies.[4] Prior to speech or any written manifesto, different modes of adornment are employed to contest society's representation of and expectation about lower-class leisure activity, morality and sexual expression. Fashion allows dancehall women[5] to challenge the patriarchal, class-based and (Christian and Rastafarian) puritanical logic operating in Jamaica. Of course, the wider context in which this articulation of social relations has taken place is that of socio-political and economic realities which includes continued anti-black racism, black nationalism and global cultural and economic restructuring. In this sense, far from fashion being meaningless, superficial and unworthy of cultural analysis, it allows working-class black women to invest their everyday lived realities with multiple meanings and processes which links them to both the spectacular fetishism of global consumerism and mass media semiosis as well as the African love of ceremonial pomp and pageantry.

The fact that dancehall women most often do not consciously adhere to this critical position in their speech, nor readily perceive their action as jamming the hegemonic syntax, is quite beside the point.[6] Phenomenology teaches us that there is often a gap between intentional action and explicit, self-aware interpretation.[7] Far from imputing a kind of rational, contestive voluntarism to dancehall women, I suggest that the significance and meaning of their action as a form of contestation is not always available for self-articulation. As such, my account and interpretation of the meaning of fashion and adornment in the culture is not wholly circumscribed by empirical enquiry into conscious explanation, speech acts, or verbalized discourse. Rather, my analysis is based on *both* empirical engagement and my own analysis of the expressive body in the culture. This body, its desires and perceptions are seldom fully disclosed within speech; rather, they are made manifest in a variety of bodily practices.

CHANGING TIMES, CHANGING STYLES

Fashion styles are always embodied and situated phenomena, reflecting and embodying social and historical changes. Prosperity, crisis and social upheaval are stitched into the fabric of every epoch. For example, the extraordinary wealth of Renaissance Europe was materially layered into the ornate and elaborate detailing of upper-class clothing. In contrast, in its rejection of the sumptuous and colorful style of the *ancien régime*, postrevolution France adopted a less ostentatious and simple cut in order to reflect newfound freedom.[8] Fashion and bodily practices became a crucial site to both express wealth in the one case and challenge old hierarchies in the other.

Among New World Africans, fashion and bodily practices have also absorbed and expressed key symbolic functions. Starting from the long revolution fomented in the hold of the slave ship, when the enslaved cut their hair into elaborate designs[9] and reaching its apogee in the Black Power movement of the 1970s, bodily practices

were as important as political manifestos in the struggle for freedom, agency and assertion of cultural identity. The "natural" Afro hairstyle, dashiki, large-hooped earrings, psychedelic skirts and patchwork miniskirts of the 1960s and 1970s signalled a rejection of European aesthetics. Fashion styles visually represented and extended the ideological affirmation and valorization of blackness and Africanity in circulation during the period. Like their North American counterparts, many Jamaicans adopted Africanized textiles, kaftans and long flowing brightly colored majestic robes, head-wraps and jewelry made from natural materials such as seashells. However, during this period, the most important challenge to the aesthetic and ethical sensibilities of the Jamaican elite came in the form of Reggae music and the wearing of dreadlocks. Many Rastafarians and Reggae fans adopted dreadlocks and the military uniform of khakis and combat trousers. These motifs not only posed a challenge to the white capitalist and Christian ideology pervasive on the island, but they also drew attention to the permanent state of warfare that characterized life in the downtown ghettos of Kingston. Rastafarian fashion, in particular the wearing of dreadlocks, performed a critique of the dominant regime, asserting an alternative cultural, ethical and aesthetic sensibility in its stead.

In the late 1970s, the rise of Edward Seaga's neo-liberal free-enterprise government heralded a new era of increased insecurity, violence and anxiety. This political turn gave rise to a corresponding cultural energy. Popular cultural expression on the island such as music, dance and clothing style moved away from the socialist, pan-Africanist eschatological project associated with the Rastafarian Reggae of Bob Marley and Michael Manley's socialist government towards what appeared to be the hedonistic, self-seeking pleasure and excess of dancehall style.[10] Because the elite found it offensive and it was not initially given airplay on national radio, dancehall music was generally produced and consumed in the open air or indoor spaces designated as dancehalls.

Dancehall music or ragga (as it is known in Britain) is reggae's grittier and tougher offspring, making use of digital recording, remixing and sampling while DJs "skank" or "toast" over dub plates.[11] To the ruling elite, the music was considered pure noise, a cacophonous drone that grated the nerves. The lyrics were considered bawdy, guttural and sexually explicit. Finally, the elite considered dancehall (especially female) dress and adornment brash and excessive, reinforcing the view that lower-class Black women were sexually permissive. As a whole, the subculture confirmed to the Eurocentrically inclined elite the immorality and degeneracy of the urban poor.[12]

In contrast to this disparagingly reductive view, dancehall culture should be viewed as a complex reminder of the continued relationship between popular expressions, commodification, urbanization, global economic and political realities and historico-cultural memory. For example, in music, older Jamaican styles and practices were revived and brought into conversation with new digital technologies and global flows of information.[13] In terms of dance, dancehall unearthed older Jamaican forms such as Dinki Mini and Mento. As the Jamaican choreographer and cultural theorist Rex Nettleford notes,

> The movements in dancehall are nothing new; in my own youth I witnessed and participated in mento sessions which forced from executants the kind of axial movements which concentrated on the pelvic region with feet firmly grounded on one spot.[14]

Dancehall fashion fits into a general "African love of pageantry, adornments and social events …"[15] The African-American folklorist Zora Neale Hurston suggested that "The will to adorn" constitutes "the second … most notable characteristic in Negro expression."[16] The will to adorn, she argued, is not an attempt to meet conventional standards of beauty, but to satisfy the soul of its creator.[17] I suggest that the desire to "satisfy the soul" and project their own aesthetics onto the world is at the core of dancehall women's sartorial practice.

DANCEHALL FASHION

In a society influenced by Christian Puritanism and the sexual conservatism of Rastafarian ideology, dancehall fashion has responded antithetically with bare-as-you-dare fashion. Unlike previous African diasporic youth subcultures, dancehall is unique in that women are highly visible. Although there are a number of prominent female dancehall music performers, women's visibility in the culture centers on their ostentatious, sartorial pageantry. The "session," "bashment" or "dance" is an occasion for visual overload, maximalism and the liminal expression of female agency. Women form "modelling posses" or rival groups, where they compete with each other at a dance event for the most risqué and outlandish clothes. Their consumption practices are largely funded through the informal sector, as hagglers (informal commercial traders), petty traders, cleaners, dancehall fashion designers or by having a "sugar daddy." Many of the outfits are designed and made by the wearer or by a local tailor. The style appears anarchic, confrontational and openly sexual. Slashed clothing, the so-called "lingerie look" (such as g-string panties, bra tops), "puny printers" (showing the outline of the genitals), Wild West and dominatrix themes, pant suits, figure-hugging short dresses and micro hot pants infamously known as "batty-riders" are favored [Figure 24].

Revealing mesh tops, cheap lace, jeans designed as though bullets have ripped into the fabric and sequined bra tops became an essential part of dancehall women's wardrobe in the 1990s. At the close of the 1980s, the dancehall female body was wrapped in bondage straps and broad long fringes or panels attached to long dresses to accentuate the fluidity of the body's movement in dance. Incompatible materials and designs were juxtaposed – velvet, lace, leather, suede, different

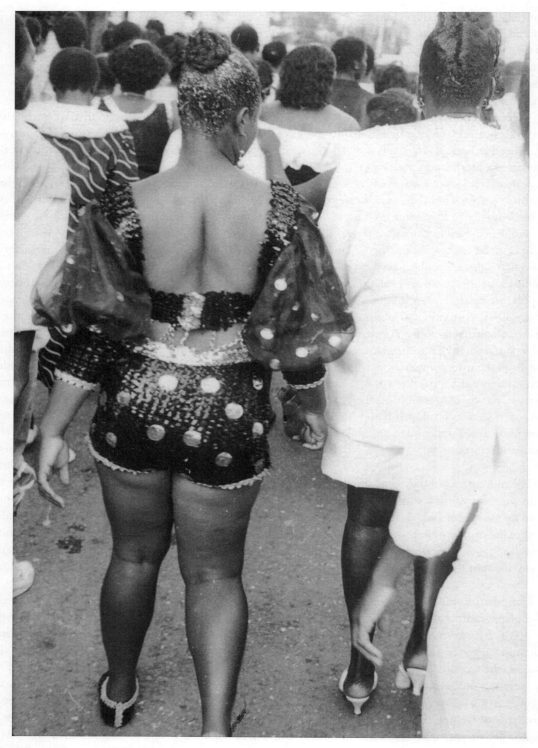

Figure 24. Batty-rider. Photo © The Gleaner Company Limited.

shades of denim, rubber and PVC, as well as animal prints such as mock snake, zebra and leopard skin, to produce an eclectic personal statement. Seemingly irreconcilable colors are combined to produce a refreshingly audacious, motile canvas on the dance floor. According to Carolyn Cooper, the sessions are the "social space in which the smell of female power is exuded in the extravagant display of flashy jewellery, expensive clothes [and] elaborate hairstyles."[18]

Hairstyle, make-up and jewelry are a key part of the dancehall look. In the late 1980s to late nineties, huge cheap and chunky gold earrings with razor-blade designs, as well as necklaces with dollar signs were worn on the ears, nose, nails, waist, and belly button as status symbols. More recently, the style has moved towards "ice" (slang for diamonds) and "bling-bling" (code for expensive jewelry and accessories). Hair is either dyed in bright colors or covered in metallic-colored wigs, weaves and extensions (platinum blonde, orange, turquoise, aubergine, pink). This style disrupts the Jamaican elite notions of "good" and "natural" hair versus "bad" and "processed" hair. In so doing, dancehall women draw attention to the artifice of African hairstyle[19] and the way "black women exercise power and choice."[20] In opposition to the Jamaican elite preference for understated beauty characterized by lightly applied make-up highlighting flawless skin, dancehall women's make-up is deliberately bright, glittery and brash. Shoe styles continue the sexual fetish theme of the clothes: laced or zipped up stilettos, knee or thigh-length boots in patent leather or "pleather" are favored for their emphasizing effects on the crotch and thighs. High-heeled strap shoes that coil round the calves towards the knees complete the image.[21]

[…]

GLOBAL AND LOCAL FLOWS

At first sight, dancehall fashion appears to be strangely dislocated from the rest of society, an orchidacious sub-culture extruded from beyond the rim of mainstream culture. Dancehall adornment springs out like an alien life form complete with its own entirely separate dynamics of existence and taste, like fungi on a tree. Dancehall fashion seems to be the very antithesis of conservative restraint and the concealed style of both official culture and Rastafarian gender coding. It appears to be totally divorced from any cultural or historical context or continuity; springing forth with mutant abundance in a flash of audaciously colored wigs, raucous screech-screaming lamé and sequined tops stretched revealingly across expanses of black flesh. And yet, this dislocated appearance is deceptive. Closer examination of dancehall style reveals deep cross-cultural and historical connections at work in its constitution, demonstrating an attunement with a hybrid array of cultural elements.

In an age of transactional flow of bodies, information, goods, mass media and images, cultural eclecticism has become the only response. Jamaica's proximity to North America, with the more than 60 American TV channels that beam into Jamaican homes, combined with the large number of Jamaicans in the diaspora, means that cultural influence and exchange is the norm. Like their counterparts in the sonic world, dancehall fashion also favors sampling, cutting and mixing in order to give birth to something different and distinct. Dancehall women have raided the global wardrobe and given it local texture. Odd and incongruous materials, imageries, accessories and patterns are combined to produce dizzying and dazzling layers of material, texture and form. Plastic, lurex, polyester, lycra, nylon are combined with leather, silk, organza lace, velvet, brocade. Late 1960s hot pants ride higher into the buttocks to reveal more than its original ever did; English granny purple-rinse hair styles become an unrecognizable, chromatic sculptured coiffure on youthful bodies; the "cut up" and bondage straps of punk were cleaned up and re-emerged as the "air-conditioned linen summer wear" designed by Sandra Campbell; Vivienne Westwood's 1976

Bondage Collection was hungrily retrieved and stripped of its Nazi associations. Punk girls' fishnet tights became the now classic mesh string vest. Fake chunky 22- carat gold evoked the tradition of goldsmith's art that flourished in the former Gold Coast of West Africa, Ghana, denuded of its royalty and hierarchy and reduced to a kitschy repetition of the original. The bridal nose ring linked to the ear by a fine delicate chain connects dancehall women to a tradition of Bollywood-esque ostentatious display. All these motifs are emblematic of the way in which dancehall women have absorbed and adapted global fashions, goods and images, and inflected them with new meanings that have made them refreshingly and uniquely Jamaican. This is what Hudita Nura Mustafa, in her account of changing fashion in Senegal, has termed the "sartorial ecumene." Sartorial ecumene refers to the "incorporation of objects and images of global origins into [local] practices and circulations involving dress and bodily adornment."[22] It is in the surface of adornment that the creative subjectivity and agency of women at the core of dancehall styling should be understood.

The fabric and cut of aspect of dancehall fashion has a direct lineage to the Jamaican masquerade tradition of Jonkonnu and "Pitchy Patchy." Here, women are clothed in strips of material gathered together to give the appearance of a jumble of loose layers of fabric. This historical connection enables us to understand a key point about dancehall culture: that it is far more closely connected to the deep fiber of the Jamaican folk tradition than the ruling elite would like to acknowledge:

> Old characters like Pitchy Patchy have their counterparts in contemporary dancehall. The best jeans (stone washed or plain) are made to look ragged with designer-looking patches of varying colours, with strategic rips or strips hanging like the organized raggedness of traditional Pitchy Patchy.[23]

Female adornment is grounded in a dense hybrid matrix of borrowings and repetitions, creating a truly diasporic culture of excess that is at once deeply embedded within a Jamaican folkloric tradition and again a manifestation of cultural borrowing and exchange from outside. Dancehall fashion is therefore a historical palimpsest, providing glimpses into layers of other historical styles, traditions and symbolic systems.

Having prowled through the international circuit of goods and images and woven them back into the local fabric, dancehall women return them to the world of consumption for further re-stitching. Dancehall fashion has quickly gathered its own international crop of sartorial disciples who raid and absorb the aesthetic reservoir of global street-wear and turn them into high fashion, by changing the context and the price and investing them with a symbolic capital that was missing in the early incarnation. Stripped of its rawness and tamed to suit European high-fashion tastes, dancehall fashion becomes an object of desire that those who are scornful of dancehall (but secretly admire it) can now wear. This is later recirculated among dancehall style aficionados to signify renewed prestige and taste in a complex feedback loop of call and response. For example, as the 1990s drew to a close, dancehall fashion connoisseurs turned to the very couture designers they inspired. Moschino and Versace are favorites among dancehall fashionistas (with their labels hanging out to show that they are wearing the "genuine" article). The issues of "original" and "copy" in reality, however, have little importance: designs, fabrics and modes of accessorizing are inscribed within a system of incessant borrowing and dialogue to the extent that it becomes futile to fixate on origin. Which came first, Pam Hogg's autumn/winter 1992/93 slashed latex body suit or the slashed t-shirts doing the rounds in Jamaica around the same time? Is Versace's gold encrusted jeans an original which the dancehall fashion aficionados imitated? The answer to these questions is impossible to resolve. The line of influence of any cultural artifact is often not obvious or explicit; in dancehall the line is a spaghetti sprawl of loops and curves. Origins and originals are the stuff of bourgeois distinction making and intellectual property rights – elements with no meaning in a world where the distinction between fake and real has little purchase. Rather, the incessant appropriation, re-appropriation and expropriation of global/local exchanges reveal the intrinsic mutuality of cultural artifacts and patterns of expression. Through dancehall's sartorial borrowing and transfer, fashion is perpetually caught up within a dynamic of differential repetition that has multiple origins.

In this article, I have argued that dancehall fashion and corporeal stylization show how women inured by life in the urban ghettos of Kingston interpret their life world, inflect it with meaning and recycle the different cultural artifacts circulating within a global economy of sartorial signs. Beneath interpretation and a semiotic analysis, however, I have indicated that dancehall styling is ultimately a question of survival; an excessively imaginative response to the class, race and gender-based normative violence of the hegemonic morality of the uptown elite. I hope to have encouraged an appreciation of the ways in which, prior to speech and lyricization, women in dancehall culture exhibit an expressive styling that ultimately should be characterized as a defiant performance of generative identity in the midst of perpetual existential crisis.

NOTES

Extracted from Bakare-Yusuf, B., 'Fabricating Identities: Survival and the Imagination in Jamaican Dancehall Culture,' *Fashion Theory* 10(4) (December 2006), pp. 461–83.

1. Stolzoff, Norman C. 2000. *Wake the Town and Tell the People: Dancehall Culture in Jamaica.* Durham, NC: Duke University Press; Cooper, Carolyn. 1993a. *Noises in the Blood: Gender and the "Vulgar" Body of Jamaican Popular Culture.* London: Macmillan.

2. Polhemus, Ted. 1988. *Bodystyles.* Luton: Lennard; Tseëlon, E. 1997. *The Masque of Femininity.* London: Sage.

3. This is not to deny that women do also contribute to the production of music as is [evidenced by] the prominence of female dancehall DJs such as Lady Saw, etc. However, through sartorial practices, a larger group of women can participate in and contribute to dancehall culture. Fashion and adornment thus becomes a democratic space which allows different categories of women to participate in the production of symbols and cultural meaning.

4. Breward, C. 1994. *The Culture of Fashion.* Manchester: Manchester University Press.

5. Not all female participants in the culture dress so flamboyantly, however. "Dancehall women" therefore refers to those women who spend a considerable amount of their time and resources attending the dancehall events, drawing attention to themselves at any event through their fashion style, which makes them stand out from the rest of the crowd. It is these women, known as dancehall "divas" or "donnets," who have aroused interest, fascination and vilification all at once, who are the central subject of this article.

6. During the fieldwork for this research it became clear that some of the subversive and transformative potential I attributed to dancehall women was not always explicitly shared by the women. Many pointed out that they had not intentionally set out to challenge hegemonic structures. Rather, they were simply dressing for themselves, and the dancehall space provided them with the opportunity to express themselves. The gap between how participants understand and explain their action and my own interpretation of their action in no way detracts from the argument. It is important to remember that Jamaican women have a long history of resisting oppressive regimes and articulating their existential positioning using a variety of media. I locate dancehall women's sartorial expression as a continuation of this history of resistance and cultural production.

7. Tseëlon, *The Masque of Femininity.*

8. Breward, *The Culture of Fashion*; Connerton, Paul. 1989. *How Societies Remember*. Cambridge: Cambridge University Press.

9. Mintz, Sidney W. and Richard Price. 1976. *The Birth of African-American Cultures: Anthropological Perspective*. Boston: Beacon.

10. Chude-Sokei, Louis. 1997. "Postnationalist Geographies: Rasta, Ragga, and Reinventing Africa." In Chris Potash (ed.) *Reggae, Rasta, Revolution: Jamaican Music From Ska to Dub*. London: Schirmer Books; Barrow, Steve and Peter Dalton. 1997. *Reggae: The Rough Guide*. London: Rough Guides.

11. Jahn, Brian and Tom Weber. 1992. *Reggae Island: Music in the Digital Age*. Kingston: Kingston Publishers.

12. It would be true to say that Dancehall music and culture have now become mainstream, but their energy, creativity and reproduction continue to be drawn from the socio-political and economic realities of the marginalized urban poor. Despite being a major Jamaican cultural export, Dancehall still occupies an ambivalent place within the Jamaican elite cultural imaginary.

13. Bilby, Kenneth. 1997. "From 'Jamaica.'" In Chris Potash (ed.) *Reggae, Rasta, Revolution: Jamaican Music From Ska to Dub*. London: Schirmer Books.

14. Nettleford, Rex. 1994. "Dance-hall, Part of the Jamaican Heritage?", *The Gleaner*, 22 July, 1C.

15. Mustafa, Hudita Nura 1998. "Sartorial Ecumenes: African Styles in a Social and Economic Context". In *The Art of African Fashion*. The Netherlands and Eritrea/USA: Prince Claus Fund and African World Press, New Jersey.

16. Hurston, Zora Neal. 1933. "Characteristics of Negro Expression." In Gena Dagel Caponi (ed.). 1999. *Signifyin(g), Sanctifyin', & Slam Dunking: A Reader in African American Expressive Culture*. Amherst: University of Massachusetts Press, p. 294.

17. Ibid.

18. Cooper, *Noises in the Blood*.

19. Mercer, Kobena. 1987. "Black Hair/style Politics." *New Formations* 3, Winter.

20. Banks, Ingrid. 2000. *Hair Matters: Beauty, Power, and Black Consciousness*, New York: New York University Press, p. 69.

21. D'Elia, Susan. 2002. "Women's Fashion in Jamaican Dancehalls." http://debate.uvm.edu/dreadlibrary/delia02.html

22. Mustafa, 'Sartorial Ecumenes,' p. 22.

23. Nettleford, Rex. 1995. "From Jonkonnu to Dancehall." *The Gleaner* (date illegible from original), 16D.

GUIDE TO FURTHER READING

Works that have been central to the concept of postmodernism include Guy Debord, *The Society of the Spectacle* (1967), Jean Francois Lyotard, *The Postmodern Condition: A Report on Knowledge* (1979), Jürgen Habermas, 'Modernity – An Incomplete Project' (1980), Ihab Hassan, 'Toward a Concept of Postmodernism,' in *The Postmodern Turn: Essays in Postmodern Theory and Culture* (1987) and Fredric Jameson, *Postmodernism, or The Cultural Logic of Late Capitalism* (1991). Essays by Habermas, Jameson, Baudrillard and others were popularized by Hal Foster in his collection *The Anti-Aesthetic: Essays on Postmodern Culture* (1983), and many anthologies and introductory books, such as Thomas Docherty (ed.), *Postmodernism: A Reader* (1993), Tim Woods, *Beginning Postmodernism* (1999) and Christopher Butler, *Postmodernism: A Very Short Introduction* (2002), have further helped to make these writings accessible.

The critical preoccupation with 'kitsch' can be traced to Clement Greenberg's influential essay 'The Avant Garde and Kitsch', written in 1939 for the journal *Partisan Review*, as well as to Frankfurt School theorists Max Horkheimer and Theodor Adorno's article 'The Culture Industry: Enlightenment as Mass Deception', in *Dialectic of Enlightenment*, originally published in 1944. In both cases the authors warn against what they perceive as the aesthetic deficiencies of popular art, an element that would be later celebrated by Pop Artists and consumers of the 'Populuxe' 1960s. See also Gillo Dorfles, ed., *Kitsch: the World of Bad Taste* (1968). In contrast, cultural theorists associated with the Centre for Contemporary Cultural Studies in Birmingham, UK, such as Stuart Hall, *Resistance Through Rituals: Youth Subcultures in Post-War Britain* (1975); Dick Hebdige, *Subculture: The Meaning of Style* (1979); and later Angela McRobbie, ed., *Zoot Suits and Second Hand Dresses: An Anthology of Fashion and Music* (1988), have viewed popular culture as a catalyst for, rather than passive receiver of creative innovation, focusing in particular on the activities of youth subcultures.

Postmodern ideas have also been influenced by writing on architecture, beginning with Jane Jacobs's alternative reading of urban planning in *The Death and Life of Great American Cities* (1961) and Robert Venturi's *Complexity and Contradiction in Architecture* (1966), both of which critique the modernist theories of architecture and the urban planning that can be traced to Le Corbusier's work in the 1920s. Charles Jencks's *The Language of Post-Modern Architecture* (1977) furthered this notion, as did Philip Johnson and Mark Wigley's exhibition and catalogue *Deconstructivist Architecture* (New York, Museum of Modern Art, 1988), which popularized the work of architects such as Frank Gehry and Zaha Hadid as inheritors and reworkings of Russian constructivism from the early twentieth century. Useful explanations of postmodernism in architecture include Diane Ghirardo, 'Introduction', in *Architecture after Modernism* (1996), and Kate Nesbitt (ed.), *Theorizing a New Agenda for Architecture: An Anthology of Architectural Theory, 1965–1995* (1996).

Theories of identity and subjectivity have also been central to concepts of postmodernism from psychoanalysis-influenced and feminist readings of film, such as Jacqueline Rose, *Sexuality in the Field of Vision* (1986), Joan Riviere, 'Womanliness as Masquerade' (1986), and Laura Mulvey, 'Visual Pleasure and Narrative Cinema' (1989), as well as from the point of view of postcolonialism or 'subaltern studies'. Key texts include Frantz Fanon, 'The Fact of Blackness,' in *Black Skin, White Masks* (1952, 1967), Edward Said, *Orientalism* (1978), Gayatri Chakravorty Spivak, 'Can the Subaltern Speak?' (1988) and Homi K. Bhabha, *The Location of Culture* (1994). The application of such thinking to design history includes, for example, Kobena Mercer, 'Black Hair/Style Politics' (1987) and Anne McClintock, 'Soft-Soaping Empire: Commodity Racism and Imperial Advertising' (1995).

For more on Italian postmodernism, see Grace Lees, 'Balancing the Object: The Reinvention of Alessi' (1997), Grace Lees-Maffei, 'Italianità and Internationalism' (2002), Penny Sparke, 'Nature, Craft, Domesticity and the Culture of Consumption: The Feminine Face of Design in Italy, 1945–1970' (1999), and Guy Julier, *The Culture of Design* (2000). For more on postmodern graphic design, see David Crowley and Paul Jobling, 'Graphic Design in a Postmodern Context: the Beginning and the End?' in *Graphic Design: Reproduction and Representation Since 1800* (1996), Paul Jobling, 'The Face' in *Fashion Spreads: Word and Image in Fashion Photography Since 1980* (1999), and Teal Triggs, 'Scissors and Glue: Punk Fanzines and the Creation of a DIY Aesthetic' (2006).

SECTION 6

Sustainable Futures, 1960–2003

INTRODUCTION

Rebecca Houze

Roughly a century after Arts and Crafts theorists had criticized the dehumanizing and wasteful excesses of industrialization, twentieth-century critics, designers, historians, manufacturers and concerned citizens again began to raise awareness of the environmental crisis that now holds our planet in peril. American biologist and writer Rachel Carson drew attention to the dangerous results of chemical pesticides in her 1962 book *Silent Spring*, which provoked public outcry and inspired a grassroots environmental movement in the United States that led to a nationwide ban on the use of DDT (dichlorodiphenyl-trichloroethane), and the establishment of the Clean Air Act of 1963 and Environmental Protection Agency in 1970. That same year the first Earth Day was celebrated. More than twenty years later, the first United Nations Earth Summit was held in Rio de Janeiro, Brazil in 1992. The rapid depletion of natural resources, mass extinction of plant and animal life and global warming that threatens to change earth's climate and destroy ecosystems around the world have been understood by many to be a direct result of the industrialism that gave birth to modern design. Numerous organizations have since been established around the world specifically to rethink design in light of new ecological awareness and reshape it for a sustainable future.

This section begins with an extract from *Operating Manual for Spaceship Earth*, written in 1969 by the visionary American architect and designer R. Buckminster Fuller, who first developed his theories of sustainability with models for 'Dymaxion' houses and cars in the 1920s and geodesic domes in the 1940s. In 'Spaceship Earth', Fuller conceives of the planet as both organic sustainer of life and technological wonder that we must care for and maintain in order for humanity continue to exist.

American social critic and journalist Vance Packard caused a sensation with his 1957 book *The Hidden Persuaders*, which claimed that the advertising industry used psychoanalytic methods to play upon our fears and desires, tempting us to buy. Packard's ideas, which implicated the designer in the corrosive and deleterious mechanism of manipulative advertising, were indicative of a growing discomfort within the design community itself. 'First Things First: A Manifesto' (1964), signed by twenty-two prominent graphic designers, including Ken Garland and Anthony Froshaug, asserted, 'we have reached a saturation point at which the high-pitched scream of consumer selling is no more than sheer noise … We think that there are other things more worth using our skill and experience on.' In 2000, 'First Things First', was revised and reissued, adding, 'Unprecedented environmental, social and cultural crises demand our attention … We propose a reversal of priorities in favour of more useful, lasting and democratic forms of communication – a mindshift away from product marketing and toward the exploration and production of a new kind of meaning.'

Packard's *The Waste Makers* (1960) was a scathing critique of America's gluttonous throwaway culture, unethical manufacturing practices, and depletion of natural resources. In the selection reproduced here, 'How to Outmode a $4,000 Vehicle in Two Years', Packard criticizes the automobile industry's manipulation of the consumption cycle through 'dynamic obsolescence'. In the 1950s, car manufacturers, he argues, finding little need for further mechanical innovation in their products, put their energies into making stylistic changes to each new model by adding different colours, squashing the body into flatter shapes, adding decorative headlights, voluptuous chrome detailing and sharper tailfins. Packard echoed Adolf Loos in his criticism of such changes, akin to the stylistic changes in women's fashions, which contributed to a more rapid devaluing of vehicles that were otherwise in good working order. Aside from the questionable ethical strategy of increasing sales through needless production, stylistic obsolescence sometimes led to manufacturing changes that were dangerous in other ways. In order to accommodate an increasingly flattened silhouette, for example, General Motors produced the Corvair with a rear-end motor. The Corvair, which became notorious for its deadly tendency to flip, was the impetus for consumer advocate Ralph Nader's influential book *Unsafe at Any Speed: The Designed-In Dangers of the American Automobile* (1965).

Austrian-American industrial designer Victor Papanek criticized the design profession for ignoring human need as well as that of the natural environment of planet earth in his collection of essays *Design for the Real World: Human Ecology and Social Change* (1971). In 'Do-it-Yourself Murder: The Social and Moral Responsibilities of the Designer', Papanek picks up on Packard's criticism of stylistic obsolescence, and argues that the responsible designer, rather than stimulating the whims of the wealthiest fraction with streamlined toasters, should find solutions to living improvements in the developing world, and among the overlooked 'minority', who actually constitute the majority of the human population. Simple irrigation pumps made of old tires, ergonomic chairs for restless schoolchildren, contraceptive packaging for the illiterate and low-cost educational television sets were among the creative design projects he supported.

Whereas Fuller, Packard and Papanek each approached design as designers or critics, Jeffrey Meikle looks at the plastics industry from the point of view of a historian. His account, based on trade and popular literature, as well as archival documents, traces the development of imitative synthetic materials, from celluloid in the nineteenth century to Bakelite in the 1930s to the explosion of industrial chemical products in the 1960s. The section extracted here, 'Material Doubts and Plastic Fallout', deals with the backlash against the plastics industry as a result of new ecological awareness. Critics of plastics warned against the expensive wastefulness of petroleum fuel, unsightly overflowing landfills, children smothered by clinging plastic laundry bags, and fatal destruction of land, air, water, plant, animal and human life as a result of toxic pollution.

By the 1980s and 1990s, our impact on the environment began to be seen as the responsibility not only of the designer or government regulation but of the consumer as well. Joel Makower's *The Green Consumer Supermarket Guide*, reminiscent of the *Whole Earth Catalogue* project, with contributions from John Elkington and Julie Hailes (1991), offered simple ways for consumers to make more educated choices about the products they purchased, from dishwashing detergents to juice boxes to batteries. By selecting items produced by companies with ethical manufacturing records, made with non-toxic ingredients and packaged in recyclable containers, consumers could exert pressure on industry to design in a more sustainable manner. In the past century we have stuffed landfills with garbage. In 'Redefining Rubbish: Commodity Disposal and Sourcing', in *Second Hand Cultures* (2003), Nicky Gregson and Louise Crewe explore what happens to the discarded trash of our throwaway culture when it becomes reabsorbed as a new type of desirable object.

As both the cause and effect of industrialization, what role will design play in the future? Today, 'green' design has become more than a fashionable trend. In the wake of human-caused environmental catastrophe, and of natural disaster insufficiently planned for, ecologically sensitive design is now the only option. Architect William McDonough sees the natural world, like R. Buckminster Fuller before him, as the model for design and as the supplier of a perpetually renewable energy source – the sun. In *The Hannover Principles* written for the 1992 Earth Summit, William McDonough summarizes the view that we are one among many species who must coexist, and that we must design 'for all children, of all species, for all time'.

30

OPERATING MANUAL FOR SPACESHIP EARTH

R. Buckminster Fuller (1969)

Our little Spaceship Earth is only eight thousand miles in diameter, which is almost a negligible dimension in the great vastness of space. Our nearest star – our energy-supplying mother-ship, the Sun – is ninety-two million miles away, and the nearest star is one hundred thousand times further away. It takes approximately four and one third years for light to get to us from the next nearest energy supply ship star. That is the kind of space-distanced pattern we are flying. Our little Spaceship Earth is right now traveling at sixty thousand miles an hour around the sun and is also spinning axially, which, at the latitude of Washington, D.C., adds approximately one thousand miles per hour to our motion. Each minute we both spin at one hundred miles and zip in orbit at one thousand miles. That is a whole lot of spin and zip. When we launch our rocketed space capsules at fifteen thousand miles an hour, that additional acceleration speed we give the rocket to attain its own orbit around our speeding Spaceship Earth is only one-fourth greater than the speed of our big planetary spaceship. Spaceship Earth was so extraordinarily well invented and designed that to our knowledge humans have been on board it for two million years not even knowing that they were on board a ship. And our spaceship is so superbly designed as to be able to keep life regenerating on board despite the phenomenon, entropy, by which all local physical systems lose energy. So we have to obtain our biological life-regenerating energy from another spaceship: the sun.

Our sun is flying in company with us, within the vast reaches of the Galactic system, at just the right distance to give us enough radiation to keep us alive, yet not close enough to burn us up. And the whole scheme of Spaceship Earth and its live passengers is so superbly designed that the Van Allen belts, which we didn't even know we had until yesterday, filter the sun and other star radiation which as it impinges upon our spherical ramparts is so concentrated that if we went nakedly outside the Van Allen belts it would kill us. Our Spaceship Earth's designed infusion of that radiant energy of the stars is processed in such a way that you and I can carry on safely. You and I can go out and take a sunbath, but are unable to take in enough energy through our skins to keep alive. So part of the invention of the Spaceship Earth and its biological life-sustaining is that the vegetation on the land and the algae in the sea, employing photosynthesis, are designed to impound the life-regenerating energy for us to adequate amount.

But we can't eat all the vegetation. As a matter of fact, we can eat very little of it. We can't eat the bark nor wood of the trees nor the grasses. But insects can eat these, and there are many other animals and creatures that can. We get the energy relayed to us by taking the milk and meat from the animals. The animals can eat the vegetation, and there are a few of the fruits and tender vegetation petals and seeds that we can eat. We have learned to cultivate more of those botanical edibles by genetical inbreeding.

That we are endowed with such intuitive and intellectual capabilities as that of discovering the genes and the R.N.A. and D.N.A. and other fundamental principles governing the fundamental design controls of life systems as well as of nuclear energy and chemical structuring is part of the extraordinary design of the Spaceship Earth, its equipment, passengers, and internal support systems. It is therefore paradoxical but strategically explicable, as we shall see, that up to now we have been mis-using, abusing, and polluting this extraordinary chemical energy-interchanging system for successfully regenerating all life aboard our planetary spaceship.

One of the interesting things to me about our spaceship is that it is a mechanical vehicle, just as is an automobile. If you own an automobile, you realize that you must put oil and gas into it, and you must put water in the radiator and take care of the car as a whole. You begin to develop quite a little thermodynamic sense. You know that you're either going to have to keep the machine in good order or it's going to be in trouble and fail to function. We have not been seeing our Spaceship Earth as an integrally-designed machine which to be persistently successful must be comprehended and serviced in total.

Now there is one outstandingly important fact regarding Spaceship Earth, and that is that no instruction book came with it. I think it's very significant that there is no instruction book for successfully operating our ship. In view of the infinite attention to all other details displayed by our ship, it must be taken as deliberate and purposeful that an instruction book was omitted. Lack of instruction has forced us to find that there are two kinds of berries – red berries that will kill us and red berries that will nourish us. And we had to find out ways of telling which-was-which red berry before we ate it or otherwise we would die. So we were forced, because of a lack of an instruction book, to use our intellect, which is our supreme faculty, to devise scientific experimental procedures and to interpret effectively the significance of the experimental findings. Thus,

because the instruction manual was missing we are learning how we safely can anticipate the consequences of an increasing number of alternative ways of extending our satisfactory survival and growth-both physical and metaphysical.

Quite clearly, all of life as designed and born is utterly helpless at the moment of birth. The human child stays helpless longer than does the young of any other species. Apparently it is part of the invention "man" that he is meant to be utterly helpless through certain anthropological phases and that, when he begins to be able to get on a little better, he is meant to discover some of the physical leverage-multiplying principles inherent in [the] universe as well as the many nonobvious resources around him which will further compoundingly multiply his knowledge-regenerating and life-fostering advantages.

I would say that designed into this Spaceship Earth's total wealth was a big safety factor which allowed man to be very ignorant for a long time until he had amassed enough experiences from which to extract progressively the system of generalized principles governing the increases of energy[-]managing advantages over environment. The designed omission of the instruction book on how to operate and maintain Spaceship Earth and its complex life-supporting and regenerating systems has forced man to discover retrospectively just what his most important forward capabilities are. His intellect had to discover itself. Intellect in turn had to compound the facts of his experience. Comprehensive reviews of the compounded facts of experiences by intellect brought forth awareness of the generalized principles underlying all special and only superficially-sensed experiences. Objective employment of those generalized principles in rearranging the physical resources of environment seems to be leading to humanity's eventually total success and readiness to cope with far vaster problems of universe.

To comprehend this total scheme we note that long ago a man went through the woods, as you may have done, and I certainly have, trying to find the shortest way through the woods in a given direction. He found trees fallen across his path. He climbed over those crisscrossed trees and suddenly found himself poised on a tree that was slowly teetering. It happened to be lying across another great tree, and the other end of the tree on which he found himself teetering lay under a third great fallen tree. As he teetered he saw the third big tree lifting. It seemed impossible to him. He went over and tried using his own muscles to lift that great tree. He couldn't budge it. Then he climbed back atop the first smaller tree, purposefully teetering it, and surely enough it again elevated the larger tree. I'm certain that the first man who found such a tree thought that it was a magic tree, and may have dragged it home and erected it as man's first totem. It was probably a long time before he learned that any stout tree would do, and thus extracted the concept of the generalized principle of leverage out of all his earlier successive special-case experiences with such accidental discoveries. Only as he learned to generalize fundamental principles of physical universe did man learn to use his intellect effectively.

Once man comprehended that any tree would serve as a lever his intellectual advantages accelerated. Man freed of special-case superstition by intellect has had his survival potentials multiplied millions fold. By virtue of the leverage principles in gears, pulleys, transistors, and so forth, it is literally possible to do more with less in a multitude of physio-chemical ways. Possibly it was this intellectual augmentation of humanity's survival and success through the metaphysical perception of generalized principles which may be objectively employed that Christ was trying to teach in the obscurely told story of the loaves and the fishes.

NOTE

Reproduced from Buckminster Fuller, R., *Operating Manual for Spaceship Earth*, Carbondale, IL: Southern Illinois University Press, 1969, pp. 49–56. Reprinted by permission of the Estate of R. Buckminster Fuller.

31

HOW TO OUTMODE A $4,000 VEHICLE IN TWO YEARS, FROM *THE WASTE MAKERS*

Vance Packard (1960)

One of the strangest, yet best recognized, secrets of Detroit is 'planned obsolescence' – a new model every year. – BUSINESS WEEK

An auto-parts dealer in Springfield, Illinois, offered me the opinion that as far as he could figure the United States motorcar had become "a women's fashion item." And an advertising executive working on a motorcar account confessed: "You want to know what sells cars today? It's style, period!" The advertisements certainly seemed to spell out his conviction. Some samples:

Ford: "Nothing Newer in The World of Style" – or later, "*Vogue* magazine says Ford is a Fashion Success."

Chevrolet: "Styling That Sets a New Style"

De Soto: "Best dressed Car of the year"

Oldsmobile: "Start of a New Styling Cycle."

When the new 1960 Pontiac was unveiled, *The New York Times* described its sculptured lines – "a horizontal V front" – and added this observation: "Emphasis is almost entirely on styling, for there are no major mechanical changes."

The automobile industry was the first major group to become fascinated with the increased sales that might be achieved by imitating the women's-fashion stylists. Decades ago, General Motors took the automotive leadership from Henry Ford I by successfully insisting that competition be on the basis of styling rather than pricing. Mr. Ford in fifteen years had brought the price of his Model T motorcar down from $780 to $290, by sticking to a basic design except for minor changes. Such fantastical dedication to the ideal of an ever-lower price tag made competition on the basis of price most unattractive. Competitors such as General Motors did not relish trying to match Old Henry in either production know-how or pricing, so they emphasized a yearly change and a variety to choose from.

In the twenties and thirties, significant technological innovations such as balloon tires, shock absorbers, and four-wheel brakes were available almost every year to captivate the public. By the early fifties, however, the automobile industry was finding itself with fewer and fewer significant technological improvements that it felt were feasible to offer the public. Consequently, at all the major automotive headquarters – Ford now included – more and more dependence was placed on styling. One aim was to create through styling "dynamic obsolescence," to use the phrase of the chief of General Motors styling, Harley Earl. The motorcar makers began "running up and down stairs," as fashion merchandiser Alfred Daniels put it.

"New" became the key word as the manufacturers sought to make car owners feel like old fuds in any vehicle more than two years old. When the 1957 motorcars were launched, Chrysler revealed that it had "The Newest New Cars in 20 Years." Nash had "The World's Newest ... Car." And

Pontiac was "Completely New From Power to Personality." A columnist for *Advertising Age* noted that Buick – which he called the least changed of the new models – had used the word "new" twenty times in an advertisement. He added: "We find it difficult to assume that such complete and utter nonsense is justified by the need to sell 7,000,000 cars in 1957. If our national prosperity is to be founded on such fanciful, fairyland stuff as this, how real and tangible can our prosperity be?"

That, indeed, seemed a fair question. And glory be to an advertising-industry man for raising it!

The intensified preoccupation with obsolescence-through-style brought new power to the automobile stylists and more than a little grumbling from engineers, who felt they were receiving less and less attention when it came to fixing the format of automobiles. General Motors' Mr. Earl defined the stylist, incidentally, as "a man who is dissatisfied with everything." At Ford, styling was taken away from engineering and made a separate department. The $200,000-a-year head of this styling department, George W. Walker – "the Cellini of Chrome" – was at one time a stylist for women's clothing. When the 1958 models were launched, he frankly conceded that he designed his cars primarily for women. "They are naturally style conscious," he said, and even though they may not drive the car in many cases they seem to have a major say in the choice of a new car.

When the president of General Motors found himself testifying before a Senate subcommittee in the late fifties, he alluded to the "application of fancification to our automobiles." At another sitting he said, "Styling has become increasingly important in determining the share of the market."

Let us pause and examine in some detail just how "fancification" and other styling devices were systematized to produce obsolescence of desirability in the traveling machines made in the United States.

To comprehend the strategic mapping going on behind all the commotion about styling, we need first of all to understand the shell game Detroit plays with the public. The body shell is crucial to obsolescence planning.

If motorcar salesmen had their way, automobile makers would issue a vehicle that at least looks brand new each year or half year. Unfortunately for them, it costs many, many millions of dollars for retooling to overhaul a motorcar's physical form in any fundamental way. Consequently, even in seeking the superficial outer appearances of change, the motorcar makers have depended to a large extent upon illusion created by changes of decoration rather than of the body shell.

As recently as 1956, the Detroit motorcar makers customarily made a major overhaul in their shell only every third year. During the two intervening annual models they simply rejiggered grilles, lights, fenders, and so on. By 1957, the industry was heading toward an overhaul of the shell every second year. One year was becoming known as the year for "basic" change and the other the year for the "trim" change.

And by 1958, insiders were whispering the news – stunning to competitors – that General Motors was going to overhaul the shells of its five motorcars every single year. Each car was to be a new car each year. General Motors was able to achieve this break-through by an interesting expedient made possible by its gargantuan size. It chose to create a new look for its five cars each year by sacrificing some of the distinctiveness in the appearance of each of the five, Chevrolet, Pontiac, Oldsmobile, Buick, Cadillac. (This was before the compacts.) In short, all General Motors cars would bear more than a little family resemblance. The bold decision was made to bring out a brand new shell each year and to use it for all five cars. Almost all models of all five cars each year would have substantially the same body. The basic body shell was to be stretched amidship about three inches for some of the big Cadillacs and Buicks. Later, there were reports that the three "luxury" compacts, which General Motors began unveiling in late 1960, would also have their own common body shell.

When General Motors' five standard-size cars for 1959 were unveiled, Joseph Callahan, the engineering editor of *Automotive News*, reported that "at least 12 important stampings are identified on all 5 cars."[1] Among the twelve he mentioned were a number of door panels, the upper back panel, three cowl panels.

"The big advantage of the common body," he explained, "is that the manufacturer of a multiple line of cars can save some of the millions it annually spends to create style obsolescence."

Obviously the major hazard in such an approach was the possible appearance of sameness in all General Motors motorcars. Action was taken to reduce this hazard by attaching different trimmings to the basic shell. Strips of painted metal were attached to the doors to produce distinctive sculptured looks. And Callahan added "Differences also were produced by using a variety of chrome trim, rear deck lids, quarter panels, bumper and bumper guards. Of course, many interchangeable parts are reworked for different cars and models. Reworking is achieved by changing the location of holes, making minor changes of shape, attaching extra pieces, etc."

Automotive insiders began speculating – and still are – whether the less gigantic Ford and Chrysler companies would be able to follow General Motors' all-new-shell-every-year program. A Senate subcommittee report on "Administered Prices" in the automobile field expressed concern about General Motors' move. It stated: "General Motors … alone has the financial resources to play this form of nonprice competition to the full: all other companies have good cause to be deeply alarmed over the future."[2]

Meanwhile, advertising journals surmised that eventually the automobile industry might be able to reach a new-car-every-six-months cycle of innovation.

How could the stylists know what shell to use when they had to design at least three years ahead of the car's unveiling? The styling experts at General Motors held an advantage in trying to anticipate – without exercising more than moderate clairvoyance – what shell or silhouette was likely to be considered smart looking by the public three years hence. General Motors bought about half of all automobile advertising. Since the silhouette had to be frozen so far in advance of unveiling, General Motors was aided in securing a favorable response from the public three years later by its superior image-building power. As the Senate report pointed out: "Because of its great sales volume it [General Motors] has an immense impact in framing consumer attitudes toward style changes." During Senate hearings George Romney, president of the then-small American Motors, which pioneered the American-built compacts, testified to General Motors' power to mold public taste when he talked about the wrap-around windshield – and the "millinery" aspect of car making. He said that if a small company had introduced the wrap-around, it probably would have been a flop. It took a big company to swing it. Familiarity, he said, begins acceptance. Mr. Romney then made this remarkable comment:

"Now, Senator, in this millinery aspect, in the fashion aspect, a company doing 45 to 50 per cent of the business can make an aspect of car appearance a necessary earmark of product acceptance by the public just as a hat manufacturer – a woman's hat manufacturer – who sold 50 per cent of the hats would have a much easier time of making all other hat manufacturers put cherries on their hats if the cherries were decided by it to be the fashion note for the year." (Mr. Romney spent several heartbreaking years trying to interest the American public in the rationality of compacts and probably succeeded only because of the dazzling logic of his case – and the fact that many American sophisticates had turned to small foreign cars for relief from Detroit's gaudy giantism. This made it psychologically safe for Americans to be seen in small cars.)

During most of the fifties, the General Motors stylists decided that the trend in silhouettes should be toward cars that were ever longer, ever lower, and ever wilder at the extremities. By 1959, one automobile executive was confessing: "In length we have hit the end of the runway." A Chicago official estimated that just getting cars back to the postwar length would release eight hundred miles of street space for parking. There was no question, however, that millions of Americans still wanted the biggest-looking car they could get, particularly if they lived in wide-open areas where parking was not a serious and chronic problem.

Detroit producers who tried to bring out cars that defied the direction in styling general Motors had set – such as Chrysler in the early fifties – were badly mauled.

By the late fifties, Poiret's law that all fashion ends in excess was indubitably being demonstrated in the automotive field. The Big Three stylists were speculating how many more inches they could lower the silhouette before snapping the human endurance and overstraining their own ingenuity. A four-wheeled vehicle can be squashed only so far. They used smaller wheels. They sacrificed rigidity. Some of them spread the wheels still further apart as the only way left to get the engine lower. Meanwhile, the hump down the middle grew. The joke spread that the front seat of the new wide, wide cars could hold two grownups and a midget. One reason General Motors accepted the revolutionary idea of putting a rear-end motor in its Corvair was that this helped solve the hump problem.

As early as 1957, *Automotive Industries* reported that the low silhouette had become so low that "many people feel we have reached bottom." It added, however, "There is a feeling that stylists are aiming ever lower." The sight line of drivers had dropped nine inches below the sight line of prewar autos. The following year, *The Harvard Business Review* carried an illuminating paper on product styling by Dwight E. Robinson, professor of business administration at the University of Washington. His investigations had taken him, among other places, to Detroit's secretive studios for styling. He reported: "Stylists recognize that the extreme limits on lowness imposed by the human physique are only a few inches away and [will] come close to realization in the 1960 models."

By 1959, Pontiac's Bonneville hardtop stood just four and a half feet high, a full foot lower than the Pontiac of a decade earlier. Some drivers of late-model makes of cars – where seats were nearly a half foot closer to the floor than they had been a decade earlier – reported they were wearing bicycle clips to keep their pant cuffs from dragging on the floor. People also began discovering that sitting in a low-seated car throws more of the weight onto the end of the spine, a more tiring position for long trips.

In July, 1959, *The Wall Street Journal* reported an astonishing incident that indicated the style swing must certainly finally be approaching its nadir. At General Motors' own annual meeting, shareholders stood up and lamented their personal difficulties in trying to work their bodies into late-model General Motors cars. One man from New Jersey exclaimed, "I bumped my knee and my head getting into" a 1959 Oldsmobile. He was received by a burst of applause. An average-sized man from Massachusetts exclaimed that he found he couldn't sit in a 1959 Buick with his hat on. And he added: "It's a disgrace for a woman to have to get in and out of such low cars."

The report commented that General Motors' Chairman Frederic G. Donner "listened impassively and without comment" to these laments.

Six months earlier, the same Mr. Donner was quoted in *Sales Management* as supporting what it referred to as "artificial obsolescence." Mr. Donner was reported stating, "if it had not been for the annual model change, the automobile as we know it today would not be produced in volume and would be priced so that relatively few could afford to own one. Our customers would have no incentive or reason to buy a new car until their old one wore out." He clearly was concerned about giving car owners "an incentive or reason" to turn in their old cars before they wore out physically.

Meanwhile, stylists were striving to justify the new low, low cars on high philosophic or sound functional grounds. A Chrysler stylist told a Detroit gathering of the Society of Automobile Engineers that the low silhouette was all a part of a broad trend to the "low look" in contemporary design. He cited everything from ranch houses to sofas. Others cited the low center of gravity in the new cars as a great aid in cornering. Actually, the banked curves of most of the recently built highways made this a puny plus factor.

As for the trend to wildness at the extremities, this was evidently related stylistically to squashing down the midsection. If you believed the motor-car advertisements, you assumed there was sound functional reason for the fantastic outcropping of tail fins on motorcars in the late fifties. The fins were said to stabilize a moving car in a crosswind. Professor Robinson commented: "I found few designers in Detroit willing to say there is much scientific support for these claims."

Instead, Professor Robinson concluded that the fins began jutting up on the drawing boards as the stylists sought to push the midsection lower and lower. He asserted: "The analogy between this squashing effect and tight lacing at the waist and expansion of the skirt in the crinoline era is al-most irresistible." He went on to say, "The tail fin – supposedly derived from the airplane tail – may be interpreted as the last resort of over-extension, an outcropping that quite seriously serves much the same purpose as the bustle or the train."

[…]

The Big Three of Detroit were spending more than a billion dollars a year to put a new dress on their cars each year. To put it another way, since the consumer of course pays in the end, the average new-car buyer was paying more than two hundred dollars extra to cover the annual cost of restyling the cars. And this did not include the actual cost of the non-functional "brightwork" or "goop" placed on the cars. That added at least another hundred dollars.

A further cost of the annual styling was the loss in quality. Laurence Crooks of Consumers Union put it this way: "The annual model change has a great deal to do with lack of quality in cars, and any speeding up of this changing… always redounds to the discredit of the cars. It takes a long time to perfect a car and get the bugs out of it."

Because of all these factors related to style change, American cars were declining in value at a precipitous rate. The Federal Reserve Bank of Philadelphia made a study of this aging problem of "second-hand sirens" and concluded that motorcars were depreciating twice as fast as they reasonably should. It explained:[3] "Because yearly model changes make a car look older than it actu-ally is, mechanically speaking, the price drops faster than the remaining mileage potential … A car four years old with roughly two-thirds of its active life left usually sells for about one-third of its original price. Variety and change accelerate obsolescence."

NOTES

Extracted from Packard, V., *The Waste Makers*, New York: D. McKay Co., 1960, pp. 78–91. © Vance Packard. Reprinted by permission of The Estate of Vance Packard.

1. *Automotive News*, December 29, 1858, p. 13.
2. *Report of the U.S. Senate Antitrust and Monopoly Subcommittee of the Committee on the Judiciary, 85th Congress, 2nd Session. November 1, 1958.* "A Study of Administered Prices in Automotive Industry," p. 85.
3. *Business Review* of the Federal Reserve Bank of Philadelphia, April 1959, p. 2.

32

DO-IT-YOURSELF MURDER: THE SOCIAL AND MORAL RESPONSIBILITY OF THE DESIGNER, FROM *DESIGN FOR THE REAL WORLD*

Victor Papanek (1971)

The truth is that engineers are not asked to design for safety. Further inaction will be criminal – for it will be with full knowledge that our action can make a difference, that auto deaths can be cut down, that the slaughter on our highways is needless waste … it is time to act. – Robert F. Kennedy

One of my first jobs after leaving school was to design a table radio. This was shroud design: the design of the external covering of the mechanical and electrical guts. It was my first, and I hope my last, encounter with appearance design, styling, or design "cosmetics." The radio was to be one of the first small and inexpensive table radios to compete on the post-war market. Still attending school part-time, I naturally felt insecure and frightened by the enormity of the job, especially since my radio was to be the only object manufactured by a new corporation. One evening Mr. G. my client, took me out on the balcony of his apartment overlooking Central park.

He asked me if I realized the kind of responsibility I had in designing a radio for him.

With the glib ease of the chronically insecure, I launched into a spirited discussion of "beauty" at the market level and "consumer satisfaction." I was interrupted. "Yes. Of course, there is all that," he conceded, "but your responsibility goes far deeper than that." With this he began a lengthy

and cliché-ridden discussion of his own (and by extension his designer's) responsibility to his stockholders and especially his workers:

Just think what making your radio entails in terms of our workers. In order to get it produced, we're building a plant in Long Island City. We're hiring about 600 new men. Now what does that mean? It means that workers from many states, Georgia, Kentucky, Alabama, Indiana, are going to be uprooted. They'll sell their homes and buy new ones here. They'll form a whole new community of their own. Their kids will be jerked out of school and go to different schools. In their new subdivision supermarkets, drugstores, and service stations will open up, just to fill their needs. And now, just suppose that radio doesn't sell. In a year we'll have to lay them all off. They'll be stuck for their monthly payments on homes and cars. Some of the stores and service stations will go bankrupt when the money stops rolling in. Their homes will go into sacrifice sales. Their kids, unless daddy finds a new job, will have to change schools. There will be a lot of heartaches all around, and that's not even thinking of my stockholders. And all this because you have made a design mistake. *That's* where responsibility really lies, and I bet that they never taught you this at school!

I was very young and, frankly, impressed. Within the closed system of Mr. G.'s narrow market dialectics, it all made sense. Looking back at the scene from a vantage point of a good number of years, I must agree that the designer bears a responsibility for the way products he designs are received at the market place. But this is still a narrow and parochial view. The designer's responsibility must go far beyond these considerations. His social and moral judgment must be brought into play long *before* he begins to design, since he has to make a judgment, an *a priori* judgment at that, as to whether the products he is asked to design or redesign merit his attention at all. In other words, will his design be on the side of social good or not.

Food, shelter, and clothing: that is the way we have always described mankind's basic needs. With increasing sophistication we have added tools and machines. [...] We have taken clean air and pure water for granted for the first ten million years or so, but now this picture has changed drastically. While the reasons for our poisoned air and polluted streams and lakes are fairly complex, industrial designers and industry in general are certainly co-responsible with others for this appalling state of affairs.

In the mid-thirties the American image abroad was frequently created by the movies. The make-believe, fairyland, Cinderella-world of "Andy Hardy Goes to College" and "Scarface" communicated something which moved our foreign viewers more, directly and subliminally, than either plot or stars. It was the communication of an idealized environment, an environment upholstered and fitted out with all the latest gadgets available.

Today we export the products and gadgets themselves. And with the increasing cultural and technological Coca-colonization of that part of the world we are pleased to think of as "free," we are also in the business of exporting environments and "life styles" of the prevalent white, middle-class, middle-income society abroad and into ghettos, poverty pockets, Indian reservations, etc., at home.

The designer-planner is responsible for nearly all of our products and tools and nearly all of our environmental mistakes. He is responsible either through bad design or by default: by having thrown away his responsible creative abilities, by "not getting involved," or by "muddling through."

I am defining the social and moral responsibilities in design. For by repeating his mistakes a millionfold or more through designs affecting all of our environments, tools, machines, shelters, and transportation devices, the designer-planner has finally put murder onto a mass production basis.

[...]

Design is a luxury enjoyed by a small clique who form the technological, moneyed, and cultural "elite" of each [South American] nation. The 90 per cent of the native Indian population which lives "up-country" has neither tools nor beds nor shelter nor schools nor hospitals that have ever been within breathing distance of the designer's board or workbench. It is this huge population of the needy and the dispossessed [with whom we are concerned]. If I suggest that this holds equally true of most of Africa, Southeast Asia, and the Middle East, there will be little disagreement.

Unfortunately, this ... applies just as easily to our own country. The rural poor, the black and white citizens of our inner cities, the educational tools we use in over 90 per cent of our school systems, our hospitals, doctors' offices, diagnostic devices, farm tools, etc., suffer design neglect. New designs may sporadically occur in these areas, but usually only as a result of market pressures, rather than as a result of either research breakthrough or a genuine response to a real need.

[...]

Can there be substantial doubt that the peoples of this world are not served by designers?

[...]

All too often designers who try to operate within the entire [design problem of a particular country or the world] find themselves accused of "designing for the minority." Apart from being foolish, this charge is completely false and reflects the misconception and misperception under which the design field operates. The nature of this faulty perception must be examined and cleared up.

Let us suppose that an industrial designer or an entire design office were to "specialize" exclusively within the areas of human needs outlined in this and other chapters. What would the work load consist of? There would be the design of teaching aids [Figure 25]: teaching aids to be used in pre-nursery school settings, nursery schools, junior colleges, colleges and universities, graduate and post-doctoral research and study. There would be teaching aids and devices for such specialized fields as adult education, the teaching of both knowledge and skills to the retarded, the disadvantaged, and the handicapped; as well as special language studies, vocational re-education, the rehabilitation of prisoners, and mental defectives. Add to this the education in totally new skills for people about to undergo radical transformation in their habitats: from slum, ghetto, or rural poverty pocket to the city; from the milieu of, say, a central Australian aborigine to life in a technocratic society; from Earth to space or Mars; from the tranquility of the English countryside to life in the Mindanao Deep or the Arctic.

The design work done by our mythical office would include the design, invention, and development of medical diagnostic devices, hospital equipment, dental equipment, surgical tools and devices, equipment and furnishings for mental

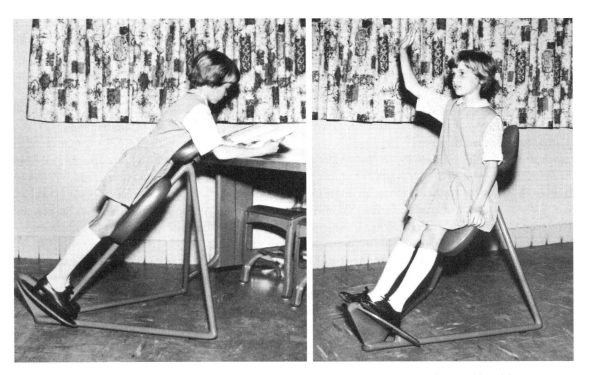

Figure 25. Perch or reclining structure to be used in classrooms in addition to regular chairs. This provides eight more positions for restless children. Designed by Steven Lynch, as a student at Purdue University, in Victor Papanek, *Design for the Real World: Human Ecology and Social Change* (1971), Toronto, New York, London: Bantam Books, 1973, pp. 52–3. Several additional photographs showing the chair in alternate positions and uses may be found in the collections of the Victor Papanek Estate.

hospitals, obstetrician's equipment, diagnostic and training devices for ophthalmologists, etc. The range of things would go all the way from a better readout of a fever thermometer at home to such exotic devices as heart-lung machines, heart pacers, artificial organs, and cyborgian implants, and back again to humble visor-like eyeglasses, reading mechanisms for the blind, improved stethoscopes and urinalysis devices, hearing aids and improved calendrical dispensers for "the pill," etc.

The office would concern itself with safety devices for home, industry, transportation, and many other areas; and with pollution, both chemical and thermal, of rivers, streams, lakes, and oceans as well as air. The nearly 75 per cent of the world's people who live in poverty, starvation, and need would certainly occupy still more time in the already busy schedule of our theoretical office. But not only the underdeveloped and emergent countries of the world have special needs. These special needs abound at home as well. "Black lung" disease among the miners of Kentucky and West Virginia is just one of a myriad of occupational ills, many of which can be abolished through relevant re-design of equipment and/or processes.

Middle and upper managerial ranks (if male and between ages of thirty-five and sixty) are a prime health-hazard group. The incidence of death from cardiovascular arrests by stroke or heart attack is frighteningly high. This loss of human lives can be ascribed to three main causes: faulty diet, a lack of exercise, and stress syndrome. Exercising equipment with built-in motivation might spare the lives of many people in this group, a group desperately needed all over the world to keep humanity going.

Basic shelters for American Indians and the Lapp population of Norway, Sweden, and Finland – and shelters (both temporary and permanent) for all men poised at the edge of an alien environment – need design and discovery. Whether it be a comparably simple shelter such as a space station or dome cities for Venus or Mars or something as complex as the complete "terraforming" of the moon, our design office will be needed here just as it is in sub-oceanic cities, Arctic factories, and artificial island cities to be anchored like so many pleasure boats in the Amazon River basin, the Mediterranean, or around the (genuine) island chains of Japan and Indonesia.

Research tools are usually "stuck-together," "jury-rigged" contraptions, and advanced research is suffering from an absence of rationally designed equipment. From radar telescopes to simple chemical beakers, design has lagged behind. And what about the needs of the elderly and the senile? And of pregnant women and the obese? What about the alienation of young people all over the world? What about transportation (surely the fact that the American automobile is the most efficient killing machine since the invention of the machine gun doesn't permit us to rest on our laurels), communication, and design for entirely new "breakthrough" concepts?

Are we still designing for minorities? The fact of the matter is that all of us are children at one point of our lives, and that we need education throughout our lives. Almost all of us become adolescent, middle-aged, and old. We all need the services and help of teachers, doctors, dentists, and hospitals. We all belong to special need groups, we all live in an underdeveloped and emergent country of the mind, no matter what our geographical or cultural location. We all need transportation, communication, products, tools, shelter, and clothing. We must have water and air that is clean. As a species we need the challenge of research, the promise of space, the fulfillment of knowledge.

If we then "lump together" all the seemingly little minorities of the last few pages, if we combine all these "special" needs, we find that we have designed for the majority after all. It is only the "industrial designer," style-happy in the seventies of this century, who, by concocting trivia for the market places of a few abundant societies, really designs for the minority.

Why this polemic? What is the answer? Not just for next year but for the future, and not just in one country but in the world. During the summer of 1968 I discovered a Finnish word dating back to medieval times. A word so obscure that many Finns have never even heard it. The word is: *kymmenykset*. It means the same thing as the medieval church word *tithe*. A tithe was something one paid: the peasant would set aside 10 per cent of his crop for the poor, the rich man would give up 10 per cent of his income at the end of the year to feed those in need. Being designers, we don't have to pay money in the form of *kymmenykset* or a tithe. Being designers, we can pay by giving 10 per cent of our crop of ideas and talents to the 75 per cent of mankind in need.

There will always be men like Buckminster Fuller who spend 100 per cent of their time designing for the needs of man. Most of the rest of us can't do that well, but I think that even the most successful designer can afford one tenth of his time for the needs of men. It is unimportant what the mechanics of the situation are: four hours out of every forty, one working day out of every ten, or ideally, every tenth year to be spent as a sort of sabbatical designing for many instead of designing for money.

Even if the corporate greed of many design offices makes this kind of design impossible, students should at least be encouraged to work in this manner. For in showing students new areas of engagement, we may set up alternate patterns of thinking about design problems. We may help them to develop the kind of social and moral responsibility that is needed in design.

NOTE

Extracted from Papanek, V., *Design for the Real World: Human Ecology and Social Change*, Toronto: Bantam Books, 1973, pp. 65–95. Copyright © 1984 Victor Papanek. Reprinted by kind permission of Thames & Hudson Ltd., London and Academy Books, Chicago.

33

MATERIAL DOUBTS AND PLASTIC FALLOUT, FROM *AMERICAN PLASTIC*

Jeffrey L. Meikle (1995)

[...]

OUT OF CONTROL

By definition the plastic industry was everything ecological activists wanted to expunge from American experience. Since the early twentieth century, promoters of industrial chemistry and synthetic materials had boasted of transcending age-old limits of traditional materials by extending scientific control over nature. During the 1920s predictions of an expanding stream of inexpensive artificial goods had suggested material abundance as a basis for a utopian democracy. By the final third of the century that transcendence threatened to drain natural resources and pollute the society that supported it by generating a flow of irrecoverable, inassimilable matter-garbage, society's excrement. Far from engendering the steady-state equilibrium once suggested by thermosetting Bakelite, industrial chemistry had ushered in a thermoplastic flux whose artificiality threatened to poison or submerge nature if it could not fully replace it. Or so it seemed.

The most eloquent ecological critic of the plastic industry, Barry Commoner, came to prominence in 1971 with *The Closing Circle: Nature; Man, and Technology.* He argued the human race had "broken out of the circle of life, converting its endless cycles into man-made, linear events."

This one-way process of divergence from nature afforded evidence of a "nearly fatal illusion" – the assumption "that through our machines we have at last escaped from dependence on the natural environment." Since that statement embodied the fundamental tenet of plastic utopianism, it was not surprising he had nothing good to say about synthetic materials. Commoner argued that of all species, human beings were "uniquely capable of producing materials not found in nature," resulting in the world's first known "intrusion into an ecosystem of a substance wholly foreign to it." Nature had no mechanisms for breaking down the "literally indestructible" plastics and integrating them into its eternal cycles. It was "sobering," he wrote, "to contemplate the fate of the billions of pounds of plastic already produced," some of it incinerated and thus polluting the air, some of it dumped in the ocean and harming marine life, the rest of it straining landfills or strewn across the landscape. Beyond that were unknown possibilities of carcinogenic plasticizers and other chemicals released during plastic's use. Dismissing the idea of a technological fix, Commoner attributed the problems not to "some minor inadequacies in the new technologies" but to "their very success in accomplishing their designed aims." Discarded plastics "clutter the landscape," he concluded, "*because* they are unnatural, synthetic substances designed to resist degradation – precisely the properties that are the basis of their technological

Quality furniture leads a charmed...and charming...life, surfaced with

Catalin LAMINATING RESINS

Figure 26. An All-Plastic Dining Room, 1963. From a Catalin Advertisement, *Modern Plastics*, December 1963. Reprinted from Jeffrey L. Meikle, *American Plastic: a Cultural History*, New Brunswick, NJ: Rutgers University Press, 1995, plate 15.

value." Survival of the human race was threatened by ignorant exploitation of an unprecedented ability "to tear the ecological fabric that has, for millions of years, sustained the planet's life."[1]

Five years later Commoner expanded his analysis by describing the economic mechanism that he argued was fueling the expansion of petrochemicals. Published shortly after the energy crisis of 1973, *The Poverty of Power* sought to explain why society was entangled in a fatal reliance on oil. Between 1946 and 1974 annual production of synthetic chemicals had risen a hundredfold from 150,000 tons to fifteen million tons. The plastic industry's share reflected an average annual growth rate between 1948 and 1970 of 15.9 percent (compared with 4.3 percent for steel). For Commoner this expansion provided a measure of earth's pollution and a sign of the bankruptcy of a way of life based on dwindling resources. In his opinion the overriding economic motive for this expansion was the petrochemical industry's reliance on the high-investment continuous flow processes of the refinery. Successful competition with labor-intensive industries like wood, wool, or leather required pushing volume to the limit and finding a use for every by-product. "By its own internal logic," he maintained, "each new petrochemical process generates a powerful tendency to proliferate further products and displace pre-existing ones." The industry tended "not so much to serve social needs as to invent them" just to keep oil flowing from wellhead to refinery to extrusion machine. Although Commoner did not call it a pyramid scheme, his description suggested a house of plastic cards soon to collapse in a mess of debris and toxic waste as oil reserves ran dry. The solution required voluntary return to labor-intensive traditional materials except in those instances – phonograph records or heart valves – where plastic marked a true innovation.[2]

Even before "whole earth" became an idea to fight for, industry watchdogs had occasionally warned that disposing of disposables might prove costly. As early as 1966 Joel Frados of *Modern*

Plastics advised readers to think constructively about the issue before "well meaning but misinformed authorities step in with homemade remedies and regulations."[3] He was writing during an explosion in the volume of plastic for packaging and other disposables – the culmination of a trend that got under way in the 1950s. In 1952 Americans had first experienced single-serving jelly "paks" of vacuum-formed sheet vinyl. Later in the decade they bought shirts packaged in clear polyethylene bags and vegetables packed in flimsy polystyrene trays or wrapped in thin film; they ate banana splits from "boats" of thin, rigid, vacuum-formed polystyrene sheet and drank coffee from Styrofoam cups.[4] The following decade witnessed polyethylene bleach and detergent bottles, polystyrene containers for cottage cheese and yogurt, recloseable polyethylene lids for cans of coffee and shortening and cat food, polyethylene squeeze tubes for suntan lotion, polyethylene swivel closures for lighter fluid cans and cosmetics, polyethylene bread bags, Styrofoam meat trays, polyethylene six-pack connectors, vinyl blister packs, green polyethylene garbage bags, and Ex-Cell-O's polyethylene-coated paper milk cartons, which eliminated annoying flakes of wax in the milk but were soon almost superseded by lightweight bottles of blow-molded polyethylene.[5] By the time Frados issued his warning, the only major consumer disposable still to appear in the next two decades was the soft drink bottle of PET (polyethylene terephthalate) developed by Du Pont's Nathaniel C. Wyeth, a maverick from the family of painters who resented that chemistry brought less recognition than art.[6] But if the major disposables were already introduced, the volume of single-use plastics continued swelling at a faster rate than plastic in general. In 1960 packaging accounted for 300,000 tons of resin, nearly 10 percent of total plastic production; in 1966, packaging increased to 1.3 million tons, nearly 20 percent of the total. By 1969 packaging absorbed nearly one quarter of all resin produced, and the tide kept rising. Frados knew what he was talking about.[7]

American consumers initially balked at the idea of disposable plastics. Throwing things away violated the image of durable quality the industry had built up since the 1930s. The few plastic packages of the 1930s, Ovaltine's Annie shakers and various cigarette boxes and cosmetic jars, won public acceptance as "premiums" that retained their value. In 1957, two years before the dry cleaning bag scare, sales managers complained about the difficulty of marketing "disposable and expendable" goods owing to a "disinclination of consumers to accept the fact that such merchandise has been designed to be, and therefore should be, discardable and destroyable." It was too bad the industry had emphasized "durability and re-use value" because now people expected them. Reeducation was necessary. As an editor announced at the National SPI [Society of the Plastics Industry] Conference of 1956, "Your developments should be aimed at low cost, big volume, practicability, and *expendability*" – with a goal of winding up "in the garbage wagon."[8]

Actually consumers took quickly to the short-term convenience of plastic packaging and throwaway products. Within a few years, however, "expendability" provoked a vocal minority who had begun to worry about environmental decay. Soon after becoming editor of *Modern Plastics* in 1968, Sidney Gross protested that the "problem of garbage" flowed not from packaging or plastics but from "our civilization, our exploding population, our life-style, our technology." It was unfortunate that plastic's 2 percent by weight of the nation's solid waste comprised "the most visible garbage, and the most lasting." All too often the public condemned plastic as a "villain" to be "exorcised from the economy."[9] It certainly seemed that way in 1970 when a member of the liberal city council of Madison, Wisconsin, proposed a ban on nonreturnable food and beverage containers and a one-dollar deposit on every returnable container. Initially considered a joke, the ordinance was taken seriously after the proposed deposit was reduced to fifteen cents. Within a year fifteen state legislatures were

considering bills to ban or limit plastic bottles or containers.[10]

Especially threatening was a tax of two cents passed in New York City in the summer of 1971 on every plastic bottle or container. After six months of opposition to the ordinance, SPI succeeded in having it declared discriminatory and thus unconstitutional. The legal battle was the first in a long series fought by the society in defense of disposable plastics, led by its attorney, Jerome Heckman.[11] Ironically, earlier that year New York's sanitation department had campaigned to convince residents to use polyethylene trash bags instead of metal garbage cans – a policy chosen after tests inspired by a successful program in Toronto. Some disposables were clearly better than others.[12]

As the industry heeded expressions of environmental dismay, sanitation engineers and plastics executives debated landfills versus incinerators for disposing of disposables. Because plastic remained inert in landfills and did not release toxic fumes through decomposition, it seemed an ideal packaging material, superior to traditional paper products. But as the prospect of overflowing landfills loomed, attention turned to incineration, and with it a fear that chemicals released by burning plastic would pollute the air, corrode incinerators, and leach into ground water. By 1970 people were discussing such options as recycling disposables and developing resins that would decompose in sunlight or in the presence of soil bacteria. Neither idea gained adherents except among environmentalists and newspaper editors. A disintegrating plastic would violate everything the industry had worked toward. Recycling, on the other hand, seemed impractical because it required sorting out dozens of different resin formulations from the general flow of garbage.[13] Not until the late 1980s did the industry take recycling seriously. The inhabitants of the United States then generated about ten million tons of plastic waste each year. That amounted to 7 percent of the annual flow of garbage *by weight,* the measure SPI typically used to minimize its impact, but it comprised a more impressive 16 to 25 percent *by volume*. With landfills dwindling, the industry adopted a system of resin codes for marking disposable containers for easier sorting. Material suppliers set up pilot projects for blending recycled materials with virgin resins and encouraged entrepreneurs to experiment with molding scrap into boards, flower pots, and other low-tech objects. By then it had long been true, as an engineering journal observed in 1979, that "plastics recycling" had "shifted from its emotional history … to an era of serious research and development."[14]

Long before that "emotional history" had run its course; however, the industry experienced a series of nonstop one-two punches during the early 1970s. The initial uproar over solid waste came to a head in 1971 with dozens of regulatory bills introduced across the country. At that time the issue that most provoked vocal opposition was not the overriding problem of garbage but the aesthetic problem of litter. With landfills nowhere near bursting, it was easier to arouse people about bleach bottles washed up on beaches and Styrofoam cups tossed along the road. While paper litter quickly disintegrated, the plastic stuff remained as a visual reminder of an inflationary culture.

[…]

If manufacturers used plastics – whether for versatility of design, durability, lower cost, greater profit, or whatever reason – then consumers had no choice but to go along. Even those who thought they despised plastic would buy it and use it, often without even recognizing it. "If we were as evil as our adversaries claim," [Sidney] Gross [editor of *Modern Plastics*] once wrote, then "we wouldn't be where we are today."[15] He would have appreciated a science fiction tale, *Mutant 59: The Plastic Eaters*, published in 1972 at the height of plastic's period of ill repute. A clever disaster novel, it described a strain of bacteria mutating after exposure to a new biodegradable plastic and thereby gaining an ability to feed on any plastic.

As solid plastic turned to slime everywhere, toys ran amok, clothes melted, heart valves malfunctioned, subway trains crashed, and an airliner dissolved in midair. "Good God, just think of it," someone declared. "Take out plastic from a modern city and what do you get – complete breakdown." Like it or not, as he put it, "we're totally dependent on it."[16] Eventually the technical experts devised methods for isolating and neutralizing the mutant bacteria, for reasserting the control that plastic had always promised. But with the melting into slime of most plastic objects, a kind of ultimate reputation for shoddiness was established. And with an irony [Norman] Mailer would have appreciated, the novel ended with a contaminated space probe landing on Mars, ready to dissolve any future expansion of plastic beyond the bounds of spaceship earth. In the real world, however, plastic's expansion continued over the next twenty years, as did the inflationary culture of which it was substance and image. The throwaway society kept on expanding as Americans learned to live with more and more of less and less. They glimpsed the outlines of a new relationship to things, or a more tenuous conception of things, as the physical yielded to the digital, the material to the immaterial, the plastic presence to the process of plasticity. As that transformation began, or as intellectuals posited such a transformation, plastic's meaning began to shift almost beyond any correlation with material things. Once again, after several decades, plastic expressed a sense of limitless shape-shifting.

NOTES

Extracted from Meikle, J. L., *American Plastic: A Cultural History*, New Brunswick, NJ: Rutgers University Press, 1995, pp. 264–76. Copyright © 1995 by Rutgers State University. Reprinted by permission of Rutgers University Press.

1. Barry Commoner, *The Closing Circle: Nature, Man, and Technology* (New York: Alfred A. Knopf, 1971), 12, 15, 127, 162–164, 185, 12.

2. Barry Commoner, *The Poverty of Power: Energy and the Economic Crisis* (New York: Alfred A. Knopf, 1976), esp. 198–210; quotations from 206–207.

3. Joel Frados, "There's Something in the Air," *MP* [*Modern Plastics*] 44 (October 1966): 89.

4. On 1950s packaging and disposables see "One Portion at a Time," *MP* 29 (May 1952): 84–85; "Flip to Close," *MP* 33 (April 1956): 119; "Plastics Applications in the Years Ahead," *MP* 33 (June 1956): 171; R. L. Van Boskirk, "The Plastiscope," *MP* 34 (October 1956): 304; and idem, "The Plastiscope," *MP* 36 (September 1958): 39–41.

5. On 1960s packaging see R.L. Van Boskirk, "The Plastiscope," *MP* 38 (May 1961): 43; "New Day for Thin-Wall Containers," *MP* 41 (May 1964): 84–88,160,162; "Coming Up-Multi-Million Lb. Market," *MP* 41 (December 1963): 93; "Packaging's Versatile Vessels," *Du Pont Magazine* 58 (January–February 1964): 12–13; "Designing Closures for a Dual Purpose," *MP* 42 (September 1964): 116–119,192, 194; R. L. Van Boskirk, "The Plastiscope," *MP* 43 (April 1966): 45, 47; "What's in Store for Polystyrene Meat Trays?," *MP* 44 (November 1966): 89–91; "Business Bulletin," *Wall Street Journal* (May 25, 1967): 1; "$65,000,000 Bet on Plastics-Paper Vs. Glass," *MP* 39 (March 1962): 87; "$65 Million Throw-Away!" *MP* 39 (June 1962): 88–91; and "Coming Market for Polyethylene: Milk Bottles," *MP* 42 (December 1964): 84–88, 162–166.

6. Wyeth's impatience with his lack of recognition as a chemist was reported by Jon Eklund, National Museum of American History, Smithsonian Institution, Washington, D.C.

7. Dominick V. Rosato, William K. Fallon, and Donald V. Rosato, *Markets for Plastics* (New York: Van Nostrand Reinhold, 1969), 6.

8. Both quotations, including direct quotation from Lloyd Stouffer, are from "Plastics in Disposables and Expendables," *MP* 34 (April 1957): 93.

9. Sidney Gross, "Garbage (2)," *MP* 47 (January 1970): 63; idem, "Garbage," *MP* 46 (April 1969): 81; and idem, "Garbage (4)," *MP* 48 (August 1971): 37.

10. Nonreturnables Face Legislative Ban in Madison, Wisconsin," *Plastics and the Environment,* no. 1 (April 3, 1970): 2–4, SPIA. See also Julian Kestler, "Localities May Tax Plastics Packaging," *MP* 48 (May 1971): 14, 16.

11. Copy of letter from Ralph L. Harding, Jr., SPI [The Society of the Plastics Industry, Inc.] executive vice president, to Executive Committee of SPI Environment Policy Committee, June 10, 1971, SPIA [The Society of the Plastics Industry, Inc., Archive, Hagley Museum and Library, Wilmington, Delaware], looseleaf notebook entitled "Executive VP-Chronological or Reading File, 1971–77" (hereafter referred to as "VP Reading File"); "Plastics Return the Ecologists' Fire," *Business Week* (July 10, 1971): 25; Julian Kestler, "New York's Plastic Container Tax Poses Grave Threat to Plastics Packaging," *MP* 48 (August 1971): 10; and idem, "What Are the Implications of the Overturning of New York City's Tax Law?" *MP* 48 (December 1971): 18.

12. "Plastics in Canada," *MP* 44 (April 1967): 106; SPI Polyethylene Refuse Bag Committee minutes, October 31, November 17, 1967, February 2, 1968, March 28, 1969, SPIA, microfilm reel 9; "Plastics Refuse Bags Get Wide Test," *MP* 46 (September 1969): 228; "Refuse Bags: How Big, How Fast, How Profitable?" *MP* 47 (February 1970): 10, 12; "New York City Goes For Plastic Refuse Bags," *Plastics and the Environment*, no. 3 (June 29, 1970): 5–6, SPIA; and a copy of Ralph L. Harding, Jr., to Charles Luce, chairman, Consolidated Edison, February 11, 1971, SPIA, VP Reading File.

13. For typical discussions see A. Stuart Wood, "Plastics' Challenge in Packaging: Disposability," *MP* 4 (March 1970): 50–54; "A Plastic for Ecologists," *Time* 95 (May 11, 1970): 86; "Plastics-Mostly PVC-Under Attack in Press," *Plastics and the Environment*, no. 3 (June 29, 1970): 1–3, SPIA; "SPI Position Paper Outlines Industry's Stand

on Coping with the Garbage Crisis," *MP* 47 (October 1970): 184; and F. Rodriguez, "Prospects for Biodegradable Plastics," *MP* 48 (September 1971): 92, 94. For technical discussions with similar conclusions see J.J.P. Staudinger, ed., *Plastics and the Environment* (London: Hutchinson, 1974).

14. Robert H. Wehrenberg II, "Plastics Recycling: Is It Now Commercially Feasible?" *Materials Engineering* 89 (March 1979): 34. For the lower estimate and a discussion of the difficulty of measuring volumes of garbage see William Rathje and Cullen Murphy, *Rubbish!: The Archaeology of Garbage* (New York: HarperCollins, 1992), 99–102. See also Robert D. Leaversuch, "Industry Begins to Face Up to the Crisis of Recycling," *MP* 64 (March 1987): 44–47; Cass Peterson, "Recycling: Making Cents of Trash," *Washington Post* Service, in *Austin American-Statesman* (June 14, 1987): D1, DB; Guy Darst, "Plastic Bottles to Carry Code for Recycling" (AP), *Austin American-Statesman* (April 9, 1988): B11; Myra Klockenbrink, "Plastics Industry, Under Pressure, Begins to Invest in Recycling," *New York Times* (August 30, 1988): 19; "Recycling: Don't Trash That Foam," *Time* 133 (January 9, 1989): 48; Barbara Rudolph, "Second life for Styrofoam," *Time 133* (May 22, 1989): 84; SPI Council for Solid Waste Solutions, "The Urgent Need to Recycle" (advertising section), *Time* 134 (July 17, 1989): 17–28; and *Plastics Recycling: Problems and Possibilities*, Serial No. 102–63, 102nd Congress, Second Session, House Committee on Small Business, Subcommittee on Environment and Employment (Washington, D.C: Government Printing Office, 1992).

15. Sidney Gross interviewed by the author, December 9, 1986. The quotation is from Sidney Gross, "Plastics Age Arrives Early," *MP* 57 (February 1980): 45.

16. Kit Pedler and Gerry Davis, *Mutant 59: The Plastic-Eaters* (New York: Viking, 1972), 109.

34

INTRODUCTION TO *THE GREEN CONSUMER SUPERMARKET GUIDE*

Joel Makower, John Elkington and Julia Hailes (1991)

Let's start with the basics: Every time you open your wallet, you cast a vote 'for' or 'against' the environment.

This is more powerful than you might imagine. First and foremost, the marketplace – whether the supermarket, hardware store, or appliance showroom – is not a democracy. It doesn't take 51 percent of people 'voting' in any one direction to affect environmental change. Far from it. In fact, a relative handful of shoppers can send shock waves through an industry simply by making good, 'green' choices.

Here's an example. In April 1990, three major tuna canning companies announced that they had made a revolutionary decision: They would stop buying tuna caught in a way that harmed dolphins. In the past, millions of dolphins a year were being needlessly killed simply because they became caught in the tuna fishermen's nets. When these three tuna companies made their announcement, they said nothing about 'protecting dolphins,' or even about 'saving the earth.' They spoke instead of 'consumer pressure.'

What's amazing about all this is that it was a relatively small number of consumers who were 'pressuring' the tuna companies – probably less than a million active individuals, according to some reports. That's less than 1 percent of the American marketplace. In fact, during the twelve months preceding the tuna companies' announcement, *tuna sales had barely changed*. And so the 'votes' of a very small number of individuals revolutionized an entire industry.

Another revolution took place a few months later. In October 1990, McDonald's Corporation announced that it was abandoning its polystyrene foam 'clamshell' hamburger boxes in favor of paper products. In making their announcement, McDonald's officials didn't claim that there was anything wrong with its plastic packages. But 'our customers just don't feel good about it,' said the company's president. 'So we're changing.' And again, while McDonald's had been the subject of consumer protests over the amount of unrecyclable trash it created, *its sales had increased during the preceding year*.

There are other, less dramatic revolutions happening nearly every day. Since Earth Day 1990, practically every consumer products company seems to have examined its products and policies through a 'green' lens, taking a hard look at how sales might be affected by American's growing concern about the impact of their purchases on the environment. Across America, companies are listening to consumers' concerns for a cleaner environment, and watching carefully the way we 'vote' with our dollars.

This book will show you how to cast votes 'for' Planet Earth whenever you shop for food and groceries. It is intended to help you sort through the often confusing world of Green Consumerism to choose products that are environmentally sound.

Why should you do this? For starters, as you'll see, some of the products we buy contribute to environmental problems. You may be surprised at the ways this can happen. For example, the manufacture of a paper towel or napkin can contribute dangerous pollutants downstream from a paper mill. The use of some aerosol products contributes to urban smog. Many products are packaged excessively in materials that are neither recycled nor recyclable. Some products are made by companies that have poor environmental records. Buying products from companies that pollute supports their lack of concern for the environment.

Make no mistake: We're not suggesting we can simply shop our way to environmental health. Part of being a Green Consumer is learning when not to buy – when more is not necessarily better … By making the right choices, you can help to minimize the pollution and waste created by many 'un-green' products and companies.

[…]

SHOPPING 'TIL WE DROP

[…] [W]e've become rampant consumers. Nearly uninterrupted economic growth has helped to create a glut of goods in the marketplace. More than 20,000 new products land on supermarket shelves every year, a rate that does not appear to be slowing down. Those products arrive in stores in an astonishing assortment of materials, sizes, and formats. It's no longer simply 'regular size' and 'family size.' From aerosols to zip tops, the possibilities have been limited only by financial and technological constraints. Plastic has helped create the packaging boom, but equally disturbing is packaging made of several materials – combinations of plastics, for example, or laminates consisting of paper, plastic, and foil. All of these present new problems and challenges when it comes time to recycle, reuse, or otherwise dispose of such trash. Ironically, some of these packaging

options – aerosols and aseptic 'juice boxes,' for example – are being presented by their creators as environmentally superior.

It's been a colorful carnival of choices. But now we're finding that along with this apparent prosperity comes some tough problems, not the least of which is how to reconcile the resources being used and the trash created by it all. We've come to expect to pay extra for convenience, but we're just beginning to fully understand how high the price tag for convenience may really be.

[…]

THE THREE RS

To help us remember what to do when shopping, the Green Consumer movement has its own set of 'Three R's': refuse, reuse, and recycle. Each of them plays a key role in our attempts to minimize the environmental problems caused by our purchases and lifestyles. Keep in mind that this is a hierarchy: they are listed in descending order of preference.

1. REFUSE

This is where the power of green is at its strongest. By refusing to buy wasteful and polluting products, you can make a powerful statement. As we have learned in other cases – most notably in the tuna industry's decision to go 'dolphin-safe', and in McDonald's decision to switch from polystyrene to paper – a few Green Consumers can send shock waves through an industry.

What should you refuse to buy? Several things:

- products packaged in many layers of packaging
- products packaged in unrecycled or unrecyclable materials
- single-use and other products that have a short life before they must be thrown away
- products that are not energy efficient

- products made by companies with poor environmental records
- products purchased from retailers that have poor environmental records
- products that make false or misleading claims about their 'greenness'

As we said before, few products are perfect. Your level of refusal to purchase some of these products will likely be influenced by the available alternatives. If a product you feel you need is available only in one form, and it is an environmentally undesirable one, you may choose to buy it anyway. But you don't have to accept this as 'the best you can get.' Consider writing the manufacturer and ask them to consider changing the product's packaging or contents to make it more environmentally responsible. Your letter will have more impact, however, if you have chosen not to purchase the product, and tell the manufacturer that.

[…]

2. REUSE

Things that may only be used once before being thrown away are an inefficient use of our precious resources. It would be ideal if the products you do buy had the longest life possible. So, it is important to buy products that can be reused over and over. Consider batteries that must be thrown away – filling landfills with a mélange of hazardous chemicals – when you can buy ones that are rechargeable hundreds of times? Why buy something that will have a short life when you can buy something that will last and last?

Some reusable things may cost a bit more to buy – rechargeable batteries, for example, are considerably more expensive than disposable ones – but over time, most of these products can more than pay for themselves. For example, a battery charger and four 'AA' batteries sell for about $15, compared to four disposable 'AA' batteries, which retail for around $3. But if you recharge the batteries only five times, you'll save enough money to recover the cost of the equipment, plus the electricity used for recharging. After that, you're ahead of the game!

Another aspect of 'reuse' is to look for products made from or packaged in recycled material. By doing this you are supporting the reuse of resources. The greater the content of recycled material, the better. Some products or packages state specifically: 'Made of 100% recycled content.' Lacking such statements, it's difficult to tell the exact amount of recycled content.

3. RECYCLE

If you have refused and reused as much as possible, a high percentage of your leftover trash should be recyclable. And it is extremely important that you make sure to recycle what's left.

Recycling is not a new idea. During World War II, it was a way of life for Americans. Everything from tin cans to scrap iron, rubber to cooking grease, was recycled to help the war effort. Everyone did his or her part to preserve the country's scarce or strategic resources. But when the war ended and the economy boomed, there was a backlash: Americans were taught by advertisers that true prosperity meant having the luxury to use things once and throw them away. Unfortunately, that notion became a way of life for many people.

Now, recycling has come full cycle. Our scarce and strategic resources are once again being associated with some of our everyday purchases – the petroleum contained in the plastic packaging we buy, for example, the bauxite and energy used to produce aluminum, the drinkable water spoiled by the effluents of paper mills, and on and on. And so, recycling has once again taken on a new importance.

Consider just a few of the benefits recycling can bring:

- Recycling a single aluminum can saves enough energy to produce 20 more cans.
- Recycling a glass bottle or jar saves 25 percent of the energy it took to produce it and cuts up to half of the pollution created manufacturing a new one.
- Using recycled paper instead of virgin paper for one print run of the Sunday edition of the *New York Times* would save the equivalent of 75,000 trees and reduce landfill waste.
- Each year, the amount of steel recycled in this country saves enough energy to meet the equivalent of the electrical power needs of the city of Los Angeles for more than eight years.

Despite these impressive statistics, Americans recycle only about a tenth of our household trash; another 10 percent or so is incinerated. The rest of the trash is tossed into landfills. In discarding our trash, we are also discarding vast amounts of raw materials – and the energy it takes to convert these materials into finished goods.

[…]

NOTE

Extracted from Makower, J., Elkington, J. and Hailes, J., 'Introduction' in *The Green Consumer Supermarket Guide*, New York: Penguin, 1991, pp. 7–58. Copyright © by John Elkington, Julia Hailes, and Viking Penguin. Used by permission of Viking Penguin, a division of Penguin Group (USA) Inc., and by Victor Gollancz, an imprint of the Orion Publishing Group.

35

REDEFINING RUBBISH: COMMODITY DISPOSAL AND SOURCING

Nicky Gregson and Louise Crewe (2003)

[...]

ENTERING THE SECOND-HAND WORLD

There are, we argue, a range of practices that determine which commodities come to enter the second-hand arena, when, and at which sites and spaces. Such strategies range from the more organized retro and car-boot trader sourcing strategies and charity sorting warehouses to the more personalized, fortuitous discarding strategies of individuals clearing out commodities to either donate to charity or retro shops or to sell on at a car-boot sale. It is important to think too, here, about temporalities of possession and disposal and the differences which exist in relation to this across different commodity groups. Some commodities are treasured, loved, never to be discarded. Others, mistakes for example, or unwanted gifts, have a very short temporality and are quickly put back into circulation. For analytical ease we will distinguish in what follows between traders' sourcing strategies which typically comprise detailed and ongoing searches for commodities to sell (i.e. akin to an occupation), and the more personalized, ad hoc casting-off and disposal strategies which individuals undertake in their homes and gardens as part of broader consumption practices.[1] Taken together, sourcing and

disposal strategies determine when and how commodities enter and leave the second-hand world. In practice of course such analytical separation rarely holds up; the boundaries between sourcing and disposal are fuzzy, unclear and ruptured; many traders work in unplanned, unorganized ways, ways which are worlds apart from conventional buying and sourcing work undertaken in formal retail spaces; many 'good housekeeping' sorting and discarding strategies are themselves highly regulated, ordered and organized in ways which approximate hard work. Sourcing, sorting and disposal strategies vary, then, not only across and between the three case-study sites, but also in terms of the levels of investment which individuals make in such practices. The spatialities of supply are complex, circular and dynamic and reveal both the connections between our study sites and the variability across them. In the following two sections we try to capture the range and complexity of ways in which things come to be in second-hand worlds, focusing first on the disposal of commodities and their deposition by individuals in second-hand spaces, and secondly on the ways in which commodities are sourced for sale in the second-hand world. We identify three key disposal dispositions and two main sourcing models, although again, as we have been at pains to emphasize, these strategies are not mutually exclusive in either time or space, but rather may occur concurrently.

DISPOSAL DISPOSITIONS

Throughout the course of our work we encountered a range of different investments in different kinds of disposal practices. These practices are in turn linked to the spatialities of disposal, as individuals make often quite complex judgments about not just how, but where, to dispose of their 'rubbish'. The spaces of disposal themselves map onto and parallel individual constructions of commodity value and judgments about appropriate disposal behaviours – that which is defined as rubbish or garbage at a particular moment in time is likely to be discarded to the bin, the skip, the tip or the landfill site. Junk, in contrast, is more likely to be hoarded, collected and, much later, either rediscovered and revalorized (by self or other), or given away, cleared out or sold, ending up in the recycling bin, the jumble sale, the car-boot sale or at the charity or retro shop. But again such valorization judgments are neither linear nor objective, but vary in time and space and are subjectively determined. There are, too, a number of evaluative layers at work here which makes it often difficult in practice to determine with any certainty the precise motivations underpinning disposal strategies. For example, while the dumping of a washing machine onto a skip might be read as the straightforward disposal of a non-functional (and therefore valueless) commodity, there is rarely, we would argue, a straightforward association between functionality and value. In the case of consumer durables, it may appear on first reading that functionality is the key determinant of value, but in fact, and as we go on to demonstrate below, such connections are far more complex and relate to a matrix of variables which include functionality but critically also involve design and aesthetic issues, so that apparently 'functional' commodities may be cast out not simply because they don't work, but because an owner's aesthetic principles have shifted – the casting out of formica units and Bakelite telephones are illustrative examples here of commodities which have been cast out (and devalorized) and subsequently re-found and revalorized not simply by repair but by design shifts too. Again, this example illustrates the complex interplay between structural and market shifts on the one hand, and design history, aesthetic taste and subjective style judgments on the other in determining the practices and spaces through which disposal occurs.

Below we argue that disposal – as a means of making space – is the primary strategy through which individuals 'cast out' and the main way in which commodities enter the second-hand world. Quite which spaces commodities are cast out to, however, depends on both the nature of the commodity and, critically, on the disposal disposition of the subject, as we go on to discuss below. For conceptual ease we identify three main disposal dispositions as a way in to tracking where commodities are cast out to.[2] These dispositions in turn have particular potency for particular commodities and particular gendered subject positions, and we thus use particular commodity groupings as lenses through which to uncover the range and variability in disposal motivations. These three dispositions we call *philanthropy, economic/political critique* and *money-making*. The three dispositions serve as an analytical framework to shape our discussion below but, again, such distinctions do not always hold up in practice: some consumers, as we go on to illustrate below, may display several disposal dispositions at different times for different commodities in different contexts. Consequently, the importance of subject position and the subject: object relation infuses the specificities of disposal strategies through time and space.

[…]

PHILANTHROPY

The first rationale we explore is based around notions of philanthropy, of casting out in order to help others deemed or imagined to be less fortunate. For certain people, participation in second-hand consumption is not something that they would ever consider – to buy cast-offs is simply not for them – but they are happy to donate their discarded goods to 'deserving' others – often via charity shops.[3] This disposition in part is described as about doing good through disposal. Sam provides one example of this practice: a 20-something secretary, she recounts how part of her good housekeeping space-making strategy is about selecting clothing for people 'less fortunate' than herself. Moreover, she is careful to ensure that this clothing is deposited at what for her are appropriate charity shops – in her case 'the Cancer shop'. This disposition, however, is not confined to those who just donate. Val both donates and purchases, and she provides one of the few instances among our respondent group for whom fund-raising imperatives over-ride pragmatism in shaping disposal practices. Indeed Val drives from one area of Sheffield to the other side of the city to deposit her goods at a shop dedicated to fund-raising for a local animal charity.

For others, casting out as philanthropy is triggered by key world events such as recent world crises in Rwanda, Kosovo and latterly, Afghanistan. Often linked to media reports and charitable appeals for donations to, for example, Romanian orphanages, this is about helping out others in distant places. Anna, for example, discusses how she prefers to give to a known cause when having a clear-out, telling how she has 'just given a whole bagful to Romania, to the orphans,' while Nicky recently donated a bag destined initially for either the nearest charity shop or the next plastic-bag drop to a door-to-door collection for Kosovo. And closer to home still are the successful 'toys for Christmas' campaigns in the UK that again depend on the philanthropic conscience of potential donors.

What we see here is the moral imperative of disposal: not only is disposal constituted as an appropriate good housekeeping practice, but part of this good housekeeping is overlain with notions of casting out appropriately, in ways that depend clearly on the identification of the deserving other. Desperate, poor and needy, the other is here constituted unproblematically, as the assumed-to-be-grateful recipient – in short as the charitable case, defined by those who are in the position to act charitably.[4]

POLITICAL AND ECONOMIC CRITIQUE

This second disposition connects with the moral economy and political critique … For some this political critique is a fairly straightforward rejection of the rampant commercialism and aggressive consumerism they see as typifying first cycle consumption. We have already seen how, prompted in part by desires toward recycling and sustainability, at least some of our interviewees mobilize narratives around global equity in order to explain their desire to dispose of commodities into the second-hand arena. Margi and Trish are clear examples of this emergent sense of a critique of first-cycle consumption:

Yes, we need to be clothed and we need to feel good about how we look, but that doesn't mean we need to impose all of this bollocks onto the world – so in away it's almost a protest against that in a way – you know, recycle to survive I think is a really good philosophy. (Margi, Derbyshire)

If you're a charity shopper, you know, everybody's junk is somebody else's treasure – you know, if I have a clear out, there might be some little nick nack, but I make the effort to go and get that bag just because I know that somewhere somebody is not going to be making money out of it … it's also about the world and recycling. (Trish, London)

More specifically, we would argue that disposal for reasons to do with political critique is particularly marked in the case of certain commodity groups. The case of children's clothing illustrates this disposal disposition particularly keenly, and it is here that we find the most developed sense of a critique of first-cycle exchange and consumption as well as the tentative stirrings of ethical consumption. Given the speed with which young children in particular outgrow clothing, individual items have a very limited temporality of individual use. And they are thus frequently disposed of to second-hand sites such as charity shops and car-boot sales in order that others might benefit (note the connections here to philanthropic dispositions). One of our interviewees, Daphne, [...] is particularly instructive in articulating this version of ethical consumption. She expressed considerable disquiet at what she sees as the extortionate cost of children's clothes in the shops and argues that it is 'not right' to charge £40 for shoes that will last children six weeks or to charge £60 for a jumper for a five-year old. Her disposal and sourcing strategies in respect of children's clothes are thus best interpreted as resistant strategies in a broader moral economy of household provisioning. And Anna too discusses the ways in which second hand clothes for babies and children circulate around friendship and kin groups 'Caroline brings her stuff from her daughters for Caroline E to check through, and Caroline E checks through it and then it's handed on to me and I check through it for my friend in York, and I parcel it all up ... it's like this big thing going on, there's no money involved but there's all this exchange'. And so while the disposal (and indeed purchase) of second-hand clothing for children serves to reproduce gendered discourses about Woman as (style-conscious) mother, nurturer and carer, it also offers scope at least for a partial reworking of these discourses. In coming to recognize that the characteristics of newness and difference need not mean the same thing as never worn and currently in the shops, women put both a subtle twist on the style conscious mother construction and provide themselves with the basis for a moral critique of the intensifying commodification of children on the high street and through the media. In short they are constituting second-hand arenas as a

way of offering nearly new, often fashionable and very cheap clothing for children, and in so doing are invoking a prototypical version of ethical consumption, for and of mothers.[5]

Although most clearly developed in relation to children's clothing, such strategies are also apparent around a few other commodities, specifically books and toys, which also have a residual life that transcends their use by their initial owner. Passing such goods on to others through the medium of second-hand sites such as charity shops and car-boot sales seems to us to approximate a consumer: object relation that is best viewed in terms of temporary possession rather than ownership. Charity shops, then, operate as a form of alternative library facility, from which books can be bought for a nominal sum and to which they can then be returned. Similarly with toys – Val for example, recounted how she put her initials on jigsaws that she had already bought/returned. Reducing the need for costly first-cycle purchase of such commodities, we argue more broadly that this form of political critique is often less about the recycling of matter and its associated environmental benefits, and rather more grounded in a narrative that desires to extend the useful life (i.e. use value) of commodities.

MONEY-MAKING

Our third disposal disposition we call money-making. This disposition is distinctly about exchange values. For some this is about making money from used commodities; for others it is about supplementing low incomes. Again, this strategy varies both across and between destinations and is acutely differentiated in terms of product category. And again, like our other strategies it is variegated by gender, so that while both women and men dispose of goods in order to make money (often to buy more) this strategy is on the whole, we would argue, apparently far more masculine than our other two strategies, and is bound up more with functionalist discourses rather than questions of embodiment, respectability or political critique.[6] First, then, at one level there is evidence of a fairly straightforward selling-to-make-money approach demonstrated by both men and women. Sophie, for example, told us

Sophie: I needed a bit of money (when I was at UCL). I was very skint so I came here (Portobello Market) and sold a few of my clothes.

Louise: A few of the vintage things you'd bought for yourself?

Sophie: Yeah, the things I felt I could just about let go. And it worked really well. I enjoyed it. I loved it. It's an addictive thing to do … (Notting Hill).

For others, as the following vendor intimates, selling at a boot sale is frequently a follow-on from participation as a buyer. Indeed, for some the motivation for buying at boot sales is primarily to stock up to sell later: 'You never know what you'll come back with, golf clubs, aromatherapy oils, ballet shoes. We've got a house stuffed full of junk. When there's enough, we'll go out and sell all over again' (Mrs Coates).

And yet for others – and primarily here we are referring to men – there is a particular logic to disposal-for-sale strategies which has its roots, we would argue, in discourses of masculinity and which, particularly in the case of car-boot-sale-disposal, serve to reproduce conventional gendered consumption practices. Involving an array of commodities encompassing primarily electrical goods, DIY tools and materials, gardening equipment, car sundries and audio goods, the critical feature of men's disposal strategies at car-boot sales is that they are governed seemingly primarily by utilitarian and instrumentalist considerations and by technical discourses. Many of these acts of disposal as moneymaking are riven through with constructions of Man as builder/repairer of the domestic form – here money-making often comes from the left overs and cast-offs of DIY projects.

[…] Others, though, are about attempting to sell on items/goods that have been 'upgraded': redundant and/or obsolete PCs and printers, personal stereos, audio systems, vinyl that has been replaced by CDs and so on.

This form of disposal continues to intrigue us. Rather than turning to philanthropic motivations, then – and give away – there is a desire to sell, to elevate exchange over use values, even when things are faulty and admitted to be. […] Why this is we can only speculate about, but we would note that rarely – if ever – did women talk about selling such faulty items, tending instead to dispose of them at 'rubbish' venues: in skips, at landfill sites and in household dustbins.

[…]

NOTES

Extracted from Gregson, N. and Crewe, L., 'Redefining Rubbish: Commodity Disposal and Sourcing', *Second-Hand Cultures*, Oxford: Berg, 2003, pp. 115–42.

1. Of course in practice sourcing and disposal strategies don't follow one another in a neat and linear sequence but are commonly run together, as individuals and traders both acquire desired commodities and dispose of unwanted things at one and the same time. It is, however, difficult to convey such continuity and multiplicity through the written word, whose order and structure is, of necessity, linear.

2. Although less common, there are two other disposal dispositions which we encountered in our research. The first we term indiscriminate jettisoning. Exemplified by Louise, this strategy involves periodic chucking-out of anything and everything in sight, including books, men's, women's and children's clothes (much of it bearing designer labels), toys, electrical items and so on. In one particular week, for example, she cleared out a cupboard and threw away a bin-liner full of almost-new childrenswear

(including hardly-worn Marese, Miniman and Gap items as well as more mass-market M&S, Adams and Debenhams labels), two cassette players, a record player, about 50 white cot and cot-bed sheets, pillow-cases and blankets, and a computer box full of sun cream, mosquito repellent and other holiday sundries. While it is interesting to speculate where Louise's junk may end up (in a landfill site to be raked over by refuse collectors perhaps), there is little more to say about this strategy in conceptual terms, save that it is indicative of overconsumption and the result of limited interest in, commitment to and time available for sorting and sifting through a range of commodities in order to evaluate their potential value to others. It is good housekeeping at its most radical and unreflexive, possession-purging on a grand scale. The final disposal disposition that we identify is the hoarder who has a reluctance to dispose of anything. This of course is not in itself a disposal strategy but it does nonetheless provide the opportunity for potential future rediscovery and revalorization. And given our comments, about the central presence of women in space-making good housekeeping practices, we suggest here that a number of men may fall into the hoarder category, using sheds and garages as repositories for 'you never know when you might need it' commodities.

3. It needs to be noted here that the philanthropic disposition connects to particular disposal sites – charity shops, charity car-boot sales and jumble sales.

4. Nicky Gregson, Louise Crewe, and Kate Brooks, 'Shopping, Space and Practice', *Environment and Planning D: Society and Space*, vol. 20, no. 5 (2000), pp. 597–617.

5. Alison Clarke, '"Mother swapping": The Trafficking of Nearly New Children's Wear', in P. Jackson et al. (eds.) *Commercial Cultures: Economies, Practices, Spaces*, Oxford: Berg, 2000, pp. 85–100.

6. It is important to acknowledge here that this argument may say rather more about the specificities of the second-hand sites we investigated, and their limitations/possibilities for money-making. Clearly, disposal through charity shops is the counter case to this disposition. But there are other second-hand sites – such as dress agencies – that are spaces where disposal is governed by money-making. And our – admittedly limited – knowledge of these sites would suggest that they are for the most part frequented by women. Moreover, it needs to be recognized that, of the sites we investigated, it was primarily car-boot sales (and market stalls) that were associated with disposal as money-making. In the case of the former, it is entirely possible that some of the arguments we make in this section say rather more about the interweavings of masculinities with class at certain car-boot sales than about the gendering of this disposal disposition.

36

THE HANNOVER PRINCIPLES: DESIGN FOR SUSTAINABILITY

William McDonough and Michael Braungart (1992)

1. Insist on the rights of humanity and nature to co-exist in a healthy, supportive, diverse, and sustainable condition.
2. Recognize interdependence. The elements of human design interact with and depend upon the natural world, with broad and diverse implications at every scale. Expand design considerations to recognizing even distant effects.
3. Respect relationships between spirit and matter. Consider all aspects of human settlement including community, dwelling, industry, and trade in terms of existing and evolving connections between spiritual and material consciousness.
4. Accept responsibility for the consequences of design decisions upon human well-being, the viability of natural systems, and their right to co-exist.
5. Create safe objects of long-term value. Do not burden future generations with requirements for maintenance or vigilant administration of potential danger due to the careless creation of products, processes, or standards.
6. Eliminate the concept of waste. Evaluate and optimize the full life-cycle of products and processes, to approach the state of natural systems, in which there is no waste.
7. Rely on natural energy flows. Human designs should, like the living world, derive their creative forces from perpetual solar income. Incorporate this energy efficiently and safely for responsible use.
8. Understand the limitations of design. No human creation lasts forever and design does not solve all problems. Those who create and plan should practice humility in the face of nature. Treat nature as a model and mentor; not an inconvenience to be evaded or controlled.
9. Seek constant improvement by the sharing of knowledge. Encourage direct and open communication between colleagues, patrons, manufacturers, and users to link long term sustainable considerations with ethical responsibility, and re-establish the integral relationship between natural processes and human activity.

The Hannover Principles should be seen as a living document committed to the transformation and growth in the understanding of our interdependence with nature, so that they may adapt as our knowledge of the world evolves.

NOTES

The Hannover Principles was originally prepared for the city of Hannover, Germany, for EXPO 2000 by William McDonough and Michael Braungart, William McDonough Architects (New York, NY), and The Environmental Protection Encouragement Agency (Hamburg, Germany). The tenth anniversary edition is a revised and updated version of the original document issued by the City of Hannover in 1992.

GUIDE TO FURTHER READING

For a thorough overview of early literature on design and sustainability, see Pauline Madge, 'Design, Ecology, Technology: A Historiographical Review' (1993). Notable among books to champion environmental responsibility in the later twentieth century was *Small Is Beautiful: A Study of Economics as if People Mattered* (1973) by British economist Ernst Friedrich Schumacher, followed by Timothy O'Riordan's *Environmentalism* (1976).

Victor Papanek continued to influence designers and public with his books *How Things Don't Work*, co-authored with Jim Hennessy (1977), *Design for Human Scale* (1983) and *The Green Imperative: Natural Design for the Real World* (1995). Architect Christopher Alexander also contributed to ideas on the relationship of people and their built structures to the natural world, most notably in *A Pattern Language: Towns, Buildings, Construction*, co-authored with Sara Ishikawa and Murray Silverstein (1977), *The Timeless Way of Building* (1979) and *The Nature of Order, Books 1–4* (2003–2004). Many of these ideas, however, had already been addressed in the 1860s and 1870s, for example, by Frederick Law Olmstead, whose essays are collected in *Civilizing American Cities: Writings on City Landscapes* (1971), and Ebenezer Howard, *To-morrow: A Peaceful Path to Real Reform* (1898), reissued in 1902 as *Garden Cities of To-Morrow*. The theme of the 2009 annual conference of the Nineteenth Century Studies Association in the United States, 'The Green Nineteenth Century', reflected the current interest in recovering theories of sustainability in those first efforts to rethink industry and the urban fabric. Lewis Mumford's 'Toward an Organic Ideology' in *Technics and Civilization* (1934), Frank Lloyd Wright's 'Prairie Architecture' (1931) and *The Natural House* (1954) show the persistence of reform ideals even as industry flourished in the first half of the twentieth century.

The particular mobilization of these issues in the 1960s and 1970s, such as in Charles Reich's *The Greening of America* (1970), was related in part to a growing awareness of the complex ecology of planet Earth, newly imagined as a fragile and beautiful entity seen in photographs taken from space. The NASA image of the earth as a swirling blue-green globe was depicted on the cover of the *Whole Earth Catalogue*, a collaborative compilation of information, published by Stewart Brand between 1968 and 1972. The goal of the project was to provide useful information and tools for individuals to help build sustainable communities. Similarly influential was British scientist James Lovelock's 'Gaia Hypothesis', named after the ancient Greek goddess of Earth, which asserted that the biosphere and physical components of our planet form a complex, interrelated, self-sustaining system. See Norman Myers, *The Gaia Atlas of Planet Management: For Today's Caretakers of Tomorrow's World* (1984). The notion of Earth as life-giving and nurturing mother found parallels as well in the burgeoning women's movement of the 1960s and 1970s.

Other prominent theorists of sustainable design in the second half of the twentieth century include Otl Aicher and Gui Bonsiepe, both of whom were affiliated with the Hochschule für Gestaltung (College of Design) in Ulm, Germany. See, for example, Otl Aicher, *Die Welt als Entwurf* (*The World as*

Design) (1991) and Gui Bonsiepe, 'Design and Democracy' (2006). The strategy of 'planned obsoles-cence' was first introduced by the American advertising pioneer Earnest Elmo Calkins in 'Advertising Art in the United States' (1936). Karrie Jacobs admonishes the graphic designer for contributing to an unsustainable industry in 'Disposability, Graphic Design, Style and Waste' (1990), while Naomi Klein resists the forces of globalized and multinational commerce in *No Logo* (2000). It is not possible to do justice to the extensive literature on or organizations devoted to sustainable design in the past two decades. A few notable English language examples include *Our Common Future*, published by the World Commission on Environment and Development (1989), *More From Less* (exhibition catalogue, London, Design Centre, 1990–1), Dorothy Mackenzie, *Green Design, Design for the Environment* (1991), and *Green Desires: Ecology, Design, Products* (exhibition catalogue, EcoDesign Foundation, University of Sydney, 1992).

Today, architects and designers such as William McDonough and Bruce Mau continue to further the cause for sustainability. See William McDonough, 'Design, Ecology, Ethics, and the Making of Things' (1993), William McDonough and Michael Braungart, *Cradle to Cradle: Remaking the Way We Make Things* (2002), as well as the catalogue for the exhibition 'Massive Change', by Bruce Mau and the Institute Without Boundaries (2004).

PART II

METHODS AND THEMES

INTRODUCTION

Grace Lees-Maffei

In 1987, leading British anthropologist Daniel Miller infamously decried the design historical project as being merely to 'locate great individuals such as Raymond Loewy or Norman Bel Geddes and portray them as the creators of modern mass culture'. Miller wasn't alone: design history has been criticized for focusing on a canon of 'good' design (mostly modernist) and for the perceived dominance of issues of production (that is, an emphasis on designs, designers and manufacturers). Design historian Jonathan M. Woodham's response to Miller and other critics of design history is included in the first section of Part II, 'Foundations, Debates, Historiography, 1980–2000'. *The Design History Reader* forms another response to such critiques. While aspects of production, the figure of the designer, a canon of greats and the concept of 'good' design are examined in various texts within the *Reader*, they are not represented within its organizational structure. Instead, following two sections that examine debates around the nature of design history and interdisciplinary examinations of design as a process of negotiations, the thematic sections that make up Part II of the *Reader* highlight themes of gender, consumption, mediation and globalization.

Part I gathers together texts that inform histories of design, and Part II demonstrates the variety of work being done in design history through thematic groupings. Following the opening section, which explores some of the foundational debates within design history about the object of study for this emerging discipline, Section 8 suggests that, rather than associating design history with the study of the object or objects, the discipline might equally be seen as centred on the examination of a range of processes, or negotiations. The texts chosen demonstrate negotiations such as those between producers and consumers, or the negotiation of the meaning of a word such as 'craft', as well as each exemplifying the ways in which design history negotiates with other disciplines and fields. The facility with which design historians use and contribute to the work of a wide range of neighbouring subjects of study is useful and productive.

Section 9 reviews issues of gender and design. A classic foundational text from Judy Attfield is followed with two examinations of modernism and gender, and the section ends by extending the understanding of gender into issues of masculinity and men's studies. The section builds on a distinction between biological sex and culturally constituted gender to question the role of gender in the design process, to explore the ways in which taste is implicated in discourses around femininity and masculinity, and to consider the central role of objects, such as clothing and cars, in the construction of gendered identities.

The role of objects in the construction of identities is also important in Section 10, on consumption. Political philosopher Marx, and sociologists Veblen and Bourdieu provide differing accounts of the role of objects in society. Semiologist, structuralist and, later, post-structuralist, Barthes examines what objects and images can mean in his study of 'Myth Today'. Clarke traces the way personal networks were exploited for commercial gain as Tupperware was distributed through the social ritual of party selling. Post-war America is further explored by Weems Jr., who reveals how large corporations moved from ignoring African-American consumers to targeting them as a market segment.

The penultimate section addresses mediation, an aspect of enquiry that has recently achieved critical mass within design history. Such an emphasis can mean examining the channels and discourses that exist between the producers and consumers of designed goods, such as advertising, advice literature and magazines (all are addressed in this section). Or, it can mean analysing the role of objects themselves as mediating between individual and society. This is a fruitful area for further work.

Another area demanding further investigation is explored in the book's last section: globalization. First, Crowley's case study of Poland's Zakopane style demonstrates the constructed nature of national design and can be used to question its utility as a unit of analysis. Avery and van Eeden each consider designed goods as evidence of the iniquities of colonialism. Weisenfeld explores a case study of aesthetic influence across nations and cultures and Bick and Chiper offer a comparative analysis of the non-Western consumption of a North American brand in a process of transculturation.

The themes represented in Part II are only several from a wide range, which it has not been possible to fit into this *Reader*. Groupings by materials are discussed in the general introduction and groupings by place are suggested in Section 12. Further themes include, for example, domesticity, which has moved from the margins to become a central concern within design history and cultural history. In the UK, the Arts and Humanities Research Council's Centre for the Study of the Domestic Interior (2002–6) was based at the Royal College of Art, Victoria and Albert Museum and the Bedford Centre for the History of Women at Royal Holloway, University of London. It brought together the scholarship of interior design history with literary studies and ethnography. Texts in the *Design History Reader* that address issues of domesticity include Reid's analysis of the Khrushchev Kitchen, Csikszentmihalyi and Rochberg-Halton's 'Most Cherished Objects in the Home', Sparke's introduction to her study of what she terms 'the sexual politics of taste', Clarke's exploration of the Tupperware party and Ferry's analysis of domestic advice.

Clearly, the placement of a text in Part II is not intended to imply that it has no contribution to make to understanding of the history of design; on the contrary, we would urge readers to reflect on the texts here as contributions to Part I as much as Part II and vice versa. The potential readings that may be traced through *The Design History Reader* are various, numerous and in your hands.

Foundations, Debates, Historiography, 1980–95

INTRODUCTION

Grace Lees-Maffei

Design history has its foundations in texts unknowingly conceived as contributions to a nascent discipline. As European functionalist design gained currency between the wars, so writers produced commentaries that promoted modernist design practice. Pre-eminent among these is Nikolaus Pevsner's 1936 book *Pioneers of the Modern Movement from William Morris to Walter Gropius* (revised and republished in 1949 as *Pioneers of Modern Design*). But, while his work was influential as a catalyst for debate and research into modern design, Pevsner's position as a starting point for design history needs to be interrogated. His focus on key figures and a limited definition of design as a professional activity proved a rich spur to critical opposition. For example, although it retained aspects of Pevsner's modernist techniques, in its use of an overarching metanarrative to mount a linear, progressive history of furniture, Siegfried Giedion's 'anonymous history' *Mechanization Takes Command* (1948) moved away from Pevsner's canonical approach to an understanding of design as being embedded in everyday things.

Mistakenly characterized by those outside the field as being hidebound by Pevsnerian modernist values, design history in Britain instead coalesced around the Design History Society in 1977, at least partly as a way of moving the critique beyond a celebration of modern movement designers towards a more inclusive understanding of design. As would-be design historians negotiated design history's genesis and future formation, a trail of self-consciously critical and reflective writings formed, mostly in the journal literature. A selection of this material, dating from 1980 to 1995, is presented in this section, and aspects of debates about the nature of design history are represented throughout the *Reader*. Questions such as 'how do we define design?' and its correlative 'what should we be writing design history about?', 'what is the wider relevance of design history beyond its own disciplinary borders?' and, particularly, 'what is the relationship between design history and design practice?' became important for understanding current and future practice in the discipline.

Informed by the British cultural studies movement centred around the University of Birmingham, Fran Hannah and Tim Putnam characterize early design history as displaying twin tendencies; neither the history of styles, nor eclecticism – the aspiration to social and historical context, assembled through dabbling in other disciplines such as business history and the history of technology – has produced satisfactory work. They advocate a design history that acknowledges the historically-specific nature of aesthetic evaluation, which replaces notions of a designer's 'innovation and influence' with deeper understanding of a designer's culture and which understands design not as a noun but rather as a series of changing processes of use.

Hannah and Putnam's account, which specifies a very British story of design history responding to the needs of UK art college education, can be compared with Clive Dilnot's transatlantic perspective to reflect upon the differences between design history as it developed in the UK and the US respectively, as can the texts by Victor Margolin and Jonathan Woodham, which also appear in this section. Dilnot's schematic 'Mapping the Field' considers the purpose, emergence and varieties of design history, with the latter placed into four spheres of interest: decorative arts, modernisms, design organisation and social relations. Dilnot extended his ideas into a second, looser and more discursive article, considering, in turn, 'Problems' and 'Possibilities', informed by contemporary art historical practice. There, Dilnot's conclusion echoes Hannah and Putnam's: he calls for debate, which relates the design 'profession to the society in which it operates'.

A readiness to harness the work of other disciplines has been a characteristic strength of design history. It is not *in spite of* but *because* design history emerged in opposition to an art historical umbrella that no longer fit its needs that it has enjoyed its interdisciplinary and multidisciplinary freedom. A significant number of the texts included in *The Design History Reader* were not conceived specifically as design historical contributions. Design history has benefitted from sharing its concerns with neighbouring disciplines including business history, the history of technology, social history, anthropology and material culture studies as well as art history and the more recent visual culture studies. This very freedom to roam means that asking questions about the disciplinary boundaries of design history is an important and rewarding exercise. Published in 1989, John A. Walker's landmark textbook *Design History and the History of Design* still remains useful. Extracted here are Walker's ideas about the scope of design history, the meaning of design, the significance of a design 'canon', the outline of a more inclusive 'production-consumption model' and the varieties of design history.

A notable contribution by Victor Margolin to these disciplinary debates argued that design history's shortcomings meant it would be better off incorporated into what he has termed 'design studies'. Adrian Forty published a reply in which he stated: 'I do not feel the need, as Margolin does, to discover a boundary for design history […] surely the discipline of history as it has developed over the last century or so already provides a perfectly satisfactory definition of the "field".' British design historian Jonathan Woodham, too, responded that design history was thriving, at least in Britain, and needed no parent discipline. As the extracts in this section make clear, the UK has developed a greater profile for design history institutionally, so that design history has been represented departmentally, with degree provision at BA, MA and PhD levels. Conversely, design history has remained marginal to art history and American studies within the US academy, although this trend is slowly changing, as Margolin discusses in his revised article, which appeared in the 2002 volume of his essays *The Politics of the Artificial*.

Scholarship proceeds collectively through questioning, disagreement and revision as well as collaboration and consensus. It is a sign of the discipline's vigour that debates about its nature and practice have continued. Design history has benefited from these foundational debates and moved on, so that the majority of design historians working today embrace a broad conception of the discipline's scope. Indeed, the transatlantic debate shown in the extracts here has been eclipsed by a global imperative for design history (discussed in section 12 of this *Reader*). And an early concern for 'good design' has become less compelling during a period in which design history seeks to challenge ideas about discrimination and pursue an inclusive definition of design within social context.

Because they have been useful, the writings extracted can be regarded as having achieved canonical status. Retrospectively, debates about what design is and what design history should be can be viewed as so much male jockeying indicative of a desire to draw boundaries, to prescribe the discipline and thereby gain mastery of it. Walker's book includes an important chapter by Judy Attfield on gender and design. The fact that Attfield's contribution is reproduced in Section 9 of this *Reader* with other gender analyses is not intended to diminish the significance of gender as a foundational issue for design history. On the contrary, it is because the editors of this volume believe that gender is absolutely fundamental as a first principle of design historical analysis that the subject has been accorded its own section for more detailed treatment than could be afforded by its appearance in this section. The remaining sections in Part II examine some of the core questions facing contemporary design history, which have emerged as a consequence of the debates represented here.

37

TAKING STOCK IN DESIGN HISTORY

Fran Hannah and Tim Putnam (1980)

What is 'design'? How, and for whom, has it existed? What is a history of design a history of? What are its distinctive problems and methods? To whom is this knowledge of any use or interest?

In the mid-1970s, when design history was emerging as a distinct area of study in Britain, these questions were much discussed. Lecturers in polytechnics and colleges of art, who had experimented for a number of years in adapting the history of art to the needs of design students and had come to think of themselves as 'design historians', felt a need to define the area of their study. To a large extent this was a definition against ruling conventions of art history; the designer was not to be considered an artist-hero; design was not to be treated as an art object. [...]

Today, half a decade later, design history seems on the surface to have achieved the status of a distinct subject specialism: it has its own degrees, conferences and publications.[1] Yet neither of these critical routes has been followed very far by very many. The empirical 'consolidation' of the subject has largely taken place around the formula of the history of design in social-economic context. All too often this means that art-conventional notions of design still pass as the substance of the subject while context amounts to an eclectic dipping into new fields. Bits of business history, history of technology or social history find their way into an account without consideration of the problems proper to those histories or even the processes by which they have become established as knowledge. 'Context' is not really established because we are still in thrall to certain categories which present themselves as the self-evident substance of any history of design. Such notions as 'designer', 'school', 'artefact', 'medium', 'style', continue to be taken as starting points even when they have been the subject of critical discourse in art history. Far from being a greener pasture free from the contradictions of art history, design history is in fair danger of becoming an academic backwater.

This would be a great shame, as the subject has many pretensions and not a small list of responsibilities. Its development in Britain, due to the nature and scope of art and design education in this country, is unique and is attracting an increasing interest overseas. [...] We want to open up the way to thinking historically about design as a complex social relation interconnected with other relations. This knowledge should involve and relate to people, and it should relate to the practical knowledge involved in making and using design. A first stage in developing this knowledge is distinguishing the different 'histories of design' extant in design history, or which need to be developed in order to meet the demands placed upon it. A critical comparison of these histories may then lead to the establishment of the History of Design which would be the appropriate object of study for design historians.

THE FORMATION OF DESIGN HISTORY ECLECTICISM

When the new Dip A.D. courses began in 1963 they contained a compulsory art historical element. This was intended as a background to the 'fine art' element of visual analysis which was considered the appropriate general theoretical study for 'designing'. The students were to study 'the major Arts in several significant periods'.[2] From the beginning the actual place of art historical work in design courses was problematical. While visual research might pretend to a general theoretical position in relation to design, art history could only escape from the deep background by becoming involved with the history of aspects of design studied on diploma courses. These are the forces which induced the development of design history, apart from those areas, chiefly related to the history of architecture, which formed part of the art history survey courses.

This increasing integration with design education was reflected in the substitution of an extended essay project or thesis for the final examination in art history. The drawing up of the guidelines for these pieces of research, the definition of their subject matter, and the criteria used to assess them embodied the embryo of a new theoretical and empirical study more directly related to the main study areas. The subjects undertaken in the theses, chosen by the students, came to include a progressively wider range of cultural artefacts, including works of popular culture hitherto disregarded by art history.

In practice the closer involvement with design students meant accommodating the media-based grouping of the design courses themselves. This pattern is quite historically specific. It derives in part from the nature of subject differentiation in British academic tradition, in part from a regard for the structure of British industry. The desire to produce designers suitable for industry has been a major factor in post-war design education and prompted numerous debates which affected course structure. Certain of these concerned the relative merits of British models of designing (which are generally organised around in-house designers) as opposed to the American system of freelance industrial design. The 'generalists' argued for inter-media courses based on study of design methods and problem analysis, while the 'specialists' claimed that a knowledge of processes for specific media was necessary until the pattern of employment itself changed.[3] [...]

In situations where design students from several areas came together, a more comprehensive coverage of design types could be undertaken. The courses depended fairly heavily on the available literature concerning architecture with a strong emphasis on the 'Modern Movement' and the Bauhaus. Pressure to include material outside that of the dominant avant-garde (partly a result of the nostalgia boom of the early 1970s) led to the inclusion of stylistic categories such as Art Deco and 1930s streamlining. [...]

Where, as was often the case, design history teaching followed the media basis of a design course, a different pattern of eclecticism emerged. The starting point was existing discussions of the 'minor' 'decorative' or 'applied' arts, together with literature written for collectors. The limitations of such accounts were all too apparent: concentration on visual or stylistic features became a sterile exercise in classification once categories of objects were treated in isolation. In addition, connoisseurship encouraged a closed system of relation between monetary and aesthetic value, divorced from the conditions in which the objects in question were made and used. [...] Chatty social history, or a narrow sociology which abstracts functions appropriate to particular product types, were integrated into media-based work while 'social and economic context' remained an aspiration. [...]

We focus on three unresolved historiographical problems in design history writing: the nature of aesthetic evaluation; innovation and influence; and 'design itself'. In each case we attempt to expose and transform categories 'given' to design history by the circumstances in which it has been created.

AESTHETIC EVALUATION

It is widely recognised that historians should make explicit their reasons for defining a subject as worthy of study. Anachronism is inevitable if what is presently considered significant cannot be contrasted and related to the orders of significance which have prevailed in other times and places. The crudest form which this problem takes in design history is the unrecognised intrusion of aesthetic evaluation. Historians have taste which cannot and need not be suppressed, but if this taste operates as an unknown and therefore arbitrary determinant of what is selected as good or significant design, then the result is indifferent design criticism rather than any kind of history.

The influences of important traditions of design writing which are anti-historical in this respect have been exorcised to a certain extent. Connoisseurship knows the periodisation of design criteria intimately in one sense, yet typically lacks a sense of the constantly shifting boundary around what is worthy of attention by the connoisseur. It is now well understood that this lack of self-consciousness derives from the fact that connoisseurship operates within boundaries of current social cachet and market valuation which it does not need or want to see. [...]

The 'Modern Movement's' peculiar combination of functionalism and aestheticism is now recognisable as a profoundly anti-historical influence.[4] [...] For example, Stephen Bayley's recent *In Good Shape*,[5] issued under the Design Council imprint, recognises the historically limited character of the 'Modern Movement', but bases its own selection of 'significant' modern design on whatever has 'style and wit'. A complex taste operates without being recognised or discussed as such. More consistent bases of selection, such as pioneering form or scale of production are surreptitiously introduced without being systematically employed. [...] Even if the principles of the ruling taste could be specified, we would still be left with little more than a document in the history of taste,

circa 1979. Covert aestheticism then provides us with our first example of misplaced substance in design history. [...]

INNOVATION AND INFLUENCE

Many monographs on great designers and schools of design are organised around a notion of fundamental innovation or extensive influence rather than an endorsement of visual values.[6] Even here, however, where an apparently more historical criterion of significance and ordering is being employed, the choice of designer or design school as an organising category often interferes with the exploration of the problems raised. There is great temptation to treat the designer or school as the substance of the discourse, whose existence is not taken as problematic, and to place the substance in context, following out selected lines of connection which are then given the name of influence or innovation. [...] Accounts which take great designers or schools as self-evident starting points [...] suffer from historical tunnel-vision. This point was made forcefully by Tim Benton in 1975, concerning the self-confirming nature of the status attributed to the Bauhaus.[7] Similar points have been made in the history of ideas and in art history.[8] A second problem with this sort of account is that the substance is a subject, an individual or collective personality, which exercises creative or free, unconditioned agency. [...] There are serious problems with identifying designers as personal agents because their work is embedded in a complex social process of historically varying form. [...]

At the most basic level, one must be able to differentiate agency from situation. [...] This does not mean that designs are not produced by real individuals but that personal creative activity operates with and through a designer's culture. Designing draws on and refers forward to a stock of knowledge and external requirements. The analysis of this culture involves:

(a) Characterising the limits of variation of what designers do: to the extent, for example, that design is a theoretical as opposed to practical activity it will be capable of being described as a set of rules rather than as a set of improvisations made by drawing on a repertoire.

(b) How does one learn to be a designer? Learning by example is clearly different from formal pedagogy.

(c) What is the place of designing in the social division of knowledge and labour involved in making things? What are the means of specification and evaluation which connect designing with its external context?

(d) What are the available means for circulation of information to and for the designer in a general cultural context, apart from those specified directly in relation to (b) and (c)? [...]

Taking the notion of design as an activity seriously involves reformulating our ideas of who or what acts, and the nature of the what that is acted upon, because it is also the acted with. In other words, because the culture is drawn through the designers, innovation and influence take place within the culture. These should be studied as processes in their own right and not employed as unproblematic criteria by which 'important' designers are selected as worthy (but necessarily incoherent) units of study. [...]

THE NATURE OF 'DESIGN'

The notion of designing as an activity may be pursued further, into the realm of 'design' the noun, which is supposed to exist in artefacts and in representations. Designing is relational in character, and these relations fix on objects, but the objects are not then fixed with an immutable significance forever. The production of design increases its complexity as a social process; the designed object enters into new relations of valuation and of consumption. Therefore a given design passes through and is defined within a plurality of relations. [...] In this way, the meaning of design is continually being historically reconstituted; it is a persistent complex of activities rather than a once and for all creation. Therefore there must be multiple histories of design. [...]

Because much design history teaching takes place in courses which see themselves as medium based (in some sense, often left implicit) powerful forces are at work to objectify categories which may rest on nothing more substantial than the industrial structure of a particular country at a particular point in time. Much of the place occupied by the notion of medium needs to be reoccupied by an analysis of production processes which include material transformation (i.e. the interaction of medium in the narrow sense and physical processes), the social division of labour and knowledge (systems of manufacture), and economic calculation as applied to design and production decisions. [...]

In our view, it is crucial that categories derived from the world of production, embedded in functional technical-economic discourses, are not allowed to usurp discussion of the significance of design in use. [...] We would look askance, therefore, at any attempt to discuss the history of design in terms of social activities or needs which did not take the existence of those categories as an historical problem, or which failed to recognise that a fundamental characteristic of design is that it exists in a multiplicity of relations, which cut across each other.

[...] What is the historical significance of stylistic analyses? Several writers have emphasised that the most important considerations in histories of design are not visual, but concern the conditions in which objects are made and used. This seems an odd opposition, for visual properties are essential to an understanding of both the production and the consumption of design. Surely what is being opposed is a notion that the history of design may be conceived as a chronology of stylistic characteristics abstracted from these, indeed from any, relations. [...] Yet it is recognised that the perception of colour, proportion and perspective are historically and culturally variable, and that the ways in which stylistic characteristics have been recognised and significant discriminations made have varied enormously. How artefacts and their representation change significance as they pass out of the conditions of their conception and production ought to be a high priority problem in design history. The variability of significance rather than the persistence of qualities should be at the forefront of analysis. What does it mean to assert a stylistic identity between a 'Louis XV' chair in eighteenth-century Paris and a 'Louis XV' chair in a twentieth-century museum? [...]

An important object of research should be to uncover and articulate means by which significance is attributed to objects, in order to open up more dimensions in the history of styles, and pose questions about the relationships between changes in valuation and changes in patterns of production and consumption. The means by which these investigations are carried out may vary, but it is possible to see lines along which work needs to be done. As the history of valuation must be read to a large extent through linguistic evidence, there is a vast amount of research to be done to establish continuities and discontinuities in descriptions and evaluations of design existing at any time or over time. The patterns then derived may be compared with changes in other patterns of usage, and, outside linguistic media, with visual evidence, in order to establish changes in significance attributed to the perceptual qualities of design.[9] [...]

Therefore, the analysis of style becomes the analysis of styles of life, of modes of use of the produced environment, both directly and indirectly. It is important not to lose either of these senses of use, although they are often, in fact, intertwined. Direct usage is what is often called utilitarian or functional; it refers to the sense in which designed objects may be said externally to constitute part of the objective conditions of a mode of living irrespective of whether they are seen as such from within that mode of life.

Indirect usage is mediated symbolically; it refers to the sense in which discrimination between design qualities is used to define boundaries between different social and cultural categories and also, within a way of life, between times, moods, activities and other dispositions. These two sorts of usage must be studied together in bounded circumstances in order to recover any convincing sense of design in historical actuality. The study of 'functions' in itself imposes a reality which has a one-dimensional rationality; the study of systems of meaning in themselves fails to recover the pattern of practical activities which make up characteristic styles of life – both types of analysis are prone to a-historical abstraction, because they do not place at the centre of the analysis the problem of how those people whose activities are being reconstructed actually ordered their lives.

[...] Research should concentrate on the relationship between visual evidence and the other sorts of evidence by which patterns of typical activities can be reconstructed. In many cases, oral history techniques will be found to fill a gap between written and 'visual' evidence, although there is a great deal of scope for reading illustration as model narrative and for culling habitual action from literary sources. Fixed systems of evidence better display the oppositions and part whole relations which seem to determine a universe of meaning but reminiscence often reveals better the real-time structure which shows how different activities were experienced as connected or disconnected. [...]

CONCLUSION

In this paper we have argued that the conceptualisation of the historical space in which design can exist for those making and using it is essential if the proto-discipline called 'design history' is to achieve maturity. It is important to recognise that this process of discussion and criticism is not an end in itself, but the means by which design history can meet its responsibilities in design education, evaluation and research, as well as make a contribution to the understanding of the produced environment, as the world we inhabit.

NOTES

1. To date, five CNAA BA (Hons) degrees with Art History, one BA and two MAs in its own right. The Design History Society publishes a newsletter. […]

2. National Council for Art Education Report, 1960 (extracts in C. Ashwin (ed.), *Art Education: Documents and Policies 1768–1975*, Society for Research into Higher Education, London, 1975).

3. D. Warren Piper (ed.), *Readings in Art and Design Education, 1: After Hornsey*, Davis-Poynter, London, 1973.

4. Of many examples: R. Venturi, *Complexity and Contradiction in Architecture*, MoMA, New York, 1966; M. Tafuri, *Architecture and Utopia*, MIT, Boston, 1977

5. S. Bayley, *In Good Shape*, Design Council, London, 1979.

6. For example, S.I.A.D., *Designers in Britain*, III, Allan Wingate, London, 1951.

7. Tim Benton, 'Background to the Bauhaus', in *Design 1900–1960* (ed. T. Faulkner), Newcastle Polytechnic, 1976.

8. Fritz Ringer, *Decline of the German Mandarins*, Harvard University Press, London, 1971; Michel Foucault, *The Archaeology of Knowledge*, Tavistock, London, 1972. See Adrian Rifkin's article in *BLOCK*, no. 3, 1980.

9. P. Bourdieu, *La Distinction, critique social du jugement*, Editions de Minuit, Paris, 1979, examines the relationship between categories of discrimination and 'objective' social indices; J. Walker, 'The Old Shoes', *BLOCK*, no. 2, and Jon Bird, in *BLOCK*, no. 3, examine means by which significance is constructed.

38

THE STATE OF DESIGN HISTORY, PART I: MAPPING THE FIELD

Clive Dilnot (1984)

THE EMERGENCE OF DESIGN HISTORY

Before 1939, there were two or three areas of design historical activity, with the exception of architecture.[1] One area was the history of the decorative arts. Largely constituted as a branch of the history of monumental architecture, especially of great houses, it included the histories of interior or garden design and the contents and furnishings of rooms. It also included the provenance-creating histories of all those objects, that is, furniture, glassware, ceramics, silver, and so forth, collected in museums, preserved in the country houses, and, above all, sold through the antiques trade and the sales room. The histories of the decorative arts are intimately related to the history of art in this area.[2] Because the histories of the decorative arts are oriented to the needs of the sales rooms as the most vital and vigorous consumers of their work, they have accomplished important achievements in detailed research. But they lacked a concept and a comprehension of design.[3] [...]

By contrast, the second embryonic form of design history, building on art and architectural history, elevated design to the highest principle. If design history has an academic antecedent, it is surely Nikolaus Pevsner's *Pioneers of Modern Design*, despite all later criticisms.[4] First published in 1936, it is animated by two powerfully linked ideas. First, design is of great importance and significance in the modern world. Second, precisely because of this, the form that designing takes in this emerging world is of social and ontological importance; so, too, is its history. [...] Scarcely formulated in his writings to any explicit theoretical extent, the conviction of the import and subtlety[5] of this relationship animates almost every sentence Pevsner wrote.[6]

History as polemic in the service of a design principle, or even history for use as functional to collecting, has lost much of its respectability or has taken on the new form of history as celebration. But the quasi-scientific detachment to which historians now sometimes pretend, was, before 1939, ruled out of court, at least for 'design history' (for what possible market could there have been for it?). [...] Design history arises, in the service of design, as a response to particular practical problems. It does not arise artificially, simply for the sake of itself. Once the problem is solved, through the assistance of history, interest in the subject tends to die down again. This tendency prompts the question, what is implied by the current simultaneous rise of a need for history on all design fronts? And, will the answer explain the otherwise puzzling absence of design history between 1936 and the late 1960s?

The reasons for this absence are many. Modernism's rampant success in colonizing both the British and American architectural establishments after 1945, undoubtedly helped by Pevsner and Siegfried Giedion,[7] was not perfectly repeated in design. When product design, in particular, took on the Modernist ethic, it did not need the historical and intellectual weight that was a necessary pre-condition for adaptation by architecture. The critical arguments such as those developed in Herbert Read's *Art and Industry* were of more impact. The same remained generally true in graphic design. Except for specialist areas, notably typography[8] and illustration, history seemed to be irrelevant for a discipline in the process of forming itself and attempting to escape the historic limitations of arts-and-crafts attitudes and its commercial art background.

Conditions were not propitious for the emergence of design history. A rampant anti-intellectualism, combined with a hierarchical dominance of the fine arts, the history of art, and the idea of 'culture' in the art and design schools, served to make discussions of design in any historical sense more or less impossible. But [...] in the 1950s and 1960s [...] design came of age; [...] The consumer revolutions of the post-war period, the institutionalization of design, the expansion of art and design education, and the explosion of youth and pop cultures, all served in different ways to highlight design and styling skills and to emphasize the new significance of the look or style of things. [...]

This cultural identification with things also marked an acceptance of industrial culture. Beginning in 1952 with the exhibition of Victorian and Edwardian decorative arts at the Victoria and Albert Museum, a gradual revival of interest occurred in the objects and history of the nineteenth and twentieth centuries. The Victorian Society was founded in England in 1957, the Society for the History of Technology in America in 1958. The decade also brought the beginnings of industrial archeology and a general popular obsession with the previously despised Victorian Age.

Pevsner's *Pioneers of Modern Design* was revised and re-issued in 1960, and in the same year, Reyner Banham's *Theory and Design in the First Machine Age* was published. Banham's book marked the beginning of a period of intensive study of Modernism and its origins, which [...] departed somewhat from the Pevsnerian model. However, [...] the emerging design history still fit easily into the traditional forms of art and architectural history writing. Pevsner's book treats painting seriously, and is written in terms of 'great men' [and] it is on individuals that the early design history was based.

This approach was not necessarily counter to the interest of the emerging design professions. The codification of professional design education in Britain in the early 1960s was accompanied by the enhanced status of designers and design. In that context, design histories that further developed the role of professional designers and design institutions were welcomed initially. However, [...] it was clear by the early 1970s that 'good design' was not a magic talisman. Modernism began to lose its appeal, and problems of design organization, technology, and the relation of design to society and to the economy came to the fore. Also, the question of design's relationship to commerce, markets, and popular taste provoked both practitioners and embryonic historians to re-examine the tenets and assumptions of a Modernist design practice and a history of design that simply reproduced the modernist story or somewhat naively documented the emergence of good design and its institutions. This rethinking of approaches set the stage for the emergence of a new design history.

THE FORMS AND VARIETIES OF DESIGN HISTORY

[...] The coherence of a design historical attitude was both slow in forming and not bound by any rigid framework or set of texts. (In that respect, even *Pioneers* has not dominantly imposed its values on present design history.) On the contrary, with the laudable aim of keeping the discipline open and relativistic, there was a notable reluctance to specify objects and subjects of study or to consider what the role of this history might be.

The major consequence of this almost accidental emergence of a history of design is that design history, in the sense of a single, organized discipline with defined aims and objects, *does not exist*.

It is thus bafflingly difficult to survey or define design history in its present state. At best, one can say that, without explicit definition or statement, the new design history is formed around four linked principles and four related absences. The principles are as follows:

- Design history is the study of the history of professional design activity.
- It is not the activity itself that forms the first layer of attention of historians, but the results of that activity: designed objects and images. (This emphasis is justified on a number of aesthetic and archeological grounds, as well as on the premise that design is a practical activity that results in a new thing or image.)
- An equally natural orientation was added to design in the nineteenth and twentieth centuries.
- Design history emphasizes individual designers. Explicitly or implicitly, they are the focus of the majority of design history written and taught today.

The absences, by contrast, are less specific, but equally present in the way the discipline operates:

- There is little explicit consideration of aims, methods, or roles of design history in relation to its actual or potential audiences.
- There is little consideration of design history's origins, except in an educational and institutional sense.
- There is a general lack of historical, methodological, or critical self-reflection. Whereas self-reflection might at the very least engender clear statements of position or clarification of aims, the ad hoc nature of most design history means that it is very difficult to define social, theoretical, or methodological presuppositions. This not to say they do not exist.

Differences of emphasis and orientation in design historical work certainly exist. These can be classified as four general traditions or approaches; however, it is important to note that these are only general attitudes or tendencies, not schools to which historians ally themselves, nor are they necessarily exclusive categories. Many historians of design cross some or all of these boundaries in the course of their work. In addition, there are four areas of work in design history that can be set out as follows:

1. A CONTINUATION OF THE TRADITIONAL HISTORIES OF THE DECORATIVE AND MINOR ARTS AS APPLIED TO THE SUBJECT MATTER OF DESIGN, DECORATION, AND EPHEMERA OF THE NINETEENTH AND TWENTIETH CENTURIES

As the recent past has become of more concern to design historians, museum directors, collectors and designers, there has also been a natural tendency to extend to the decorative arts of the nineteenth and twentieth centuries the kind of scholastic attention that, prior to 1945, was confined almost exclusively to works of the eighteenth century and earlier. This has taken a number of forms. The most dominant at present is the encounter with the world of mass culture (the break is approximately 1925). There, the orientation of the studies has shifted to a whimsical conception of popular taste and to a concern with what might be called junk antiques. Typical products of the recent histories of this genre are the enthusiastic studies of early Art Deco products, histories of fashion, and popular books on ephemera, such as Bevis Hillier's *Austerity Binge*.

What links all of these works is the patent problem of attempting to discuss issues of twentieth-century decoration within the traditional terms of the 'high' decorative arts. [...] The central issues in terms of the decorative (and one must ask whether that term can even apply to twentieth century phenomena) now are issues of style, taste, and fashion. Indeed, it is precisely works that deal centrally with these concepts that best support the attempt to write a serious history of the meaning of decorative style in the twentieth century. [...]

Yet the tradition of writing decorative history survives. Its ability to elucidate the precise provenance of an object is in considerable demand by the sales rooms, the antiques trade, and the new museums that emphasize nineteenth- and twentieth-century collections. What this tradition can give in terms of developing an understanding of design and decoration in the twentieth century remains to be seen.

[...] There is a need to construct histories of design crafts that either avoid the excesses of recent decorative histories or assimilate them into an overall model of the development of industrial design. [...] Recent work undertaken on William Morris, the Arts and Crafts Movement, and Art Nouveau [...] augments the lineage of Modernism that was first set out in Pevsner's *Pioneers*. [... These] can be considered as celebrations of a slightly different set of values, even if they are read as proto-Modernist [... and] their general development is toward an increasing examination of the social conditions in which this work was produced and its connection to theories of life and human relations.[9] [...]

2. A FOCUS ON MODERNISM

The fascination with William Morris and Arts and Crafts values is almost a Pevsnerian trademark. Later studies of Modernism, beginning with Banham's 1960 revisions on architectural history in *Theory and Design in the First Machine Age*, have stressed the period after 1900, the less immediately central aspects of the European avant-garde (Italy, Expressionism, De Stijl), and technology (electricity and building services). [... As] the Open University's third-level course on the history of modern architecture and design from 1890 to 1939 [...] concentrat[es] on the

development of the work of individual designers across their careers and across a range of conditions, it follows and also modifies the Pevsnerian tradition. Pevsnerian also is the emphasis on stylistic analysis. However, the course departs from the straightjackets of Modernist histories. The introduction contains a design case study on Norman Bel Geddes, and the course includes units on British design and the electric home, the garden cities movement, and mechanical services.

Organizing the course made evident at least two of the problems of doing design history: The abundance of potential [archival] material disclosed the lack of a conceptual framework within which to make sense of it all. [... And] the history of Modernism, which had been primarily an architectural history, cannot remain unaltered by the incorporation of the history of design. [...] A broader history of social and industrial developments [...] shifts from Modernism per se to the unraveling of its meaning and function in the present phase of capitalist development [... including] the more anonymous developments in technique, industrial production, and consumerism.

[...] As a counterpoint to Pevsner's history and European work in general, Penny Sparke in Britain and Jeffrey Meikle and Arthur Pulos in the United States are asserting the validity of American design contributions, particularly the American system of manufactures and the development of professional design consultants in the 1930s.[10] These histories [...] challenge the notion of what it is to be modern. For Pevsner this meant to have a self-conscious awareness of design's social role and its progression toward a rational universalism. Indeed, one was modern to the extent that one was aware of the significance of design as an ideal. For Americans, to be modern in the esthetic or design theoretical sense is acceptable, but of more import is to be modern in the economic and technological sense, to be in tune with the most progressive developments of American capitalism

[...]

3. A FOCUS ON ISSUES OF DESIGN ORGANIZATION

If there is a clear thread at all discernible in the history of design in industrial societies, it is that design in the process of production has become separated from the act of making and, therefore, has increasingly become a process of conceiving rather than realizing form [...] having to do not only with design questions, but also increasingly with those of company corporate policy and political or legal matters.

[...] In practice, design organization is the core concern of works as chronologically and methodologically diverse as John Heskett's *Industrial Design*, Jonathan Woodham's *The Industrial Designer and the Public*, and Penny Sparke's *Consultant Design*. [...] Natural extensions of this relation lead either to technological and industrial histories, to institutional studies, or to studies of the consumer or the design purchasing and design-affected public. In specific cases, design organization is also a subject that social and economic historians have become interested in.

4. A FOCUS ON THE SOCIAL RELATIONS OF VARIOUS KINDS OF DESIGN

Design historical and analytical developments in Europe have directly confronted this issue. For example, Wolfgang Fritz Haug has developed a theory of commodity esthetics (Warenasthetik) from a Marxist perspective [... and] Gert Selle has formulated a theory of design as an expression of social relations from a comparable perspective.[11] Both Haug's and Selle's work relate to the more general social and political aspects of art, architecture and design as manifested through the collective work of the Ulmer Verein für Kunstwissenschaft, the left-wing West German association of art and architectural historians that has been stimulating and focusing work on the sociopolitical aspects of architecture and design. This group sees the forms of art, architecture, and design as being produced within capitalism, but conversely playing a significant ideological role in capitalist culture. This group's work is directly comparable to work being produced in East Germany. [...] British and American scholars are used to attacks on the left-wing or totalitarian aspects of functionalism but Hüter and Lothar Kühne reject this view, contending that the Bauhaus and 1920s Modernism are products of a phase of the capitalist economy. [...]

Italian design history perhaps is even more cultural than social. Related to the dominance of high-level quasi-Marxist architectural history and criticism, design history and criticism in Italy attempt to grasp the difficult connection of designed material to sociocultural forms and relations. This approach is the thrust of the highly developed, theoretical essays in two exhibition catalogs: *Italy: The New Domestic Landscape*[12] and *Italian Re-evolution: Design in Italian Society in the Eighties.*[13]

[...] [This] emphasis on cultural aspects of design meaning [...] rather than design production or reception, connects Italian work to some of the new English design history, which falls on the axis between the Birmingham Center for Contemporary Cultural Studies and a group at Middlesex Polytechnic that produces the journal *Block* and runs one of the two main British Master of Arts courses in design history. The primary emphasis of this work is the study of representations, which owes its origins to the semiotic cultural criticism pioneered by Roland Barthes. [...] Dick Hebdige's work, particularly *Subculture: The Meaning of Style*, deals marginally with conventional design history, but is at the center of the relation of material culture, images, and forms of representation to social relations and processes. So, too, is the emerging feminist analysis of design. [...] Feminist design history possesses the supreme virtue of refusing the distinction between design and social life that characterizes so much design thinking, practice, and historical work.

NOTES

Extracted from Dilnot, C., 'The State of Design History, Part I: Mapping the Field', *Design Issues* 1(1) (Spring, 1984), pp. 4–23. Reprinted by permission of the author.

1. What is the different significance of history and study between architecture and design? A study that focused on this issue could provide a whole range of insights into what differentiates the practices of architecture and design in a conceptual sense.

2. In retrospect, it seems that design history's problem with art history was less the way the latter imposed its methodology on design history and more the fact that design history kept art history's methods but renounced its intellectual core, thus depriving itself of the means to give significance to the form of the things it dealt with. The histories of the decorative arts, with some exceptions, have already anticipated design history in this.

3. When historically does society begin to recognize consciously that things are designed rather than that they simply are? This seems to be a fundamental problem. It is the difference between design as a necessary but barely acknowledged moment of human praxis and 'design' as the conscious apperception and acceptance of this fact. But when and why does the latter occur?

4. Nikolaus Pevsner, *Pioneers of Modern Design* (London: Faber and Faber, 1936).

5. This is in sharp contrast to the poor caricature of Pevsner's work recently drawn in David Watkin, *Morality in Architecture* (London: Oxford University Press, 1978).

6. It certainly fires *Pioneers* and guides the series of biographic and critical articles Pevsner wrote in the late 1930s and 1940s. Many of these articles are usefully collected in Nikolaus Pevsner, *Studies in Art, Architecture, and Design*, vols. 1 and 2 (London: Thames and Hudson, 1976).

7. Giedion's influence on Modernism has been frequently commented on. Less discussed, because more problematic, is the influence of Giedion's *Mechanisation Takes Command* (London: Oxford University Press, 1948). In some ways, it would seem that this curious work has never been fully assimilated into design history.

8. The exceptions as it were prove the rule. The 1950s saw the Swiss school of typographers attempt to establish their scheme of rational design in part by reclaiming the functional heritage of the 1920s. See, for example, Karl Gerstner and Markus Kutter, *Die Neue Graphik* (The New Graphic Art) (Teufen: Arthur Niggli, 1959). But history was here wholly functional to the design enterprise.

9. See, for example, the shifts of focus from Gillian Naylor, *Arts and Crafts Movement* (London: Studio Vista, 1971), to Lionel Lambourne, *Utopian Craftsmen: The Arts and Crafts Movement from Cotswolds to Chicago* (London: Astragal Books, 1980).

10. Arthur Pulos, *American Design Ethic: A History of Industrial Design*, Cambridge: MIT, 1983; Penny Sparke, *Consultant Design: the History and Practice of the Designer in Industry*, London: Pembridge Press, 1983. Meikle's work is *Twentieth Century Limited: Industrial Design in America, 1925–1939* (Philadelphia: Temple University Press, 1979). The subject is now a highly fashionable one for design historians. However, concentration on the most overt designers (Loewy and so forth) is likely to distort considerably the wider understanding of the commercial role of design in the United States in the 1930s and its relation to the U.S. economy and society.

11. Gert Selle, *Ideologie und Utopie des Designs* (Köln: DuMont, 1968), and *Die Geschichte des Designs in Deutschland von 1870 bis heute* (Köln: Du Mont, 1978).

12. Emilio Ambasz, ed., *Italy: The New Domestic Landscape* (New York: Museum of Modern Art, 1972).

13. Piero Sartogo, ed., *Italian Re-Evolution: Design in Italian Society in the Eighties* (La Jolla, CA: La Jolla Museum of Contemporary Art, 1982).

39

DESIGN HISTORY AND THE HISTORY OF DESIGN

John A. Walker (1989)

DESIGN HISTORY AND THE HISTORY OF DESIGN

It is vital at the outset to distinguish between design history and the history of design. It is unfortunate that the same words 'design' and 'history' have to be employed, albeit in a different order, to refer to different things. In other fields the problem does not arise: the science of astronomy is clearly distinct from what it studies: the universe. Design history, it is proposed, shall be the name of a comparatively new intellectual discipline, the purpose of which is to explain design as a social and historical phenomenon. It follows that the expression 'the history of design' refers to the object of study of the discipline design history. Like art history, its immediate forbear, design history is a branch of the more general academic discipline, history. And like history itself, design history has close links with other disciplines such as anthropology, archaeology (especially industrial archaeology) and sociology.

What constitutes a discipline may be hard to grasp. It can be described briefly as the ensemble of assumptions, concepts, theories, methods and tools employed by a particular group of scientists or scholars. During the early stages of a discipline, most of these assumptions, etc., will be implicit and unconscious. When they become explicit the discipline attains self-awareness. Also, of course, disciplines are defined by the particular body of material or field of research they claim for themselves. Problems relating to the character and limits of the subject matter of design history will be discussed shortly.

The awareness that a distinct discipline exists occurs when a sufficient number of practitioners become self-conscious about their activities and begin to join together to discuss common problems and interests. It is usually at this critical conjuncture that a professional organization is formed. In Britain the Design History Society was established in 1977 even though, of course, histories of design were being written long before that date. Once an organization exists, the trappings of an academic discipline soon follow: elected officers, a newsletter, a scholarly journal, an annual conference.

Although the phrase 'the history of design' implies that there is a single, homogeneous object of study, in practice design history never supplies us with a single, complete, homogeneous account upon which we can all agree. There are always multiple histories, various histories of design. These histories are the output, the product of the discipline design history. They are physically embodied in various languages, media and forms of presentation, for example, lectures with slides, diagrams, articles, books, radio and television programmes, exhibitions.

[...]

THE WORD/CONCEPT 'DESIGN'

'Design' is a word which occurs in many contexts: a design, graphic design, fashion design, interior design, engineering design, architectural design, industrial design, product design, corporate design, design methods. It is not immediately obvious that a common essence underlies all these different usages. Ludwig Wittgenstein's notion of family resemblance may be more appropriate as a linking concept than the idea of a single essence.[1]

Like all words and concepts, 'design' gains its specific meaning and value not only because of what it refers to but also differentially, that is, via its contrast with other, neighbouring terms such as 'art', 'craft', 'engineering' and 'mass media'. This is one reason why definitions of 'design' which purport to encapsulate an essential meaning tend to be so unsatisfactory. And, like most other words, 'design' causes ambiguities because it has more than one common meaning: it can refer to a process (the act or practice of designing); or to the result of that process (a design, sketch, plan or model); or to the products manufactured with the aid of a design (designed goods); or to the look or overall pattern of a product ('I like the design of that dress').

Another reason why definitions are inadequate and provisional is that language, like everything else, is subject to historical change. The word 'design' has altered its meaning through time: during the Renaissance 'disegno' (which in practice meant drawing) was considered by art theorists such as Vasari to be the basis of all the visual arts; consequently these were often referred to as 'the arts of design'. At that time disegno described the inventive, conceptualizing phase which generally preceded the making of paintings, sculptures and so forth. All artists engaged in design as part of their creative activities, hence design was not yet considered the exclusive concern of a full-time professional. Designers as such only emerged later as a result of the growing specialization of functions which occurred in Europe and the United States as part of the industrial revolution of the eighteenth and nineteenth centuries. At least this is the generally accepted story. A different view is held by Simon Jervis whose ideas will be considered shortly. Thus, eventually, design came to mean a full-time activity undertaken by trained specialists employed or commissioned by manufacturers. The designer did not normally make the product he or she designed.

It is clear from the above that any comprehensive history of design ought to include a history of the evolution of the concept 'design' as well as a history of designers and designed goods. Such a history would need to explain the emergence of design as distinct from art and craft, and trace its subsequent development in relation to the changing status of the latter as a result of the transition from a feudal to a capitalist mode of production and the growth of industry, engineering, technology, mass production and mass media/communication. It would also need to clarify the meanings and usages of older expressions such as 'art manufactures', 'the industrial arts', 'the applied arts', 'commercial art', 'ornament' and 'the decorative arts'. An examination of the fluctuating fortunes of these terms would be valuable because changes of nomenclature are one sign of changes in material reality.

During the 1980s, when design was promoted as the solution to Britain's industrial decline, the words 'design' and 'designer' took on a new resonance. They became values in their own right. For example, people spoke of 'designer jeans' (and even 'designer drugs', 'designer socialism'). Since all jeans are designed, the adjective was redundant but its use demonstrated how 'the design' was being perceived as a desirable attribute rather than the product as a whole. One journalist described 'designer' as a marketing trigger word. Part of the same process was an emphasis on the names of particular designers – a Katherine Hamnett T-shirt, a James Stirling museum, an Ettore Sottsass sofa. This habit derived from the fine arts where the signature of the artist was the guarantee of uniqueness, authenticity, individuality and creativity. In the end what counted was not the suitability and practicality of the designed object but merely the fact that it was by such and such a famous name. The designer's label on the product became more important than the product itself.

[...]

THE CANON

Once a number of histories exist which celebrate more or less the same set of 'great' or 'pioneer' designers and their 'classic' or 'cult' objects it is fair to say that a canon has been established comparable to those canons of great artists and masterpieces found in literature, music and the visual arts. Critics of such histories do not wish to deny that there are qualitative differences between designers and between products, but they argue that the geography of a mountain range cannot be understood in terms of peaks alone. (It is surely necessary to include bad and mediocre examples in order to reveal qualitative differences by comparing them to the best.) Also, they question the process by which the canon comes into being: it is a historian's construction not a natural phenomenon and some wonder why, for example, the pantheon of designers includes so few women.

Critics of the canon suspect, too, that a simplistic conception of history underlies it, that is, the 'relay race' conception: the baton of genius or avant-garde innovation passes from the hand of one great designer to the next in an endless chain of achievement.

Few design historians have reflected on the nature of the canon and studied the critical labour involved in its reproduction. One who has is Juan Bonta. His book *Architecture and its Interpretation* (1979) traces, via a case-study of the critical reception of Mies van der Rohe's 1929 Barcelona Pavilion over several decades, the process of canonization in action. To generalize from this example: the first stage, Bonta demonstrates, is pre-canonical: the work is increasingly mentioned, praised and predictions are made in the professional literature as to its future canonical status. When a single positive interpretation/evaluation crystallizes within the scholarly community, the work attains canonical status. Bonta argues that pre-canonical interpretations are the most creative. Once the work is fixed in the canon initial insights tend to be lost or blurred as they are regurgitated by commentators at some distance from the original. Works which fail to achieve canonical status are weeded out and forgotten; they then become invisible. Canonization is followed by a dissemination phase in which the authoritative interpretation of the specialists is conveyed to a wider public via popular articles and textbooks. After this there are three possibilities: the work may become a cultural monument beyond the reach of criticism, or it may suffer a decline in reputation and be forgotten, or it may be subject to re-interpretation and re-evaluation by a younger generation of critics examining it from new perspectives.

[...]

PRODUCTION-CONSUMPTION MODEL

The bulk of the literature on design consists of 'partial' studies in the sense that there are books on designers, products, styles, design education, etc., but what is lacking is a general account of how all these specific studies interrelate and, taken together, constitute a coherent totality. A general model of the production, distribution and consumption of design can be presented diagrammatically. Such a systematic representation makes clear the logical relationships and connections between the various elements. One advantage of this kind of model is that it enables us to see at a glance where a particular study belongs and to identify those topics which currently receive little attention.

A general model is necessarily highly abstract. No doubt it would need modifying when applied to any particular country. The model is not completely ahistorical: it was designed with modern Western society in mind (1700–1980s), the era of the capitalist mode of production, so it would need to be changed drastically to apply to a tribal or feudal society. (Some degree of applicability to the latter is presumed because of the fundamental importance of production and consumption to human life.) How applicable it is to non-capitalist societies such as Cuba, China and the Soviet Union is also a moot point.

In [Figure 27] the processes of design, production and consumption are treated as a fairly autonomous system, although it is obvious that these processes take place within a wider social environment. (Therefore we should always speak about design within society, rather than design and society.)

Any specific application of the model would need to take account not only of the boundaries which ensure design's relative autonomy but also the interactions between the microsystem and its encompassing macrosystem. A general economic recession or boom would affect the sphere of design, as would more minor changes such as revisions in the laws relating to safety standards.

Within the capitalist mode of production more than one type of production occurs and some of these depart from the dominant mode. For instance, the handicraft mode typical of feudalism to some extent persists in the era of mass industrial production, even though its status vis-à-vis the dominant mode is anachronistic and marginal. Design in terms of an industrial system of manufacture, rather than craft production, is the subject of the illustration.

Orthodox Marxism employs a base/superstructure model to count for the structure of society in which a material foundation supports an ideological superstructure:

SUPERSTRUCTURE } ideology, culture
BASE } economics, technology

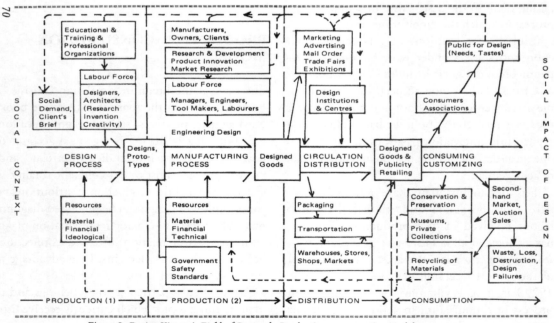

Figure 2: *Design History's Field of Research*: Production–consumption Model

Figure 27. 'Design History's Field of Research: Production-consumption Model'. Reprinted from John A. Walker, *Design History and the History of Design*, London: Pluto Press, 1989, p. 70, by permission of Pluto Press.

In the final analysis, Marxists argue, it is the base which determines what happens in the superstructure. Design cuts across the divide between these two realms because it is clearly part of the economy, part of industrial production and technology, but, equally clearly, it is an ideological phenomenon involving ideas, feelings, creativity, tastes, styles and so forth.

In [Figure 27], for the purposes of exposition and clarity, two processes of production and consumption are treated separately in a linear, sequential order, but it should be recognized that in practice the two processes are interdependent. As Marx explains in *Grundrisse*, production and consumption, together with distribution and exchange, are simply separate moments in totality, a cyclical system. Their reciprocal nature is indicated by Marx as follows:

> Without production, no consumption; but also, without consumption, no production; since production would then be purposeless … Production mediates consumption; it creates the latter's material; without it, consumption would lack an object. But consumption also mediates production, in that it alone creates for products the subjects for whom they are products. The product only obtains its 'last finish' in consumption because a product becomes a real product only by being consumed.[2]

Furthermore, each process includes its opposite; that is, in the course of production, labour-power, tools and raw materials are used up, 'consumed' (Marx calls this process 'productive consumption'). And in the course of consuming (e.g. food) human beings produce themselves (hence the term 'consumptive production').

A material which is the culmination of one process of production often serves as the raw material for a second process of production in which it is used up. It follows that whether something is regarded as production or consumption depends upon the viewpoint adopted: a computer, from the point of view of the designer, is a design tool,

an aid to production; but from the point of view of the computer manufacturer, the designer is a consumer or user of computers. Despite the duality of the two processes, Marx is inclined to assign priority to production, in part because production 'produces not only the object but also the manner of consumption'. Whether this remark still applies today is debatable: recent design and production is often said to be 'consumer led'.

POINTS TO NOTE ABOUT THE PRODUCTION-CONSUMPTION MODEL

1. The Figure is divided vertically into four sections representing different phases: production of a design; production of designed goods; distribution; consumption. The horizontal axis is thus one of time. Each process takes time and the sequence of events is logically ordered. One cycle of events is represented by the diagram. The actual length of cycles depends, of course, on the type of product being manufactured.

2. The dotted lines indicate the relative autonomy of the design realm. This signals the permeability of the boundary between micro and macro systems.

3. The reciprocal nature of production and consumption is indicated by various feedback lines which reveal, for example, the influence of the tastes of consumers upon the design process.

4. The Figure begins with the assumption that there is a social demand for design, otherwise it would not exist. This demand may be manifested by a specific commission to a designer or design team by a manufacturer, public utility or government department, or it could be a private initiative in which a designer devises a design or invention speculatively.

5. During the phase of production two labour processes occur. At the end of the first there is a design and, at the end of the second, a

designed product. Both processes mobilize various forces and resources.

6. The particular labour force – designers – brought into existence by the division of labour and specialization of knowledge need to be trained, hence the inclusion of art and design colleges, architectural schools and so on. Architects and designers also form and join various professional and trade organizations which promote and regulate their activities.

7. Resources can be divided into three categories: (1) material (premises, plant, machines, tools, raw materials); (2) financial (fees, capital, loans, income); (3) aesthetic-ideological (skills, techniques, image banks, graphic conventions, styles, earlier designs, theories such as functionalism and modernism).

8. In the Figure, the design process is separate from the manufacturing process. This represents the situation where a firm commissions a freelance designer or design team to undertake a specific task. However, in large firms such as motor car companies, design may be 'in-house', though even these usually have separate design departments. In car manufacture it is not only the vehicles which have to be designed but also the machines, the tools and the factories to make them – so engineers employed by the company or other subsidiary companies also engage in design.

9. Design is not mentioned in the distribution phase even though, of course, advertisements have to be designed, as do transportation vehicles and systems, exhibitions, shops, stores, supermarkets and mail order catalogues. This indicates that a great deal of design takes place between manufacturers, between different businesses, rather than for the public directly.

10. The consumption or reception phase. Consumers and users of designed goods are not a homogeneous mass – people are differentiated according to sex, age, race, class, religion, politics, nationality, region, occupation, language, family status, education, wealth, tastes, interests, etc. Manufacturers generally seek to 'target' potential consumers and their marketing departments use various systems of classification to assist this process, for example, crude categories AB, C1/2, DE, representing social groups according to a descending scale of income and social status. During the consumption and use of designed goods a process of 'reading', interpreting and critical evaluation can be said to take place (decoding the meanings, stylistic references, connotations and practicality of the design). Perceptual, aesthetic and emotional responses are involved. It follows that the insights of aesthetics, psychology and psychoanalysis could be fruitful at this point.

11. Finally, it is assumed that design has an effect, for good or ill, on society as a whole. Design's total impact on the quality of life is, of course, very difficult to measure, though it becomes obvious in particular instances especially when poor design results in a disaster of some kind.

12. Since the Figure represents a 'steady-state', cyclical model, it does not explain how innovation and radical change comes about. Such changes are the result of either alterations in the external environment – wars, revolutions, economic crises – or those internal to commodity production-saturated markets, customer boredom, falling sales due to the competition of rival firms.

13. Since the model only concerns itself with professional design, the designing which all people do to some extent is ignored, apart from the inclusion of customizing in the consumption phase.

[…]

VARIETIES OF DESIGN HISTORY

Having summarized the general problems of history-writing, it is now possible to look at the various ways in which design historians have approached their task. As explained earlier, histories of design vary not only because they treat different facets of the subject but also because different scholars adopt different methods and approaches. Readers will find it helpful in understanding and evaluating such texts if they can characterize and name the approach in question. Some writers give this information in the introductions to their books, others do not. Where no explicit methodological discussion occurs, it is worth scanning the index: if Marx, Engels and Gramsci are frequently cited then the chances are the book employs a Marxist approach (alternatively, it could be anti-Marxist). If the index proves unhelpful, then the text will need to be closely scrutinized and read symptomatically.

Texts can be categorized in several ways:

1. According to level and audience. Every text presumes an ideal reader or group of readers. There are specialist, academic books on design and there are also popular, journalistic ones.
2. According to the political perspective informing the text. For example, liberal, anarchist, feminist, socialist.
3. According to the underlying philosophical assumptions, for example, idealist, materialist, realist, Hegelian.
4. According to the principal academic or scientific mode of analysis employed, for example, structuralist, semiotic, functionalist, stylistic, comparative, typological, deconstructive.
5. According to the kind or school of history-writing employed, for example, humanist, social, cultural, history of ideas, Braudelian.
6. According to time or place, for example, histories of twentieth-century design, the design of particular nations or larger geographical units such as Europe.
7. According to the extrinsic discipline employed, for example, anthropology, sociology, economics, archaeology, psychology.
8. According to a materials/techniques emphasis.

Although these approaches have been listed separately, in any particular text one will generally expect to find a mix of elements. If a writer combines ideas and methods promiscuously, then one may be compelled to characterize the text as 'eclectic'.

NOTES

Extracted from Walker, J. A., *Design History and the History of Design*, London: Pluto Press, 1989. Reprinted by permission of Pluto Press.

1. On the notion of family resemblance see L. Wittgenstein, *Philosophical Investigations* (Oxford: Blackwell, 1953), paragraphs 66–7.
2. K. Marx, *Grundrisse: Foundations of the Critique of Political Economy* (Harmondsworth: Penguin Books, 1973), pp. 90–4.

40

DESIGN HISTORY OR DESIGN STUDIES: SUBJECT MATTER AND METHODS

Victor Margolin (1992)

I would argue that design history has not developed on the basis of a well-understood subject matter or a set of methods and principles to guide research. Instead it has grown as a response to the initial literature in the field, first celebrating it and then criticizing it. I think, particularly, of Sir Nikolaus Pevsner's, *Pioneers of the Modern Movement*, first published in 1936 and later revised as *Pioneers of Modern Design from William Morris to Walter Gropius*. I would like to look more closely at this book for several reasons. First, because it initially proposed a narrative for design history that has been extensively criticized by many design historians working today; and second, because it raised the question of what contribution any historical narrative can make to the understanding of design. [...]

Pevsner found the sublime in the work of Gropius and his fellow pioneers and by 1960 still believed that it embodied the true principles of design.[1] [...] It was Pevsner's entanglement of morality with subject matter that still makes his book problematic. The agenda which underlies the book excludes most of what we would accept today as appropriate subject matter for design history. Not only did Pevsner establish strict geographic limits to his investigation – its focus was Western Europe and Britain – but he also excluded all the objects of daily life used by ordinary people. For Pevsner, the study of design was an act of discrimination by which ordinary objects were separated from those which embodied an extraordinary quality. [...]

Given Pevsner's restrictive view of objects worthy of historical investigation, it is no wonder that there have been so many efforts to broaden the subject matter of design history since his book was published. In England, Reyner Banham was one of the first to promote an infatuation with popular culture, particularly that which originated in America. Banham, a member of the Independent Group, a circle of artists, architects, and critics who gathered at the Institute of Contemporary Art in London in the early 1950s, was an important link to Pevsner since he had written his dissertation, later published as *Theory and Design in the First Machine Age*, under him at the Courtauld Institute of Art.[2] [...]

In a now-classic essay, "Who is this 'Pop'?" Banham made an important connection between Pevsner's discerning approbation of modern architecture and design and the enthusiasts of popular culture.[3] [...] Although, as a critic, he wrote many articles about mass culture, Banham did not associate with the design history movement in England until the early 1970s when he contributed a volume on Mechanical Services to the Open University course on modern architecture and design and participated in a conference on design and popular culture at Newcastle Polytechnic to which he contributed a paper on American cars entitled "Detroit tin revisited." In an obituary of Banham, published in the *Journal of Design History*, Penny Sparke[4] stated the importance of this intervention. [...]

Penny Sparke is correct in attributing to Banham a seminal role in opening up the subject matter of design history. His work gave younger historians the confidence to explore the history of mass-produced goods of all kinds. But Banham provided no principles for defining design as a subject with defensible boundaries.

John Heskett brought a new set of concerns to design history when he wrote about military airplanes, tanks, and armored vehicles in a history of industrial design which was published in 1980. With a particular interest in understanding the conditions for design innovation, Heskett noted that the design of weapons was "heavily conditioned by military attitudes."[5] Opening up a line of inquiry that few design historians have followed since, Heskett declared that:

> The aesthetics of fear are rarely discussed, or even acknowledged, yet the powerful impersonal forms of military weaponry are among the most widespread and evocative images of our age.[6]

We must also note that from a feminist point of view the subject matter of design history, despite its enlargement to include popular culture and military weaponry, still seems rather narrow. Cheryl Buckley cogently argued in 1986 that:

> To date, design historians have esteemed more highly and deemed more worthy of analysis the creators of mass-produced objects … To exclude craft from design history is, in effect, to exclude from design history much of what women designed. For many women, craft modes of production were the only means of production available, because they had access neither to factories of the new industrial system nor to the training offered by the new design schools. Indeed, craft allowed women an opportunity to express their creative and artistic skills outside of the male-dominated design profession.[7]

What I have demonstrated thus far is a progressive opening up of the subject matter of design history

to include topics well beyond what Pevsner would have been willing to recognize as valid. As further material for inclusion we could cite design in Asia, Africa, Latin America, and other regions of the world outside the European and North American orbit. But even having done that, we would still be faced with the nagging problem of whether and how we might establish boundaries for the field. We already have a fragmentation into histories of craft, graphic design, and industrial design. While these divisions serve expedient purposes in the education of students who are preparing careers in one or another of the design professions, they have no legitimate correspondence to fundamental categories of design activity and are simply stop-gap measures to hold off the inevitable problem of trying to define "design" itself. […]

The point I want to make here is that "design" does not signify a class of objects that can be pinned down like butterflies. Designing is an activity that is constantly changing. How then can we establish a body of knowledge about something that has no fixed identity? From a 19th century point of view, this is a troubling question. The 19th century mind thrived on classification. During this period, great museums were built to house collections of discrete objects such as flora and fauna, high art, decorative arts, and technology. Boundaries between the natural and the artificial were clearly drawn, Art was also differentiated from craft and the two were distinguished from technology. This is the legacy that clearly informed Pevsner's history and it still continues to bedevil the rest of us today.

But today in the museum world, as in the universities, there are powerful intellectual forces that are breaking down the boundaries between fields of knowledge that once seemed immutable. […] The expansion of design history's subject matter since the mid-1930s when Pevsner published his *Pioneers* seems to be just another redrawing of the design map. Although this expansion has continued in recent years to include current material as well as new topics such as design in Asia and Latin

America, these topics have not yet contributed to a radical rethinking of the discipline.

For the most part the development of design history has remained closely tied to specific pragmatic ends, notably courses for young designers and future teachers of young designers, the preparation of museum curators, or the training of design journalists. There are no formal doctoral programs in design history anywhere in the world, although a number of individuals have received doctorates in Britain and the United States through programs of independent study. [...]

To think of design history as a discipline based on firm assumptions of what design is and how we might study its past is to ignore the dynamic crossings of intellectual boundaries that are occurring elsewhere. Given the intensity of these activities and the blurred distinctions that already exist in so much current intellectual practice, we should ask ourselves whether design history as it has been constituted up to now is a viable enterprise.

Having begun with such a limited subject matter as Pevsner provided, it is understandable that significant energy would have been expended in the postwar years to broaden the range of topics that design historians might study. Although we have begun to incorporate new material from the less developed regions of the world, we have also learned from a number of feminist historians that entire categories of objects, regardless of where they were designed or produced, are suspect because of their relation to patriarchal culture which extends across all geographical regions.

Feminism is the most powerful critique of design history thus far, although feminist historians are divided among those who have maintained a static definition of "design" and history's relation to it and those who are interested in using history to explore what a new feminist design practice might be like.[8] Despite these differences, however, feminists have had to break down the distinctions between history, theory, and criticism in order to establish a different vantage point from which to view design and design history.

But even looking at design from new vantage points we must still ask ourselves whether we are studying a specific class of things that are stabilized in categories such as industrially produced objects or whether the subject matter of design is really much broader. I think the latter is true. The history of design in the 20th century shows us that designers, unlike architects, have not worked with a set of principles and rules that have proscribed the scope of their work. Rather they have invented the subject matter of their profession as they have gone along. [...]

For several years my colleague Richard Buchanan and I have been working with the following theme,

Design is the conception and planning of the artificial, that broad domain of human made products which includes: material objects, visual and verbal communications, organized activities and services, and complex systems and environments for living, working, playing, and learning.[9]

We recognize that the artificial as a category is not fixed but is changing rapidly as human invention is turned to phenomena that were once thought to be natural. We see this in artificial intelligence, genetic engineering, and nanotechnology, for example. To grasp the significance of these new activities, we must be continually changing our understanding of what design is while we are simultaneously pre-occupied with establishing its historical narrative. [...]

What I foresee instead is that design can serve as a powerful theme around which the most diverse kinds of inquiries, related to history as well as to the contemporary situation, can be organized. Instead of developing design history as a field, or discipline as some would hope, I would prefer to think of design studies which includes history but also invites a dialogue with other specialists as well as historians.

I define design studies as the field of inquiry which addresses questions of how we make and use products in our daily lives and how we have done so in the past. These products comprise the domain of the artificial. Design studies encompasses issues of product conception and planning, production, form, distribution, and use. It considers these topics in the present as well as in the past. Along with products, it also embraces the web of discourse in which production and use are embedded.

Scholars in a number of different spheres of research are already contributing to a wider discourse about design. I have mentioned feminism and its critique of design in patriarchal culture. Mary Douglas, Grant McCracken, Daniel Miller and other cultural anthropologists have written extensively about consumption although they focus on it as a symbolic act while ignoring questions of how products are designed and made as well as how they are actually incorporated into the daily activities of users. In his important book, *Material Culture and Mass Consumption*, published in 1987, Miller was particularly critical of the kind of design history that is "intended to be a pseudo art history, in which the task is to locate great individuals such as Raymond Loewy or Norman Bel Geddes and portray them as the creators of modern mass culture."[10] (Since his book was published, however, Miller has participated in several conferences that have been sponsored or cosponsored by the Design History Society in the UK and his book has been cited by some design historians as being an important work for the field.) Miller, a cultural anthropologist, has focused his attention on the consumer and asserted, along with other anthropologists, that consumption is not a passive act but a creative project through which people put products to use in ways that were not necessarily intended by those who designed and produced them. Miller has thus broadened the context within which to study products in contemporary culture.

A good example of such a study is the catalogue *Household Choices* which was produced by the Household Choices Project in the UK.[11] It includes essays by historians, anthropologists, urbanists, and specialists in housing and features several photographic essays as well. John Murdock, in his introduction to the catalogue, noted the influence of new methods in art history and literary criticism on the study of design:

> The idea that the product, usually at the point of sale, might pass beyond the control of its manufacturer into a realm of variable understanding, interpretation and use, seemed less familiar than it had recently become to art historians, and certainly less familiar than it was to critics of written texts.[12]

This project has brought us a considerable distance from Pevsner's *Pioneers of the Modern Movement*, a book from which it differs in many ways. It does not moralize about the quality of products nor does it privilege the artifacts of the Modern Movement as worthier of our attention than others. At the same time, it does not give primacy to the designer's intentions in defining the meaning of a product. It suggests a more complex identity for the product than simply the outcome of a design process. The product is located in a situation and its meaning is created in part by its users.

I do not wish, however, to privilege cultural anthropology as the disciplinary base for design studies. It is only one of a number of established fields of study – the philosophy of technology, general systems theory, cultural studies, among them – whose scholars are now slowly beginning to recognize the significance of design in contemporary life. As I reflect on the form that design studies might take in a university setting, I do not envisage a new discipline that will close its boundaries to interventionists from elsewhere. I would follow the lead of Robert Kates who was instrumental in establishing a program on world hunger at Brown University. Instead of focusing on the problem of disciplinary boundaries, Professor Kates emphasized the definition of problems for study:

But we are not a discipline, nor should we be one, despite our proto-theory, scholarly materials, or university courses. We need to be inclusive, not exclusive; we will need new skills and insights as our current inquiries change.[13]

The challenge for those of us who study design at the end of the 20th century is to establish a central place for it in contemporary life. This requires bold new conceptions and the kind of openness Professor Kates advocates rather than the more limited thinking that has characterized much of design study thus far.

NOTES

Extracted from Margolin, V., 'Design History or Design Studies: Subject Matter and Methods', *Design Studies* 13(2) (April 1992), pp. 104–16. Copyright © 1992, with permission from Elsevier. This article was reprinted in *Design Issues* 11(1) (1995), pp. 4–15 and a revised version appeared in Victor Margolin, *The Politics of the Artificial: Essays on Design and Design Studies*, Chicago: University of Chicago Press, 2002, pp. 218–33.

1. Despite this statement in *Pioneers of Modern Design from William Morris to Walter Gropius* (Harmondsworth: Penguin, 1960), Pevsner had begun to rethink some of his views in the 1950s. See P. Madge, 'An enquiry into Pevsner's Enquiry' *Journal of Design History*, vol. 1, no. 2 (1988): 122–123.
2. D. Robbins, (ed.), *The Independent Group: Postwar Britain and the Aesthetics of Plenty* (Cambridge: MIT Press, 1990).
3. Reyner Banham, 'Who is this "Pop"?' in Banham, *Design by Choice*, (Ed. Penny Sparke) (London: Academy Editions, 1981), 94.
4. Penny Sparke, 'Obituary Peter Reyner Banham 1922–1988,' *Journal of Design History* vol. 1, no. 2 (1988): 142.
5. John Heskett, *Industrial Design* (New York and Toronto: Oxford University Press, 1988), 190.
6. Ibid.
7. Cheryl Buckley, 'Made in Patriarchy: Toward a Feminist Analysis of Women and Design,' *Design Issues*, vol. 3, no. 2 (1986): 7.
8. J. Attfield, and P. Kirkham, (Eds.), *A View from the Interior* (London, UK: The Women's Press, 1989); Sheila Levrant de Bretteville, 'Feminist Design: At the Intersection of the Private and Public Spheres,' in R. Langdon, and Nigel Cross, (Eds.), *Design and Society* (London: The Design Council, 1984), 86–93; A. Franck, 'A Feminist Approach to Architecture: Acknowledging Women's Way of Knowing,' in E. Perry Berkeley, (Ed.), *Architecture: A Place for Women* (Washington and London: Smithsonian Institution Press, 1989), 201–216.
9. Richard Buchanan and Victor Margolin, Program statement for the conference, 'Discovering Design,' held at the University of Illinois, Chicago, 5–6 November 1990.
10. Daniel Miller, *Material Culture and Mass Consumption* (Oxford, UK: Basil Blackwell, 1987), 142.
11. T. Putnam, and C. Newton, *Household Choices* (n.p: Futures Publications, 1990),
12. John Murdoch, 'Foreword,' *Household Choices*, 5.
13. Kates, W., 'The Great Questions of Science and Society Do Not Fit Neatly into Single Disciplines' *The Chronicle of Higher Education*, Section 2 (May 17, 1989): 81.

41

RESISTING COLONIZATION: DESIGN HISTORY HAS ITS OWN IDENTITY

Jonathan M. Woodham (1995)

DESIGN HISTORY AND DESIGN STUDIES

Since its emergence as a distinct field of academic study in the 1970s, design history has been subject to considerable criticism from many quarters; whether at the hands of scholars working within the general framework of the discipline but seeking to redefine radically its goals and broaden its ambit[1] or academics concerned with different academic fields, such as anthropology, who criticized trenchantly the limitations of the design historical work which they had encountered;[2] as well as others who should have been well-placed to review the position of design history as a legitimate area of pedagogy, research and publication.[3] Victor Margolin[4] falls into this latter category, particularly with regard to his 1992 article 'Design History or Design Studies: Subject Matter and Methods.'[5] The reason why I wish to draw particular attention to this text is that it misrepresents the academic health and identity of design history (at least in Britain), understates the increasing opportunities for specialist design historical study at undergraduate and postgraduate levels and largely overlooks the growing body of valuable research, exhibition and publication work in the field.[6] Secondly, since it seeks to colonize design history under the imperial umbrella of design studies (the territorial boundaries of which are seemingly endless), I would resist this on the grounds that design historians, particularly of the

modern period, are already highly conversant with the inter-disciplinary possibilities described and have little need of an aspirant parent 'discipline' to help them enter into meaningful and productive academic debate, research, or pedagogy.

At the outset of his piece, Margolin drew attention to the fact there had been a range of publications, exhibitions and conferences devoted to the design of the past; the establishment of design history societies in Britain, the United States, and Scandinavia, the launch of the Design History Society's *Journal of Design History* in Britain; as well as curriculum development on both sides of the Atlantic. However, he concluded thus:

> And yet, despite these activities, there is little to show that could gain recognition for design history as a solid field of academic study. I do not wish to take away from the benefit it has had on thousands of design students on several continents who have come to understand the wider cultural context in which designers work. But I do want to address the issue of what has or has not been accomplished to establish design history as a productive scholarly enterprise.[7]

Such a viewpoint, alongside others articulated elsewhere in the article, caused ripples of disquiet among a number of those in Britain involved with design historical research, publication, specialist teaching, and curriculum development at the undergraduate and postgraduate levels.[8] This sense of disquiet was engendered not as a result of the validity of the criticisms put forward as much as from the inaccuracy of many of the premises upon which they were based. It was, perhaps, more than coincidental that his 1992 article was placed within a journal of design studies since it followed a line of approach taken up in Margolin's introduction to an earlier publication, *Design Discourse: History, Theory, Criticism*, in which he wrote of 'Design Studies as a New Discipline.'[9] [...] It would be interesting to speculate about the extent to which this envisaged shift away from the positioning of design history as a legitimate area of academic inquiry in its own right (towards the broader umbrella of design studies) has been conditioned by its relative status and context in academic curricula in the United States. After all, in the fall of 1991, a reviewer in the North American *Design Book Review*, while acknowledging that design history was 'a relatively new discipline,' also expressed the view that it 'was well-established in Britain, but still forming in this country' and that, not surprisingly, 'the discipline has been dominated by British design historians.'[10]

THE STATE OF DESIGN HISTORY: A PARTIAL REMAPPING OF THE FIELD[11]

[...] While it is true that in Britain the genesis of design history as an academic discipline developed initially as part of a wider response to the British Ministry of Education's Coldstream and Summerson Reports of the 1960s and 1970, respectively,[12] it also is the case that such a context was perceived to be problematic in several of the earlier articles reflecting on the shortcomings of design historical practice.[13] [...]

It also is clear that design history in Britain had received a considerable shot in the arm from the growing number of courses with 'a distinct identity within academia that [were] independent of [their] relations to practice.'[14] An important

spearhead, its modernist inclinations notwithstanding, was the Open University's third-level course on the history of modern architecture and design in 1972, which was based on the research of Charlotte and Tim Benton, Adrian Forty, Reyner Banham, and others.[15] From the mid-1970s onward, a flurry of institutional activity in the higher education sector saw, over a five-year period, the establishment in Britain of a number of freestanding courses which offered honors degrees with either a distinct design historical focus; as at the Polytechnics of Manchester and Brighton;[16] or in combination with art history, film studies and architectural history; as at the Polytechnics of North Staffordshire, Newcastle upon Tyne, Leicester, Sheffield, and Middlesex.[17]

Whatever the difficulties involved in the ideology, methodological underpinning and academic direction of the new degree courses in design history established in Britain from the mid-1970s onward, Her Majesty's Inspectorate (HMI), part of the State's Department of Education and Science,[18] was strongly supportive. The conclusions were drawn on the basis of first-hand observation and consultation with the staff and students in 1986 and 1987. It was stated on the opening page that:

> Although each of the [seven] courses has a distinct identity, they all share at least two common concerns. One is a desire to extend the range of artifacts, objects and images properly regarded as legitimate material for historical study. The other is a desire to develop new theoretical frameworks of analysis and criticism which are appropriate to this extended range. One consequence has been their appeal to a wider cross-section of students than established conventional history of art students.[19]

[...]

In Britain today, the number of freestanding, distinct design history degrees has expanded considerably, including courses at the Universities of Teesside, Lancaster and Derby, the London Institute (Camberwell), and the West Surrey College of Art and Design. Many others include design historical studies within a wider modular framework. For many years also in Britain there have been a small number of Masters programs in the field, the most noteworthy being those run at Middlesex University and at the Victoria and Albert Museum in conjunction with the Royal College of Art; both have very distinct identities within the spectrum of design historical studies in Britain.[20] While Margolin may be right in stating that 'there are no formal doctoral programs in design history anywhere in the world, although there are a number of individuals who have received doctorates in Britain and the United States,'[21] he fails to acknowledge the general pattern of doctoral research in the arts and humanities in Britain. There are, in fact, established links between M.A. courses taught in design history and Ph.D. output, a trend which is likely to gather speed over the next few years.[22] There also are other ways in which design historical research work may be consolidated within institutional frameworks, although these have not reached the levels of maturity or funding that may be found in other longstanding fields of historical research. For example, a Research Assistantship program 'with a distinct identity within academia' resulting in a number of doctoral awards[23] has been in place since the early 1970s at the University of Brighton. A number of other British universities and institutions of higher education have also been active in this field. Whether the relative design historical research throughput at the doctoral level in Britain is as significant as might be desired in an academic discipline still in the process of consolidation at the highest academic levels is another matter. It should be noted that, historically, this has been due as much to the relative differentials of British government funding for research at the 'old' and 'new' universities (where design historical work almost exclusively resides); a very real problem which only has been addressed since the centralization of funding for

the expanded university sector in Britain in the early 1990s.[24]

DESIGN HISTORY: A DISCOURSE

It is difficult to see why Margolin still continues to attach such importance to the methodological limitations of Pevsner's *Pioneers of the Modern Movement* of 1936 (later revised as *Pioneers of Modern Design*) at a time when the methodological possibilities of design history have moved on considerably.[25] [...] [I]t is not as though his thesis has not been addressed elsewhere, perhaps most obviously by Herwin Schaefer in his 1970 text, *The Roots of Modern Design: the Functional Tradition in the 19th Century*.[26] Schaefer, who was acknowledged by Pevsner to have been of great assistance in the preparation of the 1949 Museum of Modern Art edition of *Pioneers*, was critical of Pevsner's undue emphasis on 'the artistic creativity of individuals,' and dwelt instead on the history of functionalism in the eighteenth and nineteenth centuries, concentrating on those strands of machine and anonymous design which he felt were lacking in Pevsner's work. [...]

Another well-known alternative to the Pevsnerian perspective is to be found in Siegfried Giedion's *Mechanization Takes Command*, published in 1948 with the subtitle 'a contribution to anonymous history.'[27] [...] Much more recently, Matthew Turner, in an attack on what he characterized as the narrow geopolitical and aesthetic base on which design history was established, proposed the exploration of registered designs as another possible means of escaping from the tyranny of 'an extremely limited range of Western cult objects.'[28] [...] Philip Pacey proposed another mode of action, contending that design history [... should examine ...] 'the prior and current activities of non-professional designers [... to avoid ...] seeming exclusively concerned with an activity associated with the industrialized, affluent West.[29]

Historiography notwithstanding it is interesting to note that Margolin appears to have overlooked the significance of Adrian Forty's book, *Objects of Desire: Design and Society*.[30] It should be remembered that the manuscript was completed in 1980 and, although not opening up a number of the key concerns articulated later by Buckley, Attfield, Kirkham and other feminist writers of design history admired by Margolin, the text is still an important marker in the demotion of the centrality of the designer in design historical accounts. Its reception in the design press was understandably cool as its readers, buoyed up by the 'Designer hype' of the 1980s, saw the notion of the 'individual creative genius' seriously undermined.[31] [...]

Daniel Miller, an anthropologist from University College, London [...] is now well known to many design historians, particularly as studies in material culture increasingly are being explored. British design historians also have contributed to Winterthur conferences in the United States which deal with many aspects of material culture, as indeed does the *Winterthur Portfolio*,[32] which contains much material of value. [...] Many people involved in design history have taken such critical perspectives on board, utilizing fresh methods and approaches, harnessing the findings of research in other fields, and revising their perspectives as appropriate. [...]

DESIGN HISTORY: A POSITIVE VIEW

Given his views about the lack of achievement of design history as a field of academic study, it is perhaps somewhat ironic that, in his efforts to validate the position of 'Design Studies as an Academic Discipline,'[33] Margolin has unwittingly made a good case for the wider recognition of the achievements of design history since it already embraces much of what is discussed. Contrary to his suggestions, design historians have taken on many of the challenges posed by other disciplines such as anthropology, cultural studies, or feminist theory, and there is a growing body of evidence to support this.

[...]

Contrary to Margolin's suggestion, most design historians have absolutely no desire 'to produce a single history of modern design,'[34] since interdisciplinary thinking has long been the province of historians, albeit conditioned by a strong sense of intellectual rigor. The *Journal of Design History*[35] has sought to promote such interdisciplinary interchange as part of its endeavor to consolidate the discipline. Its Editorial Policy states that the *Journal*:

> aims to help consolidate design history as a distinct discipline but it will not be narrowly specialist in content or sectarian in tone. The widespread recognition of the cultural significance and economic importance of design will provide a broad base on which to build and the Journal seeks to build links with other disciplines exploring material culture, such as anthropology, architectural history, business history, cultural studies, design management studies, economic and social history, and the history of science and technology.

[...]

The core of the discipline of design history is, of course, design and it is that focus which distinguishes it from other fields of historical inquiry. As with any other academic discipline, its methods and approaches are continually appraised, boundaries change and are occasionally crossed with positive results. To attempt to draw up a definitive map of design history with fixed perimeters would be to deny the distinct, positive and differing character of design historical practice of many of the centers where design history is taught and researched in Britain. To place design history under the yoke of the aspirant new discipline of design studies – however *that* may be defined – seems to be imposing a somewhat unnecessary burden.

NOTES

Extracted from Woodham, J. M. 'Resisting Colonization: Design History Has Its Own Identity' *Design Issues* 11(1) (1995), pp. 22–37, © 1995 by the Massachusetts Institute of Technology.

1. See, for example J. Attfield and P. Kirkham, eds., *A View From the Interior* (London: Women's Press. 1989); and J. Attfield, 'FORM/female FOLLOWS FUNCTION/male: Feminist Critiques of Design,' John A Walker, *Design History and the History of Design* (London: Pluto Press, 1989); A. Forty, *Objects of Desire: Design and Society 1750–1850* (London: Thames & Hudson. 1986).

2. See D. Miller, *Material Culture and Mass Consumption* (Oxford: Blackwell, 1987).

3. See, for example Denis Kelly's idiosyncratic, dispiriting, and rather unrepresentative piece entitled 'Design History: Doing It Yourself from the Picture on the Package,' *Issues* 1:2 (Winter 1990/1991), pp. 102–111. There are still others who have written from a position of relative unawareness of recent methods, content of, and research in the history of graphic design, such as T. Kalman, J. Abbot Miller, and K. Jacobs in 'Good History, Bad History' *Print* (New York, March/April 1991): 114–123.

4. A member, since its launching of the Advisory Board for the *Journal of Design History* published by Oxford University Press, Oxford, UK 1988–, he also is a co-founder and editor of *Design Issues*.

5. Victor Margolin, 'Design History or Design Studies: Subject Matter and Methods,' *Design Studies*, vol. 13, no. 2 (April 1992), p. 132. Robin Kinross, a few years earlier, also broached some of the potential difficulties inherent in the formation of design historical curricula for the practical designer in his brief polemic 'Design History's Search for Identity,' *Designer* (November 1985, London: SIAD): 12–13. Some of the problems raised in relation to the broad issue of arriving at a definition of design history stem from Kinross's and, as will be argued below, Margolin's concern to locate the subject under the umbrella of design practice. It is worth noting, however, that Kinross concluded that 'there is something to fear in a monolithic system whereby critic-historians are trained on specially-devised courses in design studies.'

6. Its value has been recognized in the national funding of research in Britain, and it would be unfortunate if Margolin's criticisms were taken at face value by any of those involved in the next evaluation in 1996.

7. Margolin, 'Design History,' 105. Immediately preceding this, he evidenced an increasing recognition of design history by design professionals through the fact that sessions were conducted by historians at national and international conferences mounted by such bodies as the Industrial Designers Society of America and ICOGRADA (the International Council of Graphic Design Historians). The fact that a Design History Working Group set up by the latter 'made little impact on the organization' may say more about it and its parent group than the significance of design historical study per se. Conversely, Reed Benhamou, in *Technology & Culture* 32:1 (January 1991): 135, wrote of the Design History Society based in Britain as having 'proved its worth by organizing a number of groundbreaking conferences and colloquia in this developing field' and that the *Journal of Design History*'s 'concept of design as a socioeconomic activity promises to unify potentially sectarian disciplines within design and to provide scholars working in the fields with a new forum for research'.

8. A forthright response was articulated by Adrian Forty in 'DEBATE: A Reply to Victor Margolin,' *Journal of Design History* 6:2 (1993): 131–132.

9. Victor Margolin (ed.), *Design Discourse: History, Theory, Criticism* (Chicago: University of Chicago Press, 1989), 4–10.

10. Bruno Gilberti, '*Design History and the History of Design*, John A. Walker, *The Meaning*

of Design, Peter Dormer,' *Design Book Review* (Fall 1991): 53–56.

11. More than a decade on from Clive Dilnot's 1983 article on 'The State of Design History I: Mapping the Field,' this is not so much an attempt to redraw a comprehensive map of design historical studies as it is to suggest that the evidence adduced by Margolin is partial and not necessarily reflective of the general methods of design history, its health and practice in Britain. A useful bibliography of some of the early debates in Britain is contained in John A. Walker, *Design History and the History of Design* (London: Pluto Press, 1989).

12. The first report of Sir William Coldstream's National Advisory Council on Art Education was published by the Ministry of Education in 1960; the joint Coldstream/Summerson Report on The Structure of Art and Design Education in the Further Education Sector in 1970 sought to introduce academic studies to practical courses in art and design as a means of upgrading them to university equivalent status.

13. F. Hannah and T. Putnam. 'Taking Stock in Design History,' *BLOCK* 3 (Middlesex Polytechnic. 1980): 26. The intellectual distance traveled between these early useful and thoughtful speculations and present practice in design history itself bears testimony to the development of design historical study and research in Britain. It is interesting to note, in the light of subsequent critiques of design history, that, among the authors Hannah and Putnam cited as potentially useful, were Berg, Bird, Bourdieu, Foucault, Douglas and Isherwood, and McKendrick and Tickner.

14. Margolin, 'Design History and Design Studies. Subject Matter and Methods,' 112.

15. Discussed by Clive Dilnot, 'The State of Design History, Part I: Mapping the Field', *Design Issues*, vol. 1, no. 1 (Spring, 1984), pp. 4–23.

16. Now the Manchester Metropolitan University and the University of Brighton, respectively.

17. Now Staffordshire University, the University of Northumbria, De Montfort University, Sheffield Hallam University, and the University of Middlesex. The content of all of these first generation courses was described in J. Griffiths, 'Where the Courses Are,' *Designer* (London: SIAD. November 1985): 14–15. Given the genesis in an ethos where such courses evolved in higher education institutions containing faculties with strong practical courses in art and design practice, one or two of them devoted a small proportion of their curriculum hours to practical work, normally of a non-assessable, diagnostic nature. This is not to say, as did Margolin, that such course do not have 'a distinct entity within academia.' Incidentally, such practical elements as originally existed have generally been downsized or abandoned altogether.

18. Responsible for the monitoring of standards in the public sector of higher education.

19. HMI, *Survey of Public Sector Degree Courses in the History of Art & Design* (London: Department of Education and Science, 1988), 2.

20. A wide range of opportunities for specialist study at the Masters level also exist at the Courtauld Institute of Art, Winchester School of Art, the University of Central England, and at other centers. A number of other courses are in the process of formulation, as at the University of Brighton.

21. Margolin. 'Design History or Design Studies: Subject Matter and Methods,' 112.

22. I understand that the M.A. Course Team at the Victoria &Albert Museum/Royal College of Art currently is considering the possibilities of instituting a formal doctoral program.

23. These have included Penny Sparke on *Theory and Design in the Age of Pop*, 1975; Suzette Worden on *Furniture for the Living-Room: An Investigation of the Interaction Between Society and Design in Britain from 1919 to 1939*, 1980; Hazel Clark on *The Designer in Early Mass Production: An Examination of the Factors influencing His Role with Special Reference to Calico Printing 1800–1850*, 1983; Lesley

Miller on *Designers in the Silk Industry in Lyons 1712–1787*, 1989; Helen Long on *The British Domestic Interior 1870–1910*, 1992; and Judy Attfield on *The Role of Design Within the Relationship Between Furniture Manufacture and its Retailing (1935–65) with Initial Reference to the Firm of J. Clarke,* 1992.

24. When the former polytechnics were given university status alongside the already existing, thus 'old' universities. Formerly, particularly in the area of research, the polytechnics were ill-served by central funding; they are now being evaluated alongside the 'old' universities, and thus are able to compete for an appropriate share of resources. As stated […] above, it would be unfortunate if Margolin's assessment of the achievements of design history was in any way instrumental in undermining the relative success enjoyed in the area in the first national research funding exercise, from which a small number of the new universities benefited.

25. It is somewhat ironic that Margolin draws his conclusions from the 1960 Pelican edition of the text which, although the central argument remained intact, incorporated a new title and a large number of changes made in the light of considerable developments in research and publication in the field since its original publication by Faber in 1936. Furthermore, its whole appearance changed following the production of the second edition in 1949 in conjunction with the Museum of Modern Art in New York, itself an ardent propagandist for architecture and design which followed the aesthetic canons of the Modern Movement. Perhaps the most striking change was in the number of illustrations which increased from 84 to 134.

26. H. Schaefer, *The Roots of Modern Design: the Functional Tradition in the 19th Century* (London: Studio Vista, 1970).

27. S. Giedion, *Mechanization Takes Command*, (Oxford: Oxford University Press, 1948).

28. M. Turner, 'Registered Design as a History of Design,' *Art Libraries Journal*, 16.3 (London 1991): 33.

29. P. Pacey, '"Anyone Designing Anything?" Nonprofessional Designers and the History of Design,' *Journal of Design History*, 5.3 (Oxford: Oxford University Press, 1992): 21.

30. A. Forty, *Objects of Desire: Design and Society 1750–1980* (London, Thames & Hudson, 1986).

31. A. Forty. 'Lucky Strikes and Other Myths,' *Designer* (London SIAD, November 1985): 16.

32. It is perhaps surprising, in this context, that more reference to North American work in this field is not made in Margolin's appraisal of design history in 'Design History or Design Studies: Subject Matter and Methods.' This is particularly so given the fact that, when he was charting the achievements of 'A Decade of Design History in the United States 1977–87' for the *Journal of Design History* 1:1 (Oxford University Press): 51–71, considerable acknowledgement was made to material culture studies at the University of Delaware and the Winterthur Museum.

33. Margolin, *Design Discourse: History, Theory, Criticism,* Chicago: Chicago University Press, 1989, esp. pp. 3–10 and pp. 285–287.

34. Margolin, 'Design History or Design Studies,' 110. A singular definition also appeared to be what several of the American participants were seeking from their British counterparts at the closed seminar on Design History at the Center for Advanced Study in the Visual Arts at the National Gallery of Art, Washington D. C. in May, 1993.

35. Published by Oxford University Press since 1988, it is the journal of the Design History Society. The author has served on its Editorial Board since its founding.

GUIDE TO FURTHER READING

Much of the associated material for this section is cited in the texts extracted. An approach to the analysis of design and culture informed by British cultural studies is articulated in Dick Hebdige's 'From Culture to Hegemony' (1979). Another early methodological intervention is Tony Fry's 'Design History: A Debate?' (1981) and his later *Design History Australia* (1988) is an essential critique. A 1995 special issue of the journal *Design Issues* collected key contributions to the debate about design history, including Jeffrey L. Meikle's 'Design History for What? Reflections on an Elusive Goal' and Victor Margolin's 'A Reply to Adrian Forty'. More recent texts questioning what design history is and should be are Meikle's 'Material Virtues: On the Ideal and the Real in Design History' (1998) and Judy Attfield's 'The Meaning of Design: Things with Attitude' (2000). A revised version of the Margolin article extracted here was printed in his book *The Politics of the Artificial: Essays on Design and Design Studies* (2002).

Further texts that exemplify the shape of the discipline include the bibliographies, dictionaries and encyclopaedias, anthologies and textbooks produced to support design historical study. Anthony J. Coulson's *A Bibliography of Design in Britain 1851–1970*, published by the Design Council in 1979, as part of its remit to promote discussion of design, provides a snapshot survey of the printed literature on design shortly after the formation of the UK Design History Society in 1977. The book's simple structure denotes its early publication within the development of the discipline: sections deal in turn with professional infrastructure (education, organisations, exhibitions, museums and collections), 'design and designers' (methods, design theory, periods, important designers) and 'Areas of design activity' (design by media, such as graphics, interiors, furniture, transport etc.). A more developed thematic approach is anticipated in the short section on contextual social history. A later US counterpoint is provided by Jeffrey L. Meikle in his 'American Design History: A Bibliography of Sources and Interpretations' (1985), which bears comparison with Victor Margolin's 'A Decade of Design History in the United States 1977–87' (1988) and its follow-up 'Design History in the United States, 1977–2000' (2002). See also Margolin's 'Postwar Design Literature: A Preliminary Mapping' (1989).

Notwithstanding its title, Simon Jervis's 1984 *Penguin Dictionary of Design and Designers* retained a decorative arts emphasis exemplified by *The Oxford Companion to the Decorative Arts* (1975, 1985) and *The Penguin Dictionary of Decorative Arts* (1977). Jervis's dictionary was superseded by Guy Julier's *The Thames and Hudson Dictionary of Design since 1900* (1993, 2004) and Mel Byars's *The Design Encyclopedia* (1994, 2004).

Anthologies of relevance to design history include Paul Greenhalgh's *Quotations and Sources on Design and the Decorative Arts* (1993), Isabelle Frank's *The Theory of Decorative Art: An Anthology of European and American Writings, 1750–1940* (2000), Ben Highmore's *The Design Culture Reader* (2008), Hazel Clark and David Brody's *Design Studies: A Reader* (2009) and Fiona Candlin and Raiford Guins's *The Object Reader* (also 2009). Specific fields of design practice are represented by Carma

Gorman's *The Industrial Design Reader* (2003) and Mark Taylor and Julieanna Preston's *INTIMUS: Interior Design Theory Reader* (2006). Architecture is the focus of Abigail Harrison-Moore and Dorothy C. Rowe's *Architecture and Design in Europe and America, 1750–2000* (2006). Writings by designers are anthologised in Gillian Naylor's *William Morris by Himself: Designs and Writings* (1988) and Mary Greenstead's *An Anthology of the Arts and Crafts Movement*: *Writings by Ashbee, Lethaby, Gimson and their Contemporaries* (2005), to name but two examples. Two anthologies prepared for the UK's Open University in the 1970s remain useful: Christopher Harvie, Graham Martin and Aaron Scharf's *Industrialisation and Culture 1830–1914* (1970) and Tim and Charlotte Benton with Dennis Sharp, *Form and Function: A Sourcebook for the History of Architecture and Design 1890–1939*, (1975).

The early design history textbooks remain the first port of call for many readers and have therefore been influential in contributing to ideas about what design history *is*. Penny Sparke's *An Introduction to Design and Culture: 1900 to the Present* and Adrian Forty's *Objects of Desire* both appeared in 1986. The following year, Hazel Conway's edited collection *Design History: A Student's Handbook* (1987) featured introductory materials-based chapters by leading design historians. It was eclipsed by John A. Walker's 1989 textbook, extracted here. Also published in 1989, Victor Margolin's *Design Discourse: History, Theory, Criticism* formed the first of a series of selections from *Design Issues*, including Dennis P. Doordan (ed.), *Design History: An Anthology* and Victor Margolin and Richard Buchanan (eds) *The Idea of Design* (both 1995). Peter Dormer's *Design Since 1945* was published in 1993. In 1996 the narrowly focussed *Design and Aesthetics*: *a Reader* appeared, edited by Jerry Palmer and Mo Dodson and the broadly based *Block Reader in Visual Culture*, edited by Jon Bird et al., which, like the *Design Issues* readers, derives exclusively from one publication. Jonathan Woodham's *Twentieth-Century Design* (1997) provided a textbook historical survey with a bibliographic essay, while Guy Julier's *The Culture of Design* (2000) set an agenda for design historians considering contemporary design issues. Further small surveys include David Raizman's *History of Modern Design* (2003) and Jeffrey L. Meikle's *Design in the USA* (2005).

SECTION 8

Objects, Subjects and Negotiations

INTRODUCTION

Grace Lees-Maffei

While some of the questions raised in Section 7 surrounded a perceived need to define design history as a discrete discipline and to delimit its field of study, this section proposes that two key defining characteristics of design history are the breadth of its understanding of design as a subject of study and its ability to utilize and contribute to a wide range of related disciplines. Design history is an umbrella discipline bringing together a range of fields determined by materials and processes, such as ceramics history, furniture history and fashion history and its breadth is extended through the influence of neighbouring disciplines, such as cultural studies, material culture studies, psychology, sociology and the history of technology. This section takes its cue from the call for contextualized understanding of design in the preceding section: the selection of texts presented here demonstrates how diverse is the design in design history.

'Design' is a verb as well as a noun; the word can refer to a process as well as an object. The 'design' studied by design historians is not confined to objects and materials: a range of processes are implicated, including the design process, manufacturing, marketing and retailing, consumption, meaning formation and practices which extend beyond objecthood into political, social, temporal, and other realms. This section showcases some exemplary object analyses, i.e. studies of a single object and studies of a type form, which also exemplify the understanding of design as a process. Motor scooters, refrigerators and Shaker furniture are all examined here as are the processes of mediation and consumption, cherishing, market-led innovation, etymology, meaning-formation, and spiritual significance. More examples of object analyses appear throughout the *Reader*. For example, of the five texts extracted in Section 1, three are object analyses. Focussing on 'an Indian basket', 'a slipware dish' and 'the Wedgwood slave medallion' respectively, these texts reveal the processes of negotiation between indigenous and settler communities in seventeenth-century America, the negotiations between local and external influences in design, manufacture and consumption of eighteenth-century vernacular ceramics, and the way a piece of jewellery could be used to denote affiliations in the largest political debate of the century.

Cultural studies practitioner Hebdige considers the way in which meaning accrues to an object through the processes of design, mediation and consumption practices. His text is a case study of how an object type can form a cogent unit of analysis. Furthermore, Hebdige's text can be used to reflect on the interplay between design history and cultural studies, especially as it developed in Britain in the 1970s and 1980s, and subsequently as popular culture studies in the US. Hebdige begins by discussing how we might go beyond Roland Barthes's structuralist and semiotic approach to analysing the symbolism of goods, as demonstrated in 'The New Citroën' (1957), to 'reconstruct the full "cultural significance" of the DS Citroen' (p. 81) in a range of contexts, which is what he does for the motor scooter.

Psychologist Mihaly Csikszentmihalyi and sociologist Eugene Rochberg-Halton collaborated on *The Meaning of Things: Domestic Symbols and the Self* (1981). They attempt to trace the processes by which particular objects become associated with personal meanings, 'cherished' and therefore distinguished from the more ordinary, perhaps disregarded, objects in the home. For design historians, this book has provided great insight into consumption practices. Consumption became a dominant concern in design history since the 1990s as is examined in more detail in section 10 of the *Reader*.

Historians of technology have made extensive studies of processes that inform the development of technologies and their application to goods and services. Ruth Schwartz Cowan's essay 'How the Refrigerator Got Its Hum' (1985) provides a case study of a process by which market forces triumphed over the best technological solution. The essay anticipated the influence of the Social Construction of Technology (SCOT) model, in which human action is shown to shape technology, rather than the reverse. Feminist historians of technology, Cowan significant among them, have illuminated the social and economic importance of the home and its technologies and provided appropriate methodologies for its study.

An emphasis upon industrialization within design history has partly effaced the importance of craft for understanding mass production and the design process. While craft history perhaps plays a disproportionately small part in *The Design History Reader*, simply because there are many other fields crowding in for attention, there is much in the *Reader* to inform understanding of both historical and contemporary craft objects. In this section, Paul Greenhalgh shows how a keyword such as 'craft' is the subject of considerable negotiation in a way that makes useful comparison with the reflections on the various meanings of 'design' in the previous section. He argues that the term craft, as it has been used at least since the Second World War, is an amalgam of three intellectual elements: *decorative art*, *the vernacular* and the *politics of work*. In the formation of this amalgam, the separation of the idea of fine from decorative art was the earliest and most important event. Greenhalgh models the utility of etymology in uncovering a process by which meanings accrue to objects, noting that 'For several decades now the major debate within the craft world has been to do with the status of the word itself' and 'A space had opened up between the actuality of practice and the discourse of classification.' While Dean (see section 1) discusses how the term 'vernacular' has been used as a historical category, Greenhalgh provides a brief sketch of how the vernacular was understood and negotiated in the past. Greenhalgh concludes that the 'commercial, institutional and creative survival' of craft practices is dependent upon achieving 'clarity and confidence' in the use of the word 'craft'.

The final extract in this section continues the exploration of craft, using the highly particularized example of the Shaker religious communities. Curator Burks reveals the Shakers to be involved in a self-conscious and continual process of negotiation with the objects and spaces that surrounded them. Shaker faith was embedded in the details of design and manufacture of their furniture and other goods. Objects were used to negotiate religious belief, and harmonize the material and spiritual realms. While the production and consumption of goods was mediated by a set of shared rules, innovations such as metric measures were incorporated into their developing traditions of working.

The texts presented here show negotiations occurring on two levels. They make clear how design history focuses on objects as ways of exploring wider processes and negotiations, between manufacturers and consumers, consumers and objects (Hebdige, Csikszentmihalyi and Rochberg-Halton), and manufacturers and retailers (Cowan). And, just as objects operate within a series of negotiations, so design history negotiates with other disciplines in order to understand the significance of those objects. These texts suggest negotiations between design history and neighbouring disciplines including cultural studies (Hebdige), the social sciences, including psychology and sociology (Csikszentmihalyi and

Rochberg-Halton), the history of technology and business history (Cowan), craft history (Greenhalgh) and museology (Burks). This section aims to draw attention, by example, to the negotiations found throughout the *Reader* and the discipline it represents.

42

OBJECT AS IMAGE: THE ITALIAN SCOOTER CYCLE

Dick Hebdige (1981)

[…]

THREE 'MOMENTS'

How then is it possible to talk simultaneously about objects and the practices which shape them, determine or delimit their uses, their meanings and their values without losing sight of the larger networks of relationships into which those objects and practices are inserted? The task becomes still more daunting if we acknowledge first that there can be no absolute symmetry between the 'moments' of design/production and consumption/use and, further, that advertising stands between these two instances – a separate moment of mediation: marketing, promotion, the construction of images and markets, the conditioning of public response. It is tempting when writing about design either to run these three moments together or to give undue prominence to one of them so that production, mediation or consumption becomes the 'determining instance' that dictates the meaning of the object in every other context. In either case, the result is more or less the same – a delicately (un)balanced sequence of relationships is reduced to a brutal set of aphorisms, e.g., masses consume what is produced in mass (where production is regarded as determining); desire is a function of the advertising image (where mediation is regarded as the determining instance); people remain human and 'authentic', untouched by the appeal of either images or objects (where consumption or the refusal of consumption is seen as determining). Clearly none of these models is sufficient in itself though each may seem appropriate in particular circumstances when applied to particular objects. It would be preferable to find a way of holding all three instances together so that we can consider the transformations effected on the object as it passes between them. […]

THE SCOOTER AS SEXED OBJECT: EARLY DAYS

The first motor scooters were manufactured in Europe in the years immediately after the First World War (though there are recorded examples of machines called 'scooters' being sold even earlier than this in the United States). From the outset, the word 'scooter' denoted a small, two-wheeled vehicle with a flat, open platform and an engine mounted over the rear wheel. The scooter was further characterised by its low engine capacity: the Autoglider (1921) had a two-and-a-half hp engine. Together these features distinguished the scooter from other categories of two-wheeled transport and marked it off especially from its more powerful, more 'primitive' (i.e., of earlier origin, more 'functional' and 'aggressive') antecedent: the motor cycle. The demarcation between motorcycle and motorscooter coincided with and reproduced the boundary between the masculine and the feminine.

Figure 28. '1946 Vespa,' in Dick Hebdige, 'Object as Image: The Italian Scooter Cycle,' *BLOCK* 5 (1981), pp. 44–6, reproduced in *Hiding in the Light: on Images and Things*, London: Comedia Routledge, 1988, pp. 77–115, p. 88.

[…]

THE 1946 VESPA

In 1946 and 1947, two new Italian scooters appeared, which eclipsed all previous models in terms of sales and served to fix the design concept of the contemporary scooter – the Vespa (Wasp) appeared first and was designed by Corriando D'Ascanio for Piaggio, formerly Piaggio Air, the company which during the War had produced Italy's only heavy bomber, the P108 B.

[…]

The design, then, made concessions to the rider's comfort, convenience and vanity (the enveloping of machine parts meant that the scooterist was not obliged to wear specialist protective clothing). In addition, the Vespa made a considerable visual impact. It was streamlined and self-consciously 'contemporary'. There was a formal harmony and a fluency of line which was completely alien to the rugged functionalism of traditional motorcycle designs. […]

D'Ascanio's Vespa established the pattern for all subsequent scooter designs and its general shape changed little over the years (the headlamp was later moved from the mudguard to the handlebars but this was the only major styling alteration).

It combined three innovations – the stub-axles, open frame, and enclosed engine – which were reproduced over the next twenty years by manufacturers in France, Germany and Britain so that, by 1966, one journalist could state authoritatively that 'there is hardly a scooter built today which does not incorporate two out of these three distinctive features'.[1] This fixing of the design concept was made possible through the phenomenal sales (by 1960, 1,000,000 Vespas had been sold, and after a slack period in the late 1960s, the oil crisis led to a market revival and in 1980 Piaggio were reported to be producing 450,000 scooters a year (see *Guardian*, 21 February, 1981)). Domination of the market led to domination of the image: the field was secured so effectively that by the mid-1960s the words 'Vespa' and 'scooter' were interchangeable in some European languages. (Traffic signs in Paris still stipulate the times when 'Vespas' can be parked.)   [...]

THE 1947 LAMBRETTA

In 1947, another scooter appeared which in its basic concept, scale and price, bore a close resemblance to the Piaggio prototype – the Lambretta produced by Innocenti of Milan. For almost twenty-five years, until Innocenti's scooter section was bought outright by the Indian Government in the early 1970s, the Lambretta range offered the most serious threat to Piaggio's lead in terms of international sales and trade recognition. By 1950, Piaggio and Innocenti had between them opened up a completely new market for cheap motorised transport. Early advertising campaigns were directed at two emergent consumer groups – teenagers and women – neither of which had been considered worthwhile targets for this class of goods before the War. A new machine had been created and inscribed in its design was another new 'invention': the ideal scooterist – young, socially mobile, conscious of his or her appearance. The scooter was defined by one sympathetic journalist as 'a comfortable, nicely designed little vehicle for people who do not care too much about the mechanical side of things'.[2] [...]

THE PRODUCTION OF CONSUMERS

The economist Paul Sweezey has outlined some of the changes associated with the development of monopoly capitalism in the post-War period: the automation of the work process; increased specialisation and diversification (spreading of risk over a wider product range); expansion of the white-collar sector; control of distribution networks; market sharing between corporations; price fixing (the self-imposed limitation of growth in productive capacity to keep prices pegged at an 'acceptable' level); imperialism (exploitation of Third World resources, domination of Third World markets); the displacement of competition from the field of price to the field of sales promotion; increased expenditure on research, design and 'market preparation'. All these developments were motivated by need: 'the profound need of the modern corporation to dominate and control all the conditions and variables which affect its viability'.[3] It is in this context that the massive expansion of the advertising and marketing industries during the period can be most clearly understood. Given the huge costs involved in producing a new line of goods, if crippling losses were to be avoided, the consumer had to be as carefully primed as the materials used in the manufacturing process. [...]

It was during this period that design became consolidated as a 'scientific' practice with its own distinctive functions and objectives. From now on, the shape and look of things were to play an important part in aligning two potentially divergent interests: production for profit, and consumption for pleasure. The investment on a previously unimagined scale in the visual aspects of design from the 1930s onwards indicated a new set of priorities on the part of manufacturers and marked another stage in a more general (and more gradual) process: the intercession of the image between the consumer and the act of consumption. [...]

THE DEMATERIALIZATION OF THE OBJECT

Scooters were presented to the public as clean, 'social appliances'[4] which imposed few constraints on the rider. Design features were cited to reinforce these claims: the panels enclosing scooter engines were easy to remove and the engines themselves were spread out horizontally to facilitate cleaning and the replacement of spares. The stub-axles made it simpler to remove the wheels and by the 1960s most scooters were designed to accommodate a spare. Elegance and comfort were selected as particularly strong selling points: the Lambretta was marketed in Britain as the 'sports car on two wheels' and a variety of accessories – windscreens, panniers, bumpers, clocks, even radios and glove compartments were available to lend substance to the luxurious image. Innocenti's promotion policies tended to centre directly on the notion of convenience: an international network of service stations manned by trained mechanics was set up to cater for the needs of a new class of scooterists who were presumed to have little interest in even the most routine maintenance (though the stereotype of the 'effeminate', 'impractical' scooterist was resisted by the scooter clubs which encouraged their members to acquire rudimentary mechanical skills, to carry tool boxes, etc.). The concept of 'trouble free scootering' was taken even further in Spain. At the height of the Continental touring craze in the late 1950s, Innocenti introduced a special mobile rescue unit called the Blue Angels to cope with Lambretta breakdowns and consumer complaints.

All these support structures can be regarded as extensions of the original design project: to produce a new category of machines, a new type of consumer. The provision of a comprehensive after-sales service can be referred back ultimately to the one basic element which distinguished the D'Ascanio Vespa from its competitors – the disappearance of the engine behind a sleek metal cowling. The sheathing of machine parts placed the user in a new relation to the object – one which was more remote and less physical – a relationship of ease. As such it formed part of what Barthes described in 1957 as the general 'sublimation of the utensil which we also find in the design of contemporary household equipment'[5] a sublimation effected through the enveloping skin which served to accentuate the boundary between the human and the technical, the aesthetic and the practical, between knowledge and use. The metal skin or clothing added another relay to the circuit linking images to objects. It was another step towards an ideal prospect – the dematerialization of the object; the conversion of consumption into life style. [...]

THE SCOOTER IN USE

Imports of foreign motorcycles and scooters into Great Britain for the first six months of 1954 – 3,318; for the first six months of 1956 – 21,125. (Figures from J. Symonds, 'Where are the British Scooters', *Design* no. 94, 1957.)

The first Italian scooters appeared in Britain in the early 1950s. [...] By the mid-1950s the Italian scooter was beginning to represent a threat to the British motorcycle industry which until World War II had dominated the international market. [...] A clash, then, between two 'official' versions of the scooter, between two divergent interests. A 'clash of opinion' between, on the one hand, a declining heavy engineering industry with a vested interest in preserving the market as it stands, with a fixed conception of both product and market, with material resources geared towards the reproduction of that market, the production of a particular design genre, with a set of established cultural values to mobilise in its defence; on the other, a design industry on the point of boom, with a vested interest in transforming the

Un mondo di sogni si schiude in vetrina.

Figure 29. 'Un Mondo di sogni si schiude in vetrina (A world of dreams is revealed in the shop-window),' in Dick Hebdige, 'Object as Image: The Italian Scooter Cycle,' Block 5 (1981), pp. 44–6 reproduced in *Hiding in the Light: on Images and Things*, London: Comedia Routledge, 1988, pp. 77–115, p. 97.

market, in aestheticising products and 'educating' consumers, with material resources geared toward the production of a new commodity – Image – with an emergent set of cultural values (a new formation of desire) to articulate and bring to fruition. The Italian origins of the scooter function differentially within the two systems. In the first, 'Italianness' defines the scooter as 'foreign competition' and doubles its effeminacy (Italy: the home of 'male narcissism'). In the second, it defines the scooter as 'the look of the future' and doubles its value as a well-designed object (Italy: the home of 'good taste').

The object splits. And is re-assembled in use …

THE SCOOTER CLUBS

By the mid-1950s, there were British branches of the Lambretta and Vespa user clubs, co-ordinated from separate offices in Central London and sponsored by the Douglas Company and the Agg Concessionaires. Both provided monthly magazines (*Vespa News*, *Lambretta Leader*, later *Jet-Set*). While these organisations were clearly modelled on the lines of the Italian clubs and served a promotional and public relations function, […] some of the larger branches had their own names – the 'Bromley Innocents', the 'Vagabonds', the 'Mitcham Goons' – their own pennants, badges and colours and, in their informal character, and strong regional affiliations, they bore some resemblance to the pre-War cycling clubs. In the 1950s and early '60s the mass rallies and organised scooter runs were a major attraction for club members. As many as 3,000 scooterists would converge on Brighton and Southend for the National Lambretta Club's annual rally where, at the service marquee, 'your Lambretta would be repaired and serviced entirely free of charge'.[6] [...] One of the socially cohesive elements at these events, at least for many of the younger club members, was a shared predilection for Italy and 'Italianate' culture. The clubs organised 'Italy in Britain' weeks to foster the connection. [...]

As more scooters came on to the market (by 1963, there were twenty-two different firms selling scooters in Britain), the emphasis shifted on to the competitive events, which tended to be dismissed by the motorcycling contingent as 'rally-type stuff of an endurance nature'.[7] It seems likely that the British scooter clubs were particularly receptive to the idea of competition because it offered a means of counteracting the stigma (of 'effeminacy' and 'shallowness') which had been attached to the sport in its earlier 'social' phase. Innocenti developed the 200cc Lambretta specifically to meet the demands of the Isle of Man Scooter Rally which, by the late 1950s, had become the most important event of its kind in Europe. Quite apart from the racing and the track events, there were [...] feats of lone heroism which were intended to display the toughness and stamina of both rider and machine.

[...]

THE MODS

During the mid-1960s, Italian scooters became wedded, at least as far as the British press and television were concerned, to the image of the mods (and rockers) – to the image of 'riotous assembly' at the coastal resorts of Southern England [...]

an army of youth, ostensibly conformist – barely distinguishable as individuals from each other or the crowd – and yet capable of concerted acts of vandalism. The mods and the scooter clubs, the 'Battle of Brighton', 1964, and the Brighton runs of the 1950s, were connected and yet mutually opposed. [...]

THE 'DRESSED' IMAGE

The first wave of modernist youth emerged in or around London in the late 1950s. Most commentators agree on certain basic themes: that Mod was predominantly working class, male-dominated and centred on an obsessive clothes-consciousness which involved a fascination with American and Continental styles. The endorsement of Continental products was particularly marked. The Dean in Colin MacInnes's *Absolute Beginners* (1959) is a 'typical' (i.e., ideal) early modernist [...] English by birth, Italian by choice. [...]

When the Italian scooter was first chosen by the mods as an identity-marker (around 1958–9 according to eye witness accounts [...]), it was lifted into a larger unity of taste – an image made up out of sartorial and musical preferences – which in turn was used to signal to others 'in the know' a refinement, a distance from the rest – a certain way of seeing the world. Value was conferred upon the scooter by the simple act of selection. The transformation in the value of the object had to be publicly marked: 'There was a correct way of riding. You stuck your feet out at an angle of forty-five degrees and the guy on the pillion seat held his hands behind his back and leant back ...'[8]

[...]

THE AESTHETICISATION OF EVERYDAY LIFE

At a more general level, Mod highlighted the emergence of a new consumer sensibility, what

Raymond Williams might call a 'structure of feeling', a more discriminating 'consumer awareness'. It was, after all, during the late 1950s when the term 'modernist' first came into use, that the Coldstream Council recommended the expansion of Design within Higher Education, that Design Departments were set up in all the major art schools, that royal patronage was formally extended to industrial design,[9] that the Design Centre itself opened in the Haymarket, that magazines like *Which?*, *Shopper's Guide*, *Home* and *House Beautiful* began publicising the ideas of 'consumer satisfaction' and 'tasteful home improvement'. And it was in 1964 when 'mod' became a household word, that Terence Conran opened the first of the Habitat shops which, according to the advertising copy, offered 'a pre-selected shopping programme ... instant good taste ... for switched on people'.[10]

The mirrors and the chromium of the 'classic' Mod scooter reflected not only the group aspirations of the mods but a whole historical Imaginary, the Imaginary of affluence. The perfection of surfaces within Mod was part of the general 'aestheticisation' of everyday life achieved through the intervention of the Image, through the conflation of the 'public' and the 'personal', consumption and display. [...]

BRIGHTON REVISITED REVISITED

In 1964, on the stately promenades of the South Coast resorts, a battle was enacted between two groups of adolescents representing different tastes and tendencies. The seaside riots provided a spectacle which was circulated as an 'event' first as news, later, as history (the film *Quadrophenia* appeared in 1979). [...]

According to a survey conducted at Margate, the mods tended to come from London, were from lower-middle- or upper-working-class backgrounds and worked in skilled or semi-skilled trades or in the service industries. (Jimmy, the hero of *Quadrophenia*, is presented as a typical mod, he works as an office boy in a London advertising agency ...) The rockers were more likely to do manual jobs and to live locally.[11] Most observers agree that mods far out-numbered rockers at the coast. When interviewed, the mods used the words 'dirty' and 'ignorant' to typify the rockers. The rockers referred to the mods as 'pansy' and 'soft'.

The clash of opinion between design and motorcycling interests, between service and productive sectors, 'adaptive' and 'outmoded' elements was translated at Brighton and Margate into images of actual violence. The rocker/mod polarity cannot be so neatly transposed into options on gender (i.e., sexist/counter-sexist). Apparently, girls occupied equally subordinate positions within both subcultures. Male mods sometimes referred to girlfriends as 'pillion fodder'. There were proportionately fewer girls driving scooters within the mod subculture than outside it in the 'respectable' scootering community ...

THE MOD REVIVAL

The scooter fanatic of eighteen to twenty really doesn't know what it is about. It isn't impossible to be Mod [in 1980], they just go about it the wrong way – a scooter was a means of transport. You didn't worship it ...

(Original Mod quoted in *Observer* Magazine, 1979)

The disappearance of the service stations, the recession, small Japanese motorcycles, compulsory crash helmets, Scooters India, the Red Brigades: the original 'network of relations' transformed over time, and with it the object, and the relationship of the user to the object. The scooter is 'undressed': all new mods are amateur mechanics. The shortage of spare parts and the collapse of the support structure of garages mean that more scooterists are forced to service and maintain their own machines.

CONCLUSION

In the *Evening Standard* (24 February, 1977), a Mr Derek Taylor, 'one of these new fashionable middle-management people', explained why he had sold his car and bought a secondhand Lambretta: '... with road tax at £4 a year, insurance £12 and petrol consumption of nearly 100mpg, I reckon I'm on to a good buy ... I still enjoy my comfort and want to get to work in a clean and presentable condition ...' The fashion paradigm is punctured by the practical scooter-man. [...] The image falls off into irony.

NOTES

Extracted from Hebdige, D., 'Object as Image: The Italian Scooter Cycle,' *BLOCK* 5 (1981), pp. 44–64, reproduced in *Hiding in the Light: on Images and Things*, London: Comedia Routledge, 1988, pp. 77–115. Copyright © 1988 Comedia Routledge. Reprinted by permission of Taylor & Francis Books, UK.

1. Jan Stevens, *Scootering*, Penguin, 1966.
2. Mike Karslake, *Jet-Set*, Lambretta Club of Great Britain, December, 1974.
3. Paul Sweezey, 'On the Theory of Monopoly Capitalism', in *Modern Capitalism and Other Essays*, Monthly Review Press, 1972. Peter Donaldson in *Economics of the Real World*, Penguin, 1973, provides some interesting statistics here on the transfer of capital in Britain during the post-war period. He writes: 'Spending on take-overs during the first half of the 1960s was something like ten times that of the 1950s ... One estimate is that the mergers movement during the 1960s must have involved the transfer of some twenty per cent of the total net assets of manufacturing industry ...'
4. 'This exquisite social appliance', a line from *We Carry On*, Innocenti promotion film, 1966.
5. R. Barthes, *Mythologies*, Paladin, 1972.
6. Mike Karslake, op. cit., 1974.
7. Jack Woods, 'Is the Scooter Making a Comeback?' in *Motorcycle Sport,* November, 1979.
8. R. Barnes, *Mods!*, Eel Pie Publishing, 1980.
9. See Fiona MacCarthy, *A History of British Design 1830–1970*, Allen & Unwin, 1979; The Design Centre opened in 1956. The Duke of Edinburgh's Prize for Elegant Design was first awarded three years later; also *The Practical Idealists*, J. & A. Blake, Lund Humphries, 1969.
10. Ibid.
11. P. Barker and A. Little, in T. Raison (ed.), *Youth in New Society*, Hart-Davis, 1966. Peter Willmott gives some interesting figures on patterns of scooter and motorcycle ownership in a working-class London borough in *Adolescent Boys of East London*, Penguin, 1966, during the mod-rocker period. Of his sample of 264 boys, one in over sixteen owned scooters (mainly in the sixteen- to seventeen-year range) whilst only one in twenty over sixteen owned a motor bike (they tended to be slightly older, seventeen to eighteen).

43

THE MOST CHERISHED OBJECTS IN THE HOME

Mihaly Csikszentmihalyi and Eugene Rochberg-Halton (1981)

To find out what the empirical relationships between people and things in contemporary urban America are, in 1977 we interviewed members of 82 families living in the Chicago Metropolitan Area. Twenty of these families lived in Rogers Park, a relatively stable community at the northern limits of the city of Chicago; the remaining were selected from the adjacent suburb of Evanston, an old and diversified city in its own right, even though it is geographically indistinguishable from Chicago. Half the families belonged to the upper-middle class, half were lower-middle class as measured by Hollingshead's occupational ratings and by level of education. In each family we talked to at least one of the children, both parents, and at least one grandparent, who often lived at a different address from the younger generations. There were 79 respondents in the youngest generation, 150 in the middle one, and 86 in the oldest generation, for a total of 315 respondents. Forty-four percent of the respondents were males. The Evanston sample was selected by street canvassing of census tracts chosen to give a stratified socioeconomic representation ranging from the poorest to the wealthiest neighborhoods in the community. The Rogers Park sample was drawn by random telephone sampling. Of the total group, 67 percent were Caucasian, 30 percent Afro-American, and 3 percent Oriental. Fifty percent of the lower SES (socioeconomic status) respondents were Caucasian, 50 percent Afro-American; the respective proportions for the upper SES groups were 87 and 13 percent. The first criterion in selecting the sample was to find families with three generations that could be interviewed, so that families with one generation living farther than one hour driving distance, or with children under 10 years of age, were excluded. [...]

Each respondent was interviewed in his or her home. The interview began with a number of questions directed at the respondent's relationship to the neighborhood, community, and the city; [...] We then asked for a description of the home itself – its atmosphere, its mood, its outstanding physical characteristics. Next, we inquired about the objects it contained: 'What are the things in your home which are special to you?'

After the respondent identified the special objects, the interviewer probed to ascertain why the object was special, what it would mean to the respondent to be without it, where it was kept, how and when it was acquired, and so forth. All responses were tape recorded and later transcribed verbatim. The word 'special' was used by the interviewer throughout the interview to mean significant, meaningful, highly valued, useful, and so on. It is less precise than these other words and thus imposes on the respondent the task of defining what constitutes the meaning of an object.

A total of 1,694 things were mentioned by the people with whom we talked; on the average, this comes to slightly more than five objects for each respondent. By examining the kinds of objects mentioned as being special, we were hoping to make a first step toward understanding how people relate to the world of artifacts around them. But clearly; it was impossible to tackle all 1,694 objects one by one. Thus we attempted to develop an empirical typology or 'grammar' by sorting these things into as many distinct categories as would preserve the commonsense, or 'emic,' characteristic of the objects. It was found that 41 categories accounted for all the objects mentioned and that each thing could be classified in one of them with at least a 95 percent accuracy. Some of these categories were much more inclusive than others: Furniture, for example, included chairs, tables, chests, sofas, and dining-room sets; TV, on the other hand, included only television sets. [...]

A similar process of classification was used to organize the reasons given why the objects were special. A total of 37 *meaning categories* were constructed, such as 'Memento,' 'Souvenir,' 'Gift,' or 'Enjoyment,' depending on whether the respondent stressed general memories or the memory of a place, the fact that the object was a gift or provided enjoyment as the reasons for cherishing the object. Because possessions actually exist in a context for the person and have multiple meanings, any one object may appear in more than one of these categories. The categories do not exhaust the range of meanings or capture the personal significance of objects for individual respondents, but they serve to uncover generally shared patterns of meaning. By using these criteria, we coded 7,875 different reasons that the objects were special; in other words, on the average, each object was coded as having four separate meanings. Interrater reliability in coding these meanings was less than for object categories but was still respectable: the agreement between two coders was approximately 85 percent for all generations. In most of the following analyses, instead of the 37 meaning categories, we shall use 11 meaning classes that resulted from combining similar categories. For instance, the categories

THE MEANING OF THINGS

Table 3.1. *Percentage of total sample mentioning at least one special object in each category (N = 315)*

Objects	Percentage
1. Furniture	36
2. Visual art	26
3. Photographs	23
4. Books	22
5. Stereo	22
6. Musical instruments	22
7. TV	21
8. Sculpture	19
9. Plants	15
10. Plates	15

Figure 30. 'Percentage of total sample mentioning at least one special object in each category (N = 315)', Mihaly Csikszentmihalyi and Eugene Rochberg-Halton, 'The Most Cherished Objects in the Home', *The Meaning of Things: Domestic Symbols and the Self*, Cambridge University Press, 1981, Chapter 3, pp. 55–89. Image on p. 58 reprinted by permission of Cambridge University Press.

'memento,' 'recollection,' 'heirloom,' and 'souvenir' were all combined in the class 'Memories.' [...]

With these preliminaries out of the way, we can now turn to our first question: What sorts of objects are significant in the lives of contemporary Americans? [Figure 30] lists the ten categories of objects that were mentioned the most by people. Taken together, they add up to about half of all the objects; the remaining 31 categories account for the other half.

[...]

FURNITURE

Not surprisingly, chairs, sofas and tables are most often mentioned as being special objects in the home (beds were classified in a separate category). After all, furniture is important in the home, it is the sine qua non without which the house would be naked and one would be ashamed to have visitors. One could say that furniture is special because it makes life at home comfortable, but then one immediately thinks of a Japanese or Hindu home, which is practically devoid of furniture but equally comfortable to its inhabitants. Clearly, the notion that chairs and tables are more comfortable in an absolute sense is not true; they are so only within a pattern of cultural habits and expectations.

Furniture presupposes a settled life-style and surplus exchange power, which can be invested in these symbols of stability. Perhaps it is only after the great silent bourgeois revolution of the late Middle Ages that furniture became a central domestic symbol, a test for the family's settledness and affluence. From the early dynasties of Egypt through the Renaissance, few homes contained any furniture. [...]

Initially, the possession of furniture was a clear sign of authority: In Ottoman Moslem culture until quite recently a couch (or divan) was still a symbol of the ruler and his court; it was on such a couch that the pasha or Raja conferred with his counselors, hence the name of Divan given to the supreme council and its 'prime minister.' In most cultures a throne has been the symbol of highest authority, and we still defer to the chairperson at a meeting.

Thus it seems that in the evolution of cultural life forms the personal ownership of furniture is a relatively recent step, one that confers authority and power to its owner. As with any other man-made object, furniture is the product of psychic activity. It takes the concentrated attention of many people to acquire the raw material and the intention to fashion it in a shape that conforms to the human body and its actions. Therefore to own furniture, again like owning other objects, means to possess other people's psychic activity. The pre-eminent place of furniture over other objects might be due to the fact that it can be displayed more easily, that it is supposed to be useful, and that it constitutes relatively heavy investments of money, and hence of psychic energy. [...]

Here is what a teenage boy says about why he selected the kitchen table and chairs as being special to him:

'Cause I can sit on 'em, eat on 'em, play on 'em, do lots of things with the chairs and table. (What would it mean to you not to have these things?) It would mean that I wouldn't have as much comfort because those chairs are very comfortable. And with another table, I couldn't play as good 'cause I love the feel of that table.

This short answer illustrates several trends in the answers of the younger generation. The meaning of kitchen furniture for this youngster revolves about the active experiences he can have by interacting with the thing; the accent is on the utilitarian, enjoyable characteristics of the objects, and the outcome refers exclusively to the respondent's own personal self. The table does not provide a link with others or with some ideal to be achieved; it only serves the momentary purposes of the user.

Among women of the middle generation, the reasons for cherishing furniture are very different. The following is an example of why one middle-aged woman finds two upholstered chairs in the living room special:

> They are the first two chairs me and my husband ever bought, and we sit in them and I just associate them with my home and having babies and sitting in the chairs with babies.

Another respondent comments on why a wicker arm chair in the living room is special to her:

> It is very old. It was given to me as a present by one of the oldest black families in Evanston. They thought I would take care of it. My brother brought it home. It belonged to some very special people, and it has been in the family for years.

Both these quotes illustrate quite a different set of meanings from the ones typically mentioned by younger respondents. Gone is the emphasis on comfort and enjoyment; one finds, instead, important memories, relationships, and past experiences. The egocentric attitude is replaced by a concern for other people: one's family or wider ethnic connections. There is an implicit sense of responsibility for maintaining a network of social ties. In general, these themes are quite typical of the women in the sample.

The same themes also appear in the answers of their husbands. In addition, the men often look at their furniture as the embodiment of a personal accomplishment, or an ideal they strive to achieve. Here is what one man says about a desk in the study:

> I made it. It's very simple, actually, it's just a door. Actually, of the things that I've made, the reason I'm fond of them is that I've made every effort to achieve simplicity. I have a passion for building things as compulsively as possible and as economical of design as possible. My wife

and I are Junkers and garbage freaks, we like to make use of things other people don't use or throw away, that are free.

In contrast to the other answers reviewed thus far, this one introduces a direct note of accomplishment, of the object embodying an abstract ideal (simplicity, economy) as opposed to personal enjoyment or social relationships. Of course [...] every category of respondents might mention any of the reasons for cherishing an object. Yet some types of reasons are more typical of some classes of respondents than of others, and this is why we use quotations from children stressing enjoyment and egocentricity, from adult women stressing social networks, and from men stressing accomplishment and abstract ideals. [...]

Generally, when grandparents mention furniture they say it is special to them for reasons similar to those that adult women, the mothers in our sample, also stress: the objects are signs of past events, of ties to family and to other people. In addition, there is also a strong concern about the object becoming a link with the younger generations; a sign representing the owner to be passed on into the future:

> (This chest) was bought by my mother and father when they were married, about 70 years ago. And they didn't buy it new, so it's practically an antique. My mother painted it different colors, used it in the bedroom. When I got it my husband sanded it down to the natural wood. It's beautiful. I wouldn't part with it for anything. And I imagine the kids are going to want it, my daughter-in-law loves antiques.

It is interesting in this case that the respondent thought it noteworthy to mention the transformations brought to the chest: Her mother painted it, her husband sanded it. These actions change the appearance of the thing while preserving its identity; they appropriate the object at different stages of its relationships by stamping the identity of the owner on its appearance. Painting and sanding are almost rituals of passage in a relationship with the object spanning two generations. In addition to the concern for continuity of relationships in the past and in the future, the oldest generation, like the youngest, often stresses the theme of comfort and personal usefulness that a favorite piece of furniture provides.

There was a total of 638 meanings given for why furniture was considered special. Of these, the largest classes referred to Memories (15 percent), Stylistic reasons (12 percent), and Experiences (11 percent). Only 5 percent of the meanings were Utilitarian, that is, focused on the usefulness of the object. The importance of the relationship between the self and the object was stressed in 17 percent of the cases; 15 percent of the time, people stressed the relationship between the object and the respondent's immediate family. Other kin and nonfamily ties were mentioned, each only about 3 percent of the time.

In the range of its significance, Furniture is quite typical of the other object categories. They tend to be considered special for a limited range of reasons: because they embody memories and experiences; because they are signs of the self and of one's family.

[...]

[ANALYSIS]

The first impression one receives in reviewing the evidence is the personal nature of the themes evoked by the objects that people surround themselves with in their homes. [Figure 31] lists the frequency with which all the meaning categories were mentioned. The two most frequent categories of meaning were the ones coded Self (mentioned by 87 percent of the respondents) and Enjoyment (mentioned by 79 percent). These two categories generally overlapped because objects providing enjoyment almost always were coded also as having reference to the personal self. When a reason was phrased: 'I like to work with these tools,' 'TV is entertaining,' 'I dig my bed,' or 'Guns. Shooting is my hobby,' it was coded in both the Self and the Enjoyment categories.

Thus the main single reason for having objects is one that might be seen as egocentric and hedonistic. It might be useful to distinguish at this point hedonistic pleasure from enjoyment. The former refers to a value derived from satisfaction that is an end in itself; it is the consummation of a feeling and not the meaning or purpose of that feeling that makes the difference. Whatever will make one 'feel good' is pleasurable regardless of what effects this has on one's other goals or on the goals of others. Enjoyment, by contrast, results from the purpose aimed at by the activity and intrinsically involves the integration of the pleasurable feeling with one's context of goals. Enjoyment, then, is a purposeful feeling inseparable from the interaction and not merely a subjective, individual sensation. It implies self-control, the development of skills in the pursuit of voluntary as opposed to spontaneous goals. [...]

The second major theme is that of kinship; **2** of the ties that bind people to each other – that provide continuity in one's life and across generations. On the whole, 82 percent of the people cherished at least one object because it reminded them of a close relative. But numbers do not begin to express the importance of kinship ties. It is the cumulative effect of hearing people talk about their parents, spouses, and children, the depth of their emotions in doing so, that is so impressive. The quotes reported earlier in this chapter should give the reader some flavor of the importance of these attachments; in later chapters we shall elaborate further on this theme.

The third theme concerns the lack of certain relationships rather than their presence. In addi- **3** tion to meanings dealing with the self, and with one's kin and friends, there could have been a third level of interactions represented in the home, a level referring to a wider area of meanings. One might have expected artifacts that reminded the owner of his or her ethnic background, political allegiance, cultural preferences and values. After

Table 3.2. *Proportion of respondents mentioning various classes and categories of meaning for cherishing special objects (N = 315)*

A. Person-related reasons	Percentage of people mentioning		B. Non-person-related reasons	Percentage of people mentioning	
1. Self	87		1. Memories	74	
			Memento		52
2. Immediate Family	82		Recollection		46
Spouse		34	Heirloom		20
We		33	Souvenir		22
Children		35			
Mother		27	2. Associations	52	
Father		20	Ethnic		9
Siblings		11	Religious		7
Grandparents		12	Collections		15
Grandchildren		7	Gifts		40
Whole Family		22			
			3. Experiences	86	
3. Kin	23		Enjoyment		79
Relatives		9	Ongoing Occasion		48
Ancestors		7	Release		23
In-laws		11			
			4. Intrinsic Qualities	62	
4. Nonfamily	40		Craft		34
Friends		24	Uniqueness		17
Associates		9	Physical		
Heroes		20	Description		46
			5. Style	60	
			6. Utilitarian	49	
			7. Personal Values	53	
			Embodiment of Ideal		24
			Accomplishment		31
			Personification		15

Figure 31. 'Proportion of respondents mentioning various classes and categories of meaning for cherishing special objects (N = 315)', Mihaly Csikszentmihalyi and Eugene Rochberg-Halton, 'The Most Cherished Objects in the Home', *The Meaning of Things: Domestic Symbols and the Self*, Cambridge University Press, 1981, Chapter 3, pp. 55–89. Image on p. 85 reprinted by permission of Cambridge University Press.

all, homes in the past were supposed to be centered around household gods, crucifixes, icons, historical pictures, flags – symbols of attachment to widely shared cultural ideals. Such objects, however, were conspicuous by their absence. Only 7 percent mentioned religious meanings, and 9 percent, ethnic ones. Political allegiance was not represented visibly in the home, except for the pictures of a few 'heroes' like John F. Kennedy or Martin Luther King. The meaning

category 'Embodiment of an Ideal,' mentioned by 24 percent of the people, was the most frequent in this area. But the ideals mentioned were often very fragmentary and idiosyncratic; the closest to a widely shared cultural ideal was perhaps the ecological consciousness symbolized by plants.

The reasons people give for cherishing their household possessions reveal a picture of the meaning of life for urban Americans that is in some respects familiar but in others, strikingly unexpected in its detail. We get a sense of a life in which immediate experience, a search for enjoyment, is important. At the same time, one feels an almost equally strong desire to remember the good times of the past and especially to preserve the relationships experienced with people very close to oneself. This search for meaning seems to proceed in almost complete vacuum of formal goals and values. This does not mean that goals and values are absent. They are often implicit in the other reasons about which respondents talk. But none of the great spiritual and ideological systems that are supposed to have moved people

in the past have left objective traces in the homes of these Americans nor has a new configuration as yet taken their place.

Another generalization that the findings suggest is the enormous flexibility with which people can attach meanings to objects, and therefore derive meanings from them. Almost anything can be made to represent a set of meanings. It is not as if the physical characteristics of an object dictated the kind of significations it can convey, although these characteristics often lend themselves to certain meanings in preference to others; nor do the symbolic conventions of the culture absolutely

88   THE MEANING OF THINGS

Table 3.3. *Distribution and percentages of meaning classes making up the object categories*

	N	%	N	%	N	%	N	%
	Furniture		Visual art		Sculpture		Musical instruments	
Memories	98	15.4	84	15.6	73	18.0	25	10.4
Associations	35	5.5	28	5.2	47	11.6	8	3.3
Experiences	69	10.8	47	8.8	36	8.9	52	21.7
Intrinsic Qualities	56	8.8	86	16.0	46	11.3	8	3.3
Style	80	12.5	56	10.4	47	11.6	15	6.3
Personal Values	27	4.2	24	4.5	22	5.4	21	8.8
Utilitarian	34	5.3	1	.2	1	.3	5	2.1
Self	106	16.6	54	10.1	47	11.6	57	23.8
Immediate Family	98	15.4	84	15.6	58	14.3	41	17.1
Kin	18	2.8	6	1.1	10	2.5	2	.8
Nonfamily	17	2.7	67	12.5	19	4.7	6	2.5
Total	638	100.0	537	100.0	406	100.0	240	100.0

	Photos		Televisions	Stereos		Books		Plants	
Memories	79	26.7	1	.6	16	7.6	29	11.3	7	4.1
Associations	5	1.7	5	2.8	7	3.3	22	8.6	7	4.1
Experiences	27	9.1	56	31.5	59	28.1	50	19.5	36	21.3
Intrinsic Qualities	49	16.6	4	2.3	4	1.9	10	3.9	13	7.7
Style	8	2.7	2	1.1	7	3.3	3	1.2	24	14.2
Personal Values	7	2.4	7	3.9	4	1.9	37	14.5	25	14.8
Utilitarian	2	.7	20	11.2	17	8.1	14	5.5	1	.6
Self	22	7.4	60	33.7	68	32.4	58	22.7	39	23.1
Immediate Family	77	26.0	17	9.6	21	10.0	19	7.4	14	8.3
Kin	13	4.4	2	1.1	2	1.0	3	1.2	1	.6
Nonfamily	7	2.4	4	2.3	5	2.4	11	4.3	2	1.2
Total	296	100.0	178	100.0	210	100.0	256	100.0	169	100.0

Figure 32. 'Distribution and percentages of meaning classes making up the object categories', Mihaly Csikszentmihalyi and Eugene Rochberg-Halton, 'The Most Cherished Objects in the Home', *The Meaning of Things: Domestic Symbols and the Self*, Cambridge University Press, 1981, Chapter 3, pp. 55–89. Image on p. 88 reprinted by permission of Cambridge University Press.

decree what meaning can or cannot be obtained from interaction with a particular object. At least potentially, each person can discover and cultivate a network of meanings out of the experiences of his or her own life.

This is illustrated in [Figure 32], where one sees that every object category can serve to convey a meaning in each meaning class. One person even cherished a TV set as a carrier of memories; and another, plants, a painting, and a sculpture for utilitarian reasons —these were the most unlikely associations between objects and meanings. All other object-meaning combinations were mentioned at least twice or more often. The process of creating signification is not entirely determined by prior cultural convention.

At the same time, [Figure 32] also indicates that although each person is free to attach any meaning to any object, in fact, some things stand for Memories much more often than others, whereas other objects recall Experiences or Personal Values more frequently. In this specialization of meaning both the object's physical characteristics and the values attributed to it in the culture at large seem to play a determining role. We have seen, for instance, that TV and stereo sets most often signify the Self; photos, the Immediate Family; and paintings, Nonfamily. Photos specialize in preserving Memories, sculptures embody Associations, and so on down the line.

[...]

In describing specific objects and meanings, we have seen that these relationships are unequally distributed. Some are characteristic of youth, others of old people; some are more prevalent among men, some among women. This suggests that the cultivation of the self might involve transactions with different types of objects, depending on one's sex role and position along the life cycle.

NOTE

Extracted from Csikszentmihalyi, M. and Rochberg-Halton, E., chapter 3, 'The Most Cherished Objects in the Home,' *The Meaning of Things: Domestic Symbols and the Self*, Cambridge: Cambridge University Press, 1981, pp. 55–89. © Cambridge University Press 1981, reprinted with permission.

44

HOW THE REFRIGERATOR GOT ITS HUM

Ruth Schwartz Cowan (1989)

THE REFRIGERATOR: GAS VERSUS ELECTRIC

All mechanical refrigerators create low temperatures by controlling the vaporization and the condensation of a liquid, called a 'refrigerant'; when liquids vaporize they absorb heat and when they condense they release it, so that a liquid can remove heat from one place (the 'box' in a refrigerator) and transport it to another (in this instance, your kitchen). Virtually every refrigerator on the market in the United States today controls the condensation and the vaporization of its refrigerant by a special electric pump known as a 'compressor.' Compression is not, however, the only technique by which these two processes can be controlled. The simplest of the other techniques is 'absorption.' The gas refrigerator is an absorption refrigerator. Inside its walls, a refrigerant (ammonia, usually) is heated by a gas flame so as to vaporize; the ammonia gas then dissolves (or is absorbed into) a liquid (water, usually), and as it dissolves it simultaneously cools and condenses. The absorption of ammonia in water automatically alters the pressure in the closed system and thus keeps the refrigerant flowing, hence making it possible for heat to be absorbed in one place and released in another, just as it would be if the flow of the refrigerant were regulated by a compressor. The absorption refrigerator, consequently, does not require a motor – the crucial difference between the gas refrigerator and its electric cousin. Indeed, with the exception of either a timing device or a thermal switch (which turns the gas flame on and off so as to regulate the cycles of refrigeration), the gas refrigerator need have no moving parts at all, hence no parts that are likely to break or to make noise. [...]

Between 1830 and 1880, dozens upon dozens of mechanical refrigerating machines were patented – machines that would make ice as well as machines that would cool large compartments without making ice. [...] By 1890, nearly every brewery in the United States had purchased a refrigerating machine to remove the heat generated during the fermentation of beer and to cool the finished product while it aged and awaited transportation. Before the nineteenth century had turned into the twentieth, meat packers were using mechanical refrigeration in the handling and processing of meat, cold-storage warehouses had begun to appear in cities, icemen were carrying manufactured ice through the streets, and refrigerated transport (which utilized manufactured ice in railroad cars and refrigerating machines on ocean-going vessels) was becoming increasingly common and less expensive. [...]

The technical obstacles to developing a domestic mechanical refrigerator were substantial: such a refrigerator would have to be small and light enough to fit somewhere in a household, automatic enough not to require constant supervision, reliable enough not to require constant servicing; and it would have to have a power source that could be operated by a totally unskilled worker. Ultimately, it would also have to be designed so that it could be mass-produced, and it would have to be safe: many of the refrigerants then in common use were either toxic or flammable, and 'ice-house' accidents were regularly highlighted in the newspapers. That a potential market existed was clear, for the use of ice and iceboxes in American households expanded drastically after 1880. In Philadelphia, Baltimore, and Chicago, over five times as much ice was consumed in 1914 as in 1880; and in New Orleans, the increase was thirteenfold; the dollar value of iceboxes manufactured in the United States more than doubled between 1909 and 1919.[1] In the early years (1910–20), neophyte manufacturers of domestic refrigerators had no difficulty finding investors willing to lend them money and large corporations willing to buy them out. Just before and after the First World War, the problems involved in initiating domestic refrigeration were technical, not financial or social, and appear to have been about as great for the absorption machine as for the compression one. Indeed, since, until about 1925, gas service was more widespread than electric service, one might guess that the absorption machine would have had the competitive edge.

THE ELECTRIC COMPRESSION MACHINE

The first domestic refrigerator actually to go into large-scale production, however, was a compression machine. The honor of being first seems to belong to A. H. Goss, then an executive of the General Motors Company; to E. J. Copeland, a purchasing agent for General Motors; and to Nathaniel B. Wales, a Harvard graduate who was an independent inventor.[2] [...] In 1917, Copeland developed a satisfactory automatic control device and a solution to the problem of gas leakage (sulfur dioxide is toxic); and in February 1918, the first Kelvinator refrigerators were sold.

[...] By 1923, fifty-six companies were already involved in the business.[3] Some of these,

such as Kelvinator and its rival, Frigidaire (which had been founded in 1916 and purchased by General Motors in 1919), were heavily capitalized and had already produced several thousand refrigerators. Other companies had just entered the field and had only test models and/or faltering finances. In those early years, compression refrigerators dominated the field; and out of the fifty-six companies, only eight were yet either well financed or well on their way to large-scale production.

Yet, in 1923, even the compression domestic machine was still in its developmental stage: the machines on the market did not inspire every middling householder to reach immediately for a checkbook. They were, to start with, expensive: the price had fallen from its original peak; but in 1923, the cheapest still ran to $450 – not an inconsiderable sum at a time when most people earned less than $2,000 a year. Furthermore, refrigerators were difficult to run. Electric utilities estimated that, once every three months, they serviced the machines that they had sold: the tubes leaked; the compressors malfunctioned; the thermostats broke; and so did the motors.[4] All these early machines were, in addition, 'separated' machines – and water-cooled ones at that. The refrigerating machinery was sold separately from the refrigerating compartment, which might well have been simply the icebox that a family had previously used; the machinery could be set up in the basement, say, and the icebox put in the kitchen. The compressor had additional work to do, since the refrigerant had to be moved a considerable distance, but it must have been a relief to householders to have the noise, the oil, and the serviceman in some remote part of the house. Water cooling (the standard technique in large commercial installations) was not convenient in the home. The water pipes froze in some locales in the winter time (turning a refrigerator back into an icebox); or the water frequently leaked into parts of the machinery where excess humidity created excess problems. [...]

In the decade between 1923 and 1933, inventions that would profoundly alter the design of domestic refrigerators did, in fact, materialize. [...] In Sweden, for example, two young engineering students, Carl G. Munters and Baltzar von Platen, figured out how to design an absorption refrigerator that would run continuously and thus would not require expensive automatic controls; this machine (the Electrolux Servel) went on the market in 1926. Engineers at Kelvinator and, later, at General Electric discovered techniques for dispensing with water as a cooling agent. In 1927, General Electric became the first manufacturer to make a hermetically sealed motor and to sell the box as an integral part of its refrigerating machinery. Within a year, other manufacturers followed suit and also began mass production of refrigerator boxes made from steel rather than from wood. In 1930, chemists at General Motors (which still owned Frigidaire) developed a series of artificial refrigerants (the Freons) that were neither toxic nor flammable; and in 1932, engineers at Servel designed an air-cooled absorption machine. By the middle years of the Depression, most of the fundamental innovations in domestic refrigeration design (with the exception of automatic defrosting, which came later) had been made.[5]

[...] The potential market for domestic refrigeration was enormous: by 1923, it was clear that every household in the United States was going to be equipped with either gas or electric service (and probably both in many places); and, thus, that if the price could be brought low enough, every household would become a potential customer for a refrigerator.[6] The potential revenues for the gas and electric utility companies would be even more enormous, since, unlike other household appliances, the refrigerator operates twenty-four hours a day. [...]

One of the manufacturers that succeeded, and whose success helped carry the compression refrigerator to dominance, was General Electric. By the 1920s, General Electric was an enormous corporation with vast resources and had its finger in almost every aspect of the electrical industry in the United States, from the design of large generating plants to the manufacture of light bulbs.[7] [...] Immediately after the First World War, G.E. found itself in poor financial condition; in 1922, the company was reorganized, and Gerard Swope was brought in as president. Swope believed that General Electric was going to have to enter the consumer electric market and, to this end, instructed A. R. Stevenson, who was then head of the engineering laboratories in the company's main headquarters in Schenectady, to review the current state of the refrigerator business.[8] [...]

Stevenson understood that General Electric would be assuming a considerable risk if it entered the refrigerator business; but he believed the risk to be worth taking for a number of reasons: he believed that there was a good chance that G.E. would be first, that the company had the resources to sustain the initial losses, that after this initial period the profits would be great, and finally that 'widespread adoption [would] increase the revenue of the central stations, [... "the utility company that is generating electricity" ...] thus indirectly benefiting the General Electric Company.'[9] G.E. stood to gain, both coming and going, from developing a successful refrigerator.

[...] During 1926, construction of an assembly line began (at a total cost of eighteen million dollars), and the design was modified again to allow for mass production. In 1927, a new department of the company was created to promote and market the machine; and within months of its establishment, the first mass-produced Monitor Tops had found their way into kitchens across the land. By 1929, fifty thousand Monitor Tops had been sold — a figure that may have been as surprising to the top management of General Electric (the company had anticipated sales of seven thousand to ten thousand per year) as it was to everyone else.[10]

General Electric stimulated sales of its refrigerators by means of outlandish advertising and public relations techniques. Franchised distributors were appointed in the major cities across the country and given exclusive rights to sell and service their territories. Rex Cole, in New York, was famous for constructing a neon sign that could be read three miles away, and for staging promotional parades. Judson Burns of Philadelphia had his new store designed in the shape of a Monitor Top. [...]

General Electric was not alone, either in these outlandish promotional schemes or in its effort to develop a successful compression refrigerator; the other major refrigerator manufacturers, just as anxious to attract consumer attention (especially during the straitened Depression years), were just as willing to spend money on advertising and promotion. The electric utility companies, which were then in a most expansive and profitable phase of their history, cooperated in selling both refrigerators and the idea of mechanical refrigeration to their customers. By 1940 the market for household refrigerators was dominated by the four manufacturers of compression machines which had at their disposal the financial resources of enormous corporations: General Electric; Westinghouse, which began to manufacture refrigerators in 1930; Kelvinator, which was then owned by American Motors; and Frigidaire, which still belonged to General Motors.[11] Cross-licensing and mass-production techniques had made it possible for the manufacturers to lower their prices; installment plans and occasional price wars had made it possible for ever larger numbers of people to purchase refrigerators. Despite the Depression, and despite the still relatively high cost of refrigerators (when compared with other household appliances), roughly 45 percent of American homes were taking advantage of mechanical refrigeration by the time we entered the Second World War.[12]

THE GAS ABSORPTION MACHINE

The manufacturers of gas absorption refrigerators were not idle during these years, but they lacked the large sums of money, the armies of skilled personnel, the competitive pressure, and the aggressive assistance of utility companies that the compression manufacturers had been able to command [...] the Common Sense Company, for example, was working with thirty thousand dollars in the same year in which Kelvinator had one million dollars.[13] [...]

By 1926, when the American Gas Association met in Atlantic City for its annual convention, only three manufacturers of gas refrigerators remained in the field; and of these three, only one – Servel – would succeed in reaching the stage of mass production.[14] [...] Thus, Servel was essentially alone: from 1927 until 1956, (when it ceased production of refrigerators), it was the only major manufacturer of gas-absorption refrigerators in the United States. Never as highly capitalized as its competitors in the field of compression machinery (G.E., after all, had invested eighteen million dollars just in its production facilities in 1927, when Servel's entire assets amounted to not more than twelve million dollars), Servel had entered the market somewhat later than the other manufacturers and was never able to compete effectively. The gas utilities, notoriously conservative companies, were defending themselves against the encroachments of electricity and were not helpful; [...] For all its virtues as a machine, the Servel, even in its peak years, never commanded more than 8 percent to 10 percent of the total market for mechanical refrigerators.[15]

The demise of the gas refrigerator was not the result of inherent deficiencies in the machine itself. [...] [T]he compression machine [...] succeeded for reasons that were as much social and economic as technical; its development was encouraged by a few companies that could draw upon vast technical and financial resources. With the exception of Servel, none of the absorption manufacturers was ever able to finance the same level of development or promotion; and Servel never approached the capabilities of General Motors, General Electric, or Westinghouse. The compression refrigerator manufacturers came on the market earlier and innovated earlier, making it doubly difficult for competing devices to succeed. The fact that the electric utilities were in a period of growth and great profitability between 1920 and 1950, while the gas manufacturers and utility companies were defensive, conservative, and financially weak, cannot have helped matters either. [...]

THE PROFIT MOTIVE AND THE ALTERNATIVE MACHINE

The case of the gas refrigerator appears, in many particulars, to be structurally similar to the cases of many other aborted or abandoned devices intended for the household. There were, at one time, dozens of different kinds of washing machine: [...] All these washing machines yielded, during the 1920s and 1930s, to the agitator within the vertically rotated drum, because of the aggressive business practices of the Maytag Company which owned the rights to that design.[16] The central vacuum cleaner, which technical experts preferred, quickly lost ground to its noisier and more cumbersome portable competitor, in part because of the marketing techniques pioneered by door-to-door and store-demonstration salesmen employed by such firms as Hoover and Apex.[17] [...]

We have compression, rather than absorption, refrigerators in the United States today not because one was technically better than the other, and not even because consumers preferred one machine (in the abstract) over the other, but because General Electric, General Motors, Kelvinator, and Westinghouse were very large, very powerful, very aggressive, and very resourceful companies, while Servel and SORCO were not. Consumer 'preference' can only be expressed for whatever is, in fact, available for purchase, and is always tempered by the price and convenience of the goods that are so available. At no time, in these terms, were refrigerators that ran on gas really competitive with those that ran on electric current.

NOTES

Extracted from Cowan, R. S., 'How the Refrigerator Got Its Hum', in D. MacKenzie and J. Wajcman (eds), *The Social Shaping of Technology: How the Refrigerator Got Its Hum*, Milton Keynes: Open University Press, pp. 202–18. © 1985. Reproduced with the kind permission of Open University Press. All rights reserved.

1. These figures come from U.S. Census Bureau data as quoted in Oscar Edward Anderson, Jr., *Refrigeration in America: A History of a New Technology and its Impact* (Princeton, N.J., 1953), pp. 114–115.
2. See 'Arnold H. Goss Ends His Life,' *Electric Refrigeration News* 25 (26 October 1938): 1, 2, 11; Anderson, *Refrigeration,* p. 195; obituary of Nathaniel B. Wales, *New York Times* (18 November 1974); J. W. Beckman, 'Copeland Tells Story of Household Refrigeration Development' *Air Conditioning, Heating and Refrigeration News* 6 (6 July 1932): 9–11; and Giedion, *Mechanization Takes Command* (New York, 1948), p. 602.
3. A. R. Stevenson's report, 'Domestic Refrigerating Machines,' can be found, in its original typewritten form, in the Technical Data Library, General Electric Company, Schenectady, N.Y., Data File 1120. The original report was dated 17 August 1923, but many appendices were added in the ensuing five years, making a document that runs to several hundred pages. I was given access to it originally and will quote from it (citing it as *(DRM – GE)* through the kindness of Dr. George Wise, Corporate Research and Development, General Electric Company, Schenectady. The pagination in various sections of the report is not sequential. The complete list of companies and the report on their products is *DRM – GE*, vol. III.
4. *Electric Domestic Refrigeration, 1924,* a report of the Electric Domestic Refrigeration Committee, National Electric Light Association (New York, 1924), p. 2, table 1.
5. Anderson, *Refrigeration*, chap. 11; 'Electrolux Inventors Receive Franklin Award,' *Gas Age* 70

(2 July 1932); 'Industry Pioneer Number,' *Air Conditioning, Heating and Refrigeration News* 19 (7 October 1936), passim.

6. See *Electric Domestic Refrigeration*, 1924, p. 2; and *The Facts About Gas Refrigeration Today*, American Gas Association (New York, 1933).

7. There is no scholarly history of General Electric; the best of the popular accounts is John Winthrop Hammond, *Men and Volts, The Story of General Electric* (Philadelphia, 1941), the copyright on which was held by G.E. See also David G. Loth, *Swope of G.E.* (New York, 1958). On the history of G.E.'s refrigerator, see *DRM – GE*, Report 2, General Survey, Historical Introduction, pp. 1–2; and Report 1, Summary and Conclusions, Audiffren, pp. 16–19, and appendices 21 and 22.

8. See Loth, *Swope* , pp. 116–18; and letter from Pratt to Swope, 17 August 1923, DRM-GE.

9. *DRM – GE*, Report 1, Summary and Conclusions, Reasons for Exploitation, p. 17.

10. 'Outline History of the General Electric Household Refrigerator,' (typescript, Public Relations Dept. G.E., Schenectady, N.Y., 1970); 'G.E. Announces New Refrigerator,' *G.E. Monogram* (October 1925): 22; Ralph Roeder, 'General Electric Refrigerators' (typescript, Public Relations Dept., G.E., Schenectady N.Y., n.d.); and T. K. Quinn, *Giant Business, Threat to Democracy, The Autobiography of an Insider* (New York, 1956), chap. 8. Quinn was in charge of the refrigerator division of G.E. during the late 1920s and early 1930s.

11. For a summary of the refrigerators that were available in the late 1930s and their relative advantages and disadvantages, see John F. Wostrel and John G. Praetz, *Household Electric Refrigeration, Including Gas Absorption Systems* New York, 1938). For the relative market share of each manufacturer, see Frank Joseph Kottke,

Electrical Technology and the Public Interest (Washington, D.C., 1944), pp. 168–70.

12. Sixteenth Census of the United States, *Housing*, 1940, vol II, General Characteristics, part I, United States Summary (Washington, D.C., 1943), p. 2.

13. DRM – GE [5], vol. III, *appendices*, especially appendices on 'Common Sense' and 'Kelvinator.'

14. 'Survey of Gas Refrigerators.' *American Gas Journal* (2 April 1927), pp. 329–34.

15. On estimates of the sales of Servel, see H. B. Hull, *Household Refrigeration*, 4th ed. (Chicago, 1933); and Don Wright, 'Gray Sees Bright Future for Gas Refrigerator', *Gas Age* 34 (March 1958): 84; and 'When Everybody Loves a Competitor,' *Business Week* (25 November 1950), p. 72.

16. On some of the different forms of washing machine, see Giedion, *Mechanization Takes Command*, pp. 562–70; as well as Edna B. Snyder, A Study of Washing Machines, University of Nebraska, *Agricultural Experiment Station Research Bulletin* 56 (Lincoln, 1931). On the tactics of the Maytag Corporation, see U.S. Federal Trade Commission, 'Kitchen Furnishings and Domestic Appliances,' vol. III of the Report on the House Furnishings Industry (Washington, 1925); and 'U.S. Supreme Court Hears Patent Suit Arguments,' *New York Times*, 20 April 1939 (25:3).

17. On the advantages of the central vacuum cleaner over the portable forms, see M. S. Cooley, *Vacuum Cleaning Systems* (New York, 1913), chap. 1. On the sales techniques of the portable vacuum cleaner manufacturers, see Frank G. Hoover, *Fabulous Dustpan: The Story of the Hoover Company* (New York, 1955); and Earl Lifshey, *The Housewares Story: A History of the American Housewares Industry* (Chicago, 1973), chap. 8.

45

THE HISTORY OF CRAFT

Paul Greenhalgh (1987)

[THE SEPARATION OF THE FINE AND DECORATIVE ARTS]

Much evidence would support the idea that it was during the Enlightenment that the status and divinity of the arts was first assessed in absolutist terms. It was then that the Academies were created. Under their auspice the system of the five fine arts, of painting, sculpture, architecture, music and poetry, was formulated and brought to maturity. In the manner of Diderot's *Encyclopédie,* what was irrational was made rational and what had little order was ordered.

[…] By the opening of the nineteenth century, a hierarchy was broadly in place. The developing infrastructure of European professional culture facilitated the further rise of academies, professional thinkers and connoisseurs, who further clarified a system from the amorphous, rolling actuality of object manufacture. The decorative arts steadily congealed into a *salon de refuse* of genres that cohered only by virtue of their exclusion. Outside the fine arts, there was no fixed nomenclature or hierarchy. Variously – and interchangeably – known as the decorative, useful, industrial, applied or ornamental arts, they struggled to maintain a place in intellectual life at exactly the time when intellectual life was being classified and consolidated in museums, academies and universities.[1]

Supporters did not accept this fate quietly. The issue of status was widely and loudly debated, so much so that it was deemed important enough to be raised and recorded at governmental level.

The following exchange between C. R. Cockerell and Richard Redgrave in a committee of 1846 exposed key aspects of the debate:

[…]

Redgrave: I conceive that the architect's art is as much addressed to the object of making poetical impressions upon the mind as that of the painter.

Cockerell: Would you say the same of design as applied to manufactures, to chintzes, to jewellery, to vases, to calico printing and china painting?

Redgrave: Even there I conceive that the power of making an impression upon the mind may be exerted as well as in the painter's art. If the poetry of invention does not enter into these designs, we shall never have proper designers.[2]

Cockerell's division […] identified high art with non-functional objects. For Cockerell, in order to be a truly disinterested vehicle of artistic ideas, a genre had to be severed from perceivable use-value. For this reason, he positions architecture alongside the decorative arts. For Redgrave, utility was irrelevant. The intention behind the creation of the object was the key to its status as art. Using a position usually associated with John Ruskin, he was arguing that art was a quality that could be applied to any object and was not genre-specific.[3] Poetry could manifest itself anywhere if the conceptual will was there. For the rest of the century, discussion on the status of the decorative arts revolved around this point. [...]

The Fine Art sections of the South Kensington International Exhibition of 1871, for example, included the following:

> Paintings of all kinds including oil, water-colour, distemper, wax, enamel, on glass and porcelain; sculpture including modelling, carving, chasing in marble, stone, wood, terracotta, metal, ivory, glass, precious stones; mosaic; engraving, lithography, photography, architectural designs and drawings, photographs of recently completed buildings, restorations and models; tapestries, carpets, embroideries, shawls, lace; designs of all kinds for decorative manufactures; reproductions, i.e. exact, full life-size copies of ancient and medieval pictures painted before 1556, reproductions of mosaics and enamels, copies in plaster and fictile ivory, electrotypes of ancient works of art.[4]

This gathering showed alternative yardsticks in operation for the measuring of fine art: the cost of production, the value of materials and the status of the patron. In the exhibition of 1871, porcelain, an expensive material selling into high markets, was a fine art, earthenware was not.

It also revealed the relative strength of the decorative arts in the nineteenth century. Compared with, say, the second half of the twentieth century, they enjoyed a healthy patronage and a substantial critical literature. A generation of designer-writers continually made the case, with considerable success. Richard Redgrave, Christopher Dresser, John Ruskin, William Morris, Walter Crane and many others wrote and spoke eloquently in their defence as arts worthy of consideration alongside all others. The decorative arts enjoyed prestige and patronage. Ruskin, always the maverick, was confident enough to place them above all other arts: 'There is no existing highest-order art but that it is decorative ...

Get rid, then, at once of any idea of decorative art being a degraded or a separate kind of art'.[5] [...]

The suffering of the decorative arts within the cultural hegemony thus had nothing to do with quality or confidence, but the abundant presence of both could not reverse the ideological tide. A space had opened up between the actuality of practice and the discourse of classification. By 1890 the category of fine art occupied a clear space on its own, and for many commentators it had narrowed its range to exclude poetry and architecture. Whilst acknowledging that there was no historical precedent for it, one writer confirmed that 'unless the context shows that it must have a wider meaning, [fine art] is taken to mean the arts of painting and sculpture alone'.[6]

[...]

THE VERNACULAR

The beginnings of vernacularism as a cultural phenomenon can be clearly identified in the writings of the Gothic revivalists in the early nineteenth century, as urbanism and industry took their inexorable toll on older forms of life. Its real significance in the present context dates from the last quarter of the century. It was of great symbolic importance to William Morris and the founders of the Arts and Crafts movement. The rural and handmade aspects of craft production arose at least partly as a result of the desire to return to the vernacular world.

There is a powerful irony, therefore, in the fact that it was the modernisation of European culture which gave the vernacular a presence on the cultural scene. [...] It supplied modernists as varied as Wassily Kandinsky and Bernard Leach with forms whilst simultaneously providing a model for anti-modernist lobby groups committed to the preservation of tradition. Socialists admired it as being an appropriate way of developing and maintaining a community; fascists admired its blood-ties and its racial Purity. It has furnished the Utopias of the left and the right in Europe and North America since the onset of mass industrialisation. Its attractiveness to all lay in the fact that it stood outside such notions as professionalism, specialisation, authorship or academicism. It could make legitimate claims to universal honesty, that most desirable of normative values. [...]

THE POLITICS OF WORK

Work was a key area of politico-economic debate during the nineteenth century. For some, work actually defined the human condition. Thomas Carlyle believed that it not only underpinned the structure of society, but also lent psychological stability to the individual. Samuel Smiles saw in it national progress. For Karl Marx, they who controlled work – the means of production – controlled the world. It was logical, if not inevitable, therefore, that work would become an issue in that most prestigious area of commodity production, the visual arts.

Marx's theory of alienation established a causal relationship between work conditions and the degradation of the human personality:

What constitutes the alienation of labour? First, that the work is external to the worker, that it is not part of his nature; and that consequently, he does not fulfil himself in his work but denies himself, has a feeling of misery rather than well-being, does not develop freely his physical and mental energies but is physically exhausted and mentally debased ...

We arrive at the result that the man (the worker) feels himself to be freely active only in his animal functions – eating, drinking, procreating, or at most also in his dwelling and in his personal adornment – whilst in his human functions he is reduced to an animal. The animal becomes human and the human becomes animal.[7]

More influential in the British and the Arts and Crafts context, John Ruskin's 'The Nature of the Gothic', published in 1851, was strikingly close in its reasoning:

You must make a tool of the creature or a man of him. You cannot make both. Men were not intended to work with the accuracy of tools, to be precise and perfect in all their actions. If you will have that precision out of them, and make their fingers measure degrees like cog-wheels and their arms strike curves like compasses, you must unhumanise them.[8]

In effect, the way that people work, the conditions they work under and the way they make things, is fundamental to the well-being of society. [...] William Morris was centrally responsible for generating out of this position what I will term a politics of craft. [...] The objects produced were a by-product of this larger ideal:

It was essential to the [capitalist] system that the free-labourer should no longer be free in his work; he must be furnished with a master having complete control of that work, as a consequence of his owning the raw material and tools of labour; and with a universal market for the sale of the wares with which he had nothing to do directly, and the very existence of which he was unconscious of. He thus gradually ceased to be a craftsman, a man who in order to accomplish his work must necessarily take an interest in it ... Instead of a craftsman he must now become a hand, responsible for nothing but carrying out the orders of his foreman.[9]

Morris, Ruskin and indeed Marx were tapping a rich vein within British social life. Rebellion against the constraints of machinery and the division of labour were far from new in the mid nineteenth century. The heritage of Luddism – resistance to mechanical and political control of the workplace – went back to the origins of the Industrial Revolution itself.[10] [...]

THE FORMATION OF A NEW SYSTEM OF THE ARTS

These three elements, *decorative art,* the *vernacular* and the *politics of work,* were brought together in the last two decades of the nineteenth century by makers and thinkers associated with the Arts and Crafts movement. [...]

In the twentieth century, all definitions and movements within the craft world were derivations from and combinations of the three elements I have described. [...] A few managed to hold the three together very much in the Arts and Crafts spirit. Amongst these were the great studio-craftspeople such as Michael Cardew, Eric Gill, Bernard Leach and Ethel Mairet. Most inheritors of the mantle, however, quite deliberately decided to settle for a partial rather than a pure model. After 1918, therefore, craft began simultaneously to expand, fragment and factionalise. [...]

The founders of the Bauhaus professed a debt to William Morris and the Arts and Crafts Movement and passionately declared that:

> Architects, sculptors, painters, we must all turn to the crafts ... There is no essential difference between the artist and the craftsman ... Let us create a new guild of craftsmen, without the class distinctions which raise an arrogant barrier between craftsman and artist.[11]

As the school settled down, however, hand-making and the vernacular were aspects of the canon that went into steep decline. [...] Emphasis on hand-making appeared to be anti-progress and the vernacular politically reactionary.

Ernest Thompson Seton, an American naturalist and folklorist, promoted the idea of a 'Woodcraft' life-style [in] his *Book of Woodcraft* (1912). [...] In 1925, the Woodcraft Folk was founded in Britain as a deliberate alternative to Baden-Powell's imperially inspired Boy Scouts. Thompson Seton and William Morris were cited as the inspiration behind the British movement, which was sponsored by the Co-operative Society and supported by the Labour Party. Combining socialism with a love of nature and the vernacular, the Woodcraft Folk were, in effect, simply making use of the idea of craft as it had been formed thirty years earlier, without recourse to the element of decorative art. [...]

The Women's Institutes passionately promoted the crafts on an amateur and semi-professional level. Craft here was a skilled pastime, or something which was in effect a rarefied form of household husbandry. This remains the single most common usage of the term. It is a vision of craft void of the original political commitment, a vernacular ruralism with pretensions to decorative art. The Women's Institutes are to do with making things in order to enhance the quality of life. They promoted and preserved the world of rural and domestic crafts. The Countess of Albemarle, a patron of the WI, recognised in 1950 that: 'We owe to William Morris and other pioneers of the Arts and Crafts Movement in the last century the spread of this doctrine that we cannot afford to let craftsmanship perish ...'[12]

The Bauhaus (craft without the vernacular), the Woodcraft Folk (craft without art) and the Women's Institutes (craft without its politics) are all examples from the inter-war period of selective visions from within the meaning of craft as it had been earlier formulated. The signs of strain between the three elements had surfaced; the confused plurality of what it was to be a craftsperson began to grow.

Craft expanded on the institutional front dramatically after the First World War. The *Arts and Crafts Yearbooks* through the 1920s cited thirteen national organisations considering themselves to be centrally involved in the crafts. Some of them, such as the Rural Industries Bureau (founded 1921), the Home Arts and Industries Association (founded 1884) and the Church Crafts League were well funded and powerful.[13] There can be no doubt that they helped form a particular vision of life in Britain. The Art Schools became more overtly concerned with craft as a constituency and museums generally awoke to the issue of craft.[14] [...] After the Second World War, and particularly after 1960, institutional recognition of the class [of craft] was complete. [...]

DESIGN

The new system was a tripartite affair – *art* – *craft* – *design* – and was largely a result of the perceived need to clarify problems of status, meaning and control of the decorative arts. As I have demonstrated, the decorative arts were an amorphous collection of practices fashioned from the disenfranchised when the original concept of fine art was formed in the eighteenth century. Towards the end of the nineteenth century a further rift began to open up within the decorative arts, between those practices connected closely with the craft ethic and those seen to be centrally part of the world of large-scale manufacturing. The latter would ultimately become collectivised as *design* [... which, like craft] began its steady rise as a distinct area of activity from the later nineteenth century. It had been formerly used as a general term which implied a drawing, a plan or a preparatory study. As with craft, it had older roots in mental activity. To have a design on something, or someone, suggested an insatiable desire.

Deriving from the Italian (Latin) word for drawing, disegno, it was used to mean drawing or preparatory study throughout the European tradition. It is especially common in this regard throughout the nineteenth century. Thus the Schools of Design established in Britain from 1836 onwards, and the endless books written on design, broadly and loosely referred to the idea of preparing a study or design for a finished piece of work. Painters or sculptors might talk about a design for a painting, as much as an engineer or a potter would refer to designs for steam engines or pots.

Steadily through the closing decades of the century its meaning began to embrace the idea of the preparation of templates for longer runs of objects: to make a design for something. It also came to imply a problem-solving activity lodged between art and science, a phenomenon akin to the Renaissance notion of the liberal arts.[15] The term industrial design was occasionally used to suggest a pattern applicable to objects manufactured in long runs, such as textiles. Again, as with craft, it would be wrong to argue that design was a distinct area of activity or a constituency within the visual arts in this period. It was not. Indeed, many writers between 1880 and 1914 used the word 'design' far more often than 'craft', and used the former virtually interchangeably with art.

It was in the twentieth century that the idea fully evolved of a designer as a professional who saw an entire process of manufacture through from drawing-board to finished artefact. It was only then that 'design' became exclusively tied to the idea of industry and designers clearly distinguished from artists and craftspeople. They are now irrevocably associated with mass production, or at least highly-mechanised production. [...]

MAKING

Arts and Crafts pioneers [...] posited that creative practice – art – was inseparably part of the physical process of making. In short, craft was premised on the understanding that *cognitive* and *manual* activity were effectively the same. Indeed, the politics of craft were premised on their congruence. However, after 1918, aestheticians and practitioners associated with the fine arts steadily legitimised the idea that the two were wholly separate realms. This had a drastic effect on the standing of craft. [...] Dominated by the seemingly everlasting heritage of Romanticism, the majority of recent thinkers have considered art to be a state of mind, an outlook, a way of seeing things rather than a way of doing things. [...] Thus, technical skill, indeed, physical process of any kind, was replaced by intellect. But [...] artistic expression *through* the making process was at the heart of craft aesthetics and politics. [...] Skill as an actual phenomenon was *far* less important than what it represented on the ideological plane. For the craftsperson it was to do with empowerment, for the avant-garde fine artist it was to do with constraint. Indeed, for followers of Duchamp and Dubuffet, the idea of the 'artist-craftsman' is a contradiction in terms. [...] The image of being *merely* a maker of things has been reinforced by the issue of function. Ornamentation has always had a role; it has rarely had a material function. The demand for function has severed the tie back to the actuality of the decorative heritage and intensified the sense that craft is a purely technical activity.

POSTSCRIPT: THE ORDER OF THINGS

How we name things determines what they are perceived to be, how they are used and thought about. How you are called is what you are. Nomenclature is the key product of the process of classification through which we order our lives. This process results in a hierarchy that is used to rank cultural produce so that value – ethical, aesthetic and economic – can be attached to classes and to individual objects within classes. Craft is a very important name.

NOTES

Extracted from Greenhalgh, P., 'The History of Craft,' in Domer, P. (ed.) *The Culture of Craft*, Manchester: Manchester University Press, 1987, pp. 20–52. Reprinted by permission of the author and Manchester University Press.

1. The history of these various other terms is outside the scope of the present chapter. I use 'decorative arts' mainly for convenience, but also because it has been the longest-standing, the most widely understood and the least ambiguous of the available terms.

2. Report of a *Special Committee of the Council of the Government School of Design*, appointed November 1846 (London, Clowes & Sons, 1847), p. 41.

3. Though he accepted further into this interview with Cockerell that painting was special and exceptional, demanding a higher intellectual calibre and artistic quality in greater degree, p. 42.

4. The international exhibitions often revealed a broad plurality. See Paul Greenhalgh, *Ephemeral Vistas: Expositions Universelles, Great Exhibitions and World's Fairs 1851–1939* (Manchester, Manchester University Press, 1988), Chapter 8.

5. John Ruskin, 'Modern Manufacture and Design', from *Sesame and Lilies, The Two Paths and The King of the Golden River* (London, Everyman, 1859), quoted from Paul Greenhalgh (ed.), *Quotations and Sources on Design and the Decorative Arts 1800–1990* (Manchester, Manchester University Press, 1993).

6. Parker, *Nature of the Fine Arts*, p. 1.

7. Karl Marx, *Extracts from the Economic and Philosophical Manuscripts*, quoted from Paul Greenhalgh, 1993, p. 35.

8. John Ruskin, *The Stones of Venice* (London, 1851), quoted from Alasdair Clayre (ed.), *Nature and Industrialization* (Milton Keynes, Open University Press, 1977), p. 255.

9. William Morris, *Art and its Producers*, The National Association for the Advancement of Art and its Application to Industry, Liverpool Conference Papers 1888 (London, 1889), p. 231.

10. See Charles Poulsen, *The English Rebels* (London, Journeyman, 1984).

11. 'The First Proclamation of the Bauhaus, 1919', quoted from Herbert Bayer, Walter Gropius and Ise Gropius (eds), *The Bauhaus 1919–1928*, exhibition catalogue, MoMA, New York (New York, 1938), p. 16.

12. From Mavis Fitzrandolph (ed.), *30 Crafts* (London, The National Federation of Women's Institutes, 1950), p. 9.

13. See Holly Tebbutt, 'The Rural Industries Bureau' (MA thesis, Royal College of Art, 1990).

14. See David Jeremiah, 'The Culture and Style of British Art School Buildings', *Point,* 1, winter 1995, pp. 34–47.

15. Rudolf Wittkower, *The Artist and the Liberal Arts*, London, University College London, 1950, p. 21

46

FAITH, FORM AND FINISH: SHAKER FURNITURE IN CONTEXT

Jean M. Burks (2008)

We are not called to be like the world; but to excel them in order, union and peace, and in good works—works that are truly virtuous and useful to man, in this life.

Father Joseph Meacham[1]

The Shaker aesthetic that evolved from the 1820s through the 1850s resulted from the intersection of religious beliefs with Worldly design traditions. Classic Shaker furniture as it emerged in the early nineteenth century combined two themes: the vernacular interpretation of the prevailing neoclassical aesthetic and the elimination of unnecessary decorative details associated with the so-called Fancy style. Because no one was born a Shaker, early craftsmen were trained in the World before converting to the faith, and they brought their skills, tastes, and awareness of current techniques with them into the community. These cabinetmakers influenced the direction of Shaker design during its formative stages, although the end result was always tempered by spiritual considerations.

SHARING SPACE

My Mother is a Joiner Wise
She builds her spacious dome
And all that trace her sacred ways
Will find a happy home

Shaker Hymn[2]

The Shakers saw their homes as the closest thing to heaven on earth, which meant that their goal was to shape the actual physical environment of the village after the traditional concept of heaven as the realm of infinite space.

[…] Built-in closets and cupboards were uncommon in single family New England houses, but the Shakers made the most of every inch of available space in each building. […] The Shakers further regulated their lives through an extensive classification system of numbers and letters to indicate the location of stored items. All buildings were assigned letter designations, such as 'D' for dwelling house, and each room, closet, and drawer was numbered, as recorded in several manuscript booklets in the collection of the Canterbury Shaker Museum Archives. This system would make it possible for a sister to be instructed to store a blanket for the summer in drawer 85, room 8, Building D. The 1837 Great Stone Dwelling at Enfield, New Hampshire, was fitted with 860 drawers, which eliminated the need for a box or a chest anywhere in the house.[3] […]

The communal nature of the Shaker way of life gathered together into gospel order many people who shared one home to live as a unified family under Christ. From a practical standpoint, it made sense to eliminate any unnecessary furnishings that would require funds or time to maintain, move, or clean. To conserve space, Shaker furnishings were designed to hang from or be built into walls and to satisfy several needs at once or to be easily portable. Pegboard, placed about six feet above the floor, was a ubiquitous feature of nearly every Shaker dwelling house or workshop room and eliminated the need for free-standing furniture that took up valuable floor space. [...]

Their dedication to order as a guiding principal finds physical expression in the design of their furniture, whose form is determined by the concepts of balance, pattern, hierarchy, and scale. Balance entails a state of equilibrium between opposing forces. Symmetry, the distribution of equivalent forms and spaces on either side of a vertical or horizontal axis, is the most common method for achieving balance. Bilateral symmetry, in which the parts on either side of the axis are mirror images of each other, is central to most eighteenth- and nineteenth-century Worldly furniture. For example, in a chest of drawers, a sideboard, or a cupboard, the case is divided visually by a vertical axis or centerline in which each half mirrors the other. Although some Shaker furniture follows this common pattern, other Shaker cabinetmakers regularly moved away from this rigidly held aesthetic and developed many asymmetrical forms, which can achieve balance by presenting equivalent but nonmatching forms on either side of a vertical or horizontal axis. Unbridled by Worldly fashion, customer whim, or the traditionally conservative apprenticeship system, Shaker craftsmen were able to create furniture to suit the community's specific needs, which often involved developing new combinations and layouts to suit the task. Counters and sewing desks are the most prominent examples of

Figure 33. Sewing Case, ca. 1830. Hancock Massachusetts. Cherry and pine with wrought iron and brass. Collection of Robert and Katharine Booth. Photo: Don Roman. Reprinted with permission.

asymmetrical arrangements seen in Shaker work furniture. Often built as long horizontal cases, they present a highly organized though asymmetrical layout with different shapes placed on either side of the center of the piece. [...]

Because of the institutional requirements of communal living, Shaker furniture often grew to monumental size and proportions not seen in Worldly design. Tailoring counters ranging from six to twelve feet long and four feet wide, trestle tables spanning over twenty feet in length, meetinghouse benches measuring 162 inches, and washstands over five feet long to accommodate several members simultaneously were not uncommon in Shaker dwelling-house, workshop, or meetinghouse spaces.

THE PURSUIT OF PERFECTION

[...] Patterns played an important part in the workshops and were developed to ensure uniformity in a variety of materials and products, both for sale to the World's people and for home use. The Shakers at Sabbathday Lake, Maine, anticipated progressive trends by adapting to the introduction of the metric measures in the United States in 1877, a system that appealed to them because it was so logical and exact. That same year, they began to mass-produce wooden dry measures, ranging from a capacity of one-tenth of a liter to twenty liters, for sale to the World. Metrics were very much in keeping with the Shaker ethic of applying the latest, most scientific Worldly ideas to their own industries. Another example of this dedication to precision is the very successful production furniture business at Mount Lebanon that commenced in the 1860s. The acceptance of machine technology and standardization of parts made assembly-line replication possible. The Shakers even numbered the chairs they made and advertised in their yearly catalogues according to size, ranging from 0 (the smallest) to 7 (the largest).

Templates enabled the Believers to make exact duplicates of many objects – from tinware to oval boxes, cloaks, bonnets, baskets, and furniture. Three cabriole leg forms, which match those on surviving tripod stands, were discovered in the eaves of the 1815 carpenters' shop at the Pleasant Hill, Kentucky, community during the twentieth-century restoration of the building. In his journal, Brother Maurice Thomas of Kentucky Hill recorded that on Wednesday, October 15, 1817, 'Micajah Bernett and my self made some patterns,'[4] a possible reference to templates for furniture parts such as these. [...]

SHUNNING SUPERFLUITY

All work done, or things made in the Church for their own use ought to be faithfully and well done, but plain and without superfluity ... Plainness and simplicity in both word and deed is becoming the Church and the people of God. Order and conveniency and decency in things temporal.

Joseph Meacham[5]

[...]

In reference to furniture, 'headings, mouldings and cornices which are merely for fancy may not be made by Believers,' as stated in the Millennial Laws.[6] Early and classic Shaker furniture exhibits restrained decorative elaborations on structural forms, such as a rounded table edge or a turned chair pommel. Moldings were used in moderation, both at mid-case and on the cornice, and these are relatively small and simple, consisting primarily of quarter-round or bull-nose-shape elements. This guiding principle finds physical manifestation in some lift-top boxes that are fitted with a single board pine plank. Either integral or applied, the edges are square and are not enhanced with the addition of complex molded pieces, as is often found in Worldly pieces of the same period. [...]

The drawers and doors of most Shaker built-in and free-standing furniture are fitted with simply turned hardwood pulls. During the period of revival and inspiration known as the Era of Manifestations or the Era of Mother's Work, strict adherence to the Millennial Orders became increasingly important. According to an entry in the *New Lebanon Ministry Sisters' Journal* on Saturday, July 4, 1831, cabinetmaker 'David Rowley has been employed for several days in taking out Brass knobs and putting in their stead wood knobs or buttons (on furniture). This is because brass ones are considered superfluous, thro spiritual communication'.[7] [...]

The distinctive design of the Shaker chair evolved from the Shakers' dual position of being in the World and yet separate from it. They refined the New England ladder-back form by eliminating the decorative turnings on the posts and stretchers and often substituting a woven wool or cotton seat for the traditional splint or rush. The resulting design is an outward expression of the Shakers' internal concepts: simplicity, utility, perfection in craftsmanship, and above all cleanliness. Ladder-back chairs were routinely suspended upside down from peg rails to prevent dust from settling on the seat. Some other early chairs were fitted with rattan cane, a natural fiber that was appealing to the Shakers because, unlike upholstered material or fabric, it resisted insect infestation. Woven cane also contributes to the physical and visual lightness, delicacy, and portability of Shaker seating furniture. To promote ease of cleaning, beds in retiring rooms were fitted with wooden wheels to make them easily moved. [...]

DEFINING FUNCTION

These people are strict utilitarians in all they do. The first inquiry is, 'will it be useful?'

David R. Lamson[8]

Although the Shakers were unaware of the aesthetic implications of Louis Sullivan's doctrine of 'form follows function,' their literature contains such phrases as 'beauty rests on utility. That which has in itself the highest use possesses the greatest beauty.'[9]

From a spiritual standpoint, the Shakers avoided decoration and ornament in material goods because it encouraged the sin of pride, which could turn the Believers' thoughts from worship to Worldly possessions. Brother Hervey Elkins wrote in 1853 that 'an arbitrary inhibition rests upon statuary, paintings, watches, jewelry of all kinds, knives of more than two blades, sofas, divans, musical instruments, and whatever gorgeous appendage would serve to feed vanity and pride, more than subserve the practical utility of civilized life.'[10]

An important motive in building a functional piece of furniture presumably often involved adapting old forms and developing new combinations over time. These include small work stands with push-pull drawers that could be accessed on either end to accommodate two sisters working simultaneously [... and] other more massive sewing desks from New Hampshire and Maine, including [one] that provided both storage space and expandable surface area for textile activities, were regularly fitted with large rectangular pull-out boards in front to facilitate cutting large pieces of material. [...]

THE PURSUIT OF PROGRESS

We have a right to improve the inventions of man, so far as is useful and necessary, but not to vain glory, or anything superfluous.

Father Joseph Meacham[11]

Forms, fashions, customs, external rules all have to bow to the fiat of evolution and progress toward that which is more perfect. This need not alarm the most conservative Believer. For unless we keep pace with the progress of the universe our individual progress will be an impossibility. We shall be whirled off at some side station and relegated to the limbo of worn-out superannuated and used-up institutions.

Oliver Hampton, Union Village, Ohio, 1887[12]

The opinions expressed by Father Joseph Meacham (d. 1796) and Oliver Hampton (1816–1901) almost a century apart confirm that the Shakers were always searching for new technologies to simplify their lives and streamline their work, unlike the Amish, with whom they are often confused. Throughout their history, the Shakers have embraced spiritual, social, and mechanical progress in every aspect of their daily work and worship. Brethren and sisters were constantly striving for perfection on an individual basis, as well as trying to make their communities mirror heavenly ideals on earth. Believers were also forward-looking in their approach to social reform. Mother Ann taught that God was both Father and Mother, which led to the belief that men and women were equal in leadership and responsibility in Shaker communities. This was clearly an innovative concept in the eighteenth century, at a time when women could not own property and legally were regarded as the possession of men. During the nineteenth century, Eldress Dorothy Durgin (1825–1898) of Canterbury, New Hampshire, was a proponent of pioneering reforms, including the introduction of musical instruments into the faith. Eldress Mary Antoinette Doolittle of Mount Lebanon edited the Shaker newspaper – whose title she changed to *Shaker AND Shakeress* – during the 1870s. The Believers were also far ahead of their time during the Civil War in their support of racial equality and pacifism, as well as in their condemnation of capital punishment at the turn of the twentieth century. [...]

Carpenters had machinery for matching boards with tongue-and-groove joints invented by Brothers Henry Bennett and Amos Bishop in 1828 probably for use on flooring and siding. An improved lathe with a screw feeder to turn broom handles more efficiently was introduced by Brother Jesse Wells in 1805, and weavers of splints and work baskets were supplied with tools devised by Brothers Daniel Boler and Daniel Crossman. The seed shops had presses for printing seed bags and herb packages, as well as the machinery for filling them.[13] The sisters' textile work was enhanced through the use of Shaker-made steam-iron stoves and commercially produced power looms, as well as hose and sweater knitting machines.

Throughout their history, the Shakers believed in sharing their inventions with the World. These included what appears to be the first wrinkle-resistant fabric, perfected by the Sabbathday Lake Shakers in the 1840s.[14] They placed cotton or wool fabric into a special press with paper that had been treated with zinc chloride and then they applied heat and pressure. The resulting fabric was shiny and smooth on the top side and was also water-resistant. According to folk legend, Sister Tabitha Babbitt of Harvard devised the circular saw in 1810; however, there is no documentation to substantiate this popular myth.[15] Brother Alonzo Hollister of Mount Lebanon lent his heated, airtight container used in the making of sugar to a visitor named Gail Borden, who conducted experiments in the Shakers' workshops, and this eventually led to his formula for condensed milk.[16]

Unfortunately, Worldly businessmen took advantage of the Shakers' generosity and profited from their ingenuity. In order to protect their own interests, the Believers patented some of their major contributions, such as Sister Emeline Hart's revolving oven in 1876 and David Parker's water-powered commercial washing machine in 1858 and his sarsaparilla lozenges in 1866.[17] However, the Society was reluctant to invoke government protection, which they regarded as a necessary evil at best, preferring to rely on the inherent quality in Shaker-made goods to attract consumers. Consequently, the number of Shaker ideas that were patented is small in relation to those that were freely shared. Perhaps the best-known example of Shaker ingenuity is Brother George O. Donnell's metal ball-and-socket mechanism or tilter for chairs submitted to the United States Patent Office in 1852.

The Shakers often took the realities of human behavior into consideration when making design decisions. They recognized the natural tendency for Believers to tip their straight chairs back on the rear posts and took pains 'to prevent wear and tear of carpets and marring of floors caused by the corners of the back posts'[18] by adding tilting buttons or swivel feet to the hind legs. They introduced this ingenious device attached to the rear legs to allow 'the chairs [to] take their natural motion of rocking backward and forward while the metallic feet rest unmoved: flat and square on the floor or carpet.'[19] [...]

Outward signs of progress continued throughout the twentieth century and into the present. The Canterbury Shakers installed battery phones throughout their village in 1904; purchased their first car, a Reo, in 1908; had electricity in 1910.[20] At this writing, the last active community at Sabbathday Lake sells their herbs on the Internet.

TEACHING TRUTH

> Be what you seem to be, and seem to be what you really are, and don't carry two faces under one hood.
>
> Father James Whittaker[21]

Shaker commercial products made for the world became widely known for exceptional quality as the sect developed a reputation for honest business dealings, trustworthiness, and fairness. [...] The same commitment to integrity is expressed by Brother Orren Haskins, in 1887, who urged his fellow Believers to avoid Worldly styles when designing Shaker-made articles:

Why patronize the out side world for gugaws in our manufactures, when they will say we have enough of them abroad? We want a good plain substantial Shaker article, yea, one that bears credit to our profession & tells who and what we are, true and honest before the world, without hypocrisy or any false covering. The world at large can scarcely keep pace with it self in its stiles and fassions which last but a short time, when something still more worthless or absurd takes its place. Let good enough alone, and take good common sense for our guide in all our persuits, and we are safe within and without.[22]

The Shakers dedicated themselves to spiritual honesty in their confession of sins, which is reflected in their devotion to 'truth to materials.'[23] Consequently, no marbling, graining, or trompe l'oeil appear; only natural wood or solidly painted surfaces are visible. More specifically, Elder Giles Avery of Mount Lebanon called the 'dressing' of plain pine furniture 'with the veneering of bay wood, mahogany or rosewood' deception and placed it in the same category as cheating.[24] [...]

The Believers' plain and functional furniture was the inevitable result of two compelling forces – a theology demanding a physical statement of gospel simplicity and a Worldly cultural environment that embraced the forms of the new neoclassical style, which was characterized by elegance of proportion and rectilinear lines. These ideas were also expressed in the reliance upon finish rather than on carved, three-dimensional ornament, and a desire either to emphasize the natural grain of the wood enhanced with varnish or to conceal plain lumber with solid but colorful pigments. In the transmission of design, geographic distance between urban high-style centers and rural areas often resulted in a simplification of overall forms and surface treatment. Country cabinetmakers tended to produce a more basic, pared-down interpretation of upscale fashions, and these were for the most part the craftsmen who brought their talents and tastes into the Shaker population when they converted to the faith. The intersection of these spiritual and secular forces resulted in classic Shaker furniture.

NOTES

Extracted from Burks, J. M., 'Faith, Form and Finish: Shaker Furniture in Context', in ed. Jean M. Burks, *Shaker Design: Out of this World*, New York: Bard Graduate Center for Studies in the Decorative Arts, Design and Culture, Shelburne VT: Shelburne Museum and London: Yale University Press, 2008, pp. 31–60. Reprinted with permission.

1. Flo Morse, *The Shakers and the World's People* (Hanover, N.H.: University Press of New England, 1987): 124.
2. June Sprigg, *By Shaker Hands* (New York: Knopf, 1975): 76.
3. Eldress Nancy E. Moore, 'Journal of a Trip to Various Societies Sept. 1854–Oct. 1854.' Western Reserve Historical Society, Cleveland. Quoted in Sprigg, 1975, p. 72.
4. 'Journal of Maurice Thomas, 1 January 1816–31 December 1817' (part 2, p.162), Wednesday, 15 October 1817, in the library of the Filson Club, Louisville, Ky. Quoted in Timothy D. Rieman and Jean M. Burks, *The Complete Book of Shaker Furniture* (New York: Abrams, 1993): 334.
5. 'Collection of Writings Concerning Church Order and Government, Copied Here by Rufus Bishop in 1859' (1791–96): 42, 45, Western Reserve Historical Society, Cleveland, VIIB: 59.
6. 'Millennial Laws of Gospel Statutes and Ordinances Adopted to the Day of Christ's Second Appearing. Revised and reestablished by the Ministry and Elders, October 1845.' pt. 3, sec. 9. Reprinted in Edward Deming Andrews, *The People Called Shakers* (New York: Dover, 1953): 256–57.
7. Quoted in Edward Deming Andrews and Faith Andrews, *Shaker Furniture* (New York: Dover, 1937): 19.
8. *Two Years' Experience among the Shakers* (West Boylston, Mass: David, Lamson, 1848): 17.
9. Andrews, *Shaker Furniture* (1937): 21.
10. *Fifteen Years in the Senior Order of Shakers* (Hanover, N.H.: Dartmouth Press, 1953): 29.
11. As quoted in Morse, *The Shakers and the World's People* (1987): *133.*
12. *The Manifesto* 17, no. 3 (1887): 57–58. Quoted in Robley Edward Whitson, ed., *The Shakers: Two Centuries of Spiritual Perfection* (New York: Paulist Press, 1983): 143.
13. Edward Deming Andrews, *The Community Industries of the Shakers* (Charlestown, Mass.: Emporium Publications, 1971): 40–44. Facsimile reprint of the *New York State Museum Handbook* 15; White and Taylor, *Shakerism* (1905): 314.
14. Beverly Gordon, *Shaker Textile Arts* (Hanover, N.H.: University Press of New England, 1980): 27.
15. See Andrews, *The Community Industries of the Shakers* (1971): 42.
16. See *Dictionary of American Biography* (New York: Charles Scribner's Sons, 1964): 457–58.
17. Edward Deming Andrews and Faith Andrews, *Work and Worship* (Greenwich, Conn.: New York Graphic Society, 1974): 157–58.
18. United States Patent Office specification, 2 March 1852, no. 8771.
19. Ibid.
20. Sprigg, *By Shaker Hands* (1975): 171.
21. Morse, *The Shakers and the World's People* (1987): 184.
22. 'Reflections, 1887,' Mount Lebanon, Western Reserve Historical Society, Cleveland, VIIA:8.
23. Constantin Brancusi, as quoted in 'The Truth in Materials' by Grace Bakst Wapner, www.chronogram.com/issue/2000/04/lucid.htm.
24. Quoted in Sprigg, *By Shaker Hands* (1975): 156.

GUIDE TO FURTHER READING

A suggested antecedent to the work in this section is the notion of type-forms, which Le Corbusier developed in *The Decorative Art of Today* (1925) from the earlier thoughts on standardization of Hermann Muthesius, explored in section 3 of this *Reader* (see also Ulrich Conrads's *Programs and Manifestoes on 20th-Century Architecture*, 1989). The text by Dick Hebdige in this section refers to Roland Barthes's approach to analysing the symbolism of goods, as demonstrated in 'The New Citroën' (1957, see section 10 of the *Reader*) and, in turn, Penny Sparke discusses Hebdige's text in the extract from her work in section 9 of the *Reader*. See also Christopher Breward's discussion of the utility of cultural studies in design history in 'Cultures, Identities, Histories: Fashioning a Cultural Approach to Dress' (1998).

Design historians have made much use of material culture studies, including Jules David Prown's 'Mind in Matter: An Introduction to Material Culture Theory and Method' (1982); *Material Culture: A Research Guide*, edited by Thomas J. Schlereth (1985), including chapters by Kenneth L. Ames on American decorative arts and household furnishings and Simon J. Bronner, on material culture study in American folkloristics, from Schlereth's 1983 special issue of *American Quarterly*; Arjun Appadurai (ed.), *The Social Life of Things: Commodities in Cultural Perspective* (1986), especially Igor Kopytoff's 'The Cultural Biography of Things: Commoditisation as Process'; Daniel Miller's *Material Culture and Mass Consumption* (1987) and Grant McCracken's *Culture and Consumption: New Approaches to the Symbolic Character of Consumer Goods and Activities* (1988). The influence of material culture studies within design history is exemplified in Judy Attfield's approach to object analysis – see *Wild Things* (2000) and *Bringing Modernity Home: Writings on Popular Design and Material Culture* (2007). Also, Louise Purbrick's *The Wedding Present: Domestic Life Beyond Consumption* (2007) and her article on the same subject (2003), and Alison J. Clarke's work, including *Tupperware: The Promise of Plastic in 1950s America* (1999) (extracted in section 10 of this *Reader*).

Further on the history of technology, Wiebe E. Bijker, Thomas P. Hughes and Trevor Pinch, *The Social Construction of Technological Systems* (1987); Carroll Pursell's contribution to Schlereth (ed.) (1985) and Barry M. Katz, 'Review: Technology and Design – A New Agenda' (1997). As well as the other chapters in Donald MacKenzie and Judy Wajcman (eds) *The Social Shaping of Technology* (1999) see Cowan's *A Social History of American Technology* (1997) and *More Work for Mother* (1983).

Those interested in Paul Greenhalgh's exploration of history through analysis of the changing meaning of words, as demonstrated here in discussion of 'craft', will find literary and cultural studies practitioner Raymond Williams's *Keywords* (1976, revised 1983) useful, and its follow-up *New Keywords*, edited by Tony Bennett, Lawrence Grossberg and Meaghan Morris, professors of sociology, communication studies and cultural studies respectively (2005). The remaining essays in *The Culture of Craft*, edited by Peter Dormer, from which the Greenhalgh essay here is taken, are useful, as are: Tanya Harrod's *The Crafts in Britain in the 20th Century* (1999); Janet Kardon (ed.), *Revivals! Diverse Traditions: The History* of *Twentieth-Century American Craft, 1920–1945* (1994); *Pioneers of Modern Craft*, edited by Margot Coatts (1997); Sue Rowley's Australian edited collection *Craft and Contemporary Theory* (1997); Glenn Adamson's *Thinking Through Craft* (2007), and three special issues of *The Journal of Design History*: *Craft, Culture and Identity* (1997), *Craft, Modernism and Modernity* (1998), both edited by Tanya Harrod, and *Dangerous Liaisons: Relationships between Design, Craft and Art*, edited by Grace Lees-Maffei and Linda Sandino (2004). Mary Butcher's 'Eel-Traps without Eels', in the former volume, provides a particularly lucid and concise case-study of the place of function in the understanding of craft objects. See also Berg's new *The Journal of Modern Craft* for developed analyses of the significance of craft.

On Shaker design see Mary Lyn Ray, 'A Reappraisal of Shaker Furniture and Society' (1973) and Beverly Gordon's 'Victorian Fancy Goods: Another Reappraisal of Shaker Material Culture' (1990); Timothy D. Rieman and Jean M. Burks, *The Complete Book of Shaker Furniture* (1993) and Stephen Bowe and Peter Richmond, *Selling Shaker* (2006).

SECTION 9

Gender and Design

INTRODUCTION

Rebecca Houze

Gender influences the production and reception of designed goods in a range of ways, as a number of design historians have shown. Feminist design history has been influenced by pioneering works of second-wave feminist cultural theory and literary studies such as Betty Friedan's *The Feminine Mystique* (1963) and Kate Millet's *Sexual Politics* (1970). One approach taken by feminist design historians has been to recuperate and champion the work of women designers or traditional areas of women's production outside the accepted canon – an approach paralleled by visual artists Judy Chicago and Miriam Schapiro in the 1970s. Another strategy has been to offer gendered critiques of designed objects, design processes, and consumption practices, such as those collected by Judy Attfield and Pat Kirkham in *A View From the Interior: Feminism, Women, and Design* (1989). Several examples of this approach have already been introduced in the *Reader*, including Debora Silverman's examination of Art Nouveau in section two and Nancy Troy's rethinking of Le Corbusier's early career in the decorative arts in section 3.

In her chapter 'FORM/female FOLLOWS FUNCTION/male: Feminist Critiques of Design', Attfield draws a distinction between feminist processes of historical inquiry and an emphasis on women designers. Attfield finds that the latter inevitably ends up confirming that women excel in 'soft' areas, such as textiles and fashion, reiterating the question first posed by art historian Linda Nochlin in her provocative 1971 essay 'Why Have There Been No Great Women Artists?' Rather, Attfield writes, a more productive feminist critique 'suggests a methodology for design history which is not based upon aesthetics or connoisseurship, but upon a concern for people'. Like Cheryl Buckley, in her influential article 'Made in Patriarchy: Towards a Feminist Analysis of Women and Design', first published in *Design Issues* in 1986, Attfield wants to examine a wider range of study based on more diverse criteria, one that challenges patriarchal interpretations of design, and which is characterized by 'a political position that seeks changes in the interest of women'.

Penny Sparke takes a slightly different approach with her valorization of feminine pleasure in the colourful, decorative and sensuous spaces and objects that have been traditionally situated outside of 'modernist' design, but which have constituted arguably more prevalent parts of women's lives. In the extract included here, from her book *As Long As It's Pink: The Sexual Politics of Taste* (1995), Sparke describes the trauma of 'the architect's wife', who, confined to the marginal spaces of her own home, quietly weeps. Her children's room was the only one 'permitted' to deviate, with its softer curtains, from her husband's strict control over the minimalist interior aesthetic. Sparke alludes to Millet's work in the subtitle of *As Long As It's Pink*, which also opens with a quotation taken from earlier French feminist Simone de Beauvoir (see *The Second Sex* (1949)), an approach that combines elements of American and mid-century French feminisms in studies of design from an historical as well as psychological point of view. Sparke's case study of the American designer Elsie de Wolfe (*Elsie de Wolfe: The Birth of Modern Interior Decoration* (2005)) is one application of this method.

Traditionally, production and consumption have been gendered simplistically in a manner which accords with the contested notion of separate spheres, in which, as a function of industrialization, men occupied the public world of work (production), and women were confined to the private world of the home (consumption). In response, gendered analyses of design have frequently been concerned with the 'feminine' realm of domesticity, as a way of redressing the imbalance favouring the 'masculine' public world of work. Attfield and Kirkham suggest, in *A View from the Interior*, that '[i]n order to validate the work of women in the field of production it is essential to assert the importance of the hand-made object produced in the small workshop or in the home itself'. In her article 'Humanizing Modernism: The Crafts, "Functioning Decoration" and the Eameses', Kirkham examines how modernist readings of Charles and Ray Eames have not accounted for the eclectic aesthetic of the couple's own home, as well as the craft influences in their furniture designs, often mistakenly attributing this aspect entirely to Ray, while refusing to acknowledge the more complex partnership that led to their many innovations. Ironically, it was William Morris, Pevsner's first 'pioneer' of modern design, and the artists associated with the Arts and Crafts Movement who first championed the progressive nature of craft. This problem is further explored in section 8 of the *Reader*.

In the past two decades, promotion of the work of women in isolation has ceded to a more holistic understanding of gender, encompassing men and masculinity, and a study of homosexual and homosocial practices. Thus, women's studies and women's history have become gender studies and gender history; this trend has attracted criticism from some feminists for, once again, removing women from the focus of analysis.

Christopher Breward questions presumptions about the 'great masculine renunciation' of fashion around the turn of the twentieth century in the extract reproduced here from his ground-breaking book *The Hidden Consumer* (1999), arguing instead that masculine identities were shaped within a complex and nuanced culture of sartorial consumption in which social and sexual anxieties were rehearsed. Breward presents this history through a reading of rich literary sources – nineteenth- and twentieth-century novels, city guides, and trade journals, which were filled with descriptions of clothing and the character traits it was believed to represent. His study looks ahead to section 10, in which the role of consumption in design history is more thoroughly discussed.

In 'Self-Made Motormen: The Material Construction of Working-Class Masculine Identities through Car Modification', Andrew Bengry-Howell and Christine Griffin use ethnographic methods to explore this particular subculture of young British men, who inscribe their own identities upon cars by erasing the signs of their original brands and meticulously changing their shape and decoration. The cars, then used for 'cruising', are highly individualized expressions of gender, defined through a combination of labour, conspicuous consumption and performance. Aspects of gender and design are explored elsewhere throughout the *Reader*, for example, in Dick Hebdige's reading of the gendered Italian motor scooter in section 8, and in Alison J. Clarke's historical account in section 10 of the Tupperware party in 1950s America.

47

FORM/female FOLLOWS FUNCTION/male: Feminist Critiques of Design

Judy Attfield (1989)

It is impossible from a consciously female perspective to attempt any kind of survey of the critiques of design, its practice or its history without questioning the assumptions which have become an established orthodoxy. So I start from a definition of design legitimated by Pevsner's *Pioneers of the Modern Movement* (1936) and which places Giedion's *Mechanization Takes Command* (1948) in its bibliography together with the Open University's *History of Architecture and Design 1890–1939* (1975). What these texts have in common is a shared definition of design which was first formulated at the height of the 'Good Design' movement, based on a set of principles which decreed that in answering functional requirements correctly, Beauty would logically follow.

Design history still suffers from its provenance in the Modern Movement, where to some extent it remains, sealed in a time lock which still considers form the effect of function, and a concept of design – the product of professional designers, industrial production and the division of labour – which assumes that women's place is in the home. Feminist perspectives offer design history a range of historical/critical methods which challenge the mainstream about how it defines design as a practice, about the parameters of what type of designed objects it should examine, about what values are given priority in assessing it, and even who it calls designers.

It is more difficult, but still necessary, to attempt a definition of 'feminist' in this context, although to do so might imply a dominant, single view of feminism. But the project here is to displace dominant definitions in order to make space for the normally silent, hidden and unformulated dimensions of design omitted in its conventional study or literature. Broadly speaking, I refer to a 'feminist perspective' as that which acknowledges that women form a group among many in a multicultural society, with different tastes, needs, values and orders of priority because of the roles they play, the type of jobs they do and the position in society they occupy through the accident of their birth. In this context, feminism is a political position which seeks changes in the interest of women. There is no ultimate agreement as to what those changes should be nor what strategies should be used to pursue them since different cultural groups of women have different interests. It is a sensitivity to this diversity which marks out the distinction between the women's liberation campaign centered in the United States in the late 1960s and early 1970s, from the wider, global women's movement.

To advocate design improvement in the environment and in products mainly used by women at present should not be taken as acceptance of the fact that such improvements can reinforce the traditional, subordinate place of women in society. (Many feminist critiques of design point out how a definition of women as a subordinate group is reinforced and made to appear natural through design.) In discussing history and applying a feminist analysis to it, it is particularly relevant to be precise about the historical construction of the term 'feminist' and the changes it has undergone. Without an awareness that change is possible there is little point in taking a feminist perspective in the first place.

[...]

THE POLITICS OF EXPERIENCE

A fundamental starting point for feminist design historians is the fact that women experience the designed world differently from men. One of the most powerful and influential critiques of town planning, Jane Jacobs' *The Death and Life of Great American Cities* (1961), caused a transformation by introducing a critical element into the writing of architectural history which until then had glorified modernism without question.[1] It was precisely her female point of view which brought out new and valuable insights in the relationship between design ideals and lived experience.[2]

Design shapes the environment and makes assumptions about women's place in terms of buildings, public spaces and transport. It also provides the imagery women use to form their identity through fashion, advertising and the media generally. It assumes that particular areas of the design profession are 'women's work'; thereby reflecting the predominant division of labour in society. Furthermore, it segregates the sexes through artifacts by endowing these with unnecessary gender definitions, while neglecting the special needs of women who want their own transport, places and spaces.[3] And, as already explained, it excludes women from the determining spheres of science, technology and industry.[4]

The role of design in forming our ideas about gender power relations often remains invisible, while at the same time it makes them concrete in the everyday world of materials goods. 'White goods' such as washing machines and electric cookers may reduce the heavy manual labour

women perform and those designed by women may satisfy their needs better than those designed by men, but such goods are still manufactured with women in mind – the implicit assumption is that it is they who will be doing the bulk of the washing and cooking, not men – hence the division of labour by gender remains unaffected by product innovation and improvement.

Design reflects our aspirations and arouses our expectations, but it is also a process and as such has a potential for transformation. Some professional feminist designers have attempted to reform gender relations through innovatory designs.[5] Feminist historians have been and are undertaking research to bring to light those designers' achievements as well as the achievements of women working in the field whose contributions remain unrecognized. It is also vital to consider the impact that women have had historically, and can continue to exert on design by means of individual and joint consumption.[6]

'WOMEN-DESIGNERS' VERSUS A FEMINIST CRITIQUE

Isabelle Anscombe's *A Woman's Touch* (1984) gives exclusive attentions to women designers who have participated in 'the history of the major design movements since the 1860s'. It helps to set the record straight by giving more emphasis to those women who did manage to penetrate the professional arena – some of them, like Charlotte Perriand[7] and Eileen Gray,[8] already known in conventional design history – but who were often overshadowed by male designers with whom they associated through professional or personal ties. However, it soon becomes clear that this 'women-designers' approach does little except confirm the prejudice that women are inferior designers except in the so-called 'feminine' areas such as the decorative arts, textiles, interior design and fashion. Even where there was an opportunity to alter the emphasis by showing how some female designers were prevented from practicing in the more exclusively male areas of design, as in the case of Eileen Gray, Anscombe fails to do so.[9]

There are other problems related to looking at women designers as the main focus. For instance, the restrictions of method in the conventional biography place them in a preset, hierarchical framework in which 'great,' usually male, designers appear. Is this really because there have been no great women designers? Since Linda Nochlin's essay on women artists, written in the early 1970s, this has become a somewhat rhetorical question.[10] Design is even less of an autonomous activity than art and needs to be examined in close relationship with the social, cultural, economic and technological conditions which have nurtured its development as a practice. However, the historiography which has produced some of the seminal works of design history has established a tradition of pioneers of modern design and an avant-garde aesthetic in which few women figure. There is an urgent need, therefore, to bring to light the work of women pioneers of design careers who, at present, face unwelcoming, male-dominated enclaves in architecture, engineering, product and industrial design, where all that is thought necessary to meet the needs of women is an equal opportunities policy.[11]

A considerable body of work has built up around an object-based study of the history of design, which avoids some of the more overtly sexist problems by not focusing on designers.[12] It also marks out for itself a methodology distinct from conventional art history in which the cult of the artist rubs off on the art work, thereby giving it a particular value distinct from the anonymous designed object. A women-designers approach is based on the traditions of such an art history and cannot cope with anonymous design. This is not to say that object-based study is innocent and neutral in matters of gender. On the contrary, a hierarchy has built up around types of objects which gives importance to industrial design and the 'machine aesthetic' – i.e. the more obviously masculine – while considering areas such as fashion as trivial and synonymous with 'feminine.' But

the limitations of a women-designers approach not only diminishes women, it also devalues design history as a discipline by using a borrowed and inappropriate methodology.[13]

A feminist critique makes it possible to look at women designers in a new light and to assess their work in the context of the history of a profession which has consistently marginalized them. It also suggests a methodology for design history which is not based upon aesthetics or connoisseurship, but upon a concern for people.

USE-VALUE AND FEMINIST CRITIQUE

Some feminist design historians are not content to satisfy academic criteria. They want their research to be of value to practicing designers. They conceive of design history as contributing to an understanding of different groups' needs as part of the design process. *Making Space* (1984) by Matrix (a feminist architects' collective) is one example of an interventionist text which seeks to bring theory and practice together and to relate knowledge of the past to the present and the future.

The problems of defining an object of study appropriate to design history have been fraught by precedents set by art history. Although feminist art history does present us with an excellent body of critique and methodology, it cannot be appropriated and applied directly to design unless we treat design as if it were art. There is some measure of agreement that it need *not* just be about the appreciation of something called 'good design,' nor the attribution of authorship to particular designers of certain cult objects, lest the whole exercise deteriorate into one of connoisseurship. But what it *should* be is less clear. Not only is there confusion over *what* should be looked at, but *why*.

A feminist perspective can be quite specific in its focus on use-value. By providing historical explanations for women's lack of visibility at the production stage, it is possible to understand better why dominant masculine values are constantly reproduced in the material world. Thus a familiar critique of design history can become part of a more general movement of reform. It is at that particular intersection – between what we think and what we do – that the transitive meaning of design as a verb, as an action, can take place.

An example of mainstream history of design, Penny Sparke's *An Introduction to Design and Culture in the Twentieth Century* (1986), avoids defining design because 'available definitions are varied, complex, contradictory and in a state of permanent flux.'[14] But by devoting her attention to industrial, mass-produced goods and the education and practice of professional designers, Sparke represents the conventional high ground of design history, traditionally associated with the mechanized and male-dominated areas of design where women only appear as passive consumers.

In her essay, 'Made in patriarchy,' Cheryl Buckley uses a critique of patriarchy and capitalism to formulate a method for a feminist history of design.[15] Patriarchy is a useful concept because it explains the dominance of masculine attributes transhistorically as a cultural phenomenon manifested by women as well as men. It serves to explain, for example, why some women contribute to the production of sexist ads which degrade women. Nevertheless, because patriarchy depends on stereotypical definitions of male/female and is basically a-historical, it represents many difficulties as an operative concept, not the least of which is the contradictory task of reconciling rather crude male/female stereotypes with a history of changing gender relations.

In matters of sexual politics where the personal is political, gender neutrality has been proposed as a strategy. In Britain it occupies a central position in recent anti-sexist education initiatives to degender activities such as sewing and woodwork, areas where design is taught in many schools. So gender neutrality has definite advantages, but there is a limit to which it can be used in the history of design when dealing with issues of sexual differentiation.

Part of the debate about what makes design different from art has been the distinction between the functional object and the merely beautiful. This value system, entirely based on the ideology of modernism, cannot be applied to non-functional or handmade objects, nor to those which do not conform to the rules of good design. This has made it impossible to deal seriously with a whole galaxy of objects, i.e. those falling outside the prescribed category of the 'modern classic.' Omitted are fashion, ephemera and many other areas of design in which women have been most prominent; this omission therefore accounts for their lack of visibility. Contemporary cultural studies, social history and anthropology have provided a way in to a less hierarchical, non-aesthetic analysis of designed objects which allows inquiry in the kind of areas which put women back into the picture and make it possible to examine popular taste. So it is not just a case of looking only at women's concerns, but of using feminism as a starting point, as a means of transcending the limitations of conventional design history.

The purpose of a feminist critique of design and its history should be to discuss women's concerns so that women do not feel segregated or excluded in any way for reasons of gender. Though there are some radical feminists who choose permanent separatism as a form of refusal, this excludes many women as well as men. A gendered view, on the other hand, is a practical way of opening a space for discussion. It forms part of a wider move away from authoritarian, patriarchal values for both men and women. It also allows women to become involved as ungendered beings – as people who consider issues beyond those of gender: i.e. race, class, age, sexuality, religion, occupation and so on.

It should not be 'Woman' who is made the special case for treatment, but the culture which subordinates people by gender, class, race, etc., and does nothing to question the attributes which position them as 'Other.' The concept of 'the Other' is one used to define the category of 'woman' in a negative relationship to the category of 'man.' ('Man' enjoys the privilege of being the norm – 'the measure of all things' – while 'woman' is that which deviates from it.) The acknowledgment of such a presence with particular needs and interests contests the privileged position of the dominant power. This includes the challenging of mainstream art which insists on purity and preserves itself from contamination of the ordinary, the everyday and the common. It will also allow traffic across the borders and the entry of the 'minor' arts, the crafts, ephemera, fashion and the popular. By transgressing the normal definition of art, it can redirect the search for an impossible, timeless 'classic' towards a more practical activity.

Design history presents a suitable case for treatment as it struggles to come to terms with its relationship to art and the all-pervasive postmodernism which threatens to shatter its confident, macho value system based on the prime importance of industrial production.

While post-modernism cannot replace the rules it shatters with anything nearly as comforting as the harmony and belief in technological progress offered by the myth of modernism, it does enable a decentered shift in the way in which we look at the world, and how we relate to it – not an unfamiliar experience to women who are accustomed to occupying the margins.[16] Feminist practice in design, history and critique offers a point at which a criterion can be constructed which doesn't refer everything back to market forces or abstract aesthetics.

NOTES

Extracted from Attfield, J., 'FORM/female FOLLOWS FUNCTION/male: Feminist Critiques of Design' in Walker, J. A., *Design History and the History of Design*, London: Pluto Press, 1989, pp. 199–225. Reprinted by permission of Pluto Press.

1. The critique of modern town planning has become associated with a simplistic, reactionary post-modernism which is only to do with styling for the market, and a loss of faith in designing as a practice concerned with people's needs. Jacobs' critique is not about the so-called 'failure of modernism' but about an interventionist approach to designing in which the designer teams up with users and works with them to achieve an environment more in keeping with their needs. Whereas Robert Venturi's *Complexity and Contradiction in Architecture* (1966) which presented an aesthetic critique of modernism and a celebration of historical styles without considering social implications has been much more influential.

2. Marshall Berman acknowledges this in his book *All that is Sold Melts into Air* (London: Verso, 1985) pp. 312–29.

3. See A. Karf, 'On a road to nowhere,' *Guardian* 8 March 1988.

4. See C. Cockburn, *Brothers: Male Dominance and Technological Change* (London: Pluto, 1983) and *Machinery of Dominance* (London: Pluto, 1985); T. Gronberg and J. Attfield (eds), *A Resource Book on Women Working in Design* (London: London Institute/Central School of Art, 1986).

5. See, for example, S. Torre, 'Space as Matrix,' *Heresies* (11) 1981 pp. 51–2; D. Hayden, *The Grand Domestic Revolution* (London: MIT Press, 1982).

6. See, for example, Suzette Worden, 'A voice for whose choice?' in Design History Society, *Design History: Fad or Function?* (London: Design Council, 1978).

7. Charlotte Benton, 'Charlotte Perriand: Un Art de Vivre,' *Design History Society Newsletter* (25) May 1985 pp. 12–15.

8. Both have been associated with Le Corbusier and have suffered from having their designs attributed to him, or having work ignored if – as in the case of Perriand – it was not done in association with him.

9. See Peter Adam's biography, *Eileen Gray* (London: Thames & Hudson, 1987).

10. L. Nochlin's essay first appeared in V. Gornick and B. Moran (eds), *Women in Sexist Society, Studies in Power and Powerlessness* (New York: Basic Books, 1971) pp. 480–510. For

an overview of feminism and art history see T. Gouma-Peterson and P. Mathews, 'The feminist critique of art history,' *Art Bulletin* LXIX (3) Sept 1987 pp. 326–57.

11. Some design departments have responded to the needs of women by adopting a policy of positive discrimination in recruitment and in access courses, but this is still uncommon. For example, the 'Women into architecture and building' course (1985–) in the Department of Environmental Design, North London Polytechnic.

12. Represented by such texts as Hazel Conway (ed.), *Design History: a Students' Handbook* (London: Allen & Unwin, 1987).

13. For example see A. Forty, 'Lucky Strikes and other myths,' *Designer* November 1985 pp. 16–17.

14. P. Sparke, *An Introduction to Design and Culture in the Twentieth Century* (London: Allen & Unwin, 1986) p. xiii.

15. C. Buckley, 'Made in patriarchy: towards a feminist analysis of women and design,' *Design Issues* 3 (2) 1987 pp. 3–15.

16. I refer here to what Hal Foster calls 'a post-modernism of resistance' which is concerned with 'a critical deconstruction of tradition, not an instrumental pastiche of pop – or pseudo-historical forms, with a critique of origins, not a return to them. In short, it seeks to question rather than exploit cultural codes, to explore rather than conceal social and political affiliations'; from his introduction to *Postmodern Culture* (London: Pluto, 1985).

48

THE ARCHITECT'S WIFE, INTRODUCTION TO
AS LONG AS IT'S PINK:
THE SEXUAL POLITICS OF TASTE

Penny Sparke (1995)

> It is evident that women's "character" – her convictions, her values, her wisdom, her tastes, her behavior – are to be explained by her situation.
>
> Simone de Beauvoir[1]

Sometimes what seem like the most trivial of tragedies are the most poignant. In Nicholas Barker's television series *Signs of the Times* (1992), television cameras entered 'ordinary' people's living spaces and asked them to talk about their lives. One woman, married to an architect for whom white walls, minimal décor and Venetian blinds were de rigueur, explained how she sometimes went into the children's bedroom – the only room in which curtains were 'permitted' – and softly wept. A middle-class woman shedding tears for curtains in her domestic space may seem absurd in today's society in which tragedies of enormous global and personal significance are beamed into our living-rooms. And yet it was a televisual moment which moved a considerable number of people, especially women. It hit a nerve.

[…]

Very little scholarly writing on consumption has addressed the question of feminine taste, or seen it as part of the broader discussion about sexual politics. Until recently cultural theorists have tended to view consumption as a form of manipulation, the commodity out to trap the unsuspecting consumer.[2] The only alternative to this essentially negative account of consumption has been that of anthropologists who have studied it as a form of social ritual, a means of achieving social cohesion.[3] However, their accounts, like those of their fellow social scientists, have underplayed the role of gender.[4] A number of social, economic and cultural historians have addressed feminine consumption as it emerged in the late-nineteenth century with the growth of department stores and mass retailing.[5] While some have perpetuated the idea that women's role in this was entirely passive, others have offered a more positive view of feminine taste, seeing it as operating outside the value judgments imposed on it by masculine culture. The evocation in these writings of the sensations of pleasure and aesthetic delight go some way towards an understanding of consumption in specifically feminine terms. While these accounts have emphasized the physical and aesthetic sites of consumption and their role in stimulating a response from consumers – a response rooted in the values of the domestic sphere – they have stopped short of a description of goods themselves as objects of feminine taste. This book takes those objects as its starting point. It bases its argument on the assumption that they alone – the curtains and the glass ornaments – have represented and embodied masculine and feminine values in action – that is, the dynamic tension between gendered values as they have moved through the cycle of production, consumption and use. Only objects experience that cycle in its entirety and only they cross the bridge between the separate spheres.

Like people, objects have lives and their meanings change in response to the different contexts within which they are found. At the same time, they carry their accrued meaning to each new context, transforming and enriching it in the process. While many scholars have tried to break the codes of objects, few have grasped the importance of the object's life span.[6] Only the British cultural theorist, Dick Hebdige, in his analysis of the Italian Vespa motor-scooter,[7] which moved from being a mainstream mass cultural object in one country to a subcultural icon in another, has made fully explicit the importance of recontextualzation in decoding objects.[8] In focusing on an object which was consumed by a predominately male subculture, Hebdige side-stepped the vital question of gender raised by the vast number of goods within mainstream mass culture which are designed and made by men in a masculine cultural setting and consumed and used by women in a feminine context. The gender relationships within mass-produced goods are complex. Within sexual politics objects have a clear role to play: like barometers, they measure the extent to which masculine values dominate culture at any one time, and feminine culture's resistance. They also reflect the way in which masculine and feminine values meet at the intersection between production and consumption, negotiating the power relationships between them.

Interestingly, the moments of feminine 'resistance,' as represented by the objects of mass production and mass consumption, have not kept in step with radical feminist action in this century. At moments of feminist achievement – the 1920s, for example – objects were often at their most masculine while at moments of feminist inactivity – the 1950s come to mind – many objects were extremely feminine. This

can be explained by the fact that mass-produced objects, which represent and embody stereotypical notions of femininity, have tended to be seen by radical feminists as oppressive constructions of patriarchal culture from which, they believe, women should free themselves if they want to achieve equality with men. The evidence from objects suggests, however, that the relationship between women and gendered goods is more complex and ambiguous than this, and that it can be seen to have liberated women as much as it has oppressed them. Any account of the relationship between gender and taste has to take place on the level of the stereotypical, rather than the actual, attributes of the two sexes. Within the epochs of modernity and postmodernity gender identity has been established to a significant extent through negotiations with the stereotypes that have been presented through the mass media. They play, therefore, a key role in the construction of gender. Within the context of feminine domesticity, stereotypical images of women and of the home were conflated and turned into a single ideal. In response to that ideal women have formed their own individual and collective identities. By incorporating, in material form, the stereotypical attributes of femininity and domesticity, objects of consumption have also played an important part in the cultural construction of gender. Through the exercise of their tastes women have selected and arranged objects in their domestic settings and in doing so have both formed and reinforced their own gender identities.

The question of how mass-produced objects are imbued with stereotypically gendered attributes is, of course, central to this discussion. Once industrialisation had removed much 'making' from the home, and standardised factory production had come to dominate the manufacture of individual items for specific customers, large numbers of goods had to be 'designed' for customers whose individual characteristics were unknown to their makers. The nineteenth-century designers and manufacturers of goods destined for the domestic sphere worked with an image of the customer, usually female, firmly in their minds, catering, as closely as possible, for her psychological, symbolic and aesthetic needs. Conscious that fashion, novelty and comfort were general requirements, they translated those concepts as faithfully as they could into goods. In doing so, they aligned the concept of design, as it functioned within production, directly with that of taste, as it operated in the arena of consumption. While the spheres of production and consumption were clearly gendered, the aesthetic values of goods on the marketplace reflected the primacy of the latter. The shift from a world in which the female consumer played a central role to one in which rationally conceived, standardised mass production began to dictate a new aesthetic and role for the domestic object came with the marriage of technological and economic modernity to cultural modernism. Motivated and justified by a commitment to democratic ideals, architectural and design modernism imposed on goods and their design a stereotypically masculine aesthetic, not only because it was undertaken by men but because it was now embedded within masculine culture. Thus taste was superseded by design which, in turn, set out to remove all aesthetic autonomy and authority from the hands of women.

The terms of the struggle, which still goes on today, as the architect's wife knows to her cost, were not simply those of the aesthetic characteristics of objects – their shape, colour and decoration – but the ways in which the two sexes used and related to objects in their everyday lives. With the separation of the spheres came a split between the realms of aesthetics and utility: within the feminine sphere objects became, first and foremost, symbols, sacrificing their utilitarian features to their symbolic functions. Thus, while a chair remained an object for sitting in, its primary function within the domestic context was not only to represent, but also to embody in a material manner, the idea of comfort.[9] In sharp contrast, within the masculine sphere, objects were defined increasingly as tools. In its attempt to assert the

pre-eminence of masculine culture, and the role of objects as its representatives, architectural and design modernism set out to rid them of their feminine content. It achieved this by removing them from the contexts for which they were intended, and by defining them instead in terms of their internal properties. Thus a modernist chair became an exercise in an examination of 'chairness' which did not take into account, and indeed forcibly set out to deny, the role of that object within the feminine, domestic context of comfort and display. Such was the power of feminine culture, however, allied to that of the marketplace within which it found a home, that the aesthetic role of the object survived and the modernist 'style' became, by the middle of this century, a familiar characteristic of the everyday environment. In turn, masculine culture embarked on a campaign intent upon devaluing and trivialising what it saw as an unacceptable 'feminisation' of modernist ideals.

While on one level the links between women, commerce and the marketplace succeeded in pulling mass-produced objects away from the exclusive control of masculine culture, on the other; they reinforced the marginalisation of feminine taste. Defined as part of mass culture, it suffered the fate of other cultural manifestations of the mass media, such as romantic novels and TV soaps; generally perceived as trivial and potentially damaging because of their sentimentality and lack of sophistication. Like them, the objects of feminine taste have, in this century, frequently been deemed inferior to those of high culture. The material culture of feminine domesticity – expressed by such reputedly 'vulgar' items as coal-effect fires, chintzy fabrics and potted plants – has frequently been singled out for condemnation or, at best, sarcasm, termed as 'bad taste' or 'kitsch'. The aesthetic and ideological opposition to modernism demonstrated by these objects served to divorce them from the world of 'legitimate' culture and its 'good taste'.

By the early years of this century, the concept of taste, once whole and feminine, was no longer a unified one. The split into 'good taste' and 'bad taste' was the result of a male-directed moral crusade which began with the mid-nineteenth century design reform movement and which moved into modernist architectural and design theory as well as modern cultural criticism. It was, in reality, little more than a thinly-disguised attempt by masculine culture to set the cultural terms of reference for modernity such that women, with their new-found power as consumers, would not take over the reins. Surprised and threatened by women's suddenly increased authority in the marketplace, masculine culture attempted to redress the balance of gender power by condemning and devaluing the alliance between aesthetic, commercial and feminine culture. In its place they posited a high cultural model which aligned itself with universal values and the pure logic of function. In his insistence on Venetian blinds rather than curtains, the architect in *Signs of the Times* was perpetuating a tradition of male domination, the puritanical control of the material environment begun over a century and half earlier. His wife did have something to cry about after all.

NOTES

Extracted from Sparke, P., 'Introduction: The Architect's Wife', in Sparke, P., *As Long As It's Pink: The Sexual Politics of Taste*, London: Pandora Press, 1995, pp. 1–12. Reprinted by permission of Rivers Oram Press.

1. Simone de Beauvoir. *The Second Sex*, (London: Penguin Books, 1972), p. 635.
2. Judith Williamson adopted this neo-Marxist position in her book *Consuming Passions: The Dynamics of Popular Culture,* (London: Marion Boyars, 1986). The writers Rosalind Williams, *Dream Worlds: Mass Consumption in late 19th Century France*, Berkeley, University of California Press, 1982, and Rachel Bowlby, *Just Looking: Consumer Culture in Dreiser, Gissing and Zola*, New York, Methuen, 1985, in their

accounts of nineteenth-century department stores, also saw women playing a passive, 'enslaved' role in this context.

3. The anthropologists, Mary Douglas (in her book written with Baron Isherwood, *The World of Goods: Towards an Anthropology of Consumption*, Harmondsworth, Penguin Books, 1978) and Daniel Miller (in his book *Material Consumption and Mass Consumption,* Oxford, Basil Blackwell 1987) have both described consumption in this positive way.
4. Many social psychologists writing about consumption, among them Peter Lunt and Sonia Livingstone in their book, *Mass Consumption and Personal Identity: Everyday Economic Experience*, Buckingham, Open University Press, 1992, have tended to underplay the role played by gender. Their book, for example, devotes only one section in one chapter (there are seven in all) to the subject of 'Shopping as a gendered activity.'
5. The most enlightening texts in this context are Rachel Bowlby's *Just Looking*, Rosalind Williams' *Dream Worlds*, and W.R. Leach's 'Transformations in a Culture of Consumption': Women and Department Stores 1980–1912,' published in *Journal of American History*, 71, Sept. 1984, pp. 319–342.
6. The discipline of semiotics, and more recently, that of product semantics, have as their goal to read objects as if they constituted a language. Their usefulness to this project is limited by their lack of involvement in the historical, socio-economic and cultural contexts of objects.
7. Dick Hebdige. 'Object as Image: the Italian Scooter Cycle In Dick Hebdige, *Hiding in the Light*, London and New York, Comedia, Routledge, 1988.
8. This theme is also dealt with by George Basalla in his article 'Transformed Utilitarian Objects,' published in *Wintherthur Portfolio*, 1982, pp. 184–201.
9. The idea that objects can be 'read' in a gendered way parallels similar ideas in other cultural arenas, among them literature (Elaine Showalter, *A Literature of Their Own*, London,

Virago, 1982); film (Laura Mulvey, 'Visual Pleasure and Narrative Cinema,' *Screen*, vol. 16, no. 3, Autumn 1975, pp. 6–18); and advertising (Diane Barthel, *Putting on Appearances: Gender and Advertising*, Philadelphia, Temple University Press, 1988).

49

HUMANIZING MODERNISM: THE CRAFTS, 'FUNCTIONING DECORATION' AND THE EAMESES

Pat Kirkham (1998)

[...]

In the early 1980s I set out to research the work of Charles (1907–78) and Ray Eames (1912–88), a husband-wife partnership whose furniture I admired. Visits to the Eames Office (their workshop cum laboratory of design which was their base for over thirty years) where I interviewed Ray and to the Eames House (where they had lived since late 1949) proved rewarding in many ways but they also brought me face to face with something I did not understand, namely the extremely carefully composed decorative arrangements of objects which I found therein [Figure 34]. They termed these arrangements of objects 'functioning decoration' and Robert Venturi claimed that they had reintroduced 'good old Victorian clutter' to interiors.[1]

Such things did not fall within the parameters of orthodox Modernist design practice by any stretch of the imagination or intellect and what had at the beginning seemed a relatively straightforward project about Modernist design, the work of one specific firm and the overdue recognition of a woman designer took on new dimensions. My project began to broaden to encompass attitudes towards the crafts in the period c. 1941–78 as I increasingly became aware of the continued influence upon their work of the Arts and Crafts Movement – usually believed dead by the Second, if not the First, World War.

Helpful to my own understanding of the more neglected areas of the work of the Eameses were the current debates about 'post-Modernism' and a greater valuation (in every sense of the word) of the crafts. The debates, with their emphasis on addition, accretion, juxtaposition, changing scales, fragmentation, wit and whimsy, cross-cultural references and the de/re-contextualization of objects and images, encouraged me to focus on such aspects in the work of the Eameses.[2] In the 1960s both the Smithsons and Robert Venturi had applauded the Eameses' 'functioning decoration', which incorporates all the above-mentioned elements, seeing it as a major development in design.[3] Nevertheless, love of crafts and joy in objects was not generally included in accounts of their work thereafter, with the notable exception of the perceptive American critic Esther McCoy.[4] I do not want to claim the Eameses for post-Modernism but rather to re-offer for serious consideration those areas of their work which were distant from, and sometimes in opposition to, minimalist Modernism which encouraged reduction, removal, and little or no decoration and banished 'clutter'.

As far as the crafts are concerned, it is difficult to find any other major US industrial designer of his generation as firmly embedded as Charles Eames in the Arts and Crafts traditions of 'right making', honesty of construction, truth to materials and joy in labour. Both he and Ray believed

Figure 34. Sofa Compact (1954) with rugs, blankets and cushion. Living room, Eames House, 1983. Photo © Pat Kirkham. Reprinted with permission.

that one of life's main objectives was 'to get as many of the rewards of life from the work you do'[5] and their workshop was very much a 'hands-on' place. A man of many practical skills as well as powerful intellect, Charles stood in the tradition of W. R. Lethaby as much as in Modernist ones. According to those who worked with him, he could turn his hand to almost any practical task and do it as well as, if not better than, anyone else in the Eames Office. He and Ray were both brought up in a school system based on Arts and Crafts ideas in the teaching of art and design but Charles learned much of what he knew about engineering and practical skills on the many jobs he did in his teenage years and early twenties. Ray frequently bemoaned her lack of 'workshop skills', a situation which she blamed on her more genteel 'female' education which left her totally untrained in the sort of technical and workshop skills used in making special tools and prototypes for their furniture, exhibitions and films.[6] It should be remembered, however, that her work as a sculptor and skills in 'femmage'[7] meant that she, as well as Charles, was happiest designing in a hands-on way.

They both felt passionately about the importance of seeing beauty in the everyday, in the 'commonplace' and many of their films aimed to convey this idea. This too had its roots in the Arts and Crafts Movement and no two people were more in tune with W. R. Lethaby's dictum that 'art' included the well-laying of a table or the making of a beautifully designed loaf of bread. Indeed, Ray could be said to have perfected the 'art' of table-laying and together they devoted a short film to the topic of bread.[8]

Charles studied architecture for two years before being asked to leave because of 'a premature enthusiasm for Frank Lloyd Wright'[9] and later confessed that he was mainly influenced by Wright's attachment to nature, especially the 'schmalzy stuff about the field and the earth ... and materials'.[10] By then – the late 1920s – he was not only an excellent photographer but was also skilled at several crafts, including pottery, lithography, printmaking and etching. During the Depression he worked when he could as an architect but in 1933–4 he left behind his first wife, his child and his architectural partner and went on an eight-month trip to Mexico.[11] There his interest in the crafts broadened considerably. He admired the rich craft traditions of Mexico and returned home with a small collection of objects of aesthetic, cultural and archaeological interest, including an ancient Toltec wand. After his second marriage in 1941 to Ray Kaiser, a woman whose passion/obsession for objects matched, if not outstripped, his own, the collection grew enormously and encompassed a wide variety of craft and other objects (see below). Many of the objects 'starred' in Eames films and many more were utilized in their 'functioning decoration'.

His years at the Cranbrook Academy of Art (1938–41), where he went on a fellowship and was later given a teaching post, augmented Charles's already considerable understanding of crafts and craft processes. Those who were at Cranbrook with him remember that Charles spent a lot of time in the ceramics and weaving studios as well as the photography and sculpture studios and the metal shop, preparing himself for a career which was based on a comprehensive understanding of materials and technologies.[12]

[...]

It is somewhat ironical that it was the most avant-garde member of the Eames partnership, Ray, who was regarded as the one pulling the male partner away from Modernism and towards the crafts and decoration. Such blame would, I suspect, have been difficult to place at the feet of a male who happened to be an avant-garde artist. But Ray was both a woman and a wife – doubly subservient and culpable in the mores of mid-century middle America. But by the time she went to Cranbrook in 1940, Ray Kaiser was an out-and-out Modernist.[13] A painter and sculptor trained at the Art Students League in New York in the 1930s under Hans Hoffman, she was part of the AAA (American Abstract Artists), a militant group of avant-garde artists wholeheartedly committed to the cause of abstract art. Clearly, the binary oppositions of female/craft and male/Modernism, which have proved useful tools in feminist critiques, do not apply here.

Had the couple met in 1938 instead of two years later, their pairing might have offered an inversion of how people later liked to categorize them. Then it would have been a case of female/Modernist and male/traditionalist; female/purist and male/eclectic. However, history often works against neat narratives and formulae. At Cranbrook Ray, who had shown an interest in decoration during her school years,[14] learned a greater appreciation of the crafts. She wove and designed rugs under the well-known designer and craftworker Marianne Strengell[15] and always displayed one of them in the Eames House. However, it is important not to make too much of this craft work because, in the early 1940s during moments when she and Charles were not jointly developing moulded plywood furniture, she chose not to work at crafts and continued in a Modernist vein as sculptor, painter and graphic designer.[16] In other words, after her four months at Cranbrook she did not substantially shift her modes or means of artistic expression. What one can say with certainty is that, by the time they married in 1941, they were both well versed in Modernism. Such a situation once again means that the binary oppositions of female/male, traditionalism/Modernism, craft/industrial, hand/machine, do not neatly 'fit' this partnership.

Although the design work of the Eameses was joint work, Ray, who was trained as an artist, was frequently not given the credit she deserved. She was, however, given more than equal credit when 'credit' was equated with blame for deviations from Modernist orthodoxy. It was she, rather than Charles, trained in architecture and who, from 1941, enjoyed an international reputation as a 'functionalist' industrial designer, who was given credit for those areas of their work, including aspects of the crafts, which were unpalatable to orthodox Modernist taste.

The importance of Ray's input into Eames furniture, especially the early furniture, is now becoming more accepted[17] yet she was given little credit at the time for furniture that was hailed as innovative largely because of its use of industrial production techniques. Two pieces of furniture stand out as different from the others in that they invoked more of a craft ethos and referenced preindustrial worlds. They were less favourably received by the design *cognoscenti* and it is no coincidence that they were the ones for which Ray was allowed credit.

The complex moulding of the plywood child's chair of 1945 was a triumph of modern machine mass production and was hailed as such [Figure 35]. However, such was the fear of anything to

Figure 35. Moulded plywood chairs for children, 1945. Eames Office. View of exhibition, 'Connections: The Work of Charles and Ray Eames', at the Sainsbury Centre, Norwich, 1978. Photo © Pat Kirkham. Reprinted with permission.

do with hand crafts or folk work in products which graced the interiors of the brave new world of 'functionalism' and machine aesthetics, that the cut-out heart motif that humanized the object while serving as a hand-hole was attacked as sentimental and 'absurdly romantic' by Arthur Drexler, the influential US design critic.[18] Although little has been written about the chair, some people considered that the cut-out heart was the result of Ray's interference in the otherwise rational and problem-solving design process with which Charles Eames and the Eames Office are associated. Ray insisted that the chair should be a joint attribution and in the 1980s recalled that Charles had been every bit as keen as she on the heart and also on producing furniture and toys for children.[19]

Today the heart is generally viewed as one of several interesting features of the chair and it is tempting for a feminist historian to play on the gender bias implicit in 'blaming' Ray, to claim it for her. She was certainly skilled in visually representing the human aspects of life. But the situation is more complicated. Their work was intensely collaborative and Charles as well as Ray knew an earlier graphic use of the cut-out heart by their friend, graphic designer Alvin Lustig.[20] It simply is not known whether it was Charles or Ray who first had the visual audacity to suggest its use on a piece of furniture. When asked Ray would always say that, like all their work, it was such a close collaboration that it was impossible to say that either one had suggested or designed any particular aspect. If it was the idea of Ray, it was certainly adopted with Charles's wholehearted backing. He was described by certain former employees as something of a 'control freak', focused to the point of selfishness in his determination to get what he wanted,[21] suggesting that he would never have allowed a design of which he did not approve to go out from the office which bore his name. They worked very closely together on each project, particularly in the early days but most of the time thereafter too, and it seems highly unlikely that they were not both extremely

committed to the design which referenced the world of the hand-crafted object and was one of their first mass-production pieces. Therefore, tempting as it is to suggest that Ray was solely responsible for this wonderfully cross-referential humanizing of a chair to be used by children by means of a well-known folk/craft motif, the closeness with which she and Charles worked and Charles's determination to have things done exactly as he wanted them do not allow this.

The walnut stool of 1960 (more properly 'stools' because four versions were originally made and three continue to be so) provides another example of a contemporary machine-made product with strong craft references [Figure 36]. It also provides a clearer case of bias against Ray and craft work on the part of critics and curators. Once again, many Modernists who knew of Charles Eames as an industrial designer of furniture and as a champion of new technologies and materials found themselves unable to accept that he would have produced an item with so many craft connotations. Ray was always upset when this piece was attributed solely to her, as was the case at the Museum of Modern Art, New York for many years and even now is the case in the Eames exhibition currently touring Europe.[22] She was happy to state that it was her idea to base the multifunctional piece which they were in the process of designing for the lobby of the *Time-Life* building, New York on an African stool which in their own home doubled as coffee table and plant stand. But she pointed out that there were many other aspects to the complex process of designing and developing that particular stool and considered that allocating to her sole 'authorship' of the piece made a nonsense of their practice, detracted from Charles's input to the design and denied the joint nature of the rest of their work.[23]

In the light of earlier remarks about the intense Modernism of Ray's approach and practice and craft processes, it does not seem unreasonable to suggest that there was some gender bias at work in an attribution to Ray of these 'pro-crafts' pieces. It was, and is, a common assumption that crafts were

Figure 36. Time-Life chair and walnut stool, 1960. Eames Office. Photo by West Dempster, 1965. © Herman Miller, Inc. Reprinted with permission.

more properly the work of women – and certainly not the business of a man who, in 1960, was regarded as *the* most prominent industrial designer in the world. The machine-turned solid walnut stool appears to have been regarded as more of a craft product than the leather and aluminium machine-made chair which was designed at the same time to go in the same lobby. This suggests a pro-Modernist bias against wood and in favour of the more obviously 'modern' aluminium which was produced by a new casting technique. Leather was by no means a modern material but the combination of black leather and metal was read as more 'modern' than figured walnut. As it was, the smooth finishes, symmetry and geometric forms of the stool could have been praised as fitting a

machine aesthetic and the fact that the tops and bottoms were identical, with only the middle sections differing, read as indicating the machine origins of this modular piece. But this recognition did not take place.[24] A final irony is that Ray spent a great deal of time working on the development of the leather and metal chair, which the Museum of Modern Art and other institutions for many years attributed to Charles alone (together with much other joint work), while only crediting her with the stool.

[…]

The Eameses did not have all the answers to humanizing design in industrializing, industrialized and 'post-industrial' worlds, far from it, but, at a period when it seemed as if science and technology held the key to those answers (a point of view held by the Eameses), their own work validated the pre-industrial, personal and the hand-made as well as the industrial, the uniform and the mass-produced. They stressed the importance of quality of manufacture, whether by hand or machine, and of joy in labour as well as the pleasures to be obtained from objects.

I hope that this article has given some insights into the ways in which their concerns for crafts and the values they thought crafts represented interrelated with their concerns as designers, educators and as communicators. A full and deep appreciation of the crafts informed the hearts, minds and eyes of these notable designers of mid-century America and it is clear that the crafts continued to have a considerable role in the post-war period of Modernist hegemony. Despite their histories, briefly recounted above, Charles, who was steeped in Arts and Crafts attitudes, was always regarded as a Modernist even though many aspects of his joint work with Ray, particularly their reconstituting in forms appropriate to Modernist interiors, decorative traditions related to modes of collecting and decorative display of the nineteenth century and earlier. That work was seen by some as 'spoiling' the purism of Modernist interiors because it added alien elements and adopted an aesthetic of addition and sometimes excess. Through an exciting cross-fertilization between a machine aesthetic and the world of small objects, it offered interesting ways of personalizing the industrially built environment and of fusing aspects of craft and machine manufacture with elements of the natural world, and remains relevant today.

NOTES

Extracted from Kirkham, P., 'Humanizing Modernism: the Crafts, "Functioning Decoration" and the Eameses', *The Journal of Design History* 11(1) (1998), pp. 15–29. Reprinted by permission of the Design History Society.

1. Pat Kirkham, *Charles and Ray Eames: Designers of the Twentieth Century*, MIT Press, 1995, p. 167.
2. Ibid., pp. 4–5.
3. Ibid., pp. 166–7.
4. Ibid., pp. 166 and 399–400.
5. Ibid., p. 8.
6. Ibid., p. 78.
7. Ibid., p. 179.
8. Ibid., pp. 6, 55, 147, 171 and 175. For the film *Bread*, see p. 144.
9. Ibid., p. 12.
10. Ibid., p. 56.
11. Ibid., pp. 16–18.
12. Joseph Giovannini, 'The Office of Charles Eames and Ray Kaiser: the material trail', in Donald Albrecht (ed.), *The Work of Charles and Ray Eames: A Legacy of Invention*, New York, 1997, p. 52.
13. Kirkham, pp. 31–44.
14. Ibid., p. 33.
15. Ibid., p. 47.
16. Ibid., pp. 38–41.
17. Giovannini, op. cit., is the first major article since the publication of my book on the Eameses to argue the importance of Ray, especially in the early years of the partnership.
18. Kirkham, pp. 216–18.
19. Ray Eames in conversation with Pat Kirkham, New York, 1987.
20. Kirkham, pp. 41–2.
21. See John Neuhart, Marilyn Neuhart, and Ray Eames, *Eames Design: The Work of the Office of Charles and Ray Eames*, New York, 1989, p. 8 and Kirkham, p. 423, note 50.
22. The stool is not currently (October 1997) on display in the Museum of Modern Art galleries. Contemporary production versions are on display in the Eames exhibition currently traveling in Europe (Vitra Design Museum, Weil-am-Rhein, Germany, until 4 January 1998, and at other venues thereafter. Contact Interpretive Programs Office, Library of Congress, Washington, DC, USA for further details). For the stool, see also Neuhart *et al.*, p. 249.
23. Kirkham, pp. 250–2.
24. Neuhart *et al.*, p. 249.

50

'IN LONDON'S MAZE': THE PLEASURES OF FASHIONABLE CONSUMPTION, FROM *THE HIDDEN CONSUMER*

Christopher Breward (1999)

THE PLAYGROUND OF CITY LIFE: CLOTHING AND THE CONVIVIALITY OF BACHELORDOM

Atkinson now comes in to put the finishing touches to his master for the morning promenade. He brings half a dozen cravats, and a whole trayful of scarf pins … Seton is to choose … puts a forefinger on a scarf of quiet grey; then again, laying it on a perfect pearl … retires to his dressing room, followed by his man. When he reappears, it is as the finished product of civilization. He is booted, hatted, gloved and generally carried out in all the details of a perfect scheme … His valet regards him with the pride of the stableman who has just drawn the cloth from the loins of a flawless horse. 'Cigarettes, Atkinson, I think. Put the cigars in the bag!' The cigarettes are in a tiny case of enameled gold, which bears an 'S' in inlaid diamond points on the lid … 'Which cane sir?' 'Let me see!' and he turns to a suspended rack at the door. There are as many canes as scarf pins. He hesitates between a trifle in snakewood, with a handle of tortoiseshell, and a slender growth of some other exotic timber, capped with clouded amber almost as pale as the pearl … Now we are out of doors, and skimming, in Seton's private hansom over the well watered roads … until we reach the flower shop in Piccadilly for the morning button hole … Our dandy looks at a whole parterre and points to one bloom, like the chess player who knows that he is pledged to the choice by touching the piece.[1]

Lynn Hapgood characterizes *No 5 John Street* as 'a world of surfaces in a text full of sensuous detail that exposes the deceitful nature of what the physical eye sees… the upper class in particular is portrayed as all surface since its concerns are with life as art, in a deliberate evasion of reality.'[2] Certainly the dressing rituals of Seton detailed above appear to conform to that commonly held notion of aristocratic dandyism as the denial of sordid realities through the deliberate manipulation of appearances, the construction of a protective and critical carapace of finely tuned sartorial exhibitionism. Yet beyond the caricaturing tendencies of the novel and the abstract definitions of dandyism, Seton's self-presentation can be seen also to link with real debates and concerns over the state of masculinity, the advances of consumerism and the problems of city life that informed an understanding of male behaviour and desire between c.1880 and 1914. In the pages of popular novels, tourist guides, journalistic accounts and advertising promotions both real and imaginary men like Seton were seen to epitomize a mood of assertive masculine acquisitiveness whose challenging potency has since been overlooked or misconstrued by historians of consumption and gender alike.

Cultural historian Richard Dellamora, in finding connections between these disruptive models and the sexual upheavals of the 1890s, conjectures the reasons for the dismissal of such characters and their significance in broader histories when he states that

> Heretofore, political historians, by which I mean male political historians, have been blind to the significance of homosexual scandal in the 1890s ... a less defensive approach by historians would acknowledge the crisis of masculinity at the time. And a less pure history, which permitted itself to be contaminated by literary scandal and gossip, would recognise how anxiety about gender roles inflects a wide range of interactions.[3]

Along with Elaine Showalter, Regenia Gagnier and others, Dellamora repositions the *fin de siècle* dandy at the centre of these interactions, in a manner which, while it illuminates the rhetorical intentions of a cosmopolitan minority, perhaps ignores the day-to-day commercial significance of his type. His rise and downfall is used portentously to reflect 'a loss of balance between the dual imperatives of leisure and work incumbent upon Victorian gentlemen. The dandy is too relaxed, too visible, consumes to excess while producing little or nothing.'[4] In the spectacular and very singular figure of Oscar Wilde, whose 1895 disgrace is generally quoted as precipitating the crisis over masculinity that informed twentieth-century attitudes towards manliness, the two models of dandy and gentlemen are seen to have become dangerously confused.[5] As Gagnier states, between the demise of his aesthetic mode in 1882 to the moment of his trial 'Wilde made the respectable sartorial choice of non-working class men: to appear as a gentleman ... in a manner which had been perfected by a dandy'.[6] In his mannered appropriation of the evening suit and other trappings of a leisured lifestyle, Wilde mocked the ideals of gentlemanliness with ultimately disastrous results. But, beyond that affront

to notions of bourgeois respectability, the dandy is held to signify very little else, perhaps because it is difficult to extrapolate broad cultural meanings from the posturings of one man, or because the close association of dandified forms of presentation and behaviour with the image projected by Wilde has succeeded in limiting their application elsewhere.

While acknowledging the unsettling effects that figures like Wilde had on the literary, legal and medical construction of sexualities, and agreeing with the necessity for revisiting the period of the 1890s as a key moment in the development of their 'modern' forms, I would argue here for a clearer recognition of the less spectacular circumstances which gave rise to an identifiable 'dandified' style as being rooted in a more popular, generalized celebration of leisured urban masculinity relatively untouched by high moral debate. The adoption of a visibly relaxed and 'non-productive' sartorial rhetoric was not in itself transgressive; only the context and manner in which it was mobilized made it so. In equating an embracing of idle display so closely with sexual dissonance, historians are in danger of obscuring or distorting similar choices made by men who identified with the status quo. Furthermore, one might claim that the metropolitan dandy drew on a thriving, self-consciously virile culture of cosmopolitan masculine consumption which had been in evidence since the 1860s at least, and which colonized wider forms of popular culture at precisely the moment that Wilde's version was acquiring its problematic sexual reputation, sending the established version into partial eclipse. The two strands of leisured display, one associated with political, sexual and social resistance, the other with a commercial engagement with the urban market place, require careful unraveling if the defining features of the latter are not to be subsumed by the polemics of the former.

The fictional figure of Seton, with his carefully judged appearance and assiduous collecting of fashionable possessions, is thus as much a reflection of what London's shops and catalogues offered the ambitious young man at the turn of the century as he is evidence of decline and decadence. His literary scopophilia may look to the obsessions of Dorian Gray in one direction, but in the other it finds a brighter resonance in the pages of Doré's illustrated price list of tailored goods. That the mannered presentation of self could simply represent an unproblematic adherence to the rules of 'smart' society in an expanded arena of consumer choices is clearly communicated in guides such as *London and Londoners*, published in 1898, where the author provided tongue-in-cheek guidance to the ways of modern society:

It is fashionable to be radical in theory and advocate women's privileges. To have an inner knowledge of all classes of society. To know the latest club scandals. To have some particular fad. To wear some particular garment different from anybody else … To telegraph always, but rarely write a letter, unless one has a secretary. To be up in the slang of the day … to know the points of a horse. To have an enormous dog in the drawing room … To know the latest music hall song … To go to Paris twice a year and at least once to Monte Carlo. Never to be in town after Goodwood or to return to it before November. To be abroad from January to March … To excel in one's special sport, fox hunting for preference, and to be able to drive a tandem. To subscribe to every journal published. To belong to a club and have some of one's letters and telegrams sent there. Always to fill one's rooms with more men than women.[7]

While such a list evidently reveled in the paradoxical nonsense of trivia, its pointed social observation map the co-ordinates of an accumulated cosmopolitan knowledge that defined the exalted status of the fashionable bachelor. In its random citation of desirable adherences it is possible to discern the more serious juxtapositions of high and low culture, reactionary posturing and avant-garde enthusiasms artistic affectation and hearty philistinism, that influenced a prevalent model of fashionable masculinity at the turn of the century. Here was a dandified position that comfortably accommodated sexual conformity, advanced tastes and commodity fetishism within its remit. Of particular significance are the references to music hall, slang, sport, new technology and travel. Beyond the expected mention of club life, gambling and hunting which would have denoted aristocratic excess in a list produced fifty years earlier, this engagement with the modernity of London, in company clearly defined as male, positioned the potential flâneur in the midst of a culture enthralled rather than repelled by the notion of masculine pleasures. More than this, the figure of the leisured London bachelor, targeted by the publishers of such guides, had himself come to symbolize a modern and fashionable position by the 1890s, as potent in commodity terms as the Gibson girl or the Dollar Princess. And, like his sisters, he was utilized by retailer and consumer as a prop upon which products and attitudes could be hung.

Aside from clothing, the elevation of certain forms of metropolitan recreations to the status of a bachelor 'specialism' had been a marked characteristic of popular writing from the mid nineteenth century. The 1860s were identified with the beginnings of a celebration of the romantic, irresponsible lifestyle associated with the cosmopolitan single man which reached its apex by 1900.[8] The twin poles of his existence, around which all other characteristics circulated and drew their influences, from political persuasion to visual appearance and interior decoration, were food and drink and the brash culture of the modern man's journal. Thus the apotheosis of the bon viveur was the man who spent his days either 'researching articles' for the popular press or reading them in the comfort of a West End restaurant or café, and his evenings at the theatre.

[…]

However, while the assertive models of masculine consumption offered by popular journals proclaimed a bullish adherence to the clean and flourishing style of the bachelor dandy, less accommodating descriptions of his appearance and behaviour on the streets and in the bars of the metropolis give some indication of the tensions implicit in the ideal. Confined to the tailoring catalogue or the society column the leisured bachelor epitomised the essence of West End fashionable poise, and offered a refreshingly positive reading of the sartorial options open to the aspirant 'man about town'. Yet so ubiquitous did his figure become from the 1880s onwards, through its reproduction in yellowback novels, advertising campaigns and stage productions, that more negative or less closed interpretations were inevitable [Figure 37]. For every clean-cut Englishman puffing the 'smart' attractions of the Arrow collar or Wood-Milne shoeshine there was a more derogatory model espousing the 'wicked' attractions of the East End or the quick fortune to be made from venture capitalism. Beyond the fixing of the bachelor type as a model for an unproblematic, if occasionally risqué, consumerism, his mediation and wider diffusion through urban culture was revealing of a more profound crisis in the nature of an English middle-class and aristocratic masculinity not entirely secure with the tenure of its hegemony.

The tendency at the turn of the century to equate certain forms of dandified appearance with an entrepreneurial crassness and betrayal of the gentlemanly ideal clearly held anti-semitic implications. Those novels which celebrated the freedom and decency of the bachelor existence were equally insistent on presenting a parody of the Jewish playboy to which the 'natural reserve' of an English sartorial style might be favourably compared. Duncan Schwann offered a formulaic caricature of the type when he recalled that his friend

> James Berners was wrapped in a fur coat, the impossible collar of which was formed of two seal skins, others giving each sleeve the appearance of muffs. On his head at an angle of forty five

degrees was set a Tyrolese hat, with a cloakroom ticket stuck in the band … He carried an ivory topped cane in his hand, a cauliflower, or was it a tomato? In his buttonhole, and a cigar, in an amber holder stuck out from the middle of his pale face … he looked like a son of a Shylock and the Queen of Sheba, dressed as a combination of stage lobster and a millionaire from the far west, with his crimson waistcoat, check suit, and the precious stones he scattered over his tie and fingers.[9]

Similarly Montague William QC was unable to resist describing the wardrobes of 'Mr Herbert Maurice – Plutocrat and son of a Jewish trader and his son Gerald' in his reminiscences on life as a London judge. Of Herbert Maurice's riding habit he noted that 'though his get up in the saddle is of the most sporting description and similar to that of all the fashionable young men of the day, there is always something outré about it'. And true to form

> On arriving at man's estate Gerald became a member of one or two second rate clubs. He smokes an enormous number of cigarettes and passes a great portion of his time at the billiard table … He wears collars that reach half way up his cheek … and trousers that cling so closely to his thin legs as to suggest difficulties in the way of getting them off … a remark he is very fond of making at the Rockingham Club is 'Hang it all, I think I ought to know a gentleman when I see one'.[10]

Further inversions of fashionable masculinity might be found in the figure of the bohemian artist, whose lack of meaningful employment and laboured manipulation of appearances set him up as a potential rival to the bachelor in the role of London flâneur.[11] Schwann dismissed him as a 'blighter who never washed, ate with his fingers and let his hair grow as long as Samson's … they slouch about Soho with seedy squash hats and seedier fur overcoats which they pinched from the

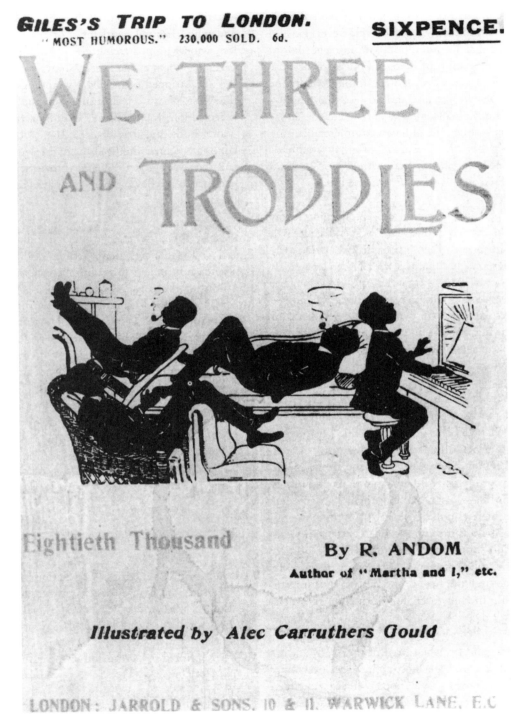

Figure 37. *We Three Troddles*, 6d novel cover, 1902. 'The figure of the bachelor presented a problematic icon which encapsulated modern attitudes to metropolitan life' in Christopher Breward, *The Hidden Consumer: Masculinities, Fashion and City Life 1860–1914*, Manchester: Manchester University Press, 1999, p. 182.

last doss house they slept in, looking like a mixture of Svengali and a rag picker'. However, he also admitted that 'a contemporary of mine at Oxford got the reputation of being a bohemian because he usually sat in a dress gown, drank Benedictine after hall, read Verlaine and possessed an engraving of the Blessed Damozel'.[12] The contradictory tensions between the pull of a commercial culture and an adherence to 'artistic' originality embodied in the bohemian also concerned the West End hatter Fred Willis, who remembered that

> The genuine bohemian was an engaging fellow but his name was one that a west end tradesman did his best to keep out of his debt book. The type took great pains with the carelessness of their dress. At this time the Austrian velour hat was making a tentative appearance … and the bohemian took to it with avidity… Worn with a flowing bow tie and a corduroy coat it gave the wearer unquestioned right of entry into the Café Royal or Rule's.[13]

More threatening still to the mannered perfection of the bachelor model were not those who set his characteristics in sharper relief, or offered alternative, sexually or socially disruptive modes of dressing and behaviour, but the limits of his own make-up and milieu, and the possibilities inherent in a wider urban culture of transgressing the commercial boundaries set up to describe his own position as the commodified embodiment of West End sophistication. Thomas Burke alluded to the risk-filled attractions of moving beyond the manufactured bonhomie and petty restrictions of Piccadilly in the search for 'authentic' pleasures when he advised that:

> It is a good tip when tired of the West, and as the phrase goes, at a loose end, to go East, young man, go East. You will spot a winner every time, if it is entertainment you seek, by mounting the first East bound omnibus that passes. For the East is eternally fresh, because it is alive. The West, like all things of fashion, is but a corpse

electrified. They are so tired these lily clad ladies and white fronted gentlemen, of their bloodless, wine whipped frivolities … Night, in the particular spots of the East… shows you life in the raw, stripped of its silken wrappings … In the West, pleasure is a business; in the East it is recreation. In the East it may be a thinner, poorer body, but it is alive … There when the lamps are lighted and bead the night with tears, and the sweet girls go by and throw their little laughter to the boys – there you have your true Bacchanale.[14]

Despite the close association of the bachelor figure with the new energies of a fashionable consumer culture, and his symbolic role as a justification for the consumption practices of men, his relentlessly cheerful and dapper persona still drew familiar moral accusations of inauthenticity, of hollow obsessions too closely tied to the feminised and enervating concerns of the West End and its emporia. Regardless of its status as a figment of the fevered imagination of the hack writer, the mythical East End offered the promise of masculine pleasure in concentrated virile form, free from the taint of business or the shop, and an arena in which bachelor identities met more dangerous connotations and ultimate resistance or mediation.

NOTES

Extracted from Chapter 5, '"In London's Maze": The Pleasures of Fashionable Consumption', in Breward, C., *The Hidden Consumer: Masculinities, Fashion and City Life 1860–1914*, Manchester: Manchester University Press, 1999, pp.170–3, 181–4. Reprinted by permission of the author and Manchester University Press.

1. R. Whiteing, *No 5 John Street* (London: Grant Richards, 1899), pp. 182–3.
2. L. Hapgood, 'Regaining a Focus: New Perspectives on the Novels of Richard Whiteing' in

N. Le Manos and M. J. Rochelson (eds), *Transforming Genres: New Approaches to British Fiction of the 1890s* (London, Macmillan and New York: Pantheon Books, 1994), p. 185.

3. R. Dellamora, 'Homosexual Scandal and Compulsory Heterosexuality in the 1890s' in L. Pykett (ed.), *Reading Fin de Siècle Fictions* (London: Longman, 1996), p. 82.

4. Ibid., p. 86.

5. A. Sinfield, *The Wilde Century: Effeminacy, Oscar Wilde and the Queer Moment* (London: Cassell, 1994); E. Cohen, *Talk on the Wilde Side* (London: Routledge, 1993); E. Showalter, *Sexual Anarchy: Gender and Culture at the Fin-de-Siècle* (London: Virago, 1992).

6. R. Gagnier, *Idylls of the Marketplace: Oscar Wilde and the Victorian Public* (Aldershot: Scolar Press, 1986), p. 67.

7. R. Pritchard (ed.), *London and Londoners: What to See; What to Do; Where to Shop and Practical Hints* (London: Scientific Press, 1898), pp. 323–4.

8. D. Shaw, *London in the Sixties by One of the Old Brigade* (London: Heinemann, 1910).

9. D. Schwann, *The Book of a Bachelor* (London: Heinemann, 1910), p. 91–2.

10. M. Williams, *Round London* (London: Macmillan & Co., 1896), pp. 118–19.

11. C. Cruise, 'Artists' Clothes: Some Observations on Male Artists and Their Clothes in the Nineteenth Century' in P. Kirkham (ed.), *The Gendered Object* (Manchester: Manchester University Press, 1996), pp. 112–21.

12. Schwann, *Bachelor*, pp. 31–4.

13. F. Willis, *101 Jubilee Road: A Book of London Yesterdays* (London: Phoenix House, 1948), p. 33.

14. T. Burke, *Nights in Town: A London Autobiography* (London: Allen & Unwin, 1915), p. 397.

51

SELF-MADE MOTORMEN: THE MATERIAL CONSTRUCTION OF WORKING-CLASS MASCULINE IDENTITIES THROUGH CAR MODIFICATION

Andrew Bengry-Howell and Christine Griffin (2007)

INTRODUCTION

This paper examines the cultural significance of the motorcar to young men who modify their cars and explores how the active process of *doing* car modification operates in the construction and maintenance of masculine identities. It draws on a study of 30 young white working-class car modifiers from the East and West Midlands and North Wales, who owned modified cars and were all associated with the British cruising scene. As a collective cultural practice, the cruising scene developed out of unauthorized gatherings of young people in modified cars, called cruises, that started occurring on car parks in retail parks and industrial estates late at night during the 1990s.[1] These gatherings provided a forum for young modified-car enthusiasts to meet and socialize, and for modified car owners to exhibit their symbolically and mechanically enhanced vehicles and engage in performative motorcar displays before an appreciative audience.[2]

[...]

THE SOCIAL AND CULTURAL MEANING OF THE CAR

Throughout its history the motorcar has been a highly gendered commodity, with a strong discursive association with men and masculinity.[3] Although a small number of women purchased and drove motorcars from the earliest days of their manufacture,[4] the cultural meaning of the motorcar has been historically constituted in terms of a symbolically powerful and normalized relationship between masculinity and technology.[5] Although this changed somewhat in the 1950s with the arrival of the family car, which was marketed for mixed use by the whole family,[6] the symbolic power of men was reproduced through the seating grid, in which the husband/father was positioned as the driver, with his wife sat by his side as a passenger and their children sat behind them in a row in the back.[7]

Since the 1960s, shifting gender relations have seen a dramatic increase in the number of female car owners and female drivers; by the end of the twentieth century 42 per cent of new cars sold in Britain were being bought by women,[8] and female drivers are projected to outnumber male drivers during the early part of the twenty-first century.[9] This has corresponded with motorcars becoming increasingly gendered, with certain makes and models specifically marketed at women, whilst others are marketed at men.[10] For women, the motorcar is constituted as a safe means of independent transportation[11] that is associated with fun, freedom and individualism.[12] For men, the motorcar continues to be constituted as a symbol of status and masculine power.[13]

YOUTH AND MOTORCARS

Since the 1950s the motorcar has been central to the cultural identities of many teenagers in western industrialised societies, where it has represented a means of escaping parental control[14] and realising personal freedom.[15] For young people who could afford it, acquiring a motorcar heralds the arrival of an important stage of transition, from dependency on public transport and private transport controlled by parents to individual car-based autonomy and independent automobility.[16] For young men, motorcar ownership holds particular cultural resonance in that it reproduces a traditional association between masculinity and technology[17] and marks a cultural rite of passage into manhood.

[...]

As a researcher, ABH [Andrew Bengry-Howell] had been interested in the cruising scene for a number of years, although prior to this particular study his knowledge in this area had been largely gleaned from cruising web sites and articles in car magazines. He had never mixed with car modifiers on a regular basis nor attended cruises, and was surprised when he first arranged to meet a small group of car modifiers to find that, with the exception of one girlfriend, the group entirely consisted of men. As he made contact with other car modifiers it became apparent that most were male, and although he did encounter a small number of women at meets and cruises he attended in the course of the study, they were almost always girlfriends of young men who owned modified cars rather than owners of modified cars themselves. As such we have constituted car modifying and cruising as predominantly masculine practices and our analysis foregrounds the significance of the motorcar to the identity work of young men.

[...]

For our participants, car modification was an inherently practical activity, which was realised through the material process of changing aspects of a motor vehicle's original design.[18] Although our research participants generally enjoyed talking about their cars and the modifications that they had made, most ascribed greater significance to the practice of doing car modifications. The significance of car modifying was constituted in terms of the physical labour invested in practices like lowering a car's suspension, fitting oversized alloy wheels, replacing a car's original panels with those from a body kit, tinting windows, enhancing an exhaust system to produce a desired sound and improve performance, and a whole range of alterations that serve to personalise a car and make it truly theirs. The process of car modification was one in which our participants deliberately attempted to extricate their cars from 'the style boundaries imposed by the manufacturer's production design'[19] and culturally produce a car to individual specifications.

[...]

To some degree the car modifiers in this study engaged in similar practices to standard car owners (i.e., they washed and polished their cars regularly, maintained and serviced them, and were careful to secure their vehicles when they were left unattended). Whereas such practices generally embody an owner's attempts to preserve a vehicle in its original condition, car modifying precipitated a very different relationship between owner and commodity. The practice of modifying a car generated a much more fixed and intimate form of ownership wherein motorcars were produced as commodities that were symbolically and uniquely associated with those who owned and modified them.[20] Car modification transformed the act of consumption into a set of practices[21] through which car modifiers produced their cars as symbolic extensions of themselves.[22]

[...]

The importance that was placed on an owner modifying their car themselves can be understood as a reflection of traditional working-class values. The sense of 'achievement' cultivated through being able to 'say' that 'you're actually building the car', and others' appreciation of the products of your labour, resonated with a working-class masculine tradition in which physical work was a source of pride[23] and personal achievement was measured in terms of doing a good job. Traditionally, working-class pride has been located within work-based settings, where it was realised through occupational roles like craftsman and other skilled workers.[24] For car modifiers, however, a sense of 'pride' and 'achievement' in manual work and its output was aligned with practices that assumed meaning though leisure and consumption within non-work-based contexts of everyday life.[25]

[…]

'IT WAS A BIT OF A CHICK CAR': TRANSGENDERED CARS AND THE PRACTICE OF 'DEBADGING'

ABH: I think it's interesting that when you chose a car you picked the Mondeo as it's not a car that is usually associated with young people

Jane: I think that people who modify cars don't really go by the adverts. If you look Novas and Corsas are advertised like a woman's car, but there are so many people that have modified them now

ABH: Presumably the things that people do to them change their meaning so that they are no longer a woman's car?

Spoiler: Make them more aggressive and all that.

ABH: So what made you want to start modifying it, was it something that you wanted to do as soon as you got the car?

Dale: I didn't think about making it a project really (right) but then (2) I had it I come to the point my sister's had about three cars (1) and she's twenty one now (right) and like my dad helped me out buying this (1) and it came to the point and I was thinking about getting rid of it (right) (1) and I said well (1) if we can make it better and we go halves on whatever I do to it then I'll keep it for (1) till it stops basically

ABH: Why did you want to get rid of it?

Dale: Don't know cos (2) it's only a 1.3 (right) cos it's a Fiesta (right) and I had some comments that it was a bit of a chick car (right) one of my ex girlfriends (1) her friends said that's a chick car that is

ABH: It's a what car?

Dale: Chick car (right) (1) a girl's car.*

The modified Novas, Corsas and Fiestas that most of our participants owned were cars that in their standard form manufacturers have primarily targeted at a female market, or at families where they have been marketed as a second car. It was within this context that the other main reason for debadging a car carried significance, as it marked the beginning of a transgendering process in which standard production-line cars that were culturally associated with women were reconfigured as cars that were associated with men. Dale explicitly constituted his incentive to modify his car in terms of a resolution to a problem that had arisen for him when a friend of his girlfriend had publicly identified his Ford Fiesta as a 'chick car'. The label 'chick car' positioned Dale as the owner of a type of car that was symbolically associated with women, and thus served to discursively undermine the cultural legitimacy of his masculinity. In response, Dale had attempted to reconcile the incongruity of being a man in possession of a woman's car by removing all the insignia from his car that identified it as being a Fiesta, and modifying the overall shape of the car with a body kit that he had seen advertised in Max Power. The symbolic work that Dale invested in modifying the physical appearance of his car amounted to a deliberate attempt to de-feminise his standard car and culturally produce it in a form more befitting for a man. This symbolic process of masculinising a car through modification was one that, for Spoiler, was represented as making a car 'more aggressive', which in Dale's case was contingent on him degendering the existing meaning of his car and deconstructing its 'chick car' status.

[...]

Within this context, the significance of practices like debadging go beyond symbolic concealment, to mark the commencement of a transformative process in which a car modifier deliberately deconstructs the material signs that define and differentiate his standard car within dominant discourse and attempts to relocate it in a non-branded symbolic world or reinvent it as their own brand. Although this play with brands and radical transformation of a common cultural commodity challenges dominant discourses of consumption, the fervent desire of car modifiers to have a unique car leads them to purchase increasingly expensive equipment and accessories, and thus serves to reinforce dominant consumption practices. As such, car modifiers' consumption practices are both conventional and unconventional, and their consumption of the motorcar serves to position them as both active consumers and producers of cultural commodities.

Studies on young people's consumption of clothes have identified the important role that brands play in identity work, with brands that carry kudos being actively sought out and those that are deemed less worthy actively avoided.[26] Within the context of current understandings of how brand associations and brand loyalties influence young people's consumption practices, young car modifiers' consumption of branded motorcars is particularly interesting. Young people's consumption practices are often said to be influenced by the symbolic, rather than intrinsic, qualities of commodities and their relative meaning within the context of their peers.[27] In the case of our participants' consumption of standard

motorcars, a range of external factors restricted them to types of motorcar that are marketed at and discursively associated with women, which carried negative associations among their peer group since they were classed as 'chick' cars.

It runs somewhat contrary to prevailing understandings of young people's consumption to suggest that young car modifiers would actively select a commodity that they and their peers viewed in negative terms, and it was within this context that debadging a car was a particularly important practice. Debadging a car served to deconstruct a car's standard feminine identity and symbolically distance it from gendered meanings that were undesirable, and to constitute it as a 'blank canvas' that could then be inscribed with idiosyncratic meanings and desired masculine cultural associations. This degendering practice embodied a symbolic attempt at resolving the contradiction of being a man in possession of a woman's car, and configuring a standard feminised motorcar as an object of masculine identity construction. Masculine identities constructed through modified cars were produced and reproduced as gendered 'configurations of practice', in which meaning was socially defined in relation to and contradistinction from models of femininity.[28]

The cultural production of meaning through car modification is an intensely creative process through which young white working-class male car modifiers discursively mark themselves out from the mass of standard-car owning subjects and materially constitute themselves as 'unique' car owning individuals. Car modification is an inherently physical practice that is creatively constituted in the 'hand-made space'[29] where the human body, tools and material objects engage. This 'space' holds particular historic significance for working-class men, whose pride and achievements have been traditionally organised around the skilful manipulation of tools, and the 'machinic pleasure',[30] sensual delight and powerful emotions derived from embodying technologies.[31] Economic change has displaced men's 'machinic pleasure' and the craft ideal from its traditional occupational setting into free time,[32] and car modification projects provide an important leisure-based opportunity for young working-class men to reconnect with a set of associations and values that have traditionally defined working-class men's lives.[33] Although most of our research participants were in paid work, they attributed relatively little importance to their occupations. Paid work was constituted as necessary in order to finance the car modification projects they undertook in their leisure time, which were the principal site of their identity construction.

The consumption-based opportunities that car modification projects offered for identity construction were predicated on young men being financially supported by their parents, and thus able to afford to invest a high percentage of their modest incomes on modifying their cars. In a British social context where protracted youth transitions[34] are said to constrain young people's opportunities for independent living by making them financially dependent on their parents,[35] the young men in our study utilised a situation that is often presented as problematic in order to construct masculine identities grounded in their consumption practices. During their protracted transition to adulthood they had relatively few financial responsibilities that might restrict their consumption. Since they were financially dependent on their parents, these young working-class men were 'free' to constitute themselves as independent, unique and individual consumers through the material construction of modified cars.

Studies of young working-class men often represent them as victims of the socioeconomic changes that have transformed Britain over the past 20 years.[36] Faced with the erosion of many occupations that were traditionally associated with working-class men, young working-class masculinity has been said to be in crisis.[37] It would be tempting within this context to constitute car modification in terms of a compensatory practice and represent our participants as socially disadvantaged on the basis of their age, social class, modest academic achievements, occupational status, limited financial resources and the localities that they reside in, or as subordinate to hegemonic masculinities.[38] This, however, would be imposing an interpretation of the meaning of car modifying for our research participants that was not supported by our data.

Whilst it could be argued that car modification is in some way compensatory, this notion along with the idea that car modifiers were in anyway disadvantaged was completely absent from our research participants' talk. On the contrary, most positioned themselves as culturally privileged on the basis of their ownership of, and ability to produce, highly conspicuous motorcars, to which they and others ascribed cultural value. Within the context of their peers and significant others who appreciated the aesthetics of a modified car, the products of a car modifier's symbolic labour were a source of considerable cultural capital.[39] Car modification enabled the participants in our study to differentiate themselves from consumers of standard cars, however prestigious, and those for whom motorcars primarily functioned as a means of transport, who were disparagingly referred to as 'A to B drivers'. Modified cars were performatively displayed as the ultimate conspicuous commodity, which embodied and culturally celebrated the practical skills and personal achievements of the individuals who had physically and symbolically laboured to produce them.

NOTES

Extracted from Bengry-Howell, A. and Griffin, C., 'Self-Made Motormen: The Material Construction of Working-Class Masculine Identities through Car Modification', *Journal of Youth Studies* 10(4) (2007), pp. 439–58. Reprinted by permission of Taylor & Francis Ltd.

Editors' Note: Parenthetical Notations in the interview refer to the length of the pause in seconds and the direction of the speaker's face.

1. Mills, M. (2000) 'All the people I know, drive like idiots', *The Guardian*, 28 April, pp. 4–5; Bengry-Howell, A. (2001) *Bigging it Up: Young Masculinities and the Symbolic Appropriation of the Car*, Unpublished MPhil Thesis, University of Birmingham, UK.

2. Ibid.

3. Flink, J. (1988) *The Automobile Age*, MIT Press, London.

4. Scharff, V. (1991) *Taking the Wheel: Women and the Coming of the Motor Age*, Free Press, New York.

5. Wajcman, J. (1991) *Feminism Confronts Technology*, Polity, Cambridge; Mellström, U. (2004) 'Machines and masculine subjectivity: technology as an integral part of men's life experiences', special issue: Masculinities and Technology, *Men and Masculinities*, vol. 6, no. 4, pp. 368–382.

6. Wernick, A. (1991) *Promotional Culture*, Sage, London, p. 72.

7. Ibid.

8. Coward, R. (1999) 'Into the driving seat', *The Guardian*, 16 November, [Online] Available at: http://www.guardian.co.uk/Columnists/Column/0,,247913,00.html (2 August 2007).

9. Silverton, P. (1999) 'Allo, Jane, gotta new motor?', *Red*, December, pp. 113–116.

10. Coward, R. (1999) 'Into the driving seat'; Silverton, P. (1999) 'Allo, Jane, gotta new motor?'

11. Hubak, M. (1996) 'The car as a cultural statement: car advertising as gendered socio-technical scripts', in *Making Technology Our Own? Domesticating Technology into Everyday Life*, eds M. Lie & K. Sorensen, Scandinavian University Press, Oslo, pp. 171–200.

12. Silverton, P. (1999) 'Allo, Jane, gotta new motor?'

13. Wajcman, J. (1991) *Feminism Confronts Technology*.

14. Pickett, C. (1998) 'Car fetish', in *Cars and Culture: Our Driving Passions*, ed. C. Pickett, Powerhouse Publishing and HarperCollins, Sydney, p. 27.

15. Bayley, S. (1986) *Sex, Drink and Fast Cars: The Creation and Consumption of Images*, Faber & Faber, London and Boston, MA.

16. Carrabine, E. & Longhurst, B. (2002) 'Consuming the car: anticipation, use and meaning in contemporary youth culture', *The Sociological Review*, vol. 50, no. 2, pp. 181–196.

17. Wajcman, J. (1991) *Feminism Confronts Technology*.

18. Bengry-Howell, A. (2005) *Performative Motorcar Display: The Cultural Construction of Young Working Class Masculine Identities*, Unpublished PhD Thesis, University of Birmingham, UK.

19. Brownlie, D., Hewer, P. & Treanor, S. (2005) 'Identity in motion: an exploratory study of conspicuous consumption among car cruisers', *Finanza Marketing e Produzione*, vol. 23, no. 3, pp. 99–107.

20. Bengry-Howell, A. (2005) *Performative Motorcar Display: The Cultural Construction of Young Working Class Masculine Identities*.

21. Willis, P., Jones, S., Canaan, J. & Hurd, G. (1990) *Common Culture: Symbolic Work at Play in the Everyday Cultures of the Young*, Open University Press, Milton Keynes.

22. Belk, R. W. (1988) 'Possessions and the extended self', *Journal of Consumer Research*, vol. 15, pp. 139–168.

23. Willis, P. (1977) *Learning to Labour*, Saxon House, Farnborough.

24. Ibid.

25. Bengry-Howell, A. (2005) *Performative Motorcar Display: The Cultural Construction of Young Working Class Masculine Identities*.

26. Miles, S., Cliff, D. & Burr, V. (1998) '"Fitting in and sticking out": consumption, consumer meanings and the construction of young people's identities', *Journal of Youth Studies*, vol. 1, no. 1, pp. 81–96; Frosh, S., Phoenix, A. & Pattman, R. (2002) *Young Masculinities: Understanding Boys in Contemporary Society*, Palgrave, London.

27. Miles et al. (1998) '"Fitting in and sticking out": consumption, consumer meanings and the construction of young people's identities'.

28. Connell, R. (2005) 'Hegemonic masculinity: rethinking the concept', *Gender & Society*, vol. 9, no. 6, pp. 829–859. See p. 848.

29. Law, J. (2001) *Machinic Pleasures and Interpellations*, Centre for Science Studies, Lancaster University, [Online] Available at: http://www.lancs.ac.uk/fss/sociology/papers/Law-Machinic-Pleasures-and-Interpellations.pdf (2 August 2007).

30. Ibid.

31. Mellström, U. (2004) 'Machines and masculine subjectivity: technology as an integral part of men's life experiences'.

32. Moorhouse, H. F. (1988) 'American automobiles and worker's dreams', *Sociological Review*, vol. 31, pp. 403–426. See p. 421.

33. Willis, P. (1977) *Learning to Labour*.

34. Furlong, A., Cartmel, F., Biggart, A., Sweeting, H. & West, P. (2003) *Youth Transitions: Patterns of Vulnerability and Processes of Social Inclusion*, Central Research Unit, Scottish Executive, Edinburgh.

35. France, A. & Wiles, P. (1997) 'Dangerous futures: social exclusion and youth work in late modernity', *Social Policy & Administration*, vol. 31, no. 3, pp. 59–78.

36. McDowell, L. (2003) *Redundant Masculinities? Employment Change and White Working Class Youth*, Blackwell Publishing, Oxford.

37. Horrocks, R. (1996) *Masculinity in Crisis*, Macmillan, London.

38. Connell, R. (1995) *Masculinities*, Polity Press, Cambridge.

39. Bourdieu, P. (1979) *Distinction: A Social Critique of the Judgement of Taste*, Routledge & Kegan Paul, London.

GUIDE TO FURTHER READING

Following *A View From the Interior: Feminism, Women and Design* (1989), attention to constructions of gender in design grew considerably. This current was reflected in a series of exhibitions on women designers held in the early 1990s: *Goddess in the Details: Product Design by Women* (Pratt Institute, 1994) examined works by Florence Knoll and Eva Zeisel; *International Women in Design* (Supon Design Group, 1993) looked at women graphic designers, such as April Greiman, Sheila Levrant de Bretteville and Rosemarie Tissi; *Women Designing: Redefining Design in Britain Between the Wars* (University of Brighton, 1994) included contributions by Hazel Clark, Cheryl Buckley and Jonathan Woodham. *Women Designing*, in particular, offered a more nuanced approach than that of Isabelle Anscombe's *A Woman's Touch: Women in Design from 1860 to the Present Day* (1984), which has been criticized, despite its important preliminary research in bringing to light the work of women who have historically been overshadowed by their male counterparts. Indeed the 'women designers' approach has also led to insightful examinations of the institutional structures that shape design, as in Martha Scotford, *Cipe Pineles: A Life of Design* (1999), and in excavations of the gender imbalance in design partnerships by Pat Kirkham, *Charles and Ray Eames: Designers of the Twentieth Century* (1998), and Rebecca Houze, 'From Wiener Kunst im Hause to the Wiener Werkstätte' (2002).

While many design historians interested in gender have focused on the producers of things, some have tried to understand the things themselves. In addition to the articles in *The Gendered Object*, edited by Pat Kirkham (1996), on topics ranging from Barbie dolls to bicycles and neck ties, examples of object-based approaches include, Rozsika Parker, *The Subversive Stitch: Embroidery and the Making of the Feminine* (1984), and Sigrid Wortmann Weltge, *Bauhaus Textiles: Women Artists and the Weaving Workshop* (1993). Research into spaces and objects that have been traditionally associated with women in recent history, such as cosmetics and the fashion show, has led frequently to particularly creative scholarship. See, for example, Melissa Hyde, 'The "Make-Up" of the Marquise: Boucher's Portrait of Pompadour at Her Toilette', (2000), and Nancy Troy, *Couture Culture: A Study in Modern Art and Fashion* (2002).

Phillipa Goodall's essay 'Design and Gender' (1983), first published in *BLOCK*, calls into question the politics of the 'home' in which women's traditionally unpaid domestic labour was gradually appropriated by the masculine world of manufacture and commerce as a result of industrialization in the eighteenth and nineteenth centuries. Drawing upon sources such as Caroline Davidson's *A Woman's Work is Never Done: A History of Housework in the British Isles 1650–1950* (1982), Goodall demonstrates that designed objects in the home, especially those associated with the kitchen and laundry, or with the eroticized space of the bathroom, as well as publications like the 1947–8 *Daily Mail Ideal Homes Book*, encoded the institutional practices of production and consumption. The subject of housework, first addressed by Christine Frederick and Margarete Schütte-Lihotzky in the early twentieth century (see section 3 of the *Reader*) was later taken up by Dolores Hayden, *The Grand Domestic Revolution:*

A History of Feminist Designs for American Homes, Neighborhoods, and Cities (1981). Ella Howard provides a useful overview of this literature in 'Feminist Writings on Twentieth-Century Design History, 1970–1995: Furniture, Interiors, Fashion' (2000–1), published in a special issue of *Studies in the Decorative Arts* on Women in Design, edited by Pat Kirkham, which coincided with the exhibition 'Women Designers in the USA 1900–2000: Diversity and Difference' (2000–1).

Sheila Levrant de Bretteville published one of the earliest feminist readings of graphic design, entitled 'Some Aspects of Design From the Perspective of a Woman Designer' (1973). See also her contribution 'Feminist Design: At the Intersection of the Private and Public Spheres', in Richard Langdon and Nigel Cross (eds) *Design and Society* (1984). Feminist readings of interior spaces and dress have also opened the door to more complex examinations of gender. Shaun Cole elaborates on Breward's investigation of masculinity, by looking more closely at homosexuality, class and dress in his book *'Don We Now Our Gay Apparel': Gay Men's Dress in the Twentieth Century* (2000). Bill Osgerby examines the masculine space of 'The "Bachelor Pad" as Cultural Icon' (2005), while Christopher Reed locates signs of subversive political resistance in the rooms decorated by Vanessa Bell and Duncan Grant in *Bloomsbury Rooms: Modernism, Subculture, and Domesticity* (2004), describing an alternative, eclectic modernism later suppressed by homophobic attitudes towards the decorative arts. For further examinations of the gendered interior, see *INTIMUS: Interior Design Theory Reader*, edited by Mark Taylor and Julieanna Preston (2006).

SECTION 10

Consumption

INTRODUCTION

Rebecca Houze

Under the influence of anthropology, ethnography and material culture studies, and a desire to move beyond a canon of designers and manufacturers, consumption has been a core focus of interest within design history. We have explored several of these areas already throughout the *Reader*, from John Styles's study of eighteenth-century England to Thomas Hine's examination of 'Populuxe' in 1950s America. Indeed, there are few areas of design history that do not touch upon consumption in some aspect. Within design history, studies of consumption have tended to be informed by ideas about the role of the 'reader' (or viewer, or user) in making meaning for cultural artifacts (texts, objects), initiated by French structuralist and post-structuralist writers such as Roland Barthes and Michel Foucault, under the influence of early twentieth-century semioticians, Ferdinand de Saussure and Charles Pierce. Such studies have further been informed by Marxist critique of the role of objects within consumer society and by postmodern theory.

It is thus fitting to begin this section with an extract from Karl Marx's 1867 essay 'The Fetishism of the Commodity and its Secret' from the first volume of *Capital*. Marx begins, 'A commodity appears, at first sight, a very trivial thing, and easily understood. Its analysis shows that it is, in reality, a very queer thing, abounding in metaphysical subtleties and theological niceties.' What is a commodity? Is it a thing? A symbol? The strangeness of the commodity, Marx demonstrates, results from the fact that it is valued for exchange rather than use. Although Marx described the 'commodity fetish' as specific to industrialized capitalist societies, the fetish more generally can be understood in both anthropological and psychoanalytical terms, as an object invested with ritual power, on the one hand, and of displaced sexual desire on the other.

A half century later, Norwegian-American sociologist Thorstein Veblen identified 'conspicuous consumption' as the act of spending on things or in ways that signify social class. In earlier, pre-industrial societies, he writes, the patriarch's power was expressed through his own clothing, possessions and consumption of expensive food and drink – luxuries that were withheld from those in his service, including wife, children and slaves. Over time, this system transformed such that a man's wealth became increasingly visible through the expenditures of his wife on household objects, clothing and leisure activities, the conspicuous wastefulness of which was reflected upon him, as provider. Although Veblen's theories were developed at the turn of the twentieth century and reflect late-Victorian spending habits, they can also be used to help us understand mid-twentieth-century Western society in which women were also frequently viewed as the chief household consumers whose decorative and sartorial expressions signified their husbands' social standing.

Roland Barthes's semiotic readings of French advertisements and expressions of popular culture in the 1950s, such as dish and laundry detergents, new plastics and the stylish Citroën D.S. car, have been extremely influential as early examples of poststructural literary criticism. In his essay 'Myth Today', informed by Saussure's theory of language as an arbitrary and culturally constructed system, Barthes suggests that visual images can be read as a type of 'speech', which mythologizes their ideological underpinnings. His reading of these images and designed objects expands upon Marx's notion of the commodity as a 'social hieroglyphic', a form, like language, which is socially constructed and distinct from nature. For Barthes, myth is 'depoliticized speech' in which the troubled history of French colonialism in Africa, for example, can be obscured by the image of a young black man in uniform, saluting, we imagine, the French flag. If myth obscures ideology, does design do so as well? In the two essays reproduced here, from *Mythologies*, the sleek and elegant '*D.S.*', the new Nautilus, becomes the '*Déesse*' (goddess) in our imaginations, just as the alchemical transformations of modern plastics evoke the world of Greek mythology and the futuristic realm of science fiction. The selections here invite a comparison with the critique of consumption in section six offered by Vance Packard and Jeffrey Meikle, whose analyses of automotive styling and the plastics industry reveal the dangerous consequences of mid-century industrial design. Excessive and irresponsible consumption has proved to be increasingly problematic, a view raised by the collection of texts in section 6 on Sustainable Futures. There, Joel Makower, John Elkington and Julia Hailes propose more environmentally friendly modes of shopping in *The Green Consumer Supermarket Guide* (1991), while Nicky Gregson and Louise Crewe analyse the recycling and reuse of discarded objects, in 'Redefining Rubbish' (2003).

Pierre Bourdieu's ethnographic survey of French consumers in the 1960s and 1970s has been useful in establishing 'taste' as a set of social relationships having to do with education, profession and family class origin. Complicating Veblen's understanding of 'conspicuous consumption', Bourdieu demonstrates that cultural capital represented by the artifacts we purchase, collect, or desire has less to do with one's own financial wealth than with one's understanding of the cultural value of music and literature, furnishings, clothing, and decorating styles, gained through education, experience, or privilege. The three case studies we've reproduced here describe variations in consumption habits among the French middle class, from the 'Grand Bourgeois', dismissive of popular style, furnishing and décor, who enumerates his eccentric, idiosyncratic collection of antiquities and special objects acquired through inheritance and travels abroad, to the university professor who enjoys shopping for antiques with his wife, but who, for financial reasons, chooses to purchase simpler, less expensive and more practical furnishings, to the young advertising executive, compelled to dress in stylish, expensive, distinctive fashions for professional appearances but whose busy domestic life with working wife and two young children does not afford the luxury of a well-appointed home or car that might match his work clothes.

This section includes several 'primary texts' that have laid a foundation for further studies of consumption from a design historical perspective, especially related to economic and social class. The final two selections go beyond these pioneering studies to make explicit the dimensions of gender and race within consumption. In her entertaining and illuminating look at Tupperware in the 1950s, Alison J. Clarke explores the developing culture of suburbia in the United States, and women's ambiguous roles as both conspicuous consumers and as arbiters of domestic taste. In 'The Ascent of the Tupperware Party' we see how the plastics company captured an enormous market by employing housewives to sell the products at informal gatherings in their homes, combining entrepreneurial spirit with sociality. Robert Weems, Jr. explores strategies of companies in the 1960s that tried to enter the African-American market by appealing to a politicized expression of racial pride. Although this may have bolstered the influence of black entrepreneurs and black media, it is also clear during this period of increasing racial tension, with riots and 'white flight' to the suburbs of American cities, that 'while desired as shoppers', African Americans were, 'often less desired by whites as classmates, co-workers, and neighbors'.

52

THE FETISHISM OF THE COMMODITY AND ITS SECRET, FROM *CAPITAL*

Karl Marx (1867)

A commodity appears, at first sight, a very trivial thing, and easily understood. Its analysis shows that it is, in reality, a very queer thing, abounding in metaphysical subtleties and theological niceties. So far as it is a value in use, there is nothing mysterious about it, whether we consider it from the point of view that by its properties it is capable of satisfying human wants, or from the point that those properties are the product of human labour. It is as clear as noon-day, that man, by his industry, changes the forms of the materials furnished by nature, in such a way as to make them useful to him. The form of wood, for instance, is altered, by making a table out of it. Yet, for all that, the table continues to be that common, every-day thing, wood. But, so soon as it steps forth as a commodity, it is changed into something transcendent. It not only stands with its feet on the ground, but, in relation to all other commodities, it stands on its head, and evolves out of its wooden brain grotesque ideas, far more wonderful than "table-turning" ever was.

The mystical character of commodities does not originate, therefore, in their use value. Just as little does it proceed from the nature of the determining factors of value. For, in the first place, however varied the useful kinds of labour, or productive activities, may be, it is a physiological fact, that they are functions of the human organism, and that each such function, whatever may be its nature or form, is essentially the expenditure of human brain, nerves, muscles, &c. Secondly, with regard to that which forms the ground-work for the quantitative determination of value, namely, the duration of that expenditure, or the quantity of labour, it is quite clear that there is a palpable difference between its quantity and quality. In all states of society, the labour-time that it costs to produce the means of subsistence, must necessarily be an object of interest to mankind, though not of equal interest in different stages of development.[1] And lastly, from the moment that men in any way work for one another, their labour assumes a social form.

Whence, then, arises the enigmatical character of the product of labour, so soon as it assumes the form of commodities? Clearly from this form itself. The equality of all sorts of human labour is expressed objectively by their products all being equally valued; the measure of the expenditure of labour-power by the duration of that expenditure, takes the form of the quantity of value of the products of labour; and finally, the mutual relations of the producers, within which the social character of their labour affirms itself, take the form of a social relation between the products.

A commodity is therefore a mysterious thing, simply because in it the social character of men's labour appears to them as an objective character stamped upon the product of that labour; because the relation of the producers to the sum total of their own labour is presented to them as a social relation, existing not between themselves, but between the products of their labour. This is the reason why the products of labour become commodities, social things whose qualities are at the same time perceptible and imperceptible by the senses. In the same way the light from an object is perceived by us not as the subjective excitation of our optic nerve, but as the objective form of something outside the eye itself. But, in the act of seeing, there is at all events, an actual passage of light from one thing to another, from the external object to the eye. There is a physical relation between physical things. But it is different with commodities. There, the existence of the things *quâ* commodities, and the value relation between the products of labour which stamps them as commodities, have absolutely no connection with their physical properties and with the material relations arising therefrom. There it is a definite social relation between men, that assumes, in their eyes, the fantastic form of a relation between things. In order, therefore, to find an analogy, we must have recourse to the mist-enveloped regions of the religious world. In that world the productions of the human brain appear as independent beings endowed with life, and entering into relation both with one another and the human race. So it is in the world of commodities with the products of men's hands. This I call the Fetishism which attaches itself to the products of labour, so soon as they are produced as commodities, and which is therefore inseparable from the production of commodities.

This Fetishism of commodities has its origin, as the foregoing analysis has already shown, in the peculiar social character of the labour that produces them.

As a general rule, articles of utility become commodities, only because they are products of the labour of private individuals or groups of individuals who carry on their work independently of each other. The sum total of the labour of all these private individuals forms the aggregate labour of society. Since the producers do not come into social contact with each other until they exchange their products, the specific social character of each producer's labour does not show itself except in the act of exchange. In other words, the labour of the individual asserts itself as a part of the labour of society, only by means of the relations which the act of exchange establishes directly between the products, and indirectly, through them, between the producers. To the latter, therefore, the relations connecting the labour of one individual with that of the rest appear, not as direct social relations between individuals at work, but as what they really are, material relations between persons and social relations between things. It is only by being exchanged that the products of labour acquire, as values, one uniform social status, distinct from their varied forms of existence as objects of utility. This division of a product into a useful thing and a value becomes practically important, only when exchange has acquired such an extension that useful articles are produced for the purpose of being exchanged, and their character as values has therefore to be taken into account, beforehand, during production. From this moment the labour of the individual producer acquires socially a twofold character. On the one hand, it must, as a definite useful kind of labour, satisfy a definite social want, and thus hold its place as part and parcel of the collective labour of all, as a branch of a social division of labour that has sprung up spontaneously. On the other hand, it can satisfy the manifold wants of the individual producer himself, only in so far as the mutual exchangeability of all kinds of useful private labour is an established social fact, and therefore the private useful labour of each producer ranks on an equality with that of all others. The equalisation of most different kinds of labour can be the result only of an abstraction from their inequalities, or of reducing them to their common denominator, viz. expenditure of human labour power or human labour in the abstract. The twofold social character of the labour of the individual appears to him, when reflected in his brain, only under those forms which are impressed upon that labour in every-day practice by the exchange of products. In this way, the character that his own labour possesses of being socially useful takes the form of the condition, that the product must be not only useful, but useful for others, and the social character that his particular labour has of being the equal of all other particular kinds of labour, takes the form that all the physically different articles that are the products of labour have one common quality, viz., that of having value.

Hence, when we bring the products of our labour into relation with each other as values, it is not because we see in these articles the material receptacles of homogeneous human labour. Quite the contrary: whenever, by an exchange, we equate as values our different products, by that very act, we also equate, as human labour, the different kinds of labour expended upon them. We are not aware of this, nevertheless we do it.[2] Value, therefore, does not stalk about with a label describing what it is. It is value, rather, that converts every product into a social hieroglyphic. Later on, we try to decipher the hieroglyphic, to get behind the secret of our own social products; for to stamp an object of utility as a value, is just as much a social product as language. The recent scientific discovery, that the products of labour, so far as they are values, are but material expressions of the human labour spent in their production, marks, indeed, an epoch in the history of the development of the human race, but, by no means, dissipates the mist through which the social character of labour appears to us to be an objective character of the products themselves. The fact, that in the particular form of production with which we are dealing, viz., the production of commodities, the specific social character of private labour carried on independently, consists in the equality of every kind of that labour, by virtue of its being human labour, which character, therefore, assumes in the product the form of value – this fact appears to the producers, notwithstanding the discovery above referred to, to be just as real and final, as the fact, that, after the discovery by science of the component gases of air, the atmosphere itself remained unaltered.

[…]

To what extent some economists are misled by the Fetishism inherent in commodities, or by the objective appearance of the social characteristics of labour, is shown, amongst other ways, by the dull and tedious quarrel over the part played by Nature in the formation of exchange value. Since exchange value is a definite social manner of expressing the amount of labour bestowed upon an object, Nature has no more to do with it, than it has in fixing the course of exchange.

The mode of production in which the product takes the form of a commodity, or is produced directly for exchange, is the most general and most embryonic form of bourgeois production. It therefore makes its appearance at an early date in history, though not in the same predominating and characteristic manner as now-a-days. Hence its Fetish character is comparatively easy to be seen through. But when we come to more concrete forms, even this appearance of simplicity vanishes. Whence arose the illusions of the monetary system? To it gold and silver, when serving as money, did not represent a social relation between producers, but were natural objects with strange social properties. And modern economy, which looks down with such disdain on the monetary system, does not its superstition come out as clear as noon-day, whenever it treats of capital? How long is it since economy discarded the physiocratic illusion, that rents grow out of the soil and not out of society.

But not to anticipate, we will content ourselves with yet another example relating to the commodity form. Could commodities themselves speak, they would say: Our use value may be a thing that interests men. It is no part of us as objects. What, however, does belong to us as objects, is our value. Our natural intercourse as commodities proves it. In the eyes of each other we are nothing but exchange values. Now listen how those commodities speak through the mouth of the economist. "Value" – (i.e., exchange value) "is a property of things, riches" – (i.e., use value) "of man. Value, in this sense, necessarily implies exchanges, riches do not."[3] "Riches" (use value) "are the attribute of men, value is the attribute of commodities. A man or a community is rich, a pearl or a diamond is valuable …" A pearl or a diamond is valuable as a pearl or a diamond.[4]

So far no chemist has ever discovered exchange value either in a pearl or a diamond. The economic discoverers of this chemical element, who by-the-bye lay special claim to critical acumen, find however that the use value of objects belongs to them independently of their material properties, while their value, on the other hand, forms a part of them as objects. What confirms them in this view, is the peculiar circumstance that the use value of objects is realised without exchange, by means of a direct relation between the objects and man, while, on the other hand, their value is realised only by exchange, that is, by means of a social process. Who fails here to call to mind our good friend, Dogberry, who informs neighbour Seacoal, that, "To be a well-favoured man is the gift of fortune; but reading and writing comes by nature."[5]

NOTES

Extracted from Marx, K., *Capital. A Critique of Political Economy*, Vol. 1, translated from the third German edition by Samuel Moore and Edward Aveling, edited by Frederick Engels. Revised and amplified according to the fourth German edition by Ernest Untermann. New York, The Modern Library, 1906, pp. 81–96. © 1906 by Charles H. Kerr & Company. The first German edition, *Das Kapital: Kritik der politischen Ökonomie*, was published in 1867.

1. Among the ancient Germans the unit for measuring land was what could be harvested in a day, and was called Tagwerk, Tagwanne (jurnale, or terra jurnalis, or diornalis), Mannsmaad, &c. (See G. L. von Maurer, "Einleitung zur Geschichte der Mark, &c. Verfassung," München, 1859, pp. 129–59.)

2. When, therefore, [Ferdinando] Galiani says: Value is a relation between persons – "La Ricchezza á una ragione tra due persone," – he ought to have added: a relation between persons expressed as a relation between things. (Galiani: Della Moneta, p. 221, V. III. of Custodi's collection of "Scittori Classici Italiani di Economia Politicia." Parte Moderna, Milano, 1803.)

3. "Observations on certain verbal disputes in Pol. Econ., particularly relating to value and to demand and supply." Lond., 1821, p. 16.

4. [Samuel] Bailey, "Money and its vicissitudes," London, 1837, p. 165.

5. The author of "Observations" and S. Bailey accuse [David] Ricardo of converting exchange value from something relative into something absolute. The opposite is the fact. He has explained the apparent relation between objects, such as diamonds and pearls, in which relation they appear as exchange values, and disclosed the true relation hidden behind the appearances, namely, their relation to each other as mere expressions of human labour. If the followers of Ricardo answer Bailey somewhat rudely, and by no means convincingly, the reason is to be sought in this, that they were unable to find in Ricardo's own works any key to the hidden relations existing between value and its form, exchange value.

53

CONSPICUOUS CONSUMPTION, IN
THE THEORY OF THE LEISURE CLASS

Thorstein Veblen (1899)

[…]

Conspicuous consumption of valuable goods is a means of reputability to the gentleman of leisure. As wealth accumulates on his hands, his own unaided effort will not avail to sufficiently put his opulence in evidence by this method. The aid of friends and competitors is therefore brought in by resorting to the giving of valuable presents and expensive feasts and entertainments. Presents and feasts had probably another origin than that of naïve ostentation, but they acquired their utility for this purpose very early, and they have retained that character to the present; so that their utility in this respect has now long been the substantial ground on which these usages rest. Costly entertainments, such as the potlatch or the ball, are peculiarly adapted to serve this end. The competitor with whom the entertainer wishes to institute a comparison is, by this method, made to serve as a means to the end. He consumes vicariously for his host at the same time that he is witness to the consumption of that excess of good things which his host is unable to dispose of single-handed, and he is also made to witness his host's facility in etiquette.

In the giving of costly entertainments other motives, of more genial kind, are of course also present. The custom of festive gatherings probably originated in motives of conviviality and religion; these motives are also present in the later development, but they do not continue to be the sole motives. The latter-day leisure-class festivities and entertainments may continue in some slight degree to serve the religious need and in a higher degree the needs of recreation and conviviality, but they also serve an invidious purpose; and they serve it none the less effectually for having a colourable non-invidious ground in these more avowable motives. But the economic effect of these social amenities is not therefore lessened, either in the vicarious consumption of goods or in the exhibition of difficult and costly achievements in etiquette.

As wealth accumulates, the leisure class develops further in function and structure, and there arises a differentiation within the class. There is a more or less elaborate system of rank and grades. This differentiation is furthered by the inheritance of wealth and the consequent inheritance of gentility. With the inheritance of gentility goes the inheritance of obligatory leisure; and gentility of a sufficient potency to entail a life of leisure may be inherited without the complement of wealth required to maintain a dignified leisure. Gentle blood may be transmitted without goods enough to afford a reputably free consumption at one's ease. Hence results a class of impecunious gentlemen of leisure, incidentally referred to already. These half-caste gentlemen of leisure fall into a system of hierarchical gradations. Those who stand near the higher and the highest grades of the wealthy leisure class, in point of birth, or in point of wealth, or both, outrank the remoter-born and the pecuniarily weaker. These lower grades, especially the impecunious, or marginal, gentlemen of leisure, affiliate themselves by a system of dependence or fealty to the great ones; by so doing they gain an increment of repute, or of the means with which to lead a life of leisure, from their patron. They become his courtiers or retainers, servants; and being fed and countenanced by their patron they are indices of his rank and vicarious consumers of his superfluous wealth. Many of these affiliated gentlemen of leisure are at the same time lesser men of substance in their own right; so that some of them are scarcely at all, others only partially, to be rated as vicarious consumers. So many of them, however, as make up the retainers and hangers-on of the patron may be classed as vicarious consumers without qualification. Many of these again, and also many of the other aristocracy of less degree, have in turn attached to their persons a more or less comprehensive group of vicarious consumers in the persons of their wives and children, their servants, retainers, etc.

Throughout this graduated scheme of vicarious leisure and vicarious consumption the rule holds that these offices must be performed in some such manner, or under some such circumstance or insignia, as shall point plainly to the master to whom this leisure or consumption pertains, and to whom therefore the resulting increment of good repute of right inures. The consumption and leisure executed by these persons for their master or patron represents an investment on his part with a view to an increase of good fame. As regards feasts and largesses this is obvious enough, and the imputation of repute to the host or patron here takes place immediately, on the ground of common notoriety. Where leisure and consumption is performed vicariously by henchmen and retainers, imputation of the resulting repute to the patron is effected by their residing near his person so that it may be plain to all men from what source they draw. As the group whose good esteem is to be secured in this way grows larger, more patent means are required to indicate the imputation of merit for the leisure performed, and

to this end uniforms, badges, and liveries come into vogue. The wearing of uniforms or liveries implies a considerable degree of dependence, and may even be said to be a mark of servitude, real or ostensible. The wearers of uniforms and liveries may be roughly divided into two classes – the free and the servile, or the noble and the ignoble. The services performed by them are likewise divisible into noble and ignoble. Of course the distinction is not observed with strict consistency in practice; the less debasing of the base services and the less honorific of the noble functions are not infrequently merged in the same person. But the general distinction is not on that account to be overlooked. What may add some perplexity is the fact that this fundamental distinction between noble and ignoble, which rests on the nature of the ostensible service performed, is traversed by a secondary distinction into honorific and humiliating, resting on the rank of the person for whom the service is performed or whose livery is worn. So, those offices which are by right the proper employment of the leisure class are noble; such as government, fighting, hunting, the care of arms and accoutrements, and the like, – in short, those which may be classed as ostensibly predatory employments. On the other hand, those employments which properly fall to the industrious class are ignoble; such as handicraft or other productive labor, menial services and the like. But a base service performed for a person of very high degree may become a very honorific office; as for instance the office of a Maid of Honor or of a Lady in Waiting to the Queen, or the King's Master of the Horse or his Keeper of the Hounds. The two offices last named suggest a principle of some general bearing. Whenever, as in these cases, the menial service in question has to do directly with the primary leisure employments of fighting and hunting, it easily acquires a reflected honorific character. In this way great honour may come to attach to an employment which in its own nature belongs to the baser sort.

In the later development of peaceable industry, the usage of employing an idle corps of uniformed men-at-arms gradually lapses. Vicarious consumption by dependents bearing the insignia of their patron or master narrows down to a corps of liveried menials. In a heightened degree, therefore, the livery comes to be a badge of servitude, or rather servility. Something of a honorific character always attached to the livery of the armed retainer, but this honorific character disappears when the livery becomes the exclusive badge of the menial. The livery becomes obnoxious to nearly all who are required to wear it. We are yet so little removed from a state of effective slavery as still to be fully sensitive to the sting of any imputation of servility. This antipathy asserts itself even in the case of the liveries or uniforms which some corporations prescribe as the distinctive dress of their employees. In this country the aversion even goes the length of discrediting – in a mild and uncertain way – those government employments, military and civil, which require the wearing of a livery or uniform.

With the disappearance of servitude, the number of vicarious consumers attached to any one gentleman tends, on the whole, to decrease. The like is of course true, and perhaps in a still higher degree, of the number of dependents who perform vicarious leisure for him. In a general way, though not wholly nor consistently, these two groups coincide. The dependent who was first delegated for these duties was the wife, or the chief wife; and, as would be expected, in the later development of the institution, when the number of persons by whom these duties are customarily performed gradually narrows, the wife remains the last. In the higher grades of society a large volume of both these kinds of service is required; and here the wife is of course still assisted in the work by a more or less numerous corps of menials. But as we descend the social scale, the point is presently reached where the duties of vicarious leisure and consumption devolve upon the wife alone. In the communities of the Western culture, this point is at present found among the lower middle class.

And here occurs a curious inversion. It is a fact of common observation that in this lower middle class there is no pretense of leisure on the part of the head of the household. Through force of circumstances it has fallen into disuse. But the middle-class wife still carries on the business of vicarious leisure, for the good name of the household and its master. In descending the social scale in any modern industrial community, the primary fact – the conspicuous leisure of the master of the household – disappears at a relatively high point. The head of the middle-class household has been reduced by economic circumstances to turn his hand to gaining a livelihood by occupations which often partake largely of the character of industry, as in the case of the ordinary business man of today. But the derivative fact – the vicarious leisure and consumption rendered by the wife, and the auxiliary vicarious performance of leisure by menials – remains in vogue as a conventionality which the demands of reputability will not suffer to be slighted. It is by no means an uncommon spectacle to find a man applying himself to work with the utmost assiduity, in order that his wife may in due form render for him that degree of vicarious leisure which the common sense of the time demands.

The leisure rendered by the wife in such cases is, of course, not a simple manifestation of idleness or indolence. It almost invariably occurs disguised under some form of work or household duties or social amenities, which prove on analysis to serve little or no ulterior end beyond showing that she does not occupy herself with anything that is gainful or that is of substantial use. As has already been noticed under the head of manners, the greater part of the customary round of domestic cares to which the middle-class housewife gives her time and effort is of this character. Not that the results of her attention to household matters, of a decorative and mundificatory character, are not pleasing to the sense of men trained in middle-class proprieties; but the taste to which these effects of household adornment and tidiness appeal is a taste which has been formed under the selective guidance of a canon of propriety that demands just these evidences of wasted effort. The effects are pleasing to us chiefly because we have been taught to find them pleasing. There goes into these domestic duties much solicitude for a proper combination of form and colour, and for other ends that are to be classed as aesthetic in the proper sense of the term; and it is not denied that effects having some substantial aesthetic value are sometimes attained. Pretty much all that is here insisted on is that, as regards these amenities of life, the housewife's efforts are under the guidance of traditions that have been shaped by the law of conspicuously wasteful expenditure of time and substance. If beauty or comfort is achieved, – and it is a more or less fortuitous circumstance if they are, – they must be achieved by means and methods that commend themselves to the great economic law of wasted effort. The more reputable, "presentable" portion of middle-class household paraphernalia are, on the one hand, items of conspicuous consumption, and on the other hand, apparatus for putting in evidence the vicarious leisure rendered by the housewife.

The requirement of vicarious consumption at the hands of the wife continues in force even at a lower point in the pecuniary scale than the requirement of vicarious leisure. At a point below which little if any pretense of wasted effort, in ceremonial cleanness and the like, is observable, and where there is assuredly no conscious attempt at ostensible leisure, decency still requires the wife to consume some goods conspicuously for the reputability of the household and its head. So that, as the latter-day outcome of this evolution of an archaic institution, the wife, who was at the outset the drudge and chattel of the man, both in fact and in theory – the producer of goods for him to consume – has become the ceremonial consumer of goods which he produces. But she still quite unmistakably remains his chattel in theory; for the habitual rendering of vicarious leisure and consumption is the abiding mark of the unfree servant.

NOTE

Extracted from Veblen, T., *The Theory of the Leisure Class: An Economic Study of Institutions,* New York: B. W. Huebsch, 1919, pp. 68–101.

54

MYTH TODAY, THE NEW CITROËN, AND PLASTIC, FROM *MYTHOLOGIES*

Roland Barthes (1957)

MYTH TODAY

What is a myth, today? I shall give at the outset a first, very simple answer, which is perfectly consistent with etymology: *myth is a type of speech.*[1]

MYTH IS A TYPE OF SPEECH

Of course, it is not any type: language needs special conditions in order to become myth: we shall see them in a minute. But what must be firmly established at the start is that myth is a system of communication, that it is a message. This allows one to perceive that myth cannot possibly be an object, a concept, or an idea; it is a mode of signification, a form. [...]

[...] Ancient or not, mythology can only have an historical foundation, for myth is a type of speech chosen by history: it cannot possibly evolve from the 'nature' of things.

Speech of this kind is a message. It is therefore by no means confined to oral speech. It can consist of modes of writing or of representations; not only written discourse, but also photography, cinema, reporting, sport, shows, publicity, all these can serve as a support to mythical speech. Myth can be defined neither by its object nor by its material, for any material can arbitrarily be endowed with meaning: the arrow which is brought in order to signify a challenge is also a kind of speech. True, as far as perception is concerned, writing and

pictures, for instance, do not call upon the same type of consciousness; and even with pictures, one can use many kinds of reading: a diagram lends itself to signification more than drawing, a copy more than an original, and a caricature more than a portrait. But this is the point: we are no longer dealing here with a theoretical mode of representation: we are dealing with *this* particular image, which is given for *this* particular signification. Mythical speech is made of a material which has already been worked on so as to make it suitable for communication: it is because all the materials of myth (whether pictorial or written) presuppose a signifying consciousness, that one can reason about them while discounting their substance. This substance is not unimportant: pictures, to be sure, are more imperative than writing, they impose meaning at one stroke, without analyzing or diluting it. But this is no longer a constitutive difference. Pictures become a kind of writing as soon as they are meaningful: like writing, they call for a *lexis*.

We shall therefore take language, discourse, speech, etc., to mean any significant unit or synthesis, whether verbal or visual: a photograph will be a kind of speech for us in the same way as a newspaper article; even objects will become speech, if they mean something. This generic way of conceiving language is in fact justified by the very history of writing: long before the invention of our alphabet, objects like the Inca *quipu*, or drawings, as in pictographs, have been accepted as speech. This does not mean that one must treat mythical speech like language; myth in fact belongs to the province of a general science, coextensive with linguistics, which is *semiology*.

MYTH AS A SEMIOLOGICAL SYSTEM

For mythology, since it is the study of a type of speech, is but one fragment of this vast science of signs which Saussure postulated some forty years ago under the name *semiology*. […]

Semiology is a science of forms, since it studies significations apart from their content. […]

Let me therefore restate that any semiology postulates a relation between two terms, a signifier and a signified. This relation concerns objects which belong to different categories, and this is why it is not one of equality but one of equivalence. We must here be on our guard for despite common parlance which simply says that the signifier expresses the signified, we are dealing, in any semiological system, not with two, but with three different terms. For what we grasp is not at all one term after the other, but the correlation which unites them: there are, therefore, the signifier, the signified and the sign, which is the associative total of the first two terms.

[…]

In myth, we find again the tri-dimensional pattern which I have just described: the signifier, the signified and the sign. But myth is a peculiar system, in that it is constructed from a semiological chain which existed before it: it is a second-order semiological system. That which is a sign (namely the associative total of a concept and an image) in the first system, becomes a mere signifier in the second. We must here recall that the materials of mythical speech (the language itself, photography, painting, posters, rituals, objects, etc.), however different at the start, are reduced to a pure signifying function as soon as they are caught by myth. Myth sees in them only the same raw material; their unity is that they all come down to the status of a mere language. Whether it deals with alphabetical or pictorial writing, myth wants to see in them only a sum of signs, a global sign, the final term of a first semiological chain. And it is precisely this final term which will become the first term of the greater system which it builds and of which it is only a part. Everything happens as if myth shifted the formal system of the first significations sideways. As this lateral shift is essential for the analysis of myth, I shall represent it in the following way, it being understood, of course, that the spatialization of the pattern is here only a metaphor:

It can be seen that in myth there are two semiological systems, one of which is staggered in relation to the other: a linguistic system, the language (or the modes of representation which are assimilated to it), which I shall call the *language-object*, because it is the language which myth gets hold of in order to build its own system; and myth itself, which I shall call *metalanguage*, because it is a second language, *in which* one speaks about the first. When he reflects on a metalanguage, the semiologist no longer needs

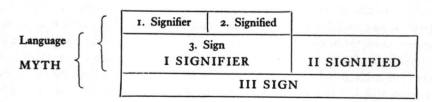

Figure 38. Table demonstrating the relationship between 'signifier,' 'signified,' and 'sign,' in Roland Barthes, *Mythologies*, (1957), translated by Annette Lavers, New York: Hill & Wang, 1994, p. 115. Reprinted by permission of Hill and Wang, a division of Farrar, Straus and Giroux, LLC, and by the the Random House Group, Ltd.

to ask himself questions about the composition of the language-object, he no longer has to take into account the details of the linguistic schema; he will only need to know its total term, or global sign, and only inasmuch as this term lends itself to myth. This is why the semiologist is entitled to treat in the same way writing and pictures: what he retains from them is the fact that they are both *signs*, that they both reach the threshold of myth endowed with the same signifying function, that they constitute, one just as much as the other, a language-object.

It is now time to give one or two examples of mythical speech. I shall borrow the first from an observation by Valéry.[2] I am a pupil in the second form in a French *lycée*. I open my Latin grammar, and I read a sentence, borrowed from Aesop or Phaedrus: *quia ego nominor leo*. I stop and think. There is something ambiguous about this statement: on the one hand, the words in it do have a simple meaning: *because my name is lion*. And on the other hand, the sentence is evidently there in order to signify something else to me. Inasmuch as it is addressed to me, a pupil in the second form, it tells me clearly: I am a grammatical example meant to illustrate the rule about the agreement of the predicate. I am even forced to realize that the sentence in no way *signifies* its meaning to me, that it tries very little to tell me something about the lion and what sort of name he has; its true and fundamental signification is to impose itself on me as the presence of a certain agreement of the predicate. I conclude that I am faced with a particular, greater, semiological system, since it is co-extensive with the language: there is, indeed, a signifier, but this signifier is itself formed by a sum of signs, it is in itself a first semiological system (*my name is lion*). Thereafter, the formal pattern is correctly unfolded: there is a signified (*I am a grammatical example*) and there is a global signification, which is none other than the correlation of the signifier and the signified; for neither the naming of the lion nor the grammatical example are given separately.

And here is now another example: I am at the barber's and a copy of *Paris-Match* is offered to me. On the cover, a young Negro in a French uniform is saluting, with his eyes uplifted, probably fixed on a fold of the tricolour. All this is the *meaning* of the picture. But, whether naively or not, I see very well what it signifies to me: that France is a great Empire, that all her sons, without any colour discrimination, faithfully serve under her flag, and that there is no better answer to the detractors of an alleged colonialism that the zeal shown by this Negro in serving his so-called oppressors. I am therefore again faced with a greater semiological system: there is a signifier, itself already formed with a previous system (*a black soldier is giving the French salute*); there is a signified (it is here a purposeful mixture of Frenchness and militariness); finally, there is a presence of the signified through the signifier.

Before tackling the analysis of each term of the mythical system, one must agree on terminology. We now know that the signifier can be looked at, in myth, from two points of view: as the final term of the linguistic system, or as the first term of the mythical system. We therefore need two names. On the plane of language, that is, as the final term of the first system, I shall call the signifier: *meaning* (*my name is lion, a Negro is giving the French salute*); on the plane of myth, I shall call it: *form*. In the case of the signified, no ambiguity is possible: we shall retain the name *concept*. The third term is the correlation of the first two: in the linguistic system, it is the *sign*; but it is not possible to use this word again without ambiguity, since in myth (and this is the chief peculiarity of the latter), the signifier is already formed by the *signs* of the language. I shall call the third term of myth the *signification*. This word is here all the better justified since myth has in fact a double function: it points out and it notifies, it makes us understand something and it imposes it on us.

[...]

Figure 39. 'La nouvelle Citroën (The New Citroën)', cover of *Paris Match*, no. 340 (October 1955). Reprinted by permission of *Paris Match*.

THE NEW CITROËN

I think that cars today are almost the exact equivalent of the great Gothic cathedrals: I mean the supreme creation of an era, conceived with passion by unknown artists, and consumed in image if not in usage by a whole population which appropriates them as a purely magical object.

It is obvious that the new Citroën has fallen from the sky inasmuch as it appears at first sight as a superlative *object*. We must not forget that an object is the best messenger of a world above that of nature: one can easily see in an object at once a perfection and an absence of origin, a closure and a brilliance, a transformation of life into matter (matter is much more magical than life), and in a word a *silence* which belongs to the realm of fairy-tales. The *D.S.* – the 'Goddess' – has all the features (or at least the public is unanimous in attributing them to it at first sight) of one of those objects from another universe which have supplied fuel for the neomania of the eighteenth century and that of our own science-fiction: the *Déesse* is *first and foremost* a new *Nautilus*.

This is why it excites interest less by its substance than by the junction of its components. It is well known that smoothness is always an attribute of perfection because its opposite reveals a technical and typically human operation of assembling: Christ's robe was seamless, just as the airships of science-fiction are made of unbroken metal. The *D.S. 19* has no pretensions about being as smooth as cake-icing, although its general shape is very rounded; yet it is the dove-tailing of its sections which interest the public most: one keenly fingers the edges of the windows, one feels along the wide rubber grooves which link the back window to its metal surround. There are in the *D.S.* the beginnings of a new phenomenology of assembling, as if one progressed from a world where elements are welded to a world where they are juxtaposed and hold together by sole virtue of their wondrous shape, which of course is meant to prepare one for the idea of a more benign Nature.

As for the material itself, it is certain that it promotes a taste for lightness in its magical sense. There is a return to a certain degree of streamlining, new, however, since it is less bulky, less incisive, more relaxed than that which one found in the first period of this fashion. Speed here is expressed by less aggressive, less athletic signs, as if it were evolving from a primitive to a classical form. This spiritualization can be seen in the extent, the quality and the material of the glass-work. The *Déesse* is obviously the exaltation of glass, and pressed metal is only a support for it. Here, the glass surfaces are not windows, openings pierced in a dark shell; they are vast walls of air and space, with the curvature, the spread and the brilliance of soap-bubbles, the hard thinness of a substance more entomological than mineral (the Citroën emblem, with its arrows, has in fact become a winged emblem, as if one was proceeding from the category of propulsion to that of spontaneous motion, from that of the engine to that of the organism.)

We are therefore dealing here with a humanized art, and it is possible that the *Déesse* marks a change in the mythology of cars. Until now, the ultimate in cars belonged rather to the bestiary of power; here it becomes at once more spiritual and more object-like, and despite some concessions to neomania (such as the empty steering wheel), it is now more *homely*, more attuned to this sublimation of the utensil which one also finds in the design of contemporary household equipment. The dashboard looks more like the working surface of a modern kitchen than the control-room of a factory: the slim panes of matt fluted metal, the small levers topped by a white ball, the very simple dials, the very discreteness of the nickel-work, all this signifies a kind of control exercised over motion, which is henceforth conceived as comfort rather than performance. One is obviously turning from an alchemy of speed to a relish in driving.

The public, it seems, has admirably divined the novelty of the themes which are suggested to it. Responding at first to the neologism (a whole publicity campaign had kept it on the alert for years), it tries very quickly to fall back on a behavior, which indicates adjustment and a readiness to use ('*You've got to get used to it*'). In the exhibition halls, the car on show is explored with an intense, amourous studiousness: it is the great tactile phase of discovery, the moment when visual wonder is about to receive the reasoned assault of touch (for touch is the most demystifying of all senses, unlike sight, which is the most magical). The bodywork, the lines of union are touched, the upholstery palpated, the seats tried, the doors caressed, the cushions fondled; before the wheel, one pretends to drive with one's whole body. The object here is totally prostituted, appropriated: originating from the heaven of *Metropolis*, the Goddess is in a quarter of an hour mediatized, actualizing through this exorcism the very essence of petit-bourgeois advancement.

PLASTIC

Despite having names of Greek shepherds (Polystyrene, Polyvinyl, Polyethylene), plastic, the products of which have just been gathered in an exhibition, is in essence the stuff of alchemy. At the entrance of the stand, the public waits in a long queue in order to witness the accomplishment of the magical operation par excellence: the transmutation of matter. An ideally-shaped machine, tabulated and oblong (a shape well suited to suggest the secret of an itinerary) effortlessly draws, out of a heap of greenish crystals, shiny and fluted dressing-room tidies. At one end, raw, telluric matter, at the other, the finished, human object; and between these two extremes, nothing; nothing but a transit, hardly watched over by an attendant in a cloth cap, half-god, half-robot.

So, more than a substance, plastic is the very idea of its infinite transformation; as its everyday name indicates, it is ubiquity made visible. And it is this, in fact, which makes it a miraculous substance: a miracle is always a sudden transformation of nature. Plastic remains impregnated throughout with this wonder: it is less a thing than the trace of a movement.

And as the movement here is almost infinite, transforming the original crystals into a multitude of more and more startling objects, plastic is, all told, a spectacle to be deciphered: the very spectacle of its end-products. At the sight of each terminal form (suitcase, brush, car-body, toy fabric, tube, basin or paper), the mind does not cease from considering the original matter as an enigma. This is because the quick-change artistry of plastic is absolute: it can become buckets as well as jewels. Hence a perpetual amazement, the reverie of man at the sight of the proliferating forms of matter, and the connections he detects between the singular of the origin and the plural of the effects. And this amazement is a pleasurable one, since the scope of the transformations gives man the measure of his power, and since the very itinerary of plastic gives him the euphoria of a prestigious free-wheeling through Nature.

But the price to be paid for this success is that plastic, sublimated as movement, hardly exists as substance. Its reality is a negative one: neither hard nor deep, it must be content with a 'substantial' attribute which is neutral in spite of its utilitarian advantages: *resistance*, a state which merely means an absence of yielding. In the hierarchy of the major poetic substances, it figures as a disgraced material, lost between the effusiveness of rubber and the flat hardness of metal; it embodies none of the genuine produce of the mineral world: foam, fires, strata. It is a 'shaped' substance: whatever its final state, plastic keeps a flocculent appearance, something opaque, creamy and curdled, something powerless ever to achieve the triumphant smoothness of Nature. But what best reveals it for what it is is the sound it gives, at once hollow and flat; its noise is its undoing, as are its colours, for it seems capable of retaining only the most chemical-looking ones. Of yellow, red and green, it keeps only the aggressive quality, and uses them as mere names, being able to display only concepts of colours.

The fashion for plastic highlights an evolution in the myth of 'imitation' materials. It is well known that their use is historically bourgeois in origin (the first vestimentary postiches date back to the rise of capitalism). But until now imitation materials have always indicated pretension, they belonged to the world of appearances, not to that of actual use; they aimed at reproducing cheaply the rarest substances, diamonds, silk, feathers, furs, silver, all the luxurious brilliance of the world. Plastic has climbed down, it is a household material. It is the first magical substance which consents to be prosaic. But it is precisely because this prosaic character is a triumphant reason for its existence: for the first time, artifice aims at something common, not rare. And as an immediate consequence, the age-old function of nature is modified: it is no longer the Idea, the pure Substance to be regained or imitated: an artificial matter, more bountiful than all the natural deposits, is about to replace her, and to determine the very invention of forms. A luxurious object is still of this earth, it still recalls, albeit in a precious mode, its mineral or animal origin, the natural theme of which it is but one actualization. Plastic is wholly swallowed up in the fact of being used: ultimately, objects will be invented for the sole pleasure of using them. The hierarchy of substances is abolished: a single one replaces them all: the whole world *can* be plasticized, and even life itself since, we are told, they are beginning to make plastic aortas.

NOTES

Extracts from Barthes, R., 'Myth Today', 'The New Citröen' and 'Plastic,' in Barthes, R., *Mythologies* (1957), translated by Annette Lavers, New York: Hall and Wang, 1994, pp. 109–59, 88–90, 97–99. Translation copyright © 1972 by Jonathan Cape Ltd. Reprinted by permission of Hill and Wang, a division of Farrar, Straus and Giroux, LLC, and by The Random House Group Ltd.

1. Innumerable other meanings of the word 'myth' can be cited against this. But I have tried to define things, not words.
2. *Tel Quel*, II, p. 191.

55

INTRODUCTION AND THE SENSE OF DISTINCTION, FROM *DISTINCTION: A SOCIAL CRITIQUE OF THE JUDGEMENT OF TASTE*

Pierre Bourdieu (1979)

INTRODUCTION

There is an economy of cultural goods, but it has a specific logic. Sociology endeavours to establish the conditions in which the consumers of cultural goods, and their taste for them, are produced, and at the same time to describe the different ways of appropriating such of these objects as are regarded at a particular moment as works of art, and the social conditions of the constitution of the mode of appropriation that is considered legitimate. But one cannot fully understand cultural practices unless 'culture', in the restricted, normative sense of ordinary usage, is brought back into 'culture' in the anthropological sense, and the elaborated taste for the most refined objects is reconnected with the elementary taste for the flavours of food.

Whereas the ideology of charisma regards taste in legitimate culture as a gift of nature, scientific observation shows that cultural needs are the product of upbringing and education: surveys establish that all cultural practices (museum visits, concert-going, reading etc.) and preferences in literature, painting or music, are closely linked to educational level (measured by qualifications or length of schooling) and secondarily to social origin.[1] The relative weight of home background and of formal education (the effectiveness and duration of which are closely dependent on social origin) varies according to the extent to which the different cultural practices are recognized and taught by the educational system, and the influence of social origin is strongest – other things being equal – in 'extra-curricular' and avant-garde culture. To the socially recognized hierarchy of the arts, and within each of them, of genres, schools or periods, corresponds a social hierarchy of the consumers. This predisposes tastes to function as markers of 'class'. The manner in which culture has been acquired lives on in the manner of using it: the importance attached to manners can be understood once it is seen that it is these imponderables of practice which distinguish the different – and ranked – modes of culture acquisition, early or late, domestic or scholastic, and the classes of individuals which they characterize (such as 'pedants' and *mondains*). Culture also has its titles of nobility – awarded by the educational system – and its pedigrees, measured by seniority in admission to the nobility.

The definition of cultural nobility is the stake in a struggle which has gone on unceasingly, from the seventeenth century to the present day, between groups differing in their ideas of culture and of the legitimate relation to culture and to works of art, and therefore differing in the conditions of acquisition of which these dispositions are the product.[2] Even in the classroom, the dominant definition of the legitimate way of appropriating culture and works of art favours those who have had early access to legitimate culture, in a cultured household, outside of scholastic disciplines, since even within the educational system it devalues scholarly knowledge and interpretation as 'scholastic' or even 'pedantic' in favour of direct experience and simple delight.

The logic of what is sometimes called, in typically 'pedantic' language, the 'reading' of a work of art, offers an objective basis for this opposition. Consumption is, in this case, a stage in a process of communication, that is, an act of deciphering, decoding, which presupposes practical or explicit mastery of a cipher or code. In a sense, one can say that the capacity to see (*voir*) is a function of the knowledge (*savoir*), or concepts, that is, the words, that are available to name visible things, and which are, as it were, programmes for perception. A work of art has meaning and interest only for someone who possesses the cultural competence, that is, the code, into which it is encoded. The conscious or unconscious implementation of explicit or implicit schemes of perception and appreciation which constitutes pictorial or musical culture is the hidden condition for recognizing the styles characteristic of a period, a school or an author, and, more generally, for the familiarity with the internal logic of works that aesthetic enjoyment presupposes. A beholder who lacks the specific code feels lost in a chaos of sounds and rhythms, colours and lines, without rhyme or reason. [...]

Although art obviously offers the greatest scope to the aesthetic disposition, there is no area of practice in which the aim of purifying, refining and sublimating primary needs and impulses cannot assert itself, no area in which the stylization of life, that is, the primacy of forms over function, of manner over matter, does not produce the same effects. And nothing is more distinctive, more distinguished, than the capacity to confer aesthetic status on objects that are banal or even 'common' (because the 'common' people make them their own, especially for aesthetic purposes), or the ability to apply the principles of a 'pure' aesthetic to the most everyday choices of everyday life, e.g.,

in cooking, clothing or decoration, completely reversing the popular disposition which annexes aesthetics to ethics.

In fact, through the economic and social conditions which they presuppose, the different ways of relating to realities and fictions, of believing in fictions and the realities they simulate, with more or less distance and detachment, are very closely linked to the different possible positions in social space and, consequently, bound up with the systems of dispositions (habitus) characteristic of the different classes and class fractions. Taste classifies, and it classifies the classifier. Social subjects, classified by their classifications, distinguish themselves by the distinctions they make, between the beautiful and the ugly, the distinguished and the vulgar, in which their position in the objective classifications is expressed or betrayed. And statistical analysis does indeed show that oppositions similar in structure to those found in cultural practices also appear in eating habits. The antithesis between quantity and quality, substance and form, corresponds to the opposition – linked to different distances from necessity – between the taste of necessity, which favours the most 'filling' and most economical foods, and the taste of liberty – or luxury – which shifts the emphasis to the manner (of presenting, serving, eating etc.) and tends to use stylized forms to deny function.

The science of taste and of cultural consumption begins with a transgression that is in no way aesthetic: it has to abolish the sacred frontier which makes legitimate culture a separate universe, in order to discover the intelligible relations which unite apparently incommensurable 'choices', such as preferences in music and food, painting and sport, literature and hairstyle. This barbarous reintegration of aesthetic consumption into the world of ordinary consumption abolishes the opposition, which has been the basis of high aesthetics since Kant, between the 'taste of sense' and the 'taste of reflection', and between facile pleasure, pleasure reduced to a pleasure of the senses, and pure pleasure, pleasure purified of pleasure, which is predisposed to become a symbol of moral excellence and a measure of the capacity for sublimation which defines the truly human man. The culture which results from this magical division is sacred. Cultural consecration does indeed confer on the objects, persons and situations it couches, a sort of ontological promotion akin to a transubstantiation. [...]

The denial of lower, coarse, vulgar, venal, servile – in a word, natural – enjoyment, which constitutes the sacred sphere of culture, implies an affirmation of the superiority of those who can be satisfied with the sublimated, refined, disinterested, gratuitous, distinguished pleasures forever closed to the profane. That is why art and cultural consumption are predisposed, consciously and deliberately or not, to fulfil a social function of legitimating social differences.

THE SENSE OF DISTINCTION

A GRAND BOURGEOIS 'UNIQUE AMONG HIS KIND'[3]

S. a lawyer aged 45, is the son of a lawyer and his family belongs to the Parisian *grande bourgeoisie*. His wife, the daughter of an engineer, studies at the Paris Political Science Institute and does not work. Their four children are at the 'best' private Catholic secondary schools in Paris. They live in a very big apartment (more than 300 square metres) in the 16th arrondissement: a very large entrance-hall, a spacious living-room, a dining-room, a study, and the bedrooms (his office is not in the apartment).

In the living-room, modern furniture (big cushions, a large couch, armchairs), antiquities,

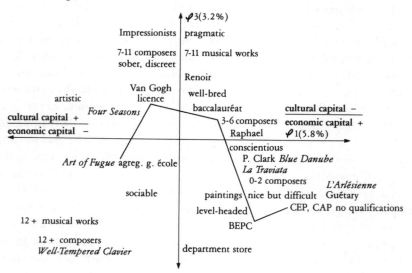

266 / *Class Tastes and Life-Styles*

Figure 13 Variants of the dominant taste. Analysis of correspondences: simplified plane diagram of 1st and 3rd axes of inertia.

This simplified diagram only includes variables which make an absolute contribution equal to or greater than 1.5%. The only illustrative variable represented is educational qualification.

Figure 40. 'Variants of the dominant taste. Analysis of correspondences: simplified plane diagram of 1st and 3rd axes of inertia' in Pierre Bourdieu, *Distinction: A Social Critique of the Judgement of Taste* (1979), translated by Richard Nice, London and Cambridge, MA: Harvard College and Routledge and Kegan Paul, 1984, p. 266. Copyright © 1984 by the President and Fellows of Harvard College and Routledge & Kegan Paul Ltd. Reprinted by permission of the publisher, and by Taylor and Francis Books, UK.

'a Greek head in stone, authentic and rather beautiful' (a wedding present), an object which the head of the household calls his 'personal altar' ('a rather attractive religious thing I managed to get off my parents' – his father collects all sorts of objets d'art, and has bought, among other things, 'all sorts of stuff, enamel-work, chalices, crosses … from a sort of Russian, a dealer'), 'a terracotta thing from the Tang dynasty', bought from an antique shop in Formosa where he went accompanied by ten specialists, several paintings, a Paul Sérusier ('It is rather charming but, that said, I'd just as soon put a modern picture in its place'), in the dining-room a Dutch still life.

[…]

'For My Personal Enjoyment'   For his country house in Burgundy, a very big one ('a thousand square metres to furnish, after all!'), almost a 'mistress', he bought furniture from 'a rag-and-bone man': 'I came across a chap, a junk dealer, who had solid wood furniture, real country-style, and I bought other bits and pieces, stuffed animals', including stuffed boars 'which outraged everyone, except me … because they are funny. Pleasure is what is fun.'

'I'm irritated by people who buy things just to show them off, to say they've got them or put them in a particular place. The value isn't what counts, it's the pleasure it gives you … I bought the boars for my personal enjoyment, or simply because I found it was funny, a joke, or because it annoyed other people.' The house is 'too damp to put a decent piano in it' but he is 'going to get a grand piano … At the casino, they are throwing out old grand pianos … perhaps they have a note or two missing.'

'Heirlooms? Don't Make Me Laugh'   The inherited objects with which he has furnished the house are of little interest to him. When his wife reminds him that there are some, he replies: 'Heirlooms? Don't make me laugh, there have been three bits of furniture.' She enumerates them: 'When we were getting married, Aunt X. popped off. I inherited a certain amount of silver: first legacy. Then there was Madame C.: second legacy. Then Mademoiselle L.: third legacy.' 'So we have a certain amount of china, old bits and pieces and furniture. Furniture has never been much of a problem for us because we inherited a certain amount. Fourth legacy, my in-laws got rid of some of their property. We got some armchairs …'

If he does not like this furniture, he 'chucks it out': 'not too much clutter'. 'You need a big enough apartment, rooms which allow you a certain inner silence, uncluttered and then on the other hand, you need rooms containing all the personal objects which are never souvenirs – they can go into the dustbin – but objects you like to have around you.' He 'detests travel souvenirs' and never brings any back ('except the thing I just mentioned, the Chinese terracotta … I've bought little knick-knacks and trinkets that we've distributed to all and sundry, but we've never cluttered ourselves up … Looking around, you wouldn't know we'd traveled. The local souvenir, bought on the spot, has no interest whatsoever'). Besides, when you're traveling, it's better to keep an open mind, 'walk around with your hands in your pockets and look around you, but without having one eye glued to a view-finder' (in the Far East, his wife recalls, 'we took photos', but, she adds, 'we looked at them, showed them round once or twice', and now they are 'at the bottom of the cupboard').

[…]

'I Have a High Opinion of Myself'   He refuses any sartorial 'refinement': 'If people want to see me, it's not for the socks I'm wearing, my pocket handkerchief or the flower in my buttonhole, or my tie. If people want to see me or invite me to dinner, they invite me as I am. In other words, I have a high opinion of myself,' he explains, taking the opportunity to indicate once again his distance both from bourgeois taste and from

the questions put to him by the sociologist (who belongs to his wife's family). He adds: 'I think that five hundred francs is quite enough for a suit, there's no point in spending a thousand francs on a suit when personally I don't give a damn.'

[...]

A 'TRULY CLASSICAL' UNIVERSITY TEACHER

Jean L., aged 36, an alumnus of the Ecole Normale Supérieure, has the *agrégation* in physics. He is now a *maître-assistant* (senior lecturer or assistant professor) in one of the Paris universities and lives in the north-western suburbs. His father (an *agrégé* in grammar) was a lycée teacher. He wife, a pharmacist's daughter, is a dentist. She teaches at the Paris Dental School and also runs her own practice.

'A Louis XIII Convent Table from the Flea Market' Preferring 'sobriety' and 'discretion', Jean dislikes 'fat cushions and heavy curtains', and 'apartments done up by interior designers.' He is 'quite sensitive to the overall harmony of an interior': 'If you're lucky enough to come across a really fine piece of furniture, you put that one piece in a corner. That's all you need for a whole room.' 'At home, until recently, we had cheap furniture that we bought when we married. A quietly modern style that wasn't unattractive. Veneered teak, quite cheap, but now the chairs are giving up the ghost ... Now we have one or two old bits of furniture that we've picked up, real antiques ... a Louis XIII convent table that someone spotted for us in the Flea Market, a Louis XIII chest that isn't bad', found in an antique shop in Amiens. 'Of course, we won't be getting any Louis XIII chairs – for one thing they're terribly expensive, and anyway, if they're genuine, they're not even solid. So we'll get some made for us in the same style but without pretending to be antique.' The decorating and furnishing of the house are mainly left to his wife who attaches a great deal of importance to them. 'She's quite expert at that, I'm not, especially as regards prices ... I enjoy it, but when all's said and done, if I were on my own I don't think I'd devote much time to it. I haven't got much of a taste for it, but my wife certainly has and in the end I do appreciate it, all the same.' His wife is very fond of old *faïence*: 'I'm always willing to accompany her if she says, "Come along, let's go and look at some porcelain." I know I'll enjoy it, I know she's much more sensitive to it than I am ... There's one thing I'd really like to buy, I haven't done so yet, but I sometimes look: it's old scientific instruments, because they used to make some remarkable things in the last century and three or four centuries back.'

[...]

A YOUNG EXECUTIVE WHO 'KNOWS HOW TO LIVE'

Michel R., an advertising executive working in a Paris agency, the son of the managing director of the French subsidiary of a leading multinational corporation, studied in a private Catholic secondary school in the 17th arrondissement and then at the Paris Political Science Institute; his wife, Isabelle, the daughter of a provincial industrialist, also went to Sciences Po and works for a weekly news-magazine. He is 30, she is 28; they have two children. They live in Paris, in a modern five-roomed apartment in the 15th arrondissement. They like things to be 'snug and cosy'. They have no interest in 'home-improvement' and have kept their apartment as they found it. 'The decoration is all the work of our predecessor. I didn't much like the green in the dining-room, it was rather gloomy, but we got used to it, and I get bored working on the place I live in.' 'I have that beading on the doors, I'd like to get rid of it. The pseudo 16th or 18th-century veneering or whatever it is all over this modern apartment is ghastly; I put up with it but it gets on my nerves,' says Michel, who has removed some of it but 'couldn't face the rest'.

[...]

'We'd Seen a Lot of Mediocre Stuff' The dining-room tables and chairs, mahogany, 18th-century English style, were bought in London as soon as they were married. 'I don't know if we'd do the same thing today ... I can't remember why we bought them, but from a bourgeois point of view they must be a good investment.' After visiting many antique shops, they 'finally chose something very expensive. It would have cost twice as much in Paris. We'd seen a lot of mediocre stuff and decided we didn't like it. Importing the furniture 'was no problem. It's exempt from customs duties. You just have to pay VAT [value-added tax].' In the living-room they have some modern and some old furniture, a bookcase from Roche-Bobois, a sofa from a shop in Le village Suisse ...

Michel's car is 'only an old Peugeot 404', whereas his bosses 'have got Jaguars, the director of the agency has an Alfa-Romeo, a Lancia'. 'From time to time, they say, "So you aren't trading it in?" They'd be relieved if I got a new car. They're afraid I'll visit clients in my car.'

'The Right Sort of Clothes for People in Advertising' Though at weekends, at home, he wears 'a filthy pair of trousers', for work he dresses with great care and elegance. He buys his suits at Barnes, the advertising man's tailor, in the rue Victor Hugo in Paris. 'They're the right sort of clothes for people who make it in advertising – English cloth, Price of Wales checks with a touch of luxury. Not the sort of thing civil servants could wear, and bank managers couldn't get away with it either. In banking you need a plain shirt; banking isn't showy whereas in advertising, people put every penny they earn into clothes ... In my business we're constantly classifying people, there are social classes, castes, and it's a matter of fitting a product to the right caste. When someone new comes to the agency, we size them up at a

glance ... A guy with a velvet suit and big lapels is compensating for something, he's not very sure of himself, he wants to make an impression.' For a while, the agency had 'a finance manager from a very modest background; when he arrived he was so badly dressed that it was bad for business ... he was dressed like a junior clerk.' 'Wearing a suit with narrow lapels, narrow bottoms, a bit short, in a loud colour with a shirt that doesn't match and a narrow tie, for example, by our standards, that's grotty.'

NOTES

Extracted from Bourdieu, P., 'Introduction,' and 'The Sense of Distinction,' in *Distinction: A Social Critique of the Judgement of Taste*, translated by Richard Nice, London and Cambridge, MA: Harvard College and Routledge & Kegan Paul, 1984, pp. 1–7, 260–317. Copyright © 1984 by the President and Fellows of Harvard College and Routledge & Kegan Paul Ltd. Reprinted by permission of the publisher, and by Taylor and Francis Books, UK.

1. Bourdieu et al., *Un art moyen: essai sur les usages sociaux de la photographie* (Paris, Ed. De Minuit, 1965); P. Bourdieu and A. Darbel, *L'Amour de l'art: les musées et leur public* (Paris, Ed. De Minuit, 1966).

2. The word *disposition* seems particularly suited to express what is covered by the concept of habitus (defined as a system of dispositions) – used later in this chapter. It expresses first the *result of an organizing action*, with a meaning close to that of words such as structure; it also designates a way of being, a habitual state (especially of the body) and, in particular, a *predisposition, tendency, propensity* or *inclination*. [The semantic cluster of 'disposition' is rather wider in French than in English, but as this note – translated literally – shows, the equivalence is adequate. Translator.] P. Bourdieu, *Outline of a Theory of Practice* (Cambridge, Cambridge University Press, 1977), p. 214, n. 1.

3. All these interviews (this one and those of the same type that follow) were carried out in 1974, with the aim of collecting, as systematically as possible, the most significant features of each of the life-styles that had emerged from analysis of the survey, which had already reached a fairly advanced stage. Given previous knowledge of the generative formula of his or her properties and practices, it was decided to lead the interviewee (who was often a relation or acquaintance of the interviewer) methodically towards the most central areas of his or her life-style (hence the heterogeneity of the themes discussed, which contrasts with the forced homogeneity of statistical survey data). This was done by supplying all the reassurances and reinforcements that are expected in ordinary life from someone in whom one 'confides'. Finally, by tightening the discourse, through alternating use of direct, semi-direct and indirect quotation, the aim has been to intensify and so make palpable the concrete image of the systematic totality, the life-style, which statistical analysis dissolves even as it brings it to light.

56

'PARTIES ARE THE ANSWER': THE ASCENT OF THE TUPPERWARE PARTY

Alison J. Clarke (1999)

By 1954 the American press described Tupperware parties as "the newest selling idea to take the country by storm."[1] *Tupperware Sparks*, the corporate in-house magazine, announced, "We're 20,000 strong!" as a network of dealers, distributors, and managers (consisting predominantly of housewives between the ages of twenty-five and forty) took the Tupperware "gospel" to the nation.[2]

[...]

'A PICNIC GROUND FOR DIRECT SELLING': THE CONSUMPTION SPACE OF SUBURBIA

In 1953 *Fortune* featured one of numerous editorials identifying suburbia as a key new consumer market: "Anybody who wants to sell anything to Americans, from appliances to zithers, must look closely at Suburbia."[3] This "big and lush and uniform" environment offered astute marketers an abundant supply of easily targeted consumers. [...]

Throughout the 1950s the suburban home became the focus for critiques and celebrations of postwar change and national identity. This culminated in 1959 with the renowned "Kitchen Debate" between Vice President Richard Nixon and Soviet Premier Nikita Sergeyevich Khrushchev at the American National Exhibition in

Moscow. A showcase for American consumer goods and technology, the exhibit featured a fully equipped model of a ranch-style suburban home, representative of the supremacy of the U.S. average standard of living. "Thirty-one million families own their own homes," asserted Nixon in his depiction of a post-war consumer republic. "America's 44 million families own a total of 56 million cars, 50 million television sets and 143 million radio sets. And they buy an average of nine dresses and suits and 14 pairs of shoes per family per year."[4] Whereas Khrushchev argued that such excessive consumption was a testament to the inferior quality of American "gadgetry," Nixon flaunted free enterprise, home ownership, and the abundance of goods as a means of diffusing class conflict and creating social cohesion.[5]

In this context Tupperware dealers were, the corporate culture stressed, "privileged to have their voices heard in the world's largest auditorium – the American living room."[6] "Direct selling," they were told by the mid-1950s, "is as American as corn on the cob. We must conduct ourselves ... in such as way that we can make our own individual communities and our country proud of the direct selling industry."[7] As archetypal postwar developments (epitomized by Levittown, Long Island, and Park Forest, south of Chicago) differed radically from older residential and urban communities, showing none of the reassuring signs of established and immutable communities, they created their own institutions and rituals, which

Figure 41. 'Brownie Wise, vice president and general manager of THP [Tupperware Home Parties], demonstrates the power of charismatic dealership as she throws a liquid-filled Wonder Bowl provocatively across the room at a crowded Tupperware party, ca. 1952' in Alison J. Clarke, *Tupperware: The Promise of Plastic in 1950s America*, Washington, DC and London: Smithsonian Institution Press, 1999, p. 97. Photo: Brownie Wise Papers, Archives Center, National Museum of American History, Behring Center, Smithsonian Institution. Reprinted courtesy of the Smithsonian Institution.

were embodied in the Tupperware party – the ideal home-based networking opportunity for a newly displaced population.

THE 'TUPPERWARE PARTY': SOCIALITY, MODERNITY, AND MASS CONSUMPTION

By 1951 the Tupperware party had captured the direct sales market by offering its overtly fashionable, fun-filled events. Regional distributorships with titles such as Patio Parties and Vogue Plastics spread the party plan network nationwide,

upgrading this established sales scheme by reconstituting it as a radically modern, leisurely, and convivial event. The Tupperware party promoted home shopping as a time-saving, sociable, and integral part of the modern homemaker's life: "Tupperware Parties are fun! You 'feel at home,' because they're informal and you shop relaxed."[8]

As a women's event, the Tupperware version of the hostess party acted as a celebratory and consciously feminine activity. With the "Modern Way to Shop," a woman could combine "a neighborly visit with armchair shopping" and improve her knowledge of household economy, by benefiting from novel recipes and homemaking tips.[9] A Get-Acquainted Set of basic Tupperware pieces initiated novices to the social relations and commodities of the Tupperware system. For more experienced party guests the introduction of new product types ensured a sustained consumer (and dealer) interest. For example, as "the latest in modern design," a set of slim-line TV Tumblers, which made their debut in 1955 under the slogan "Christian Dior isn't the only one coming out with a 'new look' these days," drew on popular references to women's fashion. Devised as "the perfect answer to beverage serving when watching your favorite TV program," the "soft-glowing" modern tumblers, which brought together the dual concerns of fashion and television culture, came equipped with Tumblemates (12-inch [30.5 centimeter] drink stirrers) and matching wagon-wheel coasters.[10]

Tupperware parties animated the product range using detailed description and highly tactile, even sensual, displays. Women were encouraged to touch and handle products. Party game sessions, in which miniature Tupperware trinkets were awarded for performance, broke down inhibitions and countered the passivity of the captured audience. With titles such as "Clothes Pin," "Waist Measurement" (best avoided if "expecting mothers are present," warned a corporate booklet), "Game of Gossip," and "Chatter," the games celebrated overtly feminine issues. Games such as "Elastic Relay," "Partner Balloon Burst," and "Grab Bag" required physical contact between party guests. Other games played at these sessions were vaguely subversive (and according to oral histories, immensely memorable), such as "Hubby," in which guests were asked to write hypothetical newspaper advertisements to sell their unwanted partners, and then they were told to swap ads and read them aloud to the group. One, for example, read: "One husband for sale. Balding, often cranky, stomach requiring considerable attention!"[11]

In addition to serving as a highly rarefied sales form, the party acted as a ritual ceremony that, while focusing on Tupperware products, was filled with social significance among maker, buyer, and user. The structure of the party plan system blurred the theoretical boundaries of several identifying categories such as domesticity and commerce, work and leisure, friend and colleague, consumer and employee. "It was developed," according to the trade journal *Specialty Salesman*, "to appeal to women who wanted to earn extra money but were too timid to use pressure or endure rebuffs in conventional selling. In party selling you never have to ring the doorbell of a dark house … guests will be coming where the party is scheduled. Every time you have a party, you earn money."[12]

Gifts and commodities abounded as the hostess offered the intimacy of her home and the range of her social relations with other women (relatives, friends, and neighbors) to the Tupperware dealer in exchange for a nonmonetary reward. The dealer, overseen by an area distributor, used the space to set up a display of products and recruit further hostesses from among the guests, benefiting from commission accrued on sales and the potential for further party reservations.

Dorothy Dealer's Dating Diary, a full-color cartoon booklet issued to potential dealers, outlined strategies of informal salesmanship, networking and "friend finding." Women were dissuaded from adopting a corporate image and encouraged to use their own social skills to "create incentive or change excuses into a positive party date." A typical scenario read:

Potential hostess: Oh, but Janice I just can't have a party … I'm right in the middle of redecorating.

Dealer: But wouldn't that be a wonderful chance for your friends to see your newly decorated home?[13]

Other scenarios included reluctant husbands less than keen on "allowing" their wives to act as hostesses to an event that would fill their home with neighborhood women and plastic pots. The *Dorothy Dealer* remedy to this problem revolved around a woman's rational appeal to her husband, reassuring him that the gifts accrued by hosting a party and the savings made through Tupperware food storage far outweighed the inconvenience.

The booklet described the benefits of "prospecting" among a wide range of people and situations (for example, the single working woman, the widow, the urban apartment dweller) and suburbia formed the focus of its attentions. The "Check List for Party Dating," asking dealers "Whom do you know?" proceeded to map out the social relations of suburbia with suggestions ranging from "Your Real Estate Agent" to "Your Neighbors, Church Members and Club Members."[14] Suburban communities were offered the Club Plan and Round Robin schemes, whereby Tupperware parties could be used to supplement the treasury funds of charitable organizations.[15] Dealers were advised, "[W]atch the society page in *your* paper and contact an officer in every club in *your* community!" and they were encouraged with proclamations such as "[I]n every block of homes, in every city and every town, in this wonderful United States of America, there are parties waiting for you."[16]

Although increased community activity provided the Tupperware home party plan with the ultimate arena, the social gathering of women had a historical precedent in the traditional American sewing circle and quilting bee, which appear inextricably bound to the concept of the Tupperware party. Middle-class leisured women gathered to sew together for charity, even if they had seamstresses and servants, within the afternoon sewing circles. It provided a legitimated focal point for a social activity and female companionship. Working-class women had less opportunity to sew on a casual basis but regularly joined the formalized gathering of the quilting bee, which according to historian Susan Strasser was well established in the 1820s as an important women's social activity.[17] Here women across the generations could exchange ideas, hints and methods in sewing and broader aspects of life, while their small children could be attended communally by the quilting party. A nineteenth-century contemporary account provided by Frances Trollope describes these affairs as "quilting frolics," noting that "they are always solemnized with much good cheer and festivity."[18]

Similarly, Tupperware parties were incorporated into the time and labor of everyday domestic economy. Morning events demanded an informal approach indicative of the kaffee-klatsch culture of suburban society, during which light refreshments, "just coffee and doughnuts or sweet rolls," were served. Tupperware parties preempted the daily habits of women as mothers and homemakers. The "second cup of coffee," for example, taken "when the younger set is finally off to school," made a splendid opportunity, Tupperware brochures reiterated, "to enjoy the company of your neighbors by inviting them over for a Tupperware Party." A Tupperware party at "a bake sale, a white elephant sale, a rummage sale or bazaar" contributed to a broader aspect of community life and informal economy.[19] Evening parties – more formal occasions requiring make-up and stylish attire – sanctioned all-female gatherings under the auspices of homemaking duties and offered a welcome escape from homebound activities. The Tupperware bridal shower party solved the potentially hazardous prospect of gift giving; "each guest contribut[ing] toward the Tupperware gift set," instead of debating "what to buy? Or making costly mistakes."[20] Similarly, the Tupperware housewarming party, organized by the local dealer and aimed in particular at newlyweds, offered "every new homeowner" the opportunity to enhance the household with the pastel, jewel-tone colors and modern designs of Tupperware. The significance of Tupperware, "so new in design and principle," as an appropriate, contemporary, feminine gift pervaded corporate literature: "When it comes to gift giving … you may be … sure that it is something she will cherish."[21]

In 1954 top-achieving party dealers working under distributorships such as Par-T-Wise Sales in Chicago, Partying Around in Connecticut, Party Progress in Detroit, and Poly Sales in Los

Angeles made weekly turnovers of between $533 and $629, with an average party attendance of twelve guests. *Tupperware Sparks* told of women grossing $200 with their first party event and achieving multiple party profits of $431 during one week.[22] Sustaining such sales figures proved more difficult as neighborhoods became saturated with the party plan. Ideally the Tupperware party operated as a serial rather than singular occasion; as gestures of reciprocity, party guests honored their hostess's hospitality by agreeing to host their own future event, thus extending the sales network. Corporate literature revealed how women might use a round of parties to amass their collection of Tupperware: "Many people attend six or seven parties without getting all the Tupperware they need and want … for after a while, almost everyone feels that they need a great deal more!"[23]

Tupperware items, from Jell-O molds to flour sifters, expanded as well as consolidated established forms of kitchen culture. Items such as Ice-Tups – do-it-yourself Popsicle molds – proved highly successful, circumventing the need for the commercial equivalents. Although aimed at mothers catering to their children's needs and desire, these products elicit highly personal and intimate memories for many women: "I'd make up the strongest daiquiri mix, you know, and freeze them up in my Tupperware and get through the whole lot of them doing my chores; oh yes, I used to stand there pressing a shirt, happily sucking on one of my Tupperware ices!"[24]

The dealer's practical demonstrations, some of which amounted to performances fusing entertainment and information, introduced unfamiliar products and reiterated the value of tried and tested favorites. Charismatic demonstration was an imperative. "We can turn a casual desire," advised the corporate literature, "into actual need by making a sale on an active visual demonstration. By demonstrating effectively we actually CREATE the need."[25]

The "Tupperware burp" (the technique of pushing the center of the seal to fully engage the lip with the edge of the bowl, creating an airtight seal) formed the focal point of all demonstrations. "I put my finger here – we call this Tupperware's magic button – press down and just 'wink' the edge of the seal. Hear that?" the dealer would ask rhetorically.[26] Elaborations included bounding a sealed Wonder Bowl full of liquid across a nervous hostess's living room or standing one-legged on an upturned canister to reveal its outstanding durability. As well as emphasizing the airtight qualities of the product, features such as the Tupperware burp justified the mode of sales. "We have chosen to sell Tupperware on the popular Home Party Plan," read a party brochure, "because we know that you will derive greater benefits from its use after you have seen its varied and distinctive features demonstrated and explained."[27] Tupperware required a currency of vocabulary to maintain its consumer vogue; party initiates showed their familiarity with the product range by deciphering an often obscure product language: Scrub-E-Z, Serve-n-Save, Hang-It-All, Fly-Bye-Swat, Square Round.

Although demonstrations and brochures suggested conventional product use, internal corporate literature aimed at dealers also acknowledged consumer appropriations and re-interpretations of the Tupperware design. Dealers used anecdotes gathered from women at parties to espouse the product's tried and tested versatility. A typical testament read, "This canister is one of the most useful storage items ever designed … my next door neighbor uses it for her crochet thread … and pulls the end of the thread out through the small opening[;] then her thread never gets soiled … and it doesn't get tangled up."[28]

[…]

NOTES

Extracted from Clarke, A. J., *Tupperware: The Promise of Plastic in 1950s America*, Washington, DC: Smithsonian Institution Press, 1999, pp. 101–12. Reprinted by permission of Smithsonian Books.

1. William G. Samroth, "How to Find, Hire, Train, Keep the All-Women Direct Sales Force," *Sales Management*, 1 May 1954.

2. "We're 20,000 Strong!" *Tupperware Sparks* 3, nos. 21–22 (October–November 1954), front cover.

3. "The Lush New Suburban Market," *Fortune*, November 1953, 129.

4. Elaine Tyler May, *Homeward Bound: American Families in the Cold War Era* (New York: Basic Books, 1988), 163.

5. Vice President Richard Nixon and Soviet Premier Nikita Sergeyevich Khrushchev, upon visiting the American Exhibition in Moscow in 1959 (which featured a model home and numerous household appliances), entered into a lengthy debate focusing on access to mass consumer goods as an indicator of true democracy. See "Nixon in Moscow: Appliances, Affluence and Americanism," in Karal Ann Marling, *As Seen on TV: The Visual Culture of Everyday Life in the 1950s*, Cambridge, Massachusetts: Harvard University Press, 1996, and "The Commodity Gap: Consumerism and the Modern Home," in Tyler May, *Homeward Bound*.

6. *Tupperware Sparks* 2, no. 3 (March 1952): 1.

7. Brownie Wise, "Welcome," rough draft of speech given at the 1955 Homecoming Jubilee, Orlando Fla., NMAH [Archives Center of the National Museum of American History, Smithsonian Institution, Washington, D.C.] 509, series 2.

8. *Tupperware: The Nicest Thing That Could Happen to Your Kitchen*, product catalog (Orlando, Fla.: THP [Tupperware Home Parties], ca. 1958), 1.

9. *Tupperware – A Household Word in Homes Everywhere!*, product catalog (Orlando, Fla.: THP, 1957), 3.

10. *Tupperware Sparks* 4, nos. 3–4 (March–April 1955): 4.

11. *Tupperware Party Games* (Orlando, Fla.: THP, 1956).

12. *Speciality Salesman*, March 1960, 7.

13. *Dorothy Dealer's Dating Diary* (Orlando, Fla.: THP, 1959).

14. "Check List: Whom Do You Know?", ca. 1951, NMAH 509, series 2.

15. The "Tupperware Club Plan" (all members present) and "Round Robin" (parties conducted individually with group members) used demonstrations as the focal point of charitable meetings and gave the dealer access to a high percentage of potential party recruits.

16. Gary McDonald, *A Timely Reminder*, THP pamphlet, 11 June 1952, and "Prospecting and Previewing," transcription from 1953 second managerial convention, NMAH 509, series 2.

17. Susan Strasser, *Never Done: A History of American Housework* (New York: Pantheon, 1982), 133.

18. Donald Smalley and Frances Trollope, eds., *Domestic Manners of the Americans* (New York: Vintage, 1960), 281–82.

19. *Tupperware – A Household Word*, 24.

20. Ibid., 23.

21. *Know-How* (Orlando, Fla.; THP, 1955), 44.

22. *Tupperware Sparks* 3, nos. 12–13 (January–February 1954): 6.

23. *Will You Be My Gold Key Hostess?* (Orlando, Fla.: THP, 1955), 1.

24. Anonymous "mall-walker," one of a group of retirees interviewed by the author, 18 November 1989, in a shopping mall in Osceola, Fla., that local walkers frequent for their early morning exercise.

25. *Tupperware Sparks* 2, nos. 6–7 (June–July 1952): 3.

26. *Market Basket Demonstration*, brochure (Orlando, Fla.: THP, 1956), 2.

27. *The Tupperware Story – A Story of Opportunity* (Orlando, Fla.: THP, 1956), 4.

28. *Dealer Guide to Demonstration* (Orlando, Fla.: THP, 1951), 8.

57

THE REVOLUTION WILL BE MARKETED: AMERICAN CORPORATIONS AND BLACK CONSUMERS DURING THE 1960s

Robert E. Weems, Jr. (1994)

The Black Freedom Movement of the 1950s and 1960s captured the attention of millions. Yet, the African-American experience during this period include more than boycotts, "sit-ins," "freedom rides," and massive protest marches. With the wartime and postwar migration from the South, African-Americans were transformed from a predominately rural people into a predominately urban people by 1960. As African-Americans streamed into American cities, or what American corporations call "major markets," U.S. businesses sought to influence the consumption patterns of these increasingly important black consumers. [...]

Before the 1960s, American corporations generally ignored African-American consumers. Most black-oriented radio stations, for example, experienced difficulties attracting advertising from large corporations; most had to demonstrate to prospective corporate advertisers the potential profitability of advertising aimed at black consumers. The establishment of the National Negro Network, Inc. (NNN) in 1954 represented one such effort.[1] The NNN was a nationwide consortium of forty two black-oriented radio stations formed to attract "blue-chip" corporate advertising. To assist this campaign, the NNN produced a daytime serial entitled "Ruby Valentine" that aired on the network's affiliates. In promoting "Ruby Valentine" to potential corporate advertisers, the NNN's promotional material declared:

Now ... for the first time in advertising history ... a singly coordinated program can take you to the heart of the 16 billion dollar American Negro market. This new selling concept offers an advertiser a rich sales frontier virtually uncultivated by national advertising.[2]

By the early sixties, as African-Americans proliferated in U.S. cities, American corporations no longer had to be convinced of the profitability of seeking black customers. This is borne out by such advertising trade journals as *Sponsor*, *Advertising Age*, and *Broadcasting*, all of which began featuring articles about the "Negro Market" and its growing importance to corporate marketers.[3] [...]

This significant black migration to northern, southern, and western cities represented not only a change of address for the migrants, but a distinct improvement in their occupational status. Between 1940 and 1960, the percentage of African-Americans in (relatively low-paying) southern agriculture work declined dramatically. Moreover, as fewer and fewer blacks worked in agriculture, the larger society – especially corporate America – slowly began to change its perception of African-Americans. By the early 1960s, blacks, once viewed as poor, rural workers with a minimum of disposable income, were seen as a market whose annual purchasing power exceeded that of Canada.[4]

Although 1960 census data demonstrated African-American gains in income and their strategic proliferation in major markets,[5] many corporations, who had previously ignored the African-American consumer market, were at a loss as to how to reach black shoppers. Consequently, advertising trade journals throughout the 1960s assisted these corporations by featuring numerous "how-to" articles concerning selling to African-Americans. [...]

Armed with insights about the psyche of black Americans, and market research data that demonstrated that blacks listened to radio more frequently that whites,[6] corporate marketers increasingly used radio advertising to reach African-American consumers. Between 1961 and 1966, American corporations, according to *Broadcasting* (another advertising trade journal), increased their advertising budget for black-oriented radio stations three-fold.[7] American corporations maximized their advertising campaigns on black-oriented radio stations by encouraging African-American radio personalities (disc jockeys) to directly market their products.[8] Because black disc jockeys were celebrities in their own right, they were ideal potential allies for white-owned businesses seeking to make inroads in a new market.

[...]

While national, regional, and local white business were accelerating their use of black-oriented radio to reach black consumers, these same companies sought as much information as possible concerning the nuances of the "Negro Market." But American racism and the legacy of racial segregation left most white businesspersons ill-equipped to understand African-American life. Consequently, many white companies had to rely upon the services of black consultants, the most influential being John H. Johnson, publisher of *Ebony* magazine, and D. Parke Gibson, president of D. Parke Gibson Associates, Inc.

Johnson had long been interested in making corporate America aware of the potential profits associated with black consumers. As early as 1947, Johnson's *Ebony* asserted that major corporations were missing lucrative opportunities by ignoring the African-American market.[9] It should be noted, however, that Johnson's observations were based upon self-interest. From the moment of its founding in 1945, *Ebony* failed to secure substantial advertising from large corporations.[10]

Nevertheless, by the early 1960s, *Ebony* had established itself as a major American magazine and John H. Johnson stood as one of the country's top executives. Moreover, Johnson's success as a publisher appeared to have been based upon his ability to gauge the mood and interests of his readers.[11] Consequently, to white corporate leaders seeking insights about black consumers, Johnson appeared to be an ideal ally. In his autobiography, *Succeeding Against the Odds*, Johnson described his consulting role to corporate America as follows:

> In the decade of the long hot summers, I held the unofficial position of special ambassador to American Whites ... Enlightened self-interest: that was my theme. I asked corporate leaders to act not for Blacks, not for civil rights, but for their corporations and themselves. For it was true then and it's true now that if you increase the income of Blacks and Hispanics and poor Whites, you increase the profits of corporate America. And if you decrease the income of the disadvantaged, you decrease income and potential income of American corporations. What it all boiled down to was that equal opportunity was good business.[12]

Johnson's advice to corporate American deserves closer examination. His theme of "enlightened self-interest" suggest a major reinterpretation of the 1960s. If corporate leaders took Johnson's message to heart, it can plausibly be argued that some of the gains associated with the Civil Rights

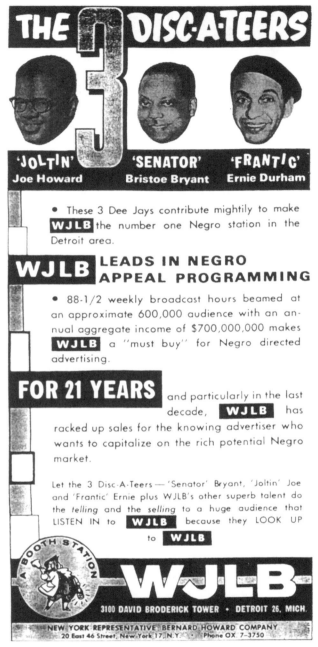

Sponsor Negro Issue (9 October 1961), 25. Courtesy of Walter Williams Library, School of Journalism, University of Missouri-Columbia.

Figure 42. *Sponsor Negro Issue* (9 October 1961), 25. Reprinted from Robert E. Weems, Jr., 'The Revolution Will Be Marketed: American Corporations and Black Consumers during the 1960s,' *Radical History Review*, 59 (Spring 1994), pp. 94–107.

Movement were based upon "conservative," rather than "liberal" impulses.

For example, during the sixties, the Congress of Racial Equality (CORE) stood in the forefront of the movement to force American corporations to use African-American models in their print and television advertising. To CORE and other civil rights organizations, this was a "social" issue.[13] However, when U.S. businesses realized that using black models increased black purchases of their products without alienating white consumers,[14] corporations gladly utilized black models in print media and on television. Johnson's concern about the "enlightened self-interest" (profits) of large white corporations appeared intimately connected with his concern about *Ebony's* financial well-being. Once he convinced corporate leaders that it was "good business" to reach more black consumers, these same corporations had to find a vehicle to do just that. Although Johnson's autobiography claims that he did not directly approach white corporate leaders about advertising in *Ebony* during the 1960s,[15] *Ebony's* advertising revenue nearly tripled between 1962 and 1969.

While Johnson urged corporate America to take a greater interest in selling to African-American consumers, D. Parke Gibson advised corporate America on how to most effectively reach black consumers. Gibson's company, established in 1960, specialized in market research and public relations consulting.[16] Gibson and his associates subsequently offered their services to a myriad of companies, including Avon Products, Inc., Coca Cola USA, Columbia Pictures, Greyhound, and the R.J. Reynolds Tobacco company.[17] Moreover, Gibson published two books about the African-American consumer market, *The $30 Billion Dollar Negro* (1969), and *$70 Billion In the Black* (1978).

An example of the advice Gibson's company gave its corporate clients appeared in the 25 July 1966 issue of *Sponsor*. Elsie Archer, director of the company's Women's Interest Bureau, published a brief article entitled "How To Sell Today's Negro Woman." Among other things, Archer offered the following insights about the black female consumer:

She wants advertising and marketing people to understand that her needs and desires are often different. For example, she does not want a blue-eyed suburban housewife telling her to use a particular product when she is faced with urban living. Particularly in the area of personal care products, advertisers should use extreme caution to avoid pricking the high sensitivity of the Negro woman ... One last word – never, never, under any circumstances refer to the Negro woman as "Negress or Negressess," a phrase guaranteed to produce an unfavorable reaction.[18]

About the same time Archer instructed corporate America on how to best reach African-American female consumers, the black community was in the throes of a dramatic shift in political orientation. Despite corporate America's increasing recognition of black consumers, as well as the passage of the Civil Rights Act of 1964 and the Voting Act of 1965, a significant proportion of African-Americans remained frustrated and angry about continuing racial injustice in the United States. The Watts Rebellion of 1965, along with the immediate popularity of the term "Black Power" in 1966, reflected a growing militancy toward, and mistrust of, white society.

The appearance of overt black nationalist sentiment during the mid 1960s initially confused corporate executives. During the early 1960s, they had been led to believe that African-Americans were preoccupied with trying to assimilate into mainstream U.S. society. For example, the 4 October 1963 issue of *Sales Management* featured an article entitled "The Negro Market: Growing, Changing, Challenging," which not only surveyed what the author believed were the basic characteristics of black consumers, but sought to project their activities into the immediate future. Considering what *actually* happened, the following prognostication turned out to be way off the mark: "Negroes will de-emphasize race consciousness and differences, and focus attention on social and cultural similarities compatible with the concept and practice of an integrated society."[19]

Despite their initial confusion, corporate markets quickly adjusted their marketing campaigns aimed at African-American consumers. Early 1960s' ad campaigns that sought to promote the image of an integrated society[20] were replaced with attempts to exploit blacks' growing sense of racial pride. The development of the "soul market" illustrates corporate America's attempt to adapt to African-American consumers' political and cultural reorientation. Corporate marketers co-opted growing black pride by extolling the virtues of African-American life and culture. Moreover, such things as "Soul Music" and "Soul Food" were promoted for both black and white consumption. From a business point of view, the "soul market" appeared to be especially profitable. Not only would corporate America reach African-Americans, but also faddish whites wanting to be viewed as "hip."

[…]

About the same time corporate America desired to make its existing products attractive to "soul brother and sisters," some white-owned companies sought to expand their black customer base by developing consumer items exclusively for African-Americans. This trend centered around the production of black personal care products. During the "Jim Crow" era, African-American entrepreneurs had monopolized the production of hair and skin products for blacks. An examination of advertisements in black newspapers during the early to mid twentieth century reveals myriad such products.[21] White corporations, because of their general disregard for black consumers, had little interest in getting a share of the black personal care products market. However, as the African-American standard of living rose during the 1960s, and as market research revealed that blacks spent a significant proportion of money on personal care products, some white-owned companies made a concerted effort to produce these goods.[22]

[…]

By the beginning of the 1970s, African-Americans were recognized as an increasingly important consumer market. Indeed, American corporations took the advice offered by trade journals and black consultants, and actively wooed prospective African-American customers. Yet, continuing racial strife clearly indicates that blacks, while desired as shoppers, are often less desired by whites as classmates, co-workers, and neighbors. Moreover, African-Americans' current annual collective spending power of between $250–300 billion has not halted the steady decline of urban black America. These ongoing problems suggest that black consumers, despite their recognized importance to the U.S. economy, cannot *buy* substantive respect and power from American corporations.[23]

NOTES

Extracted from Weems, R. E., Jr., 'The Revolution Will Be Marketed: American Corporations and Black Consumers during the 1960s,' *Radical History Review* 59 (Spring 1994), pp. 94–107. Copyright, 1994, MARHO: The Radical Historians Organization, Inc. All rights reserved. Used by permission of the publisher, Duke University Press.

1. "NNN: Negro Radio's Network," *Sponsor* (20 September 1954), 54. It is important to note that the overwhelming majority of these black-oriented radio stations were owned by white entrepreneurs. See William Barlow, "Commerical and Noncommerical Radio" in *Split Image: African-Americans In The Mass Media*, ed. Jannette L. Dates and William Barlow (Washington, D.C.: Howard University Press, 1990), 209, 214.

2. "NNN: Negro Radio's Network," *Sponsor* (20 September 1954), 46.

3. A crosssection of such articles included: C.H. Hall, "Advertisers' Guide To Marketing, 1960 Negro Market," *Printer's Ink* (30 October 1959), 246–47; "Marketing To The Negro Consumer; Special Report," *Sales Management* (4 March 1960), 36–44; "Tapping The Negro Market; Association Formed To Promote Its Value," *Broadcasting* (8 August 1960), 52; "Know-How Is Key To Selling Negro Market Today," *Sponsor Negro Issue* (9 October 1961), 9–10; H.C. Russell, "Ads Alone Won't Win Negro Market," *Advertising Age* (21 October 1963), 3; "Is There a U.S. Negro Market? *Yes* Can It Be Reached As Easily As Any Other Market? *No*", *Sponsor* (17 August 1964), 32.

4. "Know-How Is Key to Selling Negro Today," *Sponsor Negro Issue* (9 October 1961), 9.

5. "Past Decade Saw the Market Zoom," *Sponsor Negro Issue* (9 October 1961), 11–12, 33, 37.

6. "Negro Radio's Prosperous Market," *Sponsor Negro Issue*, (26 September 1960), 47; "Radio: Major Medium For Reaching Negroes," *Sponsor* (17 August 1964), 37.

7. "Advertiser Interest In Negroes Zooms," *Broadcasting* (7 November 199), 76.

8. "Know-How Is Key to Selling Negro Today," *Sponsor Negro Issue* (9 October 1961), 27; "Is There a U.S. Negro Market Today? *Yes* Can It Be Reached As Easily As Any Other Market? *No*," *Sponsor* (17 August 1964), 32; Negro Radio's 1965-Style New Sound," *Sponsor* (26 July 1965), 57.

9. John H. Johnson and Lerone Bennent Jr., *Succeeding Against The Odds* (New York: Warner Books, 1980), 229.

10. Ibid., 173, 179–80.

11. Ibid., 156–57, 287.

12. Ibid., 277–80.

13. Maurine Christopher, "CORE Seeks More Integrated Ads; Core Invites 14 Major Advertisers To Discuss Using Negroes In Ads," *Advertising Age* (9 September 1963), 1, 128; Maurine Christopher, "CORE Intensifies Drive For Negroes In Ads; Zeroes In On Pepsi-Cola Co.," *Advertising Age* (9 November 1964), 3, 71; "Boycott By Negroes?" *Printer's Ink* (23 August 1963), 5–6.

14. "Same Ad, Intelligently Done, Can Sell To Both Whites, Negroes: Bullock" *Advertising Age* (12 June 1961), 23; "Integrated Ads Not Offensive To Whites, Dallas Group Told," *Advertising Age* (14 October 1968), 31; "Use of Negro Models In Ads Won't Reduce Sales To Whites, Johnson Advises Workshop," *Advertising Age* (9 December 1968), 24; "Use of Black Models In Ads Doesn't Alter Sales Patterns, BofA [Bureau of Advertising] Reports," *Advertising Age* (9 November 1970), 52; Lester Guest, "How Negro Models Affect Company Image," *Journal of Advertising Research* (10 April 1970): 29–33.

15. Johnson and Bennett, *Succeeding Against the Odds*, 27.

16. D. Parke Gibson, "Advertising and The Dual Society: Challenge Of The Seventies," *Mediascope* 13 (August 1969): 63.

17. Ibid.

18. Elsie Archer, "How To Sell Today's Negro Woman," *Sponsor* (25 July 1966), 49.

19. Lawrence E. Black, "The Negro Market: Growing, Changing, Challenging," *Sales Management* (4 October 1963), 46.

20. Black advisors to American corporations appeared partially responsible for this development. See "Don't Contrive Integrated Ads, (John H.) Johnson Advises," *Advertising Age* (23 September 1963), 1, 111; "Help Negro In Image Effort Via Ads, [Roy] Wilkens Asks," *Advertising Age* (11 November 1963), 1, 112.

21. *The Chicago Defender*, among other African-American newspapers, featured a vast number of advertisements for personal care products (hair and skin) during this period. Most of the companies providing these products were small black-owned firms.

22. "Negro Radio's Prosperous Market," *Sponsor* (26 September 1960), 9; Raymond A. Bauer and Scott M. Cunningham, "The Negro Market," *Journal of Advertising Research* 10 (April, 1970): 10–11.

23. David H. Swinton, "The Economic Status of African-Americans: Permanent Poverty and Inequality," in *The State of Black America, 1991* (New York: National Urban League inc., 1991), 28.

GUIDE TO FURTHER READING

The diverse articles in *Acknowledging Consumption: A Review of New Studies* (1995), edited by Daniel Miller, and *The Politics of Consumption: Material Culture and Citizenship in Europe and America* (2001), edited by Martin Daunton and Matthew Hilton, reflect a range of methodologies on design topics from the French Revolution to the late twentieth century, demonstrating that the history of consumption is a wide-reaching field, which, like design history, necessarily is drawn from sociology, anthropology and studies of sign systems.

In 'Coming Up For Air: Consumer Culture in Historical Perspective', in *Consumption and the World of Goods* (1993), edited by John Brewer and Roy Porter, Jean-Christophe Agnew provides an insightful overview of the first critiques of consumption during the prosperous period of industrialization in nineteenth-century Europe and North America, including those by Karl Marx and Thomas Carlyle among others. Section 1 of the *Reader* concludes with John Styles's 'Manufacturing, Consumption and Design in Eighteenth-century England' from that same volume, which extended studies of design to the seventeenth and eighteenth centuries. Influential studies of consumption in the early modern and industrial periods include Neil McKendrick, John Brewer and J. H. Plumb, *The Birth of a Consumer Society: The Commercialization of Eighteenth-century England* (1982); Chandra Mukerji, *From Graven Images: Patterns of Modern Materialism* (1983); and Colin Campbell, *The Romantic Ethic and the Spirit of Modern Consumerism* (1987). Grant McCracken, *Culture and Consumption: New Approaches to the Symbolic Character of Consumer Goods and Activities* (1988), draws on these works as well as on histories of nineteenth-century world's fairs, advertising, fashion and the rise of the department store: Michael Miller, *The Bon Marché: Bourgeois Culture and the Department Store 1869–1920* (1981); Rosalind Williams, *Dream Worlds: Mass Consumption in Nineteenth Century France* (1982); Roland Barthes, *The Fashion System* (1967; translated 1983); Jackson Lears, *Fables of Abundance: A Cultural History of Advertising in America* (1994).

From a sociological perspective, early twentieth century writings by Max Weber (*The Protestant Ethic and the Spirit of Capitalism*, 1904–5), Werner Sombart (*Der Moderne Kapitalismus*, 1902), and Georg Simmel ('The Philosophy of Money', 1900, 1907) have been influential, especially for studies of modernism, such as in Frederic Schwartz's *The Werkbund: Design Theory and Mass Culture Before the First World War* (1996). After the Second World War, historical studies of material culture were led by Fernand Braudel, among others. Braudel was editor of the French journal *Annales*, and his book *Capitalism and Material Life 1400–1800* (1973) focuses on the early modern period of the fifteenth to eighteenth centuries, before the onset of industrialization. Braudel's work has connections to that of German sociologist Norbert Elias (*The Civilizing Process*, 1939, 1969), as well as to his contemporary, the French anthropologist Claude Lévi-Strauss, whose prolific writings on culture informed a generation of structural theorists. *The Social Life of Things: Commodities in Historical Perspective* (1986), a collection of essays edited by Arjun Appadurai, challenges the presumption that objects, or 'things' are only activated by human agency, arguing rather that objects can be invested with a power of their own – an idea noted by Marcel Mauss in *The Gift*, first published in essay form in 1923–4, and later in English translation as a book (1954), as well as by Marx in his description of the 'commodity fetish'.

Marxist critiques of consumption have been enduring, from Theodor Adorno and Max Horkheimer's 'The Culture Industry: Enlightenment as Mass Deception', in *Dialectic of the Enlightenment* (1944), to Jean Baudrillard's post-Marxist essays *The System of Objects* (1968) and *The Consumer Society* (1970). In her article 'Tu: A Cosmetic Case Study', Kathy Myers combines Marxist theories of consumption with psychoanalytic and semiotic methods, producing a reading of a British cosmetic marketing campaign that attributes as much to Sigmund Freud and Jacques Lacan as it does to Roland Barthes's demonstration that fashion exists in the realm of the written word. In their collection of essays *The Sex of Things: Gender and Consumption in Historical Perspective* (1996), Victoria de Grazia and Ellen Furlough (eds) demonstrate a variety of design methodologies. Adam Arvidsson's 'From Counterculture to Consumer Culture: Vespa and the Italian Youth Market, 1958–78' (2001) makes for an instructive comparison with the very different analysis of the Italian motor scooter provided by Dick Hebdige, and extracted in section 8 of this *Reader*. Joann d'Alisera's 'I ♥ Islam: Popular Religious Commodities, Sites of Inscription, and Transnational Sierra Leonean Identity' (2001) and John Harvey's 'Seen to Be Remembered: Presentation, Representation and Recollection in British Evangelical Culture since the Late 1970s' (2004) both examine design and consumption from the point of view of religion, a topic that was also treated by Jean Burks in her study of Shaker furniture in section 8 of this *Reader*.

SECTION 11

Mediation

INTRODUCTION

Grace Lees-Maffei

During its development, design history has examined the object, as focal concern, through the contexts in which objects are produced, mediated, used and understood. The dominance of issues of consumption in the 1990s (explored in the previous section) has been accompanied by a concern for those processes that might conveniently be gathered under the banner 'mediation'. A concern for mediation in the late 1990s and early twenty-first century is not unique to design history and is shared, for example, with cultural studies, literary studies and area studies. To study mediation is to study the phenomena which exist between production and consumption, as being fundamentally important in inscribing meanings for objects, as Dick Hebdige notes in section 8 of this book and as Jeffrey L. Meikle has noted in his article 'Material Virtues: On the Ideal and the Real in Design History' (1998).

Awareness of the role of mediating discourses in generating meanings for designed goods and processes has prompted studies that seek to find out about design through analysis of discourse (as distinct from the analysis of design *as* discourse, a discrete and very rich area of enquiry). This section explores the significance of mediation as a focus by presenting a variety of texts, each focussed upon a different type of source material: photography and film, advertising, advice literature, oral history and magazines, respectively. It begins with Walter Benjamin's 'The Work of Art in the Age of Mechanical Reproduction'. Dating from 1936, this essay has exerted a tremendous influence on cultural analysis in the twentieth century. Although as a commentary on photography and film, it falls into the group of secondary sources, its landmark status and its date mean that it has developed its own history and can now be treated as a primary source. The remaining texts in this section are presented to exemplify the mediation tendency within design history, from the late 1990s onwards. Steven Heller's essay 'Advertising, the Mother of Graphic Design' was first published in *Eye*, the graphic design magazine: consistent with its status as design journalism, it is concise, opinionated and practice-oriented. Different again are the scholarly articles by Emma Ferry and Liz Linthicum, both from *The Journal of Design History*. These texts analyse mediating sources, while also reflecting on their use. Similarly reflective is Jeremy Aynsley and Kate Forde's introduction to their anthology *Design and the Modern Magazine*, which comprises historiographic contextual survey and methodological pointers to the contribution that design history can make to the understanding of the significance of magazines, a theme being pursued across several disciplines. Rather than simply presenting exemplary studies of mediation, this section offers texts in which the emphasis is on methodological reflexivity.

Walter Benjamin's 'The Work of Art in the Age of Mechanical Reproduction' is framed by a discussion of the politics of its time, beginning with Marx and ending with fascism. The preface considers the significance of 'theses about the developmental tendencies of art under present conditions of production' for brushing aside 'outmoded concepts such as creativity and genius, eternal value and mystery' and 'for the formulation of revolutionary demands in the politics of art'. The epilogue notes that 'the logical result of Fascism is the introduction of aesthetics into political life' and its culmination in war, to which 'communism responds by politicizing art'. The main body of the essay discusses how technologies of mass production have changed the nature of art, and altered the meaning and significance of its 'aura' (this is the section reproduced here) before examining photography and film as two examples. For design historians, it offers a consideration of the value of the mass produced cultural artefacts which may be applied to the designed object. Benjamin's discussion of 'aura' forms an example of how the conditions of production determine the reception of cultural artefacts. The work of art, or, more broadly, the cultural artefact of which design is part, is, in the age of mechanical reproduction, mediated by a mass media as well as itself forming part of that media.

Heller's essay concerns two kinds of mediating discourse – advertising and graphic design – through the medium of a third, design journalism. Heller identifies reluctance among graphic designers to identify their output as associated with advertising. He responds by tracing a history of graphic design which shows the central place of advertising in its development. Not only are graphic design and advertising indivisible, they are mutually constitutive, Heller suggests. Although more recent than Benjamin's work, Heller's essay can be placed into historical context with reference to his own intro-duction to *Looking Closer 2*, the book within which it has been anthologised. Heller asserts that design criticism written by designers has blossomed to the extent that it can be identified as a trend. Within this context, Heller positions his essay as a corrective to partial versions of the past and an intervention which intends to improve contemporary discourse.

Emma Ferry's meticulous article '"Decorators May be Compared to Doctors" An Analysis of Rhoda and Agnes Garrett's *Suggestions for House Decoration in Painting, Woodwork and Furniture* (1876)' offers an empirical case study of a mediating discourse – the advice book and, particularly, the Garretts' *House Decoration* – set within sensitive and useful methodological reflection. Ferry tells us not only about a most interesting and significant advice book, but also about how it should be used by design historians. Through close reading, Ferry produces observations and conclusions that could not have been achieved with reference to any other material.

In 'Integrative Practice: Oral History, Dress and Disability Studies', Liz Linthicum proposes an affinity between design history and dress history, disability studies and oral history: 'first-hand ac-counts provide a rich source of primary material which is open to interpretation on many levels but is especially significant in recording the experiential, emotional, affective engagement with clothing as identity'. Her article fills important gaps: it places the experiential within dress history and puts dress into the foreground of disability studies. This article therefore makes a multiple contribution and demonstrates for design historians how oral history is an invaluable discourse for illuminating the practices which exist between production and consumption.

Finally, in their introduction to the anthology *Design and the Modern Magazine*, Jeremy Aynsley and Kate Forde consider not only the utility of magazines as a resource for design historical understanding, but also the specific strengths of a design historical analysis of magazines. 'Unlike design history', they note, 'cultural studies rarely engages with the circumstances of production, the design process or the material qualities of the magazines'. The essays in their book provide excellent examples.

58

THE WORK OF ART IN THE AGE OF MECHANICAL REPRODUCTION

Walter Benjamin (1936)

I

In principle a work of art has always been reproducible. Man-made artifacts could always be imitated by men. Replicas were made by pupils in practice of their craft, by masters for diffusing their works, and, finally, by third parties in the pursuit of gain. Mechanical reproduction of a work of art, however, represents something new. Historically, it advanced intermittently and in leaps at long intervals, but with accelerated intensity. The Greeks knew only two procedures of technically reproducing works of art: founding and stamping. Bronzes, terra cottas, and coins were the only art works which they could produce in quantity. All others were unique and could not be mechanically reproduced. With the woodcut graphic art became mechanically reproducible for the first time, long before script became reproducible by print. The enormous changes which printing, the mechanical reproduction of writing, has brought about in literature are a familiar story. However, within the phenomenon which we are here examining from the perspective of world history, print is merely a special, though particularly important, case. During the Middle Ages engraving and etching were added to the woodcut; at the beginning of the nineteenth century lithography made its appearance. With lithography the technique of reproduction reached an essentially new stage. This much more direct process was distinguished by the tracing of the design on a stone rather than its incision on a block of wood or its etching on a copperplate and permitted graphic art for the first time to put its products on the market, not only in large numbers as hitherto, but also in daily changing forms. Lithography enabled graphic art to illustrate everyday life, and it began to keep pace with printing. But only a few decades after its invention, lithography was surpassed by photography. For the first time in the process of pictorial reproduction, photography freed the hand of the most important artistic functions which henceforth devolved only upon the eye looking into a lens. Since the eye perceives more swiftly than the hand can draw, the process of pictorial reproduction was accelerated so enormously that it could keep pace with speech. A film operator shooting a scene in the studio captures the images at the speed of an actor's speech. Just as lithography virtually implied the illustrated newspaper, so did photography foreshadow the sound film. The technical reproduction of sound was tackled at the end of the last century. These convergent endeavors made predictable a situation which Paul Valery pointed up in this sentence:

> Just as water, gas, and electricity are brought into our houses from far off to satisfy our needs in response to a minimal effort, so we shall be supplied with visual or auditory images, which will appear and disappear at a simple movement of the hand, hardly more than a sign.

Around 1900 technical reproduction had reached a standard that not only permitted it to reproduce all transmitted works of art and thus to cause the most profound change in their impact upon the public; it also had captured a place of its own among the artistic processes. For the study of this standard nothing is more revealing than the nature of the repercussions that these two different manifestations – the reproduction of works of art and the art of the film – have had on art in its traditional form.

II

Even the most perfect reproduction of a work of art is lacking in one element: its presence in time and space, its unique existence at the place where it happens to be. This unique existence of the work of art determined the history to which it was subject throughout the time of its existence. This includes the changes which it may have suffered in physical condition over the years as well as the various changes in its ownership. The traces of the first can be revealed only by chemical or physical analyses which it is impossible to perform on a reproduction; changes of ownership are subject to a tradition which must be traced from the situation of the original.

The presence of the original is the prerequisite to the concept of authenticity. Chemical analyses of the patina of a bronze can help to establish this, as does the proof that a given manuscript of the Middle Ages stems from an archive of the fifteenth century. The whole sphere of authenticity is outside technical – and, of course, not only technical – reproducibility. Confronted with its manual reproduction, which was usually branded as a forgery, the original preserved all its authority; not so vis-à-vis technical reproduction. The reason is twofold. First, process reproduction is more independent of the original than manual reproduction. For example, in photography, process reproduction can bring out those aspects of the original that are unattainable to the naked eye

yet accessible to the lens, which is adjustable and chooses its angle at will. And photographic reproduction, with the aid of certain processes, such as enlargement or slow motion, can capture images which escape natural vision. Secondly, technical reproduction can put the copy of the original into situations which would be out of reach for the original itself. Above all, it enables the original to meet the beholder halfway, be it in the form of a photograph or a phonograph record. The cathedral leaves its locale to be received in the studio of a lover of art; the choral production, performed in an auditorium or in the open air, resounds in the drawing room.

The situations into which the product of mechanical reproduction can be brought may not touch the actual work of art, yet the quality of its presence is always depreciated. This holds not only for the art work but also, for instance, for a landscape which passes in review before the spectator in a movie. In the case of the art object, a most sensitive nucleus – namely, its authenticity – is interfered with whereas no natural object is vulnerable on that score. The authenticity of a thing is the essence of all that is transmissible from its beginning, ranging from its substantive duration to its testimony to the history which it has experienced. Since the historical testimony rests on the authenticity, the former, too, is jeopardized by reproduction when substantive duration ceases to matter. And what is really jeopardized when the historical testimony is affected is the authority of the object.

One might subsume the eliminated element in the term 'aura' and go on to say: that which withers in the age of mechanical reproduction is the aura of the work of art. This is a symptomatic process whose significance points beyond the realm of art. One might generalize by saying: the technique of reproduction detaches the reproduced object from the domain of tradition. By making many reproductions it substitutes a plurality of copies for a unique existence. And in permitting the reproduction to meet the beholder or listener in his own particular situation, it reactivates the object reproduced. These two processes lead to a tremendous shattering of tradition which is the obverse of the contemporary crisis and renewal of mankind. Both processes are intimately connected with the contemporary mass movements. Their most powerful agent is the film. Its social significance, particularly in its most positive form, is inconceivable without its destructive, cathartic aspect, that is, the liquidation of the traditional value of the cultural heritage. This phenomenon is most palpable in the great historical films. It extends to ever new positions. In 1927 Abel Gance exclaimed enthusiastically:

> Shakespeare, Rembrandt, Beethoven will make films … all legends, all mythologies and all myths, all founders of religion, and the very religions … await their exposed resurrection, and the heroes crowd each other at the gate.

Presumably without intending it, he issued an invitation to a far-reaching liquidation.

III

During long periods of history, the mode of human sense perception changes with humanity's entire mode of existence. The manner in which human sense perception is organized, the medium in which it is accomplished, is determined not only by nature but by historical circumstances as well. The fifth century, with its great shifts of population, saw the birth of the late Roman art industry and the Vienna Genesis, and there developed not only an art different from that of antiquity but also a new kind of perception. The scholars of the Viennese school, Riegl and Wickhoff, who resisted the weight of classical tradition under which these later art forms had been buried, were the first to draw conclusions from them concerning the organization of perception at the time. However far-reaching their insight, these scholars limited themselves to showing the significant, formal hallmark which characterized perception in late Roman times. They did not attempt – and, perhaps, saw no way – to show the social transformations expressed by these changes of perception. The conditions for an analogous insight are more favorable in the present. And if changes in the medium of contemporary perception can be comprehended as decay of the aura, it is possible to show its social causes.

The concept of aura which was proposed above with reference to historical objects may usefully be illustrated with reference to the aura of natural ones. We define the aura of the latter as the unique phenomenon of a distance, however close it may be. If, while resting on a summer afternoon, you follow with your eyes a mountain range on the horizon or a branch which casts its shadow over you, you experience the aura of those mountains, of that branch. This image makes it easy to comprehend the social bases of the contemporary decay of the aura. It rests on two circumstances, both of which are related to the increasing significance of the masses in contemporary life. Namely, the desire of contemporary masses to bring things 'closer' spatially and humanly, which is just as ardent as their bent toward overcoming the uniqueness of every reality by accepting its reproduction. Every day the urge grows stronger to get hold of an object at very close range by way of its likeness, its reproduction. Unmistakably, reproduction as offered by picture magazines and newsreels differs from the image seen by the unarmed eye. Uniqueness and permanence are as closely linked in the latter as are transitoriness and reproducibility in the former. To pry an object from its shell, to destroy its aura, is the mark of a perception whose 'sense of the universal equality of things' has increased to such a degree that it extracts it even from a unique object by means of reproduction. Thus is manifested in the field of perception what in the theoretical sphere is noticeable in the increasing importance of statistics. The adjustment of reality to the masses and of the masses to reality is a process of unlimited scope, as much for thinking as for perception.

IV

The uniqueness of a work of art is inseparable from its being imbedded in the fabric of tradition. This tradition itself is thoroughly alive and extremely changeable. An ancient statue of Venus, for example, stood in a different traditional context with the Greeks, who made it an object of veneration, than with the clerics of the Middle Ages, who viewed it as an ominous idol. Both of them, however, were equally confronted with its uniqueness, that is, its aura. Originally the contextual integration of art in tradition found its expression in the cult. We know that the earliest art works originated in the service of a ritual – first the magical, then the religious kind. It is significant that the existence of the work of art with reference to its aura is never entirely separated from its ritual function. In other words, the unique value of the 'authentic' work of art has its basis in ritual, the location of its original use value. This ritualistic basis, however remote, is still recognizable as secularized ritual even in the most profane forms of the cult of beauty. The secular cult of beauty, developed during the Renaissance and prevailing for three centuries, clearly showed that ritualistic basis in its decline and the first deep crisis which befell it. With the advent of the first truly revolutionary means of reproduction, photography, simultaneously with the rise of socialism, art sensed the approaching crisis which has become evident a century later. At the time, art reacted with the doctrine of *l'art pour l'art*, that is, with a theology of art. This gave rise to what might be called a negative theology in the form of the idea of 'pure' art, which not only denied any social function of art but also any categorizing by subject matter. (In poetry, Mallarmé was the first to take this position.)

An analysis of art in the age of mechanical reproduction must do justice to these relationships, for they lead us to an all-important insight: for the first time in world history, mechanical reproduction emancipates the work of art from its parasitical dependence on ritual. To an ever greater degree the work of art reproduced becomes the work of art designed for reproducibility. From a photographic negative, for example, one can make any number of prints; to ask for the 'authentic' print makes no sense. But the instant the criterion of authenticity ceases to be applicable to artistic production, the total function of art is reversed. Instead of being based on ritual, it begins to be based on another practice – politics.

[…]

VII

The nineteenth-century dispute as to the artistic value of painting versus photography today seems devious and confused. This does not diminish its importance, however; if anything, it underlines it. The dispute was in fact the symptom of a historical transformation the universal impact of which was not realized by either of the rivals. When the age of mechanical reproduction separated art from its basis in cult, the semblance of its autonomy disappeared forever. The resulting change in the function of art transcended the perspective of the century; for a long time it even escaped that of the twentieth century, which experienced the development of the film. Earlier much futile thought had been devoted to the question of whether photography is an art. The primary question – whether the very invention of photography had not transformed the entire nature of art – was not raised. Soon the film theoreticians asked the same ill-considered question with regard to the film.

[…]

X

[…] The film responds to the shriveling of the aura with an artificial build-up of the 'personality' outside the studio. The cult of the movie star, fostered by the money of the film industry, preserves not the unique aura of the person but the 'spell of the personality,' the phony spell of a commodity. So long as the movie-makers' capital sets the fashion, as a rule no other revolutionary merit can be accredited to today's film than the promotion of a revolutionary criticism of traditional concepts of art. We do not deny that in some cases today's films can also promote revolutionary criticism of social conditions, even of the distribution of property. However, our present study is no more specifically concerned with this than is the film production of Western Europe. [...]

For centuries a small number of writers were confronted by many thousands of readers. This changed toward the end of the last century. With the increasing extension of the press, which kept placing new political, religious, scientific, professional, and local organs before the readers, an increasing number of readers became writers – at first, occasional ones. It began with the daily press opening to its readers space for 'letters to the editor.' And today there is hardly a gainfully employed European who could not, in principle, find an opportunity to publish somewhere or other comments on his work, grievances, documentary reports, or that sort of thing. Thus, the distinction between author and public is about to lose its basic character. The difference becomes merely functional; it may vary from case to case. At any moment the reader is ready to turn into a writer. As expert, which he had to become willy-nilly in an extremely specialized work process, even if only in some minor respect, the reader gains access to authorship. In the Soviet Union work itself is given a voice. To present it verbally is part of a man's ability to perform the work. Literary license is now founded on polytechnic rather than specialized training and thus becomes common property.

[...]

XII

Mechanical reproduction of art changes the reaction of the masses toward art. The reactionary attitude toward a Picasso painting changes into the progressive reaction toward a Chaplin movie. The progressive reaction is characterized by the direct, intimate fusion of visual and emotional enjoyment with the orientation of the expert. Such fusion is of great social significance. The greater the decrease in the social significance of an art form, the sharper the distinction between criticism and enjoyment by the public. The conventional is uncritically enjoyed, and the truly new is criticized with aversion. With regard to the screen, the critical and the receptive attitudes of the public coincide. The decisive reason for this is that individual reactions are predetermined by the mass audience response they are about to produce, and this is nowhere more pronounced than in the film.

[...]

XIII

The characteristics of the film lie not only in the manner in which man presents himself to mechanical equipment but also in the manner in which, by means of this apparatus, man can represent his environment. [...] By close-ups of the things around us, by focusing on hidden details of familiar objects, by exploring common place milieus under the ingenious guidance of the camera, the film, on the one hand, extends our comprehension of the necessities which rule our lives; on the other hand, it manages to assure us of an immense and unexpected field of action. Our taverns and our metropolitan streets, our offices and furnished rooms, our railroad stations and our factories appeared to have us locked up hopelessly. Then came the film and burst this prison-world asunder by the dynamite of the tenth of a second, so that now, in the midst of its far-flung ruins and debris, we calmly and adventurously go traveling. With the close-up, space expands; with slow motion, movement is extended. The enlargement of a snapshot does not simply render more precise what in any case was visible, though unclear: it reveals entirely new structural formations of the subject. So, too, slow motion not only presents familiar qualities of movement but reveals in them entirely unknown ones 'which, far from looking like retarded rapid movements, give the effect of singularly gliding, floating, supernatural motions.' Evidently a different nature opens itself to the camera than opens to the naked eye – if only because an unconsciously penetrated space is substituted for a space consciously explored by man. Even if one has a general knowledge of the way people walk, one knows nothing of a person's posture during the fractional second of a stride. The act of reaching for a lighter or a spoon is familiar routine, yet we hardly know what really

goes on between hand and metal, not to mention how this fluctuates with our moods. Here the camera intervenes with the resources of its lowerings and liftings, its interruptions and isolations, it extensions and accelerations, its enlargements and reductions. The camera introduces us to unconscious optics as does psychoanalysis to unconscious impulses.

[…]

NOTE

59

ADVERTISING, MOTHER OF GRAPHIC DESIGN

Steven Heller (1995)

[…] Although graphic design as we know it originated in the late nineteenth century as a tool of advertising, any association today with marketing, advertising, or capitalism deeply undermines the graphic designer's self-image. Graphic design history is an integral part of advertising history, yet in most accounts of graphic design's origins advertising is virtually denied, or hidden behind more benign words such as 'publicity' and 'promotion.' This omission not only limits the discourse, but also misrepresents the facts. It is time for graphic design historians, and designers generally, to remove the elitist prejudices that have perpetuated a biased history.

In *Layout in Advertising* (Harper Brothers, 1928), William Addison Dwiggins, who coined the term 'graphic designer' in 1922 to define his own diverse practices of book, type, lettering, and advertising design, wrote that, 'for purposes of argument, "advertising" means every conceivable printed means for selling anything.' This suggests that advertising is the mother of almost all graphic design endeavor, except for books and certain journals. In fact, the majority of commercial artists from the turn of the century until fairly recently – from anonymous 'sho card' renderers to celebrated affichistes – were engaged in the service of advertising of one kind or another. Despite the common assertion that graphic design began with seventeenth-century Italian printing, modern graphic design is the result of the transition in the late nineteenth century from a product to a consumer culture. The move from producing (or bartering for) goods to buying mass-produced consumables created a need for printed advertising that quickly developed into a huge, dedicated industry.

Dwiggins' manual is not the only one to assert that graphic design was invented to put 'an advertising project into graphic form.' Jan Tschichold's *Die Neue Typographie,* also published in 1928, was a seminal handbook for the practitioners of *Gebrauchsgraphik,* or advertising art. This book and Tschichold's subsequent *Typographische Gestaltung* (1935), which became the basis of the modern canon, were focused not on some idealistic notion of visual communications in an aesthetic vacuum, but on dynamic new possibilities for advertising composition in an archaic and cluttered print environment. In *The Art Director at Work* (Hastings House, 1960), Arthur Hawkins, Jr., describes how such ideas influenced American advertising design: 'As competitive pressure squeezed the innocence out of advertising, [art directors] became rougher and tougher. They were usually paste-up boys … who had picked up a certain facility with a 6B pencil. Somehow, they discovered *Gebrauchsgraphik* magazine and the Bauhaus School. Their future was paved with Futura.'

By the 1920s, graphic design was synonymous with advertising design. In Germany, France, and Italy, agencies and consortia extolled the virtues of the well-designed advertising image. Lucian Bernhard and others associated with the Berliner Plakat group, under the management of printing salesman and advertising agent Ernst Growald, invented artful ways to identify and announce new products. Even the cultural avant-gardes – Futurism, Dada, Surrealism – created design forms for advertising that expressed their particular visions and ideologies. Russian constructivism's most notable graphic achievements were advertisements for films and products. The 'Productivists' Alexander Rodchenko and Lasar El Lissitzky developed ways of composing typecase design elements on an advertising page that eventually influenced layout trends in capitalist nations. In Germany the Ring, a close-knit association of radically modern designers including Kurt Schwitters, Willi Baumeister, and Piet Zwart, attempted to sell to an expanding industrial clientele a 'new advertising' based on the New Typography.

For the avant-garde, producing advertising for technologically progressive corporations, which incidentally often sponsored artistic innovation, was such a modern idea that they proudly referred to themselves as 'artists for industry' or 'advertising engineers.' Since advertising was at once the medium of progressive graphic expression and a growing industry, many of the most influential graphic design trade journals of the late 1920s and 1930s had names with advertising in their titles: *De Reclame* (the Netherlands and Germany), *Reklama* (Russia), *Gebrauchsgraphik* (Germany), *Werbung* (Germany), *Publicité* (France), *Pubblicità d' Italia* (Italy), and *Advertising Arts* (United States). Even those trade magazines that focused on printing and other aspects of commercial art featured many articles on advertising.

ICONS OF PROGRESS

'Today it is difficult to recapture the intoxicating feeling of aesthetic possibility that once surrounded national advertising,' writes Jackson Lears about the American experience of the 1920s (*Fables of Abundance,* Basic Books, 1995). 'But for a while, especially during the early years of the courtship, it seemed to many artists as if advertising embodied exhilarating energy, rather than merely impoverishment of spirit.' As the modern movements sought to redefine the place of art and the role of the artist in society, advertising was seen not only as a medium ripe for reform, but also as a platform on which the graphic symbols of reform could be paraded along with the product being sold. Within this scenario, layout (or craft) was replaced by graphic design as an artistic endeavour, the engine of *style*. Lears points out that during this period, advertising art 'became detached from the product to which it referred. "Advertising design" became a value in and of itself, without reference to the sales that design was intended to generate.' Design still served, but was no longer a slave to copy-driven campaigns.

American advertising agencies gradually shifted their preference from 'capitalist realism,' or unambiguous if mythic representation, to surrealistic imagery that imbued the commodity with a fantastic aura. Refrigerators floating in space signified the abstract notion of progress as well as the fantasy of an ethereal, modern home. Industry became the totem of the American Century and advertising extolled its monumentality through modern and moderne graphic forms. As in the Soviet idealization of the industrial state, factories, smokestacks, and gigantic bearings and gears were heroicized as icons of progress. Advertising not only sold, but it also told a tale about America's aspirations.

American advertising had traditionally been dominated by hard-sell copy, and the shift in emphasis from words to art and design did not occur overnight. But it did change precipitously thanks to Earnest Elmo Calkins, founder of the Calkins & Holden advertising agency in New York. Calkins became interested in design reform in about 1908 and instituted his new ideas by engaging some of the most widely admired magazine illustrators, including James Montgomery Flagg and J. C. Lyendecker, to render ads for common products. Later he led the field in the introduction of modern art (cubism and futurism) into advertising. He wrote profusely in trade journals and design and poster annuals and was a frequent contributor to London's *Commercial Art* annual.

In articles in general magazines, such as one titled 'Beauty the New Business Tool' *(Atlantic Monthly,* August 1927), Calkins expounded on the need for dynamic new design to help communicate the marketing innovation that became known as programmed or forced obsolescence.

Calkins, whom Jackson Lears calls the 'apostle of taste' and 'corporate connoisseur of artifice,' introduced the consumerist idea that all products – from coffee tins to automobiles – should regularly shed their surface styles as an inducement to consumers to toss out the old and purchase the new. This pseudoscience of style engineering – a kind of design-based behavior modification – forced American industrial design to shift from its quaint Victorian ornamentalism to machine-age modernism, and so encouraged the retooling of American industry. As Terry Smith states in *Making the Modern: Industry, Art, and Design in America* (University of Chicago Press, 1994), 'Advertising's parentage of U.S. type industrial design is traceable not only to their common economic purposes, but to the histories of the individuals who shaped the design profession. Most … spent the 1920s as advertising artist-illustrators. Joseph Sinel, John Vassos, Raymond Loewy, and Walter Dorwin Teague are the outstanding examples.'

These pioneering practitioners are rarely cited in graphic design histories. Likewise Calkins, who is arguably the single most important figure in early twentieth-century American graphic design, makes no more than a few cameo appearances in such significant accounts as Philip B. Meggs's *A History of Graphic Design*, Richard Hollis's *Graphic Design: A Concise History*, and R. Roger Remington and Barbara J. Hodik's *Nine Pioneers in American Graphic Design.* Yet thanks to Calkins's promotion of European modern and modernistic design, along with his invention of the creative team of copywriter and designer, graphic design grew by leaps and bounds as a service to advertising in the late 1920s, prior to the Great Depression. During the 1930s it developed into a field with its own integrity, canon, and luminaries. Although Calkins did not invent contemporary design standards, he codified them and urged their adoption. Advertising design influenced modes of editorial and institutional design until World War II; afterwards editorial design surpassed advertising in originality.

The 1950s saw the beginnings of a schism between graphic and advertising design. Modern graphic design veered from mass advertising towards corporate and institutional communications and evolved into a rarefied practice decidedly more sophisticated than advertising design of the same period. Some advertising artist/designers were celebrated for individual achievement, but as Terry Smith writes, 'advertising designed primarily by an individual artist was becoming rare enough in the United States to be remarkable, exceptional, and expensive.' Over time such advertising luminaries as did exist – E. McKnight Kauffer and A. M. Cassandre being the prime examples – were detached from the history of advertising and made into heroes of graphic design.

A kind of sociocultural stratification began to distinguish the advertising designer from the graphic designer. Today, a common view among advertising people is that graphic designers simply 'do letterheads,' while graphic designers scorn their advertising counterparts for being ignorant about type. Job or class distinctions have driven a wedge between graphic designers and advertising designers and graphic design history has perpetuated the schism. While cultural scholars, consumer theorists, and media critics have done considerable work on the social, political, and psychological role of advertising in American culture, their writings are rarely cited in graphic design literature, as if issues of consumerism and marketing have no bearing on the 'art' of graphic design. This omission can be traced back to formal prejudices.

THE FORMALIST LENS

If advertising is the function, then graphic design is the form. As Dwiggins pointed out in *Layout in Advertising*, 'The advertising piece is not an end-product; it is an intermediate step in a process. The end product of advertising is not [design] – it is sales.' Yet selling is an ignored aspect of the story contemporary graphic design historians choose to tell – after all, graphic designers are not salespeople but form-givers, which is perceived as a more culturally significant activity than being a mere advertising huckster. The problem is that an advertisement must be analyzed as a collaborative endeavor involving considerably more than just its graphics. So to avoid having to admit that graphic design has a subordinate role, the historical discourse has built up around graphic design as a formal endeavor. [...] The audience, which is rarely considered in formalist critiques of fine art, is likewise ignored in favor of aesthetic and sometimes philosophical or ideological considerations. This not only denies the public's role, but the client's as well.

In the first important historical text published in America, *A History of Graphic Design* (Van Nostrand Reinhold, second ed. 1992), Philip Meggs skirts the role of advertising. [...] In Meggs's otherwise painstaking historical account, advertising is portrayed not as the mother of graphic design, but as a midwife. While scant attention is given to the economic forces that forged the practice, certain key individuals who were nurtured by advertising are highlighted. Thus discussion of advertising is used merely to push the great master narrative along until the individual emerges from the birth canal as a graphic designer.

The problem is not that advertising cannot be read from a formalist viewpoint, but that history demands that its function and outcome be equally scrutinized. This turns the focus away from graphic design, and in order to refocus attention on their discipline, graphic design historians tend to treat advertising simply as a matter of surface. For instance, when one of Alexey Brodovitch's advertisements for the New York department store Saks Fifth Avenue is put under the historical/critical microscope, we learn about the typeface, lettering, and illustration, but not about how it functioned as a piece of advertising in a newspaper. Does consideration of its function diminish its artistic – or graphic design – value? By referring to it as 'advertising,' does the work shrink in stature from a paradigmatic piece of graphics to kitsch?

In *Nine Pioneers in American Graphic Design* (MIT Press, 1989), R. Roger Remington and Barbara J. Hodik marginalize Brodovitch's early advertising design when they write that. [...] 'He learned how to simplify the subject through analysis of the Purist painters. His posters for Martini, now in the Museum of Modern Art in New York, are among the major products of this fruitful period.' Nowhere do the authors acknowledge this work as advertising, even when they report that Brodovitch was invited to create a program in advertising design at the Philadelphia School of Industrial Design. With rare exceptions, when advertising is included in graphic design history, it is as an incidental part of the consideration of individuals and artifacts. In my own *Graphic Style: from Victorian to Postmodern* (Harry N. Abrams, 1988), the advertising artifact is treated merely as a vessel for style, not as a model from which to examine functional attributes.

Remington and Hodik do, however, take a step towards integrating advertising and graphic design in their selection of Charles Coiner, art director of the Philadelphia-based ad agency N. W. Ayer, as one of their pioneers. Coiner brought modernity to America's oldest advertising agency, introducing fine art to the repertoire and hiring some of America's leading graphic designers, such as Leo Lionni and Alexey Brodovitch, to conceive and style print ads. The authors give him full credit for his contribution to his firm's success: 'Ayer clients received forty-one awards during the first nineteen years of exhibitions by art directors ... Ayer pioneered the production of "beautiful" ads through campaigns for Cannon Mills, Caterpillar Tractor, Climax Molybdenum, French Line, Marcus Jewelers, DeBeers Diamonds, and Capehart.' Yet their text – the only contemporary study of this significant advertising pioneer (a profile appeared in *Portfolio* in 1950) — reads more as a list of achievements than an analysis of advertising's, and by extension Coiner's, role in the larger culture. Advertising is used as a backdrop to his endeavor rather than a lens through which consumer culture can be explored. Despite Coiner's inclusion, advertising remains marginalized.

Yet *Nine Pioneers* provides a key insight into how graphic design began to break from advertising during the war and how advertising designers emerged as creative forces afterwards. 'During the war, very few goods were available for consumer purchase. Advertising had nothing to sell. When the war ended, the scene changed dramatically to a buyer's market. Designers finally had the opportunity to express their ideas in the spheres of advertising and communications.' That wartime austerity offered other creative challenges to the advertising industry that were consequential to graphic design is conveniently overlooked.

Of the histories discussed here, only Richard Hollis's *Graphic Design: A Concise History* (Thames and Hudson, 1994) openly addresses the role of advertising. 'In the 1930s, it had been art directors who had established graphic design, mainly in advertising and magazine layouts.' Hollis concisely argues the importance of the 'New Advertising' — the integrated design — and concept-driven campaigns of the late 1950s and 1960s. He focuses on the key art directors — Paul Rand and Gene Federico — and campaigns such as Doyle Dane Bernbach's for Volkswagen, explaining this work as important because it made the spectator active, not passive. But Hollis's brief discussion avoids the broader implications of advertising, focusing instead on iconoclasts who are soon positioned in his narrative as graphic design exemplars.

This is the inevitable paradox of graphic design history. Since advertising is marginalized, the few acknowledged advertising design leaders must somehow be presented as graphic design leaders. For instance, the majority of work by Lou Dorfsman, the former art director of CBS

Radio and Television, is institutional and trade advertising, through which he not only set new typographic standards, but also increased business. Although the success of his ads is sometimes cited anecdotally in references to his career, Dorfsman is usually presented as either a typographer or an art director, rarely as an advertising man. Likewise Herb Lubalin, the art director of Suddler & Hennesy before branching out into editorial and type design, is routinely discussed as a typographic pioneer who, incidentally, broke new ground in pharmaceutical advertising. Analyzing such figures' design as a milestone in the marriage of type and image avoids the stigma of it being advertising. Gene Federico and George Lois, both of whom owned ad agencies, are presented as creative forces who transcended the advertising field. Federico was a great typographer, Lois a brilliant art director, and, for the purposes of design history, they achieved their status in spite of their profession.

Graphic designers have distanced themselves from advertising in the same way that children put as much space as possible between themselves and their parents. And indeed, graphic design did develop its own characteristics. American advertising was originally copy-based and unresponsive to design, and though reformers like Calkins (and later Bill Bernbach) encouraged the seamless integration of words, pictures, and design, the copy, slogan, and jingle have been the driving forces. From the turn of the century, would-be journalists and novelists were recruited as copywriters, giving the field a certain faux-literary cast. Eventually, advertising developed its own stereotypical professionals, who even today are distinct from graphic design professionals.

The tilting of the scales towards the copy-driven 'big idea' is one reason why advertising histories veer away from extensive analysis of graphic design. Another issue is quality as defined by the two fields — a great advertising campaign may not be exceptional graphic design, while a superb piece of graphic design may mask a poor advertising campaign. [...]

Although the Lucky Strike package designed by Raymond Loewy and the Eve Cigarette package designed by Herb Lubalin and Ernie Smith are featured as design artifacts, the advertising campaigns that sold the designs have been ignored. Graphic design historians are prudishly selective in what they discuss. They base decisions on ideal formal attributes – what is inherently interesting from a design perspective. They write as though consumerism is wicked – us (the canon) versus them (the mass) underscores graphic design history. Yet by eliminating advertising, design history loses rich insights into visual culture.

One of the touchstones of inclusion in graphic design histories is whether or not a work broke the stranglehold of commercial convention. Paul Rand's advertisements for Orbachs, for instance, have become part of the canon not because they were effective advertising, but because they assaulted antiquity. But this criterion is not the only way to read advertising design. Like some of the European modernists before him, Rand introduced principles of modern art into advertising, bringing the rarefied avant-garde to ordinary citizens. In *Advertising the American Dream: Making Way for Modernity, 1920–1940* (University of California, 1985), Roland Marchand describes the mainstreaming of the avant-garde as a significant marketing ploy that both introduced and made it frivolous. This important aspect of graphic design history can only be told if certain unheroic artifacts are included in the narrative. To refer to or reproduce only billboards, posters, and other aesthetically acceptable tokens of advertising is not enough.

In the 1930s, the distinction between advertising art and graphic design was virtually nonexistent. While typography was often written about as a separate aesthetic field, it was also addressed in terms of its function in advertising. Moreover, whether discussing a book jacket, record sleeve, poster, brochure, magazine, or any other form of graphic endeavor, the word 'advertising' was not regarded as derisive.

Today, advertising is not totally ignored – many trade magazines cover it – but it is rarely integrated into the broader analysis of graphic design. While certain aspects of advertising – marketing, demographics, and other pseudosciences – are less important to graphic design history, considerably more consumerist theory, media criticism, and even perceptual psychology would be useful in understanding the form and function of graphic design through the advertising lens. Likewise aesthetic theories can be applied through the lens of design to put a visually bereft advertising history into clearer focus.

During the past decade there have been calls to develop new narratives and to readdress graphic design history through feminist, ethnic, racial, postcolonialist, post-structuralist, and numerous other politically correct perspectives. There are many ways to slice a pie, but before unveiling too many subtexts, it is perhaps first useful to reconcile a mother and her child.

Advertising and graphic design have more in common than even the postmodern trend for vernacularism (or the aestheticization of timeworn artifacts) reveals. Advertising and graphic design are equally concerned with selling, communicating, and entertaining. To appreciate one, the other is imperative. But more important, if graphic design history does not expand to include advertising and other related studies, it will ultimately succumb to the dead-end thinking that will be the inevitable consequence of being arrested in a state of continual adolescence.

NOTE

Extracted from Heller, S., 'Advertising, Mother of Graphic Design', *Eye* 17(5) (1995). Reprinted courtesy of *Eye* magazine Ltd., eyemagazine.com/

60

'DECORATORS MAY BE COMPARED TO DOCTORS', AN ANALYSIS OF RHODA AND AGNES GARRETT'S *SUGGESTIONS FOR HOUSE DECORATION IN PAINTING, WOODWORK AND FURNITURE* (1876)

Emma Ferry (2003)

INTRODUCTION

[…] This article considers the best known and most popular of the 'Art at Home' series, *Suggestions for House Decoration in Painting, Woodwork and Furniture*, written and illustrated by Rhoda and Agnes Garrett in 1876.

A methodological model for considering the work of these women as professional writers is Elaine Showalter's 'gynocritical' theory,[1] an early variant of feminist criticism that concerns itself with an assessment of the specificity and difference of women's writing. Showalter has drawn on the work of historian Gerda Lerner,[2] and used the model of female culture devised by the anthropologists Shirley and Edwin Ardener.[3] The Ardeners have analysed society in terms of dominant and muted groups: women constitute a muted group, 'the boundaries of whose culture and reality overlap, but are not wholly contained by, the dominant (male) group.'[4] This model allows a reading of women's writing as 'a "double-voiced discourse" that always embodies the social, literary, and cultural heritages of both the muted and dominant.'[5] Gynocriticism, based on the Ardeners' concept of overlapping dominant-muted groups, rather than the notion of 'separate spheres', fulfils 'the need for a theory based on women's experience and analyzing women's

perception of reality.'[6] Most of the feminist critics writing within the model of gynocriticism offer an analysis of women's writing as both a response and a challenge to patriarchy.[7] This article aims to present an analysis of *House Decoration* 'as a reflection of women's repression under patriarchy, but also as a subtle and limited resistance to that patriarchy'[8] expressed through this double-voiced discourse.

Showalter has examined English nineteenth-century female novelists and the tradition of women's fiction, but this model can be extended to the domestic advice manuals written during this period. Published in 1876, *House Decoration* belongs to what Showalter identifies as the feminine phase of women's writing: 'the period from the appearance of the male pseudonym in the 1840s to the death of George Eliot in 1880'.[9] This was a time when 'women wrote in an effort to equal the intellectual achievements of the male culture, and internalised its assumptions about female nature.'[10] Significantly, Showalter also points out that the feminist content of this feminine writing is typically oblique, displaced, ironic, and subversive; one has to read it between the lines, in the missed possibilities of the text.'[11] *House Decoration* is ostensibly a text that defends and defines 'Queen Anne' style and offers advice on the decoration and furnishing of the

Figure 43. Front cover of Rhoda and Agnes Garrett, *Suggestions for House Decoration in Painting, Woodwork and Furniture* (1876). Reprinted from Emma Ferry, '"Decorators May be Compared to Doctors" An Analysis of Rhoda and Agnes Garrett's *Suggestions for House Decoration in Painting, Woodwork and Furniture* (1876)' *The Journal of Design History* 16(1) (2003), pp. 15–33. Image © The British Library Board, BL shelfmark 07943.k.32.

homes of middle-class would-be aesthetes. Read analytically, using this model of dominant-muted discourse, and set in the context of contemporary domestic design advice written by men, however, the text becomes a far more complex document that can be understood as a subversion of, rather than contribution to, Victorian domestic ideology. This presents us with:

a radical alteration of our vision. A demand that we see meaning in what has previously been empty space. The orthodox plot recedes, and another plot, hitherto submerged in the anonymity of the background. stands out in bold relief like a thumbprint.[12]

In offering an alternative reading of *House Decoration*, this article also aims to highlight the problems of using prescriptive domestic advice literature as a conventional historical source. Advice literature may be used to provide information about the Victorian period, but it can never be treated as straightforward evidence of how people lived or furnished their homes in the past. Indeed, in her introduction to the recently reissued quintessential advice book, *Mrs Beeton's Book of Household Management* (1861/2000), Nicola Humble stresses the value of studying this type of non-fictional text and adds a note of caution:

> It is precisely because they are an ephemeral, market-led form of writing that cookery books reveal so much about the features of a particular historical moment. We must remember, though, that like any other text they consist of constructed discourse, and can never be clear windows onto the kitchens of the past.[13]

Domestic design advice books therefore need to be understood both as historical documents that engage with contemporary notions of design and taste, and as a genre of Victorian narrative: they need to be placed in a context of other narratives, both historical and literary, and explored using both historical methodologies and literary theories. Thus, before identifying and discussing the muted discourse of *House Decoration* this article begins by recovering the history of Rhoda and Agnes Garrett.

R. & A. GARRETT: HOUSE DECORATORS

In analysing *House Decoration* – and indeed any form of advice literature – the notion of authorship is crucial: any advice worth buying should after all be given by someone of repute with acknowledged expertise. Rhoda and Agnes Garrett were the first English women to train in an architect's office and subsequently to work professionally as 'house decorators'. They took part in the agitation against the Contagious Diseases Acts and were both active Suffragists – Rhoda in particular was an effective public speaker.[14] [...]

Surprisingly, very little is written about the Garrett cousins. The biographical file on Rhoda

Garrett at the RIBA library simply contains a photocopy of her obituary from *The Builder*. The authors of *House Decoration* are partially 'hidden from history',[15] overshadowed by male contemporaries and their own relations.[16] Very often they have been the victims of repeated and misleading errors. In *Victorian Things* (1988), Asa Briggs, for instance, claims that: 'Agnes and Rhoda Garrett's *House Decoration* (1875), written in collaboration with Owen Jones and singing Morris's praises, had gone through six editions by 1879.'[17] That the book was published in 1876, that Owen Jones had died in 1874 and that William Morris[18] is mentioned nowhere in the text serves to demonstrate that Agnes and Rhoda Garrett are not significant enough to deserve historical accuracy. Yet contemporaries compared their breaking through 'the usual restrictions of home life ... to earn an honest independence'[19] with the struggle of Elizabeth Garrett to 'storm the medical citadel'[20] and achieve her MD in 1870.

[...]

THE 'ART AT HOME' SERIES

House Decoration belongs to the market-led phenomenon of the nineteenth-century 'Household Book'. Dena Attar's introduction to her invaluable *Bibliography of Household Books Published in Britain 1800–1914* (1987), discusses the economic and social reasons for the massive growth in the publication and sales of this literary genre. She classifies books dealing with decorating and furnishing the home as a specialized form of the domestic economy manual. This was a type that became increasingly popular in the last quarter of the nineteenth century, when not only 'decorating became an occupation open to a few women as professional employment', but for most middle-class women the changes in fashion ... meant at the least a greater self-consciousness about how their homes were furnished.'[21] [...]

Devised and edited by the Reverend William John Loftie, the 'Art at Home' series was published by Macmillan between 1876 and 1883;[22] the other titles included Mrs Orrinsmith's *The Drawing Room* (1877), Mrs Loftie's *The Dining Room* (1877 but dated 1878), and Lady Barker's *The Bedroom and the Boudoir* (1878). The Miss Garretts' 'little manual of *House Decoration*'[23] was the second volume in the series, and one of the most successful, running to six editions by 1879, with 7500 copies printed. It was planned as [Figure 44]:

an account of the more simple ways in which, without great expense a home might be made pretty and also wholesome; with designs & illustrations of furniture; the whole to consist of a kind of narrative, in which a house is described on which a great deal of money has been spent with a bad result & the simple cheap way in which the same house was made to look well.[24]

The American publishers Porter & Coates of Philadelphia also issued several of the final twelve volumes, including *House Decoration*: an early letter from Loftie to Macmillan suggests that originally Coates had commissioned *House Decoration*. [...]

Historians and literary critics, in examining advice manuals from the eighteenth century onwards, have discussed the relationship between class and gender identities. This type of didactic literature, which actively constructs a middle-class domestic female identity,[25] has been described as evidence that traditionally forms one of the buttresses of the 'separate spheres framework'.[26] Despite constructing the same middle-class urban readership as other contemporary domestic design

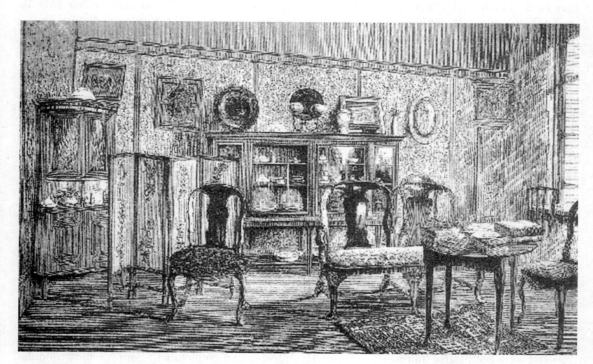

Figure 44. '"View of Drawing-Room" from *Suggestions for House Decoration*'. Reprinted from Emma Ferry, '"Decorators May be Compared to Doctors" An Analysis of Rhoda and Agnes Garrett's *Suggestions for House Decoration in Painting, Woodwork and Furniture* (1876)', *The Journal of Design History* 16(1) (2003), pp. 15–33. Image © The British Library Board, BL shelfmark 07943.k.32.

and taste manuals, including other volumes in the 'Art at Home' series, *House Decoration* remains quite distinct, and is more than domestic design advice aimed at lower-middle-class women. This 'little manual' can be read as a double-voiced discourse that in a subtle and limited manner challenges the dominant discourse of male design advice writers of the 1870s: consequently it can be interpreted as a subversion of, rather than a contribution to, domestic ideology. [...]

SUBVERTING SEPARATE SPHERES

In *House Decoration*, domestic ideology is sub-verted in two ways. First, the Garretts invert the gender identities created by Eastlake in *Hints on Household Taste*. Second, they use the text to demonstrate their professional status as trained 'house decorators' rather than domestic 'home-makers.' [...] Clearly the Garretts have appropriated the dominant discourse of Eastlake, but by reading between the lines it is possible to discern the muted discourse. Throughout, the reader of *House Decoration*, the aspiring purchaser of the services of a decorator or upholsterer, is referred to as 'he' – a 'he' just as likely to be seduced by fashion as a 'she.' [...] This can be read as an ironic inversion of flustered female consumers succumbing – rather more melodramatically – to the persuasions of the upholsterer in Eastlake's *Hints on Household Taste* (1868):

When Materfamilias enters an ordinary uphol-sterer's warehouse, how can she possibly decide on the pattern of her new carpet, when bale after bale of Brussels is unrolled by the indefatigable youth, who is equal in his praises of every piece in turn? ... The shopman remarks of one piece of goods that it is 'elegant'; of another that it is 'striking'; of a third, that it is 'unique', and so forth. The good lady looks from one carpet to another until her eyes are fairly dazzled by their hues. She is utterly unable to explain why she should, or why she should not like any of them.[27]

[...] The Garretts present their readers with the *Paterfamilias* who is resistant to change:

In the dingy and dreary solemnity of the modern London Dining Room we have but a melancholy survival of the stately hospitable-looking rooms of the last century. Yet there is no other room in the house where innovations are more grudgingly permitted, and an Englishman would suspect you of every other revolutionary tendency, if you proposed any radical changes in the colour of the walls, or in the forms and arrangements of the furniture.[28]

Women – at least women like the Garretts who have acquired the 'faculty of distinguishing good from bad design in the familiar objects of domestic life'[29] – are now positive agents of change and in-novation. [...] Whereas in 'Houses As They Are', 'the ladies of the family are told that it is now their turn to have their tastes consulted',[30] in 'Houses As They Might Be', 'the ladies of the household demand the right of having their particular tastes consulted'.[31] [...]

The Garretts are not engaged in busy idle-ness. Rather than naturally gifted amateurs, they are trained professionals working in a male-dominated world. The clearest demonstration of their professional status occurs throughout their Introduction, which begins with a reference to a paper given by J. J. Stevenson upon 'the Queen Anne Style of Architecture' in 1874.[32] By defend-ing and defining the style 'to the study of which the Miss Garretts have devoted their attention',[33] they place themselves immediately in the context of their professional life. [...]

Having thus established their stylistic ap-proach, they return to the subject of their treatise, 'the internal fittings and decorations of houses'.[34] They begin by defining their profes-sion, describing the skills of the consummate 'house decorator' who: 'Should be able to design and arrange all the internal fittings of a house, the chimney-pieces, grates, and door-heads, as well as the wall-hangings, curtains, carpets, and furniture.'[35] They perceive the 'house decorator' (i.e. R. & A. Garrett) as a professional able to judge both the total effect and the minute details of the decorative scheme, and who aims to create a 'harmonious whole'.[36] The Garretts also underline their professional status by dealing at length with the relationship between client and decorator, no doubt speaking from experience. [...]

Throughout *House Decoration* the Garretts also engage, as professionals, in contemporary design debates. In the Introduction, for example, they defend their use of antique furniture in furnishing schemes. Arguing in favour of the well-designed and constructed furniture of the days of Queen Anne ('by which courteous reader, you surely will not compel us to mean strictly the years between 1702–1714')[37] enables them to comment on the deterioration of craft skills, the alienation of the Victorian workman, and a lack of discernment in the consumer: 'The public themselves are mainly to blame. They demand cheap and showy furniture, and the only way to make furniture at once cheap and showy is to make it by machinery, and to turn the men who make it as nearly as one can into machines.'[38] Consequently, within *House Decoration* the Garretts attempt to instruct their readers in 'true artistic principles' in every area of domestic decoration, including wallpapers, colour theory, metalwork, glass-staining, embroidery, wood carving and furniture construction. Their didactic methods differ from their male contemporaries:

A great deal is said nowadays about the ignorance of the public. They have been told hitherto in a hard and dogmatic manner what they ought to admire and what they ought to avoid. A straightforward answer to a few of their whys and wherefores generally has the effect of convincing them of the reasonableness of the method pursued; and when once convinced that there is an intelligible reason for a mode of action, three-fourths of their prejudice against it vanishes.[39]

Perhaps as an ironic comment on the dogma of Christopher Dresser's *Principles of Decorative Design* (1873), they warn their readers with self-deprecating humour that all principles (and especially those of house decorators) must be taken cum grano salis [with a grain of salt]. Principles are indeed necessary, but they must be the servant of the decorator and not his master.[40] [...]

CONCLUSION

This article has demonstrated how the use of recent feminist literary and historical techniques can illuminate this double-voiced discourse, or subversive subtext, in women's writing of the late nineteenth century. In reclaiming the domestic sphere from the professional male interior designers, *House Decoration* imitates, mocks and inverts the dominant models produced by Dresser and Eastlake. [...] Highlighting the emerging professionalization of women during the last quarter of the nineteenth century, *House Decoration* becomes an important case study both for the histories of gender, taste, domesticity and design and also for the use of advice literature as historical evidence.

NOTES

Extracted from Ferry, E., '"Decorators May be Compared to Doctors" An Analysis of Rhoda and Agnes Garrett's *Suggestions for House Decoration in Painting, Woodwork and Furniture* (1876)', *The Journal of Design History* 16(1) (2003), pp. 15–33. Reprinted by permission of the Design History Society.

1. This is explained in detail in her two essays, 'Towards a feminist poetics', in M. Jacobus (ed.), *Women's Writing and Writing About Women*, Croom Helm, 1979 and 'Feminist criticism in the wilderness', in *Critical Inquiry*, vol. 8, Winter, 1981. Both essays were reprinted in E. Showalter (ed.), *The New Feminist*

Criticism: Essays on Women, Literature, and Theory, Virago Press, 1986

2. G. Lerner, *The Majority Finds Its Past: Placing Women in History*, Oxford University Press, 1979.

3. See: E. Ardener, 'Belief and the problem of women', in S. Ardener (ed.), *Perceiving Women*, Dent & Sons Ltd., 1975.

4. Showalter, 1986, p. 261.

5. Ibid., p. 263.

6. S. Spaull, Gynocriticism', in S. Mills et al., *Feminist Readings Feminist Reading*, Harvester Wheatsheaf 1989, p. 117.

7. Ibid.

8. Ibid., p. 85 on Nina Baym's *Women's Fiction: A Guide to Novels by and about Women in America 1820–1970*, Cornell University Press, 1978.

9. E. Showalter, *A Literature of Their Own* (revised and expanded edition), Virago Press, 1999, p. 13.

10. Showalter, 1979, p. 137.

11. Ibid., p. 138.

12. E. Showalter, 'Literary criticism', Review Essay, *Signs*, vol. 1, Winter, 1975, p. 435.

13. N. Humble, Introduction to *Mrs Beeton's Book of Household Management*, 1861, Oxford World Classics, 2000, pp. xv–xvi.

14. Rhoda published a lecture entitled 'The Electoral Disabilities of Women', which she delivered in the Corn Exchange, Cheltenham on 3 April 1872.

15. S. Rowbotham, *Hidden from History*, Pluto Press, 1973.

16. The literature written by and about the more famous Garretts has been invaluable in piecing together the personal histories of Agnes and Rhoda. See, for example: E. T. Cook, *Edmund Garrett: A Memoir*, Edward Arnold, 1909; M. Garrett Fawcett, *What I Remember*, T. Fisher Unwin, 1924; R. Strachey, *Millicent Garrett Fawcett*, John Murray, 1931; J. Manton, *Elizabeth Garrett Anderson*, Methuen & Co., 1965; A. Oakley, 'Millicent Garrett Fawcett: duty and determination', in D. Spender, (ed.), *Feminist Theorists: Three Centuries of Women's*

Intellectual Traditions, The Women's Press, 1983; D. Rubinstein, *A Different World For Women: The Life of Millicent Garrett Fawcett*, Harvester Wheatsheaf, 1991; B. Caine, *Victorian Feminists*, Oxford University Press, 1993, and J. Purvis & H. S. Stanley, *Votes for Women*, Routledge, 2000. This article was written before the publication of E. Crawford's study of the Garrett family, *Enterprising Women: The Garretts and their Circle*, Francis Boutle, September 2002.

17. A. Briggs, *Victorian Things*, Penguin Books, 1988.

18. The illustration of the 'Dining Room' in *House Decoration* shows Morris's 'Trellis' wallpaper. The Garretts certainly knew Morris: Rhoda's obituary in *The Englishwoman's Review*, 15 December 1882, notes that she was a committee member of the Society for the Protection of Ancient Buildings formed in 1877. She was in fact the only female committee member, and it is interesting that several of the other authors for the 'Art at Home' series, including W. J. Loftie and C. G. Leland, were involved with the SPAB. I am grateful to Dr Jenny West at the SPAB for information about Rhoda's committee attendances.

19. *The Builder*, vol. 43, 1882, p. 765.

20. See E. Moberly Bell, *Storming the Citadel: The Rise of the Woman Doctor*, Constable & Co., 1953.

21. D. Attar, *A Bibliography of Household Books Published in Britain 1800–1914*, Prospect Books, 1987, pp. 31–2.

22. I am very grateful to Robert Machesney at the Macmillan Archive for providing me with details of the full list of titles, which is as follows: Rev. W. J. Loftie, *A Plea for Art in the House* (1876); Rhoda & Agnes Garrett, *Suggestions for House Decoration* (1876); Mrs Orrinsmith, *The Drawing-Room* (1877); Rev. J. Hullah, *Music in the House* (1877); Mrs W. J. Loftie, *The Dining Room* (1877 but dated 1878); Lady Barker, *The Bedroom and Boudoir* (1878); Mrs Oliphant, *Dress* (1878); Lady Pollock, *Amateur Theatricals* (1879); C. G.

Leland, *The Minor Arts* (1880); E. Glaister, *Needlework* (1880); A. Lang, *The Library* (1881), and T. J. Ellis, *Sketching from Nature* (1883).

23. Rev. W. J. Loftie, *A Plea for Art in the Home*, Macmillan & Co., 1876, p. 29.

24. Rev. W. J. Loftie (1839–1911), correspondence with Macmillan, 1875–81. British Library, Manuscripts Collections, Reference: Add MS 55075. Letter to Macmillan dated 11 March 1876.

25. See, for example, N. Armstrong, *Desire and Domestic Fiction; A Political History of the Novel*, Oxford University Press, 1987; J. Newton, 'Making and re-making patriarchy', in S. Benstock, *Feminist Issues in Literary Scholarship*, Indiana University Press, 1987; A. Vickery, 'Golden Age to separate spheres? A review of the categories and chronology of English women's history', *Historical Journal*, vol. 36, no. 2, 1993, and E. Langland, *Nobody's Angels: Middle-class Women and Domestic Ideology in Victorian Culture*, Cornell University Press, 1995.

26. Vickery, op. cit., p. 389.

27. Eastlake, op. cit., p. 11

28. R. & A. Garrett, op. cit., p. 43.

29. C. L. Eastlake, *Hints on Household Taste*, Longman & Co., 1868, 1878, pp. 8–9.

30. R. & A. Garrett, op. cit., p. 28.

31. Ibid., p. 55.

32. *Building News*, 26 June 1874, pp. 689–92; *The Builder*, 27 June 1874, pp. 537–8.

33. Rev. W. J. Loftie, 'Advertisement, in R. & A. Garrett, op. cit., notes that the next volume of this series would be J. J. Stevenson's *Domestic Architecture* which 'will apply the same principles to the exterior that are here applied to the interior of our houses'. J. J. Stevenson's *House Architecture*, although part of Loftie's original scheme, was not issued as part of the 'Art at Home' series, being published separately in two volumes by Macmillan in 1880.

34. R. & A. Garret, op. cit.

35. Ibid., pp. 5–6.

36. Ibid., p. 6.

37. Ibid., p. 12.

38. Ibid., p. 14.

39. Ibid., p. 22.

40. Ibid., p. 14.

61

INTEGRATIVE PRACTICE: ORAL HISTORY, DRESS AND DISABILITY STUDIES

Liz Linthicum (2006)

Logic suggests that there has always been a history of clothing that has evolved around people who have been determined as 'disabled'. Bodies and psychologies, in all their variety, have always been accommodated in clothing in one designed form or another, yet studies of dress have yet to engage adequately with this subject area. There have been various perspectives that make their own reference to it, ranging from those that are dated and medically orientated – such as those from the occupational therapy,[1] ergonomics[2] and nursing[3] fields – to those that are primarily focused on consumer-oriented concerns.[4] These [...] do need to be acknowledged and recognized as forming their part within this multidimensional aspect of dress history. It is also essential, however, that the actual experiential dimensions of disabled people's interactions with clothing be at the core of historical research in this area. The following outlines some methodological, ethical and interpretative issues that have arisen during the oral history aspect of a project that has begun exploring the fertile 'inter-discipline' formed between the fields of dress studies and disability studies. [...]

PLACING USER KNOWLEDGE AT THE FOREFRONT

The oral history project centred on a highly personal aspect of people's lives that raised important issues of confidentiality. For instance, the project was more likely to benefit from a free flow of personal information if the interviewees were assured that they would not be identified by name, but by code and location. The knowledge that their identities would remain confidential also protected those who wanted to contribute to the project whilst also continuing to engage with their social circle – of which the interviewer was unlikely to have knowledge – that brought them into contact with the project in the first place, without undue pressure.[5]

The effect of preparing and using roughly similar question plans for each interview provided a structure by which responses could potentially be compared. Often, though, responses to these initial questions – such as 'What's important to you about your clothing?' – directed each interview into a surprisingly diverse range of other enquiries, which formed the basis for many of the subsequent questions that were asked, ad hoc, during the rest of each interview. Two interviewees interpreted the question 'Could I ask you to think back and tell me about the first outfit you remember wearing?' as a query regarding the clothing they first wore as newly disabled people, whereas the same question prompted others to talk about their childhood memories of clothing. Both response types offered fascinating insights into the interviewees' life views and approaches. Likewise, points of divergence echoed throughout the interviews, with specific garment types or dressing issues being mentioned by several respondents. [...]

The interviewees comprised six men and three women; three of the nine had always lived as disabled people and the other five had acquired impairments during their lives. The five in this latter group described – often by implication – a process of adjustment to life as disabled people, a process to which some of my interviewees were very accustomed whilst others were at the earlier stages:

> I didn't really bother with clothes for about a year really, just wore old clothes – I was terrified of shopping.[6] (Female respondent)

> I progressed from pyjamas to tracksuit ... a sort of upper market tracksuit, but it was still basically a tracksuit, but I felt sort of dressed, I thought, you know, I sort of gradually got to wearing trousers and ordinary clothes.[7] (Male respondent)

Despite several similarities in clothing issues brought to the interviews by both groups, the interviewees often appeared to uphold a general sense of the coping-with-adversity approach to their clothing and dressing that is portrayed in many of the older published sources.[8] This could be characterized by, for instance, this literature's repeated concern that clothing creates *camouflage* for that which has been determined as impairment, and by the strong emphasis on the 'functionality' of clothing intended for disabled people. A distinctly different attitude to clothing and dress issues was outlined by those with lifelong experiences of disability: 'My relationship with clothing is very much reflective of my relationship with myself and my self-discovery, my own self, my own identity, my own sexuality. And clothing is an important part of that journey, as it is for everybody else.'[9] [male respondent] [...]

Recognition of the contribution oral history can make in relation to reclaiming the cultural history of disability has been made by Karen Hirsch. She calls for disability issues to be included 'as an analytic category'[10] within the making of oral history. She also challenges the notion that it is 'assumed that disabled people do not have an articulate view of their circumstances that differ[s] ... from other views'.[11] These ideas, as well as her discussions that centre on the highly sensitive issue of 'interpretive authority'[12] in relation to disabled people's testimony, are examples taken from Hirsch's work that illustrate her contributions to oral history's potential to recover historical knowledge around clothing used by disabled people now and in the past.[13] The oral history material gathered for this project could be used as much for what it suggests methodologically as for what it contains. The process of oral history interviewing allowed for a more sensitive approach, enabling the research to be carried out outside now-discredited medically modelled perceptions of disabled people's realities. It also, crucially, enabled respect for individuals' own criteria for what issues mattered to them. It has been argued that by 'introduc[ing] the emotionality, the fears, the fantasies carried by the metaphors, which historians have been so anxious to write out of their formal accounts'[14] oral historians operate under 'accusations of unreliability, subjective narrative, conjecture and the essential fallibility of individual personal memory'.[15] But it is these very human traits – the 'web of feelings, attitudes and values that give meaning to activities and events'[16] – that determine oral history as a highly suitable methodology which is able to capture and respect the type of complexities that are apparent in consciously reclaiming disabled people's clothing realities.

Very often, the most informative material gathered during oral history recordings has not necessarily formed neat, accessible, broadcast-able narratives. One interviewee made a significant contribution to the project by demonstrating the ingenious adjustments – '*all my own work*'[17] – he had to make to his footwear:

So I have to have this ghastly business of toggles and laces which I lashed up myself which is not totally satisfactory, but does work a bit … you will notice that the loops on the shoe I have Snopaked to make them more obvious. As you look down under your knee everything becomes dark, of course, making it impossible to see.[18]*

He carefully demonstrated how he puts on his footwear and improvised leg support, moving his own left hand and arm with his stronger right hand in order to facilitate this complicated dressing process. The resulting two and a half minutes of recorded vocal physical effort interspersed with comment is hard to convey, in either transcription or written format and is eloquent testimony to how clothing can become not only a site for highly individual creative innovation but also a contested area which has little to do with standard, intended or medical 'solutions'. […]

Fastenings, as a problematic issue in garment design for many disabled people, are further illustrated by another interviewee:

I have had terrible times. Once I couldn't undo a coat and I had no one around me at the time, so I had to go to bed in it. I just couldn't get it off. I don't know why I couldn't … The material was too thick, couldn't cut it off.[19] (Female respondent)

A concern to place user knowledge at the forefront echoes moves in both disability studies[20] and dress studies[21] to reincorporate the body, and the issues it inherently brings with it. Recording the resonating significance of thoughts, feelings and physical efforts of people operating in intimate embodied circumstances may profoundly challenge accepted concepts of design history by foregrounding experiential contexts. The above testimonies highlight how the very 'process' of dressing, rather than an over concentration on the stylistic 'result' that dress is often implied to be, is more likely to encompass how the human endeavour of interacting with clothing has operated over the past from the 'disability' perspective. […]

INTERVIEWS AND SELF-REPRESENTATION

The importance of planning an oral history approach at the initial stage of long-term research projects became evident after one interviewee suggested that oral history interviewing could be considered as a fundamental starting tool and a sign of good practice within disability-orientated research. The value of this insight steered the very direction of my research in ways more profound than could have been initially expected. Material gathered in this initial stage underscored the approach of the entire project, as is clear in this excerpt from one of my early interviews:

I think we should be looking at things from a completely different angle. And if we look at the functionality of clothing itself and look at the fact that it's not an issue just for disabled people, it's an issue for everybody … there's a whole continuum [of approaches to/requirements from different types of clothes] which should include disabled people in a mainstream way, as opposed to this 'special needs' approach.[22] (Male respondent). […]

The material gathered during oral history interviews could allow sources themselves to influence the direction of research. […] Comments made by two interviewees in relation to identity expectations and how they had been expressed through appearance and clothing had helped to steer the project towards considering the pernicious impact of institutional life upon disabled people in the nineteenth and twentieth centuries:

I mean now it's on the wane, the use of leggings for people with learning disabilities, everyone seemed to be wearing leggings or a large number. But it says nothing about them. Nothing about the fact they very often have real ideas about what they want to wear. […] The look of a person wearing a woolly coat and a bobble hat … it's all a process of disempowerment … Your life is not shaped by you … the food you eat, the clothes you wear, the money you use, etc. etc.[23] (Male respondent) […]

Further extracts referring to mundane, everyday clothing issues have the potential to clarify, even uncover, much larger historical themes. Some standard dress-related practices carried out in many institutions have had a profound effect on how disabled people have been perceived and on how it has been assumed they have lived their lives:

'There is a whole culture of dressing disabled people as asexual; that's very strong in terms of institutionalised settings I think in many contemporaries' experiences, I remember mine particularly.'[24] (Male respondent)

The deliberate curtailment of sexual and gender expression within the old institutional settings is a deeply significant issue in the formation of institutionalized peoples' individual identities. It is an issue that recurs in other projects that have used oral history to recover disability history.[25] This negative attitude towards the sexuality of the disabled, then and now, is a major contributing factor to the way in which our culture has come to view and deal with disability itself.

COMBINING ANALYTIC STRATEGIES

[…] At an appropriate point during most of the interviews,[26] a self-help manual[27] was shown to prompt interviewees. My intention was to grant interviewees distance – considering the often personal nature of the topic – whilst they described their experience of clothing. This appeared irrelevant in practice, however, with interviewees keen to engage with the book in two very different ways. One interviewee was impressed with some of the specific ideas the book contained:

I've never seen anything like this or heard about anything like this being available in this country. And I think it would be, there are thousands of people in wheelchairs … there's a colossal market out there really, if someone could sort of latch onto it. I know everyone's got different needs and different sort of problems but you know, there are plenty of people that would benefit.[28] (Male respondent)

Another interviewee with lifelong experience of living as a disabled person took an entirely different approach:

I mean it's very well meaning. I mean it's some kind of medical approach to people's clothing … Let's have a look [turns to credits at the front of the book] Yes, it's done with an occupational therapist … they understand the issues but it's approached through the world of occupational therapists and rehabilitation and settings that actually say nothing about my home and my community and my fashion magazines and my television images and my whatever other things that inform and influence the aesthetic, design, shape of your world and your appearance within that world. And it's fine [indicating the book], but it's, it's – we need more, we [need] a lot more. A lot better. A lot more fun.[29] (Male respondent)

[…] What was also apparent from using objects to elicit responses was what can be revealed by combining oral history methods with other methodologies employed by dress studies historians, such as stringent object analysis. Another way in which the process of oral history illuminated object analysis occurred when attention was directed away from the actual content of the self-help manual during several interviews. I was struck by how inaccessible this object, and no doubt the other self-help manuals, had been: in order for it be read, assistance from another person was required to open, hold or steady the book for five out of my nine interviewees. This experience suggested that analysis of objects could be extended to consider how sources such as these operate beyond their content, in terms of how they materially manifest and interact with those for whom they are intended. [...]

'MUTUALLY INFORMATIVE DIALOGUE'

The individual life circumstances of some interviewees highlighted the need to develop a range of more inclusively refined interviewing skills. Awareness of how the researcher can affect what is being researched was a continual factor throughout all the stages of the project. For example, it became apparent during a recorded interview with a blind interviewee that using body language to convey that the interviewer was listening was of little use. Unfamiliarity with ways of verbally affirming the interviewee without undue sound interruption resulted in an unfortunately short (but nevertheless valuable) interview. This is one of many experiences that suggested the need for alternative interviewing strategies.

Biddle-Perry rightly advocates a 'mutually informative dialogue between clothing and oral historians and their research'.[30] [...] Consciously building consultative approaches into oral history projects would encourage recognition of the points at which design historians can be brought in to contribute their particular specialist insights. At the very least, interdisciplinary dialogue throws a sharp light on the position of the interviewer, encouraging a conscious reflexivity on their part and demanding clearly stated positions of expertise. My position as interviewer during the project referred to in this article was informed by several positions from within my own realm of knowledge. Fluxing between knowledge gained as a [care-giver], knowledge gained as a deaf studies student, and as a dress historian, afforded me several positions from which to begin my dialogue within that particular process.

The process of interpreting oral history material is anything but straightforward. An example of this is the knowledge that our own interpretations of oral history can create and form 'second-level narrative[s]' which, although based upon the original material we collect, result in 'reshaping ... the first'[31] and original levels of narrative, as told by the interviewees. This layering can surface in many ways, but here I shall elaborate the ethical, and the interpretative issues.

Firstly, it is vital for research of any scale to be infused with material contributed by those who are living disabled realities. The layering of a non-disabled narrative upon that which originated as a disabled one can be an obvious problem in work conducted by researchers who have no personal experience of non-standard interaction with the designed world around them. [...] [A] profound lack of development of wider, inclusive thinking – on a design level and beyond – has historically shaped our society in ways which have been profoundly negative and limiting for all of us.[32]

NOTES

Extracted from Linthicum, L., 'Integrative Practice: Oral History, Dress and Disability Studies', *The Journal of Design History* 19(4) (2006), pp. 309–18. Reprinted by permission of the Design History Society.

Editor's note: Snopake is a branded correction fluid.

1. Two examples: J. O. Yep, 'Tools for Aiding Physically Disabled Individuals Increase Independence in Dressing', *Journal of Rehabilitation*, vol. 43, no. 6, pp. 39–41; and E. H. Ahrbeck & S. E. Friend, 'Clothing: An Asset or Liability? Designing for Specialized Needs', *Rehabilitation Literature*, vol. 37, 1976, pp. 295–6.

2. For example: M. Thoren, 'Systems Approach to Clothing for Disabled Users: Why is it Difficult

for Disabled Users to Find Suitable Clothing?', *Applied Ergonomics*, vol. 27, 1996, pp. 389–96.

3. For example: M. M. Ward, 'Self-help Fashions for the Physically Disabled Child', *American Journal of Nursing*, vol. 58, 1958, pp. 526–7.

4. There is occasional work published in the American-based International Textile and Apparel Association's journal, *Clothing and Textiles Research Journal* in this area.

5. Initial interview contacts were made through Disability Action in the London Borough of Barnet, the local branch of a large national umbrella organization run by disabled people, the British Council of Disabled People, who dealt with my request with speed and enthusiasm. This led to a series of oral history interviews conducted in various locations in North and Central London, between March and June 2004, with nine adults on the theme of their realities of dressing and their relationships with clothes. I was keen that control over whom I approached for interview remained with disabled people themselves, with some contacts being made via the initial set of interviewees, who sometimes referred me on to other potential contacts. All interviewees have given formal, written permission for use of their contributions. It was important to establish a degree of confidentiality from the start of the project for several reasons.

6. Interview 04/07, 02 April 2004, Hendon.

7. Interview 04/04, 25 March 2004, Finchley Central.

8. See, for instance, Ann M. Gamwell & Florence Joyce, *A Survey of Problems of Clothing for the Sick and Disabled both in Hospital and in the Community*, ([n.p.]: Central Council for the Disabled, Disabled Living Activities Group, 1966): Disabled Living Foundation, *How to Adapt Existing Clothing for the Disabled* ([n.p]: Disabled Living Foundation, 1971): and Gillian Forbes, *Clothing for the Handicapped Child*, ([n.p.]: [n.pub.], 1972).

9. Interview 04/05, 26 March 2004, Central London.

10. K. Hirsch, 'Culture and Disability: The Role of Oral History', in R. Perks & A. Thompson (eds.), *The Oral History Reader*, Routledge, London, 1998; repr. 2003, p. 214.

11. Ibid., p. 217.

12. Ibid., p. 220.

13. Ibid., pp. 214–23.

14. R. Samuel & P. Thompson, 'The Myths We Live By', Routledge, 1990 in L. Taylor (ed.), *The Study of Dress History*, Manchester University Press, 2002, p. 244.

15. G. Biddle-Perry, 'Bury Me in Purple Lurex: promoting a new dynamic between fashion and oral history', *Oral History*, vol. 33, no. 1, 2005, p. 89.

16. S. B. Gluck & D. Patai, *Women's Words: The Feminist Practice of Oral History*, Routledge, London, 1991, p. 12.

17. Interview 04/09, 17 June 2004, Finchley.

18. Ibid.

19. 30 Interview 04/07, 02 Jul 04, Hendon.

20. See for instance: K. Lindgren, 'Bodies in Trouble: Identity, Embodiment and Disability', in B. G. Smith & B. Hutchison, *Gendering Disability*, Rutgers University Press, New Brunswick, NJ, 2004, pp. 145–65.

21. For instance, Joanne Entwistle's work on embodiment, e.g. J. Entwistle, *The Fashioned Body*, Polity Press, Cambridge, 2000, repr. 2002.

22. Interview 04/05, 26 Mar 04, Central London.

23. Interview 04/10, 26 Jun 04, Golders Green.

24. Interview 04/05, 26 Mar 04, Central London.

25. See for instance, all three parts of the 1999 BBC 2 series, *The Disabled Century*, directed by David Hevey; also, J. Campling, *Images of Ourselves; Women with Disabilities Talking*, Routledge & Kegan Paul, London, 1981; and S. Humphries & P. Gordon, *Out of Sight: the Experience of Disability, 1900–1950*, Northcote House, Plymouth, 1992.

26. This strategy was not used in the case of one interviewee who is blind.

27. R. W. Chase & M. D. Quinn, *Design without Limits: Designing and Sewing for Special Needs*, Fairchild, New York, 2003 (previously

published as M. D. Quinn & R. W. Chase, *Simplicity's Design without Limits: Designing and Sewing for Special Needs*, Drexel University, Philadelphia, 1990).

28. Interview 04/04, 25 Mar 04, Finchley Central.
29. Interview 04/10, 26 Jun 04, Golders Green.
30. G. Biddle-Perry, op. cit., p. 88.
31. K. Borland, "'That's Not What I Said': Interpretive Conflict in Oral Narrative Research', in R. Perks & A. Thomson, *The Oral History Reader*, Routledge, 1998, repr. 2003, p. 321.
32. The project, *Adorn Equip*, was an example of how this historical short-sightedness can be creatively challenged; moving beyond even issues of representation, projects such as these suggest great potential for rethinking our cultural views of disability. See http://www.adornequip.co.uk for details.

62

INTRODUCTION TO *DESIGN AND THE MODERN MAGAZINE*

Jeremy Aynsley and Kate Forde (2007)

Most commercially sold magazines result from a division of labour between editors, advertisers, journalists, illustrators, typographers, designers, art directors and, in more recent years, stylists. As such, magazine publishing is a complex area of study and the methods needed for its understanding cross a range of academic disciplines. Moreover, since magazines are composite rather than singular objects their character reflects different sources and disciplines. [...]

Perhaps because of their ambivalent status as ephemeral and potentially marginal forms, both as literature and as object, magazines have received relatively brief attention from historians concerned to identify their contribution to the design landscape. Nevertheless, design history, we suggest, is well-suited to do this, given its interest in combining immanent analysis of objects with considerations of manufacture and consumption. Indeed, the cultural and economic concerns that magazines hold in tension, their synthesis of image and text, even their three-dimensionality, are ideal territory for the interdisciplinary methods of design history. [...]

EARLY MAGAZINES AND METHODOLOGY

In order to situate the periodical in context, however, it is relevant to consider its earlier beginnings and to take a cursory glance at the history of printing. From the second half of the eighteenth century, factors such as the increase in population, expansion of trade, improved means of communication and advances in technology stimulated both the printing industry and the market. Print and typographic historian Michael Twyman deliberately omits books from his otherwise comprehensive history of printing, favouring instead the playing cards, devotional prints, reward notices, livestock sale posters, sheet music, tickets and other printed matter that flourished during the period.[1] It may be useful to see the magazine emerging from the ephemera he depicts, as much as from its more obvious precursors, the book and the newspaper. Twyman's study is also relevant for its consideration of the printing industry's historical structure, and the unsung labour force behind it. [...]

At the beginning of the nineteenth century [magazines] were fairly general productions which sought to capture as wide a market as possible by including a mixture of comment on politics, social life, fashion, etiquette, religion and morality. The earliest specialist magazines were those aimed at women. First produced during the late 1800s, they identified a readership which remains crucial today. New titles were funded by advertising for goods that simultaneously became branded commodities. These very often depended on their graphic identity in press advertisements, just as much as in point of sale and poster designs in the wider world, contributing to what historian Thomas Richards has called 'the commodity culture' of late nineteenth-century society.[2] The process of diversification of target readers has continued since then, causing the commentators Tebbel and Zuckerman to note that there is now 'no interest known to mankind which does not have at least one magazine to serve it'.[3]

Given the sheer volume of material, only a few historians have attempted to provide comprehensive surveys of the magazine industries in England and America.[4] David Reed's history of the popular magazine in Britain and America limits its terms by laying emphasis on the magazine as a manufactured product, using this as a corrective to what he regards as overly literary or personalised histories. This is the magazine as a phenomenon born of technology and commerce. Reed, therefore, describes the conditions under which such a commodity might flourish, identifying increasing urbanisation as one of the key factors. Comparing Britain's continuing industrial development in the nineteenth century (which was linked to its coal industry of the eighteenth), to America's later explosion of industrial activity, he explains how both countries' populations came to be concentrated in cities. This shift resulted in significantly lowering the unit costs of distribution for all goods, including magazines. In turn, transportation systems both within and outside the urban centres developed to make them realistic working propositions. Railway systems resulted in faster postal services, which facilitated both business communication and the dissemination of magazines. The effect of these shifts in turn stimulated a remarkable growth in education, ensured the rise of public libraries; and instilled the habit of reading in an evolving middle class.

Inevitably, such surveys deal in generalisations rather than subtleties. Nonetheless, they acknowledge the economic concerns that drive the magazine publishing industry and the precise circumstances of its manufacture – the presses, paper production, typesetting machines, colour science and advances in mechanical illustration techniques, all of which had an important impact on the speed and facility with which magazines might be produced. One such landmark technology was the first web-fed rotary perfecting press installed at *The New York Sun* in 1865.[5] The machine brought about a great acceleration in production times because rolls of paper, the web, meant faster machines which printed on both sides simultaneously. Such an example reminds us of the materiality of magazines, as does Reed's description of the race to find a suitable vegetable source for paper which until the mid-nineteenth century was extracted from cotton and rag waste. After all, it is ultimately the differing qualities of paper that are the parameters defining many aspects of a modern publication's nature. The size, strength, flexibility and porosity of the paper are all things which affect the printing process and in another significant development in magazine production was the introduction of the half-tone process as an illustrative technique. For most of the nineteenth century, wood engraving had been the basis of magazine illustrations, but it was an extremely costly and labour-intensive process. Half-tones, which use small specks of ink to create a delicate shading effect, were a radically cheaper alternative, taking hours rather than days to prepare. As an example, the high cost of engravings meant that the *Illustrated London News* cost sixpence in 1848, about half the day rate of a labourer, whereas fifty years later, the use of multiple illustrations was commonplace and the price had dropped to three pence.[6] As the century drew to a close, half-tone illustrations and, subsequently, the introduction of photography would change the appearance of magazines forever, heralding a new era dominated by the power of the image.

Magazines have often been viewed as unique historical resources for the historian because they record the incredibly complicated flow of life in a breadth of detail that is unavailable in any other medium. Tebbel and Zuckerman, for instance, point out that most of the visual images we have of America in the nineteenth century come from magazine pages that first displayed woodcuts and, in time, photography to illuminate the world. Their account of the American periodical is decidedly partisan, claiming it as possibly the 'most democratic institution the country has yet produced'.[7] The reason for their tribute is that whilst they emphasise the pivotal role that the magazine has played in promoting conformity and shaping consumer culture, they also see it as expressing the limitless interests of the most diverse population in the world. In order to demonstrate this, their wide-ranging volume covers several specialist as well as popular titles, including extensive discussions of the abolitionist press, African-American periodicals, children's magazines and story-papers. They, too, cite the emergence of the half-tone as a crucial technological factor in the magazine's history, linking it to the success of the 'muckrakers' – the magazines which flourished between 1895 and 1918 by running exposés of corruption within large corporations and government institutions. Not only were these publications sensational in content, they looked exciting and were rich with colour. Costing only a dime, instead of the usual 35 cents, they were part of a wave of magazines that was reaching a new American public with less education and less money than before.

As magazines diversified, the roles of those producing them also became more specialised. William Owen traces this division of labour in his study *Magazine Design,* citing Aubrey Beardsley as the first to be credited with the title 'art director' in the *Yellow Book* of 1894.[8] His is one of several accounts which identifies the magazine as a vehicle for the work of graphic designers, and asserts that design is a communicative rather than a decorative act.[9] Owen argues that because the early magazine lacked a unique visual format it became an ideal medium for graphic exploration. Focusing on the course of magazine design during the twentieth century, he identifies design protagonists from the fields of photojournalism, the Modern Movement in Europe and

the underground press who all had an impact on the medium. Crucially he draws attention to the difference in American and European magazine design of the 1940s. Reeling from the effects of the Second World War, Europe's publishing business lacked not only resources but the market and advertisers to pay for it. Whilst editorial design was advancing steadily in the United States, in Europe, pulp weeklies were churning out escapist fiction and magazine producers were preoccupied by the need to conserve paper. Not until the post-war boom of the 1950s did the influence of American abstract expressionism, with its generosity of colour and space, really take hold in Europe.

Studies that focus on the aesthetics of magazines often function partly as reference manuals for those working in the field and partly as manifestos for the profession. Highlighting the role of the magazine designer, they uncover what is sometimes understood as a personal struggle to relinquish traditional book and newspaper typography and to create an entirely new medium of text and pictures. As a professional designer himself, Ruari McLean's studies in typographic history, for instance, stem from a desire to elevate the reputation of the business from craft to art.[10] Whilst this approach can usefully reconstruct the creative effort involved in the production of magazines, it risks overestimating the autonomy of the designer and misreading the endeavour as a chiefly aesthetic instead of commercial enterprise.

The same charge might be levelled at histories which have focused on editors and publishing magnates.[11] Whilst the particular skills and predilections of such characters certainly affected the magazines produced under their leadership, an overemphasis on individual personalities can obscure the fact that they are working within the constraints of cultural inheritances, economic relationships and technical boundaries. Salme Harju Steinberg's study of Edward Bok (editor of the hugely successful American periodical, *The Ladies' Home Journal*) is unusual in this context. Steinberg uses Bok to explore a wider theme, namely the uneasy coexistence of reform journalism with an increasingly powerful advertising presence in the late nineteenth and early twentieth-century magazine. Steinberg never loses sight of the magazine as a double proposition, registering that its success was due to its ability to conform to the needs of both advertisers and readers. Her work identifies a relationship of compromise which is at the heart of most modern magazines.

The significance of advertising to magazines is indicated by the fact that before the advent of radio in 1920s America, the periodical press was the only way to reach a national audience. (In England newspapers as well as magazines carried advertising.) From the early nineteenth century, industrialists realised they could translate the new pursuit of reading into consuming, by building direct relationships with the market through increasingly sophisticated printed salesmanship. The interdependence of the publishing and promotional industries has ensured that many of the most insightful commentaries on modern magazine history are to be found in studies of advertising.[12] The conversion of readers to consumers has also been the subject of several recent studies, many of which focus on the magazine's cultivation of a mass female market.[13] It is a salutary thought that the only reliable figures we have concerning magazine circulation come from institutions such as the Association of American Advertisers, formed in 1899 to drag out accurate statistics from periodical publishers. In this sense, even the most objective aspects of magazine history are always and inextricably linked to the commercial sphere.

OTHER METHODOLOGIES

Moving to those studies which are predominantly concerned with the contents of magazines, they usually divide between those which analyse the text and those which give priority to images, whether in advertisements or editorial pages.[14] A number of sociologically informed interpretations have focused on how particular groups of people and sectors of society make use of magazines or how they can shape aspirations. Through such an approach, reading magazines becomes an active form of cultural production. The first inroads towards understanding magazines and valuing them as a form of literature in Britain was signalled in Richard Hoggart's seminal book, *The Uses of Literacy*, a study of working-class life, first published in 1957.[15] This tradition was continued in cultural studies by Raymond Williams, whose impressive study, *The Long Revolution* (1961) was also formative for the analysis it gave of the mechanisms of popular publishing, part of what Williams saw as a continuation of the project of the Enlightenment.[16] Williams's approach, it should be added, concentrated on the textual. An equal consideration of the visual and textual was introduced in the work of Dick Hebdige and Angela McRobbie, whose respective studies of magazines directly marketed towards youth subcultures and teenage girls applied a cultural studies approach to more contemporary material.[17] In this and much subsequent work, a fluent reading of the allure of magazines was key. Unlike design history, however, cultural studies rarely engages with the circumstances of production, the design process or the material qualities of the magazines.

[...] An enduring legacy of the Frankfurt School on interpretations of popular culture has been to disparage areas of consumption associated with the female sphere.[18] And too often in this tradition, women have been cast as passive consumers, duped by the forces of persuasion into pursuing false needs and desires. The extent to which a magazine can function as a reliable source of information rather than distraction therefore becomes a contested issue. In general, the literature on magazines varies as to whether it sees magazines as a source of manipulation of desire or fount of useful knowledge, or indeed both. Either way, it is a question that none can avoid.

With this in mind, it is possibly not surprising that women's magazines were all too often treated with a lack of seriousness in academic circles. It was not until 1970 that Cynthia White, a sociologist, published the first complete study of women's magazines, which laid down important foundations for much subsequent work.[19] The emphasis of this work was to plot the circulation histories of leading American and British magazines against broad social and cultural changes in women's lives. A central issue addressed in this study is whether magazines could be said to reflect the experience of women beyond their pages.

Through the bringing together of women's studies and literature studies, magazines have been recognised as a central element in women's lives, in work that has explored their intrinsic ambivalence. This has predominantly been through studies of individual titles, such as Jennifer Scanlon's account of the leading American women's title, *The Ladies' Home Journal*, and the thematic interpretation of how magazines engaged with issues of gender, home and leisure.[20] Interestingly, much of the pioneering work in this field has concentrated on the late nineteenth and early twentieth centuries in Britain and America – a time when many of these structures first came in to being on such a scale. These studies are concerned wherever possible to reconstruct the reader. In a work such as Ellen Gruber Garvey's, *The Adman in the Parlor: Magazines and the Gendering of Consumer Culture, 1880s to 1910s*, the approach taken is a close literary reading of the editorial pages, letter pages and the mode of address made to the reader, in the form of the advertisements.[21] Her study reveals that 'reading' was far from a passive activity. Rather, young women readers used magazines to inform their hobbies; collecting or cutting and pasting them, and incorporating their newly gained knowledge in their domestic lives in ways that magazine proprietors could not have predicted.

In turn, women's involvement as professionals in the magazine industry has also received interpretation, especially in the case of the United States. Ellen Mazur Thomson has traced the engagement of women art directors and designers in American graphic design from 1870 to 1920.[22] Michelle Bogart studied the place of women as illustrators for mainstream periodicals and the hierarchies and terms of employment in the early twentieth century.[23] And in at least one case, the life and work of a pioneering woman art director, Cipe Pineles, who was active in mid-century America as a designer of women and teenage girl magazines, has now been researched.[24]

A central concern in the literature on magazines, therefore, is their relationship with their consumers, the readers. Were readers simply recipients of what the editors or magazine proprietors fed them, or could the relationship be more complex, one of negotiation and possible dissent? While magazines were an imaginative space full of potential, did they in fact reinforce traditional stereotypes, and present deeply conservative attitudes?

[…] With translations of French theoretical writings on culture becoming available, the interpretation of magazines experienced what has been called a 'linguistic turn' in the 1970 and 1980s. In particular, Roland Barthes' writing was especially influential on a generation who were developing approaches to popular culture.[25] […] Barthes […] revealed how popular imagery can work ideologically to incorporate accepted social values and political beliefs, making them appear natural. […] Barthes and other French thinkers led more generally to a tradition of deconstruction and decoding of photographic imagery in advertising and magazines.[26] The advantage of the semiological method is that it offers ways to interpret encoded meanings in magazines and understand desire and pleasure of the text. It has been applied most successfully to systems of representation that deal with fashion, style and sexuality. The potential danger for the historian is that it can present the object of study, in this case the magazine, in a form of the continuous present while overlooking the specific circumstances of manufacture and intention.

[…] Among the empirical methods available to the design historian is what is known as content analysis, a model drawn from the social sciences and employed in media studies.[27] This can be useful if the historian of the magazine wishes to establish a representative point of view. It allows for moving beyond the interpretation of a particular issue of a magazine to establish a narrative that does justice to its changes over time. In this connection, it is useful to distinguish between a diachronic study, which seeks to explain change over time and the synchronic, which focuses on a single moment or a cross-section.[28] Most historians accept that adopting a quantitative approach can be helpful when dealing with change over time. In the case of magazines, research can start by taking a broad survey of a title and then a decision is made to pursue sampling based on regular intervals over a number of years, applying the same criteria of analysis. […]

Design historians are attentive to the changes in design layout as one of the most significant elements of a magazine. For instance, change or continuity of a title's masthead […] suggests how attitudes to the title as a whole can be conveyed. Similarly, a change of typeface or the introduction of a grid to reorganise the page layout of a magazine may be important in design history but overlooked by other kinds of interpretation. […]

Another established method within design history is to use the interview as a source of oral testimony. In Britain, many of the principal methods of gathering oral evidence for historical purposes have been outlined in Paul Thompson's work, which emphasises social history.[29] In order to establish a history of magazines, for example, interviews with key figures are sometimes the only way in which the everyday workings of a magazine can be retrieved. […]

NOTES

Extracted from Aynsley, J. and Forde, K., 'Introduction', *Design and the Modern Magazine*, Manchester: Manchester University Press, 2007, pp. 1–16. Reproduced by permission of the authors and Manchester University Press.

1. M. Twyman, *Printing: 1770–1970: An Illustrated History of its Development and Uses in England* (London: Eyre & Spottiswoode, 1970).

2. T. Richards, *The Commodity Culture of Victorian Britain: Advertising and Spectacle, 1851–1914* (London: Verso, 1991).

3. J. Tebbel and M. E. Zuckerman, *The Magazine in America, 1741–1990* (New York and Oxford: Oxford University Press, 1991), p. 244.

4. See D. Reed, *The Popular Magazine in Britain and the United States, 1880–1960* (British Library: London, 1997), and Tebbel and Zuckerman, *The Magazine in America*.

5. Reed, The *Popular Magazine*, p. 43.

6. Cited by William Owen, *Magazine Design* (London: Laurence King, 1991).

7. Tebbel and Zuckerman, *The Magazine in America*, p. 382.

8. Owen, *Magazine Design*, p.13.

9. See also, R. McLean, *Magazine Design* (London: Oxford University Press, 1969); P. Jobling and D. Crowley, *Graphic Design: Reproduction and Representation since 1800* (Manchester and New York: Manchester University Press, 1996); D. Crowley, *Magazine Covers* (London: Mitchell Beazley, 2003).

10. Ruari McLean, *Typography*, (London: Thames & Hudson, 1980); and *How Typography Happens*, (London: The British Library and Oak Knoll Press, 2000).

11. See, for instance, C. Seebohm, *The Man who was Vogue: the Life and Times of Condé Nast*, (London: Weidenfeld Nicolson, 1982), and Salme Harju Steinberg, *Reformer in the Marketplace: Edward W Bok and The Ladies'*

Home Journal, (Baton Rouge and London: Louisiana State University Press, 1979).

12. See, for instance, S. Strasser, *Satisfaction Guaranteed: the Making of the Mass Market*, (New York: Pantheon Books, 1989), and R. Marchand, *Advertising the American Dream: Making Way for Modernity 1920–1940*, (Berkeley: University of California Press, 1986).

13. M. Beetham, *A Magazine of Her Own? Domesticity and Desire in the Woman's Magazine 1800–1914*, (London: Routledge, 1996); J. Scanlon, *Inarticulate Longings: The Ladies' Home Journal, Gender, and the Promises of Consumer Culture*, (New York: Routledge, 1995); and H. Damon Moore, *Magazines for the Millions: Gender and Commerce in the Ladies' Home Journal and the Saturday Evening Post, 1880–1910* (Albany: State University of New York Press, 1994).

14. See M. Beetham, *A Magazine of Her Own?* and J. Winship, *Advertising in Women's Magazines, 1956–74*, (Birmingham: Centre for Contemporary Cultural Studies, University of Birmingham, 1980).

15. R. Hoggart, *The Uses of Literacy* (Harmondsworth: Penguin, 1958).

16. R. Williams, *The Long Revolution* (Harmondsworth: Penguin, 1965).

17. D. Hebdige, *Hiding in the Light: On Images and Things*, (London: Comedia, 1988); A. McRobbie, *Feminism and Youth Culture: From Jackie to Just Seventeen*, (Basingstoke: Macmillan, 1991).

18. W. Schirmacher (ed.), German *20th Century Philosophy: The Frankfurt School* (New York: Continuum, 2000).

19. C.L. White, *Women's Magazines 1693–1968* (London: Michael Joseph, 1970).

20. J. Scanlon, *Inarticulate Longings* and Ros Ballaster et al., *Women's Worlds: Ideology, Femininity and the Woman's Magazine* (London: Macmillan, 1991).

21. E. G. Garvey, *The Adman in the Parlor: Magazines and the Gendering of Consumer Culture, 1880s to 1910s* (Oxford: Oxford University Press, 1996).

22. E. M. Thomson, *The Origins of Graphic Design History* (New Haven and London: Yale University Press, 1997).

23. M. H. Bogart, *Artists, Advertising and the Borders of Art* (Chicago: University of Chicago Press, 1995).

24. M. Scotford, *Cipe Pineles: A Life of Design* (New York and London: W. W. Norton, 1999).

25. R. Barthes, *Mythologies,* edited and translated by A. Lavers (London: Vintage, 1993), and *Image, Music, Text,* edited and translated by S. Heath (London: Fontana, 1977).

26. See, for example, J. Williamson, *Decoding Advertisements*, (London: Marion Boyars, 1978); Sean Nixon, *Hard Looks: Masculinities, Spectatorship and Contemporary Consumption* (London: UCL Press, 1996), and P. Jobling, *Fashion Spreads: Word and Image in Fashion Photography since 1980* (Oxford: Berg, 1999).

27. J. Fiske, *An Introduction to Communication Studies* (London: Methuen, 1982).

28. E.H. Carr, *What is History?* (Harmondsworth: Penguin, 1987). For the specific implications for design history, see J.A. Walker, *Design History and the History of Design*, (London: Pluto Press, 1989), pp. 78–81.

29. P. Thompson, *Voice of the Past: Oral History* (Oxford: Oxford University Press, 1978).

GUIDE TO FURTHER READING

In addition to the work by Benjamin extracted here, landmark work on mediation, relevant to design history, includes that of Canadian media analyst Marshall McLuhan, French literary theorist Roland Barthes and British cultural studies practitioner Stuart Hall. McLuhan's work has achieved mass popularity while also informing professional media practitioners and exerting an inescapable influence upon media studies as an academic subject. See *The Mechanical Bride* (1951), a series of analyses of newspaper and magazine articles and advertisements, and *The Gutenberg Galaxy: the Making of Typographic Man* (1962), *Understanding Media* (1964) and *The Medium is the Massage* (1967), in which McLuhan suggests that the medium through which content is delivered is more important than the content itself and has an impact on learning and thinking and, ultimately, social organization. Just as McLuhan distinguished between 'hot' and 'cool' media which invite differing degrees of audience participation, so Barthes proposed that cultural texts encourage readers to respond in 'readerly' or 'writerly' ways, as a receiver or a writer of meaning respectively. Roland Barthes's essays demonstrate his shift from structuralism to poststructuralism, and have been enormously influential tools for understanding meaning within popular culture. 'The Death of the Author' (1968) and 'From Work to Text' (1971) clarify an idea, drawn from Saussurian linguistics, that cultural artefacts can accrue meaning independently from those meanings intended by their producers. Stuart Hall's 'Encoding/Decoding' (1973, 1980) similarly explicates the operation of meanings in mass culture (in this case, specifically, television).

There is a wealth of writing on advertising, so selecting a case study is a useful way of narrowing down the literature. An often-cited example is that of Tibor Kalman's work for Benetton. See Pasi Falk, 'The Bennetton-Toscani Effect: Testing the Limits of Conventional Advertising' (1997); Serra A. Tinic, 'United Colors and Untied Meanings: Benetton and the Commodification of Social Issues' (1997) and Marwan M. Kraidy and Tamara Goeddertz, 'Transnational Advertising and International Relations: US Press Discourses on the Benetton "We on Death Row" Campaign' *Media, Culture & Society* (2003).

The literature on magazines is extensive. In addition to the essays in Jeremy Aynsley and Kate Forde's *Design and the Modern Magazine*, the following are of specific design historical interest: Ellen Mazur Thomson, 'Early Graphic Design Periodicals in America' (1994); Jill Seddon, 'The Architect and the "Arch-Pedant": Sadie Speight, Nikolaus Pevsner and "Design Review"' (2007); Barbara Usherwood, 'Transnational Publishing: the Case of *Elle Decoration*' (1997); Jeremy Aynsley's '"Gebrauchsgraphik" as an Early Graphic Design Journal, 1924–1938' (1992) and 'Graphic Change Design Change: Magazines for the Domestic Interior, 1890–1930' (2005); and Jennifer Scanlon's *Inarticulate Longings: The Ladies' Home Journal, Gender, and the Promises of Consumer Culture* (1995).

On fashion magazines, particularly, see Susan Sellers, '"How Long Has This Been Going On?"', *Harpers Bazaar*, Funny Face and the Construction of the Modernist Woman' (1995) and Christopher Breward's 'Femininity and Consumption: The Problem of the Late Nineteenth-century Fashion

Journal' (1994). Also on fashion writing, see Eugenia Paulicelli in 'Fashion Writing under the Fascist Regime: An Italian Dictionary and Commentary of Fashion by Cesare Meano, and Short Stories by Gianna Manzini, and Alba De Cespedes' (2004) and Barthes, *The Fashion System* (1967).

Further analysis of the use and significance of advice books for design history is gathered in Lees-Maffei (ed.) 'Domestic Design Advice' (2003), from which Emma Ferry's article is extracted here. For a useful consideration of oral history and design history, see Linda Sandino's 'Oral Histories and Design: Objects and Subjects' (2006) and the articles in the special issue to which this forms an introduction. Other studies of mediation include Otakar Máčel's study of legal records 'Avant-Garde Design and the Law: Litigation over the Cantilever Chair' (1990); Deborah Ryan's '"All the World and Her Husband": The *Daily Mail* Ideal Home Exhibition, 1908–1939' (2000); and Michelle Jones's 'Design and the Domestic Persuader: Television and the British Broadcasting Corporations Promotion of Post-war "Good Design"' (2003).

SECTION 12

Local/Regional/National/Global

INTRODUCTION

Grace Lees-Maffei

This section takes its title from a 1994 article by Anna Calvera, a design historian working in Spain. It is used here to denote some of the contexts within which design might be understood. The places in which designs, materials, images, objects, services and other behaviours are produced condition their characteristics to some extent. This is as true of designs intended to transcend local, regional or national contexts to pursue an international agenda, as it is of vernacular design, which is defined in part by the use of local materials, practices, markets and networks (see section 1 of this *Reader*).

Design historians have produced a number of national histories of design that raise questions about the extent to which design can embody national tendencies and how typical the nation under analysis might be. The extract here from David Crowley's examination of Polish design shows something of the complexity of nationalism in design, as a group of amateurs and architects attempted to reconcile a local vernacular folk tradition with the need to find a national style, a tendency echoed in other countries at the time. In Poland, however, the effort to hone a design identity was informed by the country's history in relation to imperialist Central and Eastern Europe, and after the First World War, to capitalist Western Europe and the communist Soviet Union.

Because design history has concerned itself with a definition of design based on its separation from industrial manufacture, national design histories produced to date have reflected a bias towards Western industrialized nations. This tendency has been the subject of some critique, influenced by post-colonialist theorists such as Edward Said – whose 1978 book *Orientalism* deconstructed the Eurocentric pattern of intellectual and cultural history – and Homi Bhabha, who has employed the term 'hybridity' as an alternative to binaristic thinking about centre and margin, based around a more fluid understanding of identity and a refusal of metanarratives. Consequently, design history – like its neighbouring disciplines – has recently begun to recognize the importance of globalization as a useful focus for understanding design past and present. In the last decade, design history has benefited from the development of a number of international, cross-cultural, design history and design studies groups, conferences and symposia, facilitated through online networking tools and electronic mailing lists, which have helped to overcome geographical boundaries and spark fruitful collaborative studies.

The urgency of current efforts to globalize design history may give the erroneous impression that design itself has only recently become global. In fact, historic trade routes have ensured that designed goods have been physically transported around the globe, carrying with them international influences and enabling design dialogues between nations and cultures for centuries. For example, the silk routes used to import goods between China, North Africa and Mediterranean Europe developed from pre-historic trade and transport patterns. As well as silk and spices, blue and white porcelain was traded along the silk routes, and its history reveals the complexity of international influence trade routes engendered. Following Islamic precedents, cobalt was used in China, from the thirteenth century, to decorate white porcelain. Adorned with appropriate imagery, it was exported back to the Middle East, before becoming popular in China in the fifteenth century. Following the setting up of the British East India Company in 1600 (and the Dutch equivalent in 1602, among others), blue and white china was exported to Europe (sometimes as ballast), again using designs chosen for the export market. Persian-influenced Chinese designs became the models for European-made porcelain in manufacturing centres including Delft in the Netherlands. Delftware itself became the influence for 'English Delftware', made in England and derivative of Dutch designs. The most startling example of historic trade routes is, of course, the triangular transatlantic slave trade, which developed from the sixteenth to the nineteenth centuries. Goods shipped from Europe to Africa were bartered for slaves, who were taken to the Americas for sale, before the ships returned to Europe loaded with commodities such as sugar and tobacco and the cycle started again.

In 'Furniture Design and Colonialism: Negotiating Relationships between Britain and Australia, 1880–1901', Tracey Avery provides a finely argued account of the distinctions discernible between furniture produced in Britain for a British and colonial market and furniture produced in Australia. Such distinctions may not reside in the appearance of designed goods – Australian furniture resembled that of its British colonizer – but rather in the context of surrounding discourse through which the goods were understood.

Gennifer Weisenfeld demonstrates how Japanese designers negotiated and modified Western models of modern design. When Kaō soap was transformed from luxury product to everyday item, modernist design strategies were employed, with mixed results. While the new Kaō identity is now recognized for its importance in the history of Japanese design, it did not realize its aim of expanding the market for Kaō soap. Weisenfeld's text reverses familiar stories of Orientalism: here, the visual techniques of the modernist West are fetishized for consumption in the East.

From the international style of the 1920s and 1930s, to the iconic architecture bristling across our 'global' cities in the twenty-first century, the extent to which design can transcend local cultures and communicate globally is debatable. Many branded goods are used across the world, from László Bíró's ballpoint pens to Matthew Carter's 'Verdana' typeface, Robin Day's 'Polyprop' chair to Boeing's aircraft. But just as global brands have found success with consumers internationally, so their ubiquity has engendered a desire for products with local, regional and national associations. In 'Land Rover and Colonial-style Adventure' Jeanne van Eeden critiques an unsuccessful attempt to engage local characteristics, in a racist and sexist stereotypical representation of a colonized subject aimed, purportedly, at a knowing, politically correct audience. Van Eeden draws attention to the way in which one image can embody and propagate iniquities both past and present. The fact that the advertisement van Eeden analyses was withdrawn, and her article was published without an illustration, due to permission being denied, makes it all the more important that such material is subjected to critique.

In a global marketplace, local products and services are made available to an international audience, which alters their character and meaning. 'Swoosh Identity: Recontextualizations in Haiti and Romania' reveals how a global brand can be reinterpreted through a sociological process described by Fernando Ortiz as 'transculturation', in which an object or image acquires new resonance as a result of merging contexts. Paul B. Bick and Sorina Chiper offer a comparative analysis of cultural colonialism which goes beyond the meanings generated by the advertising and marketing campaigns of this global and controversial brand. Comparative methods are generally underused and yet they have the potential to overcome the blunt confines of national borders.

Design is not only determined by the conditions within which it is produced: design works to constitute those conditions, and it can be a tool through which to critique and alter them. The same is true of design history: critiques of the existing output of design history as having been dominated by the Europe/US nexus of industrialization remain pertinent and pressing. While the texts selected here range from Japan to Poland, Australia to South Africa and Romania to Haiti, they are not intended to provide an abbreviated global history, Rather the section showcases examples of design historical analyses that interrogate and overcome the tendency within design history to dwell upon the industrialized West, thereby contributing to both the content and methods of design history. And, as the texts in this section show, globalizing design history is important both as a way of filling in the gaps in existing histories that have ignored or excluded non-Western experience and as a way of more fully reflecting design activity, past and present. While the amount and variety of work in the existing literature that is attentive to processes of globalization is heartening, the globalization of design history remains a priority for all interested in the present and future validity of the discipline.

63

FINDING POLAND IN THE MARGINS: THE CASE OF THE ZAKOPANE STYLE

David Crowley (2001)

INTRODUCTION

The emergence and development of the Zakopane Style in Polish culture in the 1890s is a familiar story.[1] The same plot is found in different settings across Europe in the late nineteenth century. In essence, the tale hangs on the 'discovery' of vernacular culture by urban, often academically trained artists, composers and writers. Aspects of peasant life such as homes, dress and styles of ornament came to be regarded as free from the straitjacket of academicism and historicism. In the hands of its proponents, peasant culture was refined for middle-class, artistically minded consumption.[2] This pattern occurs in the history of many, if not most, Northern and Central European peoples at around the same time, though often for different reasons. It has been connected to international currents such as the fascination with what later came to be called 'Primitivism', which rippled across the continent from the 1890s, and with the rise of the discipline of anthropology.[3] But, as I will argue, consideration also needs to be made of 'local' political circumstances and, in particular, the rise of forms of 'ethnic nationalism' in the period. Anthony Smith, in his interpretation of the phenomenon, has stressed that ethnic nationalism took as its aim the formation of an ethnically defined nation capable of secession from a larger political unit such as empire.[4] [...]

As most writers reflecting on nationalism in Europe in the late nineteenth century have

observed, peoples pressing for independence from imperial rule usually based their claims to a particular 'homeland' by arguing that ancient ancestors, from whom they claimed lineage, had once inhabited this territory. As Smith has observed in his discussion of 'ethno-history', special 'poetic spaces' were often positioned at the heart of such national claims.[5] [...] The isolation of such regions, it was claimed, had preserved ancient cultural forms and ways of living from the threat of change.

It is perhaps not surprising that similar distinctions in the characterization of place have been internalized in the intellectual traditions of anthropology, a discipline that developed in Europe under the influence of nationalist thinking.[6] As Arjun Appadurai has stressed, by holding on to an internalized notion of territory, anthropology has tended to fix its subjects – typically isolated and settled native peoples – outside urban centres. Anthropology has sought out places where culture appeared to be closely adapted to a particular environment.[7] However, migration and the movement of people between city and country as well as the sometimes arbitrary nature of political boundaries complicate the neat localization of cultures. Appadurai's writings have been part of an important critique within anthropology over the last two decades that has challenged the discipline's historic blindness to the interrelations and exchanges within and between cultures.[8] New thinking has come to understand 'the field' not primarily in terms of place or territory but in terms of human relations. Thus, in the early 1990s Appadurai made the case for considering the world as 'deterritorialized ethnoscapes' whose 'culturally constructed places of identification do not often coincide with their actual physical locations'. Taking this critique as a cue, in this article I will explore the relations and processes that led to the discovery of Zakopane and the invention and dissemination of the Zakopane Style beyond the narrow limits of the Tatra region where it originated in the 1870s and 1880s. My aim is to explore the close relations and interactions between intellectual circles in Warsaw, a major metropolis in the Russian Empire, and Zakopane, a small and distant town in Austria-Hungary.

WARSAW

The Zakopane Style was, in part, the late product of a new kind of 'politics of the local' that emerged in Poland as the martyrological, romantic tradition of Polish nationalism waned from the 1860s.[9] This new political *weltanschauung* was formed by Positivism, a political philosophy designed, in this context, to maintain Polish economic and cultural life in the face of campaigns of assimilation and political repression by the powers that had partitioned Poland in the late eighteenth century. Drawing their name from Auguste Compte's Positive Philosophy and inspiration from Herbert Spencer and John Stuart Mill's utilitarian thought and Charles Darwin's theory of evolution, the Positivists argued the case for progress shaped by principles of reason, science and economic realism. They argued that revolutionary, romantic dreams of Polish patriots, which had led to doomed uprisings against Russian rule in 1831 and 1863, should be abandoned in favour of the practical construction of the economy and culture. The Poles had to develop the nation patiently, in order to press a claim on independence in a Europe undergoing dramatic economic and material change. [...]

The Warsaw Positivists included some of the most influential figures in Polish culture during the last third of the century, such as Bolesław Prus, a journalist and novelist.[10] [...] These Warsaw intellectuals held, at heart, a new vision of Polish society. National activism was now to be conducted on behalf of and by the entire mass of peoples living in the ancient lands of the former kingdom of Poland. And to 'know thy nation' became axiomatic for the patriotic Pole. Consequently, Positivism gave added impetus to the collection of folk culture and the work of ethnographers in the late nineteenth century. In the same spirit, the peasantry were to be educated to bolster their Polishness in order to be able to recognize the 'threat' of Russification and Germanization.[11]

WARSAW AND ZAKOPANE

Zakopane, in its growth and in the efforts of Polish nationalists there, offers an excellent example of Positivist enthusiasms at work on a local scale. From the 1870s until the end of the century, a steady stream of intellectuals travelled south from Warsaw to Austrian Poland, and in particular to Zakopane, to practise their Positivist creed. [...] Zakopane was the regional centre of Podhale, the northern foothills of the Tatra mountains. Populated by the Górale (highlanders), it was a very poor area of what was already one of the poorest crown lands under Austrian rule. The Górale subsisted as peasant-farmers and shepherds. The town of Zakopane mid-century was the centre of an impoverished community of peasants as well as a small imperial bureaucracy and a small business class. In 1873 [surgeon] Tytus Chałubiński, a key figure, visited Zakopane from Warsaw. He came, in the spirit of philanthropy and the regeneration of Polish society, to combat a cholera epidemic in the region.[12] This experience was a trigger for Chałubiński with other intellectuals such as the poet, Adam Asnyk, and local businessmen to found the Towarzystwo

Tartrzańskie (Tatra Society) in the same year. This self-financing organization promoted trade and industry from the region as well as the improvement of social conditions; it sought to encourage the modernization of apiculture; it lit and paved the streets of Zakopane; it established the town's telegraphic communications; and the Society's building functioned as a cultural centre for the town. In 1876 it established a Szkoła snycerska (School of Carpentry) to train local boys in this handicraft. […]

Beyond this Positivist investment in education and industry, the actions of the Tatra Society had the effect of according value to an aspect of Polish culture which had been 'invisible' throughout the century, that of a Polish peasantry, the Górale. […] For until the actions of figures such as Chałubiński, nationalist attention had been centred on the heroic, martyrological

traditions of the chivalrous Polish gentry. Political discourse in the eighteenth century had not even regarded the peasantry as 'Polish', reserving this appellation for the szlachta (gentry) and the aristocracy. The peasantry had not been considered as part of the body politic, let alone worth educating. A new definition of Polishness was emerging here, which not only saw the peasantry as holding economic potential but as a 'reservoir' of national culture.

[…] In a number of Prus's weekly columns, for example, we can find calls for architects to 'withdraw from history', i.e. from historicism and eclecticism, to find a 'national style' in 'our poor countryside', in the vernacular objects and homes of the peasantry.[13] Some kind of realizations of Prus's ambitions came in the same years when his friend, a painter and writer, Stanisław Witkiewicz, took an interest in Zakopane. In

Figure 45. 'Stanislaw Witkiewicz, with a model of the "House Under the Firs", 1896. He is on the left of this group of Górale craftsmen. Illustration from Stanislaw Eljasz Radzikowski, *Styl Zakopiański*, Kraków, 1901.' In David Crowley, 'Finding Poland in the Margins: The Case of the Zakopane Style', *Journal of Design History* 14(2) (2001), pp. 105–16, p. 110.

1886 Witkiewicz came to Zakopane as one of Chałubiński's tourists. He was much taken with the region, finding a community of like-minded intellectuals including [Władysław] Matlakowski, as well as a climate sympathetic to his tubercular condition. Most importantly, he developed a fascination with Górale buildings and their vernacular arts. He seemed to have uncovered in the Tatras a living illustration of Warsaw thinking. He was so taken with the region that in 1890 he moved, with his family, into a wooden home there.

Gathering around him a group of architects and artists, literary propagandists and Górale craftsmen, Witkiewicz set about recasting the raw materials that he found in the region into an intellectually complex decorative and architectural language in a series of villas built in the 1890s. [...] Zakopane Style homes displayed the clear influence of the local in both decoration and construction. They can, however, also be characterized by their departure from local building traditions. Whilst, for example, Witkiewicz and his colleagues made use of local types of log construction, they laid these walls on heavy rough stonework foundations. Such deviations from tradition were matters of both class and cost. Some of the largest Zakopane Style villas, such as the House Under the Firs built in 1896 for an economist and collector of folk art, Jan Gwalbert Pawlikowski, had studiously informal plans derived from essentially traditional patterns of spatial organization. The interiors used the same decorative language as that found on the exterior. And in the spirit of the *gesamtkunstwerk*, Witkiewicz and his colleagues (including his wife, Maria Pietrzkiewiczówna) designed and arranged for the manufacture of all the furnishings. By the end of the first decade of the new century, a significant number of distinctly Zakopane Style villas had been built in the vicinity of the town by seven architects, as well as a chapel (Kaplica Najświętszego Serca Pana Jezusa, 1908), hotels ('Stamary', 1905 and 'Warszawianka', 1910) and a sanatorium ('Rialto', 1897–8).

This promotion of the region transformed the economic life of the town.[14] Of equal importance was the growth of a new artistically inclined Zakopane as a kind of colony of intellectuals, a significant point of rendezvous for artists, writers and others from all three partitions (but frequently from Warsaw). The town began to take on an extraordinary national role as the Polish 'cultural capital'. In this Witkiewicz should be credited with playing an important role as a skilled propagandist for his 'new' style of design and for the Tatra region. He invested much energy in literary works and exhibitions promoting the Zakopane Style.[15] The style formed the mainstay of a broader intellectual fascination with the Tatras and the Górale. [...] Anna Sieradzka has recorded, for example, that in 1902 Bogusław Herse's shop on Senatorska Street, the most fashionable in Warsaw, announced a new collection of Górale style clothes for fashionable ladies: white blouses with lacework, short, stiff woollen waistcoats decorated with fine embroidery in richly coloured patterns and full skirts.[16] In the mid-1890s there were a number of exhibitions which displayed the Zakopane Style in Warsaw. One, held at the Muzeum Przemysłu i Rolnictwa (Museum of Industry and Agriculture), furnished Prus, as a reviewer writing in *Kurjer Codzienny*, with the opportunity to applaud work which, in part, seemed to be a vivid application of his ideas of a decade earlier.[17]

[...] Although [Warsaw] had taken on the role of the nation's capital at the end of the sixteenth century, its significance around 1900 lay in its commercial and industrial activities within the Romanov Empire, and, from the perspective of Polish nationalists, as the centre of the militant tradition that had led to uprisings in the 1830s and 1860s. Consequently, in order to control Polish terrorism Warsaw was under martial law for much of the period. It was also at the centre of the official policy of Russification. Schoolchildren, for instance, were forbidden from speaking in Polish and, somewhat surreally, in the 1880s Polish books were studied as part of the foreign language curriculum. By contrast, the Tatras offered a location where Warsaw theses could be tested in the relatively liberal conditions of Austrian rule, away from the harsh, paranoid political climate of Russian Poland. [… Warsaw] was overcrowded, enduring the twin pressures of modernity and political repression, whereas Zakopane seemed to offer a vision of an ideal world. […]

ZAKOPANE AND POLAND

[…] Advocates of the Zakopane Style […] sought to establish it as a national language of design. Witkiewicz's vigorous promotion of the Zakopane vernacular was based on a potent conceit: that the style that had been discovered in this isolated region had, in times before the partitions and before the coming of industry, been found throughout the ancient Polish lands along the Vistula. The style of wooden buildings and the applied art of the region were like a living fossil which bore the imprint of Polish culture. The march of modernity had overlooked this mountainous region, leaving peasant building and design in historical stasis. In this vein, a supporter of the style wrote in *Ateneum*, a Warsaw magazine, in 1903.

> The Górale are not at all the creators of Zakopane's style, their contribution lies in its thoughtful conservation over a long time. This style, known today as being from Zakopane, once spread widely across the whole of a Poland which Kazimierz the Great saw wooded.[18]

This conceit proved to be persuasive and was widely repeated, often in the popular press. An article in *Tygodnik Ilustrowany*, a Warsaw magazine, offers an excellent example of the way in which the national claims of the Zakopane Style were advanced.[19]

In a short article entitled 'Foundations of the Zakopane Style', its author, Julian Maszyński, took the reader on a tour through the Polish lands to an ancient sacristy in a Lublin church.

Lublin, at that time, was a poor city under Tsarist rule and was, in most respects, unlike the mountainous, peasant Podhale region. In a dusty, antediluvian room the writer discovered a seventeenth-century table, carved and painted with floral motifs and simply made. His discovery, so it seemed, was strikingly similar to the Zakopane vernacular, thereby allowing him to echo Witkiewicz. He announced:

> On the basis of the stylistic similarity between Zakopane furniture and that of this ancient age, the seventeenth century, I offer up an hypothesis, that in this age this style was found throughout the country and its relics are now preserved in those places which escaped the pursuit of novelty …[20]

[…] As the Lublin table dates from the seventeenth century, an age when Poland was not only whole but enjoyed a 'Golden Age', it reminds the reader of the nation's sovereign past. This trace of history is reinforced by the table's location in Lublin, for this article not only linked two regions divided by two empires but Lublin itself had a symbolic valency in that it lay in the central core of historic Poland. This identification of Polishness is reinforced by Maszyński's discovery in a Catholic church. Furthermore, the simplicity and purposefulness of both kinds of furniture is claimed as a Polish virtue, just as 'Organic Work' had earlier posited a new Polish pragmatism against foreign decadence and immorality. […]

The attempt to 'nationalize' the local is a paradoxical theme in the history of the Zakopane Style. […] The Górale were reified, made, in this instance, to stand for a deep vein of hitherto unknown Polish history. Yet, at the same time, they were regarded as outside history, enjoying a life untroubled by the vicissitudes of the present (vicissitudes that were all too apparent in Warsaw under the Romanovs). Furthermore, 'natural' Górale ways of life were made to stand in testimony to the notion of a pure Polishness.

Yet these ways required protection from the encroachments of modernity by the intelligentsia. In effect, the thinking of Witkiewicz and his colleagues was underscored by highly idealistic and, above all, romantic views. The paradox of the romantic 'nationalization' of Zakopane was evident to some of the Style's critics. [...]

Polish culture had to be produced for the Poles despite the nation's incorporation into the territories of its neighbours. This required making use of the media of the day, including photomechanical printing technologies and international exhibitions, to create a common culture. By such means local cultures could be rendered national. Whilst the material culture of the Zakopane region was interpreted as archaic, it was made both modern and national by its reproduction.

NOTES

Extracted from Crowley, D., 'Finding Poland in the Margins: The Case of the Zakopane Style', *The Journal of Design History* 14(2) (2001), pp. 105–16. Reproduced by permission of The Design History Society.

1. Discussion of the emergence of the Zakopane Style and its history can he found in many sources. See Jan Majda, *Góralszczyzna w twórczości Stanisława Witkiewicza*, PAN, Wroclaw, 1979; Stanisław Eljasz Radzikowski, *Styl Zakopiański*, Tow. Wydawnictwo we Lwowie, Kraków, 1901; Halina Kenerówna, *Od Zakopiańskiej szkoły przemysłu drzewnego do szkoły kenera*, Wydawnictwo Literackie. Kraków, 1978: T. Jabłońska & Z. Moździerz, *'Koliba', pierwszy dom w stylu zakopiańskim*, Zakopane, 1994; *'Stanisław Witkiewicz'*. exhibition catalogue. Muzeum Tatrzańskie, Zakopane, 1996 and 'Między Giewontem I Parnasem', exhibition catalogue, Muzeum Narodowe, Kraków. 1997.

2. The best general discussion of the vernacular revival in various national contexts is in Nicola Gordon Bowe (ed.), *Art and the National Dream: the Search for Vernacular Expression in Turn of the Century Design*. Irish Academic Press, Dublin, 1993. See also my 'The uses of peasant design in Austria-Hungary in the late nineteenth and early twentieth centuries' in *Studies in the Decorative Arts*, vol. II, no. 2. Spring 1995; Wendy Salmond, *The Arts and Crafts in Late Imperial Russia*, Cambridge University Press, Cambridge, 1996; Barbara Miller Lane, *National Romanticism and Modern Architecture in Germany and the Scandinavian Countries*, Cambridge University Press, Cambridge, 2000 and various authors in David Crowley & Lou Taylor, eds., *The Lost Arts of Europe*, Haslemere Educational Museum, Haslemere, 2000.

3. It is notable that Zakopane was the childhood home of Bronisław Malinowski and his youth was spent in the company of the family of Stanisław Witkiewicz, the greatest champion of the vernacular culture of the region. See *Kontektsy*, vol. LIV, no. 1–4, 2000. For more general sources, see Adam Kuper, *The Invention of Primitive Society: Transformation of an Illusion*, Routledge, London, 1988; Elizar Barkan & Ronald Bush (eds), *Prehistories of the Future: The Primitivist Project and the Culture of Modernism*, Stanford University Press, Stanford, 1995.

4. Anthony Smith, *National Identity*, Penguin, Harmondsworth, 1991, p. 82.

5. Smith, op. cit., p. 65.

6. See George W. Stocking, *Victorian Anthropology*, Free Press, New York, 1987.

7. Arjun Appadurai, 'Putting hierarchy in its place', *Cultural Anthropology*, vol. 3, 1988, pp. 36–50.

8. Arjun Appadurai, 'Global ethnoscapes: notes and queries for a transnational anthropology' in *Modernity at Large, Cultural Dimensions of Globalization,* University of Minnesota Press, Minneapolis, 1996, Ch. 2, pp. 48–65.

9. On the romantic conceptions in Polish historiography, see Andrzej Walicki, *Philosophy and Romantic Nationalism*, Oxford University Press, Oxford, 1982, and Jerzy Jedlicki, *A*

Suburb of Europe: Nineteenth-century Polish Approaches to Western Civilization, Central European University Press, Budapest, 1999.

10. Prus's novel *Lalka* (The Doll), Twayne, New York, 1972, is his best-known literary achievement and has been translated into English by David Welsh.

11. Russification and Germanization were the express policies of the German and Russian authorities in most cultural matters such as education. On the *Kulturkampf*, see Lech Trzeciakowski, *The Kulturkampf in Prussian Poland*, Eastern European Monographs, Boulder, CO, 1990; on Russian cultural policies, see Theodore R. Weeks, *Nation and State in Late Imperial Russia: Nationalism and Russification on the Western Frontier, 1863–1914*, Northern Illinois University Press, 1996.

12. See Ryszard Wrzosek, *Tytus Chałubiński*, Warsaw, 1970.

13. See B. Prus, 'July 1883', in *Kroniki*, VI, Panstwowe Instytut Wydawnictwo, Lwów, 1957, pp. 327–8. Prus's call was not unique: Cyprian Norwid, a Polish poet living in exile, called in the early 1850s for artists and writers to find beauty and purpose in the everyday culture of the peasantry. See my *National Style and Nation-state*, Manchester University Press, Manchester, 1992, pp. 29–30.

14. By the end of the century the adult population of the town had increased two and half times to nearly 4,500 (since 1848) and enjoyed an annual influx of tourists twice the size of the resident population. See Bronisław Chlebowski (ed.), *Slownik geograficzny krolewska polskiego*, XIV, Warsaw, 1895,

pp. 300–10; for details of the growth of tourism in the town and region, see Witold H. Paryski, 'Powstanie Zakopańskiego Ośrodka Turystycznego (do 1914 r.)', in Renata Dutkowa (ed.), *Zakopane czterysta lat dziejów*, KAW, Kraków, 1991, pp. 7–21.

15. See Stanisław Witkiewicz, 'Styl zakopiański', in *Pisma tatrzańskie*, II, Kraków, 1963.

16. Earlier Zakopane Style fashionable dress designed by Witkiewicz and a friend, Feliks Jasieński, a collector of 'Zakopanszczyzna', had been warmly applauded in the journal *Rozwój* (Progress): 'It would be a beautiful thing if Polish women would break from under the authority of Viennese and Parisian designs and welcome dress which would mark, from their appearance, national difference.' See J. Warchałowski in *Rozwój, c.1900*, unpaginated (in a book of press cuttings of Warchałowski's own journalism, Main Library of the Kraków School of Art).

17. Bolesław Prus, 'Kroniki tygodniowe', from Kurier Codzienny (24 May 1894), reproduced in Bolesław Prus, *Kroniki*, vol. XL, no. 143, Warsaw, 1964, pp. 254–8.

18. M. Brensztein, 'Styl Polski (W obronie zakopiańszczyzny jako stylu "polskiego")', *Ateneum*, 1903, no. 4, pp. 102–3. It is interesting to note that this scholarly magazine (est. 1876) was a long-standing positivist mouthpiece, edited in the 1880s and 1890s by Piotr Chmielowski, an alumnus of the Szkoła Główna.

19. Julian Maszyński, 'Zródło stylu Zakopiańskiego', *Tygodnik Ilustrowany*, no. 8, 1901, p. 145.

20. Ibid

64

FURNITURE DESIGN AND COLONIALISM: NEGOTIATING RELATIONSHIPS BETWEEN BRITAIN AND AUSTRALIA, 1880–1901

Tracey Avery (2007)

METHODOLOGIES FOR EXAMINING CROSS-CULTURAL MATERIAL CULTURE

Research on the exchange of goods between countries and cultures has focused on transfers between very different cultures; often in an imperial context between European colonizers and colonized indigenous people.[1] In Linda Young's study of the markers of gentility among the Greater British middle classes at home and abroad, the presence of mid-Victorian period furnishings indicated that things exchanged between ostensibly similar cultures such as a 'Western middle class' are assumed to be interpreted in similar ways by their geographically scattered users.[2] These groups are united by their aspiration to demonstrate a shared set of civilized behaviors, which included home furnishings and etiquette. [… Yet in Australia] style, material, construction, and patterns of wear (due to climatic changes) were often subtly different to similar objects produced and used in the British market. In researching historic objects and furnished interiors, there is a greater need to consider more pragmatic issues in the production of objects and the transfer of taste. [...]

While the overall image of the nineteenth-century Australian interior is formally and ideologically British, one result of a visual interpretation is the implication that Britain's role in the domestic furnishing of its colonies is largely hegemonic. A Western history of art and architecture based on style and taste which is formed at a European centre continues to reinforce this view, whereby countries like Australia are regarded as existing on the geographic and aesthetic margins.[3] Yet the meanings of objects and cultural ideas of home are unlikely to survive migration unchanged or, at least, unchallenged by their new environment.

[...]

IMPORTING GREATER BRITISH DESIGN: CHALLENGING BRITISH CLASS AND LABOR

The term 'Greater Britain' was often used by British and Australian writers in the late nineteenth century to describe Australia's 'familial' relationship to Britain.[4] The description of this relationship has particular resonance for meanings of home, domesticity, and civilized society. [...] Retailers in Australia procured British furniture by establishing themselves as agents for various British firms that specialized in the 'wholesale and export' market. While an agency structure might suggest that Australian retailers chose their preferred stock from a catalog, comments in some manufacturing journals in the 1880s suggest that many goods were sent speculatively by British firms. The consignment system also caused some consternation when the goods were 'not wanted' in the colonial market.[5] In the furniture trade, for example, an 1894 interview with the East End furnishers Saul Moss & Co., in the *Furniture Gazette* noted:

> Australia's imports have almost dropped to zero, and the opinion was expressed that our Colonial furniture trade in that particular quarter has almost terminated. For many years past we have sent so much common-class and old-fashioned goods to Australia that the colonials have for some time been manufacturing on their own account ...[6]

Offering the colonies goods predefined as common-class, suggests that Britons assumed that this was the class of goods 'wanted' by Australians. Yet Britain's apparent reluctance to send more middle-class and better-class furniture also suggests an inability to imagine the social mobility of migrants when they became financially successful in Australia. This conflict in the minds of Britons was expressed in 1881 by a review of the stand of

THE CABINET MAKER, MAY 2, 1881.

FURNITURE AT THE MELBOURNE EXHIBITION.

By Messrs. W. H. ROCKE & CO., 36—42, Collins Street, East Melbourne and 85, Gracechurch Street, E.C.

Figure 46. 'Furniture at the Melbourne Exhibition by Messrs. W. H. Rocke & Co., *Cabinet Maker and Art Furnisher*, May 2 1881', in Tracey Avery, 'Furniture Design and Colonialism: Negotiating Relationships between Britain and Australia, 1880–1901,' *Home Cultures* 4(1) (2007), pp. 69–92.

the Melbourne furnishing firm Rocke & Co., at the Melbourne International Exhibition:

> It might naturally be imagined that in a 'young country' the reception rooms would receive lavish attention, but that 'anything would do for the bedroom.' We must confess to astonishment in inspecting the class of furniture 'turned out' by the Melbourne manufacturers … this [is a] new era of independence in colonial cabinet work.[7] [...]

In the early nineteenth century, many better-class pieces [of furniture] were inlaid with expensively hand-cut veneers. Later in the century, a combination of machine veneers and cost cutting through the proliferation of sweated labor in England meant that the quality appearance of veneered items in fact disguised faulty construction. Design historian Adrian Forty has drawn on Henry Mayhew's chronicling of London's furniture laborers in the mid-nineteenth century to show how the development of machine-cut veneers coincided with the cheap production of previously high-class goods.[8] Prior to the employment of circular saws powered by steam in the 1830s, thin veneers were only applied to relatively expensive, 'high-class cabinet work,' as they were cut by hand.[9] The new machine technology achieved thinner veneers at a faster rate; thin veneers could be applied to a cheap-deal carcass, putting the work of hand sawyers and traditional cabinet makers at a competitive disadvantage.[10] One destination for cheaply veneered furniture was Australia, and it was here that the appearance of gentility was let down by other factors concealed in its design and production.

IMPORTED BRITISH DESIGN VERSUS AUSTRALIAN LOCAL CONDITIONS

In the late 1880s and early 1890s, British and Australian literature on the furnishing trades warned British furniture manufacturers of their potential loss of market leadership. The *Cabinet Maker and Art Furnisher* published a detailed report on the particular needs of the Australian market, as the manufacturers were 'in need of a little reliable information as to the character of the home life in the Colonies, and the most suitable class of goods to send out to meet the demands and exigencies of that life.'[11] This was no list of visual likes and dislikes, but a comprehensive account of practical, economic, cultural, and political considerations that were affecting consumption choices of colonists from a range of classes and professions. The reported concerns included the fact that people moved frequently to follow work opportunities and sold their furniture at auction to avoid expensive removal costs. Furniture had to be robust in order to survive the initial sea transport and subsequent landing conditions, due to substantial changes in temperature and humidity. Poor packing and lifting veneers exposed the goods as poor quality in terms of performance: [...]

> The usual bread-and-butter goods so well known to Colonial importers – inlaid, veneered and only half-constructed – are not at all the kind of furniture to withstand rapid transitions of temperature changes. [...] As a rule, Colonial-made furniture is substantially constructed on simple lines, in solid wood (never veneered).[12]

In Britain veneered pieces were by then associated with Georgian revival styles and popular in middle-class circles. By saying that plainer styles in solid timbers were preferred for their performance, Australians were challenging some British ideas about the propriety of styles as understood in architectural terms. [... This] could be seen as a practical move rather than a predominantly stylistic preference.

In terms of class itself, there is a difficulty in equating British and Australian definitions of 'middle class' by ownership of property and goods. While, for example, newspapers such

Brisbane Courier did use the British language of class for property and furnishings, the class signifiers of house size and number of servants, had vastly different economic realities in the colonies of Australia. A greater demand for labor in Australia meant that houses cost more to build and servants cost more to keep.[13] Moreover, in 1889, the same piece of furniture in London cost two and a half times more in Australia.[14] Again, there is a trap in reading the class of an Australian owner against a British standard when examining the visual record of a furnished interior. For example, a room furnished with a certain standard of items in Australia, could, due to cost, appear to represent consumers of a lower income and social level than in Britain.

CRITICAL CONSUMPTION: CLASS, ECONOMICS, AND THE POLITICS OF LABOR

Magee and Thompson (2003) considered whether the economic relationship between Britain and its settler societies was based on the dominion markets being 'soft,' i.e., accepting of whatever Britain produced due to a form of imperial loyalty. Contrary to a show of loyalty, in the period 1881–1903 they found that Australians increasingly spent less of their incomes on imported British goods.[15] While their research methods focused on trends in trade figures alone, they did suggest that 'cultural' factors and local conditions might explain numerical trends, and drew on research into specific manufacturing industries to support their claims.[16] The furnishing industries were not referred to, but the present study examined some of the cultural reasons why local furniture gained greater recognition among local consumers.

Broadly speaking, Australians made suites of furniture that looked British in form and style. Yet, as the following account from a Brisbane furnishing firm suggests, local people were made aware of economic and labor issues carried by furniture at this time:

Everybody has read something of the frightful 'sweating' carried on in the East end of London … Some of the defenders of this terrible system try to make out that if the English manufacturers stopped it England would lose (sic) her trade. MESSRS. ALFRED SHAW & CO … find that English furniture is so wretchedly upholstered that no reliable firm would dare to send it away as it is received. Much of what they handle has to be unripped and restuffed, for order as they may, the English 'sweaters' use all sorts of rubbish instead of hair … England will have to brighten up her honesty if she wants to maintain her manufacturing supremacy… But this penny-wise and pound-foolish English system … encourages native industry better than a 20 per cent tariff. SHAW'S have rapidly expanded the room where at first they only pieced together the imported articles … into a goodly sized workshop wherein skilled artisans make furniture of every description from the original wood and by the aid of … machinery. Those who are Nationalist enough to desire Queensland-made suites can be well accommodated here. In fact the liking of everybody can be satisfied unless they like and must have goods which Chinamen have had something to do with … the head of the firm … will not keep a stick of Chinese furniture …[17]

Standardization of form and application of ornament meant that materials and designs could be easily replicated; yet the construction and 'finishing' of furniture could be used to entice or fool the consumer, particularly those in the colonies who ordered 'sight-unseen.' Shaw's go on to say that bentwood furniture is more suitable to local needs:

Of all furniture used in this semi-tropical climate the Austrian bentwood is naturally the most popular. Not only is it light, but being wholly screwed together without any glue being used in any part, it lasts until worn out and gives universal satisfaction …[18]

These two statements from Messrs Shaw & Co., suggest that the quality of workmanship and an intimate knowledge of the effects of the local climate are effectively presented as reasons to buy from them. Beyond appearance, performance is the feature that matters to consumers, and in fact, distinguishes the local from the imported productions.

To create a deeper niche for themselves in the colonial market, European Australian furniture makers attempted to marry the desire for a British design appearance with some display of colonial nationalism by using timbers 'native' to Australia.[19] Queensland, with diverse varieties of subtropical hardwoods and softwoods, was keen to demonstrate to Britain just what could be achieved with these natural resources.[20] Prior to more widespread concerns about competition with Chinese labor, local exhibitions in Queensland had been promoting the use of native timbers. At the annual Royal National Association Exhibition in Brisbane in 1879, it was reported that the section of furniture made from Queensland timber had thirty-three entries and demonstrated that, 'The principal objects of the exhibition are to encourage and foster local industries ... and these ends are not furthered by a large display of imported goods.'[21] Though, here too, was an instance of the dilemma between British design styles and the tenuous place of Australian timber in the hierarchy of domestic suitability. A suite of drawing-room furniture '... made on the premises, of Queensland oak ...' had been 'stained black and gold,' conforming to the Aesthetic fashion of the period but negating the visibility of the local material.[22]

CIVILIZED FURNITURE: CLASS DYNAMICS AND THE LABOR OF RACE

[C]ompetition with Chinese furniture makers had a largely economic basis. The colonies were said to pay better wages to workers than their equivalent in Britain, while the Chinese workers were paid much less.[23] Furniture made by Chinese firms could be sold at as much as a third less than that made by the colonial worker.[24]

But the great fact which operates in favour of the imported article is that it cannot possibly be of Chinese production. It may perhaps be the result of 80 hours' work per week in a London garret, and be an excellent specimen of what the sweating system can produce, but at all events it bears not the taint of the detested Chinese, and to this the majority of Colonial buyers is an all-sufficient recommendation.[25]

[...] For furniture manufacturers in Britain and Australia, the principal design issue concerned the deceptive nature of the copy: Chinese-made furniture reportedly, not '... differing in any way in appearance from the European work' could not be detected by the public.[26] The ways in which support or rejection of Chinese labor was handled in Queensland centered on varying ideas of nationhood and civilization. According to one parliamentarian arguing against anti-Chinese legislation, those in favor of the bill, '... seemed to be possessed of a terrible fear lest they should have undue competition in their labour markets by that alien race [...].'[27] The Minister for Justice again attempted to position the Chinese in opposition to the white man: '... it was a matter between two classes of civilization, the European and the Chinese, as to whether they could co-exist in the colonies ...'[28]

Colonial consumers of different classes were said to exercise different choices [...]:

There is, of course, a strong feeling amongst the better classes against buying Chinese furniture, this enabling legitimate firms to do away altogether with that class of work, many making capital out of the advertised fact that 'no Chinese goods are kept in stock.'[29]

[...] However, the poorer classes in Australia had been advised to purchase furniture by Chinese

Australians, precisely to give the correct appearance. A Melbourne publication for 'housekeepers on small incomes' gave details of two bedroom suites composed of the same set of items, but available at different total cost; the lower-priced suite differed specifically by the inclusion of Chinese-made items.[30] [...] It seems that the Chinese Australians continued to produce European-style furniture, as around 1900, the Australian makers of European origin stamped their goods 'European Labour Only'.

CONCLUSION

This case study has considered how a British visual design language for home furnishings was not received as intended by its colonial market. The links between style and class in furniture, and the transposition of their meaning *en route* to Australia, has provided an example of visually similar designed objects that became vehicles for vastly different meanings. [...] By detecting unsuitable labor – poor English workmanship or undesirable Chinese labor – Australian businesses presented 'nationalist' sympathies through a characteristic that cannot easily be seen in an object. Stoler has noted that redefining aspects of European cultural practice allowed colonial Europeans to 'maintain the social distinctions of imperial control.'[31] [...]

Current postcolonial inquiries and material culture studies explain an object's multiple meanings, e.g., the bunya pine bedroom suite can represent local distinctiveness and an international taste for bedroom suites in exotic timbers. However, the tensions attached to a re-stuffed sofa are hidden when that item is sent from British to its settler societies. [...] [W]hen appearances were roughly equal, competitors in this marketplace resorted to marketing concealed points of difference. Linda Young's argument for a Greater British middle-class gentility based on a common appearance among furnishings is not in doubt. More, this research suggests that the achievement of the appropriate furnished 'British'

domestic interior in Australia involved certain reassignments of meaning around style, labor, and materials. Consequently, colonial consumption in Australia was actively negotiated, and not passively accepted, by government, manufacturers, and homemakers. [...]

NOTES

Extracted from Avery, T., 'Furniture Design and Colonialism: Negotiating Relationships between Britain and Australia, 1880–1901', *Home Cultures* 4(1) (2007), pp. 69–92.

1. Barringer, Tim and Tom Flynn (eds), *Colonialism and the Object: Empire, Material Culture, and the Museum*, London and New York: Routledge, 1998; Howes, David, ed., *Cross-cultural Consumption: Global Markets, Local Realities.* London and New York: Routledge, 1996.
2. Young, Linda, *Middle-class Culture in the Nineteenth Century: America, Australia and Britain.* Basingstoke and New York: Palgrave Macmillan, 2003.
3. Fry, Tony, 'A Geography of Power: Design History and Marginality.' *Design Issues* 6(1) (1989): 15–30. For overviews on design history in Australia, see Fry, Tony, *Design History Australia: A Source Text in Methods and Resources.* Sydney: Hale & Iremonger and the Power Institute of Fine Arts, 1988; and McNeil, Peter, 'Rarely Looking in: The Writing of Australian Design History, c.1900–1990.' *Journal of Australian Studies* 44 (1995): 48–63.
4. The term comes from the book by Charles Wentworth Dilke, 1868, *Greater Britain: A Record of Travel in English-speaking Countries during 1866 and 1867.* London, Macmillan.
5. 'Trade in Australia.' *British Mercantile Gazette* February 16 1885: 20–1.
6. *Furniture and Decoration* vol. 5, no. 10, October 1894: 155–6. While the drop in trade could also be partly due to the Australian recession of 1892–3, the implication that wholesalers had

been sending inappropriate classes of goods seems valid.

7. 'Furniture at the Melbourne Exhibition. Messrs W.H. Rocke and Co.'s exhibits.' *Cabinet Maker & Art Furnisher*, April 1881: 176.

8. Mayhew, 'Fancy Cabinet Makers of London,' *Morning Chronicle*, August 8, 1850 in Forty, Adrian, *Objects of Desire: Design and Society since 1750*. London: Thames and Hudson, 1986, pp. 56–7; Mayhew, Henry, *London Labour and the London Poor*, 4 vols. London, 1860.

9. Forty, 1986, p. 56. Joy has evidence for their use in 1829, and notes the machine's invention in 1805. Also, Joy has more on the negative connotations of veneer, due to the initial use of cheap carcasses, in Dickens' *Our Mutual Friend* (1864–5) and *The Pickwick Papers* (1836–7): Joy, Edward T. 1977. *English Furniture 1800–1851*. London: Sotheby Parke Bernet Publications, pp. 227–228.

10. Forty, 1986, p. 56.

11. 'Our Trade in Australia,' *Cabinet Maker and Art Furnisher*, October 1889, p. 90.

12. 'Our Trade in Australia', 1889, p. 90.

13. Jordan, Kerry, 'Houses and Status: The Grand Houses of Nineteenth Century Victoria', Unpublished PhD thesis, University of Melbourne, 2003, pp. 35–6, p. 47.

14. 'Our Trade in Australia', 1889, p. 90.

15. Magee, Gary B. and Andrew S. Thompson, 'Complacent or Competitive? British Exporters and the Drift to Empire.' University of Melbourne, 2003. Department of Economics, Research Papers, no. 889. Melbourne: University of Melbourne. For a more extensive consideration of British imperial economic relationships, see Thompson, Andrew S., *The Empire Strikes Back? The Impact of Imperialism on Britain from the Mid-Nineteenth Century*. Harlow and New York: Pearson Longman, 2005.

16. Magee and Thompson, 2003, pp. 1–33. They draw on a diversity of research into British companies that showed how those companies approached the dominion markets; some modified their products and others made no concessions.

17. *Boomerang* August 18 1888: 15 (Advertisement).

18. Ibid.

19. In colonial Australia the term 'native' was used to describe natural products and those European Australians born in Australia, i.e., 'native-born.'

20. Frederick Manson Bailey, *Queensland Woods with a brief popular description of the trees, their distribution, qualities, uses of timber, &c, &c*. Brisbane, Warwick and Sapsford, 1888. This was a revised edition for the Melbourne Centennial Exhibition of 1888 and listed 538 woods. The earlier edition had been produced for the Colonial and Indian Exhibition of 1884 in London.

21. 'Furniture, etc.,' *Brisbane Courier*, May 31, 1879, p. 6.

22. Ibid.

23. Coghlan, T. A., *Statistical Register for 1901 and Previous Years*. Sydney: Government of the state of New South Wales, 1903, p. 1101.

24. 'Our Trade in Australia', 1889, p. 91.

25. Ibid. pp. 90–1.

26. Ibid., p. 91.

27. F. T. Brenthall, Queensland Legislative Council, 'Chinese Immigration Restriction Bill,' Official Record of the Debates of the Legislative Council, vol. LIV, 1888: 115.

28. Minister for Justice, Andrew Joseph Thynne, Queensland Legislative Council, 'Chinese Immigration Restriction Bill' *Official Record of the Debates of the Legislative Council*, vol. LIV, 1888: 116.

29. 'Our Trade in Australia', 1889, p. 91.

30. Old Housekeeper, *The Australian Housewives' Manual: A Book for Beginners and People with Small Incomes*, 2nd edn. A. H. Massina, Melbourne, 1885.

31. Stoler, A. L., 'Rethinking Colonial Categories: European Communities and the Boundaries of Rule.' *Comparative Studies in Society and History*, vol. 31, no. 1 (1989), p. 155.

65

"FROM BABY'S FIRST BATH": KAŌ SOAP AND MODERN JAPANESE COMMERCIAL DESIGN

Gennifer Weisenfeld (2004)

When Nagase Tomirō opened his Western sundries shop in Tokyo in 1887, cosmetic soap used for the face and body was not commonly seen in the average Japanese household, and neither hand washing nor hair washing was the general custom in Japan that each is today. Now known as Kao Corporation, the company is one of the leaders in the Japanese health and beauty industry, and has played a central role in the transformation of the daily hygiene and cosmetic practices of the Japanese nation over the last century. [...] Kaō designers were able to maximize the marketing effectiveness of their advertising compositions through the skillful application of modernist pictorial techniques, which highlighted product special features and critical elements of brand identity. [...]

Kaō targeted several consumer groups, with upper and middle-class urban women initially constituting the major portion of the company's national consumer base. In the democratization process, the target clientele was expanded to include blue-collar women and their families. Advertising was integral to the creation of a national society and advertisers stood among a range of competing interests, both public and private, who were attempting to mold the sphere of women. [...] The high profit margin on cosmetic goods was a major incentive for manufacturers, although initially half of this profit was cycled back into advertising.[1] Nagase composed all the early copy and layouts for Kaō promotional material. He was a close friend of American F. W. Eastlake, founder of Tōkyō Eigo Gakuin (Tokyo English Academy) in 1890, and Eastlake was a crucial source for up-to-date examples of advertising from Europe and the United States. From the beginning, soap's image, name, and packaging were considered of preeminent importance in its effective marketing to the Japanese. [...] Early advertisements concentrated on featuring the product itself, emphasizing its unsurpassed quality, hygienic and cosmetic efficacy, and modern stylishness.[2] [...]

At the time Kaō entered the market, regular lower-grade soap was referred to as *arai sekken* (cleaning soap), while more refined (often scented) cosmetic soap was known as *kao arai* (kao, meaning "face," and *arai*, meaning "to clean"). Desiring to associate the company's domestically produced soap with cosmetic applications for the face, Nagase Tomirō experimented with a variety of homophones for the word face (*kao*) when selecting characters for the product brand-name. Advertising copy announcing the product launch explained that the combination of the characters for flower and king, creating the sound "ka-ō," referred to the pristine beauty and heavenly fragrance of the peony, commonly known as the "king of a hundred flowers." Chinese poets such as Li Bai, the text went on to explain, associated the peony with the legendary Tang dynasty beauty Yang Gui Fei (719–756), who was immortalized in the poetry of Bo Juyi for her fair, snow white complexion – a complexion that use of the Kaō product promised to help reproduce.[3] As a result, this poetic, Sinicized brand-name aurally evoked the majestic image of a clean and beautiful face and served as an inspiration for the pictorial and typographic expression of company designers. The calligraphic brand-name typography was later codified and used everywhere, including promotional delivery trucks, billboards along railway lines, and electrically illuminated signboards on top of city buildings.[4]

Nagase reinforced the Kaō brand identity as a facial cosmetic product by choosing for the company trademark the image of a crescent moon with a face uttering the words "kaō soap" in a cloud of bubbles [Figure 47]. Pictorial images associated with shining were consistently popular for use in trademarks in Japan because they were thought to imbue commercial products with auspicious associations, specifically, the illumination of heaven and the gods.[5] Most such images included one of the "three shining symbols" of the moon, star, and sun. While Nagase is credited with selecting the crescent moon logo (which was initially combined with a star), in fact, a number of years prior to his registration of the Kaō logo, the image was already associated with imported soaps, most notably the popular product Ivory soap, marketed widely by Proctor and Gamble from 1879. The crescent moon was also associated with the cycles

Figure 47. 'Kaō soap advertisement, source unknown, 1894. Tokyo, Kao Corporation.' In Gennifer Weisenfeld, '"From Baby's First Bath": Kaō Soap and Modern Japanese Commercial Design', *The Art Bulletin* 86(3) (September 2004), pp. 573–98, p. 575. Reprinted by permission of Kao Corporation.

of the month and, by extension, the ocean tides and women. [...]

By 1930, there were over 17 million women between the ages of fifteen and sixty-four in Japan, and even the limited marketing data available from the prewar period indicates the importance of women consumers as a market for new Western-style health and beauty products like soap.[6] Keen to attract this large pool of consumers, Kaō Soap Corporation and many other corporate advertisers found it beneficial to link their marketing strategies to the public policy objectives of the patriarchal Japanese state, which was already engaged in an effort to mold women of varying ages into educated consumer subjects. [...] As a commodity, cosmetic soap straddled the line between health and beauty, revealing a dual identity allied to both practical hygiene and luxury consumption.

In 1911, close to two thousand soap manufacturers registered for trademarks.[7] While leading the field, Kaō still competed with imported brand-name cosmetic products, such as Japan Lever Brothers' Velvet soap, whose advertisements featured a majestic seated female figure clad in a Greco-Roman-style flowing gown (the allegorical "Japania" perhaps). And Kaō went head-to-head with high-quality domestic products such as Mitsuwa soap, produced by Marumi-ya, and Shiseido soap. Both manufacturers relied heavily on decorative promotional graphics in the style of Art Nouveau (and later Art Deco) to conjure up luxurious images of elegant women and graceful floral motifs. Mitsuwa soap drew from the graphic sensibility of renowned Czech designer Alphonse Mucha, and Shiseido, whose broad array of cosmetic products extended from face tonics and creams to powders and perfumes, employed a delicate, linear style akin to that of Aubrey Beardsley, which featured willowy, fashionable young women with stylish coiffures in well-appointed modern interiors in combination with the company's delicate signature trademark, the camellia.[8]

Rampant unregulated and unauthorized price slashing in the mid-1920s combined with severe retail competition, however, caused additional problems for Kaō that sapped profits and eventually prompted radical rethinking of the company's business policies. When the second Nagase Tomirō took over as company president in 1927, just two years after the company went from being a limited partnership to a corporation, he began a thorough overhaul of the company's production, management, promotion, and distribution strategies. This included a radical change in Kaō soap's marketing, from a high-class luxury item to a mass-market daily consumer good, which also meant cutting the price per unit by a third, to ten sen apiece.

"NEW AND IMPROVED KAŌ"

In 1931 the company mounted a massive new advertising campaign for its lower-priced commodity, called "New and Improved Kaō" (*Shinsō Kaō*), which was overseen by the newly hired pioneering art director Ōta Hideshige (1892–1982), considered one of the first professional "art directors" in Japan.[9] [...] The vast amount of innovative design produced for the New Kaō campaign and related subsequent campaigns into the 1930s constitutes the company's major contribution to the development of the commercial design field in Japan. [...] One message this conveyed implicitly was that even through a commodity as mundane as a bar of soap, every man or woman could tap into an international culture of modernity. This was certainly the message the Japanese government communicated to its imperial subjects, so Kaō's modernist advertising reinforced official ideologies of hygiene praxis.[10] [...] This included several overarching thematic copy phrases that appeared on series of advertisements, of which undoubtedly the most memorable is "From baby's first bath, Kaō." This simple, yet affecting phrase was a direct call to mothers to implement the new rituals of cleanliness at home to insure the wellbeing of their children – the future of the nation. [...]

[...] From the 1920s, most major Western design trade publications were known in the Japanese commercial art community, and the information they presented played a critical role in the instrumentalization of modernist styles.[11] In an age of lax or nonexistent copyright laws, Japanese publishers reissued foreign images with impunity, providing a rich encyclopedia of styles and mediums for local reference and adaptation. Many of the copious journal illustrations were accompanied by translated excerpts from original publications and/or editorial comments by Japanese theorists. The advertising design trade journal *Kōkokukai* (*Advertising World*), for example, was one of the most important agents in mediating this kind of information, frequently excerpting material from the German design journal *Gebrauchsgrafik*, the French *Publicité*, and the British publications *Commercial Art* and *Modern Publicity*. [...]

Ōta recommended to the planning division and production conference the unknown Hara Hiromu's (1903–1986) bold, modern red package design, launching an illustrious career that established Hara as one of the most important and powerful graphic designers in Japan until his death in 1986.[11] [...] Although Hara was not yet well known for his design projects, he was familiar to many as a translator and author of essays on graphic art, particularly typography. He was responsible for translating the important European text *Die neue Typographie* (*The New Typography*) by Jan Tschichold from German into Japanese in 1928. Hara was drawn to the powerful cinematic montage aesthetics of famed Russian director Sergei Eisenstein and revolutionary designers Rodchenko and Lissitzky. He later employed these in his highly acclaimed photomurals promoting Japanese tourism, which were installed in the prize-winning Sakakura Junzō Japanese Pavilion at the Paris 1937 International Exposition and in the pages of the Japanese wartime propaganda journal *Front*.

[...] The full-page newspaper advertisement that kicked off the "New and Improved Kaō" campaign, which ran in all the major Japanese newspapers, featured a striking photographic image shot from overhead by commercial photographer Kanamaru Shigene (1900–1977), director of the small commercial photography studio Kinreisha.[12] This was, incidentally, one of the earliest examples of a full-page photographic newspaper advertisement in Japan [Figure 48].

Kanamaru's photograph showed a crowd of company employees standing outside the production factory holding up banners and energetically raising their hands in triumph. The copy, reminiscent of Proctor and Gamble's endorsement for Ivory soap, read "Today is the day of New and Improved Kaō, 99.4% pure, net price 10 sen a piece."[13] [...] [It] also clearly drew from triumphal images of industry and social revolution emanating from the Soviet Union in widely circulated propaganda journals such as the *USSR in Construction*, designed by Rodchenko and Lissitzky.[14] At first glance, this might seem an odd choice of inspiration for depicting production under a capitalist system. Yet [...] as hard as Soviet designers tried to distance themselves from embourgeoisement, according to Leah Dickerman, in the context of the Soviet Union's New Economic Policy implemented in the early 1920s, it was increasingly difficult to distinguish "Soviet labor from the alienated labor of capitalism, the revolutionary commodity from the commodity fetish, and Soviet technology from the oppressive machines of the industrial revolution."[15]

Many Japanese manufacturers positioned themselves as progressive producers in terms of their technologized, precision manufacturing and their high-quality products, which were marketed as bringing a healthy new life to the Japanese collective in line with state objectives. Thus, in Kaō's case, this conflation of labor and capital in a burst of revolutionary victory presents the company at the core of the imagined community of the nation, surrounded by concentric rings of enthusiastic consumer subjects. [...]

Figure 48. 'Kanamaru Shigene, photographer, Kaō soap advertisement launching the "New and Improved Kao" campaign (*Shinsō Kaō*), run in all major Japanese newspapers, March 1931. Tokyo, Kao Corporation.' In Gennifer Weisenfeld, '"From Baby's First Bath": Kaō Soap and Modern Japanese Commercial Design' *The Art Bulletin* 86(3) (September 2004), pp. 573–98, p. 582. Reprinted by permission of Kao Corporation.

One brightly colored advertising image that ran in *Betsu kenkon* (*Another Universe*), a little-known literary journal with proletarian leanings published in Korea, shows a square-shouldered worker, confidently looking to his side as he surveys a vast industrial complex. [...] While unlike the profoundly racialized images in British imperialist soap advertising Anne McClintock has identified, the Kaō image similarly alludes to the politics of empire building through imperialist expansionism on the Asian peninsula and continent.[16] It annexes what is presumably Korean labor, or elides the difference between Japanese and Korean labor, superimposing Japanese hygiene practices onto the colony as part of the colonial civilizing mission. A standard Kaō message calls out to the viewer above the product brand-name, "Number One in the Orient" – a position the Japanese Empire was also increasingly claiming for itself. [...]

While most of the photography for the New Kaō campaign has not been attributed, a number of images are reliably credited to the now-famous photographer Kimura Ihee (1901–1974), [...] a founding member of the celebrated avant-garde photography journal *Kōga* (G: Lichtbild; E: Photograph) which ran from 1932 until the end of 1933, spotlighting international developments in modernist photography. [...] In one newspaper advertisement from the first half of 1931, Kimura, taking his cue from Soviet designer Rodchenko, created a dramatically skewed grid of electrical wires and poles cutting across the metropolitan skyline, an aesthetically pleasing formalist composition that is simultaneously a meditation on the technological nature of modern daily life and, presumably, its attendant grittiness. A promotional balloon seen in the background pushes its way through the grid pulling a text trailer reading "New and Improved Kaō." The bubble-shaped balloon humorously reinforces the copy on the right that reads, "Not one bubble wasted." [...] The image of the bubble further reinforced a crucial sales point for the product, reliable sudsing. [...]

Kaō show-window designs spatialized the promotional elements of the company's print advertising on the commodity stage of the retail environment, enticing and structuring the gaze of the passing consumer. [...] [S]uch displays tried to reproduce the excitement of the urban factory environment in the consumer theater to underline the company's image of productivity and the product's high quality. Moreover, as the text in one display read, this kind of production and, by extension, consumption constituted "soap patriotism."

Another Kaō show window set Hara's new Western-style typography and figures of schoolchildren with anthropomorphized moon faces and Kaō soap backpacks in a pristine bathroom, a dream environment that surely catered to the desires of upwardly mobile Japanese consumers. Employing the hygienic image of a brightly lit, Western-style tiled bathroom, an incursion that famed novelist Tanizaki Junichirō lamented bitterly in his notorious essay "In Praise of Shadows" on Japanese toilet aesthetics (1937), Kaō aimed at those who aspired to modernize their homes and have private baths, although most Japanese homes did not have private baths until long after World War II. And even in the fervor for modernization, the Western-style bath with foaming bubbles shown in the Kaō fantasy was unlikely to have replaced the beloved Japanese *o-furo* used primarily for soaking – and collective soaking at that.

Unfortunately, no amount of creative energy expended in the "New and Improved Kaō" campaign was able to counter the ravages of the Great Depression's worldwide economic downturn. [...] It was also quickly apparent to Nagase that the working-class consumers that he and Ōta had hoped to attract were not flocking to Kaō soap, as the reality of the average worker's hygiene situation was far removed from the ideal Euro-American model Kaō followed.

[...]

MODERNISM, SOAP, AND THE NATION

A ghostly photogram of two overlapping hands emerges from a black background. The text above counsels, "First wash your hands" because "Disease comes not from your mouth, but from your hands."[17] Here the photogram is used to produce an X-ray-like vision. Reinforcing the scientific image, the X-ray simulates the visual penetration of the hands, as if it were a medical instrument. [...] The luminous whiteness of the spotlighted hands metaphorically implies disinfection, but the defensive position of the extended crisscrossed fingers wards off approaching germs, ominously portending future contamination. Such Kaō corporate advertisements reveal the subtle (and not so subtle) ways in which modernist pictorial strategies could be effectively instrumentalized to commodify new rituals of cleanliness and to aestheticize new consumer products.

The fine line separating high art from the market economy was quickly eroding. And whether they employed upbeat pictures of frolicking children or anxious ones of tainted hands, these diverse designs skillfully constructed images of national domesticity in line with gendered discourses on hygiene.

In 1934 the journal *Kōkokukai* excerpted in English a text by American Frank H. Young from *Modern Advertising Art*.[18] [...] To gain better "attention value" in a competitive emerging national market, consumer-oriented Japanese companies like Kaō had to rely heavily on the applied aesthetics of advertising design to construct a distinctive corporate identity in the mass media. One critic noted in a review in 1933 that Kaō's advertisements splendidly expressed a "Kaō whiff" that made them immediately identifiable, specifically referring to the company's extensive use of photography, which stood out against the predominantly hand-drawn images of other advertisers.[19] Kaō's strategy was part of a worldwide upsurge in modernist advertising design that

Young observes was also just taking hold in the United States.

In his short commentary, Young admits that lower-class consumers might not appreciate modernist techniques and might perhaps require more conventional approaches in marketing. In a bid to prove the contrary, Nagase, Ōta, and their staff, believing that modernism was exactly what represented a new democratic ideal in Japanese society, used modernist form to appeal to working-class and middle-class consumers, maintaining the high-style design of the product to preserve brand loyalty. The lowering of the product's price and the "New and Improved Kaō" campaign democratized Kaō soap, transforming it into a mass-market commodity. [...]

By the 1930s, touting the modern virtues of quality, purity, value, and health, Kaō was no longer positioning itself as merely a product manufacturer but instead sought to mold the daily lives of imperial consumer subjects to promote a healthy and productive nation. One ad from the back cover of a 1933 issue of the general-interest magazine *Hinode* (*Sunrise*) boldly exclaimed, "Scholars say that the use of soap is a barometer of the culture of a first-world nation," explicitly identifying soap consumption as a sign of a highly developed civilization.[20] To emphasize the point further, the designer superimposed bar charts comparing national soap consumption rates using units depicting hands washing onto the same disembodied hand-washing image in the background. This collage aestheticizes rituals of cleanliness and visually reinforces the image of Kaō soap's utility in matters of national hygiene by inserting the product into a seemingly scientific statistical framework. In this image, the United States is shown representing the highest level of consumption and Japan the lowest. Soap use was thus presented as profoundly connected to national identity and tied to Japan's quest for global status.[21]

[...]

NOTES

Extracted from Weisenfeld, G., '"From Baby's First Bath": Kaō Soap and Modern Japanese Commercial Design', *The Art Bulletin* 86(3) (September 2004), pp. 573–98. Reproduced by permission of the author.

1. From 1892, Kaō joined up with the advertising firm Mannensha, established just two years earlier, buying all the company's Kansai-area advertising through the agency. Kaō also often exhibited or participated in competitions at the various industrial expositions, both nationally and those sponsored by metropolitan governments like Tokyo. Kaō soap consistently won prizes at these expositions. Nihon Keieishi Kenkyūjo and Kaō Kabushiki Kaisha Shashi Hensanshitsu, *Kaō-shi 100-nen*, (Tokyo: Kaō Kabushiki Kaisha, 1993) 30–31, 57.

2. Nagase had well-known doctors endorse his product and commissioned famous writers to write Chinese poetry about it. Ibid., 24.

3. Aramata Hiroshi, *Kōkoku zuzō no densetsu* (Tokyo: Heibonsha, 1989), 111.

4. Nagase was an early pioneer of advertising strategy and quickly recognized the significance of the newly expanding railroad network for promotional purposes. By 1896, he had installed a Kaō signboard at each station along the Tokaido train line. *Kaō-shi 100-nen*, 31.

5. It is also important to note that in Buddhist imagery the moon has connotations of purification, and moon viewing is associated with spiritual visualization. I would like to thank an anonymous reader for bringing these connections to my attention.

6. Nihon tōkei kyōkai, ed., *Nihon chōki tōkei sōran*, vol. 1 (Tokyo: Nihon tōkei kyōkai, 1987), 80–81; and Louisa Rubinfien, "Commodity to National Brand: Manufacturers, Merchants and the Development of the Consumer Market in Interwar Japan," Ph.D. diss., Harvard University, 1995, 136.

7. Ochiai Shigeru, *Kaō kōkoku shi, jō-ge gappon* (Tokyo: Kaō shiryōshitsukan, 1989), 60.

8. For some examples of contemporary soap advertising designs by Kaō's competitors, see Tōkyō Ato Direkutazu Kurabu, *Nihon no kōkoku bijutsu: Meiji, Taishō, Shōwa*, 3 vols. (Tokyo: Bijutsu Shuppansha, 1967–68), vol. 2, 108–9, 112, 114, 130–31, 206, 208–11. In the 1930s, Shiseido designers also experimented with modernist photography and montage aesthetics in their advertising designs.

9. Tagawa Seiichi, *Front: Sensō no gurafizumu* (Tokyo: Heibonsha, 1988), 22.

10. The Japanese Infectious Diseases Prevention Law (Densenbyō yobō hō) promulgated in 1897 was an important milestone in establishing a government policy on public sanitation and hygiene. Subsequent laws and hygiene campaigns sought to inculcate official regimes of hygiene directly into the domestic sphere.

11. For a full account of Hara's career, see the recent work of Kawahata Naomichi, *Hara Hiromu to bokutachi no shin kappanjutsu* (Tokyo: Transart, 2002).

12. The Kaō company history indicates that advertisements ran in seventeen newspapers around the country, twelve in northeastern Japan, two in western Japan, and the remaining papers scattered in other regions. Advertising was largely concentrated in several major news organizations. For Tokyo it was *Jiji shinpō* and the *Tōkyō asahi shinbun*, in the Kansai area it was the *Ōsaka asahi shinbun* (which became the *Asahi shinbun* in 1889) and *Ōsaka mainichi shinbun* (which became the *Ōsaka Nippō* in 1888). *Kaō-shi 100-nen*, 30–31.

13. The catchphrase 99.4% pure was taken from Proctor and Gamble's copy for Ivory soap, which was used as a demonstration of its purity and high quality. *Kaō-shi 100-nen*, 102.

14. A practitioner, theorist, and educator who taught photography at Nihon University for most of his career, Kanamaru was closely attuned to cultural developments abroad, particularly in Germany and the Soviet Union. He amassed a sizable collection of foreign design trade journals. Kanamaru owned

numerous issues of the *USSR in Construction*: nos. 1–4, 5 (English and French), 6, 10, 11, 12 (1931), 8 (French, 1932), 10 (1932), 7 (July 1933). For an overview of Kanamaru's career and his copious publications, see the Nihon University Photography Division Festschrift published in his honor, *Kanamaru Shigene Sensei koki kinen* (Tokyo: Kanamaru Shigene Sensei koki kinen jimukyoku, 1974). Kanamaru's entire private library collection is now archived at Nihon University. I would like to take this opportunity to express my profound appreciation to Kaneko Ryūichi for introducing me to this archive and to Professors Hara Naohisa, Takahashi Norihide, and the entire staff and faculty of the photography division of Nihon University, who generously allowed me to study the Kanamaru materials.

15. Leah Dickerman, "The Propagandizing of Things," in *Alexandr Rodchenko* (New York: Museum of Modern Art, 1998), 66.

16. Both Anne McClintock and Juliann Sivulka have convincingly argued that in the Euro-American context, soap and the discourse of cleanliness were fundamentally implicated in the ideologies of imperialism and white supremacy. See Anne McClintock, "Soft-Soaping Empire," in *Imperial Leather* (London: Routledge, 1995), 207–31.

17. *Tōkyō asahi shinbun* 1934.

18. Frank H. Young, "Modern Advertising Art," *Kōkokukai* 11, no. 7 (July 1934): 76.

19. Aobun Doko [pseud.], "Kōkoku sunbyō," *Kōkokukai* 10, no. 3 (Mar. 1933): 29.

20. American soap manufacturers like B. T. Babbitt connected the notions of cleanliness through soap use and civilization in advertising copy as early as the 1890s. Babbitt's promotion for Best soap on a direct-marketing trade card ran, "Soap for All Nations," "Cleanliness is the scale of civilization." Juliann Sivulka, *Stronger than Dirt: a Cultural History of Advertising Personal Hygiene in America, 1875–1940,* (Amherst, N. Y.: Humanity Books, 2001) 103.

21. A related newspaper advertisement from the same year that similarly employs bar charts to show Japan's low standing in terms of soap use reveals the economic rather than moral subtext of this hygiene discourse. "This is the truth!" it exclaims. "Sickness is the most uneconomical!" This advertisement is pictured in Aka Enpitsu ko [pseud.], "Kōkoku sunbyō," *Kōkokukai*, 10, no. 6 (June 1933): 28.

66

LAND ROVER AND COLONIAL-STYLE ADVENTURE

Jeanne van Eeden (2006)

INTRODUCTION

In December 2000, a three-page advertisement for the Land Rover Freelander was published in a range of glossy magazines in South Africa. These magazines, aimed primarily at the leisure and so-called men's market, included *African Environment and Wildlife*, *Car*, *Complete Fisherman*, *Complete Golfer*, *Getaway*, *GQ*, *House and Garden*, *Leisure Wheels*, *Men's Health*, *Out There* and the international issue of *Time*. For the purposes of the arguments in this article, it is significant that the advertisement was not found in upmarket magazines such as *Tribute*[1] or *Ebony* that are aimed primarily at a black market and that generally focus on 'luxury items, and cars not carried at all by the other black magazines.'[2]

Produced by the South African advertising agency TBWA Hunt Lascaris, the first page of the advertisement shows a Himba[3] woman from Namibia standing in a barren saltpan; the picture plane is divided into two equal horizontal areas, namely sky and earth, and forms the backdrop for all three pages. She wears traditional animal skin garments and ornaments, and is naked from the waist up. Although she is thin and conforms to westernized ideals concerning beauty, her elongated breasts are propelled sideways in a ridiculous manner. The second and third pages of the advertisement show that this distortion of her breasts has been caused by a rapidly passing Land Rover 4×4 Freelander that envelops her legs in a cloud of dust.[4] She ostensibly 'admir[es] the product'[5] by allowing her eyes to follow the movement of the Freelander. The body copy on the second and third pages reads: 'The new more powerful Freelander. The 130 kW, 240 Nm V6 or the 82 kW, 260 Nm Td4 diesel, both available with 5 speed steptronic transmission. The only thing tougher will be deciding on which one you prefer.' [...]

In capitalist societies, advertisements are considered to be instrumental in reproducing social structures and maintaining myths by establishing 'structures of meaning'[6] that reflect ideological ways of perceiving the world. Advertising images therefore stem from sets of power relations and enlist cultural codes, stereotypes, myths and ideologies in their social production of meaning. Although advertisements generally 'depict particular mythologies or stereotypical ideals of "the good life" ... [based on] representations of gender, class and race',[7] the polysemic potential of representations should be borne in mind. Deborah Root states that the former colonies of the West are frequently represented by means of advertising images that are rich with colonial connotations, such as unbounded sexuality, luxury, power and adventure.[8] I hope to show that the Himba advertisement is an example of how advertising can appropriate such discourses and keep certain representations in cultural circulation, even though these may be in the form of pastiche or parody. [...]

In order to understand the discomfort that the Himba advertisement elicited, it is necessary to understand some of the context of colonial rule in Namibia. Namibia, then known as South West

Africa, was colonized by Germany between 1884 and 1918, and this period is characterized by the usual iniquities perpetrated by the politics of imperialism. The majority of the Europeans who visited the region during that time did so in their capacity as explorers, missionaries and hunters. Colonial rule was characterized by the violent suppression of the indigenous peoples; it is estimated that as many as 65,000 Herero (who include the Himba) were exterminated during their revolt against the Germans between 1904 and 1907. It is significant, in terms of the Himba advertisement, that the Germans were subsequently accused of destroying tribal culture and of exploiting women and children for financial gain.[9] In 1915, during World War I, South Africa ejected Germany from the region and Germany renounced sovereignty in the Treaty of Versailles. In 1920, the League of Nations granted South Africa mandate over the territory, which was surrendered with the gaining of Namibian independence in 1990.

The Himba are nomadic cattle herders who live in parts of Northern and Western Namibia, southern Angola and Botswana.[10] Unlike other indigenous peoples in Namibia, the Himba generally had little contact with westerners. During colonial times, the region where they lived was declared a reservation and access was restricted by the subsequent South African apartheid government. Only when Namibia became independent in 1990 did regions such as Kaoko in Western Namibia become popular tourist destinations,[11] particularly for South Africans. Because the Himba did not relinquish their traditions or mode of dress,[12] they are considered one of the last so-called unspoilt, traditional peoples of Africa.[13] [...]

LAND ROVER AND THE ADVERTISING STANDARDS AUTHORITY

There has been an intimate relationship between Western Namibia (the setting of the Himba advertisement) and Land Rover since the early 1950s, when it became the preferred leisure vehicle that enunciated gendered notions of travel, exploration and adventure.[14] Although the Managing Director of Land Rover in South Africa, Moira-Anne Moses, protests that they 'wouldn't want Land Rover to be only a white male product' (suggesting that it essentially still is), my reading of the Himba advertisement is based on the reality that '[t]raditionally most Land Rover owners have been male, and most still are'.[15] The assumption that is made in this analysis that the driver is a (white) male is defensible in terms of the overwhelmingly white market segment that has been able to afford the Land Rover, and because Land Rover has been coded as an adjunct of the myth of masculinity for many decades. This does not invalidate Bertelsen's viewpoint that since 1994, democracy in South Africa has increasingly been redefined as the individual freedom of (black) people to participate in the act of consumption, merely that this tendency has not yet been discernible in the culture surrounding Land Rover.[16]

The Advertising Standards Committee, a sub-section of the South African Advertising Standards Authority (ASA) met on 7 December 2000 to consider the complaints lodged against the Himba advertisement by members of the public, the Human Rights Commission, the Commission on Gender Equality and the Namibian Ministry of Foreign Affairs, Information and Broadcasting. The advertisement was subsequently ruled to be in breach of the International Code of Advertising Practice, and was withdrawn in April 2001. All the magazines that had carried the initial advertisement were obliged to print a statement from the ASA explaining the retraction, the costs of which were carried by Hunt Lascaris. Moreover, Namibian government officials considered requesting redress for the damage perpetrated against the Himba by means of the advertisement.[17]

The Himba advertisement elicited indignation on many counts. Whereas the Namibian government objected to the exploitation of a minority ethnic group, namely the Himba,[18] Mogam Moodliar, head of the South African Human Rights Commission's legal department felt that '[i]t demeans women generally, depicting them as sexual objects. The [breasts] are not in [their] natural form. They are tilted in a certain direction as a result of the speed of the Land Rover'.[19] The Namibian Campaign on Violence against Women and Children believed that the advertisement contravenes the Namibian constitution.[20] Diane Hubbard of the Legal Assistance Centre in Windhoek, the capital of Namibia, commented that the image is 'tremendously insensitive, poking fun at the Himba's traditional dress. It smacked of the same kind of exploitation that occurred during colonial times. Would a white woman in a bathing costume have been given the same treatment?'[21] Indeed, some critics pointed out that the advertisement operated in the same tradition of objectification and exploitation to which the Khoi woman Sarah Baartman had been subjected in the early nineteenth century.[22] In addition to racism and sexism, which are inextricably linked,[23] the advertisement was also accused of encouraging 'people using 4×4 vehicles to drive recklessly through the Himba's remote ancestral grazing and burial grounds.'[24]

Following deliberations with Hunt Lascaris, the ASA articulated four issues in their judgment:

- When viewed against the diverse population and culture of South Africa the advertisement is irresponsible, as it does not contribute towards the work of gender and racial healing essential to the building of a new society.
- The manner in which the female figure is depicted is exploitative and constitutes racial stereotyping.[25]
- It is not the nudity in the advertisement but the misuse, abuse and distortion of the woman's nudity that violates human dignity. [...]
- The insensitive portrayal of the Himba woman is discriminatory and makes a mockery of African culture thereby perpetuating gender and cultural inequality.

Representatives from Hunt Lascaris responded to charges regarding the 'cultural pornography' of the image by stating that it had been conceived as a 'a harmless parody and exaggeration designed to amuse the consumer'[26] and explained that a multiracial pilot study had found it inoffensive. [...] Hunt Lascaris further declared that consumers of 'motor vehicles would likely view the advertisement on a humorous basis [as hyperbole] and would merely conclude that there is a quicker version thereof'.[27] As Bertelsen points out, advertisements are inherently parasitic and make opportunistic use of jokes and puns.[28] A common defence against offensive imagery is therefore that it is 'only entertainment', which obscures the reality that entertainment (and advertisements) operate on an ideological level and have the capacity to inscribe racist or sexist meanings.[29]

Moira-Anne Moses attempted to justify why the Himba image had been chosen:

> We wanted to keep an African context and were obviously a little hesitant [about this advertisement], but research showed it was perceived in the light it was intended ... We withdrew it immediately there were complaints. It was not our intention to offend people.[30]

Moses noted, however, that '[q]uite a lot of *men* phoned in to say that they had enjoyed the ad and people who were offended should not be so sensitive'.[31] Hunt Lascaris insisted that they had not exploited the Himba woman as she had given her consent and was apparently aware of the manner in which her photograph would be used. Her face was replaced, however, by that of an employee at the advertising agency before the whole image was digitally manipulated.[32] [...]

TRAVEL AND COLONIAL-STYLE ADVENTURE

The metonymic association of woman with the African landscape reverberates throughout the nineteenth century, when exploration was established as 'an exclusively masculine act, a moment of penetration into a suggestively feminized [and empty] locale'.[33] But this practice did not end with decolonization. [...] Pritchard and Morgan point out that the '"masculine", "technological" west and north turns its gaze to consume tourism delights in the "natural" "feminine" landscapes of the south and east';[34] this meeting of opposites is also enacted in the Himba advertisement.

Colonial-style adventure, which is conventionally based on the notion of white privilege, is explicitly referred to in many contemporary advertisements and commodities, and words such as 'discover' are coded to reflect this.[35] Accordingly, Land Rover's choice of names such as Defender, Discovery, Freelander and Range Rover play on ideas of 'defence, freedom, territory, and ... mobility.'[36] [...]

One of the objectives of colonialism was the imperative to dominate and tame the Other. [...] [C]olonial discourse thus constructed the colonized 'as a fixed reality which is at once an "other" and yet entirely knowable and visible'.[37] The Other was invariably fetishized in fantasy images that operated on the principles of metaphor and metonymy,[38] fashioning ambivalent stereotypes of attraction and repulsion that still inform the cultural politics of identity. [...] There are many contemporary examples of exploitative representations of black women in South African advertisements, travel literature and tourist postcards. In these representations, women are the signifiers of absolute difference – racial, sexual and cultural. Although these examples are generally not as shocking as the Himba advertisement, they constitute a visual lexicon that has been naturalized by its continual use. Stuart Hall consequently alerts us to the fact that 'how things are represented and the "machineries" and regimes of representation in a culture do play a constitutive, and not merely a reflexive, after-the-event, role'.[39]

EXPEDITION DISCOURSE AND THE 'GENTLEMAN'S SAFARI'

In order to understand some of the further cultural resonances that I believe operate in the Himba advertisement, it is helpful to refer to two types of adventure travel that flourished in Western Namibia (specifically in the Kaoko region) during the twentieth century. First, the 'expedition discourse' was a predominantly visual discourse comprising photographic records of 'the technical conquest of an unfriendly natural surrounding by male-groups', in which hazardous car journeys featured prominently.[40] The inhospitable terrain of Western Namibia was consequently established as a stage for masculine heroism and a testing ground for western technological supremacy.[41] It can therefore be argued that the Himba advertisement was sited in a colonialist landscape to reinforce the notions of masculinity, freedom, modernity, status and a leisure lifestyle already attached to the Land Rover.[42] [...]

Second, from the 1950s onwards, the so-called Herrensafari or gentlemen's safari became established in Namibian society. [...] The Herrensafari was a privileged form of leisure and colonial travel only available to those in possession of a 4×4 vehicle. [...] Henrichsen points out that the main activity of the Herrensafari was driving, thereby not only enacting the physical control of space by leisure adventurers, but also emphasizing their symbolic temporary escape from an urban middle-class milieu[43] [and] technological supremacy. [...]

BINARY OPPOSITIONS

Ashcroft explains that binary oppositions established power relations and sustained 'the violent hierarchy on which imperialism is based and which it actively perpetuates'.[44] Binary oppositions are mutually exclusive, and because they attach positive values to only one of the pair, they naturalize ideological meanings. [...] The manner in which the advertisement is structured, with the Himba woman on the left of the picture plane and the Land Rover on the extreme right, seems to validate a reading in terms of binary opposition.

The first set of binaries gravitates around the notion of a western paradigm and includes the following: white/black; first world/third world; West/Africa;[45] North (Euro-America)/South (Africa); colonizer/colonized; centre/margin; self/other; modernity/pre-modernity; technological/pre-technological; civilization/primitivism; present/past; and fast, change/slow, changeless. [...] [T]he Himba woman is positioned not only as the conventional Other of the white European male, but also specifically of the South African male at whom this advertisement is targeted. This is suggested by the linguistic sign of the number plate on the Freelander: the initials GP signify Gauteng Province, which connotes wealth, culture and technology in the industrial and financial hub of South Africa. [...] The second set of binaries involves conventional gendered constructs, and includes the following: male/female; culture/nature; urban/rural; exploring the land/of the land; empowered/disempowered; active/passive; strong/weak; public/domestic; and action/reaction. [...]

NOTES

Extracted from van Eeden, J., 'Land Rover and Colonial-Style Adventure', *International Feminist Journal of Politics* 8(3) (2006), pp. 343–69. Copyright © 2006 Routledge, reprinted by permission of Routledge (Taylor & Francis Group, http://www.informaworld.com).

Editor's note: This article was not illustrated with figures in its original form for reasons of copyright permission.

1. Annie Coombes notes that *Tribute* is a 'glossy magazine aimed at a middle-class black entrepreneurial readership', Coombes, A. E., *History after Apartheid: Visual Culture and Public Memory in a Democratic South Africa*, Durham, NC: Duke University Press, 2003, p. 12.

2. Bertelsen, E., 'Ads and Amnesia: Black Advertising in the New South Africa', in Nuttall, S. and Coetzee, C. (eds) *Negotiating the Past: The Making of Memory in South Africa*, Cape Town: Oxford University Press, 1999, pp. 221–41, p. 230. The recently launched South African magazine *Blink* (subtitled 'The key to being a man') targets upmarket black male readers and carries an advertisement for the Land Rover Range Rover (*Blink*, February 2005, pp. 88–9). However, the Freelander and Range Rover are not coded in precisely the same manner and have different connotations since the Range Rover has limited on-road performance ('Land Rover: The Fifty Year Miracle Origin of the Species', 1997, Available at http://landrover.co.za/company/heritage/com_heri.asp (accessed 17 October 2002).

3. The use of the Himba woman as a stereotype of Africa is common; another example with a similar context is an advertisement for Britz 4×4 rentals that features a Himba woman and three images of 4×4s. The text reads: 'Self-drive ... into the wilderness and see the parts of southern Africa you only dreamed of'. *Getaway*, December, 2004, p. 306.

4. It is strange that her skirt does not seem to move in response to the speed of the Freelander. The notion of speed has traditionally been coded as an adjunct of male success and sexual power (Bayley, S., *Sex, Drink and Fast Cars: The Creation and Consumption of Images*, London: Faber, 1986, p. 31), and supports the assumption made in this article that the driver of the Freelander is a male figure.

5. Keeton, C., 'Icon of Adventure.' Available at http://www.leadership.co.za/issues/nov/articles/landy.html, 2001, p. 1 (accessed 8 October 2002).

6. Williamson, J., *Decoding Advertisements*, London: Boyars, 1978, p. 12.

7. Wallis, B., *Art after Modernism: Rethinking Representation*, Boston, MA: David R. Godine, 1984, p. xv.

8. Root, D., *Cannibal Culture: Art, Appropriation, and the Commodification of Difference*, Boulder, CO: Westview, 1996, p. 25.

9. Grobler, J., 'Still No Redress for Hereros.' *Mail & Guardian*, 13–19 March 1998, p. 7; 'Herero to File Atrocity Claims against Germany', *Mail and Guardian*, 22 January 2003, p. 12.

10. The Himba are part of the Herero who currently number about 100,000 out of the total population of Namibia of less than 2 million.

11. Rademeyer, R., 'Ons Lyk Mos Nie So Nie!', Available at http://www.news24.com/Beeld/Wereld/0371_957122,00.html , 2000, p. 2 (accessed 30 July 2003).

12. The Himba dress of animal skins and bodily adornment by animal fat and ochre have become iconic for the tourism industry.

13. Rademeyer, 2000, p. 2; Pillinger, C., 2001, 'Land Rover's U-Turn Over "Racist and Sexist" Advert', available at http://www.millennium-debate.org/suntel28jan6.htm (accessed 30 July 2003). It is ironic that this 'innocence' is confirmed by the fact that very few Himba saw the advertisement under discussion, as they are not the target market at which the product is aimed.

14. See Henrichsen, D., 'Pilgrimages into Kaoko: Herrensafaris, 4 x 4s and Settler Illusions', in Miescher, G. and Henrichsen, D. (eds) *New Notes on Kaoko*, Basel: Basler Afrika Bibliographien, 2000, pp. 159–85.

15. Keeton, 2001, p. 1.

16. Bertelsen, 1999, p. 228. See note 3. [...]

17. Pillinger, 2001, p. 2.

18. Rademeyer, 2000, p. 1.

19. Jacobs, C., 'Land Rover Boobs with Racy Ad Campaign', *Sunday Times*, 10 December 2000, p. 3.

20. Rademeyer, 2000, p. 1.

21. Pillinger, 2001, p. 1.

22. Sarah Baartman was taken from Cape Town to Europe in 1810 and [...] exhibited as a so-called oddity because of her physical appearance (particularly her breasts and sexual organs). [...]

23. hooks, b., *Yearning: race, gender, and cultural politics*, Boston, MA: South End Press, 1990, p. 57.

24. This accusation is ironic given Land Rover's ostensible commitment to conservation and environmental issues. Keeton 2001; Pillinger, 2001, p. 2.

25. The charges of racism in the advertisement were also projected onto the advertising industry in general in South Africa, which was alleged to be 'still white and racist.' Donaldson, A., 'How to Keep Abreast in Advertising – and Other Matters', 2000, p. 1. Available at http://www.suntimes.co.za/2000/12/10/insight/in06.htm (accessed 15 June 2003).

26. Jacobs, 2000, p. 3.

27. TBWA Hunt Lascaris' Justification Document, 2000.

28. Bertelsen, 1999, pp. 226–8.

29. See Wolf, M. J., *The Entertainment Economy: How Mega-Media Forces Are Transforming Our Lives*, New York: Times Books, 1998.

30. Keeton, 2001, p. 1.

31. Farquhar, J. 'Playing with Fire.' *Advantage with Advertising Age: A Compelling Insight into Media and Advertising*, 8 January 2001, p. 22.

32. Van Wyk, E., 'An Investigation of the Objections that the ASA (Advertising Standards Authority) Presented for the Retraction of the December 2000 Land Rover Freelander Advertisement.' Unpublished research paper, University of Pretoria, Pretoria, 2001.

33. Bunn, D. 'Embodying Africa: Woman and Romance in Colonial Fiction', *English in Africa*, vol. 15, no. 1 (1988), pp. 1–28, p. 1, p. 7). Travel writing was established as a decisively gendered trope, in which the '[e]xplorer-man paints/possesses newly unveiled landscape-woman.' Pratt, M. L. *Imperial Eyes: Travel Writing and Transculturation*, London: Routledge, 1992, p. 213.

34. Pritchard, A. and Morgan, N. J. 'Privileging the Male Gaze: Gendered Tourism Landscapes', *Annals of Tourism Research*, vol. 27, no. 4 (2000), pp. 884–905, p. 892, p. 894.

35. Root, 1996, p. 133, p. 148.

36. Henrichsen, 2000, p. 178.

37. Bhabha, H. K., 'The Other Question: The Stereotype and Colonial Discourse', *Screen* 24 (6 (1983), pp. 18–36, 23.

38. Bhabha, 1983, p. 29.

39. Hall, S., 'New Ethnicities' in Morley, D. and Chen, K.-H. (eds) *Stuart Hall. Critical Dialogues in Cultural Studies*, London: Routledge, 1996, pp. 441–49, p. 443.

40. Miescher, G. and Rizzo, L. 'Popular Pictorial Constructions of Kaoko in the 20th Century', in Miescher and Henrichsen, eds., 2000, pp. 10–47, p. 34).

41. Henrichsen, 2000, p. 180.

42. Ibid. p. 176.

43. Ibid. p. 160, 167–8. Henrichsen, (p. 166) believes that the Herrensafari was a ritualized form of temporary escape from modernity that was necessary specifically during the fraught political circumstances contingent upon the practices of colonialism in Namibia.

44. Ashcroft, B., 'Globalism, Post-Colonialism and African Studies', in Ahluwalia, P. and Nursey-Bray, P. (eds) *Post-Colonialism: Culture and Identity in Africa*, New York: Nova Science Publishers, 1997, pp. 11– 26. p. 14.

45. Brantlinger (1985: 199) affirms the presence of the constructed binary opposition between the West (self) and Africa (Other). Brantlinger, P., 'Victorians and Africans: The Genealogy of the Myth of the Dark Continent', *Critical Inquiry* vol. 12 (1985), pp. 166–203.

67

SWOOSH IDENTITY: RECONTEXTUALIZATIONS IN HAITI AND ROMANIA

Paul B. Bick and Sorina Chiper (2007)

INTRODUCTION

Any critical analysis of signs must begin with a discussion of the broad social climate in which those signs are produced, embedded, circulated, and consumed. Zygmunt Bauman has suggested that one of the hallmarks of late modern global capitalism is the ultimate replacement of real competition with symbolic competition.[1] [...] In our frustration with this new framework, we tend to focus inward, on the continuous and ultimately meaningless re-tooling of personal identity through ever-changing forms of self-improvement, education and obsessive physical fitness – pastimes that Christopher Lasch referred to as 'harmless in themselves', but 'elevated to a programme and wrapped in the rhetoric of authenticity and awareness', thus signifying a 'retreat from politics'.[2]

For virtually every imaginable self, there are purchasable signs to help express and project this identity. [...] While effecting and affecting the construction of social identities, brands are themselves affected in the process. The identity of a brand, as it originates in the issuing culture, can be challenged over the broad territory where it comes into contact with local values, mentalities, taboos, symbols, historical experiences, or *lebenswelt* (life-worlds).

[...] [A]s Naomi Klein has suggested, corporate branding is predicated on the co-construction of false communities.[3] From the very beginning, the goal of Nike's promotional strategy was simply to infuse the brand with the meaning of greatness and achievement, and then to repackage and promote its iconography and products as the embodiment of athletic success. [...] The irony, of course, is that [...] no actual achievement is required to join the new 'cloakroom peg communities', to use Bauman's term, nothing but the simple act of buying and displaying, and thus asserting one's pledge to a mystifying sign.[4]

THE SWOOSH IN ROMANIA AND HAITI

Our research data from Iasi (Romania), and Port au Prince (Haiti), have revealed that the swoosh is as ubiquitous on the fringes of global capitalism as it is in the American heartland. But the form and function of the swoosh in these marginal places tend to be manifested differently than they are in the United States. [...] This article is less concerned with how Nike uses the swoosh to promote its brand than in how people traditionally excluded from the identity-for-purchase paradigm appropriate its iconography and map its prior text onto unique cultural frames. [...]

First, we should mention that there are several levels of recontextualization, each achieved at various degrees of modality, thereby enriching the meanings of the swoosh as a global corporate sign with values emerging from the local cultures. For example, we found the swoosh in a wide variety of contexts, ranging from counterfeit bags, shoes, T-shirts, automobile stickers, motorcycles, lottery banks and stores, to emplacements as graffiti, and as a decorative element on tombs, in rural Haiti. The most conspicuous of these recontextualizations is the phenomenon of brand counterfeiting. Within the 'contractual' paradigm presented by Nike, 'purchase' – the exchange of monetary value for identity – is the crucial action at the nexus of co-construction, and those willing and capable of meeting this purchase requirement are granted community membership, with its pre-packaged identity and universally recognized signifying emblems of greatness and achievement as their reward.

Through mechanical or manual reproduction, cracks emerge in this paradigm of mediated actions which contradict Nike's contractual implications without destroying the 'aura' of the sign. The brisk exchange of counterfeit goods in both Haiti and Romania represents a form of 'first-order' contradiction. The fact that fake goods sell so well suggests that the order of exchange dictated by Nike is neither inviolable nor essential. The product itself, or rather the authenticity of its origin, is not necessarily an indispensable component of the sign, and in spite of a substitution by obviously inauthentic products, satisfactory identity co-construction can still take place.

Whereas in Haiti the common counterfeit Nike products are bags, in Romania they are mostly clothes, and the more conspicuous the swooshes, the better [Figure 49]. Via counterfeits, the swoosh becomes available to anyone, to the haves and the have-nots, to connoisseurs and to people who totally ignore the corporate projected identity of the brand image. In places like Haiti and Romania, where there is hardly any above-the-line advertising, the swoosh resonates less with the fitness culture, as it does in the US, and it takes on vague, discontinuous meanings. In Romania, people associate it with a 'V' for victory, with a horizontal 'J' (Michael Jordan's initial), with the tick with which teachers mark pupils' notebooks to show that their homework is good, with a reversed, rotated comma, or with a token of good luck.

We believe that the ubiquity and auratic nature of the swoosh derives both from the mythically seductive allure of the American success culture, and from the intrinsic visual appeal of the sign as such. Since 1971, when the swoosh was created by Caroline Davidson, it has evolved from a sharp, even threatening and aggressive tone towards a smooth, balanced, rounded and seductive shape. The salience of the sign comes from its simplicity and fluidity, from its vectoring from the realm of what Kress and Van Leeuwen have termed the given, the known, and the grounded to the ideal, the new, and the possible.[5] Uncluttered, lowly modal, contrastive and immediately recognizable, the swoosh is now promoted as a logo without an anchoring text, thus making it accessible and identifiable in illiterate or non-English-speaking cultures.

At a psychological level, what Nike has managed to achieve is to create a cultural artifact that impacts on the mind as a natural object, reshaped, *through recontextualizations, into a cultural symbol where the local symbolic capital weaves into the global sign-value of the swoosh*. The naturalness of the sign and its simple, organic appeal justify its application as a thing of beauty, as a decorative element, a tattoo or a piece of jewelry. The reproduction of the swoosh as a golden earring, for example, supports the idea of its visual appeal, and turns it from a two-dimensional image into a three-dimensional object, as a step to a further recontextualization: the swoosh becomes embodied when someone actually wears it, physically blending its identity into that of the wearer.

At the opposite end of this materialization of the swoosh, as a sign object whose role of status indexicality is enhanced by the material that it is made of, namely gold, lies the abstraction of random, hand-reproduction of the swoosh

Figure 49. 'Romanian man wearing a counterfeit Nike jacket.' In Paul B. Bick and Sorina Chiper, 'Swoosh Identity Recontextualizations in Haiti and Romania', *Visual Communication* 6(1) (2007), pp. 5–18, p. 9. Photo: Sorina Chiper.

as graffiti. The simplicity of the sign makes it easily inscribed without special skills or tools. A form of transgressive discourse, graffiti appears in strikingly similar contexts in both Haiti and Romania. [...] [T]he hand-reproduction of the swoosh on the outside wall of the Economics building of the 'Al. I. Cuza' University of Iasi is an interesting case of discourse in space, or geosemiosis.[6] The sign is on a side wall, at eye level, large enough to be spotted from a distance. On its left, we can read the word 'boboc' and the figure '2004[2004]'. In its syntagmatic relationship with the accompanying text, on the left, the swoosh functions as both an identifying marker

for the generation of freshmen in 2004, and as a self- assertive qualifier ('we are the best'). A closer look at the graffiti reveals that it is applied on top of an older layer of signs, thus making a metadiscursive statement not only about the way in which no piece of discourse is ever a trace on a tabula rasa, but also about the changes in what count as fashionable and topical labels for people or places.

The swoosh [...] from the wall of a house in rural Haiti, stands alone, and ambiguous in terms of what it expresses, as discourse in place, encapsulating, nevertheless, the visual essence of the sign, reduced to a disembodied, dematerialized shape. In a ludic gesture, a waving tail attached to the outlined swoosh further emphasizes the notion of movement and velocity. Framed by two windows, the tailed swoosh looks like a kite, fragile and rudimentary, yet heading for the sky, and symbolically evoking a wish to exit the debilitating condition of poverty.

The fact that these two representations are so similar suggests that there is a minimal set of requirements necessary to recall the essence of the swoosh, and that these requirements will naturally emerge in similar ways within a given discursive genre. The curve, angles and vectoring of the shape itself are conjured in a similar manner under the technical and social constraints of the graffiti genre. An even higher level of abstraction is achieved in the graffiti swoosh on the gate of a garage in Iasi where the swoosh is reduced to its most skeletal form, as a bare curved line, capturing the simplicity and the fluidity of the sign's shape, while immediately evoking the icon and its entailments.

These various degrees of abstraction that the sign undergoes raise an interesting question: if we think of prior text as being a whole entity, a complete swoosh, how much prior text is required in a recontextualization in order to evoke its essential essence? Clearly, vectoring, angle and the line of movement comprise its quintessential core.

[…]

A GRAVE IN RURAL HAITI

As is often the case with 'found' discourses, we can only know very little of the specific context of production of the grave. […] We ignore, for example, who built the grave, or why they made the specific material and discourse choices that have shaped the grave in its current form. What we can know beyond doubt is its special location, outside the southern Haitian town of Camp Perrin, approximately 180 km south of Port au Prince, and that its size, placement and construction are typical of other graves in the area.

Haitian graves tend to be built above ground, usually of cinderblocks and cement, and covered in a textured aggregate veneer, as can be seen in the tomb in the picture. They are often, but not always, painted, usually in light pastel colors, or white, and they are occasionally adorned with shapes, symbols or texts in addition to the expected linguistic information which indicates who is buried inside. The images adorning graves range from simple decorative geometric shapes to 'veve' voodoo symbols, Christian imagery, corporate iconography or combinations of these forms. Graves are often constructed in advance of their use, whenever possible, so it is quite common that the person who designed the grave will eventually be one of its end-users. The graves are often modular, and supplementary crypts can be added to them subsequently. Larger family graves, therefore, tend to be composed of numerous crypts, stacked and arranged like shipping containers around a central marker or under a kind of unifying shelter. Occasionally, for wealthier families, graves will be assembled inside small structures, like mausoleums, with simple visual burial discourses adorning the outside. Thus, graves, and some of their characteristics, such as the quality of their construction and the level of upkeep, serve as status markers in the community indicating wealth, property and family cohesion.

Graves are frequently located on or near family homesteads for both practical and psychological reasons. First, for many generations, the presence of family graves tends to deepen a perception of land ownership in areas where deeded or legal ownership of property is rare. Second, this practice has led to a psychological expectation and desire to have departed loved ones conspicuously nearby. Like the home itself, graves become key sites of family identity co-construction.

The nature of burial practice in Haiti, the social conventions and material technologies used in these practices, tend to dictate and limit the types of discourses that can be found there, while they define these discourses as part of yet another unique genre. For example, because of the varieties of materials used in grave construction and the social phenomenon of widespread illiteracy in Haiti, written memorials on gravestones are very rare, while the form remains an ideal hosting site for visual iconography.

On the grave [...] we have two crypts, side by side, joined under a large headstone on which we might expect to find, and do find, burial discourse. On top of the headstone is a larger cross, which serves both to identify the structure as a Christian burial site and to mark the site as sacred. So, it is within this production context at the level of compositionality that this text appears, in a decidedly interdiscursive turn.

TEXT ON THE GRAVE

A close-up of the inscription on the tomb reveals that the swoosh and the word Nike are woven into the same compositional space with the usual identifying linguistic data found on burial markers [Figure 50]. This dramatic recontextualization necessarily imparts sacred meanings, or deepens the existing sacralization of the swoosh, while the presence of the swoosh simultaneously commodifies the sacred context. The swoosh is accompanied by its corporate parent name but in this particular context it stands apart from any other co-textual imagery. The logo comprises a kind of pure identifying center – a plaque of light and color on a sea of flat grey stone. Rather than identifying the grave – serving as linguistic

Figure 50. 'Close-up of the grave outside Camp Perrin, Haiti.' In Paul B. Bick and Sorina Chiper, 'Swoosh Identity: Recontextualizations in Haiti and Romania', *Visual Communication* 6(1) (2007), pp. 5–18, p. 15. Photo: Paul B. Bick.

anchor – as one would expect from a marker of this size, shape and location, this one, by virtue of its sharp modality, brightly contrasting color and texture, and unexpected content, reverses our expected salience patterns. The grave itself becomes simply a platform for the presentation of the logo.

This specific swoosh is a warm and comforting version of the icon – thick-bodied, gracefully curved, pale blue and lying at rest on its side, but conveying a sense of gentle rolling, like a Caribbean wave, with its long end open and bleeding out into the new and the unknown. The naturally seductive and appealingly hopeful shape is enhanced by these small details. This image itself is slightly off center to the right and its components all vector gently yet steadily to the right as well. The cumulative compositional modality at the site of the text suggests a confident consciousness – a hopeful desire to believe that what lies beyond the grave, and beyond the immobilizing poverty of Haiti, is something beautiful, positive, attainable and worth imagining.

Joined as it is by the name of its corporate parent, the image is, to a certain degree, less ambiguous than it would be as just a swoosh alone. […] [T]he word NIKE is quite large and pronounced, set in bold, highly contrastive uppercase block lettering. What's more, it is actually carved into the face of the gravestone, as is the accompanying swoosh. In contrast, the deceased's name has been applied somewhat carelessly in the lower portion of the frame in a non-contrastive light blue and set in a combination of upper and lower case and cursive script. The man's name actually runs off the frame in an illegible scrawl. So while the corporate name and logo are permanent features in this context, the name of the deceased is merely painted, a temporary feature. The overarching compositional modality, then, is one of contrast between the permanence of the sign and the transience of the individual. People are born and die … Nike is here to stay.

CONCLUSION: CONSUMPTION OF THE SWOOSH IDENTITY

Taken together, Haitian and Romanian recontextualizations of the swoosh suggest a kind of reclamation of public space and an ownership of signs that is rarely seen in the developed world.

If all interdiscursive recontextualization amounts to a mythologizing of existing signs, as Barthes suggests,[7] and if signs always retain the power they have been invested with, then the sanctification of signs across cultural frontiers is to be expected not as an aspect of the commodity theology that Nike sells, but as a local re-imagining of personal identity in a global context. This is not to say that the Haitians fail to understand the meaning of Nike, but that they have added meaning to interdiscursive imagery in ways appropriate to the specific socio-historical context in which it is needed.

The swoosh's multiple and idiosyncratic recontextualizations diminish its social status indexicality, while multiplying its array of symbolic meanings and its iconic variations. They reference Barthes' idea that the form in which a sign is recontextualized does not completely suppress its source meaning, it only 'impoverishes it, puts it at a distance, holds it at one's disposal'.[8] Everything that Nike is, or has been, remains within the swoosh, regardless of how many layers of recontextualization, how many orders of semiological distance, separate a 'use' from its 'source'. In other words, status indexicality survives in palimpsest.

One way to look at how a thing means is to look at what it needs to mean in a given context. In order to understand desire we must first comprehend what is missing. Bauman has suggested that what the losers in global capitalism suffer most is a crippling lack of mobility.[9] Abject poverty represents a complete and utter absence of movement, be it physical, social or spiritual. The freedom to move and its various forms of absence sit at the center of the widening polarization between rich and poor. While poverty is stagnation in total, and at its worst entails a lack of hope that freedom will ever be possible, mobility has become the stratifying hallmark of ever-illusive prosperity and real freedom. The question is: does the swoosh bridge this gap or merely highlight it? Within the context of this widening breech, the swoosh may be employed here as a kind of living icon of that mobility and freedom, a sacred homage to the reality-defying lightness of a soaring Michael Jordan, and a spiritual link, however fragile, to the hope and prosperity of the mythical American promised land, where everything moves with speed and grace, and everyone wears real Nike shoes.

The form of orthodox totemism hegemonically re-enacted by Nike is subverted by the chaotic appropriations, inscriptions, embodiments or emplacements of the swoosh in countries where the sanctioned corporate propaganda is not directly heard. In Haiti and Romania, the swoosh joins local cultural and symbolic capitals functioning as a sign and an object at the same time, freely crossing boundaries between nature and culture, between the sacred and the profane, between abstraction and materiality.

To place a swoosh on building walls, on tombs, or on one's body, is definitely a form of totemic bricolage, a sort of primitive worship of new-capitalism idols which reached this status in the collective consciousness not through a consistent metaphysical ideology but through the insidious seduction practices that support corporate hegemony. Ironically, however, the consecration of the swoosh is paralleled by an unconscious protest against corporate hegemony which can be manifested in sacred contexts. The decontextualized swoosh of Nike is turned from a potential totem of the liquid modern age into a convenience object, a collective symbol that anyone can feast on, and whose rhetoric is embedded in the new context where the sign is reproduced. The sacred swooshes of Haiti defy the social stratification that comes with corporate totemism, and celebrate the freedom and joy of escaping the local dimension by joining a symbolic, u-topic community that relishes in sign consumption and production.

NOTES

Extracted from Bick, P. B. and Chiper, S., 'Swoosh Identity: Recontextualizations in Haiti and Romania', *Visual Communication* 6(1) (2007), pp. 5–18, copyright © 2007 by SAGE Publications. Reprinted by permission of Sage.

1. Bauman, Zygmunt, *Freedom,* Milton Keynes: Open University Press, 1988, pp. 57–8.
2. Christopher Lasch, *The Culture of Narcissism*, New York: Warner, 1979, pp. 29–30 cited in Bauman, Zygmunt, *The Individualized Society*, Cambridge: Polity, 2001, p. 150.
3. Klein, Naomi, *No Logo*, New York: Picador, 1999, pp. 6–7.
4. Bauman, Zygmunt, *Community: Seeking Safety in an Insecure World*, Cambridge: Polity, 2001, p. 16.
5. Kress, Gunther and Van Leeuwen, Theo, *Reading Images: The Grammar of Visual Design*, London: Routledge, 1996, p. 208.
6. Scollon, Ron and Scollon, Suzie Wong, *Discourses in Place: Language in the Material World*, London: Routledge, 2003, p. 2.
7. Barthes, Roland, *Mythologies*, New York: Hill and Wang, 1972, pp. 109–21.
8. Barthes, 1972, p. 118.
9. Bauman, Zygmunt, *Identity: Conversations with Benedetto Vecchi*, Cambridge: Polity, 2004, p. 97.

GUIDE TO FURTHER READING

Landmark texts in the development of postcolonialism that have influenced design historical thinking include Edward Said's *Orientalism* (1978), Homi Bhabha's *The Location of Culture* (1994) and Fernando Ortiz's *Cuban Counterpoint: Tobacco and Sugar* (1940, trans. 1947). The influence of postcolonialism within design history is seen in Jeremy Aynsley's *Nationalism and Internationalism: Design in the Twentieth Century* (1993), John MacKenzie's 'Orientalism in Design' in *Orientalism: History, Theory and the Arts* (1995) and Tim Barringer and Tom Flynn (eds), *Colonialism and the Object: Empire, Material Culture and the Museum* (1998). Also from 1998, see 'Race and Ethnicity in American Material Life', a special issue of the *Winterthur Portfolio*, including Theodore C. Landsmark's 'Comments on African American Contributions to American Material Life'. Ortiz, particularly, has informed Anna Calvera (2005), and Rose Cooper and Darcy White (2005) have provided a useful account of doing design history informed by Ortiz's concept of transculturation. The work in cultural studies of Paul Gilroy (1993) is also influential within design history.

The *Journal of Design History* has sought to globalize its contents, as discussed in a special issue in 2005. There, Jonathan Woodham's article 'Local, National and Global: Redrawing the Design Historical Map' employed a bibliometric approach to stating the problem of a Western bias in design history organizations and publications. It also included Victor Margolin's influential 'A World History of Design and the History of the World'. The following issue featured Anna Calvera's article 'Local, Regional, National, Global and Feedback: Several Issues to Be Faced with Constructing Regional Narratives' (2005), from which this section takes its title.

David Crowley's *National Style and Nation-State: design in Poland from the vernacular revival to the International Style* (1992) continues the story of Polish design to examine the impact of modernism on the popularity of the Zakopane Style. See also Crowley's article 'Building the World Anew: Design in Stalinist and Post-Stalinist Poland' (1994) and Andrzej Szczerski's 'Sources of Modernity: The Interpretations of Vernacular Crafts in Polish Design around 1900' (2008). Crowley refers to the influential *Nations and Nationalism since 1780* (1990) by E. J. Hobsbawm.

Tracey Avery's article extracted here is informed by a body of Australian design history which includes Tony Fry's *Design History Australia* (1988). European and American debates occurring during the same period as the one Avery analyses are reviewed in section 2 of this *Reader*.

Further reading on Japan's national aesthetic includes Penny Sparke's 'From Pre-Modern to Modern: Japanese Industry, Society and Design after 1945' (1987), Lise Skov's 'Fashion Trends, Japonisme and Postmodernism, Or "What is so Japanese about Comme des Garçons?"' (1996), Brian Moeran's 'The Orient Strikes Back: Advertising and Imagining Japan' (1996) and Brian J. McVeigh, 'How Hello Kitty Commodifies the Cute, Cool and Camp' (2000).

Van Eeden's 'The Colonial Gaze: Imperialism, Myths, and South African Popular Culture' appears in a special issue on South African design produced by *Design Issues* in 2004. An influential study of the representation of Africa as a continent for British consumption is Annie E. Coombes's *Reinventing Africa: Museums, Material Culture and Popular Imagination in Late Victorian and Edwardian England* (1994). See also Timothy Mitchell's 'Orientalism and the Exhibitionary Order' (1992). Daniel J. Sherman's 'Post-Colonial Chic: Fantasies of the French Interior, 1957–62' (2004) provides a case study analysis of the commodification of African arts as primitivism in interior design in post-colonial France.

While most of the material in the *Reader* derives from, or concerns, British and US design history, there is much to inform understanding of wider European design. German material in the *Reader* includes Gottfried Semper's view of the Great Exhibition, Hermann Muthesius and Henry van de Velde's 'Werkbund Thesis and Antithesis', Nikolaus Pevsner on Peter Behrens, Gillian Naylor on the Bauhaus, Gert Selle on kitsch, Karl Marx on commodity fetishism and Walter Benjamin on 'The Work of Art in the Age of Mechanical Reproduction'. Texts concerning French design history include Debora Silverman's analysis of 'The 1900 Paris Exposition', Nancy Troy on Le Corbusier, Peter Lloyd and Dirk Snelders on Philippe Starck, writings by French theorists Jean Baudrillard and Roland Barthes and sociologist Pierre Bourdieu. Europe beyond France and Germany is represented in the *Reader* by David Crowley's study of Poland's Zakopane style, the discussion of Romania in Paul Bick and Sorina Chiper's analysis of Nike, the contribution by Adolf Loos informs understanding of the development of Austrian design and Susan Reid's account of the Khrushchev kitchen examines a country split between Europe and Asia.

A further case study is found in the attempts to bring together global and national design traditions in Newell and Sorrel's ill-fated corporate redesign of British Airway's tailfins in 1997. It attracted criticism both for tokenism and for failing to 'fly the flag'. See Mary Jo Hatch and Majken Schultz's 'Bringing the Corporation into Corporate Branding' (2003) and Crispin Thurlow and Giorgia Aiello's 'National Pride, Global Capital: A Social Semiotic Analysis of Transnational Visual Branding in the Airline Industry' (2007). A recent analysis of relevant branding is Daniel J. Huppatz's 'Globalizing Corporate Identity in Hong Kong: Rebranding Two Banks' (2005).

ILLUSTRATIONS

CONTRIBUTORS

Judy Attfield (1937–2006) was a designer and design historian and Leverhulme Emeritus Fellow at Winchester School of Art, University of Southampton, UK.

Tracey Avery is a PhD candidate in the Faculty of Architecture, Building and Planning at the University of Melbourne and a Curatorial and Heritage Consultant in Melbourne, Australia.

Jeremy Aynsley is Professor of History of Design at the Royal College of Art, London, UK. His research interests are in late-nineteenth- and twentieth-century design in Europe and the United States, with a special focus on design in Germany.

Bibi Bakare-Yusuf is an independent scholar currently based in Nigeria. Her research focuses on gender and youth cultures in the African world, embodiment and cultural creativity and feminist theory.

Peter Reyner Banham (1922–88) was a renowned architectural historian and critic of design, born in Britain and a long-time resident in the United States.

Roland Barthes (1915–80) was a French writer and theorist who made a significant contribution to semiotic, structuralist and poststructuralist cultural analysis.

Jean Baudrillard (1929–2007) was a French cultural theorist, sociologist, and philosopher whose work is associated with postmodernism and poststructuralism.

Andrew Bengry-Howell is based in the Department of Psychology at the University of Bath, UK, where he researches youth identities and consumption.

Walter Benjamin (1892–1940) was a German Jewish writer and cultural critic, associated with the Frankfurt School, whose materialist analysis of mass culture has been immensely influential.

Paul B. Bick is based in the Department of Anthropology at the University of Illinois, Chicago, USA. He has degrees in English and linguistics.

Pierre Bourdieu (1930–2002) was a leading French sociologist who held the Chair of Sociology at the Collège de France and made significant studies of, among other things, taste, class, social mobility and academia.

Michael Braungart is Professor at Leuphana University of Lüneburg, Germany and founding principal at McDonough Braungart Design Chemistry, Charlottesville, Virginia, USA.

Jean M. Burks is senior curator, Shelburne Museum, Vermont, USA, and has written extensively on Shaker furniture.

Sorina Chiper is based at the 'Al. I. Cuza' University of Iasi, Romania. Her research interests include American autobiography, professional communication, social, cultural and visual anthropology and the Roma minority in Romania.

Alison J. Clarke is Professor in Design History at the University of Applied Arts Vienna, Austria. Her research interests include the anthropology of design, dynamics of style change, materiality and practice, consumption and material culture.

Shaun Cole is a freelance curator, writer and lecturer, and Arts and Cultural Enterprise Manager at Queen Mary, University of London, UK. He was formerly Head of Contemporary Programmes at the Victoria and Albert Museum in London.

Becky Conekin is Senior Research Fellow in Historical and Cultural Studies, London College of Fashion, UK.

Ruth Schwartz Cowan is a historian of science, technology and medicine, and Janice and Julian Bers Professor in the Department of History and Sociology of Science at the University of Pennsylvania, Philadelphia, USA.

Louise Crewe is Professor of Human Geography at the University of Nottingham, UK. Her research explores issues of consumption, retailing, commodification, value and disposal.

David Crowley is Deputy Head of the Department of Design History at the Royal College of Art, London, UK. His research spans Polish art and architectural history from 1860 to the present day, the art and design of the Cold War and Modernism in architecture and graphic design since 1920.

Mihaly Csikszentmihalyi is a Hungarian psychologist, C. S. and D. J. Davidson Professor of Psychology and Management and Director of Quality of Life Research Center at Claremont Graduate University, USA.

Matthew Denney combines work for Duke's auctioneers in Dorset, UK with teaching at Sotheby's Institute, London.

Darron Dean developed his interest in ceramic history, from his PhD on the pottery industry 1650–1720, into a concern for broader issues around household consumption.

Clive Dilnot is Professor of Design Studies at Parsons The New School for Design, New York, USA. He has worked at the School of the Art Institute in Chicago, the Graduate School of Design and Carpenter Center for the Fine Arts at Harvard University and in the United Kingdom, Asia and Australia.

John Elkington is an authority on corporate responsibility and sustainable development. His many projects and roles include a visiting professorship at the Doughty Centre for Corporate Responsibility at the Cranfield University School of Management, UK.

Emma Ferry is Senior Lecturer in Visual Culture in the School of Creative Arts, University of the West of England, Bristol, UK.

Kate Forde is Assistant Curator at the Wellcome Collection, London, UK. She has worked for a number of public arts institutions including the Tate, the V&A and the Metropolitan Museum of Art, New York.

R. Buckminster Fuller (1895–1983) was an American designer, engineer, architect and futurist philosopher who invented the Geodesic dome and the Dymaxion car. His innovative work has been highly influential on contemporary ideas about the potential of design.

Paul Greenhalgh is Director and President of the Corcoran College of Art and Design, Washington, DC, USA. He was previously President of NSCAD University (Nova Scotia College of Art and Design) and Head of Research at London's Victoria & Albert Museum.

Nicky Gregson is Professor in the Department of Geography at the University of Sheffield, UK. Her research interests span consumption and material culture, second-hand goods, materiality and practice, disposal and waste.

Christine Griffin is Professor of Social Psychology and Head of the Psychology Department at the University of Bath, UK. Her main research interests are consumption and identity, gender relations and youth research.

Mary Guyatt is Curator at the Garden Museum, London, UK. She was previously based in the Education Department at the Victoria and Albert Museum.

Julia Hailes MBE is a sustainability consultant to industry and a writer and speaker on environmental issues. She is the author of *The New Green Consumer Guide* (2007).

Eugene Halton is Professor of Sociology and American Studies at the University of Notre Dame, USA. His contribution to this reader is under the name Eugene Rochberg-Halton.

Fran Hannah was Principal Lecturer at the School of History and Theory of Visual Culture at Middlesex University, UK.

Dick Hebdige is a British sociologist and Director of the Interdisciplinary Humanities Center and Professor at the University of California, Santa Barbara, USA.

Steven Heller is co-chair of the MFA Designer as Author Department at the School of Visual Arts, New York City. He was an art director at the *New York Times* for more than thirty years.

John Heskett is a British design historian and Professor in the School of Design, Hong Kong Polytechnic University. His current research asks how design creates economic value and the role of this in design policy in governments and corporations.

Thomas Hine is a design critic and author of five books on culture and design, including studies of packaging, consumption and 1970s style.

Rebecca Houze is Associate Professor of Art History at Northern Illinois University, Dekalb, USA, and a specialist in Austrian and Hungarian design. Her current research explores the concept of 'dress' as complex site for the expression of cultural and aesthetic identity in the Dual Monarchy of Austria-Hungary, from the late nineteenth century to the First World War.

Steven Izenour (1940–2001) was an American architect and principal in the Philadelphia firm Venturi, Scott Brown & Associates.

Pat Kirkham is Professor at the Bard Center for Studies in the Decorative Arts, New York, USA. She was previously Professor of Design History and Cultural Studies at De Montfort University, Leicester, UK.

Grace Lees-Maffei is a British design historian and Senior Lecturer in the History and Theory of Design and Applied Arts at the University of Hertfordshire, UK, where she coordinates the tVAD research group in its work on relationships between text, narrative and image.

Liz Linthicum has taught at Winchester School of Art, the University of Southampton, UK. Her research into disabled people's interaction with clothes is informed by her previous work as a caregiver, and at the Centre for Deaf Studies at the University of Bristol.

Peter Lloyd is Senior Lecturer in Design and Head of the Design Group at the Open University, UK. His research interests include, design ethics, storytelling in the design process, design in the media, and video assisted learning in design.

Adolf Loos (1870–1933) was an Austrian architect and cultural critic who worked primarily in Vienna.

Nicolas P. Maffei is an American design historian and Senior Lecturer in Critical Studies at Norwich University College of the Arts, UK. His research focuses on design in America between the two world wars.

Joel Makower is a writer, speaker, and strategist on corporate environmental practices, clean technology and green marketing, and an authority on business and the environment.

Victor Margolin is Professor Emeritus of Design History at the University of Illinois, Chicago, USA.

Karl Marx (1818–83) was a German political philosopher whose ideas shaped the history of world political systems.

William McDonough is an architect and author who has been integral to the socially responsible design movement. He is also a partner at William McDonough + Partners.

Jeffrey L. Meikle is Professor of American Studies and Art History at the University of Texas, Austin, USA. His research interests range from American industrial design to postcards and the Beat generation.

William Morris (1834–96) was a British designer, writer and poet and leading figure in the British Arts and Crafts Movement. He set up the firms Morris, Marshall, Faulkner & Co. and Morris and Co. and founded the Society for the Protection of Ancient Buildings.

Hermann Muthesius (1861–1927) was a German architect, designer and writer. He wrote *Das Englische Haus* (1904–11) and was co-founder of the Deutscher Werkbund.

Gillian Naylor is an independent scholar and was Professor of the History of Design at the Royal College of Art, London. During the 1950s she wrote for *Design* magazine.

Vance Packard (1914–96) was a journalist and author of books that confronted and critiqued a variety of social phenomena in twentieth-century America including advertising, planned obsolescence and social and business hierarchies.

Victor Papanek (1927–99) was a designer and educator who made a key contribution to the literature and practice of socially responsible and ecologically minded design.

Sir Nikolaus Pevsner (1902–83) was a renowned German-born British historian of art and architecture whose best-known work was the forty-six volume guide *The Buildings of England*.

Tim Putnam was Professor of History of Material Culture at the Universities of Middlesex and Portsmouth, UK. His research interests focus on design, economic development and cultural change. He is a founding member of *The Journal of Design History* and currently chairs its editorial board.

Susan E. Reid is Reader in Russian Visual Arts at the University of Sheffield, UK. She has research interests in mid-century Soviet modernity and modernism, in material and visual culture, and in gender issues in the context of the Cold War, as well as in the relation between state, art and design specialists, and audience and popular taste.

John Ruskin (1819–1900) was a British author and critic of society and architecture and an enormously influential figure in Victorian culture, especially the Arts and Crafts Movement.

Denise Scott Brown is an architect, writer, teacher and planner. She is principal in the firm Venturi, Scott Brown and Associates, Philadelphia, USA.

Gert Selle is Professor Emeritus of Art Education at the University of Oldenburg, Germany. His writing has challenged conceptions about the designer's role in taste-formation.

Gottfried Semper (1803–79) was a German architect, theorist and writer. Following his participation in Dresden's May uprising of 1849, he fled to Paris and London, where he wrote and contributed to the Great Exhibition of 1851 before returning to the continent and continuing to work in Switzerland, Austria, and Germany.

Debora L. Silverman is University of California President's Chair in Modern European History, Art, and Culture at UCLA in Los Angeles, USA.

Adam Smith (1723–90) was a Scottish philosopher whose writings on economics have been highly influential in modern thought. He was Chair of Moral Philosophy at the University of Glasgow, 1752–63.

Dirk Snelders is based in the Department of Marketing, Product Innovation and Management in the School of Industrial Design Engineering at the Technical University Delft, Netherlands.

Penny Sparke is a leading British design historian and Pro-Vice Chancellor (Research and Enterprise) at Kingston University, UK. She has taught at the University of Brighton and the Royal College of Art, UK.

John Styles is Research Professor in History at the University of Hertfordshire, UK. He was previously based at the Victoria and Albert Museum.

Nancy Troy is Chair of the Art History Department at the University of Southern California, Los Angeles, USA. Her research and teaching interests span modern European and American art, architecture, design, and visual culture between about 1850 and 1950.

Laurel Thatcher Ulrich is 300th Anniversary University Professor of History at Harvard University, USA. Her research interests are early American social history, women's history and material culture.

Thorstein Veblen (1857–1929) was an influential Norwegian-American economist and sociologist. He taught at a number of institutions in the US and was a founder of The New School in New York City.

Henry van de Velde (1863–1957) was a Belgian architect, designer and writer who worked in Belgium, the Netherlands and Germany. He was co-founder of the Deutscher Werkbund.

Jeanne van Eeden is Professor and Head of the Department of Visual Arts at the University of Pretoria, South Africa.

Robert Venturi is an architect and principal at Venturi, Scott Brown and Associates. He has taught at Yale University and the University of Pennsylvania and is an author of *Complexity and Contradiction in Architecture* (1966).

John A. Walker is a historian and theorist of art and design. Until his retirement in 1999, he was Reader in Art and Design History at Middlesex University, UK.

Gennifer Weisenfeld is Associate Professor in the Department of Art, Art History and Visual Studies at Duke University, USA. She is a specialist in nineteenth- and twentieth-century Japanese Art and Design.

Jonathan M. Woodham is leading figure in the development of the history of design as an academic discipline over the past three decades. He is Professor of the History of Design and Director of the Design History Research Center at the University of Brighton, UK.

Frank Lloyd Wright (1867–1959) was a leading American architect, designer and writer. Unusually prolific, he is credited with having developed a distinctly American architecture.

BIBLIOGRAPHY

Adamson, G., *Thinking Through Craft*, Oxford: Berg, 2007.

Adamson, G. (ed.), *The Craft Reader*, Oxford: Berg, 2009.

Adorno, T., and M. Horkheimer, 'The Culture Industry: Enlightenment as Mass Deception', in *Dialectic of the Enlightenment* (1944), trans. John Cumming, New York: Continuum, 1972, pp. 120–67.

Agnew, J.-C., 'Coming Up For Air: Consumer Culture in Historical Perspective', in J. Brewer and R. Porter (eds), *Consumption and the World of Goods*, London, New York: Routledge, 1994, pp. 19–39.

Aicher, O., *Die Welt als Entwurf* (*The World as Design*), trans. Michael Robinson, Berlin: Ernst & Sohn Verlag, 1991.

Alexander, C., *The Timeless Way of Building*, New York: Oxford University Press, 1979.

Alexander, C., *The Nature of Order, Books 1–5*, Berkeley, CA: Center for Environmental Structure, 2003–2005.

Alexander, C., S. Ishikawa and M. Silverstein, *A Pattern Language: Towns, Buildings, Construction*, New York: Oxford University Press, 1977.

Ames, K. L., 'The Stuff of Everyday Life: American Decorative Arts and Household Furnishings' in Schlereth, T. J. (ed.), *Material Culture: A Research Guide,* Lawrence, KS: University Press of Kansas, 1985.

Anscombe, I., *A Woman's Touch: Women in Design from 1860 to the Present Day*, London: Virago, 1984.

Appadurai, A. (ed.), *The Social Life of Things: Commodities in Cultural Perspective*, Cambridge: Cambridge University Press, 1986.

Arvidsson, A., 'From Counterculture to Consumer Culture: Vespa and the Italian Youth Market, 1958–78', *Journal of Material Culture* 5(3) (2001), pp. 251–74.

Attfield, J., 'FORM/female FOLLOWS FUNCTION/ male: Feminist Critiques of Design', *Design History and the History of Design*, London: Pluto Press, 1989, pp. 199–225.

Attfield, J. (ed.), *Utility Reassessed: the Role of Ethics in the Practice of Design*, Manchester: Manchester University Press, 1999.

Attfield, J., 'The Meaning of Design: Things with Attitude', in *Wild Things: the Material Culture of Everyday Life*, Oxford: Berg, 2000, pp. 11–43.

Attfield, J., *Bringing Modernity Home: Writings on Popular Design and Material Culture*, Manchester: Manchester University Press, 2007.

Attfield, J. and P. Kirkham (eds), *A View From the Interior: Feminism, Women, and Design*, London: The Women's Press, 1989.

Auslander, L., 'The Courtly Stylistic Regime: Representation and Power under Absolutism', in *Taste and Power: Furnishing Modern France*, Berkeley, CA: University of California Press, 1996, pp. 35–74.

Avery, T., 'Furniture Design and Colonialism: Negotiating Relationships between Britain and Australia, 1880–1901', *Home Cultures* 4(1) (2007), pp. 69–92.

Aynsley, J., '"Gebrauchsgraphik" as an Early Graphic Design Journal, 1924–1938', *The Journal of Design History* 5(1) (1992), pp. 53–72.

Aynsley, J., *Nationalism and Internationalism: Design in the Twentieth Century*, London: Victoria & Albert Museum, 1993.

Aynsley, J., 'Graphic Change: Design Change: Magazines for the Domestic Interior, 1890–1930', *Journal of Design History* 18(1) (2005), pp. 43–59.

Aynsley, J. and K. Forde, 'Introduction', *Design and the Modern Magazine*, Manchester: Manchester University Press, 2007, pp. 1–16.

Bakare-Yusuf, B., 'Fabricating Identities: Survival and the Imagination in Jamaican Dancehall Culture', *Fashion Theory* 10(4) (December 2006), pp. 461–83.

Banham, R., 'All That Glitters Is Not Stainless' in R. Banham (ed.), *The Aspen Papers: Twenty Years of Design Theory from the International Design Conference in Aspen*, London: Pall Mall Press, 1974, pp. 155–60.

Banham, R., *Theory and Design in the First Machine Age*, New York: Praeger, 1960.

Banham, R., 'A Throw-Away Aesthetic' (*I.D.* March 1960) in P. Sparke (ed.), *Design By Choice*, London: Academy Editions 1981, pp. 61–5.

Barringer, T. and T. Flynn (eds) *Colonialism and the Object: Empire, Material Culture and the Museum*, London: Routledge, 1998.

Barthes, R., 'Myth Today', 'The New Citroën' and 'Plastic', in *Mythologies* (1957), translated by A. Lavers, New York: Hall & Wang, 1994, pp. 88–90, 97–9, 109–59.

Barthes, R., 'The Rhetoric of the Image' (1964), 'The Death of the Author' (1968), 'From Work to Text' (1971) in S. Heath (ed. and trans) *Image Music Text*, London: Fontana, 1977, pp. 32–51, pp. 142–8, pp. 155–64.

Barthes, R., *The Fashion System* (1967), trans. Matthew Ward and Richard Howard, Berkeley and Los Angeles, CA: University of California Press, 1983.

Baudrillard, J., 'The Ecstasy of Communication', in *The Anti-Aesthetic: Essays on Postmodern Culture* (1983), H. Foster (ed.), translated by John Johnston, New York: The New Press, 1998, pp. 126–34.

Baudrillard, J., *The System of Objects* (1968), trans. James Benedict, London: Verso, 1996.

Baudrillard, J., *The Consumer Society: Myths and Structures* (1970), London: Sage Publications Ltd, 1998.

Bel Geddes, N., *Horizons*, Boston: Little, Brown, & Company, 1932.

Bengry-Howell, A. and C. Griffin, 'Self-made Motormen: The Material Construction of Working-class Masculine Identities through Car Modification', *Journal of Youth Studies* 10(4) (2007), pp. 439–58.

Benhamou, R., 'Imitation in the Decorative Arts of the Eighteenth Century', *The Journal of Design History* 4(1) (1991), pp. 1–13.

Benjamin, W., 'The Work of Art in the Age of Mechanical Reproduction' (1936) in H. Arendt (ed.), *Illuminations*, New York: Schocken Books, 1969, pp. 217–54.

Bennett, T., L. Grossberg and M. Morris (eds), *New Keywords: A Revised Vocabulary of Culture and Society*, Oxford: Blackwell, 2005.

Benton, T., C. Benton with D. Sharp, *Form and Function: a Sourcebook for the History of Architecture and Design 1890–1939*, London: Crosby, Lockwood, Staples, in association with the Open University Press, 1975.

Berg, M., *The Age of Manufactures, 1700–1820*, London: Fontana, 1985.

Berman, M., *All That is Solid Melts into Air: the Experience of Modernity*, London: Verso, 1982.

Betts, P., 'The Politics of Post-Fascist Aesthetics: West and East German Design in the 1950s', in R. Bessel and D. Schumann (eds), *Life After Death: Violence, Normality and the Reconstruction of Postwar Europe*, Cambridge: Cambridge University Press, 2003, pp. 291–321.

Betts, P., *The Authority of Everyday Objects: A Cultural History of West German Industrial Design*, Berkeley, CA: University of California Press, 2004

Betts, P., 'Building Socialism at Home: The Case of East German Interiors', in K. Pence and P. Betts (eds), *Socialist Modern: East German Everyday Culture and Politics*, Ann Arbor, MI: University of Michigan Press, 2008, pp. 1–34.

Bhabha, H. K., *The Location of Culture*, London and New York: Routledge, 1994.

Bick, P. B. and S. Chiper, 'Swoosh Identity: Recontextualizations in Haiti and Romania', *Visual Communication* 6(1) (2007), pp. 5–18.

Bierut, M., J. Helfand, S. Heller, and R. Poynor (eds), *Looking Closer 3: Classic Writings on Graphic Design*, New York: Allworth Press, 1999.

Bijker, W. E., 'The Social Construction of Bakelite: Toward a Theory of Invention', in W. E. Bijker, T. P. Hughes and T. Pinch (eds), *The Social Construction of Technological Systems: New Directions in the Sociology and History of Technology*, (1987) Cambridge, MA and London: MIT Press, 1989, pp. 159–87.

Bing, S., 'Wohin treiben wir? (Where are we going?)' *Dekorative Kunst* 1 (1897–8), pp. 1–3, 68–71, 173–77, in T. Benton and C. Benton with D. Sharp, *Form and Function: A Source Book for the History of Architecture and Design 1890–1939*, London: Granada Publishing in association with the Open University Press, 1975, pp. 19–20.

Bird, J., B. Curtis, M. Mash, T. Putnam, G. Robertson, S. Stafford and L. Tickner (eds) *The BLOCK Reader in Visual Culture*, London and New York: Routledge, 1996.

Bonsiepe, G., 'Design and Democracy', *Design Issues* 22(2) (Spring 2006), pp. 27–34.

Bourdieu, P., *Distinction: a Social Critique of the Judgement of Taste*, (1979), trans. Richard Nice, London and Cambridge, MA: Harvard College and Routledge & Kegan Paul, 1984.

Bowe, S. and P. Richmond, *Selling Shaker, The Commodification of Shaker Design in the Twentieth Century*, Liverpool: Liverpool University Press, 2006.

Brand, S., *Whole Earth Catalogue*, a collaborative compilation of information, Menlo Park, California (1968–1975, *The Last Whole Earth Catalogue: Access to Tools*, Harmondsworth: Penguin, 1971, 1975).

Braudel, F., *Capitalism and Material Life 1400–1800*, New York: Harper & Row, 1973.

Breward, C., 'Femininity and Consumption: The Problem of the Late Nineteenth-Century Fashion Journal', *Journal of Design History* 7(2) (1994), pp. 71–89.

Breward, C., 'Cultures, Identities, Histories: Fashioning a Cultural Approach to Dress', *Fashion Theory* 2(4), (1998), pp. 301–14

Breward, Christopher, '"In London's Maze": the Pleasures of Fashionable Consumption', in *The Hidden*

Consumer: Masculinities, Fashion and City Life 1860–1914, Manchester: Manchester University Press, 1999, pp.170–3, 181–4.

Bronner, S. J., '"Visible Proofs": Material Culture Study in American Folkloristics', *American Quarterly* 35(3) (1983), pp. 316–38.

Brookes, M., 'What Aspen Knows is All the Questions', *Design* (215) (1966), pp. 25.

Buckley, C., 'Made in Patriarchy: Towards a Feminist Analysis of Women and Design', *Design Issues* 3(2) (Fall 1986), pp. 3–14. Reprinted in Victor Margolin (ed.), *Design Discourse: History, Theory, Criticism*, Chicago: University of Chicago Press, 1989, pp. 251–62.

Bullivant, L., '"Design for Better Living" Public Response to Britain Can Make It', in P. Sparke (ed.), *Did Britain Make It? British Design in Context 1946–86*, London: The Design Council, 1986, pp. 145–55.

Bullock, N., 'First the Kitchen, then the Façade', *Journal of Design History* 1(3–4) (1988), pp. 177–92.

Burks, J. M., 'Faith, Form and Finish: Shaker Furniture in Context', in *Shaker Design: Out of this World*, ed. J. M. Burks, Bard Graduate Center for Studies in the Decorative Arts, Design and Culture, New York and the Shelburne Museum, Shelburne, VT, New Haven, CT and London: Yale University Press, 2008, pp. 31–60.

Butcher, Mary, 'Eel-Traps without Eels', *Craft, Culture and Identity*, Tanya Harrod (ed.), special issue of *Journal of Design History*, 10(4) (1997), pp. 417–29.

Butler, C., *Postmodernism: A Very Short Introduction*, Oxford and New York: Oxford University Press, 2002.

Byars, M., *The Design Encyclopedia*, New York: Museum of Modern Art, 1994, 2004.

Calkins, E. E., 'Beauty the New Business Tool', *Atlantic Monthly*, August 1927,

Calkins, E. E., 'Advertising Art in the United States', *Studio Yearbook*, London: The Studio, 1936. Reprinted in M. Bierut, J. Helfand, S. Heller and R. Poynor (eds), *Looking Closer 3: Classic Writings on Graphic Design*, New York: Allworth Press, 1999, pp. 63–6.

Calvera, A., 'Local, Regional, National, Global and Feedback: Several Issues To Be Faced with Constructing Regional Narratives', *Journal of Design History* 18(4) (2005), pp. 371–83.

Campbell, Colin, *The Romantic Ethic and the Spirit of Modern Consumerism*, Oxford: Basil Blackwell, 1987.

Candlin, F. and R. Guins (eds), *The Object Reader*, New York and London: Routledge, 2009.

Carson, R., *Silent Spring*, Boston, MA: Houghton Mifflin, 1962.

Clark, H. and D. Brody, *Design Studies: A Reader*, Oxford: Berg, 2009.

Clarke, A., *Tupperware: The Promise of Plastic in 1950s America*, Washington, DC: Smithsonian Institution Press, 1999.

Clemm, S., '"Amidst the Heterogeneous Masses": Charles Dickens's *Household Words* and the Great Exhibition of 1851', *Nineteenth-Century Contexts* 27(3) (2005), pp. 207–30.

Coatts, M. (ed.), *Pioneers of Modern Craft*, Manchester: Manchester University Press, 1997.

Cole, S., 'Homosexuality, Class and Dress', *'Don We Now Our Gay Apparel': Gay Men's Dress in the Twentieth Century*, Oxford: Berg, 2000, pp. 15–31.

Conrads, U., *Programs and Manifestoes on Twentieth-century Architecture*, trans. Michael Bullock, Cambridge, MA: MIT Press (1964) 1989.

Conway, H. (ed.), *Design History: A Student's Handbook*, London: Unwin Hyman, 1987.

Coombes, A. E., *Reinventing Africa: Museums, Material Culture and Popular Imagination in Late Victorian and Edwardian England*, New Haven, CT and London: Yale University Press, 1994.

Cooper, R. and D. White, 'Teaching Transculturation: Pedagogical Process', *The Journal of Design History* 18(3) (2005), pp. 285–92.

Coulson, A. J., *A Bibliography of Design in Britain 1851–1970*, London: The Design Council, 1979.

Cowan, R. S., 'How the Refrigerator Got Its Hum', *The Social Shaping of Technology: How the Refrigerator Got Its Hum*, ed. Donald MacKenzie and Judy Wajcman, Milton Keynes: Open University Press, 1985, pp. 202–18.

Cowan, R. S., *A Social History of American Technology*, New York: Oxford University Press, 1997.

Cowan, R. S., *More Work for Mother*, New York: Basic Books, 1983.

Crowley, D., *National Style and Nation-State: Design in Poland from the Vernacular Revival to the International Style*, Manchester: Manchester University Press, 1992, pp. 102–32.

Crowley, D., 'Building the World Anew: Design in Stalinist and Post-Stalinist Poland', *Journal of Design History* 7(3) (1994), pp. 187–203.

Crowley, D., 'Finding Poland in the Margins: The Case of the Zakopane Style', *Journal of Design History* 14(2) (2001), pp. 105–16.

Crowley, D. and P. Jobling, 'Graphic Design in a Postmodern Context: the beginning and the end?' in *Graphic Design: Reproduction and Representation Since 1800*, Manchester: Manchester University Press, 1996.

Crowley, D. and J. Pavitt (eds), *Cold War Modern*, London: V&A Publishing, 2008.

Crowley, D. and S. E. Reid (eds), *Style and Socialism: Modernity and Material Culture in Post-War Eastern Europe*, Oxford: Berg, 2000.

Csikszentmihalyi, M. and E. Rochberg-Halton, 'The Most Cherished Objects in the Home', *The Meaning of Things: Domestic Symbols and the Self*, Cambridge: Cambridge University Press, 1981, pp. 55–89.

Cunningham, P. A., *Reforming Women's Fashion, 1850–1920: Politics, Health, and Art*, Kent, OH: Kent State University Press, 2003.

Curtis, B., 'One Continuous Interwoven Story (The Festival of Britain)', in J .Bird, B. Curtis, M. Mash, T. Putnam, G. Robertson, S. Stafford and L. Tickner (eds), *The Block Reader in Visual Culture*, London and New York: Routledge, 1996, pp. 209–20.

d'Alisera, J., 'I ♥ Islam: Popular Religious Commodities, Sites of Inscription, and Transnational Sierra Leonean Identity', *Journal of Material Culture* 6(1) (2001), pp. 91–110.

Daunton, M. and M. Hilton (eds), *The Politics of Consumption: Material Culture and Citizenship in Europe and America*, Oxford: Berg Publishers, 2001.

Davidson, C., *A Woman's Work is Never Done: A History of Housework in the British Isles 1650–1950*, London: Chatto & Windus, 1982.

Dean, D., 'A Slipware Dish by Samuel Malkin: An Analysis of Vernacular Design', *Journal of Design History* 7(3) (1994), pp. 153–67.

de Beauvoir, S., *Le Deuxième Sexe* (1949), translated as *The Second Sex*, New York: Knopf, 1953.

Debord, G., *The Society of the Spectacle* (*La société du spectacle*, 1967), trans. Donald Nicholson Smith, New York: Zone Books, 1994.

de Bretteville, S. L., 'Feminist Design: At the Intersection of the Private and Public Spheres', in R. Langdon and N. Cross (eds), *Design and Society: the proceedings of the Design and Society Section of an International Conference on Design Policy held at the Royal College of Art, London, 20–23 July 1982: a Conference Organised by the Department of Design Research at the Royal College of Art in collaboration with the Design Research Society and The Design Council*, London: Design Council, 1984.

de Bretteville, S. L., 'Some Aspects of Design From the Perspective of a Woman Designer' (1973). Reprinted in M. Bierut, J. Helfand, S. Heller, and R. Poynor (eds), *Looking Closer 3: Classic Writings on Graphic Design*, New York: Allworth Press, 1999, pp. 238–45.

Defoe, D., *The Complete English Tradesman*, Gloucester: Sutton Publishing, 1987 (1727).

de Grazia, V., and E. Furlough (eds), *The Sex of Things: Gender and Consumption in Historical Perspective*, Berkeley, CA: University of California Press, 1996.

Denney, M., 'Utility Furniture and the Myth of Utility 1943–1948', in *Utility Reassessed: The Role of Ethics in the Practice of Design*, Judy Attfield (ed.), Manchester: Manchester University Press, 1999, pp. 110–24.

Derrida, J., *Of Grammatology* (*De la Grammatologie*, 1967), trans. Gayatri Chakravorty Spivak, Baltimore, MD and London: The Johns Hopkins University Press, 1974.

De Vidas, A. A., 'Containing Modernity: The Social life of Tupperware in a Mexican Indigenous Village', *Ethnography* 9(2) (June 2008), pp. 257–84.

Dilnot, C., 'The State of Design History Part I: Mapping the Field', *Design Issues* 1(1) (1984), pp. 3–23.

Dilnot, C., 'The State of Design History Part II: Problems and Possibilities', *Design Issues* 1(2) (1984), pp. 3–20.

Docherty, T. (ed.), *Postmodernism: A Reader*, New York: Columbia University Press, 1993.

Doordan, D. P. (ed.), *Design History: An Anthology*, Cambridge, MA: MIT Press, 1995.

Dorfles, G. (ed.), *Kitsch: the World of Bad Taste*, New York: Bell Publishing Company, 1968.

Dormer, P., *Design since 1945*, London: Thames & Hudson, 1993.

Dormer, P. (ed.), *The Culture of Craft*, Manchester: Manchester University Press, 1987.

Drucker, J., *The Visible Word: Experimental Typography and Modern Art, 1909–1923*, Chicago: University of Chicago Press, 1994.

Dwiggins, W. A., *Layout in Advertising*, New York: Harper Brothers, 1928

Edwards, S., 'Factory and Fantasy in Andrew Ure', *Journal of Design History* 14(1) (2001), pp. 17–33.

Elias, N., *The Civilizing Process* (*Über den Prozeß der Zivilisation*, 1939), English translation, 2 vols, Oxford: Blackwell (1969) 1982.

Fagge, R., 'From the *Postscripts* to Admass: J.B. Priestley and the Cold War World', *Media History* 12(2) (2006), pp. 103–15.

Falk, P., 'The Bennetton–Toscani Effect: Testing the Limits of Conventional Advertising' in Mica Nava, Andrew Blake, Iain MacRury and Barry Richards (eds), *Buy This Book: Studies in Advertising and Consumption*, London: Routledge, 1997, pp. 64–86.

Fanon, F., 'The Fact of Blackness' (1952), in *Black Skin, White Masks,* New York: Grove Press, 1967.

Faurschou, G., 'Fashion and the Cultural Logic of Postmodernity', *Body Invaders: Panic Sex in America*, ed. A. Kroker and M. Kroker, New York: St Martin's Press, 1987, pp. 78–93.

Ferguson, R., M. Gever, T. T. Minh-ha, and C. West (eds), *Out There: Marginalization and Contemporary*

Cultures, New York: New Museum of Contemporary Art, and Cambridge, MA: MIT Press, 1990.

Ferry, E., '"Decorators May be Compared to Doctors": An Analysis of Rhoda and Agnes Garrett's *Suggestions for House Decoration in Painting, Woodwork and Furniture* (1876)', *Journal of Design History* 16(1) (2003), pp. 15–33.

'First Things First: A Design Manifesto' (2000), signed by J. Barnbrook, N. Bell, A. Blauvelt, H. Bockting, I. Boom, S. Levrant de Bretteville, M. Bruinsma, S. Cook, L. van Deursen, C. Dixon, W. Drenttel, G. Dumbar, S. Esterson, V. Frost, K. Garland, M. Glaser, J. Helfand, S. Heller, A. Howard, T. Kalman, J. Keedy, Z. Licko, E. Lupton, K. McCoy, A. Mevis, J. A. Miller, R. Poyner, L. Roberts, E. Spiekermann, J. van Toorn, T. Triggs, R. VanderLans, B. Wilkinson, published in *Adbusters, The AIGA Journal, Blueprint, Émigré, Eye, Form, Items* (Fall 1999–Spring 2000).

Fleming, J. and H. Honour, *The Penguin Dictionary of Decorative Arts*, London: Allen Lane, 1977.

Forty, A., 'Festival Politics', in Mary Banham and Bevis Hillier (eds), *A Tonic to the Nation: The Festival of Britain 1951*, London: Thames & Hudson/V&A, 1976, pp. 26–38.

Forty, A., *Objects of Desire: Design and Society 1750–1980*, London: Thames & Hudson, 1986.

Forty, A., 'A Reply to Victor Margolin', *The Journal of Design History* 6(2) (1993), pp. 131–2. Reprinted in *Design Issues* 11(1) (1995), pp. 16–18.

Foster, H. (ed.), *The Anti-Aesthetic: Essays on Postmodern Culture*, Port Townsend, WA: Bay Press, 1983.

Foucault, M., 'What is an Author?' (1969), trans. Josué V. Harari, in David Lodge, *Modern Criticism and Theory: A Reader*, London and New York: Longman, 1988, pp. 197–210.

Frank, I. (ed.), *The Theory of Decorative Art: An Anthology of European and American Writings, 1750–1940*, trans. David Britt (Bard Graduate Centre for Studies in the Decorative Arts, Design & Culture), Yale University Press, 2000.

Frederick, C., *The New Housekeeping: Efficiency Studies in Home Management*, Garden City, NY: Doubleday, Page & Co., 1914.

Friedan, B., *The Feminine Mystique*, New York: Norton, 1963.

Fry, T., 'Design History: a Debate?' in *Block* (5) (1981), pp. 14–18.

Fry, T., *Design History Australia: A Source Text in Methods and Resources*, Sydney, Australia: Hale & Iremonger and the Power Institute of Fine Arts, 1988.

Fry, T., 'A Geography of Power: Design History and Marginality', *Design in Asia and Australia*, special issue of *Design Issues* 6(1) (1989), pp. 15–30. Reproduced

in *The Idea of Design: A* Design Issues *Reader*, ed. V. Margolin and R. Buchanan, Cambridge, MA and London: MIT Press, 1995, pp. 204–18.

Fuller, R. B., 'The Case for a Domed City', *St. Louis Post-Dispatch*, September 26, 1965, pp. 39–41.

Fuller, R. B., *Operating Manual for Spaceship Earth*, Carbondale, IL: Southern Illinois University Press, 1969.

Garland, K., 'First Things First: A Manifesto' (1964), signed by K. Briggs, R. Carpenter, R. Chapman, G. Cinamon, A. Clift, H. Crowder, I. Dodd, G. Facetti, R. Fior, A. Froshaug, K. Garland, J. Garner, B. Grimbly, B. Higton, G. Jones, I. Kamlish, S. Lambert, I. McLaren, C. Rawlence, W. Slack, G. White, E. Wright, published in *Design, The Architects' Journal, The SIA Journal, Ark, Modern Publicity, Guardian,* 24 January 1964.

Ghirardo, D., 'Introduction', in *Architecture after Modernism*, London: Thames & Hudson, 1996, pp. 7–42.

Giedion, S., *Mechanization Takes Command*, New York: Oxford University Press, 1948.

Gilroy, P., 'Wearing Your Art on Your Sleeve: Notes Towards a Diaspora History of Black Ephemera', from *Small Acts: Thoughts on the Politics of Black Cultures*, London: Serpent's Tail, 1993 and reproduced in ed. R. Guins and O. Z. Cruz, *Popular Culture: A Reader*, London: Sage, 2005, pp. 495–503.

Goddess in the Details: Product Design by Women (exhibition catalogue, New York, Pratt Manhattan Gallery), New York: Association of Women Industrial Designers, 1994.

Goodall, P., 'Design and Gender', *BLOCK* (9) (1983), pp. 50–61

Gordon, B., 'Victorian Fancy Goods: Another Reappraisal of Shaker Material Culture', *Winterthur Portfolio* 25(2/3) (Summer–Autumn, 1990), pp. 111–29.

Gorman, C. (ed.), *The Industrial Design Reader*, New York: Allworth Press/The Design Management Institute, 2003.

Greenberg, C., 'The Avant Garde and Kitsch', *Partisan Review* 6(5) (Fall 1939), pp. 34–49.

Green Desires: Ecology, Design, Products (exhibition catalogue, EcoDesign Foundation, University of Sydney, 1992).

Greenhalgh, P., 'The History of Craft', in P. Dormer (ed.) *The Culture of Craft*, Manchester: Manchester University Press, 1987, pp. 20–52.

Greenhalgh, P., *Ephemeral Vistas: The Expositions Universelles, Great Exhibitions, and World's Fairs, 1851–1939*, Manchester: Manchester University Press, 1988.

Greenhalgh, P., 'Introduction', *Modernism in Design,* ed. P. Greenhalgh, London: Reaktion Books, 1990, pp. 1–24.

Greenhalgh, P., *Quotations and Sources on Design and the Decorative Arts,* Manchester: Manchester University Press, 1993.

Greenhalgh, P., 'The English Compromise: Modern Design and National Consciousness, 1870–1940' in W. Kaplan (ed.), *Designing Modernity: The Arts of Reform and Persuasion 1885–1945,* London: Thames & Hudson and Miami, FL: The Wolfsonian, 1995.

Greenhalgh, P. (ed.), *Art Nouveau 1890–1914,* exhibition catalogue, London: Victoria & Albert Museum and Washington, DC: National Gallery, 2000

Greenhalgh, P., 'The Style and the Age', in Paul Greenhalgh (ed.), *Art Nouveau 1890–1914,* exhibition catalogue, London: Victoria & Albert Museum and Washington, DC: National Gallery, 2000, pp. 14–33.

Greenstead, M. (ed.), *An Anthology of The Arts and Crafts Movement: Writings by Ashbee, Lethaby, Gimson and their Contemporaries,* Aldershot: Lund Humphries, 2005.

Gregson, N. and L. Crewe, 'Redefining Rubbish: Commodity Disposal and Sourcing', *Second Hand Cultures,* Oxford: Berg, 2003, pp. 115–42.

Gropius, W., 'Programme of the Staatliches Bauhaus in Weimar' (1919) and 'Principles of Bauhaus Production [Dessau]' (1926), in Ulrich Conrads (ed.), *Programs and Manifestoes on Twentieth-century Architecture,* Cambridge, MA: MIT Press, 1971, 2001, pp. 49–53, pp. 95–7.

Guyatt, M., 'The Wedgwood Slave Medallion: Values in Eighteenth-Century Design', *The Journal of Design History* 13(2) (2000), pp. 93–105.

Habermas, J., 'Modernity – An Incomplete Project' (1980), in Hal Foster (ed.), *The Anti-Aesthetic: Essays on Postmodern Culture,* Port Townsend, WA: Bay Press, 1983, pp. 3–15.

Hall, S., *Resistance Through Rituals: Youth Subcultures in Post-War Britain,* Birmingham: The Centre, 1975.

Hall, S., 'Encoding/Decoding' (originally published as 'Encoding and Decoding in Television Discourse', 1973), in *Culture, Media, Language: Working Papers in Cultural Studies, 1972–79,* Birmingham: Centre for Contemporary Cultural Studies, University of Birmingham, 1980, pp. 128–38.

Hamilton, R., 'Persuading Image', *Design* (134) (1960), pp. 28–32.

Hannah, F. and T. Putnam, 'Taking Stock in Design History', *BLOCK* (3) (1980), pp. 25–33, reproduced in *The BLOCK Reader in Visual Culture,* London: Routledge, 1996, pp. 148–66.

Harrison-Moore, A. and D. C. Rowe (eds), *Architecture and Design in Europe and America, 1750–2000,* Oxford: Blackwell, 2006.

Harrod, T. (ed.), *Craft, Culture and Identity,* special issue of *Journal of Design History* 10(4) (1997).

Harrod, T. (ed.), *Craft, Modernism and Modernity,* special issue of *Journal of Design History* 11(1) (Spring 1998).

Harrod, T., *The Crafts in Britain in the 20th Century,* London: Yale University Press for the Bard Graduate Center for Studies in the Decorative Arts, 1999.

Harvey, C. and J. Press, *William Morris: Design and Enterprise in Victorian Britain,* Manchester: Manchester University Press, 1991.

Harvey, J., 'Seen to Be Remembered: Presentation, Representation and Recollection in British Evangelical Culture since the Late 1970s', *Journal of Design History* 17(2) (2004), pp. 177–92.

Harvie, C., G. Martin and A. Scharf, *Industrialisation and Culture 1830–1914,* London: Macmillan, 1970.

Hassan, I., 'Toward a Concept of Postmodern', in *The Postmodern Turn: Essays in Postmodern Theory and Culture,* Columbus, OH: Ohio State University Press, 1987.

Hatch, M. J. and M. Schultz, 'Bringing the Corporation into Corporate Branding', *European Journal of Marketing* 37(7/8) (2003), pp. 1041–64.

Hawkins, A. Jr., *The Art Director at Work,* New York: Hastings House, 1959.

Hayden, D., *The Grand Domestic Revolution: A History of Feminist Designs for American Homes, Neighborhoods, and Cities,* Cambridge, MA: MIT Press, 1981.

Hebdige, D., 'From Culture to Hegemony', *Subculture: the Meanings of Style,* London: Methuen & Co., 1979, pp. 5–29.

Hebdige, D., 'Object as Image: The Italian Scooter Cycle', *Block* 5 (1981), pp. 44–64, reproduced in *Hiding in the Light: on Images and Things,* London: Comedia Routledge, 1988, pp. 77–115.

Heller, S., 'Advertising: Mother of Graphic Design', *Looking Closer 2: Critical Writings on Graphic Design,* ed. M. Bierut, W. Drenttel, S. Heller and D.K. Holland, New York: Allworth Press, 1997, pp. 112–19.

Heskett, J., 'The "American System" and Mass Production', *Industrial Design,* New York and Toronto: Oxford University Press, 1980, pp. 50–67.

Hewitt, J., 'Good Design in the Market Place: The Rise of Habitat Man', *The 60s,* special issue of *Oxford Art Journal* 10(2) (1987), pp. 28–42.

Highmore, B., 'Richard Hamilton at the *Ideal Home Exhibition* of 1958: Gallery for a Collector of Brutalist and Taschist Art', *Art History* 30(5) (November 2007), pp. 712–37.

Highmore, B., *The Design Culture Reader*, London: Routledge, 2008.

Hill, S. H., *Weaving New Worlds: Southeastern Cherokee Women and Their Basketry*, Chapel Hill, NC: University of North Carolina Press, 1997.

Hillier, B., *Austerity/Binge: The Decorative Arts of the Forties and Fifties*, London: Studio Vista, 1975.

Hine, T., *Populuxe*, New York: Alfred A. Knopf, 1987.

Hitchcock, H. R. and P. Johnson, *The International Style*, New York Museum of Modern Art, 1932.

Hobsbawm, E. J., *Nations and Nationalism since 1780*, Cambridge: Cambridge University Press, 1990.

Hollis, R., *Graphic Design: A Concise History*, London: Thames & Hudson, 1994.

Horkheimer, M. and T. Adorno, 'The Culture Industry: Enlightenment as Mass Deception', in *Dialectic of the Enlightenment* (1944), trans. J. Cumming, New York: Continuum, 1972, pp. 120–67.

Hounshell, D. A., *From the American System to Mass Production, 1800–1932: The Development of Manufacturing Technology in the United States*, Baltimore, MD: Johns Hopkins University Press, 1984.

Houze, Rebecca, 'From "Wiener Kunst im Hause" to the Wiener Werkstätte: Marketing Domesticity with Fashionable Interior Design', *Design Issues* 18(1) (Winter 2002), pp. 3–23.

Howard, E., *To-morrow: A Peaceful Path to Real Reform* (1898), reissued in 1902 as *Garden Cities of To-Morrow*, London: S. Sonnenschein & Co., Ltd., 1902.

Howard, E., 'Feminist Writings on Twentieth-Century Design History, 1970–1995: Furniture, Interiors, Fashion', *Women Designers in the USA, 1900–2000*, Pat Kirkham (ed.), special issue of *Studies in the Decorative Arts* 8(1) (Fall–Winter 2000–1), pp. 8–21.

Huppatz, D. J., 'Globalizing Corporate Identity in Hong Kong: Rebranding Two Banks', *Journal of Design History* 18(4) (2005), pp. 357–69.

Hyde, M., 'The "Make-Up" of the Marquise: Boucher's Portrait of Pompadour at Her Toilette', *The Art Bulletin* 82(3) (September 2000), pp. 453–75.

Jackson, A., 'Labour as Leisure: The Mirror Dinghy and DIY Sailors', *Journal of Design History* 19(1) (2006), pp. 57–67.

Jackson, F., 'The New Air Age: BOAC and Design Policy 1945–60', *Journal of Design History* 4(3) (1991), pp. 167–85.

Jackson, L., 'New Imagery', in *The New Look: Design in the Fifties*, London: Thames & Hudson, 1998, pp. 85–100.

Jacobs, K., 'Graphic Design, Style and Waste', *AIGA Journal of Graphic Design* 7(4) (1990), reprinted in Michael Bierut, William Drenttel, Steven Heller and D.K. Holland (eds), *Looking Closer: Critical Writings on Graphic Design*, New York: Allworth Press, 1994, pp. 183–90.

Jacobs, J., *The Death and Life of Great American Cities*, New York: Vintage Books, 1961.

Jameson, F., *Postmodernism, or The Cultural Logic of Late Capitalism*, Durham, NC: Duke University Press, 1991.

Jencks, C., *The Language of Post-Modern Architecture*, New York: Rizzoli, 1977.

Jervis, S., *The Penguin Dictionary of Design and Designers*, Harmondsworth: Penguin, 1984.

Jobling, P., 'The Face' in *Fashion Spreads: Word and Image in Fashion Photography Since 1980*, Oxford: Berg Publishers, 1999.

Johnson, P. and M. Wigley, *Deconstructivist Architecture*, New York: Museum of Modern Art, 1988.

Jones, M., 'Design and the Domestic Persuader: Television and the British Broadcasting Corporations Promotion of Post-war "Good Design"', *Journal of Design History* 16(4) (2003), pp. 307–18.

Jones, O., *The Grammar of Ornament*, London: Day & Son, 1856.

Julier, G., *The Culture of Design*, London: Sage, 2000.

Julier, G., *The Thames and Hudson Dictionary of Design since 1900*, London: Thames & Hudson, 1993, 2004.

Kaplan, W. (ed.), *Designing Modernity: The Arts of Reform and Persuasion, 1885–1945*, London: Thames and Hudson and Miami, FL: the Wolfsonian, 1995.

Kaplan, W. (ed.), *The Arts and Crafts in Europe and America: Design for the Modern World*, Los Angeles, CA: Los Angeles County Museum of Art, 2004.

Kardon, J. (ed.), *Revivals! Diverse Traditions: the History of Twentieth-Century American Craft, 1920–1945*, catalogue of an exhibition held at the American Craft Museum, New York, October 20, 1994 to February 26, 1995, New York: Harry N. Abrams, Inc. in association with the American Craft Museum, 1994.

Katz, B. M., 'Review: Technology and Design – A New Agenda', *Technology and Culture* 38(2) (April 1997), pp. 452–66.

Kirkham, P. (ed.), *The Gendered Object*, Manchester: Manchester University Press, 1996.

Kirkham, P., 'Humanizing Modernism: the Crafts, "Functioning Decoration" and the Eamses', *Journal of Design History* 11(1) (1998), pp. 15–29.

Kirkham, P., *Charles and Ray Eames: Designers of the Twentieth Century*, Cambridge, MA: MIT Press, 1998.

Kirkham, P., *Women Designers in the USA 1900–2000: Diversity and Difference*, New York: Bard Graduate

Center for Studies in the Decorative Arts, Design, and Culture, 2000.

Klein, N., *No Logo: Taking Aim at the Brand Bullies*, New York: Picador, 2000.

Kopytoff, I., 'The Cultural Biography of Things: Commoditisation as Process', in Arjun Appadurai (ed.), *The Social Life of Things: Commodities in Cultural Perspective*, Cambridge: Cambridge University Press, 1986, pp. 64–91.

Kraidy, M. M. and T. Goeddertz, 'Transnational Advertising and International Relations: US Press Discourses on the Benetton "We on Death Row" Campaign' *Media, Culture and Society* 25 (March 2003), pp. 147–65.

Kramer, Elizabeth, 'Master or Market? The Anglo–Japanese Textile Designs of Christopher Dresser', *The Journal of Design History* 19(3) (2006), pp. 197–214.

Landsmark, T. C., 'Comments on African American Contributions to American Material Life, *Race and Ethnicity in American Material Life*, special issue of *Winterthur Portfolio* 33(4) (Winter 1998), pp. 261–82.

Lears, T. J., *Fables of Abundance: A Cultural History of Advertising in America*, New York: Basic Books, 1994.

Le Corbusier, 'Type–Needs, Type–Furniture', *The Decorative Art of Today* (*L'art décoratif d'aujourd'hui*, 1925), trans. James Dunnett, Cambridge, MA: MIT Press, 1987, pp. 69–78.

Le Corbusier, *Towards a New Architecture* (*Vers une architecture*, 1924), London: Architectural Press, 1927.

Lees, G., 'Balancing the Object: the Reinvention of Alessi', *things* 6 (1997), pp. 74–91.

Lees-Maffei, G., 'Italianita and Internationalism: the Design, Production and Marketing of Alessi s.p.a.', *Modern Italy* 7(1) (2002), pp. 37–57.

Lees-Maffei, G. (ed.), *Domestic Design Advice*, special issue of *Journal of Design History* 16(1) (2003).

Lees-Maffei, G. and L. Sandino (ed.), *Dangerous Liaisons: Relationships between Design, Craft and Art*, special issue of *Journal of Design History* 17(3) (2004).

Lichtman, S. A., 'Do-It-Yourself Security: Safety, Gender, and the Home Fallout Shelter in Cold War America', *Journal of Design History* 19(1) (2006), pp. 39–55.

Linthicum, L., 'Integrative Practice: Oral History, Dress and Disability Studies', *Journal of Design History* 19(4) (2006), pp. 309–18.

Lloyd, P. A., and D. Snelders, 'What was Philippe Starck thinking of?' *Design Studies* 24(3) (2003), pp. 237–53.

Loewy, R., *Never Leave Well Enough Alone*, New York: Simon & Schuster, 1951.

Loos, A., 'Ornament and Crime' (1908) in A. Loos, Ornament and Crime: Selected Essays, trans. Michael Mitchell, Riverside, CA: Ariadne Press, 1998, pp. 167–76.

Lupton, E. and A. Miller, 'Deconstruction and Graphic Design: History Meets Theory', A. Blauvelt (ed.), special issue of *Visible Language* 28(4) (Fall 1994), pp. 346–66. Reprinted in E. Lupton and J. A. Miller, *Design Writing Research: Writing on Graphic Design*, London: Phaidon, 1996, pp. 2–23.

Lyotard, J. F., *The Postmodern Condition: A Report on Knowledge* (*La Condition Postmoderne: Rapport sur le Savoir*, 1979), Minneapolis: University of Minnesota Press, 1984.

MacCarthy, F., *William Morris: A Life for Our Time*, London: Faber & Faber, 1994.

Máčel, O., 'Avant-Garde Design and the Law: Litigation over the Cantilever Chair', *Journal of Design History* 2(3) (1990), pp. 125–44.

Mackenzie, D., *Green Design, Design for the Environment*, London: Laurence King Publishing, 1991.

MacKenzie, D. and J. Wajcman (eds), *The Social Shaping of Technology: How the Refrigerator Got Its Hum*, Milton Keynes: Open University Press, 1985.

MacKenzie, J. M., 'Orientalism in Design' in *Orientalism: History, Theory and the Arts*, Manchester and New York: Manchester University Press, 1995, pp. 105–37.

Madge, P., 'Design, Ecology, Technology: A Historiographical Review', *Journal of Design History* 6(3) (1993), pp. 149–66.

Madge, P., 'An Enquiry into Pevsner's "Enquiry,"' *The Journal of Design History* 1(2) (1988), pp. 113–26.

Maffei, N. P., 'The Search for an American Design Aesthetic, From Art Deco to Streamlining', in C. Benton, T. Benton and G. Wood, *Art Deco 1910–1939*, London: V&A Publications, 2003, pp. 361–9.

Maguire, P. J. and J. M. Woodham (eds), *Design and Cultural Politics in Postwar Britain: the Britain Can Make It Exhibition of 1946*, London and Washington: Leicester University Press, 1997.

Makower, J., J. Elkington and J. Hailes, 'Introduction', in *The Green Consumer Supermarket Guide*, New York: Penguin, 1991, pp. 7–58.

Manzini, E., 'Objects and Their Skin' in P. Sparke (ed.), *The Plastics Age: From Modernity to Post-Modernity*, London: Victoria and Albert Museum, 1990, pp. 115–27.

Marchand, R., *Advertising the American Dream: Making Way for Modernity, 1920–1940*, Berkeley, CA: University of California Press, 1985.

Margolin, V., 'A Decade of Design History in the United States 1977–87', *Journal of Design History* 1(1), (1988), pp. 51–72.

Margolin, V., 'Postwar Design Literature: a Preliminary Mapping', *Design Discourse: History, Theory, Criticism*, Chicago and London: University of Chicago Press, 1989, pp. 265–87.

Margolin, V. (ed.), *Design Discourse: History, Theory, Criticism*, Chicago: University of Chicago Press, 1989.

Margolin, V., 'Design History and Design Studies', *Design Studies* 13(2) (1992), pp. 104–16.

Margolin, V., 'A Reply to Adrian Forty', *Design Issues* 11(1) (1995), pp. 19–21.

Margolin, V. and R. Buchanan (eds), *The Idea of Design*, Cambridge, MA: MIT Press, 1995.

Margolin, V., *The Struggle for Utopia: Rodchenko, Lissitzky, Moholy-Nagy, 1917–1946*, Chicago: University of Chicago Press, 1997.

Margolin, V., 'Design History in the United States, 1977–2000', in *The Politics of the Artificial: Essays on Design and Design Studies*, Chicago: University of Chicago Press, 2002, pp. 127–86.

Margolin, V., 'A World History of Design and the History of the World, *Journal of Design History* 18(3) (2005), pp. 235–43.

Marx, K., 'The Fetishism of the Commodity and its Secret' *Capital* 1, London: Verso, 1976, pp. 163–77.

Massey, A., 'The Independent Group as Design Theorists', in N. Hamilton (ed.), *From Spitfire to Microchip: Studies in the History of Design from 1945*, London: Design Council, 1985, pp. 54–8.

Massey, A., 'The Independent Group: Towards a Redefinition', *The Burlington Magazine* 129 (April 1987), pp. 232–42.

Massey, A., *The Independent Group: Modernism and Mass Culture, 1945–59*, Manchester: Manchester University Press, 1995.

Mau, B. and the Institute without Boundaries, *Massive Change*, London: Phaidon Press Limited, 2004.

Mauss, M., *The Gift: Forms and Functions of Exchange in Archaic Societies* (*Essai sur le don, forme archaïque de l'échange*, 1923–24), English translation New York: Norton, 1954.

McClintock, A., 'Soft-Soaping Empire: Commodity Racism and Imperial Advertising', in *Imperial Leather: Race, Gender and Sexuality in the Colonial Contest*, London: Routledge, 1995, pp. 207–31.

McCracken, G., *Culture and Consumption: New Approaches to the Symbolic Character of Consumer Goods and Activities* (1988) Bloomington and Indianapolis, IN: Indiana University Press, 1990.

McDonough, W., 'Design, Ecology, Ethics, and the Making of Things' (1993), in K. Nesbitt (ed.), *Theorizing a New Agenda for Architecture: An Anthology of Architectural Theory 1965–1995*, New York: Princeton Architectural Press, 1996, pp. 400–7.

McDonough, W. and M. Braungart, *The Hannover Principles. Design for Sustainability*, William McDonough + Partners and McDonough Braungart Design Chemistry, 1992, 2003, http://www.mbdc.com/ref_publications.htm.

McDonough, W. and M. Braungart, *Cradle to Cradle: Remaking the Way We Make Things*, New York: North Point Press, 2002.

McKendrick, N., 'Josiah Wedgwood: an Eighteenth-Century Entrepreneur in Salesmanship an Marketing Techniques', *The Economic History Review*, new series 12(3) (1960), pp. 408–33.

McKendrick, N., 'Josiah Wedgwood and Cost Accounting in the Industrial Revolution', *The Economic History Review*, new series 23(1) (April 1970), pp. 45–67.

McKendrick, N., J. Brewer and J. H. Plumb, *The Birth of a Consumer Society: the Commercialization of Eighteenth-Century England*, London: Europa, 1982.

McLuhan, M., *The Mechanical Bride: Folklore of Industrial Man*, New York: Vanguard Press, 1951.

McLuhan, M., *The Gutenberg Galaxy: the Making of Typographic Man*, Toronto: University of Toronto Press, 1962.

McLuhan, M., *Understanding Media: the Extensions of Man*, New York: McGraw-Hill, 1964.

McLuhan, M. and Q. Fiore, *The Medium is the Massage: an Inventory of Effects*, New York: Touchstone, 1967.

McRobbie, A. (ed.), *Zoot Suits and Second Hand Dresses: An Anthology of Fashion and Music*, Boston: Unwin Hyman, 1988.

McVeigh, B. J., 'How Hello Kitty Commodifies the Cute, Cool and Camp', *Journal of Material Culture* 5(2) (2000), pp. 225–45.

Meggs, P. B., *A History of Graphic Design*, New York: Van Nostrand Reinhold, 1983.

Meikle, J. L., 'American Design History: A Bibliography of Sources and Interpretations', *American Studies International* 23(1) (1985), pp. 3–29.

Meikle, J. L., 'Design History for What? Reflections on an Elusive Goal', *Design Issues* 11(1) (1995), pp. 71–5.

Meikle, J. L., 'Material Doubts and Plastic Fallout', *American Plastics: a Cultural History*, New Brunswick, NJ: Rutgers University Press, 1995, pp. 242–76.

Meikle, J. L., 'Material Virtues: On the Ideal and the Real in Design History', *Journal of Design History* 11(3) (1998), pp. 191–9.

Meikle, J. L., *Design in the USA*, Oxford: Oxford University Press, 2005.

Mercer, K., 'Black Hair/Style Politics', *New Formations* 3 (1987), pp. 33–44. Reprinted in R. Ferguson, M. Gever, T. T. Minh-ha and C. West (eds), *Out There: Marginalization and Contemporary Cultures*, New York: New Museum of Contemporary Art, and Cambridge, MA: MIT Press, 1990, pp. 247–64.

Miller, D., *Material Culture and Mass Consumption*, Oxford: Blackwell, 1987.

Miller, D. (ed.), *Acknowledging Consumption: a Review of New Studies*, London and New York: Routledge, 1995.

Miller, M., *The Bon Marché: Bourgeois Culture and the Department Store 1869–1920*, Princeton, NJ: Princeton University Press, 1981.

Millet, K., *Sexual Politics*, Urbana, IL: University of Illinois Press, 1970.

Mitchell, T., 'Orientalism and the Exhibitionary Order', in N. B. Dirks (ed.), *Colonialism and Culture,* Anne Arbor, MI: University of Michigan Press, 1992, pp. 289–318.

Moeran, B., 'The Orient Strikes Back: Advertising and Imagining Japan', *Theory, Culture and Society* 13(3) (1996), pp. 77–112.

More from Less, exhibition catalogue, London: Design Centre, 1991.

Moriarty, C., J. Rose and N. Games, *Abram Games, Graphic Designer: Maximum Meaning, Minimum Means*, Lund Humphries/Princeton Architectural Press, 2003.

Morris, W., 'The Ideal Book', an address given 19 June 1893 to the Bibliographical Society, London, *Transactions of the Bibliographical Society* 1 (1893). Also reproduced in M. Bierut, J. Helfand, S. Heller and R. Poynor (eds), *Looking Closer 3: Classic Writings on Graphic Design*, New York: Allworth Press, 1999, pp. 1–5.

Mukerji, C., *From Graven Images: Patterns of Modern Materialism*, New York: Columbia University Press, 1983.

Mulvey, L., 'Visual Pleasure and Narrative Cinema', *Screen* 16(3) (1989), pp. 6–18.

Mumford, L., 'Toward an Organic Ideology', in *Technics and Civilization*, New York: Harcourt, Brace & Co., 1934.

Muthesius, H. and H. van de Velde, 'Werkbund Theses and Antitheses' (1914), in U. Conrads, *Programs and Manifestoes on 20th-century Architecture*, Cambridge, MA: MIT Press, 2001, pp. 28–31.

Myers, K., 'Towards a Theory of Consumption: Tu – A Cosmetic Case Study', *Block* 7 (1982), reprinted in *The BLOCK Reader in Visual Culture*, London and New York: Routledge, 1996, pp. 167–86.

Myers, N., *The Gaia Atlas of Planet Management: For Today's Caretakers of Tomorrow's World*, Garden City, NY: Anchor Press/Doubleday, 1984.

Nader, R., *Unsafe at Any Speed: The Designed-In Dangers of the American Automobile*, New York: Grossman, 1965.

Nava, M., A. Blake, I. MacRury and B. Richards (eds), *Buy This Book: Studies in Advertising and Consumption*, London: Routledge, 1997.

Naylor, G., 'From Workshop to Laboratory' *The Bauhaus Reassessed: Sources and Design Theory*, London: The Herbert Press, 1985, pp. 144–64.

Naylor, G., *William Morris by Himself: Designs and Writings*, Boston: Little, Brown and Co., 1988.

Nesbitt, K. (ed.), *Theorizing a New Agenda for Architecture: An Anthology of Architectural Theory, 1965–1995*, New York: Princeton Architectural Press, 1996.

Nochlin, L., 'Why Have There Been No Great Women Artists?' (1971), in *Women, Art, and Power and Other Essays*, New York: Harper & Row, 1988, pp. 145–78.

Olmstead, F. L., *Civilizing American Cities: Writings on City Landscapes*, ed. S. B. Sutton, Cambridge, MA: MIT Press, 1971.

O'Riordan, T., *Environmentalism*, London: Pion, 1976.

Osborne, H., *The Oxford Companion to the Decorative Arts*, Oxford: Oxford University Press, (1975) 1985.

Ortiz, F., *Cuban Counterpoint: Tobacco and Sugar*, trans. Harriet De Onís, Durham, NC: Duke University Press, 1995 (first published as *Contrapunteo cubano del tabaco y el azúcar*, 1940).

Osgerby, B., 'The "Bachelor Pad" as Cultural Icon: Masculinity, Consumption, and Interior Design in American Men's Magazines, 1930–65', *Journal of Design History* 18(1) (2005), pp. 99–113.

Packard, V., 'How to Outmode a $4,000 Vehicle in Two Years', *The Waste Makers*, New York: D. McKay Co., 1960, pp. 78–91.

Palmer, J. and M. Dodson (eds), *Design and Aesthetics: A Reader*, London and New York: Routledge, 1996.

Papanek, V., 'Do-It-Yourself Murder: the Social and Moral Responsibility of the Designer', *Design for the Real World: Human Ecology and Social Change* (1971), Toronto, New York, London: Bantam Books, 1973, pp. 65–95.

Papanek, V., *How Things Don't Work*, co-authored with Jim Hennessy, New York: Pantheon, 1977.

Papanek, V., *Design for Human Scale*, New York: Van Nostrand Reinhold Co., 1983.

Papanek, V., *The Green Imperative: Natural Design for the Real World*, London: Thames & Hudson, 1995.

Parker, R., *The Subversive Stitch: Embroidery and the Making of the Feminine*, London: Women's Press, 1984.

Paulicelli, E., 'Fashion Writing under the Fascist Regime: an Italian Dictionary and Commentary of Fashion by Cesare Meano, and Short Stories by Gianna Manzini, and Alba De Cespedes', *Fashion Theory* 8(1) (March 2004), pp. 3–34.

Pevsner, N., 'The Modern Movement before Nineteen-fourteen', *Pioneers of Modern Design: from William Morris to Walter Gropius*, London: Penguin, 1975 (First published as *Pioneers of the Modern Movement*, London: Faber, 1936; second edition New York: Museum of Modern Art, 1949; third revised edition London: Pelican Books, Penguin), p. 179 ff.

Porter, W., 'Toledo Wheels: the Design Story of Willys-Overland, the Jeep, and the Rise of the SUV', in *The Alliance of Art and Industry: Toledo Designs for a Modern America*, Toledo, OH: the Toledo Museum of Art, 2002, pp. 109–28.

Prown, J. D., 'Mind in Matter: An Introduction to Material Culture Theory and Method', *Winterthur Portfolio* 17(1) (1982), pp. 1–19.

Pugin, A. W., *True Principles of Pointed or Christian Architecture: Set Forth in Two Lectures Delivered at St Marie's, Oscott*, London: J. Weale, 1841.

Purbrick, L., 'South Kensington Museum: The Building of the House of Henry Cole', in M. Pointon (ed.), *Art Apart: Art Institutions and Ideology across England and North America*, Manchester: Manchester University Press, 1994, pp. 69–86.

Purbrick, L., 'Wedding Presents: Marriage Gifts and the Limits of Consumption, 1945–2000', *Journal of Design History* 16(3) (2003), pp. 215–28.

Purbrick, L., *The Wedding Present: Domestic Life Beyond Consumption*, Aldershot: Ashgate, 2007.

Pursell, C. W. Jr., 'The History of Technology and the Study of Material Culture' *American Quarterly* 35(3) (1983), pp. 304–15.

Pursell, C. W., Jr., 'The History of Technology and the Study of Material Culture', in T. J. Schlereth (ed.), *Material Culture: a Research Guide*, Lawrence, KS: University Press of Kansas, 1985, pp. 113–26.

Raizman, D., *History of Modern Design*, London: Laurence King, 2003.

Ray, M. L., 'A Reappraisal of Shaker Furniture and Society', *Winterthur Portfolio* 8 (1973), pp. 107–32.

Reed, C., *Bloomsbury Rooms: Modernism, Subculture, and Domesticity*, New Haven, CT: Yale University Press, 2004.

Reich, C., *The Greening of America: How the Youth Revolution is Trying to Make America Livable*, New York: Random House, 1970.

Reid, S. E., 'The Khrushchev Kitchen: Domesticating the Scientific-Technological Revolution', *Journal of Contemporary History* 40(2) (2005), pp. 289–316.

Remington, R. R. and B. J. Hodik, *Nine Pioneers in American Graphic Design*, Cambridge, MA: MIT Press, 1989.

Ribeiro, A., *Dress in Eighteenth-century Europe, 1715–1789*, New Haven, CT: Yale University Press, 2002.

Rieman, T. D., and J. M. Burks, *The Complete Book of Shaker Furniture*, New York: Harry N. Abrams, Inc., Publishers, 1993.

Riviere, J., 'Womanliness as Masquerade', *International Journal of Psycho-Analysis* 9 (1929), pp. 303–13. Reprinted in *The Inner World and Joan Rivière: Collected Papers*, A. Hughes (ed.), London: Karnac, 1991, pp. 89–101.

Roche, D., *The Culture of Clothing: Dress and Fashion in the "Ancien Régime"*, translated by Jean Birrell, Cambridge and New York: Cambridge University Press, 1994.

Rose, J., *Sexuality in the Field of Vision*, London: Verso, 1986.

Rowley, S. (ed.), *Craft and Contemporary Theory*, St Leonards, Australia: Allen & Unwin, 1997.

Rubin, E., 'The Form of Socialism without Ornament: Consumption, Ideology, and the Fall and Rise of Modernist Design in the German Democratic Republic', *Journal of Design History* 19(2) (2006), pp. 155–68.

Rubin, E., *Synthetic Socialism: Plastics and Dictatorship in the German Democratic Republic*, Chapel Hill, NC: University of North Carolina Press, 2008.

Ruskin, J., 'The Nature of Gothic' (1853), in *The Stones of Venice 2, The Sea Stories*, in *The Complete Works of John Ruskin* 10, E. T. Cook and Alexander Wedderburn (ed.), London: George Allen, 1904, pp. 180–269.

Ryan, D. S., '"All the World and Her Husband": The *Daily Mail* Ideal Home Exhibition, 1908–1939' in Andrews, M. and M. M. Talbot (eds), *'All the World and Her Husband': Women in 20th Century Consumer Culture*, London: Cassell, 2000, pp. 10–22.

Said, E., *Orientalism*, New York: Vintage Books, 1978.

Salisbury, H. E., 'Nixon and Khrushchev Argue In Public As US Exhibit Opens; Accuse Each Other Of Threats', *The New York Times*, 25 July 1959, p. 1.

Sandino, L., 'Oral Histories and Design: Objects and Subjects', *Oral Histories and Design*, L. Sandino (ed.), special issue of *Journal of Design History* 19(4) (2006), pp. 275–82.

Saumerez Smith, C., 'The Rise of the Designer', *The Rise of Design: Design and the Domestic Interior in*

Eighteenth Century England, London: Pimlico Press, 2000, pp. 118–33.

Scanlon, J., *Inarticulate Longings: The Ladies' Home Journal, Gender, and the Promises of Consumer Culture*, New York: Routledge, 1995.

Schlereth, T. J., 'Material Culture and Cultural Research', in T. J. Schlereth (ed.) *Material Culture: a Research Guide*, Lawrence, KS: University Press of Kansas, 1985, pp. 1–34.

Schwartz, F., *The Werkbund: Design Theory and Mass Culture Before the First World War*, New Haven, CT and London: Yale University Press, 1996.

Scotford, M., *Cipe Pineles: A Life of Design*, London: W. W. Norton & Co., 1999.

Seddon, J., 'The Architect and the "Arch-Pedant": Sadie Speight, Nikolaus Pevsner and "Design Review"', *Journal of Design History* 20(1) (2007), pp. 29–41.

Seddon, J. and S. Worden (eds), *Women Designing: Redefining Design in Britain between the Wars*, Brighton: University of Brighton, 1994.

Selle, G., 'There is No Kitsch, There is Only Design!' *Design Issues*, 1(1) (1984), pp. 41–52.

Sellers, S., '"How Long Has This Been Going On?" *Harpers Bazaar*, Funny Face and the Construction of the Modernist Woman', *Visible Language* 29(1) (Winter 1995), pp. 12–35.

Semper, G., 'Science, Industry and Art: Proposals for the Development of a National Taste in Art at the Closing of the London Industrial Exhibition' (1852), in *The Four Elements of Architecture*, trans. H. F. Mallgrave and W. Herrmann, Cambridge: Cambridge University Press, 1989, pp. 130–67.

Sherman, D. J., 'Post-Colonial Chic: Fantasies of the French Interior, 1957–62', *Art History* 27(5) (2004), pp. 770–805.

Silverman, D., 'Conclusion: the 1900 Paris Exhibition', *Art Nouveau in Fin-de-Siècle France: Politics, Psychology and Style*, Berkeley and Los Angeles, CA: University of California Press, 1989, pp. 284–314.

Simmel, G., *The Philosophy of Money* (*Philosophie des Geldes*), Leipzig: Duncker & Humblot, 1900, 1907, trans. Tom Bottomore and David Frisby, revised edition, London: Routledge, 2004.

Skov, L., 'Fashion Trends, Japonisme and Postmodernism, Or "What is so Japanese about Comme des Garçons?"', *Theory, Culture and Society* 13 (1996), pp. 129–51.

Smith, A., 'Of the Division of Labour' from *An Inquiry into the Nature and Causes of the Wealth of Nations*, London: Methuen & Co. Ltd., ed. Edwin Cannan, (1776) fifth edition, 1904, book I, chapter 1.

Smith, T., *Making the Modern: Industry, Art and Design in America*, Chicago: University of Chicago Press, 1993.

Sombart, W., *Der Moderne Kapitalismus*, 2 vols, Leipzig: Duncker & Humblot, 1902.

Sparke, P., *An Introduction to Design and Culture: 1900 to the Present*, edition 2.0, London: Routledge, 2004 (first published London: Unwin Hyman, 1986).

Sparke, P., 'From Pre-Modern to Modern: Japanese Industry, Society and Design after 1945', in *Japanese Design*, London: Michael Joseph, 1987, pp. 34–49.

Sparke, P., 'Plastics and Pop Culture', in P. Sparke (ed.), *The Plastics Age: From Modernity to Post-Modernity*, London: Victoria and Albert Museum, 1990, pp. 93–103.

Sparke, P., 'Introduction: The Architect's Wife', in *As Long As It's Pink: the Sexual Politics of Taste*, London: Pandora Press, 1995, pp. 1–12.

Sparke, P., 'Nature, Craft, Domesticity and the Culture of Consumption: The Feminine Face of Design in Italy, 1945–1970', *Modern Italy* 4(1) (1999), pp. 59–78.

Sparke, P., *Elsie de Wolfe: the Birth of Modern Interior Decoration*, New York: Acanthus Press, 2005.

Spivak, G. C., 'Can the Subaltern Speak?' in Cary Nelson and Larry Grossberg (eds), *Marxism and the Interpretation of Culture*, Oxford: Oxford University Press, 1988, pp. 217–316.

Stokes, R. G., 'Plastics and the New Society: the German Democratic Republic in the 1950s and 1960s', in David Crowley and Susan E. Reid (eds) *Style and Socialism: Modernity and Material Culture in Post-War Eastern Europe*, Oxford: Berg, pp. 65–80.

Styles, J., 'Manufacturing, Consumption and Design in Eighteenth Century England', in Brewer, J. and R. Porter (eds), *Consumption and the World of Goods* (1993), London: Routledge, 1994, pp. 527–54.

Sudjic, D., *Cult Objects*, London: Paladin, 1985.

Sullivan, L., 'The Tall Office Building Artistically Considered' (1896), in *Louis Sullivan: The Public Papers* (ed.), Robert Twombly, Chicago: University of Chicago Press, 1988, pp. 103–12.

Supon Design Group, Inc., *International Women in Design*, New York: Madison Square Press, 1993.

Szezerski, A., 'Sources of Modernity: The Interpretations of Vernacular Crafts in Polish Design around 1900', *Journal of Modern Craft* 1(1) (2008), pp. 55–76.

Taylor, M. and J. Preston (eds), *INTIMUS: Interior Design Theory Reader*, London: Wiley, 2006.

Thomson, E. M., 'Early Graphic Design Periodicals in America', *Journal of Design History* 7(2) (1994), pp. 113–26.

Thurlow, C. and G. Aiello, 'National Pride, Global Capital: A Social Semiotic Analysis of Transnational Visual Branding in the Airline Industry', *Visual Communication* 6(3) (2007), pp. 305–44.

Tinic, S. A., 'United Colors and Untied Meanings: Benetton and the Commodification of Social Issues', *Journal of Communication* 47(3) (1997), pp. 3–23.

Triggs, T., 'Scissors and Glue: Punk Fanzines and the Creation of a DIY Aesthetic', *Journal of Design History* 19(1) (January 2006), pp. 69–83.

Troy, N., 'The *Coloristes* and Charles-Edouard Jeanneret' *Modernism and the Decorative Arts in France: Art Nouveau to Le Corbusier*, New Haven, CT: Yale University Press, 1991, pp. 103–58 (extracts).

Troy, N., *Couture Culture: A Study in Modern Art and Fashion*, Cambridge, MA: MIT Press, 2002.

Tschichold, J., *Typographische Gestaltung*, Basel: Benno Schwabe, 1935.

Tschichold, J., *The New Typography*, (*Die Neue Typographie*) (1928), trans. Ruari McLean, Berkeley: University of California Press, 1995.

Ulrich, L. T., 'An Indian Basket, Providence, Rhode Island, 1676', *The Age of Homespun*, New York: Knopf, 2001, pp. 41–74.

Ure, A., 'The Factory System', in *The Philosophy of Manufacturers, or, An Exposition of the Scientific, Moral, and Commercial Economy of the Factory*, London: C. Knight, 1835, pp. 14 ff.

Usherwood, B., 'Transnational Publishing: the Case of *Elle Decoration*' in M. Nava, A. Blake, I. MacRury and B. Richards (eds), *Buy This Book: Studies in Advertising and Consumption*, London: Routledge, 1997, pp. 178–91.

Van Doren, H., 'Streamlining: Fad or Function?' *Design*, 1 (October 1949), pp. 2–5.

Van Eeden, J., 'The Colonial Gaze: Imperialism, Myths, and South African Popular Culture', *South African Design*, special issue of *Design Issues* 20(2) (Spring 2004), pp. 18–33.

Van Eeden, J., 'Land Rover and Colonial-Style Adventure', *International Feminist Journal of Politics* 8(3) (2006), pp. 343–69.

Veblen, T., 'Conspicuous Consumption', *The Theory of the Leisure Class* (1899), London: Unwin Books, 1970, pp. 60–80.

Veenis, M., 'Consumption in East Germany: the Seduction and Betrayal of Things', *Journal of Material Culture* 4(1) (1999), pp. 79–112.

Venturi, R., *Complexity and Contradiction in Architecture*, New York: Museum of Modern Art, 1966.

Venturi, R., D. Scott-Brown and S. Izenour, *Learning from Las Vegas: The Forgotten Symbolism of Architectural Form*, Cambridge, MA and London: MIT Press (1972) 1977.

Vickery, A., 'Women and the World of Goods: a Lancashire Consumer and her Possessions, 1751–81' in Brewer, J. and R. Porter (eds), *Consumption and the World of Goods*, (1993) London, New York: Routledge, 1994, pp. 274–301.

Wainwright, C., 'The Legacy of the Nineteenth Century' in P. Greenhalgh (ed.), *Modernism in Design*, London: Reaktion Books, 1990, pp. 26–40.

Walker, J. A., *Design History and the History of Design*, London: Pluto Press, 1989.

Weber, M., *The Protestant Ethic and the Spirit of Capitalism* (1904–5), trans. T. Parsons, New York: Schribner's, 1958.

Weems, R. E. Jr., 'The Revolution Will Be Marketed: American Corporations and Black Consumers during the 1960s', *Radical History Review* 59 (Spring 1994), pp. 94–107.

Weisenfeld, G., '"From Baby's First Bath:" Kaō Soap and Modern Japanese Commercial Design', *The Art Bulletin* 86(3) (September 2004), pp. 573–98.

Whiteley, N., 'Pop, Consumerism, and the Design Shift', *Design Issues* 2(2) (1985), pp. 31–45.

Whiteley, N., 'Toward a Throw-Away Culture. Consumerism, "Style Obsolescence" and Cultural Theory in the 1950s and 1960s', *The 60s*, special issue of *Oxford Art Journal* 10(2) (1987), pp. 3–27.

Williams, R., *Keywords; a Vocabulary of Culture and Society*, New York: Oxford University Press, 1976, revised 1983.

Williams, R., *Dream Worlds: Mass Consumption in Nineteenth Century France*, Berkeley, CA: University of California Press, 1982.

Woodham, J. M., 'Resisting Colonization: Design History Has Its Own Identity', *Design Issues* 11(1) (1995), pp. 22–37.

Woodham, J., *Twentieth-Century Design*, Oxford: Oxford University Press, 1997.

Woodham, J. M., 'Local, National and Global: Redrawing the Design Historical Map', *The Journal of Design History* 18(3) (2005), pp. 257–67.

Woods, T., *Beginning Postmodernism*, Manchester: Manchester University Press, 1999.

World Commission on Environment and Development, *Our Common Future*, Oxford: Oxford University Press, 1989.

Wortman Weltge, S., *Bauhaus Textiles: Women Artists and the Weaving Workshops*, London: Thames & Hudson, 1993.

Wright, F. L., 'Prairie Architecture' (1931), in Edgar Kaufmann and Ben Raeburn (eds), *Frank Lloyd Wright: Writings and Buildings*, New York: Meridian, 1960, pp. 37–55.

Wright, F. L., 'The Art and Craft of the Machine' (1901), in Edgar Kaufmann and Ben Raeburn (eds), *Frank Lloyd Wright: Writings and Buildings*, New York: Meridian, 1960, pp. 55–73.

Wright, F. L., *The Natural House*, New York: Horizon Press, 1954.

INDEX

Note: *italic* page numbers denote references to illustrations.